Magical Realism

MAGICAL REALISM

Theory, History, Community

Edited with an Introduction by

LOIS PARKINSON ZAMORA

AND WENDY B. FARIS

DUKE UNIVERSITY PRESS *Durham & London 1995*

Third printing, 2000
© 1995 Duke University Press
All rights reserved
Printed in the United States of America on acid-free paper
Typeset in Berthold Bodoni by Tseng Information Systems.
Library of Congress Cataloging-in-Publication Data
Magical realism : theory, history, community / edited, with an
introduction, by Lois Parkinson Zamora and Wendy B. Faris.
Includes bibliographical references and index.
ISBN 0-8223-1611-0 (alk. paper). — ISBN 0-8223-1640-4 (pbk. :
alk. paper)
1. Magic realism (Literature)   2. Fiction—20th century—History
and criticism.   3. Spanish American fiction—20th century—History
and criticism.   I. Zamora, Lois Parkinson.   II. Faris, Wendy B.
PN56.M24M34   1995
809.3'937—dc20   94-47223 CIP

To Friendship

CONTENTS

IV. Community

ACKNOWLEDGMENTS

We are grateful to Lilia Carpentier for the rights to translate Alejo Carpentier's essays, "On the Marvelous Real in America" and "The Baroque and the Marvelous Real"; to the editors of *Twentieth Century Literature* for permission to reprint Scott Simpkins' essay, originally titled "Magical Strategies: The Supplement of Realism," in *Twentieth Century Literature* 34, 2 (1988): 140–54; to the Women's Studies Program of the University of Maryland for permission to reprint P. Gabrielle Foreman's "Past-On Stories: History and the Magically Real, Morrison and Allende On Call," *Feminist Studies* 18, 2 (1992): 369–88; and to Auburn University for permission to publish a revised version of John Burt Foster's "Magic Realism in *The White Hotel:* Compensatory Vision and the Transformation of Classic Realism," *Southern Humanities Review* 20, 3 (1986): 205–19.

The following essays, some in slightly different versions, were originally published in these collections: Franz Roh, "Realismo mágico: Problemas de la pintura más reciente," *Revista de Occidente* 16 (April, May, June 1927): 274–301; Angel Flores, "Magical Realism in Spanish American Fiction," *Hispania* 38, 2 (1955): 187–92; Luis Leal, "El realismo mágico en la literatura hispanoamericana," *Cuadernos Americanos* 43, 4 (1967): 230–35; Stephen Slemon, "Magic Realism as Post-Colonial Discourse," *Canadian Literature* 116 (1988): 9–24; Rawdon Wilson, "The Metamorphoses of Space: Magic Realism," in *Magic Realism and Canadian Literature*, ed. Peter Hinchcliffe and Ed Jewinski (Waterloo, Ontario: University of Waterloo, 1986), 61–74; Patricia Merivale, "Saleem Fathered by Oskar: Intertextual Strategies in *Midnight's Children* and *The Tin Drum*," *Ariel* 21, 3 (1990): 5–21.

To our contributors, for their patience and good humor, we are especially grateful.

LOIS PARKINSON ZAMORA
AND WENDY B. FARIS
Introduction: Daiquiri Birds and
Flaubertian Parrot(ie)s

A quota system is to be introduced on fiction set in South America. The intention is to curb the spread of package-tour baroque and heavy irony. Ah, the propinquity of cheap life and expensive principles, of religion and banditry, of surprising honour and random cruelty. Ah, the daiquiri bird which incubates its eggs on the wing; ah, the fredonna tree whose roots grow at the tips of its branches, and whose fibres assist the hunchback to impregnate by telepathy the haughty wife of the hacienda owner; ah, the opera house now overgrown by jungle. Permit me to rap on the table and murmur "Pass!" Novels set in the Arctic and the Antarctic will receive a development grant. — Julian Barnes, *Flaubert's Parrot* [1]

Barnes has got it just right. His parodic pastiche of magical realism moves back and forth, as do many of the literary texts we consider here, between the disparate worlds of what we might call the historical and the imaginary. Propinquity — Barnes' word — is indeed a central structuring principle of magical realist narration. Contradictions stand face to face, oxymorons march in locked step — too predictably, Barnes insists — and politics collide with fantasy. In his reference to religion and banditry, and to the miraculous impregnation of the hacienda owner's haughty wife (clearly the kind of magical realist image he wishes would go away), Barnes implies that bad politics has become an expected ingredient of the form. His images reflect the popular perception of magical realism as a largely Latin American event.

In ridiculing the forms and conventions of magical realism, Barnes helps us distinguish them. As in all effective parody, he turns the form against itself, uses its conventions to critique its conventions. His hyperbole parodies the hyperbole of magical realism, for excess is a hallmark of the mode. His distillation of characters into types suggests the shift in emphasis in magical realism from psychological to social and political concerns. His refusal to sign on for the baroque "package tour" suggests the style of the cabin decor in many of these textual cruises. His comic curse on magical realism declares that its conventions have become ossified, tedious, overripe.

Julian Barnes is fun to argue with because his prescription ("Pass!") is so self-consciously reductive. He invites refutation, because the resources of magical realist narrative are hardly exhausted. On the contrary, they have been enabling catalysts for the development of new national and regional literatures and, at the same time, a replenishing force for "main-stream" narrative traditions. Readers know that magical realism is not a Latin American monopoly, though the mastery of the mode by several recent Latin American writers explains Barnes' association. It is true that Latin Americanists have been prime movers in developing the critical concept of magical realism and are still primary voices in its discussion, but this collection considers magical realism an international commodity. Almost as a return on capitalism's hegemonic investment in its colonies, magical realism is especially alive and well in postcolonial contexts and is now achieving a compensatory extension of its market worldwide. Furthermore Barnes' parodic suggestion that magical realism is a *recent* glut on that market ignores its long history, beginning with the masterful inter-weavings of magical and real in the epic and chivalric traditions and continuing in the precursors of modern prose fiction—the *Decameron, The Thousand and One Nights, Don Quixote.* Indeed, we may suppose that the widespread appeal of magical realist fiction today responds not only to its innovative energy but also to its impulse to reestablish contact with traditions temporarily eclipsed by the mimetic constraints of nineteenth- and twentieth-century realism. Contemporary magical realist writers self-consciously depart from the conventions of narrative realism to enter and amplify other (diverted) currents of Western literature that flow from the marvelous Greek pastoral and epic traditions to medieval dream visions to the romance and Gothic fictions of the past century.

It is a temptation to run Barnes' risk, to polarize the distinction between realism and magical realism in order to define the latter. In fact, realism and magical realism often spring from coherent (and sometimes identical) sources. Consider the magical departures from realism by such master realists as Gogol, James, Kafka, Flaubert. Indeed, Barnes might have noticed that beside his daiquiri bird, mentioned in the passage quoted above, perches Flaubert's parrot, the presiding spirit and eponymous hero, as it were, of Barnes' own wonderful book, *Flaubert's Parrot*. Barnes' title refers to Flaubert's short story, "A Simple Heart." In this story, Flaubert writes of the maidservant Felicité, whose banal reality eventually admits a transcendental parrot: "To minds like hers the supernatural is a simple matter."[2] In the magical realist texts under discussion in these essays, the supernatural is not a simple or obvious matter, but it *is* an ordinary matter, an everyday occurrence — admitted, accepted, and integrated into the rationality and materiality of literary realism. Magic is no longer quixotic madness, but normative and normalizing. It is a simple matter of the most complicated sort.

An essential difference, then, between realism and magical realism involves the intentionality implicit in the conventions of the two modes. Several essays in our collection suggest that realism intends its version of the world as a singular version, as an objective (hence universal) representation of natural and social realities — in short, that realism functions ideologically and hegemonically. Magical realism also functions ideologically but, according to these essays, less hegemonically, for its program is not centralizing but eccentric: it creates space for interactions of diversity. In magical realist texts, ontological disruption serves the purpose of political and cultural disruption: magic is often given as a cultural corrective, requiring readers to scrutinize accepted realistic conventions of causality, materiality, motivation.

Ironically, the dichotomy encoded in the critical term "magical realism" positions its users outside of the world portrayed in the "magical realist" texts we wish to enter, for the term implies a clearer opposition between magic and reality than exists within those texts. For the characters who inhabit the fictional world, and for the author who creates it, magic may be real, reality magical; there is no need to label them as such. We will do well, then, to test the term magical realism against such alternative terms as metaphoric realism or mythic realism, as one of the following essays proposes. Texts labeled magical realist draw upon cultural systems that are no less "real" than those upon which traditional literary realism draws — often non-Western cultural systems that privilege mystery over empiricism, empathy over technology, tradition over innovation. Their primary narrative investment may be in myths, legends, rituals — that is, in collective (sometimes oral and performative, as well as written) practices that bind communities together. In such cases, magical realist works remind us that the novel began as a popular form, with communal imperatives that continue to operate in many parts of the world. Or, where these practices (and communities) have been occulted or supplanted, magical realist writers may revitalize them in their fictions. A number of the writers discussed here self-consciously recuperate non-Western cultural modes and nonliterary forms in their Western form (the novel, the short story, the epic poem), among them Toni Morrison, Salman Rushdie, Juan Rulfo, Derek Walcott. So, too, Gabriel García Márquez insists that he is a social realist, not a magical realist: one of his characters in *One Hundred Years of Solitude* confirms this amplification of the realm of the real by observing, "If they believe it in the Bible . . . I don't see why they shouldn't believe it from me."[3]

How, then, are we to proceed, distanced as we are by our own term from the very texts we wish to approach? Comparative literature can be an effective medium for deconstructing ideologically charged dichotomies, including that of "magic" and "real." Our aim in soliciting discussions of a wide variety of texts and traditions is to establish the viability of magical realism as a significant contemporary international mode and to encourage attention to local contrasts, to cultural and political divergences. The authors of the essays in this collection recognize in a variety of ways the contradictions between the critical label and the literary practice of magical realism, as well as the dangers of appropriation, colonization, domestication inherent in their analytical activity. They are at pains, in general, not to monumentalize magical realism as *the* postmodern or *the* postcolonial mode or to propose marginality as some new (disguised) mainstream. Indeed, a collective discussion like ours, which features six recent Nobel prize winners—García Márquez, Paz, Morrison, Kawabata, Walcott, Oe—as well as such diverse and widely read writers as Rushdie, Allende, Barthelme, Rulfo, to name only a few, suggests that magical realist practice is currently requiring that we [re]negotiate the nature of marginality itself.

Amidst complex definitional and conceptual questions, the authors of these essays recognize that, by whatever name, magical realism is an important presence in contemporary world literature. Because they treat texts from many countries and cultures, they create a complex of comparative connections, avoiding separatism while at the same time respecting cultural diversity. Included here are references to Eastern, African, and indigenous American mythological and expressive traditions as well as to European traditions, and to works that self-consciously depart from European traditions. So the following essays, like the texts they treat, circulate eccentrically: their arguments overlap, but they do not revolve around a single ideological or geographical center.

Within this eccentric comparative context, each essay offers generalizing theoretical formulations, as well as specific discussion of particular literary works. Rather than providing a comprehensive geographical or linguistic survey of magical realism, the essays tend to illustrate the strength of the mode by intensive textual analyses. They show that magical realist writers are reading and responding to each other across national and linguistic borders in ways that have influenced individual works and encouraged the recent development of magical realist subjects and strategies. The essays on contemporary literature describe various formal and thematic interactions among the literary texts they treat, interactions that suggest the existence of a flourishing trend, perhaps one that will eventually be recognized as a movement. On the other hand, the essays that look back to earlier periods of literary history may suggest that magical realism is less a trend than a tradition, an evolving mode or genre that has had its waxings and wanings over the centuries and is now experiencing one more period of ascendency. The challenge of these latter essays is to articulate the differences between current literary manifestations of magical realism and their many magical precursors.

In the diversity of texts and traditions they discuss, the authors of these essays remind us that a literary genre is both a formal and a historical category. As a group, the essays address the synchronic relations of a particular magical realist work within its own cultural context and beyond its borders, as well as the diachronic relations of the texts that comprise an on-going generic tradition. Together, they allow us to evaluate the formal capacities of magical realism to express a variety of cultural and historical conditions. Ortega y Gasset said of a writer's choice of literary genre that it reflects "at one and the same time a certain thing to be said and the only way to say it fully."[4] In their use of magical realist devices to enhance the expressive potential of their chosen genre, the authors considered here confirm (and complicate) Ortega's assertion.

In surveying the definitions of magical realism in the following essays, we sight several repeating elements. The essays generally agree that magical realism is a mode suited to exploring—and transgressing—boundaries, whether the boundaries are ontological, political, geographical, or generic. Magical realism often facilitates the fusion, or coexistence, of possible worlds, spaces, systems that would be irreconcilable in other modes of fiction. The propensity of magical realist texts to admit a plurality of worlds means that they often situate themselves on liminal territory between or among those worlds — in phenomenal and spiritual regions where transformation, metamorphosis, dissolution are common, where magic is a branch of naturalism, or pragmatism. So magical realism may be considered an extension of realism in its concern with the nature of reality and its representation, at the same time that it resists the basic assumptions of post-enlightment rationalism and literary realism. Mind and body, spirit and matter, life and death, real and imaginary, self and other, male and female: these are boundaries to be erased, transgressed, blurred, brought together, or otherwise fundamentally refashioned in magical realist texts. All of the essays in this collection address the negotiations of magical realism between these normative oppositions and alternative structures with which they propose to destabilize and/or displace them.

Magical realism's assault on these basic structures of rationalism and realism has inevitable ideological impact, another point upon which these essays agree. Magical realist texts are subversive: their in-betweenness, their all-at-onceness encourages resistance to monologic political and cultural structures, a feature that has made the mode particularly useful to writers in postcolonial cultures and, increasingly, to women. Hallucinatory scenes and events, fantastic/phantasmagoric characters are used in several of the magical realist works discussed here to indict recent political and cultural perversions. History is inscribed, often in detail, but in such a way that actual events and existing institutions are not always privileged and are certainly not limiting: historical narrative is no longer chronicle but clairvoyance. As Denis Donoghue states in a review of Carlos Fuentes' magical realist tales, *Constancia and Other Stories for Virgins*, the pluperfect subjunctive is often more used (and useful) than the past perfect.[5] John Erickson, in the essay he contributes here, summarizes this aspect of magical realism by calling it "a corrosion within the engine of system," an admission of the exceptional that subverts existing structures of power.

Implied in this formulation are other subversions and repositionings: of the Cartesian identification of truth with human consciousness; of rationalist notions of the probable and predictable relations of cause and effect; of the reader's relation to the text and the text's relation to the world. These issues and others are examined in the essays that follow. Here, let us simply cite Henry James, who warns against "the peril of the unmeasured strange," stating that to make his stories of the supernatural work, he needed to juxtapose them to another history, to "the indispensable history of somebody's *normal* relation to something."[6] But this notion, too, is unsettled by magical realist texts because within them magic is often accepted as our "indispensable history" of "*normal* relations" to everything. The world is altered and enriched accordingly.

We have divided our volume into four parts: Foundations, Theory, History, Community. In our first section, we include essays published in 1927, 1949, and 1975 by two writers who were especially influential in developing the concept of magical realism. They are the German art critic and historian Franz Roh and the Cuban novelist Alejo Carpentier. Roh and Carpentier formulate two issues that have become essential in the theory and practice of magical realism: the imaginary and the autochthonous.[7] Roh speculates about the quotients of the real and the imagined and more particularly about the status of the object in Post-Expressionist painting in the twenties in Europe; Carpentier posits a particular affinity between the real and the imaginary in Latin America. Carpentier calls this experience *lo real maravilloso americano*, a term and concept that Amaryll Chanady will refer to in her essay as Carpentier's "territorialization of the imaginary." Roh's emphasis is on aesthetic expression, Carpentier's on cultural and geographical identity. Despite their different perspectives, Roh and Carpentier share the conviction that magical realism defines a revisionary position with respect to the generic practices of their times and media; each engages the concept to discuss what he considers an antidote to existing and exhausted forms of expression. We also include early and widely cited literary critical studies by Angel Flores and Luis Leal, on magical realism in Latin America.

The other essays in this first section provide an explanatory history of these foundational essays. Irene Guenther's historical overview surveys the ways in which Franz Roh's term of Magic Realism, overlapped with and was ultimately eclipsed by *Neue Sachlichkeit*, the New Objectivity, during the Weimar Republic. Guenther also considers the routes by which Roh's art historical formulation found its way to Latin American writers in the 1920s and, thirty years later, into the transnational discourse of literary criticism. Amaryll Chanady builds on her own seminal study of the narrative dynamics of magical realism, *Magical Realism and the Fantastic: Resolved Versus Unresolved Antimony* (1985), to investigate how Western rationalism is subverted, mimesis displaced by poesis, in the work of Latin American writers and critics — Carpentier, Flores, and Leal among them. She argues that they use the resources of European Surrealism even as they modify them in their efforts to articulate a theory of magical realism as a New World phenomenon. In the essay that follows Chanady's, Scott Simpkins places Roh, Carpentier, and Flores in their philosophic and cultural contexts. Using these early discussions of magical realism as his point of departure, he analyzes the generic strategies employed by two literary magicians, Borges and García Márquez, and their influence on many of their contemporaries.

We have said that our essays circulate eccentrically, that they belie a single, controlling center. It is, however, plausible to say that they orbit around three thematic centers, and the following three sections — Theory, History, Community — are grouped accordingly. The essays in our second section theorize magical realism. Wendy B. Faris proposes a conceptual framework for the mode. She establishes a set of distinguishing characteristics for magical realism as an international movement and in so doing argues for its central place in any consideration of postmodernism. Equally broad in focus, Theo D'haen's essay also explores definitional questions. His survey of the history of the term itself traces the radical revisions and recenterings of magical realism in an international context.

Rawdon Wilson and Jon Thiem begin to particularize these theoretical issues by focusing on the nature of space in magical realist texts. Wilson observes the interactions among distinct worlds proposed within the text and finds their shifting relations — the "metamorphoses of space" — to be a primary source of counterrealism. In a related argument, Jon Thiem points to the interactions between the textual world and the world outside the text, that is, the interactions between the characters' world and the reader's. Thiem identifies a magical realist narrative process, which he calls the "textualization of the reader," whereby the assumed boundaries between the fictional world and the reader's world are magically transgressed. The reader's reality, and the characters' fictionality, are called into question by this process of "textualization," as Thiem demonstrates in a group of texts by Julio Cortázar, Michael Ende, Italo Calvino, and Woody Allen, among others.

Concluding the theory section is Jeanne Delbaere-Garant's call for closer definition of the critical concept of magical realism. She argues that magical realism is useful as a generic marker only if we make distinctions about the particular sources and motivations of "magic" in a given text. She investigates psychological, mythical, and grotesque elements that unsettle the assumptions and practice of literary realism in works by the postcolonial writers Angela Carter, Jack Hodgins, and Janet Frame, with reference to Michael Ondaatje and Wilson Harris as well.

The essays in the history section are also concerned with the nature of magical realism as a literary mode. However, their focus narrows somewhat as they concentrate on the practice of individual writers in particular historical and political territories. John Burt Foster's essay on D. M. Thomas' *The White Hotel* begins this exploration by developing the concept of "felt history," or the magical bodily echoes of external events — a useful concept with which to understand magical realism as a mode that bears witness to our era. P. Gabrielle Foreman compares Toni Morrison's *The Song of Solomon* and Isabel Allende's *The House of the Spirits*, arguing that both, in their different ways, use magic to recuperate the real, that is, to reconstruct histories that have been obscured or erased by political and social injustice. Richard Todd looks at novels by Graham Swift, Peter Carey, and Mordecai Richler that present alternative national histories of England, Australia, and Canada. These novels contain narrator/historians who self-consciously undermine the "facts" of history by means of a variety of "magical" narrative strategies in order to provide the structural freedom necessary to perform their own dramatic histories.

Patricia Merivale's essay on Salman Rushdie's *Midnight's Children* and Günter Grass' *The Tin Drum* shows how the characters in these novels are "handcuffed to [the] history" of European colonialism and world war in this century. Merivale is also interested in *literary* history: she traces the clear lines of influence that connect Rushdie to Grass and the parallel ways in which their narratives resist the "facts" they record. Steven Walker analyzes what is, perhaps, the most controversial magical realist text of all, Salman Rushdie's *The Satanic Verses*. Illustrating the often-mentioned affinities between magical realism and Jungian psychology, Walker uses the Jungian archetype of the *puer aeternus* to illuminate the novel's engagement of the unconscious mind.

David Mikics' essay considers magical realist devices of transculturation and identity formation, that is, the potential of magical realism to imagine a coherent postcolonial collectivity — specifically, in the Caribbean, in the poetry of Derek Walcott and the fiction of Alejo Carpentier. Mikics' essay argues that history and community are inseparable cultural constructs, especially in colonized regions of the world. At the outset of his discussion of the Caribbean, Mikics states that magical realism "realizes the conjunction of ordinary and fantastic by focusing on a particular historical moment afflicted or graced by this doubleness. Since magical realism surrounds with its fabulous aura a particular, historically resonant time and place, the theory of magical realism must supply an approach to history, not merely literary genre." In the community of Caribbean cultures, Mikics argues, magical realism is a self-consciously historical form.

The fourth section focuses our attention on issues of community. The essays in this section suggest that magical realism, in contrast to the realism upon which it builds, may encode the strengths of communities even more than the struggles of individuals. Societies, rather than personalities, tend to rise and fall in magical realist fiction. Stephen Slemon's essay shows how magical realist devices serve postcolonial communities. He focuses on four anglophone Canadian authors, situating them in their postcolonial cultures and also connecting them to indigenous New World cultures. In so doing, Slemon observes how the competing codes of realism and fantasy mirror, and thus begin to deconstruct, colonial cultural programs. John Erickson addresses postcolonial communities in another part of the world. His subject is North African narratives of French expression, in particular, Abdelkebir Khatibi's *Love in Two Languages* and Tahar ben Jelloun's *The Sand Child*. These writers use the strategies of magical realism to create a counterdiscourse, and a countercommunity, to distance and critique colonizing power structures in Morocco. Susan Napier's essay on modern Japanese literature uses magical realism to construct a comparative poetics. The theory and practice of magical realism provides the comparative context in which Napier analyzes the intriguing admixture of Western magical realist innovations and Japanese traditions in recent Japanese fiction.

Melissa Stewart, in her essay on the problems and delights of cities in the work of U.S. writers William Kennedy, John Cheever, and Donald Barthelme, demonstrates, this time in an urban context, the ways in which magical realism promotes the integration of rational and irrational domains. Lois Parkinson Zamora discusses a hemispheric American literary territory, comparing the traditions of romance in the United States and magical realism in Latin America. The frequent appearance of ghosts in these traditions allows her to compare cultural constructions of the self and literary constructions of character in a variety of works of American fiction. These last two essays — one on visible cities, the other on ghost towns underground—confirm the communal force of magical realist fiction.

Notes

1 Julian Barnes, *Flaubert's Parrot* (New York: McGraw Hill, 1984), p. 104.

2 Gustave Flaubert, "A Simple Heart," in *Three Tales*, trans. Robert Baldick (New York: Penguin, 1961), p. 39.

3 Gabriel García Márquez, *One Hundred Years of Solitude*, trans. Gregory Rabassa (1967; New York: Avon Books, 1970), p. 277.

4 José Ortega y Gasset, *Meditations on Quixote*, trans. Julián Marías (New York: W.W. Norton, 1961), p. 113.

5 Denis Donoghue, "Safe in the Hands of the Uncanny," *New York Times Book Review*, April 8, 1990, p. 15.

6 Henry James, "Preface to *The Altar of the Dead*" (volume 17 in the New York edition), in *The Art of the Novel: Critical Prefaces* (Boston: Northeastern University Press, 1984), p. 256.

7 For a comparative history of the development of these terms and concepts in various European cultural traditions, see Jean Weisgerber, "La Locution et le concept," in *Le Réalisme magique: roman, peinture et cinéma*, ed. Jean Weisgerber (Lausanne: L'Age d'Homme, 1987), pp. 11–32. Seymour Menton discusses Post-Expressionism in light of Franz Roh's formula in *Magic Realism Rediscovered: 1918–1981* (Philadelphia: Art Alliance Press, 1983).

P A R T   I

Foundations

FRANZ ROH

Magic Realism: Post-Expressionism

Editors' Note

Writing in German in 1925 to champion a new direction in painting, Franz Roh originates the term Magic Realism to characterize this new painting's return to Realism after Expressionism's more abstract style. With the term, Roh praises Post-Expressionism's realistic, figural representation, a critical move that contrasts with our contemporary use of the term to signal the contrary tendency, that is, a text's *departure* from realism rather than its reengagement of it. According to Roh, the "convulsive life" and "fiery exaltation" of Expressionism have yielded to the representation of vigorous life in a "civil, metallic, restrained" manner. He describes the ways in which the Post-Expressionist painting of the 1920s returns to a renewed delight in real objects even as it integrates the formal innovations and spiritual thrust of Expressionism, which had shown "an exaggerated preference for fantastic, extraterrestrial, remote objects." In his statement in the preface to his book, "with the word 'magic,' as opposed to 'mystic,' I wished to indicate that the mystery does not descend to the represented world, but rather hides and palpitates behind it," he anticipates the practice of contemporary magical realists.

Roh's 1925 essay was translated into Spanish and published by José Ortega y Gasset's influential *Revista de Occidente* in Madrid in 1927; it was also published in Spanish in expanded form as a book in the same year.[1] We provide a translation of the widely circulated *Revista de Occidente* article here. The actual influence of Roh's art-historical argument on the literary practice of magical realism is taken up by Irene Guenther in the essay following Roh's.

I attribute no special value to the title "magical realism." Since the work had to have a name that meant something, and the word "Post-Expressionism" only indicates ancestry and chronological relationship, I added the first title quite a long time after having written this work. It seems to me, at least, more appropriate than "Ideal Realism" or "Verism," or "Neoclassicism," which only designate an aspect of the movement. "Superrealism" means, at this time, something else. With the word "magic," as opposed to "mystic," I wish to indicate that the mystery does not descend to the represented world, but rather hides and palpitates behind it (as will become clear in what follows). — Frauenkirch, Davos, March 1925.[2]

The New Objects

The phases of all art can be distinguished quite simply by means of the particular *objects* that artists perceive, among all the objects in the world, thanks to an act of selection that is already an act of creation. One might attempt a history of art that would list the favorite *themes* of each era without omitting those whose absence would be equally meaningful. Of course, this would only give us the foundations for a system of characteristics; nevertheless, it would constitute the elementary, indeed the only fruitful, groundwork for wider research. There is, however, a second path open to research on objects. That other way, which transcends the thematic statistics I have just mentioned, would strive to determine, for example, whether an era notoriously fond of painting the heads of old people chose to paint old people as withered or lymphatic. None of this research concerns form. Only later begins the formal operation that reworks preceding layers. In the same way, in reverse fashion, particular objects can have an obscure and inexplicable influence over particular methods of painting. But that would catapult us into an unknown realm of historico-artistic research.

We will indicate here, in a cursory way, the point at which the new painting separates itself from Expressionism *by means of its objects*. Immediately we find that in its reaction to Impressionism, Expressionism shows an exaggerated preference for fantastic, extraterrestrial, remote objects. Naturally, it also resorts to the everyday and the commonplace for the purpose of distancing it, investing it with a shocking exoticism. Many religious themes suddenly appeared in our country, which had been so secular until then; the ultimate religious symbols (which the church rarely modifies) were employed with sudden daring. If a picture portrayed a city, for example, it resembled the destruction produced by volcanic lava and not just a play of forms or the booty of an agitated cubism. If the theme was erotic, it often degenerated into savage sensuality. If devilish men were depicted, they had the faces of cannibals. If animals appeared, they were horses of a heavenly blue or red cows that, even in their objective reality, had to carry us beyond what we could experience on earth. If a painter wanted to sing the exuberance of southern provinces in a landscape, he came up with the tropics of an extraterrestrial world where men of our race burned like piles of paper under dry flames of color. But above all (as in Chagall's work) animals walked in the sky; behind the transparent brain of the viewer, also present in the picture, appeared towns and villages; overly vehement and heated heads popped like corks from overflowing bottles; grandiose chromatic storms flared through all these beings; and the farthest reaches of the pictures appeared mysteriously close to the foregrounds.

The Expressionist serials and reviews were called *The Last Judgment, Fire, Storm, Dawn*. These titles are enough to reveal the world of objects favored at that time.

But let us glance at the pictures reproduced at the end of this book.[3] It seems to us that this fantastic dreamscape has completely vanished and that our real world re-emerges before our eyes, bathed in the clarity of a new day. We recognize this world, although now—not only because we have emerged from a dream—we look on it with new eyes. The religious and transcendental themes have largely disappeared in recent painting. In contrast, we are offered a new style that is thoroughly of this world, that celebrates the mundane. Instead of the mother of God, the purity of a shepherdess in the fields (Schrimpf). Instead of the remote horrors of hell, the inextinguishable horrors of our own time (Grosz and Dix). It feels as if that roughshod and frenetic transcendentalism, that devilish detour, that flight from the world have died and now an insatiable love for terrestrial things and a delight in their fragmented and limited nature has reawakened. One could say that once again a profound calm and thoughtfulness prevails, a calm that is perhaps a prelude to a new flight, launched with a more mature knowledge and earthly substance. Humanity seems destined to oscillate forever between devotion to the world of dreams and adherence to the world of reality. And really, if this breathing rhythm of history were to cease, it might signal the death of the spirit.

Reactionaries believe unequivocally that with the new art such a moment has arrived. But considered carefully, this new world of objects is still alien to the current idea of Realism. How it stupefies the rearguard and seems to them almost as inappropriate as Expressionism itself! How it employs various techniques inherited from the previous period, techniques that endow all things with a deeper meaning and reveal mysteries that always threaten the secure tranquility of simple and ingenuous things: excessively large bodies, lying with the weight of blocks on a skimpy lawn; objects that don't imitate the least movement but that end surprisingly real, strange mysterious designs that are nevertheless visible down to their smallest details!

All heads, hands, bodies, objects that express "convulsive life," "fiery exaltation"; in short, anything nervous has become suspect in this new art, for which nervousness represents *wasted* forces. Truly vigorous life is imagined to be civil, metallic, restrained. We don't need to describe in detail the kinds of men, women, children, animals, trees, and rocks that we produced in the past.

Finally, the new art does not belong to the series of initial artistic phases that includes Expressionism. It is a movement of decantation and clarification that was fortunate enough to find right at the start an almost exhausted artistic revolution that had begun to discover new avenues. In addition, these circumstances habitually express themselves in a more measured group of themes. Is this the way to reconcile art and the people (largely through the reestablishment of objectivity)? The future will tell. History, of course, always shows that the bottom layer of the population, which experiences the monotony of hard labor, is more easily touched by discrete and prudent works than by lofty and inspired ones. *Biedermeier* painting, whose serene grandeur, barely exhausted even now, was always threatened by vulgar bourgeoisification; it has forced us to see the danger that prudent art courts when it caters to contemporary taste.

Objectivity

Objectivity is not equally important in all the arts. Music does not reproduce objects; it creates out of nothing, given the fact that its phenomena do not really attempt to refer to nature. Architecture does not attempt that reference either. But during the development of Expressionism, painting, which has somehow almost always held on to nature, went as far as it could toward rejecting its representative, imitative meaning; specific objectivity was suspected of lacking spirituality; in Futurism, the objective world appeared in an abrupt and dislocated form. On the other hand, Post-Expressionism sought to reintegrate reality into the heart of visibility. The elemental happiness of seeing again, of recognizing things, reenters. Painting becomes once again the mirror of palpable exteriority. That is the reason to speak of a New Realism without in any way alluding to the instinctive attitude that characterized previous Realisms in European art. The viewers who continue to prefer that attitude do not feel satisfied with this new "frigid, unanimated" Realism.

An example will explain what we mean by objectivity. When I see several apples on a table, I receive an extremely complex sensation (even without leaving the plane of aesthetic intuition). I am attracted not just by the breath of exquisite colors with which Impressionism entertained itself; not just by the varied designs of spherical, colored, and deformed shapes that captivated Expressionism. I am overcome by a much wider amalgam of colors, spatial forms, tactile representations, memories of smells and tastes; in short, a truly unending complex that we understand by the name of *thing*. Compared with Post-Expressionism's integrative attitude, Impressionism and Expressionism seem outmoded simplifications, limiting themselves now to fulgurations of chromatic surface, now to abstractions of stereometry and color; they steal the seductive integrity of objective phenomena from the viewer. But when painting returns to a full objectivity, all those relations and feelings that we do not find in pure harmonies of color and form reappear. It is clear that only after art had become abstract could feeling for the object, which had been dragged all over like a vague, vacuous and unsubstantial rag, flower again. Only then could the object again constitute a fundamental emotion and require a corresponding representation. After art has been spiritualized, objectivity once again becomes the most intense pleasure of painting.

We must admit that the world created like this in its most tangible reality offers us the fundamental artistic feeling of *existence* for the first time. But let us not forget (as we often have recently) that we can only become aware of the objective world if to these tactile impressions we add impressions of color and form, ordered according to a principle that is also valid for living. Of course the new art does not restore objectivity by using all sensory potential *in the same way:* what it principally evokes is a most prolific and detailed *tactile feeling*.

We may use the most varied circumstances to illustrate this idea. For Impressionism, that the world consisted of objects was an "obvious" fact not worth much attention; for the Impressionists, then, painting delighted in giving maximal value and meaning to chromatic texture, which floated in the air. Expressionism also considered the existence of objects to be patently "obvious" and looked for meaning in powerful and violent *formal rhythms;* vessels into which man's spirit (that of either an artist or a man of action) could pour everything. But the most recent painting attempts to discover a more general and deeper basis, without which the two previous enthusiasms could not have succeeded. Before, people were not at all devoted to the object: they took the exterior world which art molds and shapes for granted. In making what was formerly accepted as obvious into a "problem" for the first time, we enter a much deeper realm, even though some of the results may seem inadequate to us. This calm admiration of the magic of being, of the discovery that things already have their own faces, means that the ground in which the most diverse ideas in the world can take root has been reconquered—albeit in new ways.

The new art has been maligned for its rough drawing and "penetrating" execution. This criticism does not take account of the possibility of feeling existence, of making it stand out from the void; that a solidly modeled figure crystalizes itself, as if by a miracle, emerging from the most obscure source. Here, perhaps, the background is the last frontier, absolute nothingness, absolute death, from which something emerges and vibrates with energetic intensity.

This seems to be a more important viewpoint than the "objectivity" everyone keeps evoking. The latter doesn't acknowledge that radiation of magic, that spirituality, that lugubrious quality throbbing in the best works of the new mode, along with their coldness and apparent sobriety.

The great abstract system of Expressionism had tended more or less toward mural painting, in which a free rhythm filled broad surfaces that would affect the spectator from afar. But with Post-Expressionism, easel painting, pictures with frames, easily transportable works that delighted many tastes besides those of postmedieval Europe are enjoying a renaissance. Now, when a piece of imitated "reality" hangs on the wall it only makes sense if it starts from and then (consciously or unconsciously) transcends the representation of a window, that is, if it constitutes a magical gaze opening onto a piece of mildly transfigured "reality" (produced artificially).

This idea of a picture on a wall is prospering and increasing in popularity again. The clash of true reality and apparent reality (of the actual room with the visionary realm of the painting) has always had an elemental attraction. This enchantment is enjoyed now in a new way. Such a juxtaposition of reality and appearance was not possible until the recuperation of the objective world, which was largely lacking in Expressionism. Expressionism appeared to have already rejected the image of real nature in favor of an exclusively spiritual world.

With this new movement painting distances itself from the Expressionists' rivalry with music. Already with Kandinsky, painting had felt obliged to take second place to music because music unfolded in time and consequently had great expanses at its command, whereas easel painting continued to be an art of simultaneity. Painting could only contain a few measures, as it were, that could be embraced by a glance in a short space of time — a space of time in which a consummate condensation could be achieved nonetheless. Such a condensation evokes in the viewer the desire and even the need to remain for a long time in front of this instantaneous vision enclosed in a few measures, whereas an art of successive time (like music, the novel, drama, film) never ceases to insert new figures. This was a disadvantage for painting; unlike music, in the majority of countries and periods painting compensated for this shortcoming by synthesizing its concerns: painting became not only a harmonious form of expression but also a representation of objects, something that music could never really be. Thus, painting makes use of keys that can open in the viewer all the exciting emotions that come only from representing the object. The Expressionist way of seeing, according to which the only "true artistic and spiritual" technique was composition, the placing and design of lines and colors but not the portrayal of objects, was impossible to maintain. That way of seeing forgets that the sphere, expressive in and of itself, made of pure forms and colors, embodies a completely different meaning when it refers to object A and changes entirely if the same combination of forms refers to object B. A very simple example: a harmony of color and form, applied to the heart of a cabbage, embodies a completely different meaning when it is applied to a female nude; because in the second instance, without even considering other factors, there emerges an erotic meaning that the cabbage can never assume. Imagine the innovations that such a wide-ranging and original combination immediately imply. Furthermore, as far as expression goes, the (positive) darkness of an abstract form means something completely different from the (positive) darkness of a given object.

The Futurism of Severini, Boccioni, and Carrà had already recognized this when (as I have said) in the midst of a general confusion of purely compositional strokes, objects suddenly emerged, created, like voices from another world, only to disappear immediately. Many people dismissed this as something of no consequence; but the truth is that it produced an effect as stimulating as it was odd. So, just as with futurism, the miracle of *realistic depiction* appeared quickly in the midst of abstraction, only to lose itself again, so Post-Expressionism offers us the miracle of *existence in its imperturbable duration:* the unending miracle of eternally mobile and vibrating molecules. Out of that flux, that constant appearance and disappearance of material, permanent objects somehow appear: in short, the marvel by which a variable commotion crystallizes into a clear set of constants. This miracle of an apparent persistence and duration in the midst of a demoniacal flux; this enigma of total quietude in the midst of general becoming, of universal dissolution: this is what Post-Expressionism admires and highlights. For Expressionism, the deepest meaning, the reason it erects this world of permanent bodies as a symbol, lies in building something that by means of its very persistence resists eternal fluidity. Post-Expressionism faithfully raises a pane of glass in front of a light and is surprised that it doesn't "melt," that it doesn't inevitably transform itself, that it is accorded a brief stay in eternity. It is the same feeling that motivates the invocation of norms, of ethical and even political positions, from either the right or the left. And this is not a result of intimate inertia; it is the glimmer from which the *élan vital* (the previous generation's philosophy of life) cannot save us. So then, New Objectivity is something more than the simple respect for the objective world in which we are submerged. In addition, we see juxtaposed in harsh tension and contrast the forms of the spirit and the very solidity of objects, which the will must come up against if it wishes to make them enter its system of coordinates. The spirit cannot show itself in the open with such facility and speed as Expressionism thought it could; in the end, Expressionism aimed at disrupting the world as it existed in the structure of the Self, which in turn resisted such disruption. At least this is how New Realism, Ideal Realism, understands the Expressionist generation. It is true, says the New Realism, that Expressionism has broken with individualism in directing meditation toward the basic fundamentals of all human sensation; but it hasn't abandoned subjectivity (a collective subjectivity) at all, because the very consistency of the world has degenerated almost entirely into the special rhythms of the collective subject.

One could say of Cubism, as a basic comparison, that it painted what we might call pre-forms, primordial forms, categories of human perception, at the same time that it depicted perceived matter. Likewise, it can be said that without losing sight of its own modeling force (we are still dealing with the very definite means of composition that it employs) today's art proposes to catch reality as such, instead of evading it with a sudden and inspired stroke. This new art is situated resolutely between extremes, between vague sensuality and highly structured schematics, as true philosophy may be located between ingenuous realism and exalted idealism.

In order to clarify the situation of this art in relation to the world of objects, we can compare it not only to the kind of man who contemplates and knows but also to a new kind of man of *action*. The end of the nineteenth century, including Impressionism, gave many men a new capacity for enjoyment, a new sense of smell and even a new knowledge of *existing* reality. The Expressionist generation rightly contrasted such men with another kind of man who imposes ethical norms, who constructs the future according to preconceived plans, a utopian who scorns mere knowledge of past life, a nobler and more audacious kind of man who truly moves the world and who — even indirectly — has always pushed it decisively in the direction of its evolution. The most recent art corresponds, however, to a third class of man who, without losing anything of his constructivist ideals, nonetheless knows how to reconcile that desire with a greater respect for reality, with a closer knowledge of what exists, of the objects he transforms and exalts. This kind of man is neither the "empirical" Machiavellian politician nor the apolitical man who listens only to the voice of an ethical ideal, but a man at once political *and* ethical, in whom both characteristics are equally prominent. The new position, if it survives, will exist on a middle ground not through weakness but, on the contrary, through energy and an awareness of its strength. It will be a sharp edge, a narrow ledge between two chasms on the right and the left.

The Proximity of the Object as Spiritual Creation

Painting now seems to feel the reality of the object and of space, not like copies of nature but like another creation. We have already seen that Expressionism in its last stages was very enamored of the "spiritual." This recent painting could not, then, fall back into amorphous sensuality, although here and there it does court that danger. It manifests its interior point of departure more purely than does nineteenth-century Realism, revealing its compositional structure with a different kind of clarity. It continues to approach the ultimate enigmas and harmonies of existence through a hidden stereometry. It also believes that Being consists of fundamentally simple forms and that in the best modern works these forms are metallic and quiescent. The new idea of "realistic depiction" as it is rigorously conceived wishes to make such forms concretely evident in nature rather than in the abstract. To depict realistically is not to portray or copy but rather to build rigorously, to construct objects that exist in the world in their particular primordial shape. The old Aristotelian idea of imitation had already gained a spiritual quality. For the new art, it is a question of representing before our eyes, in an intuitive way, *the fact, the interior figure, of the exterior world*. This mattered very little to Expressionism.

The point is not to discover the spirit beginning with objects but, on the contrary, to discover objects beginning with the spirit; for that reason, one accords consummate value to the process in which spiritual form remains large, pure, and clear. This second objective world thereby rigorously resembles the first, the existing world, but it is a purified world, a referential world. We have already seen that we cannot leap out of the existing world and jump into the free spaces of pure spirit, as Expressionism often tried to do. Post-Expressionism, in holding to existing exteriority, wants to say clearly that we have to shape the world we find in front of us.

This is how we must understand what today's historical situation shows us so extraordinarily well: that the invention and re-establishment of the object can reveal to us the idea of creation. It is well known that the nineteenth century rarely attempted anything other than extrinsic imitation, and hence it had to remain seated in front of nature or works of art or plaster casts, limiting itself in the end to copying the object before its eyes. When, in violent reaction to this, Expressionism had crystallized the object's exclusively *internal* aspect, the unusual opportunity of looking at *the object close up* from the other side had arrived; in other words, the opportunity of reconstructing the object, starting exclusively from our interiority. Thus, returning to the previous example of the apples, today we could say that the fantastic apples of Expressionism may belong to a better world because it is simpler and more circumscribed, but that they lack true existence. Speaking in moral terms, we could almost say that the Expressionist ideal has not been realized because of the tragic fact that creating the best always means a compromise with what already exists.

The way in which the restorative process of this new painting operates here is quite clear. A painter like Schrimpf, who attempts to create the exterior world with the utmost precision, considers it very important not to paint outdoors, not to use a model, to have everything flow from the interior image to the canvas. That is why he paints his landscapes in his studio, almost always without a model or even a sketch. Nevertheless, he repeatedly insists that the landscape be definitively, rigorously, a *real* landscape that could be confused with an existing one. He wants it to be "real," to impress us as something ordinary and familiar and, nevertheless, to be magic by virtue of that isolation in the room: even the last little blade of grass can *refer to* the spirit. That is the painter's aim—of course, he doesn't always achieve it. Only when the creative process achieves its goal from the inside out can it generate new views of reality, which is at most built in pieces, never imitated as a whole.

The opposite side of this double-sided art that struggles between opposites appears in the painting of Kanoldt, for example, who builds his landscapes out of Italian cities because he feels certain of their spiritual content, working whenever possible in nature, outside. Thus he accentuates and intensifies the power of the object.

As long as Post-Expressionism works with this dialectic, it will be open to a thousand spiritual possibilities. But if it degenerates into a simple external imitation (as can easily happen in this difficult attempt at objectification), it will become less significant and painting will find itself trampled to death by those marvelous machines (photography and film) that imitate reality so incomparably well.

The New Space

As we have previously suggested, the partisans of nineteenth-century sensuous Realism reject the new painting's Realism as schematic, intellectual, constructed, inert, frigid. In fact, what happens is that the *feeling of space* has changed. To understand that change, we will compare the latest styles of landscape painting. The Impressionists represented space from the perspective of air, of vaporous atmosphere: that is, they gasified and shattered color on the intervening atmosphere. But in attempting to create a shimmering colored vapor to fill the whole picture, and in conceiving of the whole world as a chromatic veil, what Impressionism actually achieved was a flattening of space. Matter visualized in form and color was caught as in a gaseous substance on the picture plane. It was impossible to say whether this matter was projected by an object situated *behind* the intervening surface or by an object *in front of* this projection screen. Thus, in the age of Impressionism people talked a great deal about the value of the *visual plane,* so much did its theory owe to a contemporaneous current of classicism (Fiedler, Hildebrand). But after Expressionism the demands of the surface decreased. The desire for spatiality re-emerged, bringing with it a certain ambiguity. Painters felt depth to be primary and placed everything obliquely to emphasize the force of foreshortening. The canvas, which was made to reveal extended surface qualities in both Impressionism and Impressionist classicism (Hildebrand did not understand sculpture except as a continuation of bas relief, a conception in which he was basically wrong), was deepened, hollowed out, and filled with depressions and elevations. But it was always a matter of adjacent spaces that invaded and assaulted the foreground. Furthermore, all the foreshortened figures appeared to move forward rather than backward (something that could have happened in the middle- and backgrounds as well). However, every foreshortened figure could be given a different trajectory. From that principle the rough and often ferocious aggressivity of purely Expressionist paintings emerged.

In adopting a classical position again, the most recent painting conciliates and synthesizes the decisive elements of these three possibilities that have appeared in the history of art. The best new landscapes reveal a constant surface, to which is added a certain forward thrust (in this case as if the painter were "displaying" the shape for us), but they also make use of distance. Thus in the same way that (as we will see shortly) the delight in the juxtaposition of small and large is felt again, so another polarity and juxtaposition is also reestablished: I refer to the juxtaposition of the far and the near, which in the new painting are reconciled and face each other. This meeting is now asserted more purely and not, as in Impressionism, through intermediate veils and vaporizing, dissolving, conciliating atmospheres. It could be said that the new landscapes, like the landscapes of the fifteenth and sixteenth centuries, move vigorously forward, at the same time that they recede into the far distance. In Post-Expressionism the bird's-eye view, which Expressionism reapplied but which Impressionism prohibited because it sacrificed the flatness of the picture plane, embodies that double meaning. They must have sensed at some point — so the Expressionists proudly declared of their landscapes — how to penetrate deeply into the distance, how to "really" enter into the picture. These words manifest the exalted feeling of reality that makes the picture a suggestive spatial unity, whose floor invites footsteps. These landscapes on the wall no longer try (as those by Marees did) to spring from surface force, from the continuous feeling of the wall, as we have said elsewhere.

Art tries over and over again to picture the whole volume of space, making it felt through its division into three dimensions. While the Gothic (including painting) expresses extension primarily as an upward thrust, the Renaissance deliberately extends volume horizontally in order to savor it fully. In contrast, as is well known, the Baroque attempts to throw it all into the vortex of depth. With a charm that goes unrecognized today, the best fifteenth-century painting establishes a calm juxtaposition between breadth of surface and depth of field. This juxtaposition produces a magnificent intensity that contrasts, on the one hand, with the era of Raphael and Titian, and, on the other, with the nineteenth century (at least during its second half), where we find only the rigors of surface with no compensating factors. Today we see a renewed sensitivity to the dynamics of depth and direction, a sensitivity that is a distinguishing feature of Post-Expressionism.

Recall, finally, that in both its horizontal extensions and its elevations, Expressionism searches for a secret geometry. That is why we can say that (to the advantage of the new painting) Expressionism has still not disappeared.

Smaller than Natural (Miniature)

The rigorous dedication to the object functions in very different ways in the most recent art, but it almost always manifests itself in miniature form. It seeks to endow the viewer, who is frequently too cursory and careless in his knowledge of the world and in his idealism, with a penetrating and meticulous lucidity.

By miniature we mean a fine and exact painting, executed on a very small surface; a painting whose decisive character typically comes from its minimal exterior dimensions. Though it is true that the narrowness of the surface compels all representation to search for smallness from within, this is no more than the extrinsic and superficial concept of miniature. The *intrinsic* miniature (which can encompass also very large paintings, a typical example of which is Altdorfer's *Battle of Alexander*) is art produced by attempting to locate *infinity* in small things. This is the idea of the miniature that takes its inspiration from a *special way of intuiting the world* and, as such, can apply to all the arts, even music. Its opposite pole is another feeling for life, which animates monumental art, an idea that applies equally to all the arts. This idea of monumentality is not limited to external dimensions either. Thus, for example, *The Lacemaker* by Vermeer is a little painting the size of a plate that nevertheless produces the impression of a poster the size of a house. The miniature and the monument are two poles situated beyond the development of styles, at a distance from known spiritual models. For this reason they must be investigated on their own terms. Vermeer has painted a small object, the bust of a woman, and Altdorfer, in contrast, a gigantic battlefield with a panoramic view of the mountains. In order to understand the aesthetic means used here, it is not enough to say that the "monumental" painter seeks the foreground while the other represents distances with his small shapes. It is more important to notice that the "monumental" man piles up shapes in large groups while the "microscopic" one establishes the largest possible number of subdivisions. When the latter does not have a multipartite object in front of him, like thickets of leaves or fibers of grass or human masses spread out over the horizon, then he carves, separates, and divides the foreground. (The painting by Vermeer I mentioned above can be sketched perfectly well by accenting the small parts, without objects branching off into space in the way we see them, for example, in the well-known reproduction by Unger, who altered Vermeer's formal continuity, converting it into the prolixity of the nineteenth century.)

The spiritual type of painting that seeks what is powerful becomes caricature by virtue of its emphatic presentation and its statuesque turgidity. The other type, which cultivates the profound meaning of the diminutive, usually plunges us into tedious minutia that scatter and confuse our attention. In the best periods, both possibilities almost always coincide, which is what happened in the late Gothic period, even at the point when it was already becoming the Renaissance. (One of the most timeless examples is Dürer, especially in his copper engravings.) Expressionism tended exclusively toward the monumental; Post-Expressionism again becomes the triumphal synthesis of both tendencies. However, the tension between the two possibilities should never be suppressed. In this way Post-Expressionism avoids (consciously or unconsciously) any central "organic" line that would divide these modes of representation; on the contrary, it tends to weave them together. Thus in wide compositions we find the world of smallness ensconced at regular intervals, so to speak. At other times the hostility of the two opposing tendencies remains. Schrimpf insolently knocks large bodies down on the smallness of grass, thereby juxtaposing its diminutive fibers with the vigor of the human form. Or again, a painter may enjoy positioning a powerfully foregrounded *near* shape in front of dimunitive details in the *distance,* as the southern Italians of the quattro-cento liked to do, when the minutiae of the late Gothic coexisted genially with the massed volumes of the Renaissance.

The extent to which the miniature can express maximum power *all by itself* can be explained by thinking of the greatest spectacle that nature offers us, a sight that contains the smallest units, almost simple points placed on the prodigious surface width of the picture: *the spectacle of the starry sky, through which we experience infinity.*

The desire for precision and refinement motivated both the Construc-tivists and their sworn enemies the Verists. So that even when the theme is abstract (as in Léger, Feininger, Schlemmer), we see a sharper, more minute, cleaner structure than in the first five years of Expressionism. We must distinguish this phenomenon from Post-Expressionism's tendency— which I described earlier—to reappropriate the real world in painting. We could say that in this new painting the very system of categories has been refined, gaining in clarity, richness, and precision.

Two types of miniatures take on completely contradictory meanings in the different styles of Expressionism, a phenomenon that we need to note here, although we will reserve the study of these different styles for later. In Grosz and Dix this miniaturism tries to present the *horrible side* of the world in the crudest manner and in all its minute detail, but still without any political overtones. Later comes the political meaning, and it attempts to give us a microscopic image of social ills, to put them under the very noses of the bourgeoisie, who usually refuse to look at such disagreeable sights. In contrast, Schrimpf and Spiess celebrate the intimacy of everyday life with precise fidelity; they conceive of the world as a handful of grass, an anthill, and wish once again to evoke the long-forgotten and exquisite quality of the diminutive in art.

In addition, an erroneous judgment has been hanging over all this, namely that in representing small things one necessarily falls into spiri-tual pettiness. I have already mentioned Altdorfer's *Battle of Alexander.* Divided into a thousand little pieces, it is something final and definitive, in exactly the same way as *The Last Judgment* conceived on a large scale by Rubens or Michelangelo. In science the same thing applies: the planetary microcosm of the atom is a mystery in the end, no less than the macro-cosm of astronomy. Now then, both kinds of miniaturist painting (the one that reconciles us to the world, and the one that tries to horrify us) imply an orientation toward the infinity of small things, of the microcosm. One must, therefore, be very careful not to apply the criteria of Impressionism and Expressionism automatically and, basing ourselves on their fluctuating and monumental characters, deprecate this faithful devotion to small things, this "nitpicking," as Dürer put it. This "nitpicking" is, in fact, like the slow steps of a magnificent parade and reveals a profound new meaning.

The most recent painting coincides with Expressionism in painting pictures of vast scope. But while Expressionism was entirely consumed with this effort, Postexpressionist paintings open the way to meticulous expression. *Now* is when we really draw near to the painting of the late Middle Ages, often allegedly without a motif, from which Expressionism took the geometric plan of large scale composition. On entering the church, the ensemble of an altar painting unfolded its essential meaning at a hundred paces, and then, as the distance diminished, revealed little by little the new world of the very small in successive planes of details, details that were symbolic of all true *spiritual* knowledge of the world because they always remained subordinate to the total structure. Thus the viewer could satiate himself with minutiae, with the thickness and density of all cosmic relationships. Perhaps many Postexpressionist pictures offer the appearance of something slow and laborious at first sight; but eventually, after we have absorbed them, they offer us secret delights and intimate charms that the pure unifying idealism of abstract art never even imagined. Impressionism and Expressionism aspired to an exciting, surprising, suggestive art that with their vast grids aimed at stimulating man's fantasy, his personal associations, and his creations. But the latest painting wants to offer us the image of something totally finished and complete, minutely formed, opposing it to our eternally fragmented and ragged lives as an archetype of integral structuring, down to the smallest details. Someday man too will be able to recreate himself in the perfection of this idea.

Translated by Wendy B. Faris

Translator's Notes

1 Roh's original work is *Nach-Expressionismus, Magischer Realismus: Probleme der neuesten Europäischen Malerei* (Leipzig, Klinkhardt and Biermann, 1925). Roh takes up the issue of definition again in a later article, "Ruckblick auf den Magischen Realismus," in *Das Kunstwerk* 6, 1 (1952): 7–9. In Spanish the

book is Franz Roh, *Realismo mágico, post expresionismo: Problemas de la pintura europea más reciente*, trans. (from the German) Fernando Vela (Madrid: Revista de Occidente, 1927); the article is "Realismo mágico: Problemas de la pintura europea más reciente," trans. Fernando Vela, *Revista de Occidente* 16 (April, May, June 1927): 274–301. This translation is from the Spanish. I have consistently capitalized the term Magic Realism in accordance with art historical usage.

2 Preface to the book cited above, from which this essay is excerpted.

3 At the end of the book from which this essay is excerpted are a series of about ninety reproductions of paintings. The first several pages consist of comparative pairings illustrating the contrast between Expressionism and Magic Realism. Kandinsky is juxtaposed with Carrà, Delaunay with de Chirico and Citroen, Metzinger with Schrimpf, and Schmidt-Rottluf with Mense. Other painters whom Roh includes in the group of new Magic Realists are Schottz, Spies, Borje, Herbin, Miró, Nebel, Huber, Grosz, Dix, Picasso, Davringhausen, Galanis, etc.

IRENE GUENTHER

Magic Realism, New Objectivity, and the Arts
during the Weimar Republic

In 1920, leading critics and artists perceived Expressionism as having
nothing more to say. It was resolutely pronounced "*tot,*" dead.[1] The "child"
anxiously awaiting to take Expressionism's place, however, needed a "real
name."[2] This proved problematical because the child, the artistic trend
nipping at the heels of Expressionism even before 1920, defied easy cate-
gorization. At the time, no one viewed this new trend as a movement; no
cohesive artists' groups formed, and the artists themselves proposed no
theories except for a few disparate pronouncements. The one tendency
that seemed to hold the child together was its complete repudiation of
Expressionism, but this renunciation did not hold up in the ensuing art
historical discourse.[3] The child did not even embody one coherent style,
but instead comprised numerous characteristics, new ways of seeing and
depicting the familiar, the everyday. It was, in effect, *ein neuer Realismus*
(a new Realism).[4]

To complicate matters, the child was not given a simple name to con-
note its chronological place in art history, as Roger Fry had done with
"Post-Impressionism." Rather, it was baptized twice within a very short
timespan—*Magischer Realismus* (Magic Realism) by the German art historian Franz Roh,[5] and *Neue Sachlichkeit* (New Objectivity)[6] by the German
museum director Gustav Hartlaub.[7] More complications ensued. From the
outset, Hartlaub viewed his child as having two distinct characteristics, a
right-wing, sometimes idyllic, Neoclassicist trait[8] and a left-wing, political, Veristic one.[9] Roh, although acknowledging these variations, at first
analyzed his child in more aesthetic, stylistic terms.[10]

Hartlaub's New Objectivity quickly eclipsed Roh's Magic Realism in the
art world, in part because of the famous *Neue Sachlichkeit* exhibition of
1925. Roh's term did not reappear until a new interest in the Weimar Re-

public and German art of the time gave rise to a flurry of publications and exhibitions beginning in the 1960s.

From that time on, art historians began dissecting the movement in Marxist vs. non-Marxist terms,[11] by geographical location, artistic characteristics, political affiliation, and social content, sometimes separating Magic Realism from New Objectivity, sometimes treating them as one.[12] And sometimes, both terms were thrown out, as divergent aspects of the movement were subsumed under the rubric *Realismus* or Realism.[13] However, as discussed in the subsequent essays in this volume, Magic Realism found its way into literature in diversified forms. Pictorial in origin, the term eventually became a widely used literary concept.

In order to bridge the gap between Roh's artistic formulation and its literary connotations, an historical context and aesthetic explanation of the term are needed. Because of the fluidity of boundaries, the ambiguity of definitions, and the sometimes untraceable transformation of concepts, conjecture and fact have intertwined in the history of Magic Realism and its eventual dissemination. In effect, Roh's artistic child of the 1920s has become a present-day historian's nightmare.

The concept of *"magischer Idealismus"* (magical idealism) in German philosophy is an old one.[14] Novalis, at the end of the eighteenth century, wrote of a "magical idealist" and a "magical realist" in the realm of philosophy.[15] It is, however, with Franz Roh's 1925 publication, *Nach-Expressionismus, Magischer Realismus: Probleme der neuesten Europäischen Malerei* (Post-Expressionism, Magic Realism: Problems of the Newest European Painting), that the term *Magischer Realismus* (Magic Realism) was employed in an artistic context.[16] Two years earlier, Gustav Hartlaub had announced his intention of organizing an exhibit based on the theme of *Neue Sachlichkeit* (New Objectivity), a project also brought to fruition in 1925, the same year that Adolf Hitler's book, *Mein Kampf* (My Struggle), was published. It is to Roh's Magic Realism that we will first turn our attention.

From the outset, Roh did not place any special value on his term Magic Realism. The new art style that he saw emerging all over Europe[17] "needed a real name," an aesthetic descriptive alongside its time referent, *Nach-Expressionismus* (Post-Expressionism). Magic Realism seemed preferable to Ideal Realism, Verism, and Neoclassicism, since each of those designated only a part of the whole (preface, n.p.). Yet, Roh felt ambivalent about employing the term from the start.

Moreover, Roh never gave a concise definition of Magic Realism. His

1925 work, however, contains a list of characteristics and adjectives sprinkled throughout with which he formulated his conception of the new art. In his book, Roh insists on a "cold cerebral approach" (27) by the artist and on the "intellectual statism" of the work (69). The term "magic" as opposed to "mystic" is meant to imply that the "secret" should not enter into the realistically depicted world, but should hold itself back behind this world (preface, n.p.). Objects, depicted in their minutiae, appear as "strange shadows or phantoms" (25). Elsewhere, Roh writes of an "inner spiritual texture" in all of its purity (37)[18] and a "matter of clarity" by which the structure of the composition is unveiled (36).

The world of painted objects Roh describes does not "reproduce" nature through instinct, but "recreates" it (36). Reality is "reconstructed" through "spiritual" phenomena (37). This drive for a "spiritual reconstruction" proceeds in tandem with the artist's conviction of the problematical character of the objective, palpable, phenomenal universe (29). Sometimes, when the empirical no longer suffices, it "yields with astonishment before the magic of Being" (29–30). "Magic" in this sense, Roh explains, suggests neither a return "to the spiritual" in an "ethnological" sense (30, 38)[19] nor to a "demonic irrationalism" or "naive vitalism" (68). Instead, "magic of Being" refers to "an authentic rationalism" which "venerates" as a "miracle" the "world's rational organization"—"*ein Magischer Rationalismus*," a magical rationalism (67–68).

In his 1925 book, Roh listed twenty-two characteristics of the new Post-Expressionist art in contrast with those of Expressionism (119–20). By 1958, when Roh published *Geschichte der Deutschen Kunst von 1900 bis zur Gegenwart* (published in English as *German Art in the Twentieth Century*) he had reduced the characteristics to fifteen. He had also replaced the heading *Nachexpressionismus* [*sic*] with *Neue Sachlichkeit*, in recognition that his terms *Magischer Realismus* and *Nach-Expressionismus* had been eclipsed by Hartlaub's *Neue Sachlichkeit*. They are as follows:

EXPRESSIONISM	NEW OBJECTIVITY
1. Ecstatic subjects	Sober subjects
2. Suppression of the object	The object clarified
3. Rhythmical	Representational
4. Extravagant	Puristically severe
5. Dynamic	Static
6. Loud	Quiet
7. Summary	Thorough

8.	Close-up view	Close and far view
9.	Monumental	Miniature
10.	Warm (hot)	Cold
11.	Thick color texture	Thin paint surface
12.	Rough	Smooth
13.	Emphasis on the visibility of the painting process	Effacement of the painting process
14.	Centrifugal	Centripetal
15.	Expressive deformation	External purification of the object[20]

Roh also provided a list of artists whose works were included in his book as well as a supplemental list of painters not included, but whose works exemplified certain tendencies of Magic Realism (133–34).[21] Subjects most often painted include the city square, the metropolis, still lifes, portraits, and landscapes (125–27). Clearly, it was not the subject matter that made this art so different. Rather, it was the fastidious depiction of familiar objects, the new way of seeing and rendering the everyday, thereby "creating a new world view," that inspired the style. As New Objectivity artist Grethe Jürgens noted, "It is the discovery of a totally new world. One paints pots and rubbish piles, and then suddenly sees these things quite differently, as if one had never before seen a pot. One paints a landscape, trees, houses, vehicles, and one sees the world anew. One discovers like a child an adventure-filled land. One looks at technological objects with different eyes when one paints them or sees them in new paintings."[22]

The goal of this post-World War I art was a new definition of the object, clinically dissected, coldly accentuated, microscopically delineated. Over-exposed, isolated, rendered from an uncustomary angle, the familiar became unusual, endowed with an *Unheimlichkeit* (uncanniness) which elicited fear and wonder. The juxtaposition of "magic" and "realism" reflected far more the monstrous and marvelous *Unheimlichkeit* within human beings and inherent in their modern technological surroundings, of which both Freud and de Chirico wrote,[23] than "the psychological-philosophical ideas of Carl Jung," as Seymour Menton has asserted.[24] Roh later recalled, "For a while, one was so in awe of objects that they received new, secret meanings as pictures. Objectivism as spiritual creation."[25]

Originally, both Roh's Magic Realism and Hartlaub's New Objectivity denoted the same thing: a mode of art that had come into being with the

1. Ludwig Meidner, "Burning City," 1913. (St. Louis Art Museum, Morton D. May Bequest)

demise of Expressionism and the aftermath of World War I. It was an art that was firm in compositional structure and was, once again, representational. In reaction to Expressionism's apocalyptic visions (figure 1), heated color palette, utopian message, and the shattering disillusionment which followed the war, this post-Expressionist art concerned itself with the tangible real, the familiar. After the emotional fervor of Expressionism, as well as the horrors of the war and subsequent German Revolution, artists searched for "soberness" and "freedom from all sentimentality." [26]

Already in 1914, however, the artist Ludwig Meidner pleaded with his fellow artists to return to painting the magnificent and the unusual, the monstrous and the dramatic inherent in tumultuous city streets, train stations, factories, and nights in the big city. [27] He cautioned them not to resort to the techniques of the Impressionists from the 1870s and 1880s, like Camille Pissaro or Claude Monet, since these would be inadequate tools with which to depict the contemporary world. Artists would do best to forget these previous methods. Instead, they should develop new techniques, learn to see more intensively and more correctly than had their Impressionist precursors in order to penetrate reality in all of its depths.[28] What, by 1918, Meidner described as an emerging "fantastic, ardent Naturalism" was, in fact, the beginning of a decisive new Realism in the paintings of the 1920s;[29] a Realism that was labeled Magic Realism by Roh and New Objectivity by Hartlaub.

In 1919 an announcement appeared in *Das Kunstblatt* that noted the appearance of a new Italian journal, *Valori Plastici*, under the editorship of Mario Broglio, which "fights with enthusiasm for the newest art." Painters whose works were reproduced included Giorgio de Chirico, Giorgio Morandi, and Roberto Melli. Carlo Carrà, who had recently published his book, *Pintura Metafisica* (Metaphysical Paintings), received center stage. The announcement continued: "Characteristic of this whole group of younger artists is a singular, extreme Verism which applies a correct, hard drawing suppressing any individual style. In Germany, as one knows, George Grosz and Heinrich Davringhausen are on the same road."[30]

The *arte metafisica* (metaphysical art) of de Chirico and Carrà greatly influenced German artists like Max Ernst, George Grosz, and Anton Räderscheidt.[31] De Chirico exhibited in Italy for the first time in 1919. Already by the end of that year, Max Ernst had seen reproductions of the Italian's works at Galerie Goltz in Munich, which had a copy of the journal *Valori Plastici*. His reaction to de Chirico's paintings was one of sheer amazement.[32] Broglio's art gallery, also called *Valori Plastici*, put together traveling exhibits of the *Scuola Metafisica* paintings. Several of these shows came to Germany in 1921 and had an enormous impact there.[33] In recent years, de Chirico's works of the pre-war period have been considered "forerunners of Magic Realism"[34] as well as the principal precursors of Surrealism;[35] his influence has been assessed as greater than any other painter on the artists of New Objectivity.[36]

De Chirico's bleak new world (figure 2), with its appearances of objects isolated and mysterious, his pictorial vision of modern man's alienation and disorientation, were recognized by Franz Roh as extremely important in the development of Magic Realism. He included two paintings by de Chirico and Carrà in his *Nach-Expressionismus, Magischer Realismus* book. It is especially in de Chirico's evocation of *Unheimlichkeit* (uncanniness, eeriness), his clarity of color, his precision and ordering, his use of sharp contrasts, his ability to make "the real appear unreal, the unreal real"[37] that he most coincides with those tendencies of New Objectivity

2. Giorgio de Chirico, "The Enigma of a Day," 1914. (Museum of Modern Art, New York, New York, James Thrall Soby Bequest)

art which Hartlaub enumerated in his exhibition catalog[38] and with those artists Roh labeled Magic Realists.[39]

In 1921 Roh saw the new artistic developments in full bloom at the early summer exhibitions of the Munich galleries. Especially at the Galerie Goltz, he noted that "the works do not only have a high quality, but present the new European trend in painting in which we are presently engaged: the trend toward a new objectivism, the rejection of all . . . [those] techniques which many contemporaries in the aftermath of Impressionism are still using. 'The pulsating life' has finally become an impossible metaphor, and any sort of Baroqueness like Greco appears strange to us. Everything shall appear solidly rounded and limited, but not in the direction of Matisse and others of the last decade. Instead of heavy conglomerates, there is a sharpened cleanliness, even minute articulation with internal drawing."[40]

What was taking shape, according to Roh, was a phenomenon on a European scale. In retrospect, he termed it a "movement which had as its goal a new definition of the object. Suddenly, once again, the depth-attraction of object accentuation was discovered. . . . In contrast to the expressive urge of sensibility, one now coldly accentuated the inner law of the objects in our surroundings . . . objects . . . in no way banal and obvious," but which "deserve to be gazed at in wonder and to be created anew."[41] Artists were reaching for the magic, the mystery behind the real.

In 1922, Paul Westheim, art historian and editor of *Das Kunstblatt*, published responses to a questionnaire he had sent out to authors, artists, art historians, museum directors, and critics. Westheim posed questions concerning the end of Expressionism and the appearance of the "New Naturalism" that was being debated in studios and in literature. Was this "New Naturalism" only a slogan or was it, indeed, something essential, vital? Did the new trend, "the child," warrant attention, a real name? Respondents included Wilhelm Pinder, Clive Bell, Alfred Döblin, Ernst Ludwig Kirchner, Adolf Behne, Wassily Kandinsky, Alexander Archipenko, and Gustav Hartlaub.

Opinions and descriptions of the new artistic manner varied widely. Pinder wrote, "the end of fruitful styles does not mean death but rather transformation. . . . Expressionism is not totally alienated from nature, Naturalism is not alienated from expression." Meidner advocated, within a religious framework, a "more deliberate [reflective] approach toward nature. . . . Greater respect for the object—I remind myself everyday!" Behne perceived the "Neo Naturalism" as a "demand by mostly the nouveaux-riches . . . the materialists. They long for a materialistic, naturalistic, objective art."

Kandinsky responded to Westheim's questionnaire, stating that the "period of the coming Realism will bring: freedom from conventionalism, narrowness and hate, enrichment of sensitivity and vitality. . . . Realism will serve abstraction. We, the abstract artists, will some day be seen as the champions of absolute art." Alfred Döblin asserted that "propagandizing a new 'Naturalism' would not help, just as it had not helped other developments. . . . Art comes not from knowing, but from being. . . . We are not in need of art products, but rather manifestations of life. . . . The being of the artist is the foundation of art . . . [and] indicate[s] . . . *that* one is and *what* one is."[42] Rudolf Grossmann thought it "more important to paint a good picture in all innocence than to stir up again the controversy about some ism; or should again the drum be rolled in order to interest a bored public and to force them to take a stand?"

In his response, Hartlaub reviewed the splintering of Expressionism, how the second and third generation of Expressionists, "mostly irreligious," "disappointed and worn out by the war, revolution, and post-war period, broke down. . . ." In the new art, he saw "a right, a left wing. One, conservative towards Classicism, taking roots in timelessness, wanting to sanctify again the healthy, physically plastic in pure drawing after nature . . . after so much eccentricity and chaos. . . . The other, the left, glaringly contemporary, far less artistically faithful, rather born of the negation of art, seeking to expose the chaos, the true face of our time, with an addiction to primitive fact-finding and nervous baring of the self. . . . There is nothing left but to affirm it [the new art], especially since it seems strong enough to raise new artistic willpower."[43]

Less than a year after responding to Westheim's questions, Hartlaub's affirmation of the new art began in earnest. Recently instated as director of the Mannheim Kunsthalle, he announced his intention to curate a show of this Post-Expressionist art. The actual opening of the large *Neue Sachlichkeit* exhibition took place in 1925, at the same time Roh's book on *Magischer Realismus* appeared. The child now had two names.

For the exhibit, Hartlaub wanted to assemble artists who rejected "impressionistically vague and expressionistically abstract" art and whose work was "neither sensuously external nor constructively internal"; artists "who have remained true or have returned to a positive, palpable reality" in order to reveal the truth of the times.[44] Building on his response to Westheim's questionnaire, Hartlaub also wanted to display the two strains he had observed developing within this broad movement toward Realism. In the Neoclassicist conservative wing, artists would include the French à la Picasso's 1916–24 paintings, André Derain, and Auguste Herbin; the Italians congregating around the *Novecento* of Milan, those grouped with *Valori Plastici* in Rome, the *Scuola Metafisica* painters Giorgio de Chirico

and Carlo Carrà; and the German painters, especially those residing in Munich, like Georg Schrimpf, Carlo Mense, and Alexander Kanoldt. Artists in the politically committed Verist wing would be represented by Otto Dix, George Grosz, Rudolf Schlichter, and others.[45]

Although there were stylistic variants among the artists, and conceptual differences between the two art historians, both Roh and Hartlaub tried to highlight the common denominators in order to present this post-Expressionist art as a unit. Roh, in fact, assisted Hartlaub with his exhibition by making available a list he had compiled of artists he thought best demonstrated the characteristics of Post-Expressionism.[46] Even so, he felt uncomfortable with Hartlaub's term *Neue Sachlichkeit* and "avoided" it "in order to imply" that he was not referring to "the more neutral Realism of Courbet and Leibl."[47]

Roh was not the only one who feared that the new trend toward realism and Naturalism would draw too much from the art of the late nineteenth century. Several of the respondents to Westheim's 1922 *Das Kunstblatt* questionnaire regarding the New Naturalism voiced the same concern.[48] Paul Fechter's assessment of the new art, however, published only a few months later in the same journal, was essentially correct. *Neue Sachlichkeit* was a "fanatical Naturalism," not a reactionary movement which duplicated the "softness," "peacefulness," and "tranquility" of the earlier paintings.[49]

Especially in the German context, *Neue Sachlichkeit* was an art of its time: the visible world of urban life,[50] night life (figure 3), crowded streets, dirty cities, workers, machines, and factories, as well as of the alienated individual placed in a modern world he could neither fathom nor control.

It was an art that reflected the turbulent fourteen-year life of the Weimar Republic (1919–33); an art of a demoralized Germany reeling from its devastating loss in World War I, its subsequent revolution, and the worst monetary inflation in history that peaked by early 1924, when one American dollar was worth more than 40 trillion marks. It was an art of the first years of the struggling Republic (1919–23); an art of controlled bitterness that festered as the hopes and idealism of 1918 were dashed by the early 1920s, and the dreams of a better society gave way to resignation and cynicism.

This art also depicted the middle period of superficial calm (1924–29),

3. Otto Dix, "Metropolis," triptych (top, left and right wings; bottom, center piece), 1927/28. (Galerie der Stadt, Stuttgart)

an era of growing confidence brought about, in part, by the restructuring of war reparation payments with the Dawes Plan and the end of the French occupation of the Ruhr. It was an art that portrayed bourgeois smugness, political and economic stabilization, and further industrialization before the disastrous depression years (1929–33).

As the economic situation worsened and politics radicalized, the Weimar Republic slowly and agonizingly collapsed. While the center parties, voting increasingly conservatively, opted for law and order, the numerous right-wing and left-wing groups tore themselves and each other apart. Few looked up from the fray long enough to see the threat of the Third Reich, sense the magnitude of this peril, and somehow prevent the young Republic's demise. By April 1933, Hitler's "cultural cleansing" was in full swing. Books were burned, paintings destroyed; sides had to be chosen. Objectivity in art was now out of the question. Artists had to find new means by which to express the best and the worst that was Germany.

In the 1920s, however, the term and the style *Sachlichkeit* or objectivity appeared constantly.[51] *Sachlich* had been used earlier, in 1900, by Hermann Muthesius, the head of the German Werkbund, to oppose the nonfunctional, often prodigal decoration of architectural historicism and *Jugendstil*.[52] The term began to be applied to the newer architecture, which was functional, honest, and simplistic in design.[53]

By 1925, *sachlich* appeared pervasively in relation to the new mode of factual, objective journalism of Egon Kisch; in the cleaner, less-complicated style of shop-window display; in the photographs by Hans Finsler and August Sander;[54] in science; and even, in modified form, in some of the new philosophical and social theories.[55] Thomas Mann suggested in 1920 that schools should teach objectivity—"love for objects, passion for objects, fulfillment from them is the source of all formal brilliance"—as the best means by which "to educate the youth of an unrhetorical people for beautiful expression."[56] In music a "clearer form and an objectivity" emerged in reaction to the "soulful pollution of the previous hyperexpressive epoch."[57] Not surprisingly, *"Es liegt in der Luft eine Sachlichkeit"* (There's Objectivity in the Air), by the famous lyricist/composer duo Marcellus Schiffer and Mischa Spoliansky, made a quick rise up the popular song charts in 1928.

In art, this new attitude and economy of expression, with variations in theme and terminology, became the "dominant style" by 1925.[58] The more conservative strain of *Neue Sachlichkeit* "triumphed" in Austria. Painters like Rudolf Wacker, Sedlacek, Herbert Ploberger, Herbert von Reyl, and Klemens Brosch oriented themselves mostly with respect to German artists in Munich like Kanoldt, Schrimpf, and Mense, but created more disturbing images than the idyllic, somewhat sentimental ones prevalent in the Munich circle. The Austrian Rudolf Wacker, rather than choosing between a certain realism or beauty, opted for a synthesis—beauty in realism.[59]

In Russia, the new art was called Constructivism.[60] In France, Fernand Léger termed his painting style after 1918 *"Réalisme Nouveau"* (New Realism), Picasso began his classicist period in 1916, Georges Braque renounced Cubism, and Jean Cocteau appealed for a *"rappel à l'ordre"* (an appeal to order). André Derain and other avant-gardists heeded the call.[61] By 1931 the French painter Pierre Roy was declared a Magic Realist.[62]

Italian painters in the *Valori Plastici* and *Novecento* groups also advocated a return to rational, ordered painting.[63] Whereas some artists ran into difficulties with the totalitarian governments of the 1920s and 1930s, the Italian had little trouble under the Fascists. In fact, *Il Duce* Mussolini was one of the main speakers at the first exhibit of *Novecento Italiano* in Milan in 1923.

Works of the 1920s and 1930s by the Flemish painters A. Carel Willink and Pyke Koch, and the American artists Edward Hopper, Charles Demuth, Charles Sheeler, and later Grant Wood also reflected some of the same *sachlich*, Magic Realist tendencies.[64] In the catalog for the 1943 New York Museum of Modern Art exhibition "American Realists and Magic Realists," Lincoln Kirstein explicitly linked the American art works on display to German *Neue Sachlichkeit* of the 1920s.[65] The Magic Realist Pierre Roy, who exhibited frequently and successfully in the United States, may very well have helped spread Franz Roh's formulations. By 1927 *Neue Sachlichkeit*, according to French art critic Waldemar George, was deemed "Americanism . . . a cult of purpose, the naked fact, the preference for functional work, professional conscientiousness and usefulness."[66]

In Germany, this return to a tangible objective reality dominated all other painting styles. For the most part, *Neue Sachlichkeit* artists discerned the visible world with a cool, analytical approach, a new matter-of-factness, and sobriety. Certainly, there were some artists who tended slightly toward sentimentality, idyllic escapism, or an Henri Rousseau naive style, like Georg Schrimpf (figure 4) and Carlo Mense, but their starting point was always the microscopic analysis of objective reality. Alex-

4. Georg Schrimpf, "Landscape in the Bavarian Forest," 1933. (Bayerische Staats-gemäldesammlungen, Munich)

ander Kanoldt, with his sharp focus and precise representations, evoked imagined objects that seemed to appear from within his still lifes (figure 5) and petrified vistas. Other artists in this more conservative vein invoked a clear, timeless Classicism. Industrial or urban landscapes, sometimes barren of human life, were painted by Carl Grossberg (figure 6) and Franz Radziwill (figure 7).

Christian Schad, an exemplar of what was meant by New Objectivity, produced the most photographic, most meticulously painted works. Far from sentimentality, he painted portraits of fellow artists and writers with a scrupulous objectivity, an icy detachment. His subjects seemed frozen in time, alienated from the world and totally alone in their solitude (figure 8). Yet, Schad's "no-comment" objective paintings cry out, their subjects overwhelmed by the almost unbearable stillness and isolation of their silent sphere.

Contrasting this more conservative and objective aesthetic of New Objectivity was the socially conscious aspect that Hartlaub termed "Verism." The generally left-wing Verists were best represented by George Grosz, Otto Dix, Georg Scholz, Rudolf Schlichter, and Otto Griebel. In their concise, hardheaded art, they gave voice to post-World War I Germany, the tormented political theater of the Weimar Republic, the instability of German society, and the desperate disquietude of the time.

5. Alexander Kanoldt, "Still Life II," 1926. (Staatliche Kunstsammlungen, Gemäldegalerie Neue Meister, Dresden)

6. Carl Grossberg, "Bridge over Schwarzbachstrasse Wuppertal," 1927. (Von der Heydt-Museum, Wuppertal)

Some of these artists became politically active, as well. Grosz and Schlichter helped to organize the *Rote Gruppe* (Red Group), an organization of Communist artists that joined the KPD[67] in 1924. Others became involved with the *Assoziation revolutionärer bildender Künstler Deutschlands* (Association of Revolutionary German Fine Artists), founded in Berlin in 1928. The ARBKD's aim was "to promote the class struggle, and [its art] will correspond in style and content to the needs of the workers." Within a year, there were sixteen branches of the ARBKD in Germany, with over 800 members.[68] All wanted to make an impact with their art and, thereby, improve society.[69]

Dix went after his subject with a barely checked ferocity in order to get to the *unheimliche Wahrheit* (the uncanny truth) that lay behind it (figure 9).[70] In one of the few theoretical pronouncements by *Neue Sachlichkeit* artists, Dix wrote, "For me, anyway, what is new about this painting is that the subject matter is broader. . . . [I]n any case, the object remains primary and the form will first take shape through the object. That is why I have always placed such significance on the question of whether I can move as close as possible to the thing that I see, because *what* is more important to me than *how*! The *how* has to develop out of the *what*."[71]

With the belief that *"der Mensch ist ein Vieh"* (man is a beast) fueling his ire and his art, Grosz fought against the pervasive complacency, pettiness, and social inequity that, to him, characterized modern German society (figure 10). "My art was to be my arm, and my sword," Grosz later recounted, "pens that drew without a purpose were like empty straws."[72]

7. Franz Radziwill, "Back Buildings in Dresden," 1931. (Hessisches Landesmuseum, Darmstadt)

8. Christian Schad, "Portrait of Dr. Haustein," 1928. (Fundación Colección Thyssen-Bornemisza, Madrid)

9. Otto Dix, "Match Seller I," 1920. (Staatsgalerie, Stuttgart)

His weapon served him well. With poison in his pen, Grosz drew some of the most powerfully indicting political statements of the period.

It is in this *Tendenzkunst* (tendentious or politicized art)[73] of the Verists that inner commitment sometimes won out over dispassion, despite the determination to record the facts objectively. The suggestion has been made that in the Verists' polemics, "the expressionist fire still burned."[74] The difference was that these artists painted with a severe Realism that chided, even accused, but did not resort to the sometimes overt emotionalism, moral rectitude, or messianic fervor of their Expressionist counterparts.

Hartlaub was accused by a contemporary of being "a pastor of art sitting on an ethical judge's throne" because he rejected Verism's focus on the repulsive.[75] And while it is true that few of the Verists' searing political works hung in Hartlaub's exhibition, the ones that were displayed became objects of criticism by a conservative public that accused the Verists, especially Dix and Grosz, of "degeneracy" and "art bolshevism." By the time the exhibition traveled to Dresden, Hartlaub had revised his catalog essay in order to deemphasize the left-wing, right-wing comparisons

10. George Grosz, "Gray Day," 1921. (Staatliche Museen zu Berlin—Preussischer Kulturbesitz, Nationalgalerie, Berlin)

he had made of *Neue Sachlichkeit* painters. The murmurs of "degenerate" art in 1925, however, served as little forewarning for what lay ahead when the Nazis came to power.

Despite the diverse strands of *Neue Sachlichkeit*, there were certain common bonds. All the New Objectivity painters tended to employ themes from the modern environment and the patterns of daily life. Art became, once again, "the mirror of palpable exteriority." [76] More exacting than the camera lens, the artist painted everything with equal sharpness, even the background (figure 11). [77] Virtually no brushstrokes were visible; the finish was smooth as enamel. [78] Objects were scrutinized in their minutiae. Artists "painted inwards from the outside" [79] to get to the invisible. With surgical probing, a deeper layer—the magic and the *"unheimlich"* (uncanny) behind the real—was revealed.

Altogether, 124 works by 32 artists were displayed in Hartlaub's long-awaited exhibit *"Neue Sachlichkeit: Deutsche Malerei seit dem Expressionismus"* (New Objectivity: German Painting since Expressionism), with 9 additional paintings by Max Beckmann inserted later. [80] The exhibition, which began in Mannheim in June 1925, traveled with variations to Dresden, Chemnitz, Erfurt, Dessau, Halle, and Jena. In the following years, *Neue Sachlichkeit* exhibits also appeared in Berlin (1927), Hannover (1928), Amsterdam (1929), and under the title *"Neue deutsche Romantik"* (New German Romanticism) in Hannover (1933). [81]

Reviews ranged from the complimentary—"remarkably agreeable," [82] "finally answers in full the questions posed in Westheim's 1922 New Naturalism circular" [83]—to the disparaging—"an unappealing affair . . . this art of calculation without a soul." [84] Regardless of the differing opinions, Hartlaub's exhibition became famous and the term *Neue Sachlichkeit* well-known.

Beginning in 1933, the Hitler regime pronounced "degenerate" those artists and architects who did not in some way espouse the party line, who did not design buildings that exuded the "true Germanic spirit" or paint works that reflected aspects of the sacrosanct Nazi ideology. Just as the architects of the Third Reich were intent on halting "the unhealthy exaggerations of an objectivity which has toppled over the brink" in modern building [85] and, so, closed the Bauhaus in 1933, modern art was also under siege. Although there actually were very few Jews in the visual arts, in contrast to their far greater presence in theater, film, and literature, the Nazis created the impression that modern painting was also heavily "Jew-

11. Wilhelm Heise, "Fading Spring," 1926. (Städtische Galerie im Lenbachhaus, Munich)

ish" and, therefore, in need of artistic and racial cleansing.[86] Henceforth, all areas of cultural activity were to be *Judenrein,* free of Jews.

Although *Neue Sachlichkeit* had reached its peak and was on the wane by the early 1930s,[87] the Third Reich allowed certain strains of the art to flourish while stamping out whatever life was left in the politicized vein of the movement. Among the more idyllic, romantic artists of *Neue Sachlichkeit,* some found it fairly easy to mold their work in accordance with the Nazi *Blut und Boden* (blood and soil) cultural doctrine, with its preference for an exaggeratedly idealized and heroic realism.[88]

Georg Schrimpf of the Munich circle continued to exhibit and sell his works throughout the Nazi years, even selling two of his landscapes to Nazi official Rudolf Hess, and was professor at the Staatliche Kunstschule Berlin-Schöneberg (State Art School, Berlin Schöneberg) from 1933 to 1938.[89] Carl Grossberg's paintings of industrial landscapes were also acceptable to the Nazis. Franz Radziwill became a National Socialist party member and was given a professorship at the Düsseldorf Academy; only in 1938 was he denounced by Nazi officials and forbidden to exhibit.[90] Adolf Ziegler, mentioned in Roh's 1925 supplemental list of Magic Realist artists,[91] was named president of the Nazi Reichskammer der bildenden Künste (Third Reich's Chamber of the Fine Arts) in December 1936. Ziegler, who painted in a heavily derivative, academic style, became Hitler's favorite artist and was best known for his pictures of nude women; therefore, his nickname "Reich Master of German Pubic Hair."[92] Clearly, certain aspects of this more conservative strain of Magic Realism — clarity, occasional sentimentality, nonpolitical subject matter — could be, and were, appropriated by the cultural ideologues of the Nazi party.

The left-wing political artists and, of course, all Jewish artists were particular targets of the Nazi cultural cleansing. Numerous painters, including Max Beckmann, Max Ernst, Otto Dix, and George Grosz were denounced as "bolshevists" or "*Kunstzwerge*" (art dwarfs) by the Reichskulturkammer (Third Reich's Chamber of Culture), headed by Joseph Goebbels. Often prohibited from painting and fired from teaching positions, their works were destroyed or displayed for ridicule in vicious "*Entartete Kunst*" (Degenerate Art) shows or *Schandausstellungen* (Abomination Exhibitions). Hartlaub was fired from his job as museum director in Mannheim. Roh, accused of being a "cultural bolshevist," was taken to the Dachau concentration camp in 1933. Through the intercession of the highly respected art historian Wilhelm Pinder, Roh was eventually released from confinement. Thirty years later, still deeply disturbed by the purges of the 1930s, Roh wrote a book on the Nazis' cultural barbarism entitled "*Entartete*" *Kunst* ("*Degenerate*" *Art*) (1962).[93]

Although declared "degenerate" by Nazi standards, Roh's *Nach-Expressionismus, Magischer Realismus* of 1925 enjoyed considerable success not only at the time of its publication, but especially as his painterly stylistic formulations were appropriated and transformed into literary concepts. The book was translated partially into Spanish in José Ortega y Gasset's *Revista de Occidente* in Madrid in 1927[94] and published in its entirety later in the same year.[95] However, the Spanish edition curiously reversed Roh's German title. By placing *realismo mágico* first, *post expresionismo* second, Magic Realism was granted a privileged position from the outset.

Roh's concepts were influential in Latin America, especially in the field of literary criticism and the work of Arturo Uslar-Pietri and Enrique Anderson Imbert. Directly and indirectly, Roh's formulations also affected Johan Daisne and Hubert Lampo in the Netherlands, Ernst Jünger in Germany, as well as authors and art critics in Italy.[96]

Yet, almost from its first appearance in 1925 and certainly in the ensuing years, Roh's pictorial term *Magischer Realismus* was obscured by
Hartlaub's *Neue Sachlichkeit*. Not until recently has Magic Realism re-
appeared and been used fairly consistently in connection with the art of
the 1920s. It has been suggested that the term's very belated reappearance
is due in part to the fact that Magic Realism had "occasionally compromised itself . . . with Nazi Neo-Classicism."[97]

Post-World War II politics also had much to do with the survival or disappearance of both terms as art historical categories. While the left-wing,
socially committed Verists were promoted to the ranks of the revered in
post-war East German discourse, the more conservative aspects of *Neue
Sachlichkeit* were criticized for reflecting bourgeois dominance and capitalistic stabilization. Conversely, the painters of *Neue Sachlichkeit* were
scarcely, if at all, considered in West Germany after 1945,[98] where abstraction and a rehabilitated and reworked Expressionism reigned during the
cold war years. Not until a vigorously resurgent interest in Realism began
in the early 1960s did the West show much interest in the Magic Real-
ism/New Objectivity of the 1920s.

Even though Roh discussed at length the reasons why Picasso's Neo-
classicism, Fernand Léger's *Réalisme Nouveau,* and particularly Rousseau's Naive School were important influences on Magic Realism, the term
was, and still is, rarely used in French art criticism. Some art historians
have argued that its under-utilization in France is largely due to its over-
shadowing by the Surrealist movement, which became increasingly successful in the late 1920s.[99] The Vichy government's collaboration with the
Third Reich during the German occupation of France from 1940 to 1944 —
its agreement with many Nazi cultural policies, albeit in varying forms;
its resolve to rid France of "cultural decadence"; and its nod, like that of
the Nazis, to certain artists earlier categorized as Magic Realists (André
Derain, for instance, who was "acceptable" to and worked with both the
Vichy and German governments) — may also explain the virtual absence of
Magic Realism/New Objectivity from French art historical discourse.[100]

Arguably, the recent interest in Realism in its many modern variants, as
well as the popularity of the term as applied to a genre of contemporary
literature, has aided Magic Realism's reemergence in art criticism.

How was the German pictorial term Magic Realism appropriated by literary critics and writers? A few definitive answers can be found; gaps and

conjecture, however, abound. In *Nach-Expressionismus, Magischer Realismus*, Roh only gave a summary analysis of Magic Realism in the written word. His subject was, after all, painting. According to him, two literary tendencies were apparent — one which he linked to Rimbaud, the other he attached to Zola, using as further examples Carl Sternheim, Heinrich Mann, Georg Kaiser, Berthold Brecht, and Walter Mehring. That is all; Roh dispensed with the literary question in a few lines.[101] Yet, since 1925, the literary community has adopted Roh's term, sometimes stressing mutual affinities, but more often appropriating the concept for its own purposes. This appropriation of a pictorial term by literary critics has been facilitated by the pliant meanings of both "magic" and "realism" and the ambivalence with which Roh first presented Magic Realism.

The Austrian Alfred Kubin spent a lifetime wrestling with the uncanny, the *unheimlich* in the real. An artist and writer whose power lay in his graphic depiction of a world suffused with the monstrous and grotesque, Kubin was in certain ways an important precursor of traits found in Magic Realism. Although his drawings in no way resemble works of the Magic Realists, and his graphic style is not in any sense "realistic," Kubin's concepts do provide a direct link between literary narrative and graphic art.

In 1909 Kubin published *Die andere Seite* (*The Other Side*), a novel illustrated with fifty-two drawings. In it, Kubin set out to explore the "other side" of the visible world — the corruption, the evil, the rot, as well as the power and mystery. The border between reality and dream remains consistently nebulous; *Unheimlichkeit* (uncanniness) pervades the novel, which takes place in the capital city of Dreamland in Asia. Kubin also illuminated "the other side" in "this side of things" in his disquieting illustrations in order to render the duality of existence and, thereby, achieve a unified double vision, a conjunction of the invisible essence of reality.

While writing the book, Kubin stated that he "gained . . . the mature insight that it is not only in the bizarre, exalted, and strange moments of existence that the highest values lie, but that which is painful, indifferent, everyday, and irrelevant contains the same mysteries." This was, in fact, "the principal meaning of the book."[102] Kubin, who became the foremost Austrian graphic artist of the twentieth century, received enthusiastic acclaim for *Die andere Seite* and exerted significant influence on subsequent German and Austrian literature.[103] The German writer Ernst Jünger was one of many who was deeply affected by Kubin's work.

Jünger, an essayist, novelist, and poet who had strong ties to the right-wing, anti-democratic forces in Germany, began corresponding with Kubin in 1929 because of his admiration for Kubin's drawings and literary formulations in *Die andere Seite*. He was particularly interested in Kubin's binary concept — the invisible and the visible, the interior and the exterior in the existence of things, and the fusion of the two. Jünger cited Kubin often in his personal journals and also wrote an analysis of Kubin's art for the *Hamburger Nachrichten* in 1931.

Jünger's interest in art was also influenced by Franz Roh. Roh's "magic," the uncanny inherent in or behind the object detectable only by objective accentuation, isolation, and microscopic depiction, Jünger translated into literary "stereoscopy," the profound sense of the miniscule uncovered through precise examination, and "magic rationalism." These same terms were used by Roh in his seminal work of 1925.[104]

The first time Jünger employed the term Magic Realism was in a 1927 article entitled "*Nationalismus und modernes Leben*" (Nationalism and Modern Life).[105] He described "paintings of Magic Realism . . . [in which] each of the lines of the external world is conjured up with the exactness of a mathematical formula, the coldness of which is illuminated and reheated in an inexplicable manner, as if by transparency, by a magical background."[106]

In his combination dream-diary and daily journal, *Das abenteuerliche Herz* (The Adventurous Heart) (1929), Jünger wrote, "Magic Realism in painting succeeded in expressing the inherent precision of the world of machines even better than the machine itself. No wonder — must not the *idea* of precision itself necessarily be more precise than precision itself?"[107] Although Roh's terminology does not appear in Jünger's second version of *Das abenteuerliche Herz* (1938),[108] the concept clearly underlies the work, thereby placing the theoretical formulations of Magic Realism into German literature.[109] It has been suggested that the effect of Jünger's own prose "lies in its unimpeded clarity as an expression of a mode of thinking that knows no compromise and, at the same time, in its power to follow and uncover the underlying magic."[110]

Jünger was friends of the painters Max Ernst and René Magritte, and while in France during the German occupation also became acquainted with French artists who did not flee but remained, like Picasso and Braque. Ernst, who was on Roh's list of Magic Realists, had moved to Paris from Germany in 1922 and became prominent in the Surrealist movement there; Picasso also appeared on Roh's 1925 list. Although no definitive link can be established, perhaps Jünger's travels to France and his friendships with French cultural luminaries helped propagate the locution and formulation of Magic Realism.

Along with *Magischer Realismus*, the term *Neue Sachlichkeit* also appeared in German literary criticism of the 1920s to describe certain contemporary literary tendencies as well as precursors of the style. The influential writer W. E. Süskind published an article in 1927 on the deceased Danish writer and poet Herman Bang (1857–1912), whose work had been rediscovered when the S. Fischer Verlag edited a six-volume collection of his writings in 1926–27. In describing Bang's work and more recent German *Neue Sachlichkeit* literature, Süskind wrote, "*Neue Sachlichkeit* means this exactly: a different way of seeing, a changed scale of importance regarding the impressions. New is this objectivity insofar as it is more serving, more impersonal than any earlier Realism. It is a 'monstrous' objectivity, one which is uncanny [*unheimlich*], while in reality the objects speak for themselves and the artist only gives his hand, his brush, his pen, his reflecting memory and conscience."[111]

The term was also used in reference to the writing of Alfred Döblin. Referring to Döblin's *Berlin Alexanderplatz: Die Geschichte vom Franz Biberkopf* (Berlin Alexanderplatz: The Story of Franz Biberkopf) (1929), a critic wrote, "The *Neue Sachlichkeit* as a school, or more correctly as 'schooling', had already, in the years and days preceding, been proclaimed and demonstrated by Döblin; Döblin himself brought forth its most significant realization."[112] Döblin's work made a great impact on Günter Grass, who has been labeled a Magic Realist in recent years. At a 1968 literary colloquium honoring Döblin ten years after his death, Grass referred to him as his teacher (*Lehrer Döblin*) and thanked him for his influence. Grass went on to say that he could not imagine his own style of prose without Döblin's work as model and ended by stating, "I come from Döblin. . . ."[113]

During the Third Reich, the dominant aesthetic in German literature as in all the arts was *Blut und Boden* (blood and soil). However, beginning in 1948 and with increasing rapidity thereafter, articles appeared which employed Magic Realism as a literary concept. Ranging from "*Magischer Realismus?*" in the journal *Aufbau* to "*Über den 'Magischen Realismus' in der heutigen deutschen Dichtung*" (1949) and "*Die Wirklichkeit hat doppelten Boden. Gedanken zum Magischen Realismus in der Literatur*" (1952), Magic Realism became an established term, with varying definitions, in German literary criticism.[114]

In more recent years, numerous German writers have been categorized as Magic Realists, a reflection of the appropriation of the pictorial term by literary critics. The fact that Magic Realism has been applied to such diverse Austrian/German authors as Franz Werfel, Alfred Döblin, Thomas Mann, Ernst Jünger, Franz Kafka, Robert Musil, Heimito von Doderer, Hermann Kasack, and Günter Grass illuminates how imprecise and rife with ambiguities the concept is.

Two years after Roh's publication in 1925, *realismo magico* appeared in Italy. Massimo Bontempelli, organizer of the journal *900*, introduced the term in an article dated 1927, in which he wrote about "this 'magical realism' [*realismo magico*], which we could take as a rough definition of our tendency." [115] Even before 1927, Bontempelli described certain characteristics of *realismo magico* in the first four issues of *900* and used the term in a literary as well as artistic context. Whether Bontempelli borrowed the term from Roh cannot be definitively ascertained, but a few links can be found. Bontempelli collaborated on *Der Querschnitt*, an important German artistic and literary journal in which essays regarding modern art appeared and in which Hartlaub announced his 1925 Mannheim exhibit. This journal appeared in France for the first time beginning in 1921, and in other European countries with increasing regularity thereafter. [116] Furthermore, the writer Georg Kaiser, who was listed in Roh's book as a Magic Realist, helped edit a few issues of *900*.

Bontempelli's own formulation of Magical Realism at times coincided with Roh's (reconstructing or creating objects, reflecting on the "*pittura metafisica*" [metaphysical paintings] of de Chirico, making overtures toward a certain Classicism). Differences, however, are as numerous as similarities. Still, the fact that the term was the same — *Magischer Realismus* and *realismo magico* — and, probably of greater importance, that *900* was published in French and Italian, and distributed in both countries, helps to establish how Roh's pictorial term came to be widely known throughout Europe, albeit with variant formulations.

The term Magic Realism also made its way to the Netherlands and Belgium, especially through the writer Johan Daisne. In his 1942 novel *De trap van steen en wolken*, Daisne employed words like *fantastisch-realistisch* (fantastic realistic). By 1943, after having read an article about Bontempelli in the Belgian journal *Le Nouveau Journal*, Daisne had adopted the concept *Magisch-realisme* (Magical Realism). He used the term frequently after that time, arriving at the following formulation:

"Dream and reality constitute the two poles of the human condition, and it is through the magnetism [attraction] of these poles that magic is born, especially when a spark shoots forth, the light of which catches a glimpse of transcendence, a truth behind the reality of life and dream."[117]

Introduction of Roh's Magic Realism to Latin America occurred through the Spanish translation and publication of his book by the *Revista de Occidente* in 1927. Within a year, Magic Realism was being applied to the prose of European authors in the literary circles of Buenos Aires.[118] The unprecedented cultural migration from Europe to the Americas in the 1930s and 1940s, as the muses fled the horrors of the Third Reich, might also have played a role in disseminating the term. Over one-fifth of the 500,000 exiles who fled Germany, Czechoslovakia, and Austria between 1933 and 1941 settled in Central and South America.[119] Included in this exodus were dozens of cultural luminaries. Paul Westheim, the well-known German art historian, editor of *Das Kunstblatt*, and one of the leading proselytizers for "the New Realism," along with numerous artists, writers, and critics, found refuge in Mexico. Others found safe havens in Brazil, Cuba, and Venezuela. Although some of these *émigrés* returned to Europe immediately following the war, Westheim stayed on in Mexico, writing several art historical books, including *La Calavera* (The Skeleton) in 1953.[120] Conjecture aside, it is in Latin America that the concept was primarily seized by literary criticism and was, through translation and literary appropriation, transformed.

Arturo Uslar-Pietri, who had known Bontempelli in Paris and had traveled to Italy during the debates over *Novecentismo*, in 1948 defined "Magic Realism" as "a poetical divination or a poetical negation of reality."[121] Alejo Carpentier, a participant in the French Surrealist movement of the 1930s, expounded upon *lo real maravilloso americano* (the American marvelous real) in 1949. And in 1955 Angel Flores christened "magical realism" that which Jorge Luis Borges had termed *fantástico* in the 1940s. To add to the confusion, others began identifying Magic Realism with Carpentier's "marvelous real."

Franz Roh's actual influence on the contemporary literary genre, magical realism, is debatable, so transmuted have his pictorial formulations become. Mutual affinities can be found in de Chirico's and Carrà's *metafisica* (metaphysical); German artists' *Neue Sachlichkeit* (New Objectivity); Roh's *Magischer Realismus* (Magic Realism), *Unheimlichkeit* (uncanniness), and the *Geheimnis* (mystery, secret) behind the depicted world;

the *fantástico* (fantastic) of Borges; the *Magisch-realisme* (Magic Realism) of Daisne; the magical realism of Flores; *lo real maravilloso americano* (the American marvelous real) of Carpentier; Bontempelli's "other dimension" in *realismo magico* (Magic Realism); Jünger's "magical background," "magical rationalism," and "stereoscopy"; and Kubin's "other side of this reality." Despite the many similarities, divergences are numerous, as the subsequent essays illustrate.

Perhaps these transformations are partly due to the problems inherent in linguistic and cultural translations. Moreover, the ambivalence with which Roh first introduced *Magischer Realismus*, the term's virtual eclipse by Hartlaub's *Neue Sachlichkeit*, and the various, sometimes conflicting, styles attributed to the rubric *Magischer Realismus/Neue Sachlichkeit* exacerbated the confusion. Additionally, the binomial Magic Realism and the expansive, ambiguous meanings allocated to each of the two words certainly facilitated the flourishing of succeeding variants. Arguably, deviations are also due to the doubtful possibility of establishing clear parallels between the visual arts and the literary arts. In his comprehensive study of *Neue Sachlichkeit* in literature, Helmut Lethen declined to use Roh's term *Magischer Realismus* as well as Roh's "important art historical book . . . in order to avoid the temptation to use for the analysis of literature suggestive analogies from the visual arts."[122] Lethen just might have a point. As this essay has suggested and the editors of this volume have noted, "It is a simple matter of the most complicated sort."

Notes

1 See, for instance, Wilhelm Hausenstein, *Die Kunst in diesem Augenblick* (reissued Munich: Prestel Verlag, 1960), p. 265. Wilhelm Worringer, 1920 lecture published in *Künstlerische Zeitfragen* (Munich: Bruckmann, 1921), p. 18. See also Oscar Sandner, *"Sachlichkeit als (Österreichische) Möglichkeit"* in Oswald Oberhuber, ed., *Abbild und Emotion: Österreichischer Realismus, 1914–1944* (Vienna: Edition Tusch, 1984), p. 124. A few recent art historians, like Wieland Schmied and Seymour Menton, have given the beginning date for Magic Realism as 1918. All translations in this essay are the author's, with special thanks to the family.

2 Franz Roh, *Nach-Expressionismus, Magischer Realismus: Probleme der neuesten Europäischen Malerei* (Leipzig: Klinkhardt & Biermann, 1925), preface, n.p., *"Das Kind einen wirklichen Namen haben musste.*

3 For a contemporary argument against the "end of Expressionism," see Paul Fechter, *"Die nachexpressionistische Situation"* in *Das Kunstblatt* 7 (1923): 321,

in which Fechter argued that he did not share Hausenstein's and Worringer's opinion about the death of Expressionism. Rather, he saw only the end of a first phase of Expressionism, which was protesting and anti-Impressionistic in nature, while a second, 'New Naturalism' phase of the Expressionist movement was beginning. For a recent argument, see Emilio Bertonati, "Neue Sachlichkeit in a Wider Cultural Context" in Louise Lincoln, ed., *German Realism of the Twenties: The Artist as Social Critic* (Minneapolis: Minneapolis Institute of Arts, 1980), pp. 57–59. For a view that "no movement stood as diametrically opposed to Expressionism as New Objectivity . . . no direction was so much 'anti-Expressionism'," see Wieland Schmied, *Neue Sachlichkeit und Magischer Realismus in Deutschland 1918–1933* (Hanover: Fackelträger-Verlag, 1969), p. 13.

4. This is, in fact, the name many art historians today use to describe the various painterly tendencies of the 1920s and early 1930s.

5. Franz Roh, *Nach-Expressionismus, Magischer Realismus*. Roh states in a later article that he came up with the term Magic Realism already in 1924 as a name for the post-WWI art movement. See Roh's *"Rückblick auf den Magischen Realismus"* in *Das Kunstwerk* 6, 1 (1952): 7–9. Although Roh's *Magischer Realismus* has been translated and employed in literary criticism as magical realism, most art and cultural historians have translated the term as Magic Realism. Roh did not give *Magischer Realismus* a prefix (*Der magische Realismus* — magical realism), which would have narrowed its reference, but rather chose the wider, more encompassing form to serve as a rubric for the multiplicity of tendencies found in this new art.

6. Although there are several definitions for *"Sachlichkeit"* — "matter-of-factness," "reality," "relevance," "functionalism," "practicality," "impartiality," "objectivity" — *"Sachlichkeit"* will be translated as "objectivity" in this essay since that is the meaning most often used when referring to the art of the 1920s.

7. Hartlaub made his intention clear to install an exhibit entitled *"Die neue Sachlichkeit"* in a letter dated July 11, 1923. Preceding this, he had sent out a circular on May 18, 1923 to artists, critics, art historians, and dealers that investigated the possibilities of a *Neue Sachlichkeit* exhibition. See Gustav Hartlaub, *"Werbendes Rundschreiben,"* Mannheim, May 18, 1923. Hartlaub's celebrated exhibit finally opened in Mannheim on June 14, 1925. Inconsistencies in capitalization of the term "Neue Sachlichkeit" in these notes reflect those in the publications themselves.

8. See Brigid S. Barton, *Otto Dix and Die neue Sachlichkeit* (Ann Arbor: UMI Research Press, 1981), p. 65, wherein she counters Hartlaub's approach by asserting, "although the Verists were politically liberal, the Neoclassicists were not conservative in a political sense but in a stylistic one." In my research, the few New Objectivity artists who did manage to work through the Nazi years were indeed in this politically conservative, Neoclassicist wing.

9. See Hartlaub's *"Werbendes Rundschreiben,"* Mannheim, May 18, 1923.

10 In his 1925 work, Roh isolated several groups within the Realist movement, three of which he considered peripheral (Impressionist-inspired colorists, Expressionists such as Max Beckmann, and Constructivists like Oskar Schlemmer) and four which he considered central (the Classicists, the Verists, the naive "Rousseau school" painters, and the Italians of *Valori Plastici*). See Frank Roh, *Nach-Expressionismus, Magischer Realismus*, pp. 73–96. By 1958 Roh distinguished three groups of German Magic Realists by geography and by their diverging aesthetic qualities (Northern and Eastern Germany, aggressive social critics, art engagé; Southern Germany, Munich, melancholy, influenced by early de Chirico; detailed painted idylls, influenced by Henri Rousseau). See Franz Roh, *German Art in the Twentieth Century* (Greenwich: New York Graphic Society, 1968), pp. 71–72.

11 Marxists link *Neue Sachlichkeit* with the rational, industrialized, and often dehumanized capitalistic art of the middle class during the stable years of the Weimar Republic. This art, they assert, "reflected traits of the technical attitude of the modern manager, of the view towards reality, as it originated from capitalistic rationalization." Marxists associate Verism with the political left-wing, which was producing "proletarian-revolutionary art." See Ursula Horn, "'Neue Sachlichkeit'—Richtung oder Sammelbegriff?" in *Bildende Kunst* 20, 9 (1972): 429–33. For a concise, leftist overview of the contemporary and present art historical debates surrounding *Neue Sachlichkeit*, see Jost Hermand, "Unity within Diversity? The History of the Concept 'Neue Sachlichkeit'" in Keith Bullivant, ed., *Culture and Society in the Weimar Republic* (Manchester: Manchester University Press, 1977), pp. 166–82.

12 See Roland März, Introduction, *Realismus und Sachlichkeit: Aspekte deutscher Kunst 1919–1933* (Berlin: Staatliche Museen zu Berlin, 1974), wherein he analyzes *Neue Sachlichkeit* using five subdivisions based on political ideologies (Berlin Dada, Verism, *Neue Sachlichkeit*, proletarian-revolutionary, political Constructivism). Wieland Schmied argues for five different aspects of Realism, categorized by location and style. See Wieland Schmied, *Neue Sachlichkeit und Magischer Realismus in Deutschland, 1918–1933*, p. 31.

13 The many titles in the footnotes of this essay exemplify the numerous exhibitions and publications in recent years as well as the various names given to this predominant artistic mode of the 1920s.

14 See Manfred Frank, "*Die Philosophie des sogenannten 'magischen Idealismus'*" in *Euphorion* 63 (1969).

15 Novalis, *Allgemeines Brouillon*, 1798–99, in G. Schulz, ed., *Werke* (Munich: C. H. Beck, 1969), p. 479. The same has been noted in Jean Weisgerber, *Le Réalisme magique: roman, peinture et cinéma* (Brussels: L'Age d'Homme, 1987), p. 11.

16 The translation provided in this volume is of the 1927 excerpt published in Spanish in the *Revista de Occidente*.

17 Roh, *Nach-Expressionismus, Magischer Realismus*, p. 3. Subsequent references to this work are cited parenthetically in the text.

18 When *"das Geistige"* is used in German, it is translated as either "the intellectual" or "the spiritual" depending on context. For more on the controversy regarding *"das Geistige,"* see Peg Weiss, *Kandinsky in Munich: The Formative Jugendstil Years* (Princeton: Princeton University Press, 1979), pp. 140–41. See also Bruno Bettelheim, *Freud and Man's Soul* (New York: Alfred A. Knopf, 1982).

19 See also Franz Roh, *"Rückblick auf den Magischen Realismus,"* p. 7.

20 Franz Roh, *German Art in the Twentieth Century*, p. 71. This is the 1968 English publication of his 1958 book *Geschichte der Deutschen Kunst von 1900 bis zur Gegenwart* (Munich: Verlag Bruckmann, 1958).

21 Of the fifty-two artists listed by Roh, only twenty-four are still recognized in art historical discourse, and of those, only eighteen are assessed as "important" artists. Several are no longer even considered New Objectivity/Magic Realism painters, but have been relegated to different categories like Surrealism and Futurism; for instance, Pablo Picasso, Max Beckmann, André Derain, Max Ernst, Carlo Carrà, Gino Severini, and Joan Miró. Of the sixty artists on Roh's supplemental list, only eighteen are usually included in the history of art, less than ten of whom are deemed "important" artists. The rest are largely forgotten.

22 Grethe Jürgens, *"Rezepte zum erspriesslichen Besuch einer Kunstausstellung"* in *Der Wachsbogen* 5/6 (1932). Reproduced in Uwe M. Schneede, ed., *Die zwanziger Jahre: Manifeste und Dokumente deutscher Künstler* (Cologne: DuMont Buchverlag, 1979), pp. 144–45; and in Wieland Schmied, *Neue Sachlichkeit und Magischer Realismus in Deutschland 1918–1933*, pp. 252–53.

23 See Sigmund Freud, *"Das Unheimliche"* in *Imago* 5/6 (1919). Also in Sigmund Freud, *"Das Unheimliche"* in *Psychologische Schriften*, Studienausgabe Band IV (Frankfurt: S. Fischer, 1970), p. 259f. Giorgio de Chirico, *"Über die metaphysische Kunst"* in Wieland Schmied, ed., *Wir Metaphysiker. Gesammelte Schriften* (Berlin: Propyläen, 1973). For more on de Chirico, see Jean Clair, *"Das 'Metaphysische' und die 'Unheimlichkeit'"* in Ingo F. Walther, ed., *Realismus: Zwischen Revolution und Reaktion, 1919–1939* (Munich: Prestel-Verlag, 1981), pp. 26–35.

24 Seymour Menton, *Magic Realism Rediscovered, 1918–1981* (Philadelphia: Art Alliance Press, 1983), p. 13. Although it is true that Jung's ideas were increasingly accepted after World War I, as were Freud's, I found virtually no references to Jung or Jungian ideas in any of the numerous artists' notebooks and diaries of the period 1918–1928, by which time Magic Realism/New Objectivity had fully developed. In fact, the early German experimental psychologists and Gestaltists were referred to with far more frequency. See also Jean Clair, *"Das 'Metaphysische' und die 'Unheimlichkeit'"* in Ingo F. Walther, ed., *Realismus: Zwischen Revolution und Reaktion, 1919–1939*, pp. 26–35. Furthermore, Jung's

term *"participation mystique"* (mystical participation) to which Menton refers seems, in my opinion, to counter what Roh wrote in his preface: " 'magical' as opposed to 'mystical.' " See Franz Roh, *Nach-Expressionismus, Magischer Realismus*, preface, n.p.

25 Franz Roh, *"Rückblick auf den Magischen Realismus,"* p. 7.

26 Wieland Schmied, *Neue Sachlichkeit und Magischer Realismus in Deutschland 1918–1933*, p. 13.

27 Meidner was not the only one. See Emilio Bertonati, *Aspekte der Neuen Sachlichkeit* (Florence: Centro DI, 1968), in which he argues that New Objectivity did not come about after Germany's collapse in the First World War, but earlier, especially in the works of George Grosz.

28 Ludwig Meidner, *"Anleitung zum Malen von Grossstadtbildern"* in Uwe M. Schneede, ed., *Die Zwanziger Jahre: Manifeste und Dokumente Deutscher Künstler*, pp. 110–11.

29 Ibid., p. 110.

30 *Das Kunstblatt* 2 (1919): 319.

31 Wieland Schmied, " *'Pittura Metafisica' und 'Neue Sachlichkeit': Die Geschichte einer Inspiration"* in Ingo F. Walther, ed., *Realismus: Zwischen Revolution und Reaktion 1919–1933*, pp. 20–25.

32 Michael Koch, *"Neue Sachlichkeit — Magischer Realismus: Der Beitrag Münchens zur nachexpressionistischen Malerei und Graphik"* in Christoph Stölzl, ed., *Die Zwanziger Jahre in München* (Munich: Münchner Stadtmuseum, 1979), pp. 121–39.

33 Other Italian painters, not connected with *Valori Plastici* or the *Scuola Metafisica*, were also very influential on German artists, in particular Gino Severini and Felice Casorati. Space, however, does not permit further analysis. See Seymour Menton, *Magic Realism Rediscovered, 1918–1981*, pp. 45–55; Robert Schmitt, ed., *Neue Sachlichkeit und Realismus: Kunst zwischen den Kriegen* (Vienna: Kulturamt der Stadt Wien, 1977), especially pp. 154–56. An in-depth analysis of the Italian developments can be found in Ingo F. Walther, ed., *Realismus: Zwischen Revolution und Reaktion 1919–1939*, pp. 48–105.

34 Seymour Menton, *Magic Realism Rediscovered*, p. 45.

35 See Massimo Carrà, ed., *Metaphysical Art* (New York: Praeger, 1971), especially Ewald Rathke, "Magical Realism and the Metaphysical" and Patrick Waldberg, "Surrealism and the Metaphysical." For more on the links between *Neue Sachlichkeit* and Surrealism, see Wieland Schmied, *"Die neue Wirklichkeit — Surrealismus und Sachlichkeit"* in Stephan Waetzoldt and Verena Haas, eds., *Tendenzen der Zwanziger Jahre*, 3d ed. (Berlin: Dietrich Reimer Verlag, 1977), pp. 4/1–4/36. For the argument that "foremost, Magic Realism originated from the Dada movement," see Paul Ferdinand Schmidt, *Geschichte der modernen Malerei* (Stuttgart: Kohlhammer Verlag, 1957), pp. 257–63. The ob-

servation has been made that Magic Realism's boundaries were so "fluid that a Dadaist could just as well have become a painter of New Objectivity (Grosz) as a Surrealist (Max Ernst). After all, they have the same church fathers in common, like de Chirico and Carlo Carrà." Oscar Sandner, "*Sachlichkeit als Österreichische Möglichkeit*" in Oswald Oberhuber, ed., *Abbild und Emotion: Österreichischer Realismus, 1914–1944*, p. 121.

36 See Wieland Schmied, "*Neue Sachlichkeit* and German Realism of the Twenties" in Louise Lincoln, ed., *German Realism of the Twenties: The Artist as Social Critic* (Minneapolis: Minneapolis Institute of Arts, 1980), p. 42. See also Hans Georg Meyer, "*Die Neue Sachlichkeit*" in Henning Rischbieter, *Die Zwanziger Jahre in Hannover, 1916–1933* (Hanover: Kunstverein Hannover, 1962).

37 James Thrall Soby, *Giorgio de Chirico* (New York: Arno Press, 1966, reprint ed.), p. 25.

38 Gustav Hartlaub, *Neue Sachlichkeit: Deutsche Malerei seit dem Expressionismus* (Mannheim: Städtische Kunsthalle Mannheim, 1925), p. 2.

39 Franz Roh, *Nach-Expressionismus, Magischer Realismus*, pp. 133–34.

40 Franz Roh, "*Ausstellungen*" in *Das Kunstblatt* 6 (1921): 286–87.

41 Franz Roh, "*Rückblick auf den magischen Realismus*," pp. 7–9.

42 Emphasis mine.

43 Paul Westheim, "*Ein neuer Naturalismus?? Eine Rundfrage des Kunstblatts*" in *Das Kunstblatt* 9 (1922).

44 Gustav Hartlaub, "*Werbendes Rundschreiben.*"

45 Hartlaub was not able to assemble works of these various European artists. In the exhibition itself, almost all of the paintings displayed were by German artists.

46 Franz Roh, *Nach-Expressionismus, Magischer Realismus*, p. 134.

47 Franz Roh, "*Rückblick auf den Magischen Realismus*," p. 7.

48 Paul Westheim, "*Ein neuer Naturalismus??*" in *Das Kunstblatt* 9 (1922).

49 Paul Fechter, "*Die nachexpressionistische Situation*," in *Das Kunstblatt* 7 (1923): 324.

50 Perhaps that is why the term Urban Realism has been added to the plethora of labels used to describe this art of the 1920s. See Eberhard Roters et al., *Berlin 1910–1933* (New York: Rizzoli, 1982), p. 114.

51 For more on the history of the term *Sachlichkeit*, see Fritz Schmalenbach, "The Term '*Neue Sachlichkeit*'" in *Art Bulletin* (1940). See also Fritz Schmalenbach, *Die Malerei der Neuen Sachlichkeit* (Berlin: Gebr. Mann, 1973).

52 My thanks to Dr. Peter Guenther for this observation.

53 See Heide Berndt, "*Ist der Funktionalismus eine funktionale Architektur? Soziologische Betrachtung einer architektonischen Kategorie*" in H. Berndt, A. Lorenzer, K. Horn, *Architektur als Ideologie* (Frankfurt: Edition Suhrkamp, 1968); Ingo F. Walther, ed., *Realismus: Zwischen Revolution und Reaktion 1919–1939*,

esp. pp. 322–72 on architecture and design; Barbara Miller Lane, *Architecture and Politics in Germany, 1918–1945* (Cambridge: Harvard University Press, 1968).

54 Franz Roh also experimented with photography in the 1920s, and in 1929 became coeditor with Jan Tschichold of *Foto-Auge*, the first book on experimental, artistic photography in Germany.

55 Michael Schwarz, ed., *Georg Scholz: Ein Beitrag zur Diskussion realistischer Kunst* (Karlsruhe: Badischer Kunstverein e.V., 1975), esp. pp. 124–25.

56 Quoted in Fritz Schmalenbach, *Die Malerei der Neuen Sachlichkeit*, p. 33.

57 *Das Kunstblatt* 7 (1923).

58 Seymour Menton, *Magic Realism Rediscovered, 1918–1981*, p. 27.

59 Oscar Sandner, "*Sachlichkeit als (Österreichische) Möglichkeit*" in *Abbild und Emotion: Österreichischer Realismus, 1914–1944*, pp. 121–32.

60 Waldemar George, "*Frankreich und die Neue Sachlichkeit*" in *Das Kunstblatt* 11 (1927): 388–97.

61 Kenneth Silver, *Esprit de Corps: The Art of the Parisian Avant-Garde and the First World War, 1914–1925* (Princeton: Princeton University Press, 1989). See also Linda Nochlin, "Return to Order" in *Art in America* (September 1981): 82–83, 209–11, in which she analyzes the Realism in art of the 1920s and 1930s as a European "return to order." For an argument against viewing the style as such, see for instance Ingo F. Walther, ed., *Realismus: Zwischen Revolution und Reaktion 1919–1939.*

62 Waldemar George, "*Pierre Roy et le Réalisme Magique*" in *Renaissance* (March 1931): 86–95.

63 For the Italian development, see Robert Schmitt, ed., *Neue Sachlichkeit und Realismus: Kunst zwischen den Kriegen*, pp. 154–57.

64 For an analysis of Realism/New Objectivity in the United States, see Ingo F. Walther, ed., *Realismus: Zwischen Revolution und Reaktion 1919–1939*, pp. 246–75; for the Netherlands and Belgium, see pp. 170–91.

65 Dorothy C. Miller and Alfred Barr, eds., *American Realists and Magic Realists* (New York: Museum of Modern Art, 1943).

66 Waldemar George, "*Frankreich und die Neue Sachlichkeit*" in *Das Kunstblatt* 11 (1927): 395.

67 The KPD was the German Communist party.

68 Diether Schmidt, ed., *Manifeste Manifeste, 1905–1933*, Band I (Dresden: VEB Verlag der Kunst, 1965), pp. 26–30. See the last picture in the photograph section between pp. 304–5 of the ARBKD in Dresden, demonstrating against the increasingly reactionary cultural politics of the time with their banners, *"Wir revolutionären Künstler kämpfen gegen jede Kulturreaktion!"* (We revolutionary artists are fighting against every cultural reaction!). The Manifesto of the ARBKD is in Wieland Schmied, *Neue Sachlichkeit und Magischer Realis-*

mus 1918–1933, p. 258. For other examples of artists' political activism during the 1920s, see Uwe M. Schneede, *Realismus zwischen Revolution und Machtergreifung, 1919–1933* (Stuttgart: Württ. Kunstverein, 1971), pp. 5–6. A chronology of art and politics during the Weimar Republic is given in Schneede, pp. 34–41. See also John Willett, *The New Sobriety, 1917–1933: Art and Politics in the Weimar Period* (London: Thames and Hudson, 1978); Christine Hoffmeister, ed., *Revolution und Realismus. Revolutionäre Kunst in Deutschland, 1917 bis 1933* (Berlin: Staatliche Museen zu Berlin, 1978); Walter Laqueur, *Weimar: Die Kultur der Republik* (Frankfurt: Verlag Ullstein GmbH, 1976), esp. pp. 214–33.

69 For more on Verism, see Jost Hermand and Frank Trommler, *Die Kultur der Weimarer Republik* (Munich: Nymphenburger Verlagshandlung, 1978), pp. 368–74.

70 Helen Adkins, "*Neue Sachlichkeit—Deutsche Malerei seit dem Expressionismus*" in *Stationen der Moderne: Die bedeutenden Kunstausstellungen des 20. Jahrhunderts in Deutschland* (Berlin: Berlinische Galerie, 1988), p. 221.

71 Otto Dix, "*Das Objekt ist das Primäre*" in *Berliner Nachtausgabe*, December 3, 1927. Reproduced in Uwe M. Schneede, ed., *Die Zwanziger Jahre: Manifeste und Dokumente deutscher Künstler*, p. 138. Emphasis mine.

72 George Grosz, *A Little Yes and a Big No* (New York: Dial Press, 1946), p. 163.

73 In German, *Tendenzkunst* is an art "which expresses political opinions and ideological presuppositions, an art which is politically committed, an art which is a tool in class warfare, and an art which is propaganda." See Beth Irwin Lewis, *George Grosz: Art and Politics in the Weimar Republic* (Madison: University of Wisconsin Press, 1971), p. 92. In English, "tendentious" is sometimes given a negative connotation. I, therefore, have used "politicized" rather than "tendentious."

74 Emilio Bertonati, "Neue Sachlichkeit in a Wider Cultural Context" in Louise Lincoln, ed., *German Realism of the Twenties: The Artist as Social Critic*, p. 59. See also Franz Schulze, "Cold Facts" in *Art in America* (September 1981): 143–47.

75 Paul F. Schmidt, "*Die deutschen Veristen*" in *Das Kunstblatt* 8 (1924): 367–73, in which Schmidt argued that the Verists were the most independent group within the new art movement. Moreover, the Verists had taken the most decisive step toward opposing Expressionism because they had revolutionized form and content equally. They also represented the strongest contrast to the French artists. See also Emilio Bertonati, *Die neue Sachlichkeit in Deutschland* (Munich: Schuler Verlagsgesellschaft, 1974), p. 19, for more on Hartlaub's stance.

76 See Franz Roh's translated excerpt "The New Objects" in this volume.

77 Wieland Schmied, "*Neue Sachlichkeit. Der deutsche Realismus der Zwanziger Jahre*" in *Sammlung Berlinische Galerie. Kunst in Berlin von 1870 bis Heute* (Berlin: Berlinische Galerie, 1986), pp. 113–14. Figure 11 is cited as "Selbst

bildnis am Basteltisch (Self-Portrait at the Hobby Table), 1926, in Ingo F. Walther, ed., *Realismus Zwischen Revolution und Reaktion, 1919–1939*, p. 40, rather than as "Verblühender Früling" (Fading Spring) as cited herein by the Städtische Galerie im Lenbachhaus.

78 See Georg Scholz, *"Die Elemente zur Erziehlung der Wirkung im Bilde"* in Uwe M. Schneede, *Die zwanziger Jahre*, pp. 141–43, wherein Scholz describes the techniques used to achieve the painterly qualities of *Neue Sachlichkeit* art.

79 Remark made by the painter Ernst Thoms in Roland März, Introduction, *Malerei der Neuen Sachlichkeit* (Leipzig: 1984), p. 7f. Quoted in Bärbel Schrader and Jürgen Schebera, *The "Golden" Twenties: Art and Literature in the Weimar Republic* (New Haven: Yale University Press, 1988), p. 151. See also Georg Grabenhorst, *Ernst Thoms* (Göttingen: Musterschmidt Verlag, 1965).

80 Again, it should be noted that Hartlaub was not able to exhibit works from all over Europe as he had hoped, but assembled mainly art by German painters.

81 For more on the Mannheim exhibit, see Helen Adkins, *"Neue Sachlichkeit — Deutscher Malerei seit dem Expressionismus"* in *Stationen der Moderne: Die bedeutenden Kunstausstellungen des 20. Jahrhunderts in Deutschland*, pp. 216–35; Uwe M. Schneede, *Realismus zwischen Revolution und Machtergreifung, 1919–1933*, p. 10. In the exhibition catalog, Hartlaub thanked Roh for his assistance. For information on the traveling exhibitions in the 1920s and *Neue Sachlichkeit* exhibits of the 1960s, see Wieland Schmied, *Neue Sachlichkeit und Magischer Realismus in Deutschland 1918–1933*, pp. 259–61.

82 W. E. Oeftering, *"Kunsthalle Mannheim. Ausstellung 'Neue Sachlichkeit'"* in *Badische Presse*, August 1, 1925.

83 *Das Kunstblatt* 9 (1925): 266–68.

84 J. A. Beringer, *"Die neue Sachlichkeit"* in *Karlsruher Tageblatt*, August 3, 1925.

85 Bärbel Schrader and Jürgen Schebera, *The "Golden" Twenties: Art and Literature in the Weimar Republic*, pp. 164–65.

86 My thanks to Dr. Peter Jelavich for this observation.

87 See Franz Roh, *"Rückblick auf den magischen Realismus"* in *Das Kunstwerk*, pp. 8–9, for his opinion as to why *Neue Sachlichkeit-Magischer Realismus* slowly died out while abstraction came to dominate the modern art movement.

88 See Berthold Hinz, *Art in the Third Reich* (New York: Pantheon Books, 1979). A similar cultural purging took place in the Soviet Union. Stalin "cleansed" the Soviet Union of its flourishing modern art movement, thereby eradicating Constructivism. State-sponsored art, officially known as Socialist Realism ("the most coarsely idealistic kind of art ever foisted on a modern audience," according to art critic Robert Hughes), took its place. This Soviet art was very similar to that of the Third Reich — cultural propaganda, rabidly nationalistic, taken to its "heroic" extreme.

89 Christoph Stölzl, ed., *Die Zwanziger Jahre in München* (Munich: Münchner Stadtmuseum, 1979), p. 128.

90 See Seymour Menton, *Magic Realism Rediscovered, 1918–1981*, pp. 26–44; Helen Adkins, *"Neue Sachlichkeit—Deutsche Malerei seit dem Expressionismus"* in *Stationen der Moderne*, pp. 216–35; also in *Stationen der Moderne*, pp. 276–313; Stephanie Barron, ed., *"Degenerate Art": The Fate of the Avant-Garde in Nazi Germany* (Los Angeles: Los Angeles County Museum, 1991).

91 Franz Roh, *Nach-Expressionismus, Magischer Realismus*, p. 134.

92 Berthold Hinz, *Art in the Third Reich*, p. 38. My thanks to Dr. Peter Jelavich for his comments regarding Ziegler.

93 After World War II, Roh was reinstated by the Allies as professor of art history at the University of Munich. He also edited an art journal as well as wrote several more art history books, numerous exhibition reviews, and many articles. Throughout the post-war years until his death in 1965, Roh zealously continued his efforts on behalf of modern art in Germany. For more on Franz Roh, see Joan M. Lukach, *Hillay Rebay: In Search of the Spirit in Art* (New York: George Braziller, 1983), pp. 280–82; Carola Giedion-Welcker, *Schriften 1926–1971: Stationen zu einem Zeitbild* (Köln: Verlag M. DuMont Schauberg, 1973), pp. 146–48. Franz Roh, *"Entartete" Kunst: Kunstbarbarei im Dritten Reich* (Hanover: Fackelträger-Verlag, 1962).

94 *Revista de Occidente* 48 (June 1927): 274–301.

95 Franz Roh, *Realismo mágico, post expresionismo: Problemas de la pintura europea más reciente* (Madrid: Revista de Occidente, 1927).

96 See Jean Weisgerber, ed., *Le Réalisme magique: roman, peinture et cinéma*, esp. pp. 15–21.

97 Ibid., pp. 11–12.

98 See Jost Hermand, "Unity within Diversity? The History of the Concept '*Neue Sachlichkeit*'" in Keith Bullivant, ed., *Culture and Society in the Weimar Republic*, esp. 169–76.

99 See, for instance, Seymour Menton, *Magic Realism Rediscovered, 1918–1981*.

100 See Irene Guenther Bellomy, *Art and Politics During the German Occupation of France, 1940–1944*, unpublished thesis, University of Houston, 1992.

101 Franz Roh, *Nach-Expressionismus, Magischer Realismus*, pp. 108–11.

102 Alfred Kubin, *Die andere Seite: Ein phantastischer Roman. Mit einer Selbstbiographie des Künstlers* (München: Müller, 1917); the autobiographical preface, *"Aus meinem Leben"* in this 1917 edition and in Ulrich Riemerschmidt, ed., *Alfred Kubin: Aus meinem Leben. Gesammelte Prosa mit 73 Zeichnungen* (Munich: Deutscher Taschenbuch Verlag, 1977). See Alfred Kubin, *The Other Side*, English ed. (New York: Crown Publishing, 1967), with autobiography now as appendix. See also Alfred Kubin, *"Die Blätter mit dem Tod [Ein Totentanz]"* (Berlin: Bruno Cassirer, 1918); Alfred Kubin, *"Fünfzig Zeichnungen"* (Munich: Albert Langden, 1923).

103 Philip H. Rhein, *The Verbal and Visual Art of Alfred Kubin* (Riverside: Ariadne Press, 1989). See also Gregor Sebba, Introduction, *Kubin's Dance of Death and*

Other Drawings (New York: Dover Publications, 1973); *Alfred Kubin, 1877–1959*, exhibition catalog (New York: Serge Sabarsky Gallery, 1970); Paul Raabe, "A Documentary Biography" in *Alfred Kubin 1877/1977*, exhibition catalog (Munich: Edition Spangenberg, 1977), pp. 7–30.

104 Franz Roh, *Nach-Expressionismus, Magischer Realismus*, pp. 67–68.

105 Ernst Jünger, *"Nationalismus und modernes Leben"* in *Arminius. Kampfschrift für deutschen Nationalismus, 8* (1927–28): 4–6.

106 Ibid., p. 5.

107 Ernst Jünger, *Das abenteuerliche Herz* (1929) in *Werke*, Band 3 (Stuttgart: E. Klett, 1960–65); Ernst Jünger, *Sämtliche Werke*, Band 9 (Stuttgart: Klett-Cotta, 1978).

108 Ernst Jünger, *Das abenteuerliche Herz* (Hamburg: Hanseatische Verlagsanstalt, 1938).

109 See Volker Katzmann, *Ernst Jüngers Magischer Realismus* (Hildesheim-New York: Georg Olms Verlag, 1975). Also consult Chr. Van de Putte, *De Magisch-Realistische romanpoëtica in de Nederlandse en Duitse literatuur* (Louvain: Ed. Nauwelaerts, 1979); Wolfgang Rothe, ed., *Die deutsche Literatur in der Weimarer Republik* (Stuttgart: Phil. Reclam junior, 1974); Gerhard Loose, *Ernst Jünger, Gestalt und Werk* (Frankfurt am Main: V. Klostermann, 1957); Horst Denkler, *"Die Literaturtheorie der Zwanziger Jahre: Zum Selbstverständnis des literarischen Nachexpressionismus in Deutschland—Ein Vortrag"* in *Monatshefte 59, 4* (Winter 1967): 305–19; Horst Denkler, *"Sache und Stil. Die Theorie der "Neuen Sachlichkeit" und ihre Auswirkungen auf Kunst und Dichtung"* in *Wirkendes Wort 18, 3* (May–June 1968): 167–85.

110 Fritz Martini, *Deutsche Literaturgeschichte von den Anfängen bis zur Gegenwart*, 7th ed. (Stuttgart: Alfred Kröner Verlag, 1955), p. 561.

111 W. E. Süskind, *"Herman Bang und Wir"* (1927), reprinted in Peter de Mendelssohn, *S. Fischer und sein Verlag* (Frankfurt: S. Fischer Verlag, 1970), p. 1091.

112 Ibid., p. 1092.

113 Berhard Zeller, ed., *Alfred Döblin, 1878–1978* (Marbach: Kössel-Verlag GmbH, 1978), pp. 519–21.

114 G. Pohl, *"Magischer Realismus?"* in *Aufbau* 4 (1948): 650–53; Leonard Forster, *"Über den "Magischen Realismus" in der heutigen deutschen Dichtung"* in *Neophilologus* 34 (April 1950): 86–99; *"Die Wirklichkeit hat doppelten Boden. Gedanken zum Magischen Realismus in der Literatur"* in *Aktion*, September 1952.

115 Massimo Bontempelli, "Analogies" in *900 (Novecento)* 4 (Summer 1927): 9. Quoted in Chr. Van de Putte, *De Magisch-Realistische romanpoëtica in de Nederlandse en Duitse literatuur*, p. 33.

116 Alex Vömel, *"Alfred Flechtheim, Kunsthändler und Verleger"* in *Imprimatur; ein Jahrbuch für Bücherfreunde*, 1967, pp. 90–96.

117 Quoted in French in Jean Weisgerber, *Le Réalisme magique*, p. 17.

118 See Marguerite C. Suárez-Murias, ed., *Essays on Hispanic Literature—Ensayos de Literatura Hispana: A Bilingual Anthology* (Washington, D.C.: University Press of America, 1982), p. 99, wherein is given a reference to Enrique Anderson Imbert's personal account of the history of the "fabulous magical realism," beginning in 1925 in Germany to 1927 in Hispanic America, and its subsequent development. See Arturo Uslar-Pietri, *Letras y hombres de Venezuela* (Madrid: Editorial Mediterraneo, 1978), p. 287; Enrique Anderson Imbert, *El realismo mágico y otros ensayos* (Caracas: Monte Avila, 1976), pp. 11–12. See also Jean Weisgerber, *Le Réalisme magique*, p. 18.

119 Herbert A. Straus, "Jews in German History: Persecution, Emigration, Acculturation" in Herbert A. Strauss and Werner Röder, eds., *International Biographical Dictionary of Central European Emigrés, 1933–1945* (Munich: K. G. Sauer, 1983), vol. 2, part 1, a–k, pp. xi, xii.

120 Paul Westheim, *La Calavera* (Mexico, D.F.: Fondo de Cultura Economica, 1953).

121 Jean Weisgerber, *Le Réalisme magique*, p. 18; Marguerite C. Suárez-Murias, ed., *Essays on Hispanic Literature*, p. 99.

122 Helmut Lethen, *Neue Sachlichkeit, 1924–1932: Studien zur Literatur des 'Weissen Sozialismus'* (Stuttgart: J.B. Metzlersche Verlagsbuchhandlung, 1970), p. 193, n. 32.

ALEJO CARPENTIER
On the Marvelous Real in America

Editors' Note

Alejo Carpentier refers to the German art critic Franz Roh, and contemporary literary critics refer to both Carpentier and Roh as they devise their own theories of magical realism. Perhaps the northern European origins of Roh's formulation and its dissemination in Latin America by the Spanish *Revista de Occidente* served to spur Carpentier to his aggressively American discussion of the mode. In the two essays included here, Carpentier devises his own term, *lo real maravilloso americano,* to describe what he argues is a uniquely American form of magical realism. As opposed to European Surrealism, a movement in which Carpentier had participated in the 1930s in France, Carpentier's "marvelous American reality" does not imply a conscious assault on conventionally depicted reality but, rather, an amplification of perceived reality required by and inherent in Latin American nature and culture. It was Carpentier's conviction, strongly felt by the late thirties, formally codified in 1949 in the first essay included here, and elaborated interartistically in 1975 in the second, that *lo real maravilloso americano* differed decidedly in spirit and practice from European Surrealism. In Latin America, Carpentier argues, the fantastic is not to be discovered by subverting or transcending reality with abstract forms and manufactured combinations of images. Rather, the fantastic inheres in the natural and human realities of time and place, where improbable juxtapositions and marvelous mixtures exist by virtue of Latin America's varied history, geography, demography, and politics — not by manifesto.

Part of the first essay that we include here served to preface Carpentier's first novel, *El reino de este mundo* (*The Kingdom of this World,* 1949); we have translated an expanded version of that prologue, which was published in 1967 in a collection of Carpentier's essays, *Tientos y diferencias* (Approaches and Distinctions). The second essay was originally given as a lecture in 1975, and collected in 1981 in *La novela hispanoamericana en vísperas de un nuevo siglo* (The Hispanic American Novel on the Eve of a New Century).

I

Là-bas tout n'est que luxe, calme et volupté. Invitation to a voyage. Something remote. Something distant or different. *La langoureuse Asie et la brulante Afrique* of Baudelaire. . . . I'm back from the People's Republic of China. I became aware of Peking's very real beauty, its black houses and intensely orange ceramic tiled roofs where fabulous domestic fauna romp: small guardian dragons, curled griffins, graceful zoological household gods whose names I haven't learned. I lingered, astonished, in one of the patios of the Summer Palace, in front of stones mounted and displayed on pedestals, to be contemplated as art objects. They affirm absolutely a notion of *nonfigurative* art that is ignored in declarations of principles by nonfigurative Western artists: a magnification of Marcel Duchamp's readymade, a hymn of textures and fortuitous proportions, a defense of the *right* of the artist — detector of realities — *to choose* certain subjects or materials that have never been touched by human hands, that transcend their own limits with an original beauty that is the beauty of the universe. I have admired Nanjing's architectural subtlety, reserved and yet airy, and Nandang's strong medieval Chinese walls, bordered in white above the austere darkness of the breaker walls. I have lost myself in Shanghai's teeming crowds, those gymnastic, comical crowds who live in a city where the corners are round, in a city unaware of the West's angular corners. I have watched from the city's sea walls for hours as sampans with squared sails passed by; and later, flying above the country at a very low altitude, I was able to understand the enormous role that clouds and haze, motionless fog and mist play in the prodigious imagery of Chinese landscape painting. Contemplating the rice fields and seeing the work of laborers dressed in braided rushes, I also understood the role of the tender greens, pinks, and yellows in Chinese art, and the painter's shading chalks. And yet, in spite of having spent hours at the corner stands where glasses of hot water are served, and at the fish counters watching the fish whose colors blur in the enveloping motion of their lightly fanning fins; after having listened to the stories of storytellers whom I do not understand; after having stood in awe before the beauty and proportions of the Peking museum's masterpiece, a wondrous armillary sphere that is mounted upon four dragons and portentously combines the harmonious geometry of heavenly bodies with the heraldic curling of telluric monsters; after having visited the old observatories, bristling with amazing apparatus for sidereal measurements, the implications of which elude our Keplerian notions; after having bundled myself up against the somber cold of the great seaports and the almost feminine Pagoda Tower in Shanghai, that enormous and delicate corncob of windows and sharp eaves; after having marveled at the clocklike efficiency of the puppet theaters, I return to the West feeling somewhat melancholy. In spite of my deep interest in what I have seen, I am not sure that I have understood. In order to really understand—and not with the passivity of either a simpleton or a tourist, which in fact, I was—it would have been necessary to learn the language, to have clear ideas regarding one of the most ancient cultures in the world: to understand the clear speech of the dragon and the mask. I was greatly entertained, of course, by the incredible acrobatics of the creators of a theater that is classified for Western consumption as *opera*, when it is really nothing less than the chimerical fulfillment of what *total theater* has tried to achieve—an obsession for the most part unsatisfied by our playwrights, directors, and set designers. But the acrobatics of the interpreters of those operas, works that never thought of themselves as *operas*, were merely the complement to a language that will remain inaccessible to me for the rest of my days. They say that Judith Gautier mastered the ability to read Chinese by the age of twenty. (I don't believe she "spoke Chinese," because *Chinese* as such is never spoken; the Peking dialect, for example, is not understood one hundred kilometers outside of Peking, nor does it have anything to do with the picturesque Cantonese language or the semi-meridional dialect of Shanghai, although the written form for all of these languages is the same, so that communication is possible.) But as for me, I know that my remaining years of existence are too few to give me a true and exact understanding of Chinese culture and civilization. For that, I would need an *understanding of texts*, those texts inscribed on the steles that rest upon the stone shells of enormous tortoises—symbols of longevity, I was told—moving without movement, so ancient that no one knows their date of birth, ruling over aqueducts and fields, inhabitants of the outskirts of the great city of Peking.

II

I'm back from the world of Islam. I felt pleasantly stirred by landscapes so quiet, so well-defined by the hands of pruners and sowers, so foreign to any superfluous bit of vegetation—there are only rose bushes and pomegranate trees, watered by some underground source—that in them, I sensed the grace of some of the finest Persian miniatures; yet, truth be known, I now find myself far away from Iran and cannot know with absolute certainty whether the miniatures I recalled had anything to do with all this. I walked through silent streets, losing myself in the labyrinths of windowless houses, escorted by the fabulous smell of mutton fat so characteristic of central Asia. I was amazed by the diverse manifestations of an art that knows how to transform itself and how to play with materials and textures, triumphing over the formidable stumbling block of a prohibition—still very much observed—against depicting human figures. In terms of a love for textures, serene geometrical symmetries and subtle reversals, it seemed to me that Muslim artists showed signs of imagining an inventive abstraction equaled only by the small, marvelous patio inside the temple at Mitla, which one may contemplate in Mexico. (In these cases, true art is rigorously *nonfigurative*, maintaining a lofty distance from the place where polemics are based on tired and worn-out *realisms*). . . . I was acutely aware of the slender minarets, the polychromed mosaics, and the potent sonority of the *gazl;* the thousand-year-old pre-Koran taste for unleavened bread that falls of its own weight just as it's taken from the baker's oven. I flew over the Aral Sea, so strange, so foreign in its forms, colors, and contours, yet so similar to Baikal Lake, which amazes me with its surrounding mountains, its zoological rarities, with all that those remote places share: extension, limitlessness, repetition, the endless *taiga* exactly like that in our own jungles, the endless Yenisei River, five leagues wide (I quote Vsevolod Ivanov) after rains like those that swell the Orinoco until it also overflows its banks five or six leagues. . . . Upon my return, I was invaded by the great melancholy of one who wanted to understand but understood only partially. To understand the Islamic culture that I had barely glimpsed, I would have had to know one of the languages spoken there, or to have heard of some literary antecedent (something more substantial, to be sure, than *The Rubaiyat* read in Spanish or the wanderings of Aladdin or Sinbad or the music from *Thamar* by Balakirev or *Scheherezade* or *Antar* by Rimski-Korsakov) or be familiar with their philosophy, if indeed any philosophy functions as such in the great gnomic literature of that vast world where certain atavistic principles continue to weigh heavily on minds, even though certain political contingencies have been discarded. But he who yearned for understanding understood only partially because he never learned the language or languages spoken there. He confronted hermetic tomes in the bookstores, with titles drawn in arcane signs. I would have liked to learn those signs. I felt humiliated by the same ignorance that I feel in Sanskrit or classical Hebrew—languages that, by the way, were not taught in the Latin American universities of my adolescence, where even Greek and Latin were subjects regarded suspiciously by a freshly minted pragmatism that placed them alongside other idle, intellectual pastimes. I was aware, however, that to understand the Romance languages, the Latin American had only to live with them for a few weeks. (I would verify that fact upon my arrival in Bucharest.) Thus, seeing before me the unintelligible signs that were painted every morning across the headlines of the local newspapers, I felt something similar to perpetual discouragement, realizing that life wouldn't give me enough time (do twenty years of study mean one really *knows* the subject?) to arrive at an integrated, well-founded, universal vision of what Islamic culture is in its different parts, forms, geographical dispersions, dialectical differences, etc. I felt diminished by the true greatness of all that I had seen, but this greatness did not give me a report of its exact measurements or its real motives. It did not give me, upon returning from such extensive wanderings, the means to express to my own people what was universal in its roots, presence, and current transformations. For that, I would have had to possess certain indispensable knowledge, certain keys that, in my case and in the case of many others, would have required specialized study, the discipline of virtually an entire lifetime.

III

On the way back from my long voyage, I found myself in the Soviet Union where, despite my inability to speak the language, my sense of incomprehension was entirely alleviated. The magnificent architecture of Leningrad, at once baroque, Italian, Russian, was pleasing to me before I ever saw it. I knew those columns. I knew those astragals. I knew those monumental arches opening up buildings, reminiscent of Vitruvius and Viñola, and perhaps also of Piranesi; Rastrelli, the Italian architect, had been there after much strolling through Rome. The rostral columns that rose along the Neva were my personal property. The Winter Palace, deeply blue and foaming white, with its Neptunian, aquatic baroque [*barroquismo*], spoke a language well known to me. Over there, over the water, Peter and Paul's Fortress showed me its profile, a domesticated silhouette. And that's not all: Diderot's friend and patroness was Catherine the Great. Miranda, the Venezuelan precursor of the American Wars of Independence, was Potempkin's friend. Cimarosa lived and composed in Russia. In addition, Moscow University carries the name of Lomonosov, author of "Ode to the Northern Lights," one of the best examples of a certain kind of eighteenth-century poetry, scientific and encyclopedic, qualities that link it—more through its spirit than its style, of course—with Fontenelle and Voltaire. Pushkin made me think of *Boris Godunov;* I revised an unmusical French translation about thirty years ago at the request of a singer who had to play the role at the Columbus Theater in Buenos Aires. Turgenev was Flaubert's friend ("the most foolish man I ever met," he used to say in admiration). I discovered Dostoevsky in an essay by André Gide. I read Tolstoy's stories for the first time around 1920, in an anthology compiled by the Mexican Department of Education. Whether well translated or not, Lenin's *Philosophical Notebooks* speak to me of Heraclitus, Pythagoras, Leucippus, and even of "the idealist with whom one gets along better than with the stupid materialist." A performance at the Bolshoi (with an equestrian statue of Peter the Great in the scenery) reminds me of a visit to the far rooms with the high ceilings at the Heritage Museum. There, I find myself in the company of Ida Rubinstein in the strange portrait that Serov painted of her, at once affectionate and cruel; and also in the company of Sergei Diaghilev and Anna Pavlova, who—starting in 1915 and returning afterward every year to Havana—showed Cuba the transcendental techniques of classical dance. Continuing along, a vast retrospective exposition of Roerich jumps out at me unexpectedly, Roerich, the set designer and librettist of Stravinsky's *Rite of Spring,* who questioned Western music's principles of composition. . . . In Leningrad, in Moscow, I found once again in the architecture, in the literature, in the theater, a *perfectly intelligible* universe, intelligible despite my own deficiencies in technical and mechanical understanding of what is situated outside my own cultural territory. (How difficult it was for me one day in Peking to understand the reasoning of a Tibetan lama whose intention it was to correlate Tantrism with Marxism, or that extremely intelligent African man who not long ago in Paris spoke to me of magical tribal rites in terms of historical materialism.) I am increasingly convinced that a single lifetime is not enough to learn, understand, explain the fraction of the globe that destiny assigns a man to inhabit—although that conviction does not absolve him of an immense curiosity to see everything beyond the limits of his own horizons. But curiosity is rarely rewarded with complete *understanding.*

IV

There is no city in Europe, I believe, where the drama of the Reformation and Counter-Reformation has inscribed itself in more lasting and eloquent gestures than in Prague. On the one hand, the hard and heavy-set Tyn Church, bristling with needles, the Bethlehem Chapel with its steep roof dressed in austere, medieval slate tiles, where the vertical and terrible words of Jan Hus would one day resound; on the other hand, the curling, enveloping, almost voluptuous baroque of the Church of Our Savior in the Clementine school at the end of the Charles Bridge, opposite the daring ogives on the other bank, displays a sumptuous jesuitical scenery—more like a theater than a church—populated with saints and apostles, martyrs and doctors, all jumbled together in a choreographed assembly of stoles and miters—bronze on white, dark tones on gold—proclaiming the momentary victory of Rome's Latin over the nationalistic language spoken by the people of Prague, the language of psalms and Taborite hymns. . . . Above, in the citadel, the windows of the famous defenestration; below, on the *Mala Straná*, Waldstein's palace where the last great condottiere had the entire deafening symphony of the Thirty Year's War sculpted on the smooth ceiling of his reception hall, with profuse configurations of bugles, drums and sackbuts jumbled together with the harnesses, plumes, and standards of bellicose allegories. There I can understand better the spirit that led Schiller, in the first part of his famous trilogy, to the strange feat of writing a drama without protagonists in which the characters are referred to as "some Croatians," "some uhlans," "a bugle player," "a recruit," "a Capuchin," "a noncommissioned officer." But that's not all. Though the Reformation and Counter Reformation are present in the stones of Prague, its buildings and spaces also speak to us of a past forever suspended between the extreme poles of real and unreal, fantastical and verifiable, contemplation and action. We know that Faust, the alchemist, makes his first (imaginary?) appearance in Prague, where future generations would handle Tycho Brache's astronomical instruments, which were exact or nearly so, before visiting the house of that stargazer named Johannes Kepler, not to mention those who searched for the philosopher's stone, those who prepared hermetic mercury—their street is still preserved, complete with retorts and kilns, in the city of Charles the Great. So many things here evoke the legend of the Golem, that automaton forced to work for the benefit of a wise rabbi on the periphery of the Jewish cemetery and the superb synagogues. And the most extraordinary thing is that the old Jewish cemetery, with its dramatic steles dating back to the sixteenth and seventeenth centuries, standing side by side, or one behind the other, haphazardly, as though they were up for auction—in a late March that illuminated the Hebraic inscriptions with brushstrokes from the North wind—coexists on equal terms with the narrow Stavovske theater where one day in 1787, Mozart's *Don Giovanni* had its opening night, a Faustian work, a eucharist play [*auto sacramental*] composed, strangely enough, by that genius in an Age of Reason that firmly refused to believe in guests turned to stone, even though quite close by, bronze bishops and doctors danced in the sumptuous theological scenery of the Clementine Church. There are no mute stones in Prague for those who know how to listen. To this listener, from every corner, from every intersection, like Chamisso's character, present in every fortuitous encounter, in every debate that moves from literature to politics, there emerges the still, velvety, shadowless silhouette of Franz Kafka, who "attempted to describe a battle" and without meaning to, gave us—metaphorically, indirectly—the most stupendous sense of Prague's atmosphere, experienced in all its mystery and possibility. In 1911 Kafka says in his *Diary* that he is moved by a vision of stairs to the right of the Czech bridge: he perceives "through a small triangular window" (only in that asymmetric city, where every manifestation of fantastic architecture is to be found, could there be a *triangular window*) all of the grace and the baroque vitality of that flight of stairs ascending toward the illustrious window of the defenestration. . . . From Kafka, leaping into the past in an imaginary, timeless diligence, we arrive in Leipzig. Awaiting us there is the organ behind which Anna Magdalena, greatly moved, discovered that terrible presence, the inspired dragon Johann Sebastian, and we remember that there the Passions were first sung with very few voices and minimal orchestras. These works concern us most directly because for two hundred years they have not stopped growing, swelling with ever greater numbers of musicians, crossing the Atlantic to the shores of America in scores, performances and recordings, their *allegros* suggesting to Héctor Villa-Lobos the name of *bacchianas* for his compositions inspired by the *allegro* (continuous movement, *perpetum mobile*) of the Brazilian or Bahian rhythms. . . . From Leipzig the imaginary diligence carries us—with its coachman sounding the trumpet that Mozart and even Mörike knew so well—to Goethe's Weimar to the house where monstrous replicas of Greek sculptures await us, sculptures executed in heroic dimensions worthy of being placed in a temple if the author of *Faust* had not stood them in his scanty Weimer estate in rooms so tiny that house guests were obliged to turn sideways to get past a chessboard. These enormous Greek divinities, helter-skelter and up to their ears in the small rooms in the house in Weimar, remind me of the sort of eponymous rhetoric commonly used in the vestibules of government buildings in Latin America, where presiding statues swell, widen, elevate and exalt heroes to two or three times their actual size, even to the absurd extreme of a Statue of the Republic in the Havana Capital Building with breasts of bronze that weigh a ton, its dimensions so stupidly cyclopean that by its side, the poor giant Kafka would go completely unnoticed.

V

The Latin American returns to his own world and begins to understand many things. He discovers that although Don Quixote by rights belongs to him, he has learned words in the "Speech to the Shepherds" that go back through the ages to *Works and Days*. He opens up Bernal Díaz del Castillo's great chronicle and finds himself before the only honest-to-goodness book of chivalry that has ever been written—a book of chivalry where the evil doers are lords [*teules*] one could see and touch, where unknown animals are real, unknown cities are discovered, dragons are seen in rivers and strange mountains in snow and smoke. Without realizing it, Bernal Díaz bested the brave deeds of Amadís of Gaul, Belianis of Greece, and Florismarte of Hircania. He had discovered a world of monarchs crowned with the plumes of green birds, vegetation dating back to the origins of the earth, food never before tasted, drink extracted from cacti and palm trees, but he did not realize that in such a world, events tend to develop their own style, their own unique trajectories. Latin Americans drag a legacy of thirty centuries behind them, but in spite of a record of absurd deeds and many sins, we must recognize that *our style* is reaffirmed throughout *our history*, even though at times this style can beget veritable monsters. But there are compensations. Melgarejo, the tyrant from Bolivia, can make his horse Holofernes drink buckets of beer. During that same epoch in the Caribbean Mediterranean, José Martí appears and is capable of writing one of the best essays about the French impressionists that has ever appeared in any language. Central America, with its illiterate populations, produces a poet—Ruben Darío—who transforms all poetry written in Spanish. There is a man there who, a century and a half ago, explained the philosophical postulates of alienation to slaves emancipated only three weeks earlier. There is a man there (we cannot forget Simón Rodríguez) who created systems of education inspired by *Emile,* where it was thought that all students had to do was learn to read in order to ascend socially by virtue of their understanding of books—which is to say, their understanding of codes. There is a man whose aim was to develop Napoleonic strategies of war using lancers riding broken down mounts without saddles or stirrups. There is the Promethean loneliness of Bolívar at Santa Marta, the nine-hour battles waged with bladed weapons in the lunar landscape of the Andes, the towers of Tikal, the frescoes rescued from the Bonampak jungle, the lasting enigma of Tihuanaco, the majesty of the acropolis at Monte Albán, the abstract—absolutely abstract—beauty of the temple at Mitla, with its variations on visual themes so totally alien to the figurative impulse. The list could go on forever.

I will say that my first inkling of the marvelous real [*lo real maravilloso*] came to me when, near the end of 1943, I was lucky enough to visit Henri Christophe's kingdom—such poetic ruins, Sans-Souci and the bulk of the Citadel of La Ferrière, imposingly intact in spite of lightning and earthquakes; and I saw the still-Norman Cape Town, the Cap Français of the former colony, where a house with great long balconies leads to the palace of hewn stone inhabited years ago by Pauline Bonaparte. My encounter with Pauline Bonaparte there, so far from Corsica, was a revelation to me. I saw the possibility of establishing certain synchronisms, American, recurrent, timeless, relating this to that, yesterday to today. I saw the possibility of bringing to our own latitudes certain European truths, reversing those who travel against the sun and would take our truths to a place where, just thirty years ago, there was no capacity to understand or measure those truths in their real dimensions. (Pauline Bonaparte—like the Venus of Canova—was, for me, a *lazarillo* and a guide as I felt my way, groping at first toward essays exploring characters like Billaud-Varenne, Collot d'Herbois, and Víctor Hugues who, seen in an American light, would later animate my *Siglo de las luces* [translated as *Explosion in a Cathedral*].) After having felt the undeniable spell[1] of the lands of Haiti, after having found magical warnings along the red roads of the Central Meseta, after having heard the drums of the Petro and the Rada, I was moved to set this recently experienced marvelous reality beside the tiresome pretension of creating the marvelous that has characterized certain European literatures over the past thirty years. The marvelous, sought in the old clichés of the Brocelianda jungle, the Knights of the Round Table, Merlin the sorcerer and the Arthurian legend. The marvelous, inadequately evoked by the roles and deformities of festival characters—won't young French poets ever get tired of the *fête foraine* with its wonders and clowns, which Rimbaud dismissed long ago in his *Alchimie du verbe?* The marvelous, manufactured by tricks of prestidigitation, by juxtaposing objects unlikely ever to be found together: that old deceitful story of the fortuitous encounter of the umbrella and the sewing machine on the dissecting table that led to ermine spoons, the snail in a rainy taxi, the lion's head on the pelvis of a widow, the Surrealist exhibitions. Or even now, the literary marvelous: the king in Sade's *Julieta,* Jarry's supermacho, Lewis' monk, the horrifying machinery of the English Gothic novel: ghosts, immured priests, lycanthropes, hands nailed to a castle door.

The result of willing the marvelous or any other trance is that the dream technicians become bureaucrats. By invoking traditional formulas, certain paintings are made into a monotonous junkyard of sugar-coated watches, seamstresses' mannequins, or vague phallic monuments: the marvelous is stuck in umbrellas or lobsters or sewing machines or whatever on a dissecting table, in a sad room, on a rocky desert. Poverty of the imagination, Unamuno said, is learning codes by heart. Today there are codes for the fantastic based on the principle of the donkey devoured by the fig, proposed as the supreme inversion of reality in *Les Chants de Maldoror,* codes to which we owe "children threatened by nightingales," or André Masson's "horses devouring birds." But observe that when André Masson tried to draw the jungle of Martinique, with its incredible intertwining of plants and its obscene promiscuity of certain fruit, the marvelous truth of the matter devoured the painter, leaving him just short of impotent when faced with blank paper. It had to be an American painter—the Cuban, Wilfredo Lam—who taught us the magic of tropical vegetation, the unbridled creativity of our natural forms with all their metamorphoses and symbioses on monumental canvases in an expressive mode that is unique in contemporary art. Faced with the unsettling imaginative poverty of a Tanguy, for example, who has spent twenty-five years painting the same stony larvae beneath the same gray sky, I feel moved to repeat a phrase that made the first batch of Surrealists proud: *Vous qui ne voyez pas, pensez à ceux qui voient* [You who can't see, think of those who can]. There are still too many "adolescents who find pleasure in raping the fresh cadavers of beautiful, dead women" (Lautréamont), who do not take into account that it would be more marvelous to rape them alive. The problem here is that many of them disguise themselves cheaply as magicians, forgetting that the marvelous begins to be unmistakably marvelous when it arises from an un-expected alteration of reality (the miracle), from a privileged revelation of reality, an unaccustomed insight that is singularly favored by the unex-pected richness of reality or an amplification of the scale and categories of reality, perceived with particular intensity by virtue of an exaltation of the spirit that leads it to a kind of extreme state [*estado límite*]. To begin with, the phenomenon of the marvelous presupposes faith. Those who do not believe in saints cannot cure themselves with the miracles of saints, nor can those who are not Don Quixotes enter, body, soul, and possessions, into the world of Amadís of Gaul or Tirant le Blanc. Certain phrases of Rutilio about men transformed into wolves from *The Labors of Persiles and Segismunda* turn out to be prodigiously trustworthy because in Cervantes' time, it was believed that people could suffer from lupine mania. Another example is the trip a character makes from Tuscany to Norway on a witch's blanket. Marco Polo allowed that certain birds flew while carrying ele-phants in their claws. Even Luther saw a demon face to face and threw an inkwell at its head. Victor Hugo, exploited by sellers of marvelous books, believed in apparitions because he was sure that he had spoken with Leo-poldina's ghost in Guernsey. For Van Gogh, his faith in the sunflower was enough to fix his revelation upon the canvas. Therefore, it seems that the marvelous invoked in disbelief—the case of the Surrealists for so many years—was never anything more than a literary ruse, just as boring in the end as the literature that is oneiric "by arrangement" or those praises of folly that are now back in style. (This does not mean that I agree with those who support a return to realism—a term that now implies a slavishly politi-cal agenda.) All they do is to substitute the tricks of the magician for the worn-out phrases of academics or the eschatological glee of certain exis-tentialists. But clearly there is no excuse for poets and artists who preach sadism without practicing it, who admire the supermacho because of their own impotence, invoke ghosts without believing that they answer to incan-tations, who establish secret societies, literary sects, vaguely philosophical groups with saints and signs and arcane ends that are never reached, with-out being able to conceive of a valid mysticism or to abandon the most banal habits in order to bet their souls on the terrifying card of faith.

This seemed particularly obvious to me during my stay in Haiti, where I found myself in daily contact with something that could be defined as the marvelous real. I was in a land where thousands of men, anxious for freedom, believed in Mackandal's lycanthropic powers to the extent that their collective faith produced a miracle on the day of his execution. I had already heard the prodigious story of Bouckman, the Jamaican initiate. I had been in the Citadel of La Ferrière, a work without architectural precedent, its only forerunner Piranesi's "Imaginary Prisons." I breathed in the atmosphere created by Henri Christophe, a monarch of incredible zeal, much more surprising than all of the cruel kings invented by the Surrealists, who were very much affected by imaginary tyrannies without ever having suffered a one. I found the marvelous real at every turn. Furthermore, I thought, the presence and vitality of this marvelous real was not the unique privilege of Haiti but the heritage of all of America, where we have not yet begun to establish an inventory of our cosmogonies. The marvelous real is found at every stage in the lives of men who inscribed dates in the history of the continent and who left the names that we still carry: from those who searched for the fountain of eternal youth and the golden city of Manoa to certain early rebels or modern heroes of mythological fame from our wars of independence, such as Colonel Juana de Azurduy. It has always seemed significant to me that even in 1780, sane Spaniards from Angostura would throw themselves into the search for El Dorado and that, in the days of the French Revolution—long live Reason and the Supreme Being!—the Compostellan Francisco Menéndez would walk through the land of Patagonia searching for the enchanted city of the Caesars. Focusing on another aspect of this theme, we can see that whereas in Western Europe folk dancing, for example, has lost all of its magical evocative power, it is hard to find a collective dance in America that does not embody a deep ritual sense and thus create around it a whole process of initiation: such are the dances of Cuban *santería* or the prodigious African version of the Corpus festival, which can still be seen in a town called San Francisco de Yare in Venezuela.

In the sixth song of Maldoror, there is a moment when the hero, pursued by all the police in the world, escapes an "army of agents and spies" by adopting the shapes of diverse animals and making use of his ability to transport himself instantaneously to Peking, Madrid, or Saint Petersburg. This is "marvelous literature" in full force. Yet in America, where nothing like this has been written, Mackandal lived and was endowed with the same powers by the faith of his contemporaries, who with his magic fomented one of the strangest and most dramatic uprisings in history. Maldoror—Ducasse himself admits it—is nothing more than a "poetic Rocambole." Maldoror left behind only an ephemeral literary school. The

American Mackandal, on the contrary, leaves an entire mythology, preserved by an entire people and accompanied by magic hymns still sung today during voodoo ceremonies.[2] (It is also a strange coincidence that Isidore Ducasse, a man who had an exceptional instinct for the poetic fantastical, happened to be born in America and that he should boast so emphatically at the end of one of his poems of being *le montevidéen*.) Because of the virginity of the land, our upbringing, our ontology, the Faustian presence of the Indian and the black man, the revelation constituted by its recent discovery, its fecund racial mixing [*mestizaje*], America is far from using up its wealth of mythologies. After all, what is the entire history of America if not a chronicle of the marvelous real?

Translated by Tanya Huntington
and Lois Parkinson Zamora

Notes

Alejo Carpentier, "De lo real maravilloso americano," in *Tientos y diferencias* (Montevideo: Arca, 1967), pp. 96–112. The final part of this essay was published as the prologue to *The Kingdom of this World* in 1949; the parameters of the earlier text are noted in Carpentier's first footnote.

1 I turn here to the text of the prologue for the first edition of my novel *The Kingdom of this World* (1949), which did not appear in later editions, even though I still consider it to be, except for certain details, as pertinent now as it was then. Surrealism no longer constitutes for us a process of erroneously directed imitation, as it did so acutely even fifteen years ago. However, we are left with a very different sort of *marvelous real*, which is growing more palpable and discernible and is beginning to proliferate in the fiction of some young novelists on our continent.

2 See Jacques Roumain, *Le Sacrifice du Tambour Assoto*.

ALEJO CARPENTIER

The Baroque and the Marvelous Real

You all know the title of the talk I've proposed to give today on two elements that, in my opinion, enter decisively into the nature and meaning of Latin American art, of this Latin America, America *mestiza*,[1] as José Martí called it, which Madame Vice President of this athenaeum has just evoked with her words of introduction: "The Baroque and the Marvelous Real." It is a theme rich in vicissitudes and one about which I don't want to try your patience, so I will begin without preamble, in a somewhat dry and perfunctory manner, with a few dictionary definitions.

Before I begin to talk about the baroque, I would like to settle a linguistic dispute: what is the baroque? Everybody talks about the baroque, everybody knows more or less what the baroque is or can feel the baroque. The same thing happens with Surrealism. Today, everybody knows what Surrealism is, everybody says after witnessing an unusual occurrence: "How surreal." But if we go back to the basic text on Surrealism, to André Breton's *First Manifesto*, written in 1924, we must face the fact that the definition given by the founder of this movement hardly corresponds to what happened later. Breton himself was incapable of defining what he was doing, although he knew very well what he was going to do. Let's turn to the dictionaries. Let's start with the *Petit Larousse*. We are told: "Baroque: neologism. Synonym of Churrigueresque. Gallic in its extravagance." But we look for *barroquismo*[2] and are told: "Neologism, extravagance, bad taste." In other words, the baroque betrays Gallic characteristics and is identified exclusively with the architecture of a man named Churriguera, who was not the best representative of the baroque period but rather of a kind of mannerism; this does not explain anything at all, because the baroque is something multiple, diverse, and enormous that surpasses the work of a single architect or a single baroque artist.

Let's turn to the *Dictionary of the Royal Academy*. Under *baroque* we are told: "Style of ornamentation characterized by the profusion of volutes, scrolls, and other adornments in which the curved line predominates. Also applicable to painted and sculpted works in which both the movement of figures and the division of segments are excessive." Frankly, the academic gentlemen of the Spanish Royal Academy couldn't have come up with a poorer definition.

Turning to a similar dictionary, we find that we are given these synonyms for the baroque: "Overladen, mannerist, Gongorist (as though it were shameful to be Gongorist!), euphemistic, conceptualist," and again "Churrigueresque," and (but this simply isn't possible!) "*decadent.*"

Every time they speak to me of "decadent" art, I fall into a state of blind rage, for this business about decadence, when a certain art is called decadent, has been systematically applied to a multitude of artistic manifestations that, far from representing decadence, represent cultural summits. For many years, the French impressionists, Cézanne, Manet and others, were classified as decadent. In Beethoven's time, the masters of composition forbade their students to listen to or study the works of Beethoven because they were decadent. The atonal composers were called decadent. When we pick up a music historian such as Riemann from the beginning of the twentieth century, he tells us that all music written after Wagner is decadent. (When Debussy went to Russia at the turn of the century to conduct his works, the great master Rimsky-Korsakov—who was no fool—upon seeing that his students were enthusiastic about the works of the brilliant French innovator, told them: "Well, go and listen if you want to, but let me warn you that you run the risk of getting used to it." In other words, he spoke of Debussy's music just as one might say to a friend: "Smoke opium if you like, but be careful; it's addictive." In this case, the baroque would have been "decadent" as well.)

There have been attempts to define the baroque as a style. There have been those who have tried to enclose it within the boundaries of a particular style. Eugenio d'Ors, who doesn't always completely convince me of his artistic theories but who is certainly extraordinarily insightful in some of his essays, tells us in a famous essay[3] that what the baroque displays is, in fact, a kind of creative impulse that recurs cyclically throughout history in artistic forms, be they literary or visual, architectural or musical; and he gives us a very fitting image by saying that there is a baroque spirit, just as there is an imperial spirit. That spirit, arising through the centuries, can be equally attributed to Alexander, Charlemagne, or Napoleon. There is an eternal return to the imperial spirit, historically speaking, just as there is an eternal return of the baroque in art through the ages, and this baroque, far from signifying decadence, has at times represented the culmination, the maximum expression and the richest moment of a given civilization. As an example, I would like to use someone whom I will mention later on, namely François Rabelais, the brilliant French Renaissance humanist who, in the five volumes of his prodigious novel, *Gargantua et Pantagruel,* gave us what is perhaps the most complete, extraordinary, and juicy expression that the fullness of the French language can provide. Rabelais, who was the prince of French baroque artists, represents the pinnacle of French literature because, although certain comparisons are dangerous, it is evident that his great book of Gargantua is unique in all of French literature, situated on the same pinnacle of exceptions and prodigious feats as *Don Quixote, The Divine Comedy,* and all of Shakespeare's plays. Rabelais is the culmination of French culture and Renaissance humanism, and he was a profoundly baroque writer. An inventor of words, an enricher of the language who, when he lacked verbs, gave himself the luxury of inventing them, and when he did not have adverbs, invented those as well.

According to Eugenio d'Ors—and it seems to me that his theory is irrefutable in this respect—the baroque must be seen as *a human constant.* Thus, a fundamental error to be erased from our minds: the generally accepted theory that the baroque is an invention of the seventeenth century.

For most people, the words "baroque art" refer to a certain kind of very ornamental architecture from the seventeenth century, like that of Borromini in Italy, or a kind of sculpture with extraordinary movement and expansive forms like that of Bernini, whose most representative work, a definitive and complete baroque work, is the famous "Ecstasy of Saint Teresa," one of the culminating pieces of universal sculpture. Those who see the baroque as pejorative, as a sort of strange phenomenon or mannerism—because it is true that there were certain minor strains of baroque mannerism in the seventeenth century—contrast it to another concept. What concept is this? So-called classicism.

Now if the word "baroque" is taken in its generally understood sense, or the word "Surrealism" is understood according to Breton's definition, and these definitions still cannot explain Surrealism or the baroque, then I must say that "classicism" is the hollowest word of all, the most meaningless term that could possibly occur to anyone. Let's turn once again to the dictionary. The *Larousse* says: "Something outstanding and worthy of imitation. Applicable to a writer or work that is considered to be the model for any type of literature," and cites examples like Calderón or Lópe de Vega. We're in trouble already, because if any writer represents the baroque in the Spanish language besides Quevedo and Góngora, that it is Calderón. And those who have read one of Calderón's most famous works, *El médico de su honra*, will recall the passage in which Doña Mencía tells the story of a young knight who is accidentally thrown from his steed, one of the most frequently anthologized fragments in all baroque poetry.

In the *Dictionary of the Royal Academy*, we are told: "*Classicism:* Literary or artistic system, based on the imitation of the Greek and Roman models. Used in contrast to Romanticism." Where does this leave us? Classicism is *that which copies Roman and Greek models.* But in another dictionary, we are told that classicism can be copied from Calderón, who was baroque. As you see, the word classicism has no meaning or impact whatsoever. And I would say that as all *imitation* is academic, so all academies are governed by rules, norms, and laws. Classicism is academic, and all that is academic is conservative, vigilant, obedient, and therefore the declared enemy of innovation, of anything that breaks rules and norms.

In short, to attempt to understand what people are trying to tell us when they talk about classicism, there is no better way than to choose examples everyone knows, characteristic examples of things that we all have engraved on the retina of our memories. Let's consider three monuments representative of what is considered to be classical, three monuments that have constituted an academic style and as such, have created the norms to be imitated. These three archetypal monuments would be the Parthenon, Herrera's Escorial, and the palace at Versailles.

Now then, these works are characterized by a central axis with proportionally smaller lateral axes. Those of us who read Vignola in our architecture courses know that when copying the façades of those Greek temples, the Parthenon and the Erechtheum, the first step we took was to draw the central axis from which the frontispiece sloped away to either side, dividing the entablature in two. Each column had its lateral axis, and each axis was proportionally removed from the central axis in a kind of Pythagorean cross-section that divided the building into two equal and symmetrical parts.

In the architecture of Versailles, the Escorial or the Parthenon, there is something very important, which is that empty spaces, naked spaces,

spaces without ornamentation are in and of themselves as important as adorned spaces or the shafts of grooved columns. If we begin to look at those great naked planes in the Parthenon or Versailles, their boundaries marked by columns, we see that their value is in their proportions: they create a sort of geometrical harmony in which filled and vacant spaces are equally important. In the Parthenon, the space between the columns is as important as the columns themselves. I would go so far as to say that the column serves to mark the boundaries of empty spaces, the spaces of air. Somehow, in the structure of the Greek temple or Herrera's Escorial, the construction is complemented by vacant space, by space without ornamentation whose beauty resides precisely in its circumscription, in its expression of an emotion, an impression of severe, majestic beauty stripped of every superfluous element—all corresponding to a kind of linear geometry.

We have, on the other hand, the baroque, a constant of the human spirit that is characterized by a horror of the vacuum, the naked surface, the harmony of linear geometry, a style where the central axis, which is not always manifest or apparent (in Bernini's Saint Teresa it is very difficult to determine a central axis), is surrounded by what one might call "proliferating nuclei," that is, decorative elements that completely fill the space of the construction, the walls, all architecturally available space: motifs that contain their own expansive energy, that launch or project forms centrifugally. It is art in motion, a pulsating art, an art that moves outward and away from the center, that somehow breaks through its own borders. A typical example of the baroque can be found in Bernini's cathedral, Saint Peter's in Rome. Every time I see that explosion of forms, that explosion of vaults, that seemingly static luminescence surge from the ground through the frame that encloses it, I think of those paintings by de Chirico in which suns are stuck in cages, caged suns. To me, Bernini's Saint Peter's Cathedral is just that: a caged sun, a sun that expands and explores the columns that circumscribe it, that pretend to demarcate its boundaries and literally disappear before its sumptuousness. In the Cathedral of Toledo, behind the main altar in the ambulatory, there is a gigantic, proliferating sculpture, a sculpted composition that rises to the uppermost skylights, where the baroque sculptor has not just hung the figures that descend toward us (angels falling, men falling, saints falling in prodigiously choreographed motion, life-sized figures): he has persuaded form to collaborate with light. The light entering through the skylights combines with the sculpture in such a way that, depending on the time of day, all of the figures seem to move. In my opinion, herein resides one of the most beautiful baroque archetypes I could ever contemplate.

Going back to what we were saying about seeing the baroque as a human constant that absolutely cannot be limited to an architectural, aesthetic, and pictorial movement originating in the seventeenth century, we discover that the baroque has flourished in all ages, sporadically at times, and at times as the main characteristic of a culture. To cite clearly typical examples that everyone knows, I'll say that the baroque—and this is obvious—flourishes in all aspects of Indian culture: in the distant temples and grottoes of India there are meters and meters, if not kilometers, of more or less erotic bas-reliefs that are formally baroque and erotically baroque because of the imbrication of figures, the constant arabesques, the presence of what we called a moment ago a series of proliferating foci—in groups and individually, dancing and always united, interlocked like plants—foci that extend to infinity. There comes a moment when the bas-relief ends, but it could easily continue to cover incredible distances with its accumulated energy, if only there were more surface to sculpt.

We've spoken of Hindu sculpture. What about the Cathedral of St. Basil the Beatified in Moscow? Is it not a perfect example of baroque architecture, with its domed cupolas of different colors? Where is the central axis of St. Basil's, which everyone has seen in photos? Where, in that play of cupolas? Is there any symmetry of colors or forms? The Cathedral of St. Basil in Moscow is, I would say, one of the most extraordinary examples of the Russian baroque. In Prague, an entirely baroque city, the sculptures on the Charles Bridge form a legion, as do the figures of bishops and saints and doctors of the church, who are almost dancing in spite of the heavy bronze, who fly in spite of the weight of the material; in the Church of Saint Clementine, at the entrance of the Charles Bridge, there is a veritable theological ballet that unfolds before our eyes in an absolutely baroque style. Later, it will be the Viennese baroque in the time of Maria Teresa and the Emperor Joseph II; take Mozart's *Magic Flute*, if you will, where the baroque lives in the scenery, in the meaning of the work and the music itself—one of the masterpieces of the universal baroque from every point of view.

Now then, I have spoken of the baroque as an art that fears a vacuum, that flees from geometrical arrangements, from the space of, say, Mondrian (white surfaces, dark surfaces, above all clear surfaces, or surfaces upon which one appreciates the quality of the materials). You will ask me: "And what about the Gothic? Because that, after all, is also the nature of the Gothic." Take, for example, the façade of the Cathedral at Chartres, or the façade of Notre Dame Cathedral in Paris. We discover porticoes and we discover that in all of the elements of their façades not one space is left unfilled; there are figures of demons, of Judgment Day, scenes from the Bible, figures of different kinds mixed together.

And yet in the Gothic period, something also happens that Eugenio d'Ors noted very clearly. D'Ors establishes the difference between a human constant such as the baroque and what he calls *historical styles*. It is evident that the Romantic and Gothic periods are historical styles; the Gothic period responded to a historic moment that was superseded by the Renaissance, deprived of its architecture, relegated to the past. Absurd is he who tries to erect today, in 1975, a gothic cathedral by copying the best models. It would be a useless, absurd pastiche, bearing no relation to anything whatsoever. On the other hand, the baroque spirit can reappear at any moment and does, in fact, reappear in many of the creations of today's most modern architects, because it is *a spirit* and not a *historical style*. To conclude his argument, d'Ors tells us: "You may have observed that there is no Gothic style in literature." Whereas there is, of course, a baroque style in literature. And turning to tangible, visible examples (using ones that everybody knows), we realize that Aeschylus or Sophocles or Plato or Livius Andronicus or Cicerone, the Frenchman Racine or Bossuet or the Voltaire who wrote tedious and forgotten tragedies in Alexandrines (the by-product of Racine's classical tragedies that obeyed the rules of the Aristotelian unities and survive solely as literary curiosities for students of literature and the erudite) — we realize that not one of the authors I have just mentioned could assimilate himself to the baroque. They do not have a baroque style, nor is it possible to find in one of Plato's dialogues or in a tragedy by Aeschylus the essence and spirit of the baroque. On the other hand, all of Indian literature is baroque, and all of Iranian literature, including that monumental epic, the *Book of Kings*, by Firdousí, is baroque; and skipping through the centuries, we find ourselves in Spain among those peaks of baroque literary style, *The Dreams* [*Los Sueños*] of Quevedo, the eucharist plays [*autos sacramentales*] of Calderón, the collected poems of Góngora, and the collected prose of Gracián. The proof that there exists a baroque spirit is Cervantes, the contemporary of some of the authors I have just mentioned, who does not seem baroque to us.

Don Quixote is obviously not baroque in terms of style, although Cervantes, at times in the *Exemplary Tales* [*Novelas emplejares*] and above all in the *Interludes* [*Entremeses*], shows himself to be baroque, just as Lope also occasionally tends toward the baroque.

In Italy, the emperor of the baroque is Ariosto in his *Orlando Furioso*. In England, Shakespeare clearly approaches a baroque spirit in his tumultuous, profuse, apparently disordered theater without empty surfaces or dead moments, where each scene in itself is a proliferating cell, subordinate to the action of the next. Shakespeare is full of short, extraordinary scenes that are small units in themselves, inserted within the greater whole of the tragedy. If he isn't baroque in *Julius Caesar* or *Timon of Athens*, he is supremely baroque in Act V of *Midsummer Night's Dream*.

I mentioned Rabelais a moment ago. In his work, which carried the French language to its highest, fullest, most extraordinary expression, there are already fragments that—let's say—foresee the baroque. There is a very interesting episode in the third book of *Gargantua and Pantagruel*, as the vicar of Meudon titled his masterpiece. And there is, in this third book, a completely imaginary episode in which Rabelais invents a story (Rabelais invented everything). The story goes that one day Philip of Macedon decided to attack the city of Corinth. Diogenes lived in Corinth, Diogenes the skeptic, Diogenes the misanthrope, Diogenes in his barrel. Naturally, given his philosophic attitude toward life, he is not a man who cares whether Philip of Macedon takes the city or not. But suddenly— Rabelais invents this—Diogenes acquires the vice of patriotism. When he sees troops coming closer to the city, he gets into his barrel and starts it rolling, causing such devastation, knocking down every means of defense, that he ends up bringing about the retreat of Philip of Macedon's soldiers with his barrel.

Rabelais, who tells us this story in two pages in order to adumbrate for us the arms carried by Philip of Macedon, uses seventy nouns, seventy words (a catalog of the arms carried by the enemy), so that the devastation caused by Diogenes' barrel requires *seventy-two* consecutive verbs in order to say that it "destroys," "breaks," "shatters," "pierces," "terminates," "burns," "upsets," etc.; seventy-two verbs in two pages to tell us of the devastation caused by Diogenes' barrel.

As we go on, we find that Romanticism, which in the *Dictionary of the Royal Academy* is contrasted to classicism and academism, is completely baroque. It had to be baroque, since Romanticism, which is generally illustrated by the absurd moonlit engraving and the character who composes verse, isolated from the world in which he lives, that is, the character who "lives in the clouds," who was really nothing of the sort: the Romantic man was action and vigor and movement and will and declaration and violence. He breaks away from the Aristotelian unities in the theater, finishes off classical French tragedy (in France, anyway), demands the rights of man to proclaim his interior being and exteriorize his passions, invents Sturm und Drang, that is, an atmosphere of "storm and desire." And let's not forget that those Romantics who were seen by the bourgeoisie of the era as lost souls, loonies [*gente en la luna*], people incapable of logical thought (because, of course, their morals, ethics, and politics were incompatible with the bourgeois conformity of the era) were, in fact, men of action and men who expressed action. Almost all of them were involved in the first utopian movements. We must not forget that Delacroix, the most important Romantic painter, was the one who left us the true painting of the *Parisian Barricades*, a revolutionary painting that can be placed next to Picasso's *Guernica*. And don't forget that the young Wagner was driven out of Munich for being an anarchist, or that Lord Byron died in Missolonghi in an ardent attempt to liberate Greece.

We find, in the Romantic period, that Novalis, for example, offers us a completely baroque novel, namely *Heinrich von Ofterdinger*. The second *Faust* by Goethe is one of the most baroque works in all literature; Rimbaud's *Illuminations* (see the first poem in *Illuminations*, "After the Flood") is a masterpiece of baroque poetry. *Les Chants de Maldoror* by Lautréamont—and Lautréamont called himself "the Montevidean" because he was born in Montevideo and was very proud of having been born in America—is a monument to baroque poetics. Marcel Proust (especially Marcel Proust, and here again we recall Eugenio d'Ors, who was right on so many points in his essay) Marcel Proust gives us one of the great moments of universal baroque prose, prose in which are inserted—as d'Ors notes—parenthetical asides, further series of proliferating cells, sentences within sentences that have a life of their own and sometimes connect to other asides that are also proliferating elements. I believe that there is no page more beautifully baroque in all of Proust's gigantic novel than that episode in *The Captive* where the protagonist, the narrator, who is Proust himself, is lying in Albertine's bed in the morning and listening to the cries of the vendors passing in the street below, and with that marvelous power of intertwining thoughts and concepts by means of his prodigious knowledge, Proust writes that these cries can be related by their melodious inflections and the ways they modulate their voices to medieval liturgical chants. And not only they, but the dog groomer, the birdseed seller, the scissor sharpener, all those who come to sell their small household articles evoke for him not only the Gregorian chant but also certain fragments of Debussy's *Pelléas et Mélisande,* and suddenly Proust constructs, using those lowly street cries, one of the pages in which he plays vertiginously with time, relating the shout of a woman selling birdseed and the cry of a woman selling sweets or slices of fruit to the great medieval liturgical chant and the Ambrosian chant. This is also the baroque, just as the development of Surrealism was totally baroque.

Academism is characteristic of settled times that are complete, sure of themselves. The baroque, on the other hand, arises where there is transformation, mutation or innovation: I don't need to remind you that on the eve of the Soviet Revolution, the one who represented Russian poetry was Vladimir Mayakovsky, whose work is a monument of the baroque from start to finish, his plays as well as his poetry. The baroque always projects forward and tends, in fact, to a phase of expansion at the culminating moment of a civilization, or when a new social order is about to be born. It can be a culmination, just as it can be a premonition.

America, a continent of symbiosis, mutations, vibrations, *mestizaje,* has always been baroque: the American cosmogonies, where we find the *Popol Vuh,* where we find the books of the *Chilam Balam,* where we find all that has been discovered and studied recently in the works of Ángel Garibay and Adrián Recinos, with all of the cycles of time delineated by the appearance of the cycles of the five suns. (According to ancient Aztec mythology we would now be in the era of Quetzalcóatl's sun). Everything that refers to American cosmogony—and America is big—corresponds to the baroque.

Aztec sculpture could never be seen as classical sculpture—think of the great heads of Quetzalcóatl at Teotihuacán,[4] think of the ornamentation of the temples. It's baroque; of course it's baroque, with its geometries of both straight and curved lines, its particular fear of empty surfaces. There is almost never even a meter of empty surface in an Aztec temple. During a two-year excavation in the area of Teotihuacán, archaeologists recently discovered some delightful residences of Aztec nobles dating back to before the Conquest. Imagine the archeologists' surprise to find the walls covered with highly refined paintings representing the daily life of the time: their pools, gardens, sports, banquets, children's games, pastimes, women's lives, daily life, all of this represented in a series of paintings that can only be described as baroque. They project the most authentic baroque spirit.

The *Popol Vuh*, I repeat (and those who have read it are aware of this) is a monument to the baroque; so is Nahuatl poetry, which was unknown until thirty years ago and was brought to light by the work of Garibay, who has so far given us eleven first-rate pre-Conquest poets in an extremely copious anthology that fills two heavy volumes. It is the most baroque, the most brilliantly baroque poetry one can imagine, with its polychromatic images, its interweaving and merging elements, the richness of its language. The "Goddess of Death" at the Museum of Mexico[5] is a monument to the baroque, a female figure covered with entwined snakes. And there is (I always cite this as an example) what I consider to be the amplified baroque in America: the temple at Mitla. Mitla, near Oaxaca, gives us, in a façade of marvelously balanced volumes, a series of boxes of the same size in which each develops an abstract composition different from the one before; that is, the work is no longer symmetrical; each one of those boxes—there are eighteen of them—is a proliferating cell of a baroque composition inserted into a baroque ensemble. I cannot, when I contemplate the façade at Mitla, help recalling the thirty-three variations of Diabelli's theme by Beethoven, in which Beethoven offers us thirty-three monumental variations stemming from an initially innocuous theme that a fashionable critic recently declared to be thirty-three sonorous objects rather than musical variations. The boxes at Mitla are eighteen plastic objects. In the same vein, when I see these compositions at Mitla, I also think of Schoenberg's *Variations* for orchestra.

I know that this resemblance, established across the centuries, between the temple at Mitla and Schoenberg's *Variations*, may seem arbitrary. But in fact, there exists a spiritual resemblance between the two things that again validates d'Ors' theory.

Neither the Romanesque nor the Gothic periods reached America; in other words, two *historical styles* that performed a central role in the development of the artistic culture of the old continent are entirely unknown to us. The Gothic has not reached us simply because in some city, in 1920, it occurs to an architect with bad taste to make a false Gothic cathedral. Neither the romanesque nor the Gothic arrived in America. What did arrive was the plateresque, a type of baroque, though perhaps with more atmosphere—with more elegance, let's say—than the Churrigueresque baroque. Ah! But when the Spanish plateresque arrives in the ships of the conquerors, what does the craftsman who knows the secrets of the Spanish plateresque find? An Indian work force that, having already built and sculpted and painted with baroque spirit, adds to the Spanish plateresque its New World baroque materials, baroque imagination, baroque zoological motifs, baroque botanical motifs and floral motifs, and so we reached the heights of glory of baroque architecture, the American baroque whose most prodigious examples are the church in Tepotzotlán in Mexico (where a central, pyramidal, and very high cupola shows us the most enormous accumulation of proliferating cells imaginable, where the play of light is similar to that of the Cathedral in Toledo), the façade of San Francisco de Ecatepec in Cholula, where baroque materials are added to baroque forms through colors, tiles, and mosaics; the famous chapel in Puebla, baroque in white and gold, where a celestial concert appears and angels make their appearance playing the lute, harps, the clavichord, all of the great instruments of the Renaissance; the árbol de la vida [tree of life] in Santo Domingo in Oaxaca, a monumental baroque composition covering the vaulted ceiling, a great, expanding tree whose branches are entwined with figures of angels, saints, human figures, figures of women, all blending into the vegetation. Then there is the baroque that we find in Ecuador, Peru and in a much more modest fashion on the façade of the Cathedral in Havana, one of the most beautiful baroque façades to be found in the New World.

And why is Latin America the chosen territory of the baroque? Because all symbiosis, all *mestizaje*, engenders the baroque. The American baroque develops along with *criollo*[6] culture, with the meaning of *criollo*, with the self-awareness of the American man, be he the son of a white European, the son of a black African or an Indian born on the continent — something admirably noted by Simón Rodríguez: the awareness of being Other, of being new, of being symbiotic, of being a *criollo;* and the *criollo* spirit is itself a baroque spirit. To this effect, I would like to recall the grace with which Simón Rodríguez, who brilliantly saw these realities, reminds us in a passage from his writings of the men who speak Spanish and yet are not Spanish, the men who legislate and litigate in Spanish and yet are not Spanish, because they are *criollos*. Simón Rodríguez adds: "We have *huasos* [peasants], Chinamen and *bárbaros* [barbarians], gauchos, *cholos* and *guachinangos* [people of mixed Indian and Spanish blood], blacks, browns and whites, mountain- and sea-dwellers, Indians, *gentes de color y de ruana* [people of color and people wearing *ruanas*], tanned, mulatto and *zambos* [black Indians], *blancos porfiados y patas amarillas* [stubborn whites and yellow shanks] and a world of crossbreeds: *tercerones*, quadroons, octaroons and *saltatrás* [throwbacks]."[7] With such variety, each contributing its version of the baroque, we intersect with what I have called "the marvelous real."

And here a new linguistic quarrel arises. The word "marvelous" has, with time and use, lost its true meaning, and lost it to the extent that the words "marvelous" or "the marvelous" produce a conceptual kind of confusion as serious as that caused by the words "baroque" and "classical." Dictionaries tell us that the marvelous is something that causes admiration because it is extraordinary, excellent, formidable. And that is joined to the notion that everything marvelous must be beautiful, lovely, pleasant, when really the only thing that should be gleaned from the dictionaries' definitions is a reference to the *extraordinary*. The extraordinary is not necessarily lovely or beautiful. It is neither beautiful nor ugly; rather, it is amazing because it is strange. Everything strange, everything amazing, everything that eludes established norms is marvelous. The Gorgon with her snaky locks is as marvelous as Venus arising from the waves. Deformed Vulcan is as marvelous as Apollo; Prometheus tortured by the vulture, Icarus crashing to earth, and the goddesses of death are all as marvelous as triumphant Achilles, Hercules, conqueror of the Hydra, or goddesses of love (which in all religions and mythologies appear paired off with goddesses of death). Furthermore, the creators of the marvelous take charge of telling us what they thought about the marvelous. And what man has ever done more for the marvelous than the one who has overpopulated our minds since childhood with figures belonging to the world of the marvelous? Charles Perrault, author of the *Mother Goose* stories, inventor of "Tom Thumb," "Sleeping Beauty," "Blue Beard," "Puss in Boots," "Little Red Riding Hood," etc., stories that have accompanied us since childhood. In the preface to his stories, Perrault says something that defines the marvelous. He speaks of fairies and tells us that fairies would just as soon spew diamonds from their mouths when they are in a good mood as reptiles, snakes, serpents, and toads when they are angered; and we mustn't forget that the most famous fairy from all the medieval tales, who led up to Perrault and whom Perrault recovers, is the fairy Melusina (what a beautiful name!) who was an abominable monster with the head of a woman and the body of a serpent, and yet she belongs to the marvelous. Perrault tells us a horrendous, terrible tale in the story "Tom Thumb," the one where the ogre, instead of beheading the seven small brothers who arrived asking for shelter in his home, cheerfully and mistakenly beheads his seven daughters and then goes to bed. This horrendous, terrible scene belongs to the marvelous — as does the incest that also appears in Perrault.

So we should establish a definition of the marvelous that does not depend on the notion that the marvelous is admirable because it is beautiful. Ugliness, deformity, all that is terrible can also be marvelous. All that is strange is marvelous.

Now then, I speak of the marvelous real when I refer to certain things that have occurred in America, certain characteristics of its landscape, certain elements that have nourished my work. In the prologue to the first edition of my book *The Kingdom of this World*,[8] I define what I think the marvelous real to be. But at times people say to me, "We have something that has been called *magical realism;* what is the difference between magical realism and the marvelous real?" If we stop to take a look, what difference can there possibly be between Surrealism and the marvelous real? This is very easily explained. The term magical realism was coined around 1924 or 1925 by a German art critic named Franz Roh in a book entitled *Realismo mágico,* published by the *Revista de Occidente.*[9] In fact, what Franz Roh calls magical realism is simply Expressionist painting, and he is careful to choose examples of Expressionist painting that have nothing to do with concrete political agendas. Don't forget that in Germany at the end of World War I, a time of misery and difficulty and drama, a time of general bankruptcy and disorder, an artistic tendency named *Expressionism* appears. One of the most authentic representations of Expressionism is Bertolt Brecht's first play, *Baal.* However, there is combat there, sarcasm, a social agenda, just as there was a social agenda in the play by Karel Capek that created the character of the robot, just as there was a social agenda in the play by Georg Kaiser that had characters named *first man, second man, first lady in black, green lady, red lady,* or in the piece by Capek with *robot one, robot two, robot three;* that is to say, depersonalized characters who created a certain atmosphere of criticism and polemics, expounding more or less revolutionary ideas, etc.

Not Franz Roh: what he called *magical realism* was simply painting where real forms are combined in a way that does not conform to daily reality. And on the cover of the book appears the *Douanier,* Rousseau's famous painting in which we see an Arab sleeping peacefully in the desert, a mandolin to one side, with a lion standing there and a moon in the background; that is magical realism because it is an unrealistic image, impossible but fixed there nonetheless. Another painter whom Franz Roh liked very much and identified as magical realist was the painter Balthus, who painted perfectly realistic streets, stripped of all poetry and all interest: houses without character, little roofs, white walls and in the middle of those streets without atmosphere or air or anything to remind us of the lessons of the Impressionists, some enigmatic figures pass by each other without speaking, engrossed in their diverse, unrelated tasks. A picture of a street full of people, and yet deserted for want of communication among them. Franz Roh also considered that Chagall was a magical realist, with his painted cows flying through the sky, donkeys on rooftops, upside-down people, musicians among the clouds—elements of reality but transferred to a dreamlike atmosphere, an oneiric atmosphere.

As far as Surrealism is concerned, we shouldn't forget that Surrealism pursued the marvelous through books and through prefabricated objects. Breton said in his manifesto: "All that is marvelous is beautiful, only the marvelous is beautiful." However, we must also remember that when Breton spoke of the marvelous, like Perrault, he did not consider that the marvelous was admirable because it was beautiful but because it was strange. When he cites the classics in his *First Manifesto*, or those that end up as Surrealist classics, he begins with the totally macabre book, Young's *Nights*, followed by Swift, one of the cruelest and most terrible writers produced by eighteenth-century England, with the famous episode of the butcher shop that sold the flesh of children. Then he speaks of Edgar Allan Poe, who is not always pleasant; on the contrary, he is often necrophagous and macabre. Breton also speaks of Baudelaire, who sang equally of carrion and women, who sang of the poor masses just as he sang of the invitation to the voyage or the immense sea; Jarry, cruelly polemic; Roussel, and many others.

Now then, if Surrealism pursued the marvelous, one would have to say that it very rarely looked for it in reality. It is true that for the first time the Surrealists knew how to see the poetic force of a window display or a market, but more often their fabrication of the marvelous was premeditated. The painter who stood before a canvas would say, "I'm going to make a painting with strange elements that create a marvelous vision." You have all seen Surrealist painting and know that it is undoubtedly very successful painting, but on its canvases everything is premeditated and calculated to produce a sensation of strangeness; I would cite as a typical example the soft clocks by Salvador Dalí, those clocks made of taffy dripping over the edge of a terrace. Or else, that other canvas by a Surrealist painter that shows a perfectly banal staircase with doors opening onto a hallway. On those stairs there is only one strange element. There is a *visitor*. It is a snake meandering up the steps. Where is it going? What is its purpose? No one knows. A mystery. A *manufactured* mystery.

On the other hand, the marvelous real that I defend and that is our own marvelous real is encountered in its raw state, latent and omnipresent, in all that is Latin American. Here the strange is commonplace, and always was commonplace. The stories of knighthood were written in Europe but they were acted out in America because even though the adventures of Amadis of Gaul were written in Europe, it is Bernal Díaz del Castillo, who in *The True History of the Conquest of New Spain* gives us the first authentic chivalric romance. And constantly—we must not forget this— the conquerors saw very clearly aspects of the marvelous real in America; here I want to recall Bernal Díaz's phrase as he contemplates Tenoch-titlán/Mexico City for the first time and exclaims, in the middle of a page written in an absolutely baroque prose: "We were all amazed and we said that these lands, temples and lakes were like the enchantments in the book of Amadís." Here we have the European man in contact with the American marvelous real.

How could America be anything other than marvelously real, if we recognize certain very interesting factors that must be taken into account? The conquest of Mexico occurs in 1521, when François I ruled France. Do you know how big the urban area of Paris was under François I? Thirteen square kilometers. In Garnier's *Universal Atlas*, published less than one hundred years ago, we are told that the metropolitan area of Madrid was twenty kilometers in 1889 and that the area of Paris, capital of capitals, was eighty kilometers. When Bernal Díaz del Castillo laid eyes for the first time on the panorama of the city of Tenochtitlán, the capital of Mexico, the empire of Montezuma, it had an urban area of one hundred square kilometers—at a time when Paris had only thirteen. And marveling at the sight, the conquerors encountered a dilemma that we, the writers of America, would confront centuries later: the search for the vocabulary we need in order to translate it all. I find that there is something beautifully dramatic, almost tragic, in a sentence written by Hernán Cortés in his *Cartas de Relación* [Letters from Mexico] addressed to Charles V. After attempting to tell the king what he has seen in Mexico, he acknowledges that the Spanish language is too narrow to identify so many new things and says to Charles V: "As I do not know what to call these things, I cannot express them." And of the native culture, he says, "There is no human tongue that can explain its grandeurs and peculiarities." In order to understand and interpret this new world, a new vocabulary was needed, not to mention — because you can't have one without the other — a new optic.

Our world is baroque because of its architecture — this goes without saying — the unruly complexities of its nature and its vegetation, the many colors that surround us, the telluric pulse of the phenomena that we still feel. There is a famous letter written to a friend by Goethe in his old age in which he describes the place near Weimar where he plans to build a house, saying: "Such joy to live where nature has already been tamed forever." He couldn't have written that in America, where our nature is untamed, as is our history, a history of both the marvelous real and the strange in America that manifests itself in occurrences like these that I'll recall quickly. King Henri Christophe, from Haiti, a cook who becomes the emperor of an island and who, believing one fine day that Napoleon is going to reconquer the island, constructs a fabulous fortress where he and all of his dignitaries, ministers, soldiers, troops could resist a siege of ten years' duration. Inside, he stored enough merchandise and provisions to last ten years as an independent country (I refer to the Citadel of La Ferrière). In order that this fortress have walls capable of resisting attacks by the Europeans, he orders that the cement be mixed with the blood of hundreds of bulls. That is marvelous. Mackandal's revolt, which makes thousands and thousands of slaves in Haiti believe that he has lycanthropic powers, that he can change into a bird or a horse, a butterfly, an insect, whatever his heart desires. So he foments one of the first authentic revolutions of the New World. Benito Juárez's little black carriage, in which he transports the whole nation of Mexico on four wheels over the country's roads, without an office or a place to write or a palace to rest, and from that little carriage he manages to defeat the three most powerful empires of the era. Juana de Azurduy, the prodigious Bolivian guerrilla, precursor of our wars of independence, takes a city in order to rescue the head of the man she loved, which was displayed on a pike in the Main Plaza, and to whom she had borne two sons in a cave in the Andes. Auguste Comte, the founder of positivism, is worshiped even today in Brazilian churches. While Rousseau's *Emile* never led to the establishment of a European school, Simón Rodríguez founded a school in Chuquisaca based on the principles of that famous book, thus accomplishing in America what Rousseau's admirers in Europe could not. One night in Barlovento I stumbled upon a popular poet named Ladislao Monterola who didn't know how to read or write but, when I asked him to recite one of his compositions, gave me his own deca-syllabic version of the *Chanson de Roland*, the history of Charlemagne and the peers of France. In our nineteenth-century history, there are many more interesting figures, secondary figures who leave minor Scottish kings like Macbeth far behind. There is a Latin American dictator in the mid-nineteenth century who, after having had a brilliant start, falls prey to a phobia of betrayal and persecution and who systematically gets rid of his most faithful ministers, his best generals, his relatives, his brothers, his sisters and even his own mother, until only he remains, absolutely alone, on the top of a mountain, surrounded by an army made up of the crippled, the aged, and children. This is a story, in my opinion, more extraordinary than that of Macbeth. There are also the lives of conspirators on this continent whose novels have not yet been written and who are much more interesting than conspirators such as Pío Baroja's Aviraneta.

If our duty is to depict this world, we must uncover and interpret it ourselves. Our reality will appear new to our own eyes. Description is inescapable, and the description of a baroque world is necessarily baroque, that is, in this case the *what* and the *how* coincide in a baroque reality. I cannot construct a so-called classical or academic description of an *árbol de la vida* from Oaxaca. I have to create with my words a baroque style that parallels the baroque of the temperate, tropical landscape. And we find that this leads logically to a baroque that arises spontaneously in our literature. Modernist poetry is the first great literary school that we offered to the world, and our Modernismo transformed Spanish poetry in Spain, profoundly marking the work of, say, Valle Inclán. What, then, is modernism, especially in its first stage, if not extremely baroque poetry? Such is Darío's entire early period. And there is also a baroque that reaches the absurd, becoming an excessive scrawl, as in the poetry of a Herrera y Reissig. José Martí, so direct, so eloquent, so explicit in his political discourse, when he lets his pen go and writes for pure pleasure, as he did in the anthropological study he dedicated to Charles Darwin's memory, we have a marvelous example of baroque style. His fundamental essay, "Our America," where all of the problems of America are defined in few pages, is also a marvelous example of baroque style. The works that taught my generation—*The Vortex* [*La vorágine*] with which you are all familiar— are perennially baroque. And how could *The Vortex* be otherwise when the jungle is nothing if not baroque? I hardly need to mention that Rómulo Gallegos' *Canaima* is a baroque novel. There are, for example, descriptions of flowing water in *Canaima*, water leaping from waterfall to waterfall, moving from one pool to another, water that jumps, flows backward, intermingles. There is a masterful page where he speaks of unnavigable rivers in motion, of water that is perpetually becoming, constantly furious, bursting, rising, destructive—one of the most admirable baroque pages ever to flow from the pen of that great Venezuelan novelist. Compare the water of Gallegos to the water that Paul Valéry paints for us in *Le Cimetière marin* [Seaside Cemetery]: calm, harmonious, peaceful, tame water. Given what he sees, Gallegos is baroque, and the most baroque of his novels is, in my opinion, *Canaima*, because it's a matter of expressing a baroque world.

Asturias, writing from the thirties to the fifties more or less, forms a link between Gallegos' generation and mine. In Asturias, the influence of the *Popol Vuh*, the books of *Chilam Balam*, and the *Book of the Cachikeles* is a constant. All great mythologies, the great cosmogonies of the new continent, inspire the images in his prose.

The baroque that you are familiar with in the contemporary Latin American novel, which is often called the "new novel," or the "boom"— and the "boom," as I have said before, is not a concrete thing nor does it define anything—is the result of a generation of novelists still alive today who are producing works that translate the scope of America from its cities to its jungles and fields in a wholly baroque fashion.

As far as the marvelous real is concerned, we have only to reach out our hands to grasp it. Our contemporary history presents us with strange occurrences every day. The mere fact that the first socialist revolution on the continent should occur in the country least likely to sustain a revolution—I say "least likely" in the *geographical* sense—is a strange event in contemporary history, a strange event added to many strange events that, to our credit, have occurred in American history from the Conquest to the present, and with magnificent results. But faced with strange events that await us in that world of the marvelous real, we must not give up and say, as Hernán Cortés said to his monarch: "As I do not know what to call these things, I cannot express them." Today, we know the names of these things, the forms of these things, the texture of these things; we know where our internal and external enemies are. We have forged a language appropriate to the expression of our realities, and the events that await us will find that we, the novelists of Latin America, are the witnesses, historians, and interpreters of our great Latin American reality. We have prepared ourselves for this, we have studied our classics, our authors, and our history. In order to express our moment in America, we have sought and found our maturity. We will be the classics of an enormous baroque world that still holds the most extraordinary surprises for us and for the world.

Translated by Tanya Huntington
and Lois Parkinson Zamora

Translators' Notes

Lecture given in the Caracas Athenaeum on May 22, 1975; published in Spanish in Alejo Carpentier, *La novela latinoamericana en vísperas de un nuevo siglo* (Mexico City: Siglo XXI, 1981), "Lo barroco y lo real maravilloso," pp. 111–32.

1 *mestizo:* descending from different races, generally caucasian and native American.

2 Carpentier uses the noun *barroquismo*, as well as *barroco*, with the connotation of "baroque-ish" or "baroque-ness." We have translated *barroquismo* as "baroque" throughout.

3 Carpentier refers to d'Ors' book *Lo barroco*, which he likely read in the French edition: Eugenio d'Ors, *Du Baroque*, trans. Agathe Rouart-Valéry (Paris: Editions Gallimard, 1935).

4 Carpentier refers to the ceremonial center of San Juan de Teotihuacán as an Aztec city but, in fact, it had been abandoned by 850 A.D., whereas the Aztec capital, Tenochtitlán — now Mexico City — was founded only in 1325. The Aztecs claimed the Teotihuacanos as ancestors.

5 Carpentier refers to the monolithic Aztec sculpture of Coatlique in the Museum of Anthropology in Mexico City.

6 We leave this word untranslated, because "creole" in English might suggest Louisiana culture to some U.S. readers. In fact, both words — *criollo* and creole — refer to the racial and cultural mixing that produces new cultures.

7 Here follows a list of vernacular describing the great variety of racial mixings (*las castas*) in colonial Latin America. Literal translations are misleading, for these idiomatic terms do not refer literally to their object but rather metaphorically to a racial category. We nonetheless give literal translations to suggest some of the cultural assumptions inherent in these metaphors, and provide synonyms where literal translation is impossible.

8 The reference is to the preceding essay, "On the Marvelous Real in America."

9 Roh's name in the Spanish edition of this essay appears as "Roth," no doubt an error made when Carpentier's lecture was transcribed; We have substituted the correct spelling throughout. Here, Carpentier refers to Roh's book, a partial translation of which begins this volume.

ANGEL FLORES
Magical Realism in Spanish American Fiction

Spanish American literature has been studied mostly through the thematic or biographical approach. The thematic approach has dwelt on geographical settings, classifying the works of fiction as "novels of the pampa," "novels of the sierra," and "novels of the selva." The biographical approach, on the other hand, has surveyed the literary production chronologically — "novel of the Colonial period," "novel of the Period of Independence," "novel of the Mexican Revolution," etc. — supplementing historical considerations with biographical notes on the writers of each of the periods. However interesting these approaches may be in relating literature to ecological patterns or to history, they have contributed but little to *literary* criticism. They have not been very helpful, for instance, in evaluating the intrinsically aesthetic merits of a work and have paid little or no attention to the complex problems of form, composition, and stylistic trends. Such classificatory terms as "Romantic," "Realistic," "Naturalistic," "Existentialist" do circulate in their writings but in rather superficial, desultory, or indiscriminating ways. We are told, for instance, that Echeverría was a "Romantic" poet, disregarding completely his *El Matadero* [The Slaughterhouse], a precursory masterpiece of Naturalism; or that *Doña Bárbara* and *La vorágine* [The Vortex] were robust specimens of Realism, overlooking their romantic tirades and psychological distortions. Hence the frequency with which one meets in university theses such titles as "Romantic, Realistic and Naturalistic Elements in the Novels of Rómulo Gallegos and José Eustasio Rivera" and "El romanticismo esencial del realista José Rivera" ["The Essential Romanticism of the Realist José Rivera"]. Had the line of analysis followed a more rigorous examination into the emotional and stylistic peculiarities, it could have been ascertained that, at least in Latin American prose fiction, it is difficult if not impossible to categorize faithfully each movement. Even in those works which are taken as typical of certain schools or movements, classification fails. Jorge Isaacs' *María* cannot be dismissed as a Romantic novel pure and simple: the novel ends, as a matter of fact, with such detailed, concretely realistic pictures as the Salomé episode and the homeward travelogue. In these penultimate and final sections there is almost as much realism as there is romanticism. The romantic and realistic persist side by side too in Güiraldes, in Lynch, in Payró, in Quiroga. Perhaps during one rather fleeting moment, with no significant consequences, one influence, in this case Zola's, seemed preponderant: Antonio Argerich's *Inocentes o culpables* [Innocent or Guilty] (1884), Lucio V. López' *La gran aldea* [The Big Village] (1884), Eugenio Cambaceres' *Sin rumbo* [Drifting] (1885), Julián Martel's *La Bolsa* [The Stock Market] (1890). But even here one need only read carefully *Sin rumbo,* for instance, to observe that the author is leaning on the *theories* of Naturalism, its Achilles' heel, rather than imitating Zola's epic art. Cambaceres' Zolaism is surface veneer. His style moves toward a somewhat lyrical staccato — precursory, one may say, of Vargas Vila's.[1] Another man whose name has been associated with Zola's is Baldomero Lillo. Obviously there is some similarity due to the thematic affinity between *Sub terra* and *Germinal,* both dealing with the plight of the coal miners, but the multiple romantic strands (pathetic overtones, fateful coincidences, etc.) hovering over Lillo's pen constantly belie his Naturalism. One can survey the works of one novelist after another with the same result: that in Latin America Romanticism and Realism seem bound together in one afflatus. "Costumbrismo" ["local color realism"], flowering as constantly in Spain as in Latin America, reveals over and again the mixture of romantic-realistic elements. From the clumsy *Periquillo Sarniento* [The Itching Parrot], the earliest full-blown American novel, to *El machete,* a seminal moment in Colombian fiction, the ambiguity persists. Posada, like Lizardi, seems to hesitate between tough "machismo" and bland tearfulness: the term romantic realist or realistic romanticist, either way, fits either one of them. Evidently the roots of this ambivalence are psychological, and they lead all the way back to the great Spanish tradition, to writers and painters of the past, like Fernando de Rojas, Lope, Quevedo, El Greco, Cervantes, Goya, Pérez Galdós. And then again, much of it can be ascribed to the unstable economic and social milieu of the writers of Spain and Latin America which forces them to improvisation. The conditions of life are so difficult that they are unable to devote the time and travail required for all memorable achievements, with the result that their output is heterogeneous, often careless.

Recently Dudley Fitts told us how "depressed" he felt by the "ineptitude, uncertainty, imitativeness, sentimental histrionics" ("all add up to tedium") of Spanish and Latin American fiction. He recalled "the amused despair of the late John Peale Bishop, who had spent . . . months plowing through Latin American novels and short stories: he found them invincibly second-rate, and noted that the Spanish genius, at least in this hemisphere, spoke convincingly only in verse and the essay." And then Fitts added: "He should have excepted the Argentinians Jorge Luis Borges and Eduardo Mallea, however: their fiction can hold its own with the best."[2] However caustic and iconoclastic, Fitts' remarks do have a disconcertingly truthful ring, for in the field of fiction Latin America is unable to boast of any titans. His exceptions, Borges and Mallea, may sound strange to more than one specialist in Latin American affairs, but they are the choice of an extremely sensitive poet, a perceptive critic equally versed in ancient and contemporary literatures, a talented translator of the Greek classics and compiler of an anthology of contemporary Latin American poetry. On proposing Borges and Mallea as exceptions, he is relieving those writers of his charges of "ineptitude, uncertainty, imitativeness, and sentimental histrionics" for, emphatically, they are not second-raters. The occasion did not force Fitts to explain Borges' and Mallea's uniqueness. Since, independently of Fitts, I reached, years ago, similar conclusions, I shall endeavor to suggest the general trend in which these and other brilliant contemporary Latin American novelists and short story writers are located. This trend I term "magical realism."

Finding in photographic realism a blind alley, all the arts—particularly painting and literature—reacted against it and many notable writers of the First World War period came to rediscover symbolism and magical realism. Among them were geniuses of the stature of Marcel Proust and Franz Kafka and the latter's counterpart in painting, Giorgio de Chirico. Theirs was to a large extent a rediscovery, because some of the stylistic and expressive utterances found in Kafka, for instance, were writ large in numerous nineteenth-century figures: in the Russians (especially the Gogol of "The Nose," "Shponka and his Aunt," and other short stories, and of course Dostoevsky), in the German Romantics (Hoffmann, Arnim, Kleist, the Grimm brothers), and in Strindberg, Stifter, and to some extent in Poe and Melville. In his laboriously precisionist way Kafka had mastered from his earliest short stories — "The Judgment" (1912), "Metamorphosis" (1916) — the difficult art of mingling his drab reality with the phantasmal world of his nightmares. In his *Journal*, André Gide saw this peculiar fusion of dream and reality in Kafka: "I could not say what I admire the more: the 'naturalistic' notation of a fantastic universe, but which the detailed exactitude of the depiction makes real in our eyes, or the unerring audacity of the lurches into the strange. There is much to be learned from it."[3]

The novelty therefore consisted in the amalgamation of realism and fantasy. Each of these, separately and by devious ways, made its appearance in Latin America: realism, since the Colonial Period but especially during the 1880s; the magical, writ large from the earliest — in the letters of Columbus, in the chroniclers, in the sagas of Cabeza de Vaca — entered the literary mainstream during Modernism. An exciting note of wonderment and exoticism filled as much the tales of Rubén Darío (many of them published in Chilean newspapers in 1889) as the *Relatos argentinos* [Argentine Tales] of Paul Groussac written between 1886 and 1921, the *Cuentos malévolos* [Malevolent Stories] (1904) of Clemente Palma, the truly fabulous narratives of Leopoldo Lugones' *Las fuerzas extrañas* [Strange Powers] (1906), and the variegated production of Horacio Quiroga. Obviously the most persistent influence then was Edgar Allan Poe, either directly or via his admirers, especially the French decadents grouped as "Los raros" ["the odd ones"] by Darío: Baudelaire, Barbey d'Aurevilly, Villiers de l'Isle Adam, etc. This imaginative writing found its way into the twentieth century and is discernible in the prose experiments of many gifted poets: in Mexico, in Jaime Torres Bodet's *Margarita de niebla* [Margarita of the Mists] (1927) and *Proserpina rescatada* (1931), in Xavier Villaurrutia's *Dama de corazones* [Queen of Hearts] (1928), in Gilberto Owen's *Novela como nube* [The Novel as Cloud] (1928), and in Salvador Novo's *Return ticket* (1928); in Peru, in Abraham Valdelomar's novels and in *El caballero Carmelo y otros cuentos* [Sir Carmelo and Other Stories] (1918), and in Martín Adán's *La casa de cartón* [*The Cardboard House*] (1929); in Argentina, most especially in those nightmares of anarchy and tumult entitled *El juguete rabioso* [The Furious Toy] (1926), *Los siete locos* [*The Seven Madmen*] (1929), and *Los lanzallamas* [The Flamethrowers] (1931) by Roberto Arlt.

However, all these productions, which depend so utterly on atmosphere, mood, and sentiment, and which often look toward the rococo figurations of the French Jean Giraudoux and the Spanish Benjamín Jarnés, differ from the cold and cerebral and often erudite storytelling which concerns us here. For the sake of convenience I shall use the year 1935 as the point of departure of this new phase of Latin American literature, of magical realism. It was in 1935 that Jorge Luis Borges' collection *Historia universal de la infamia* [*A Universal History of Infamy*] made its appearance in Buenos Aires, at least two years after he had completed a masterly translation into Spanish of Franz Kafka's shorter fiction. Not that we intend to limit his extremely complex genius to one influence; he the most literate writer in the whole of America, whose works reflect so many and so divergent personalities: Chesterton, H. G. Wells, Arthur Machen, Marcel Schwob, Ellery Queen, plus the erudite army unearthed so facetiously by María Rosa Lida de Malkiel, but Kafka's impact on him has been the most profound and revealing. With Borges as pathfinder and moving spirit, a group of brilliant stylists developed around him. Although each evidenced a distinct personality and proceeded in his own way, the general direction was that of magical realism. Stimulated by Borges, the Chilean María Luisa Bombal began publishing about this time her oneiric stories in Buenos Aires: *La última niebla* [*House of Mist*] (1935), and the same year as her *La amortajada* [*The Shrouded Woman*] (1937), Silvina Ocampo published *Viaje olvidado* [*Forgotten Journey*] and Luis Albamonte, *Fusilado al amanecer* [Shot at Sunrise]. From then magical realism has grown in an exciting crescendo. Suffice it here to declare that the decade 1940–50 saw its most magnificent flowering. During these ten fruitful years Latin America produced prose fiction comparable to the best in contemporary Italy, France, or England. The year 1940 saw the appearance of Adolfo Bioy Casares' *La invención de Morel* [*The Invention of Morel*], the first full-length novel of fantasy in Latin American letters. Reminiscent of the early H. G. Wells, its style has the hard, translucent quality of Kafka. At the same moment Albamonte published his most ambitious novel, *La paloma de la puñalada* [The Dove and the Stabbing]; Enrique Wernicke, a collection of short stories, *Hans Grillo*, and a novel, *Función y muerte en el cine A.B.C.* [Show and Death at the ABC Movie Theatre]; the Mexican Andrés Henestrosa, the charming *Retrato de mi madre* [Portrait of My Mother]; and Borges, Silvina Ocampo, and Bioy Casares compiled the timely and broadly influential *Antología de la literatura fantástica* [*The Book of Fantasy*]. In the following year Borges gave us his memorable "El jardín de los senderos que se bifurcan" ["The Garden of Forking Paths"], which imposed magical realism in many corners throughout Latin America. That year

José Bianco made his debut with a brilliant tour de force, *Sombras suele vestir* [*Shadow Play*], in the style of Henry James, and Eduardo Mallea published one of his outstanding achievements, *Todo verdor perecerá* [*All Green Shall Perish*], in which a rural tragedy is lifted to new artistic levels. Soon thereafter Alfredo Pippig gave us his amazing tales *La resurrección de X.X.* [The Resurrection of X.X.], and Bianco, his intense novel *Las ratas* [*The Rats*] (1943), quite Gidean in penetration and stylistic virtuosity. With Borges, Mallea, Bianco, Silvina Ocampo, and Bioy Casares, the nucleus felt strong. The momentum reached Cuba (Novás Calvo, Ramón Ferreira, Labrador Ruiz); Mexico (Juan José Arreola, Francisco Tario, María Luisa Hidalgo, Juan Rulfo); Ecuador (Vera, Adalberto Ortiz); Chile (Subercaseaux, Chela Reyes, Mariyán, the Huidobro who in the 1920's had practiced Ultraism); Uruguay (Felisberto Hernández, Amorim, Onetti). And in Argentina a galaxy flourished: Alberto Girri, Norah Lange, Estela Canto, Manuel Peyrou, Enrique Anderson Imbert, Santiago Dabove, Carmen Gándara, Mario Lancelotti, Julio Cortázar. Astonishing were the varieties of utterance, the magnificent originality. For instance, *El estruendo de las rosas* [*Thunder of the Roses*] by Manuel Peyrou and *El túnel* [*The Tunnel*] by Ernesto Sábato appeared the same year, 1948, as *Nadie encendía las lámparas* [No one lit the lamps, translated as *Piano Stories*] by the Uruguayan Felisberto Hernández and *Varia invención* [*Various Inventions*] by the Mexican Juan José Arreola. The publication of this brilliant storyteller's *Confabulario* (1952) coincided with that of Francisco Tario's *Tapioca Inn* and Ramón Ferreira's *Tiburón* [Shark].

Meticulous craftsmen all, one finds in them the same preoccupation with style and also the same transformation of the common and the everyday into the awesome and the unreal. They all will subscribe to Chirico's dictum: "What is most of all necessary is to rid art of everything of the known which it has held until now: every subject, idea, thought and symbol must be put aside. . . . Thought must draw so far away from human fetters that things may appear to it under a new aspect, as though they are illuminated by a constellation now appearing for the first time."[4] It is predominantly an art of surprises. From the very first line the reader is thrown into a timeless flux and/or the unconceivable, freighted with dramatic suspense: Bioy Casares' *The Invention of Morel*: "Today, on this island, a miracle happened. The weather suddenly grew very warm. . . ."[5] Borges' "La lotería de Babilonia" ["The Lottery in Babylon"]: "Like all men in Babylon, I have been proconsul; like all, a slave. I have also known omnipotence, opprobrium, imprisonment. Look: the index finger on my right hand is missing. Look: through the rip in my cape you can see a vermilion tattoo on my stomach. It is the second symbol, Beth"; and his "Las ruinas circulares" ["The Circular Ruins"]: "No one saw him disembark in the unanimous night, no one saw the bamboo canoe sinking into the sacred mud, but within a few days no one was unaware that the silent man came from the South and that his home was one of the infinite villages upstream, on the violent mountainside where the Zend tongue is not contaminated with Greek and where leprosy is infrequent."[6] Arreola's "El guardagujas" ["The Switchman," in *Confabulario*]: "The stranger arrived at the deserted station out of breath. His large suitcase, which nobody carried for him, had really tired him out."[7] Sábato's *The Tunnel*: "It should be sufficient to say that I am Juan Pablo Castel, the painter who killed María Iribarne. I imagine that the trial is still in everyone's mind and that no further information is necessary."[8] And, finally, Mallea's *Sala de espera* [The Waiting Room]: "Windows opaque and engine at full steam, the 11:40 express whistled and roared through the dark country station."[9] Notice the affinity of all these opening sentences with those of *The Trial* by Franz Kafka: "Someone must have been telling lies about Joseph K., for without having done anything wrong he was arrested one fine morning"; or that of *The Stranger* by Albert Camus: "Mother died today. Or, maybe, yesterday; I can't be sure"; or that galvanizing one of Kafka's *The Metamorphosis:* "As Gregor Samsa awoke one morning from a troubled dream, he found himself changed in his bed to some monstrous kind of vermin." From then on the narrative moves smoothly, translucently, bound for an infinite, timeless perspective — timeless because despite the noun *morning* in *The Trial* and *The Metamorphosis* there stands the modifier, *one — one morning —* just as in *The Stranger* the *today* becomes *today or maybe yesterday; I can't be sure.* Time exists in a kind of timeless fluidity and the unreal happens as part of reality. The transformation of Gregor Samsa into a cockroach or bedbug (Kafka uses the imprecise "monstrous vermin") is not a matter of conjecture or discussion: it happened and it was accepted by the other characters as an almost normal event. Once the reader accepts the *fait accompli,* the rest follows with logical precision. Nowhere is the story weighed down with lyrical effusions, needlessly baroque descriptions, or "cuadros de costumbres," all of which mar the composition of *Doña Bárbara* and *La vorágine,* for instance. The practitioners of magical realism cling to reality as if to prevent "literature" from getting in their way, as if to prevent their myth from flying off, as in fairy tales, to supernatural realms. The narrative proceeds in well-prepared, increasingly intense steps, which ultimately may lead to one great ambiguity or confusion, "Verwirrung innherhalb der Klarheit," *to a confusion within clarity*, to borrow a term used by the Austrian novelist Joseph Roth in a slightly different context.[10] All the magical realists have this in common, as well as their repudiation of that mawkish sentimentalism which pervades so many of the Latin American classics: *María, Cumandá, Aves sin nido* [*Birds without a Nest*]. The magical realists do not cater to a popular taste, rather they address themselves to the sophisticated, those not merely initiated in aesthetic mysteries but versed in subtleties. Often their writings approach closely that art characterized by Ortega y Gasset as "dehumanized." Their style seeks precision and leanness, a healthy innovation, to be sure, considering the flatulence of so many reputed writers in Latin American fiction (Larreta, Dominici, Reyles). Besides, their plots are logically conceived, either well-rounded or projected against an infinite perspective as in Kafka's "Wall of China" or Chirico's *Melancholy and Mystery of a Street*. This, too, is a healthy innovation, since Latin American plots have usually been either elephantine and sprawling, as in [Agustín Yañez's] *El mundo es ancho y ajeno* [*Broad and Alien is the World*], or unwieldy and clumsily assembled, as in *Periquillo Sarniento*. This concern of the magical realists for the well-knit plot probably stems from their familiarity with detective stories, which Borges, Bioy Casares, Peyrou, and other magical realists have written, translated, or anthologized. Their mathematical precision and perspicacity may account for their strong aversion to all flabbiness, either stylistic or emotional.

Never before have so many sensitive and talented writers lived at the same time in Latin America—never have they worked so unanimously to overhaul and polish the craft of fiction. In fact their slim but weighty output may well mark the inception of a genuinely Latin American fiction. We may claim, without apologies, that Latin America is no longer in search of its expression, to use Henríquez Ureña's felicitious phrase—we may claim that Latin America now possesses an authentic expression, one that is uniquely civilized, exciting, and, let us hope, perennial.

Notes

[Editor's note: Italicized titles in brackets indicate works that have been translated into English.]

A paper read at the Spanish 4 Group Meeting of the 69th Annual Meeting of
the MLA, New York, December 27–29, 1954.

1 After this was written I was pleased to discover the following statement by the
   poet and critic Arturo Cambours Ocampo in his recent vol. *Indagaciones sobre
   literatura argentina* [*Approaches to Argentine Literature*] (Buenos Aires: Alba-
   tros, 1952), p. 76: "The spiritual position of the writers of the literary generation
   of the 1880s was not absolute and cannot be defined absolutely. It seems to me
   that this problem has been exaggerated. The works of even the most rebellious
   writers tell us at every turn that a supple romanticism was still beating in their
   hearts. . . . Romanticism is present on the elegant and poetic pages of Eduardo
   Wilde's autobiographical *Aguas abajo* [Downstream] and *Tiempo perdido* [Lost
   Time]; in the spare, melancholic description of Lopez's *La gran aldea* [The Big
   Village]; and even in the most *naturalistic* moments in Eugenio Cambaceres'
   work, we see a ray of spiritual optimism that does not conform in any way to
   the label of 'positivist' often used to describe this generation." (Editors' translation, emphasis the author's.)

2 *Hudson Review* 7, 3 (Autumn 1954) 454–59.

3 *Journal* (New York: Knopf, 1951), 4:42, entry for August 28, 1940.

4 James Thorp Selby, *The Early Chirico* (New York: Dodd, Mead, 1941), p. 21.

5 Adolfo Bioy Casares, *La invención de Morel* (1940); *The Invention of Morel*,
   trans. Margaret Sayers Peden (Austin: University of Texas Press, 1964), p. 9.

6 Jorge Luis Borges, "The Lottery in Babylon," trans. John M. Fein, and "The
   Circular Ruins," trans. James E. Irby, from *Ficciones* (1944), in *Labyrinths*
   (New York: New Directions, 1962), pp. 30, 45.

7 Juan José Arreola, "The Switchman," trans. George D. Schade, from *Confabulario* (1952), in *Confabulario and Other Inventions* (Austin: University of Texas
   Press, 1964), p. 77.

8 Ernesto Sábato, *El túnel* (1948); *The Tunnel*, trans. Margaret Sayers Peden
   (London: Jonathan Cape, 1988), p. 1.

9 Eduardo Mallea, *Sala de espera* (Buenos Aires: Editorial Sudamericana, 1953),
   p. 1, editors' translation.

10 Joseph Roth, *Antichrist*, trans. William Rose (New York: Viking, 1935), p. 23.

LUIS LEAL

Magical Realism in Spanish
American Literature

In his article on "Magical Realism in Spanish American Fiction," Professor Angel Flores proposes the year 1935 as marking the birth of magical realism.[1] For Flores, Jorge Luis Borges' book *A Universal History of Infamy*, which appeared that year, marks the new trend in Hispanic American narrative. According to Flores, Borges' work reflects the influence of Kafka, whose stories the author of the *Aleph* had translated and published two years earlier.[2] "In his laboriously precisionist way," says Flores, "Kafka had mastered from his earliest short stories—'The Judgment,' (1912) 'Metamorphosis' (1916)—the difficult art of mingling his drab reality with the phantasmal world of his nightmares. . . . The novelty therefore consisted in the amalgamation of realism and fantasy. Each of these, separately and by devious ways, made its appearance in Latin America: realism, since the Colonial Period but especially during the 1880s; the magical, writ large from the earliest—in the letters of Columbus, in the chroniclers, in the sagas of Cabeza de Vaca . . ." (112).

Flores also considers the works of the Argentines Bioy-Casares, Silvina Ocampo, Mallea, Sábato, Bianco, and Cortázar, the Chilean María Luisa Bombal, the Cubans Novás Calvo and Labrador Ruiz, the Mexicans Arreola and Rulfo, and the Uruguayan Onetti as belonging to magical realism. Flores finds in these writers the following distinguishing characteristics: a preoccupation with style and an interest in transforming "the common and the everyday into the awesome and the unreal" (114). And he adds: "Time exists in a kind of timeless fluidity and the unreal happens as part of reality" (115). He cites as an example the case of Gregor Samsa, whose transformation into a cockroach or a bedbug is accepted "as an almost normal event" (115).

Professor Flores does not offer a formal definition of magical realism in

his study but he does say that its practitioners "cling to reality as if to prevent 'literature' from getting in their way, as if to prevent their myth from
flying off, as in fairy tales, to supernatural realms. The narrative proceeds
in well-prepared, increasingly intense steps, which ultimately may lead to
one great ambiguity or confusion. . . . All the magical realists have this
in common, as well as their repudiation of that mawkish sentimentalism
which pervades so many of the Latin American classics: *María, Cumandá,
Aves sin nido*" [*Birds without a Nest*] (116). And then he adds: "Often their
writings approach closely the art Ortega y Gasset called 'dehumanized.' . . .
Besides, their plots are logically conceived. . . . This concern of the magical realists for the well-knit plot probably stems from their familiarity with
detective stories, which Borges, Bioy Casares, Peyrou, and other magical
realists have written, translated, or anthologized" (116).

I have cited Professor Flores' essay at length because, incredible as it
may seem, this is until now the only study of magical realism in Hispanic
American literature. His was a voice in the desert, though since then the
term has been used repeatedly without being precisely defined.

I do not agree with Professor Flores' definition of magical realism because it seems to me that he includes authors who do not belong to the
movement. Neither do I agree that the movement was started by Borges
in 1935 and flowered between 1940 and 1950. I will explain why.

The term "magical realism" was first used by the art critic Franz Roh
to designate the pictorial output of the Postexpressionist period, beginning around 1925. Roh explains the origin of the term by saying that with
the word "magical," as opposed to "mystical," he wished to emphasize
that "the mystery does not descend to the represented world but rather
hides and palpitates behind it."[3] In Hispanic America, it seems to have
been Arturo Uslar Pietri who first used the term in his book *Letras y hombres de Venezuela* [The Literature and Men of Venezuela] (1948), where
he says: "What became prominent in the short story and left an indelible
mark there was the consideration of man as a mystery surrounded by realistic facts. A poetic prediction or a poetic denial of reality. What for lack of
another name could be called a magical realism."[4] After Uslar Pietri, Alejo
Carpentier has paid this phenomenon the most attention. In the prologue
to his magical realist novel *The Kingdom of this World* [*El reino de este
mundo*] (1949), he makes this interesting observation: "the marvelous —
he says — begins to be unmistakably marvelous when it arises from an unexpected alteration of reality (the miracle), from a privileged revelation

of reality, an unusual insight that particularly favors the unexpected richness of reality or an amplification of the scale and categories of reality, a reality thus perceived with special intensity by virtue of an exaltation of the spirit that leads it to a kind of extreme state [*estado límite*]." [5]

So we see that magical realism cannot be identified either with fantastic literature or with psychological literature, or with the surrealist or hermetic literature that Ortega describes. Unlike superrealism, magical realism does not use dream motifs; neither does it distort reality or create imagined worlds, as writers of fantastic literature or science fiction do; nor does it emphasize psychological analysis of characters, since it doesn't try to find reasons for their actions or their inability to express themselves. Magical realism is not an aesthetic movement either, as was modernism, which was interested in creating works dominated by a refined style; neither is it interested in the creation of complex structures per se. [6]

Magical realism is not magic literature either. Its aim, unlike that of magic, is to express emotions, not to evoke them. Magical realism is, more than anything else, an attitude toward reality that can be expressed in popular or cultured forms, in elaborate or rustic styles, in closed or open structures. What is the attitude of the magical realist toward reality? I have already said that he doesn't create imaginary worlds in which we can hide from everyday reality. In magical realism the writer confronts reality and tries to untangle it, to discover what is mysterious in things, in life, in human acts. This is what Arturo Uslar Pietri, Miguel Angel Asturias, Alejo Carpentier, Lino Novás Calvo, Juan Rulfo, Félix Pita Rodríguez, Nicolás Guillén and other short story writers, novelists, and poets do in their works. In his story "Secret Weapons" ["Las armas secretas"], Julio Cortázar has the narrator say, "strange how people are under the impression that making a bed is exactly the same as making a bed, that to shake hands is always the same as shaking hands, that opening a can of sardines is to open the same can of sardines ad infinitum. 'But if everything's an exception,' Pierre is thinking . . ." [7]

Magical realism does not derive, as Professor Flores claims, from Kafka's work. In the prologue to *The Metamorphosis* Borges makes the astute observation that the basic characteristic of Kafka's stories is "the invention of intolerable situations." And we might add: if, as Professor Flores notices, in Kafka's story the characters accept the transformation of a man into a cockroach, their attitude toward reality is not magic; they find the situation intolerable and they don't accept it. In the stories of Borges himself, as in those by other writers of fantastic literature, the principal trait is the creation of infinite hierarchies. Neither of those two tendencies permeates works of magical realism, where the principal thing is not the creation of imaginary beings or worlds but the discovery of the mysterious relationship between man and his circumstances. The existence of the marvelous real is what started magical realist literature, which some critics claim is *the* truly American literature.[8]

In contrast to avant garde literature, magical realism is not escapist literature. The English critic Collingwood, in speaking of art as magic in his book *The Principles of Art*, says:

> What is important to the aesthetician is the re-emergence of a very old kind of aesthetic consciousness: one which reverses the painfully taught lesson of nineteenth-century criticism, and instead of saying "never mind about the subject; the subject is only a *corpus vile* on which the artist has exercised his powers, and what concerns you is the artist's powers, and the way in which he has here displayed them," says "the artist's powers can be displayed only when he uses them upon a subject that is worthy of them." This new aesthetic consciousness involves a dual vision. It regards the subject as an integral element in the work of art; it maintains that in order to appreciate any given work of art one must be interested in its subject for its own sake, as well as in the artist's handling of it.[9]

This interest in theme, a central characteristic of magical realism, is what unifies the works in this movement, whether they be popular or more elite examples.

In Rómulo Gallegos' novel *Cantaclaro* (1934) we find a young man from Caracas who is attracted to the plains and who soon becomes disillusioned. During one significant scene he confronts the old plainsman Crisanto Báez, whom he considers his inferior, and dares to insult him. The plainsman says to him with great dignity: "Look, young man. I don't know how to explain myself very well, but you'll manage to get my point. . . . You keep trying to understand what is beyond your grasp . . . You hear the buzzing of the bees — since you mentioned them — and, moving up the social scale, you hear us too, but you will never listen to the prayer of the Lonely Soul because your intelligence suppresses it."[10] For Don Crisanto the unreal seems to be part of reality, and he accepts it. And the same thing happens with the characters in the novel *Pedro Páramo*, where none of them "suppresses" the existence of suffering souls. But Rulfo goes even further than that, capturing reality from the dead narrator's point of view. His poetic vision of reality, expressed in verbal forms taken from popular language, gives his work a magical tone.

In magical realism key events have no logical or psychological explanation. The magical realist does not try to copy the surrounding reality (as the realists did) or to wound it (as the Surrealists did) but to seize the mystery that breathes behind things. In Pita Rodríguez's story "Alarico the Potter" the belongings of the mysterious character who wears an enigmatic ring disintegrate when he dies; in Carpentier's "Journey to the Seed" time flows backward at the exact moment when the old black gardener twirls his staff; in Carpentier's *The Lost Steps*, the protagonist, returning to the jungle, is unable to find the arm of the river through which he had gone from the present to the past, from modern civilization, where life has lost its meaning, to a primitive American paradise. Let us keep in mind that in these magical realist works the author does not need to justify the mystery of events, as the fantastic writer has to. In fantastic literature the supernatural invades a world ruled by reason. In magical realism "the mystery does not descend to the represented world, but rather hides and palpitates behind it." [11] In order to seize reality's mysteries the magical realist writer heightens his senses until he reaches an extreme state [*estado límite*] that allows him to intuit the imperceptible subtleties of the external world, the multifarious world in which we live.

Translated by Wendy B. Faris

Originally published as "El realismo mágico en la literatura hispanoamericana," *Cuadernos americanos* 43, 4 (1967): 230–35.

1 Angel Flores, "Magical Realism in Spanish American Fiction," *Hispania* 38 (1955), 187–192. (Subsequent page references are to the reprint of Flores' essay in this volume.) Spanish translation of Flores' essay by Miguel Rodríguez Puga: "El realismo mágico en la ficción narrativa hispanoamericana," *Et Caetera*, Guadalajara, México, VI, 23–25 (July 1957–March 1958), 99–108.

2 Franz Kafka, *La metamórfosis*. Translation and prologue by Jorge Luis Borges (Buenos Aires: Editorial Losada, 1943). I am not aware of the 1933 edition mentioned by Flores.

3 Cited by Juan Eduardo Cirlot, *Diccionario de los ismos* 2nd ed. (Barcelona, 1956), p. 365. [Franz Roh, "Magical Realism: Postexpressionism," trans. Faris, this volume, p. 16.] Roh's book was translated into Spanish by Fernando Vela

and published by the Revista de Occidente: *Realismo mágico* (Madrid, 1927). Review by Antonio Espina in the *Revista de Occidente*, XVI (1927), pp. 110–113.

4 Trans. note: See Arturo Uslar Pietri, *Letras y hombres de Venezuela* (1948; Mexico City: Fondo de Cultura Económica, 1949), pp. 161–62.

5 Alejo Carpentier, "On the Marvelous Real in America," trans. Huntington and Zamora, this volume, pp. 85–86.

6 Leal refers here to the Hispanic American movement of "Modernismo," to be distinguished from European and North American modernism, and closer to symbolism.

7 Julio Cortázar, *Las armas secretas* (Buenos Aires, 1959), p. 185. [*The End of the Game and Other Stories*, trans. Paul Blackburn (New York: Harper and Row, 1978), p. 248.]

8 Arturo Uslar Pietri, Angel Flores, Alejo Carpentier. See the essay by the latter: "De lo real maravillosamente americano," *Tientos y diferencias* (México, 1946), pp. 115–35. Trans. Huntington and Zamora, in this volume, pp. 75–88.

9 R. C. Collingwood, *Los Principios del Arte* (México: Fondo de Cultura Económica, 1960), p. 74. [*The Principles of Art* (1938; Oxford: Clarendon, 1964), p. 71].

10 *Obras completas de Rómulo Gallegos* (Madrid, 1958), p. 822.

11 Franz Roh, cited by Juan Eduardo Cirlot in his *Diccionario de los ismos*, 2nd edition (Barcelona, 1956), p. 365.

AMARYLL CHANADY

The Territorialization of the Imaginary in Latin America: Self-Affirmation and Resistance to Metropolitan Paradigms

In *Control of the Imaginary: Reason and Imagination in Modern Times*, the Brazilian literary theorist and critic Luiz Costa Lima investigates what he calls the "scandalous prohibition" of fiction, that is, the systematic control of the imaginary by the dictates of a restrictive conception of mimesis based on verisimilitude, decorum, and imitation of consecrated masters and legitimated models, the "parameters of a pragmatic reason geared to the most routine aspects of daily life" and morality.[1] This control of the imaginary replaces the Christian cosmological centering in the sixteenth century, when the "cult of a reason incarnating permanent, universal laws came in service to, and at the same time was the desideratum of, political centralization" (31). Medieval theocentrism gives way to the centrality of reason, which leads to the evacuation of *poiesis* from the concept of *mimesis*, thus deforming the Aristotelian notion by restricting subjectivity to the imitation of an external reality in accordance with the precepts of hegemonic rational paradigms. During the Romantic period, the expression of individual subjectivity, rebellion against established society, and self-reflection accompanying the contemplation of nature challenged this control of the imaginary.

In Latin America, however, Romanticism was characterized neither by speculative self-reflection nor by the questioning of hegemonic models, but by sentimentality and detailed observation of nature. Costa Lima states: "Observation did not find its ground, so to speak, in a subject who would convert nature into a means of stimulating and ordering the reading of himself or herself; its ground resided instead in the object observed, in the land that was to be replaced on the written page" (162–63). The prevalence of description in Brazilian Romanticism, which precluded a radical break with realism, can be attributed partly to the European insistence on the exceptional nature of New World geography and partly to the Latin American strategies of identity-construction that emphasize regional specificities. The New World imaginary is subsequently controlled by the requirement that it express national identity in accordance with the precepts of European positivism, which stress detailed observation and objective knowledge of the referent. Costa Lima cites the example of Euclides da Cunha, who advocates the "marriage of science and art" in human thought (166); the writer thus "remains riveted to the external reality of facts or to the internal reality of sentiments, to hide the stigma of fiction," a situation that continues today with testimonial narrative (199).

Costa Lima's discussion of Brazilian literature, with its implications extending to Latin American literature in general, is a particularly enlightening point of departure for a reconsideration of what has frequently been considered during the past three decades as the authentic literary expression of Latin America: magical realism. How can we reconcile the fictional world of Gabriel García Márquez, populated by characters ascending to heaven amidst bedsheets, mysteriously levitating while drinking cups of chocolate, and turning into snakes or puddles of pitch, a world benighted with deluges lasting several years and yellow flowers falling from the sky, with the claim that New World fiction is subject to a control of the imaginary based on the mimetic representation of the continent's reality, especially bearing in mind the importance of positivism in Latin America? Do we accept Jochen Schulte-Sasse's challenging argument in his Afterword to *Control of the Imaginary* that Costa Lima's inclusion of *poiesis* within *mimesis* ignores the claims of the artistic imagination to subvert and go beyond the hegemonic paradigms regulating mimesis, as is evident not only in the major texts of German Romanticism and in Coleridge's distinction between pedestrian fancy and innovative imagination but in the artistic endeavor in general? Magical realism would thus be a particularly successful manifestation of *poiesis* as opposed to *mimesis*. The fact that Costa Lima does not mention magical realism may be an indication of the problematic status of this literary mode alongside a theory emphasizing the opposite of what magical realism seems to represent.

With this apparent contradiction as a point of departure, I will examine two texts that have been particularly significant for the conceptualization and academic popularization of magical realism. The first is Angel Flores' "Magical Realism in Spanish American Fiction" (1955).[2] The second is Luis Leal's critical rejoinder in "El realismo mágico en la literatura hispanoamericana" (1967). (Both essays are included in this volume.) Considering Leal's categorical rejection of Flores' arguments, it is ironic that Leal's title is an almost exact translation of the latter's English title.[3] These essays were the first to treat the subject and have been very influential on later critics, who have repeatedly quoted and discussed their definitions. A careful analysis of these definitions in the light of the concept of control of the imaginary enables us to effect a rereading of the literary mode and its confusing and contradictory theorization.

Even a brief perusal of Flores' essay "Magical Realism in Spanish American Fiction" reveals the situation of his text as a "peripheral" production concerned with validating and even advertising the literary output of a formerly colonized society. Countering Dudley Fitts' derogatory remarks concerning the "ineptitude, uncertainty, imitativeness, sentimental histrionics" of Latin American fiction, which the Anglophone critic considered "invincibly second-rate," Flores justifies Latin America's lack of "great" literature with the claim that "conditions of life are so difficult that [Hispanophone writers] are unable to devote the time and travail required for all memorable achievements, with the result that their output is heterogeneous, often careless"; since 1935, however, magical realism has sprung up in the wake of Borges' fiction inspired by Kafka (although he points out that Borges' "extremely complex genius" was heir to other influences as well), producing "brilliant contemporary novelists and short story writers," especially in the decade 1940–50, which saw the "most magnificent flowering" of magical realism in "prose fiction comparable to the best in contemporary Italy, France, or England."[4] With respect to Mallea's *Sala de espera* [The Waiting Room], Flores points out "the affinity of all these opening sentences with those of *The Trial*, by Franz Kafka" (115). Magical realist fiction repudiates "that mawkish sentimentalism which pervades so many of the Latin American classics," "seeks precision and leanness," has "well-rounded plots" and a "strong aversion to all flabbiness, either stylistic or emotional," thus forming a marked contrast to traditional Latin American fiction, with its "flatulence" and "elephantine and sprawling," "unwieldy and clumsily assembled" plots (116). He concludes his essay with the remark that "[n]ever before have so many sensitive and talented writers lived at the same time in Latin America—never have they worked so unanimously to overhaul and polish the craft of fiction" (116). Flores' observation that the "magical realists do not cater to a popular taste, rather they address themselves to the sophisticated, those not merely initiated in aesthetic mysteries but versed in subtleties" (116), explicitly sums up the dominant preoccupation of his discussion: to reject the hierarchical dichotomy between civilization and barbarism—the European metropolis imbued with centuries of culture, and the New World ex-colonies evolving on a lower plane of cultural refinement—by demonstrating the acceptibility of Latin American literature in its present state of evolution within the universal canon.

What is particularly relevant to our problematic of the imaginary is Flores' rejection of "needlessly baroque descriptions or 'cuadros de costumbres'" ["local color realism"] (115), and his citation of Arturo Cambours Ocampo's laudatory reference to Argentine works not characterized by positivism (117, n. 1). In spite of his emphasis on the influence of Kafka, Flores points out that Latin American "imaginative writing" already existed before 1935 (he mentions the "magical" elements of Columbus' and Cabeza de Vaca's writings and the "note of wonderment and exoticism" of Rubén Darío's stories at the end of the nineteenth century), but that it differs from the "cold and cerebral and often erudite storytelling" (113) of the magical realists, whose art consists in "the amalgamation of realism and fantasy" and, in the case of writers such as Kafka, "the difficult art of mingling his drab reality with the phantasmal world of his nightmares" (112). Although the common denominator between exoticism, wonderment, the oneiric, and the supernatural is supposedly "imaginative writing," it would be simplistic to consider Columbus' reports, written according to the hegemonic paradigms of his time, as partaking of the same kind of imaginary, or even having the same function, as the "cold and cerebral" narratives of authors such as Kafka and certain Latin American magical realists. In spite of the fact that many of the early chronicles seem just as fictional to us now as do García Márquez's novels, contemporary "imaginative" writers consciously produce literature deviating from the canons of realism with its hegemonic paradigms of interpreting the world, thus differing significantly from the chroniclers. The following explanation of the function of magical realism clarifies Flores' conception of imaginative writing:

> Meticulous craftsmen all, one finds in them [the magical realists] the same preoccupation with style and also the same transformation of the common and the everyday into the awesome and the unreal. They all will subscribe to Chirico's dictum: "What is most of all nec-

essary is to rid art of everything of the known which it has held until now: every subject, idea, thought and symbol must be put aside. . . . Thought must draw so far away from human fetters that things may appear to it under a new aspect, as though they are illuminated by a constellation now appearing for the first time." (114)

The affinities between these lines and the emphasis on innovation of all avant-garde artistic movements are obvious (the notion of defamiliarization developed by the Russian Formalist Victor Shklovsky is particularly relevant in the case of magical realism): Flores thus situates magical realism as a universal phenomenon having nothing to do with the chronicles of the New World.[5] The latter, however, provide him with descriptive *topoi* that differ from the models of positivistic description of nature in the nineteenth century.

Magical realism is, of course, also subject to a certain control. According to Flores, the "practitioners of magical realism cling to reality as if to prevent 'literature' from getting in their way, as if to prevent their myth from flying off, as in fairy tales, to supernatural realms" (115–16). This is a rather puzzling observation in view of the fact that Gregor Samsa's transformation into an insect in "The Metamorphosis," a narrative mentioned by Flores as belonging to the magical realist mode, is certainly supernatural, as are the plots of the works of several Latin American authors enumerated by Flores. This "confusion" between magical realism and the fantastic has been repeatedly criticized. But what is particularly problematic is the apparent contradiction between the definition of magical realism as "an amalgamation of realism and fantasy" that includes narratives such as "The Metamorphosis" and the stipulation that the "practitioners of magical realism cling to reality."

We may find a partial solution to this contradiction by considering the emphasis on the innovative character of the imaginary by avant-garde writers. Fairy tales cannot be considered magical realist because they adhere to relatively uniform plot structures, as Vladimir Propp demonstrated in 1928,[6] an inevitable moral resolution of the Manichean conflict of the characters,[7] and a classifiable number of motifs that have been cataloged by folklorists since the beginning of the century. The rigid fairy-tale form effectively restricts the imaginary to well-defined models, even more than the strictures of realism. Coleridge's distinction between fancy and the imagination as that between the manipulation of "fixities and definites" and the idealizing and unifying creative endeavor, which Jochen Schulte-Sasse compares with that between *mimesis* and *poiesis*,[8] is also relevant to Flores' differentiation between magical realism and the fairy tale.

But Flores' assertion that the practitioners of magical realism cling to "reality as if to prevent literature from getting in their way" has more radical implications, which Luis Leal will treat more explicitly in his 1967 essay. The Cuban Alejo Carpentier's legitimation of the marvelous in Latin American art by his argument that Latin America possesses a marvelous reality does not apply to Flores' notion of magical realism, which includes European fiction. However, Carpentier's rejection of the marvelous in French Surrealist writing, which, he claims, is obtained by literary artifice and based on stock motifs — resembles Flores' exclusion of the fairy tale, and his comment about literature not "getting in the way" of magical realism. Although Flores' treatment of magical realism emphasizes the aesthetic and thus appears limited to the discussion of a literary mode, his comment on the presence of reality in magical realism indicates a general indictment of traditional forms of mimesis. Magical realism does not occupy a distinct area of literary production separate from that of mimetic writing, as does the marvelous domain of fairy tales, where the laws of logic and verisimilitude are constantly infringed without affecting our "normal" perception of reality, in a temporary suspension of disbelief. On the contrary, the mode challenges realistic representation in order to introduce *poeisis* into *mimesis*, a condition which Costa Lima advocates for a more satisfactory expression of our modernity.

A more serious contradiction surfaces toward the end of Flores' essay, where he claims that the new imaginative writing marks "the inception of a genuinely Latin American fiction" and that "Latin America now possesses an authentic expression, one that is uniquely civilized, exciting and, let us hope, perennial" (116). If magical realism is described as imaginative and innovative fiction that has assimilated the most modern narrative and stylistic techniques, and can be found in Kafka as well as Borges, it cannot be "genuinely Latin American" or the "authentic expression" of the continent. Two of the main strategies for the discursive constitution of cultural identity and the desire for metropolitan recognition in the "periphery" (I am using this ethnocentric term to emphasize the nature of the critic's predicament in the light of hegemonic values) are juxtaposed in Flores' article: valorizing the national culture by demonstrating that it is equivalent and even in some aspects identical to that of the metropolis and valorizing it by emphasizing its difference. What we see in Flores' final lines is what I would call a territorialization of the imaginary. A particular manifestation of international avant-garde fiction is ascribed to a particular continent in an act of appropriation that is not adequately justified in the argumentation of the essay. This justification had, however, already been carried out by Alejo Carpentier in his 1949 prologue to *The Kingdom of this World* (*El reino de este mundo*), but the author's writings were apparently unknown to Flores, who does not mention him.

Before returning to Carpentier's virulent territorialization of the imaginary, I will examine Luis Leal's refutation of Flores' definition of magical realism, which he considers too inclusive. According to Leal, magical realism comprises neither the fantastic nor the "psychological," neither oneiric nor "hermetic" literature, nor even Surrealism, and cannot therefore be traced back to the influence of Kafka. Leal defines magical realism as an "attitude towards reality" that consists of the "discovery of the mysterious relation between man and his circumstances." [9] In order to perceive the "mysteries of reality, the magical realist writer heightens his senses to an extreme state [*estado límite*] that allows him to intuit the imperceptible subtleties of the external world, the multifarious world in which we live" (123). He gives the example of Crisanto Báez, an uneducated rural inhabitant in Rómulo Gallegos' novel *Cantaclaro* (1934), who explains to the young man from the capital that his "intelligence" prevents him from hearing the prayer of the "lonely spirit" (122). Modern education conforming to the paradigms of enlightened reason thus restricts and impoverishes the character's perception. Leal adds that in magical realism the main events have no logical or psychological explanation. Though this statement is also relevant to the fantastic fictions of Kafka, for example, and thus does not provide criteria for distinguishing between magical realism and the fantastic, what is significant in Leal's remarks is the emphasis on the inadequacy and irrelevance of rational paradigms for the elucidation of fictional events. Whereas Flores stresses fantasy as an essential impetus for the creation of innovative fiction, Leal explicitly rejects the limitations imposed by reason.

Although the significance of both essays lies in the valorization of the imaginary, their arguments proceed in different ways and attribute a different status to fiction. For Flores, magical realism is a literary mode that is brandished as part of Latin America's credentials for being accepted by the cultural establishment of the metropolis, even though, as I have pointed out above, his emphasis on the presence of "reality" has more far-reaching implications. For Leal, magical realism, which he calls an "attitude," problematizes what Niklas Luhmann calls the "functionally differentiated society"[10] that has liberated the imaginary, as Schulte-Sasse perceptively pointed out, while relegating it to an autarkic institutionalized sphere of art. Such institutionalization limits its influence on other spheres (social, political) and condemns it to a compensatory function: despite the apparent liberation of the imaginary, the institutionalization of art since the end of the eighteenth century has effected a more devastating control than that exercised by decorum and reason.[11]

Particularly significant in this respect is Leal's distinction between magical realism and the fantastic: the magical realist writer "does not need to justify the mysterious nature of events, as the writer of fantastic stories has to. In fantastic literature the supernatural invades a world ruled by reason" (123). As several critics have pointed out, the fantastic, in the restricted sense of textually explicit antinomy between the laws of reason and supernatural beliefs, emerged in the eighteenth century, when rational explanation and empirical observation had relegated archaic paradigms to an inferior status.[12] In these fantastic fictions, the premises of a frequently exaggerated rationalist discourse affirming hegemonic paradigms of the Enlightenment are deconstructed by the description of apparently supernatural events and constant reference to the fear of the protagonist in the face of the inexplicable. Although this type of fantastic narrative is highly contradictory — affirming and challenging rational models — its main emphasis is on the rationalizing activity of a subject searching for cognitive mastery of the unknown and reconciliation of experience with scientific paradigms. Leal's preoccupation is thus primarily epistemological not aesthetic, even though he admiringly quotes Collingwood's definition of aesthetic consciousness as including thematic content. As demonstrated by his reference to the restrictive rationalist character of the fantastic and his remark that the artist captures the mystery of reality, Leal challenges the artist's subjection to rational paradigms not only in his literary activity (liberated from rational constraints by its institutionalization as a sphere separate from that of cognition) but also in his apprehension of reality in general. For Leal, magical realism is an "attitude towards reality," not a literary mode or technique.

Leal's shift in emphasis has complex filiations. Rejecting Flores' claim that magical realism can be largely explained by the influence of Kafka,

Leal traces the emergence of the mode to Franz Roh's 1925 essay on postexpressionism in painting, Uslar Pietri's 1948 discussion of the Latin American narrative as a "poetic negation of reality,"[14] and Carpentier's prologue to *The Kingdom of this World,* in which he introduced the term *lo real maravilloso* (the marvelous real). Leal even adopts Carpentier's assertion of the existence of a marvelous reality, but does not categorically territorialize it in Latin America, as Carpentier did. The latter ascribed the new Latin American literary expression, which he termed baroque and considered the appropriate style of the contemporary Latin American novelist, to the existence of a uniquely New World marvelous reality, characterized by an impressive geography, cultural and racial miscegenation, early chronicles fictionalizing the continent, and a turbulent political situation. The existence of a marvelous reality legitimated and territorialized a literary marvelous, which Carpentier opposed to the literary artifice of European writers of fantastic and surrealist literature. García Márquez effects an analogous legitimation and territorialization when he explains that Latin America, "that boundless realm of haunted men and historic women," that "outsized reality," "nourishes a source of insatiable creativity" more adequate for the representation of the continent's excesses than the "rational talents" of Europe.[13] But although Carpentier's, Leal's, and García Márquez's legitimation of the imaginary is couched in ontological terms (Latin America *is* marvelous), the surrealist filiations of their treatment of the imaginary indicate a more complex epistemological problematization that acquires a particular significance in the context of Latin America's status as a colonized society.

The argumentative model of Flores' plea for international recognition resembles in certain respects that of discourses produced by colonial writers in their demand for independence. The hegemony of metropolitan values, institutional systems, and conceptual paradigms leaves the colonies three main alternatives for legitimating their autonomy: demonstrating that the similitude between colonizer and colonized invalidates any justification of the colonial enterprise; insisting on their right, as well as the colonizer's right, to difference; and categorically rejecting the paradigms of the colonizer in order not only to demand autonomy and respect for their difference, but also to claim their superiority. An example of the first would be Huamán Poma's argument at the beginning of the seventeenth century that the Incas were already Christian before the Spanish conquest, thus rejecting any legitimation of the colonial enterprise on the grounds of evangelization.[15] The second alternative is illustrated by the Cuban essayist José Martí toward the end of the nineteenth century. Basing his argument on the specificity of Latin America, which he attributes to several factors, including racial heterogeneity (his expression "our mestizo America" was subsequently to become a catchword for numerous intellectuals), Martí advocated the development of local systems and the rejection of foreign models: "The European university must give way to the American university."[16] He also criticized the binary opposition between "university reason" and "rural reason" (313), civilization and barbarism, and argued that it should be replaced by that between "false erudition and nature" (310), the latter defined as "everyone's reason in everyone's things" (313). Here the emphasis is explicitly on the rejection of intellectual paradigms considered inadequate in the context of Latin American society. Reason and knowledge are consequently relativized in a general questioning of the claims to universality of Western traditions.

The Latin American delegitimation of metropolitan models received a significant theoretical impetus after 1939, when Ortega y Gasset's philosophy of "circumstantialism," with its criticism of the claim to universality of German idealist philosophy and insistence on the contingent nature and historicity of philosophical paradigms, became very influential in Latin America, especially in Mexico. It was there that his disciple José Gaos directed the "Seminar for the Study of Thought in Spanish-Speaking Countries," which was to stimulate the philosophical writings of major Mexican thinkers such as Leopoldo Zea.[17]

The third argument for autonomy, one based not on the claim of similitude, or difference and equality but on superiority, took two radically different forms before and after independence. In the period immediately preceding and following independence, numerous Latin American writers had insisted on the necessity that the New World countries reject retrograde peninsular paradigms and adopt more efficient means of economic management and government. By portraying a New World Adam working the land and contributing to the development of the continent, they valorized progress while depicting the colonial heritage in a pejorative light;[18] the claim of difference and equality was thus transformed into an assertion of difference and superiority. Toward the end of the nineteenth century, however, the colonial object of criticism was replaced by the newly emerged neocolonial one to the north, which contributed to a widespread rejection of the tenets of positivism. One of the most virulent denunciations of the new hegemonic values is José Vasconcelos' 1925 essay entitled *The Cosmic Race (La raza cósmica)* in which he mocked what he qualified as North American cultural and spiritual barbarism and exalted Hispanic taste and spirit. According to this Mexican educator and essayist, the age of reason, epitomized by North American civilization, was to be replaced eventually by a vastly superior age of taste, to be brought about by the Latin American fifth race, amalgam of the four other races. He opposes "fantasy, the supreme faculty" and "constant inspiration" of the new race to the "rule, norm and tyranny" of the age of reason.[19] The antipositivistic subversion of the neocolonial hierarchy between the newly emerged world power to the north and Latin America also constitutes the explicit goal of Rodó's 1900 essay *Ariel,* in which Latin America is symbolized by the spiritual Ariel in Shakespeare's *The Tempest,* while the United States is compared to Caliban, the uncouth cannibal. In *The Labyrinth of Solitude (El laberinto de la soledad,* 1950), the Mexican poet and essayist Octavio Paz pointed out that European reason had not managed to solve any of the world's problems; on the contrary, it had led to the creation of totalitarian societies, an argument that had already been developed by Max Horkheimer and Theodor Adorno during their 1944 exile in California. According to Paz, "the dreams of reason are intolerable" and its mirrors multiply "torture chambers."[20] In other essays, Paz explains that Mexico had always imitated foreign models, especially those of progress and positivism, until the Revolution of 1910, which ultimately led to a greater autonomy in the constitution of national identity.[21]

It is hardly surprising that Latin American intellectuals questioned the European rational canon. One of the criteria for the conceptual "Calibanization" of the colonized was their supposed absence of reasoning faculties. Sixteenth-century Spanish clerics debated whether the Indian had a soul; Hegel, in his *Philosophy of History,* described the indigenous inhabitant of the New World as the eternal infant, immature, lazy, and (in this respect worse than the European child) totally incapable of mental and psychological development; and ethnographers established a binary opposition between European civilization with its consciousness of historical heritage and ability to engage in self-analysis and "primitive" culture with its spontaneity and lack of self-reflexivity, thus arguing that European scholars were indispensable for the understanding of the social and political organization of primitive societies.[22] Even Tzvetan Todorov, who denounces the barbarity of the Spanish conquest and colonization, ascribes the relative facility of the conquest to the superior semiotic capacity of the Europeans, arguing that the ability to interpret and create complex sign systems indicates mental development.[23]

Claiming that a Latin American (or generally Hispanic) philosophy was different but equal to the Franco-German tradition, and even criticizing the claim to universality of European philosophical systems, became a means of questioning one of the main criteria of Western superiority. Leopoldo Zea recently remarked in a study entitled *Discourse from the Perspective of Marginalization and Barbarism* (*Discurso desde la marginación y la barbarie*, 1988) that Europe is the real Caliban, because of its cruel domination of its colonies, and that the fictitious Caliban was actually a projection of Europe's own negative qualities. Zea also refers to various contemporary challenges to the philosophical canon within the European intelligentsia and the criticism of the monolithic *logos* by poststructuralist thinkers such as Jacques Derrida. So the marginal Caliban is situated in the center, and Prospero is "Calibanized."[24] Referring to the writings of Chatelet, Zea explains that European hegemonic paradigms are "nomadized" by metropolitan thinkers who reject universalism in favor of heterogeneity, individuality, and the concrete. The periphery's insistence on difference is thus compared to the attack on the canonical conceptualization and constitution of knowledge within the metropolis.

It is against this complex background of the colonized subject's rebellion against imposed models, the resistance of the newly independent Latin American countries to neocolonial domination and the European philosophical delegitimation of metaphysical and epistemological paradigms that we must situate certain twentieth-century literary practices. Artists have frequently been considered subversive figures, challenging official dogma in spite of the various mechanisms of control. Bakhtin establishes a filiation between the modern novel and the Menippean tradition of satirizing dominant figures and systems, in which the narrative is transformed into a polyphonous integration of subversive discourses, as opposed to the epic, which functions as a foundational narrative affirming official values and versions of history. Fredric Jameson's concept of "national allegory," or literature in which individual actions allegorize national concerns (which he considers characteristic of all Third World writing),[25] bears obvious resemblances to that of epic narrative (which, in spite of generic differences, emphasizes national preoccupations, not necessarily in the modern sense). Latin American intellectuals have frequently emphasized the ideological dimension of literature, even going so far as to consider formal and stylistic brilliance as "ancillary," or instrumental and secondary, with respect to the political and social content.[26] As Hernán Vidal convincingly argues, Latin American writers have not always endorsed hegemonic paradigms; on the contrary, a significant counterhegemonic current has characterized Latin American writing since the time of the Conquest.[27] Modern forms of the novel radically problematize the Bakhtinian distinction between epic and novelistic strategies. Narratives that emphasize cultural specificity and difference, identity construction and self-affirmation in the context of neocolonialism frequently exhibit a foundational function analogous to that of the epic, and may *also* be highly critical of dominant paradigms.

The marvelous real (*lo real maravilloso*), for example, must be interpreted partially in this light. Alejo Carpentier was greatly influenced by his contacts with French Surrealists, who criticized, among other things, certain philosophical canons. Pierre Mabille, for example, considered the Western empirical attitude toward reality restrictive and dehumanizing and advocated a "marvelous" approach akin to that of the magico-mythic *Weltanschauung* of primitive societies.[28] In Carpentier's prologue to *The Kingdom of this World,* the Cuban author coins the expression *lo real maravilloso* in an obvious reference to the French Surrealists' exhortation that reality should be considered as marvelous. And Carpentier's depiction of the female indigenous protagonist in *The Lost Steps* (1953) as a spontaneous, natural woman living in a community untouched by the corruption of modern society involves a nostalgic utopian recreation of an idealized past indubitably influenced by the European pastoral mode, exoticism, and disenchantment with modern society.[29] But it is simplistic to criticize the Cuban author for imitating metropolitan conventions and identifying with European preoccupations. His concept of the marvelous real acquired an entirely different function from that of the Surrealist marvelous. Whereas the Surrealists criticized a hegemonic intellectual and literary canon in their own society and looked toward the European Other for inspiration in a movement largely inspired by exoticism, Carpentier also used the concept of the marvelous real as a marker of difference in a Latin American discourse of identity rejecting European influence. As I have remarked earlier in my discussion of the legitimation and territorialization of the imaginary in Latin America, the Surrealist quest for the marvelous is portrayed by Carpentier as artificial, while the authentic marvelous is presented as one of the main characteristics of the Latin American continent: the novelty of its "discovery" in 1492, the fictionalization of the New World by the Spaniards, the impressive dimensions of rain forests and rivers, the presence of heterogeneous racial groups. What was considered by Breton's group as a more authentic relation to reality and criticism of dominant values and conceptual paradigms is in turn criticized by Carpentier as literary artifice, as just another manifestation of the lifeless and cerebral modern European spirit. In order to believe, adds Carpentier, one must have faith.[30]

This apparently paradoxical rejection of those whose influence is obvious can be considered a symbolic parricide due to the inevitable anxiety of influence of formerly colonized societies. But what is significant is the criterion for establishing a distinction between French Surrealism and the Latin American marvelous real. Critics such as Roberto González Echevarría have noted the influence of Spengler's *Decline of the West* on Carpentier, and in particular criticism of the self-reflexive European intellect and his valorization of the nonreflexive and thus more "authentic" subject in primitive societies.[31] Carpentier's rearrangement of the "normal" chronology in *The Kingdom of this World* involves more than poetic license and structural experimentation. It challenges the dominant historiographical paradigm based on empiricism, and replaces it with one that does not correspond to what is traditionally regarded as truth, but which produces meaning in what Carpentier considers a far more effective way. It is not merely a question of fictionalizing history by adapting "facts" to the fictitional plot, extrapolating and supplying invented characters and situations, as is the case in most historical novels. Carpentier creates a different chronology whose structure illustrates one of the dominant themes of the novel, eternal return and the cyclical notion of time of "primitive" mentalities. Chronological historiographical "reality" is only one of the infinite number of truths, and maybe not even the most effective one.[32] Carpentier's transformation of aleatory events into a signifying network characterized by meaningful correspondences reminds us of Borges' distinction between the conception of reality as ruled by chance and a magico-mythic worldview in which everything is related, just as in fictional narratives. The Otherness of "primitive mentality" discussed by the metropolitan intellectuals and especially the French Surrealists is appropriated by Latin American magical realists in their narrative strategies of identity construction. This has inevitably contributed to their enormous success in Europe.

Another interesting parallel between the criticism of canonical concepts of reason by members of European artistic movements and that illustrated by Latin American literary forms is the resemblance of the Surrealists' attack on empirical reason to the implication of the Argentinian novelist Julio Cortázar's theory of "figures," which he describes (in *Hopscotch*) as a way of being "where everything has value as a sign and not as a theme of description."[33] Cortázar's creation and conceptualization of these "figures" is also somewhat analogous to Carpentier's chronological manipulation in *The Kingdom of this World*. According to some Surrealists, the perception of an event should not be considered as an empirical and objective observation but the linking of one element with others previously encountered. It is not the particular event, therefore, but the perceived relationship among events that gives meaning to the experience. This criticism of empirical knowledge, obviously influenced by phenomenology, implies at the same time a questioning of the canonical conception of representation according to which a supposedly stable given is amenable to objective semiotization. The idea of an objective and unchangeable reality that one can supposedly apprehend and represent is replaced by the emphasis on perception as the subjective creation and production of a new reality of the imagination.[34]

The subject of Cortázar's *62: Model Kit* is not merely Parisian society and the peregrinations of Argentinian expatriates but the way in which the protagonist produces meaning from the diverse stimuli surrounding him.[35] A rare Châteaubriand steak triggers a network of associations related to the color red, blood, and the torture and murder of young women by the Hungarian countess Bathory. Reality is not an empirical given but a constantly changing "constellation" or group of figures that is the product of the individual imagination. Cortázar's short story entitled "Letter to a Young Lady in Paris" develops a different strategy.[36] The protagonist, who is left in charge of a friend's apartment in Buenos Aires, vomits innumerable rabbits that proceed to destroy the carefully kept home of his absent friend. Instead of describing the events as a product of hallucination triggered by the protagonist's resentment of the material comfort of the young lady, the narrative presents them as actually occurring. Contrary to traditional fantastic fiction, in which the laws of nature and the supernatural are presented as antinomian, Cortázar's story juxtaposes them without any problematization. He rejects a rational explanation of the events as the product of the protagonist's imagination in what would then be a patently

oneiric or hallucinatory account, as well as the treatment of the supernatural in the canonical fantastic, in which the apparently inexplicable
events produce disbelief and fear in the observer/narrator. Jaime Alazraki
has coined the term neofantastic for this kind of narrative.[37] Here again, it
is important to eschew the pejorative implications of traditional influence
studies, which would trace Cortázar's fantastic fiction to sources such as
Kafka's "The Metamorphosis" (written, by the way, by an author who was
on the margin in several respects, as has been pointed out by Deleuze
and Guattari).[38] Rather, one might reread the obvious filiation from the
perspective of Brazilian *modernismo,* whose proponents criticized naive
imitation and advocated "anthropophagia," or selective cannibalism, in
which only those elements considered desirable are incorporated. In other
words, we must examine why Cortázar chose to emphasize the subjective creation of reality and subvert the canonical fantastic rejection of the
supernatural and simultaneous "seduction of the uncanny," to use Louis
Vax's expression.[39] The fact that his writings also demonstrate great interest in oriental philosophical and religious systems indicates that Cortázar
is engaged in a general relativization of hegemonic Western models.

In the case of magical realist narratives that attempt to recreate an autochthonous worldview, one can also establish the importance of European
influence. The Guatemalan author Miguel Angel Asturias, for example,
first became acquainted with the indigenous legends of his own country
during his studies in Paris and developed a style that demonstrates his
knowledge of modern literary techniques such as expressionism and Surrealism. In spite of his territorialization of magical realism, which, he
claims, has "a direct relationship to the original mentality of the Indians,"
Asturias explains that "it is similar to what the Surrealists around Breton
wanted."[40] Although it is obvious that his representation of the indigenous
population is conditioned by a European perspective, Asturias' magical
realism subverts the canons of ethnographic representation. The dichotomization between the nonreflexive primitive society and the Western eth-
nographer's discourse of knowledge is dissolved by a novelistic discourse
in which there is an attempt, albeit imperfect and artificial, to represent
an indigenous worldview by means of a non-European focalizer. The novel
Men of Maize (*Hombres de maíz,* 1949), for example, does not give us an
ethnographic account, accompanied by lengthy explanations, or even a
regionalist and *costumbrista* depiction of the quaint customs and religious
practices of the indigenous protagonists.[41] In spite of the lack of indige-

nous voices in a polyphonic narrative in the Bakhtinian sense, Asturias' novel produces a worldview different from the Western one and presents it as equally valid. Unlike the traditional fantastic narrative (in the restricted sense defined by Tzvetan Todorov)[42] in which the supernatural is portrayed as unacceptable and threatening to the world of reason, magical realism in Asturias juxtaposes two worldviews without establishing a hierarchy between them, thus relativizing the dominant Western rational paradigm.

While it is obvious that the previously mentioned Latin American novelists and short-story writers were marked by their familiarity with modern European literary movements and techniques, metropolitan exoticism and fetishization of the European Other, their creative "cannibalization" has produced a rich literary corpus that is widely appreciated not only for its formal and stylistic mastery but also for its originality. But what is important to point out is that the development of the literary modes associated with the neofantastic and magical realism that have emerged in the second half of the twentieth century in Latin America cannot be attributed by a naive essentialist argument to the supposed marvelous reality of the continent or ascribed to the unidirectional flow of metropolitan influence. It is conditioned by various factors, such as a critical stance with respect to canonical rational and especially positivistic paradigms in the context of neocolonial resistance, the tradition of the artist's vindication of the imagination and subversion of hegemonic models, the French Surrealists' indictment of restrictive empirical knowledge and valorization of non-European mentalities, the appropriation of the indigenous Other as a marker of difference, and the general delegitimation of values and conceptual frameworks of the past few decades.

Notes

1 Luiz Costa Lima, *Control of the Imaginary: Reason and Imagination in Modern Times*, trans. Ronald W. Sousa (Minneapolis: University of Minnesota Press, 1988), pp. 4, 24.

2 Angel Flores, "Magical Realism in Spanish American Fiction," *Hispania* 38, 2 (May 1955): 187–92. (Subsequent page references are to the reprint of Flores' essay in this volume.)

3 Luis Leal, "El realismo mágico en la literatura hispanoamericana," *Cuadernos americanos* 26, 4 (julio-agosto 1967): 230–35. (Subsequent references are to Wendy B. Faris' translation, included in this volume.)

4 Flores, "Magical Realism in Spanish American Fiction," pp. 110–11, 113.

5 For a detailed study of defamiliarization in the fiction of García Márquez, see Kenrick E. A. Mose, *Defamiliarization in the Works of Gabriel García Márquez* (Lewiston, N.Y.: Edwin Mellen Press, 1989).

6 Vladimir Propp, *Morphology of the Folktale* (Austin: University of Texas Press, 1968).

7 See Claude Brémond, "Les bons récompensés et les méchants punis," in *Sémiotique narrative et textuelle*, ed. Claude Chabrol (Paris: Larousse, 1973), pp. 96–121.

8 Costa Lima, "Control of the Imaginary," pp. 220–21.

9 Leal, "Magical Realism in Spanish American Literature," p. 122 in this volume.

10 Niklas Luhmann, *The Differentiation of Society*, trans. Stephen Holmes and Charles Larmore (New York: Columbia University Press, 1982).

11 Costa Lima, "Control of the Imaginary," pp. 215–20.

12 See Irène Bessière, *Le récit fantastique: La poétique de l'incertain* (Paris: Larousse, 1974), for her explanation of the emergence of the fantastic in the Enlightenment, her examination of the antinomious nature of the mode, in which natural and supernatural logic are explicitly opposed, and her definition of the fantastic as "thetic" (affirming the reality of the apparently supernatural events) as opposed to the nonthetic fairy tale.

13 Gabriel García Márquez, "The Solitude of Latin America," Nobel lecture, 1982, trans. Marina Castañeda, in *Gabriel García Márquez and the Powers of Fiction*, ed. Julio Ortega (Austin: Univ. of Texas Press, 1988), pp. 88–89. See also García Márquez, "Fantasía y creación artística en América Latina y el Caribe," *Texto crítico* 14 (1979): 3–8.

14 Arturo Uslar Pietri, *Letras y hombres de Venezuela* (1948; Mexico City: Fondo de Cultura Económica, 1949), p. 162.

15 See Roger A. Zapata, *Guamán Poma, indigenismo y estética de la dependencia en la cultura peruana* (Minneapolis: Institute for the Study of Ideologies and Literature, 1989).

16 José Martí, "La universidad europea ha de ceder a la universidad americana," in *Nuestra América*, vol. 1 of *Antología mínima* (Havana: Editorial de ciencias sociales, 1972), p. 311.

17 For a general overview of this subject, see José Luis Abellán, *La idea de América: origen y evolución* (Madrid: Ediciones ISTOMO, 1972).

18 For a more detailed treatment of this subject, see Hernán Vidal, *Socio-historia de la literatura colonial hispanoamericana: tres lecturas orgánicas* (Minneapolis: Institute for the Study of Ideologies and Literature, 1985), esp. chap. 3.

19 José Vasconcelos, *La raza cósmica (The Cosmic Race)*, ed. and trans. Didier Jaen (Los Angeles: California State University, 1979), p. 27.

20 Octavio Paz, *The Labyrinth of Solitude*, trans. Lysander Kemp (1950; rev. ed. New York: Grove Press, 1985), p. 212.

21 However, in "Critique of the Pyramid" (1970) in *The Labyrinth of Solitude*, pp. 284–325, Paz attributes his country's continuing barbarism to the legacy of the Aztecs, whose coldly calculating cruelty accompanied by fanaticism paralleled that of the worst European institutions, such as fascism and the Inquisition.

22 For a critical discussion of the development of ethnography, see Michel de Certeau, *L'Ecriture de l'histoire* (Paris: Gallimard, 1975). A specific examination of the dichotomization characterizing European representations of its Other in colonialist fiction is carried out by Abdul R. JanMohamed in "The Economy of Manichean Allegory: The Function of Racial Difference in Colonialist Literature" (*Critical Inquiry* 12, 1 (1985): 59–87, and *Manichean Aesthetics: The Politics of Literature in Colonial Africa* (Amherst: University of Massachusetts Press, 1983).

23 Tzvetan Todorov, *The Conquest of America*, trans. Richard Howard (New York: Harper & Row, 1987). For an analysis of the ethnocentric paradigms underlying Todorov's study, see Deborah Root, "The Imperial Signifier: Todorov and the Conquest of Mexico," *Cultural Critique* 9 (1988): 197–219.

24 Leopoldo Zea, *Discurso desde la marginación y la barbarie* (Barcelona: Anthropos, 1988), p. 274.

25 Fredric Jameson, "Third-World Literature in the Era of Multinational Capitalism," *Social Text* 15 (1986): 65–88. Jameson's categorical characterization of Third World literature as allegorical and his dichotomization of the First and the Third World has been criticized by Aijaz Ahmad in "Jameson's Rhetoric of Otherness and the 'National Allegory'," *Social Text* 17 (1987): 3–25.

26 For a discussion of this subject, see Roberto Fernández Retamar, *Caliban and Other Essays*, trans. Edward Baker (Minneapolis: University of Minnesota Press, 1989), esp. pp. 74–99, in which the Cuban essayist criticizes the pejorative attitude toward Latin American testimonial fiction and the blind acceptance of metropolitan aesthetic canons.

27 Hernán Vidal, *Socio-historia de la literatura colonial hispanoamericana: Tres lecturas orgánicas* (Minneapolis: Institute for the Study of Ideologies and Literature, 1985).

28 Pierre Mabille, *Le miroir du merveilleux* (Paris: Minuit, 1940).

29 Alejo Carpentier, *The Lost Steps*, trans. Harriet de Onís (1953; New York: Farrar, Straus and Giroux, 1992).

30 Irlemar Chiampi, in "Carpentier y el surrealismo," *Revista Língua e Literatura* 9 (1980): 155–74, examines the striking similarities between Carpentier's criticism of Surrealism and the critical attitude of French Surrealists such as Pierre Mabille, whom the Cuban critic knew well but does not mention in his writings.

31 Roberto González Echevarría, "Isla a su vuelo fugitiva: Carpentier y el realismo mágico," *Revista Iberoamericana* 40, 86 (Jan.–March 1974): 9–64.

32 For an analysis of North American and Latin American fictitional subversions of the positivistic historical consciousness, see Lois Parkinson Zamora, "The Usable Past: The Idea of History in Modern U.S. and Latin American Fiction," in *Do the Americas Have a Common Literature?*, ed. Gustavo Pérez Firmat (Durham: Duke University Press, 1990), 7–41, in which she refers to "the ebb and flow (not a single progress) of culture, the intermingling of various cultural currents (not a single, impelling source), and the expansive flow of individual and communal historical experience in expressive forms (both narrative and musical)" (36–37) in the fiction of Willa Cather and Carlos Fuentes, arguing that the conceptions of history in the United States and Latin America are not as radically different as is sometimes supposed.

33 Julio Cortázar, *Hopscotch*, trans. Gregory Rabassa (1963; New York: Avon, 1966), p. 489.

34 For a more detailed discussion of what Breton called "le hasard objectif" (objective chance), or subjective linking of previous sign and subsequent event in an individual creation of "excess" meaning, see Jacqueline Chénieux-Gendron, *Le surréalisme* (Paris: Presses Universitaires de France, 1984), esp. pp. 111–20.

35 Julio Cortázar, *62: A Model Kit*, trans. Gregory Rabassa (1962; New York: Avon, 1973).

36 Julio Cortázar, "Letter to a Young Lady in Paris," in *End of the Game and Other Stories*, trans. Paul Blackburn (1978; New York: Harper & Row, 1978), pp. 39–50.

37 Jaime Alazraki, "Neofantastic Literature—A Structuralist Answer," in *The Analysis of Literary Texts: Current Trends in Methodology*, ed. Randolph D. Pope (Eastern Michigan University, Ypsilanti: Bilingual Press, 1980), pp. 286–90.

38 Gilles Deleuze and Felix Guattari, *Kafka—pour une littérature mineure* (Paris: Minuit, 1975).

39 Louis Vax, *La séduction de l'étrange: Étude sur la littérature fantastique* (Paris: Presses Universitaires de France, 1965).

40 "Hearing the Scream: A Rare Interview with the Surprise Nobel Prize Winner—Miguel Angel Asturias," *Atlas* 14, 6 (Dec. 1967): 58.

41 Miguel Angel Asturias, *Men of Maize*, trans. Gerald Martin (1949; New York: Delacorte Press, 1975).

42 Tzvetan Todorov, *Introduction á la littérature fantastique* (Paris: Seuil, 1970).

SCOTT SIMPKINS

Sources of Magic Realism/Supplements to Realism in Contemporary Latin American Literature

Magic realism seems plagued by a distinct dilemma, a problem arising primarily from its use of supplementation to "improve" upon the realistic text. The source of this nagging difficulty can be attributed to the faulty linguistic medium that all texts employ, and even though the magic realist text appears to overcome the "limits" of realism, it can succeed only partially because of the frustrating inadequacies of language. The magical text appears to displace these shortcomings through a textual apparition, but this appearance itself illustrates the representational bind which hampers its desired success. And thus the magic realists, always trying to overcome textual limitations, continuously fall short of their numinous goal.

In *Don Quixote*, Cervantes offers an appropriate example of the textual strategies employed in magical texts, and their ultimate failure, as Sancho betrays the creaky machinations that fool the less-wary reader (Don Quixote himself, in this instance). Sancho, after all, is not deceived by "magic" — although Don Quixote insists otherwise.

Jorge Luis Borges and Gabriel García Márquez contribute further to this supplemental discourse by examining the condition of textual magic itself in their own writings. Largely because of his close ties with the fantastic, the designation of Borges as a magic realist has created critical dissension, although he is credited by some critics as one of the major early influences on the contemporary magic realism movement which has flourished internationally since the early part of this century.[1] And, indeed, Borges' presence surfaces throughout a great deal of the magical strategies employed by the many practitioners of this textual sleight of hand. Moreover, his work also anticipates several of the major textual concerns which have developed among the generations of writers who have followed him. As Robert Scholes observes in *Fabulation and Metafiction*, the "opposition between language and reality, the unbridgeable gap between them, is fundamental to the Borgesian vision, and to much of modern epistemology and poetic theory."[2]

Even the term "magic realism" has engendered disagreement since Franz Roh introduced it into artistic discourse in the mid-1920s through the German phrase *Magischer Realismus,* a "countermovement" in art through which "the charm of the object was rediscovered."[3] When his *Nach-Expressionismus (Magischer Realismus): Probleme der neuesten Europaischen Malerei,* published in German in 1925, was translated and disseminated in Spanish through the *Revista de Occidente* two years later, his articulation of this new sensibility in art doubtlessly had a strong influence on Latin American writers searching for a suitable means to express the "marvelous reality" unique to their own culture.[4] In *German Painting in the Twentieth Century,* Roh later schematized the differences between Expressionism and Postexpressionism (which he associates with magic realism), but his focus upon the visual arts reduces the usefulness of his charted oppositions in a literary context. (These oppositions are considered in detail in Irene Guenther's essay in this volume.)

Roberto González Echevarría, in *Alejo Carpentier: The Pilgrim at Home,* traces the historical development of this concept from Roh to Carpentier's *lo real maravilloso* and his connection with Surrealism to Angel Flores' influential but limited 1955 essay, "Magical Realism in Spanish American Fiction."[5] González Echevarría maintains that the term arose from an "effort to account for a narrative that could simply be considered fantastic" (109). The magic realist text "does not depend either on natural or physical laws or on the usual conception of the real in Western culture" because it is "a narrative . . . in which the relation between incidents, characters, and setting could not be based upon or justified by their status within the physical world or their normal acceptance by bourgeois mentality" (109). But, again, the allowance of the fantastic within this realm has led some critics, such as Luis Leal, to assert that

> magical realism cannot be identified either with fantastic literature or with psychological literature, or with the surrealist or hermetic literature that Ortega describes. Unlike superrealism, magical realism does not use dream motifs; neither does it distort reality or create imagined worlds, as writers of fantastic literature or science fiction do; nor does it emphasize psychological analysis of characters, since

it doesn't try to find reasons for their actions or their inability to express themselves.[6]

These differences in boundaries offer yet another example of the difficulties involved in defining the limits of any period or genre. "The formula" for delimiting magic realism "has been used by many [critics] . . . as though they will find comfort in a concept with universal validity, like classicism, or Romanticism, or (even) realism," Emir Rodríguez Monegal observes, adding that "Es necesario insistir en el peligro de esta utilización general de una fórmula que . . . tiene de todo menos de universal" [It is necessary to insist on the danger of general use of a formula that . . . is anything but universal].[7] As Fredric Jameson remarks, however, the term "magic realism" — despite its shortcomings — "retains a strange seductiveness."[8]

The similar interests of surrealism have also led to critical confusion regarding the concept of magical realism, especially since several writers have produced works strongly suggestive of both. In his book-length study of Alejo Carpentier, for example, González Echevarría stresses both Carpentier's ties with Surrealism and those elements which set him apart distinctly as a magic realist, and he suggests that even Carpentier's identification of "marvelous American reality" points to his preference for an ontological outlook toward the textual enterprise favored by Latin Americans, as opposed to the phenomenological, European stance proffered by Roh. González Echevarría states:

> The Latin American writer preferred to place himself on the far side of that borderline aesthetics described by Roh — on the side of the savage, of the believer, not on the ambiguous ground where miracles are justified by means of a reflexive act of perception, in which the consciousness of distance between the observer and the object, between the subject and that exotic other, generates estrangement and wonder.[9]

Yet, both González Echevarría and Rodríguez Monegal, in "Lo real y lo maravilloso en *El reino de este mundo*,"[10] note that Carpentier — and several other magic realists — chose to move away from some of the more restrictive tenets of Surrealism and turn toward what has become known as magic realism. González Echevarría contends that "in spite of his fascination with Surrealism at one time in his life, Carpentier never completely succumbs to Breton and his theories. On the contrary, Carpentier endeavors to isolate in his concept of the 'marvelous' something which would be exclusively Latin American" (123). Others such as Borges and García Márquez, however, have departed from Surrealism far more substantially than Carpentier.

Despite the various critical disagreements over the concept of magic realism, one element which does recur constantly throughout many magic realist texts, and therefore points to a unifying characteristic, is an awareness of the ineluctable *lack* in communication, a condition which prevents the merger of signifier and signified. Perhaps the problem with this type of supplementation is really nothing more than that of a rigorous, but overwhelmingly frustrated, endeavor to increase the likelihood of *complete* signification through magical means, to make the text—a decidedly unreal construct—become real through a deceptive seeming. Rosemary Jackson suggests that "the issue of the narrative's internal reality is always relevant to the fantastic, with the result that the 'real' is a notion which is under constant interrogation," and this seems to be the case. Use of the "real," in terms of signification, actually appears to eliminate the difference between the construct and the object it somehow reconstructs. Despite its undeniable artificiality, a superrealist painting of an apple, for example, may appear more "real" than an impressionistic rendition of one.[11]

Gabriel García Márquez, on the other hand, is a member of the generation of textual magicians to follow Borges (since Borges had a twenty-five-year head start). Like Borges, García Márquez employs a variety of supplemental strategies in an attempt to increase the significative force texts seem able to generate. In one of a series of interviews published as *The Fragrance of Guava*, he maintains that "realism" (he cites some of his realistic novels as examples) is "a kind of premeditated literature that offers too static and exclusive a vision of reality. However good or bad they may be, they are books which finish on the last page."[12] A "realistic" text is hardly a satisfactory mode, much less an accurate presentation of the thing in itself, García Márquez contends, because "disproportion is part of our reality too. Our reality is in itself out of all proportion" (60). In other words, García Márquez suggests that the magic text is, paradoxically, more realistic than a "realistic" text. And this realism is conjured up by a series of magical supplements—such as those found in his *One Hundred Years of Solitude*.

To Jameson, Carpentier's concept of the "marvelous real" establishes a stance distinctly antithetical to the notion of supplementation as an active component of magic realism. Carpentier's "strategic reformulation" of the label of magic realism through the term *real maravilloso* produces "not a realism to be transfigured by the 'supplement' of a magical perspective," Jameson claims, "but a reality which is already in and of itself magical or fantastic."[13] But, with this assertion, Jameson seems to neglect the transmission and portrayal of the marvelous, an act effected through a textual medium which is clearly a supplementation of the agency of realism.

For someone who has said he would rather be a magician than a writer, García Márquez meets his desires half way by being both in *One Hundred Years of Solitude*.[14] Despite the many magical events (flying carpets, living dead, accurate portents, telekinesis, etc.), García Márquez claims he "was able to write *One Hundred Years of Solitude* simply by looking at reality, our reality, without the limitations which rationalists or Stalinists through the ages have tried to impose on it to make it easier for them to understand" (*Fragrance* 59–60). In effect, he is arguing that the magical text operates virtually as a corrective to traditional tenets of mimesis, incorporating those unreal elements which in themselves antithetically ground reality.

One Hundred Years of Solitude offers numerous examples of magical supplementation amid the description of approximately a century in the history of one family, a genealogy which recounts fantastic occurrences as though they were quite commonplace.[15] Generations of characters, beginning with the marriage of José Arcadio Buendía and Ursula Iguarán, also encounter the bizarre aspects of "real" life in the inherently supernatural tropics. Early in the novel, for instance, José Arcadio realizes that his plan to found a new village—Macondo—"had become enveloped in a web of pretexts, disappointments, and evasions until it turned into nothing but an illusion."[16] This unreal reality is reinforced further as a contagion of amnesia infects the entire village. But a plan is developed to label everything in Macondo so that its increasingly forgetful inhabitants can remember reality by writing it, a strategy which reveals the unseen fantastic element behind writing and its magical ability to create a reality.

As the amnesia worsens, the villagers' situation parallels the seemingly universal—and also realistic—dilemma that accompanies language's indeterminacies: "Thus they went on living in a reality that was slipping away, momentarily captured by words, but which would escape irremediably when they forgot the values of the written letters" (53). In the amnesia episode, accordingly, García Márquez discusses this decidedly realistic concern through a magical layer, a supplemental strategy that may enchance, through its own theatricality, the force of an otherwise common-place development, boosting its significative show in the process through a transcendent power.

To prevent an overwhelming sense of disbelief, magic realists present familiar things in unusual ways (flying carpets, Nabokovian butterflies, mass amnesia, and so on) to stress their innately magical properties. By doing this, magic realists use what the Russian Formalists called defamiliarization to radically emphasize common elements of reality, elements that are often present but have become virtually invisible because of their familiarity. And through a process of supplemental illusions, these textual strategies seem to produce a more realistic text. But whether this endeavor succeeds is another matter.

Borges' "The Garden of Forking Paths" offers a distinct illustration of this point. Within its detective-story framework, his story describes a magical novel (*The Garden of Forking Paths*) which, through a play of textual supplementation, attempts to encompass infinite linguistic possibilities. The story revolves around Ts'ui Pên's labyrinthian novel, first thought to be, as his grandson Yu Tsun describes it, "an indeterminate heap of contradictory drafts" because it consists of a nearly endless series of events which involve the same characters in different roles.[17] But a sinologist, Stephen Albert, whom Yu Tsun plans to murder, discovers another hermeneutical path through this textual maze. Albert claims that Ts'ui Pên's novel is designed to create a multinarrative which saturates its textual capacity and thus achieves the desired state of complete signification. This textual strategy of magical supplementation seems to include everything, thereby overcoming the seemingly unavoidable linguistic lack.

Or does it? It is possible that Ts'ui Pên overlooks a basic problem concerning the text itself by taking its textuality for granted without calling its own provisional status into question. Ts'ui Pên (not unlike the Surrealists) tries to subvert and overcome the text, but fails because he ironically remains bound by textual restraints. Still, this strategy, which reveals the desire to increase signification, to embrace the fluttering essence of illumination, always ends—because it begins—in loss. Therefore, a magical text such as Ts'ui Pên's can never enforce a center by remaining forever decentered. Yet Borges (through Ts'ui Pên) forces the reader, as does Sterne in *Tristram Shandy*, to consider the properties often unknowingly granted to texts while they surreptitiously reveal a certain absence that usually goes unnoticed. If this absence is taken further, multiplied in a self-consciously reflexive manner as in *The Garden of Forking Paths*, the text seems to encompass everything and lack nothing—although finally it can't. But the magical attempt is there: bypassing the commonplace unity found in most realistic texts, the magical text tries to go beyond, to make the necessary swerve that Harold Bloom discusses in a different context, a *clinamen* away from the shortcomings associated with "realistic" texts.[18]

This plan appears to produce an "infinite text" such as the one Ts'ui Pên tries to create, even though its use of a static medium (language) constantly hampers its signification. Borges does manage to focus the reader's attention upon textual processes, producing as a result the defamiliarization which seems to form a major tenet of magic realism. And, the consciously polyscenic text portrays more accurately an important aspect of reality, for there are always many different viewpoints of something at any given moment.

In Borges' story, for instance, Yu Tsun is not only a narrator; he is also concurrently an English professor, a prisoner, a friend (albeit newly acquired) to Albert, a spy for the Germans, an assassin, and a character in Ts'ui Pên's novel (as his actions magically duplicate those of several fictive pasts). Like the Cubists who tried to show several perspectives of objects in order to capture three-dimensional essences, Borges constructs a multiperspective text which appears to cover all fictional possibilities. Still, of course, this inherently faulted construct cannot go beyond its frustrating limitations as a linguistic text.

The stress here on the textual element of magic realism is not incidental, because its semiotic dysfunction may be caused by the medium magic realists use: language. Many theorists of the fantastic, in fact, identify the contemporary concern with language's shortcomings as a symptom of the modern temperament. To them, magical texts are one way of supplementing not only the failures of the modern text, but also the inadequacies of what is now called the postmodern condition (perhaps exemplified by existential thought) as well. Christine Brooke-Rose contends that this epistemological crisis has led to new desires in textual generation, revaluations of textual properties, and a poetics of defamiliarization. "The burden of this meaningless situation being unbearable, we naturally escape, and easily, into our more familiar reality, endowed with significance by our desire, whatever it might be, and displace the meaningless situation into a mere backdrop, apocalyptic no doubt, but a backdrop we cease to see."[19] Perhaps magic realism's goal is to return our focus to the backdrop of textual reality, its production and function, by defamiliarizing it.

Consequently, the supplemental strategies used by magic realists may be geared toward "improving" the realistic text, a movement which realizes itself by exploiting language's ability to represent reality through fictive constructs. Borges' "fictions and inventions," for example, "move language *toward* reality, not away from it," Robert Scholes contends.[20] The textual project of magic realism, then, is displayed through its linguistically bound attempt to increase the capabilities of realistic texts. Yet this same strategy is necessarily undermined by the problematical nature of language. Borges' "The South" demonstrates this dilemma well as its protagonist, Juan Dahlmann, tries to use a magical text (*The Thousand and One Nights*) to direct his reality, to fictionally write (and rewrite) his existence. "To travel with this book, which was so much a part of the history of his ill-fortune, was a kind of affirmation that his ill-fortune had been annulled"; the narrator says, "it was a joyous and secret defiance of the frustrated force of evil."[21] But Dahlmann catches on to the lack amid this solely textual reality, a drawback that undoes its effectiveness.

As his train ride continues, Dahlmann abandons the book for the more real (though slightly less magical) magic of everyday life, and the narrator comments: "The magnetized mountain and the genie who swore to kill his benefactor are—who would deny it?—marvelous, *but not so much more* than the morning itself and the mere fact of being. The joy of life distracted him from paying attention to Scheherezade and her *superfluous miracles*. Dahlmann closed his book and allowed himself to live" (170, emphasis added). Here the narrator reveals the immanent failure of magical artifices as textual supplements: the magical text is not *much more* magical than reality itself, and to go too far beyond these natural perimeters seems an unnecessary and ineffective diversion. Dahlmann's observations suggest that even a more subtle magic still falls prey to this representational dilemma, although admittedly to a lesser extent. In fact, the diversion of a textual reality moves subjects farther away from reality itself, as Dahlmann, for instance, finds he cannot name the "trees and crop fields" he passes, "for his actual knowledge of the countryside was quite inferior to his nostalgic and literary knowledge" (170–71). The fictive reality, rather than offering a more accurate reality, actually distances itself away from what could be called "actual" reality. Thus when Dahlmann is later accosted by "some country louts," he "decided that nothing had happened, and he opened the volume of *The Thousand and One Nights*, by way of suppressing reality" (173). The magical text, in this manner, overturns its *assumed* corrective nature and instead apparently displaces the reality it was thought to somehow enhance and reground.

Angel Flores traces the inception of magic realism during this century to a reaction to the "blind alley" of photographic realism, a textual approach that may undermine its effectiveness through its literality. Realism, in effect, produces a text plagued by the ordinary, the *too real*. And imagination, another aspect of the "real," is given short shrift at best. As Borges' narrator in "The Secret Miracle" says, compared with his imagination, "the reality was less spectacular."[22] Brooke-Rose identifies the particularly modern element of this concern by noting that "the sense that empirical reality is not as secure as it used to be is now pervasive at all levels of society. Certainly what used to be called empirical reality, or the world, seems to have become more and more unreal, and what has long been regarded as unreal is more and more turned to or studied as the only "true" or "another equally valid" reality.[23] Amid this worldview, concludes Brooke-Rose, it is not at all surprising that the "inversion of real/unreal is perfectly logical."

Within this arena of uncertainty, magic realism demonstrates its hopeful scheme to supplement the realistic text through a corrective gesture, a means to overcome the insufficiencies of realism (and the language used to ground realism). Alain Robbe-Grillet describes his use of some imaginary seagulls that closely parallels this situation: "The only gulls that mattered to me . . . were those which were inside my head. Probably they came there, one way or another, from the external world, and perhaps from Brittany; but they had been transformed, becoming at the same time somehow more real *because* they were now imaginary."[24] This use of imagination claims to supplement reality by heightening its distinctive elements through ideal imagination, the essence and not necessarily the vehicle. Borges' use of imaginary authors and works, a practice also found in such magical writers as Jonathan Swift and Flann O'Brien, demonstrates this textual strategy as he creates a new reality through imagination, a reality which becomes "more real" (to return to Robbe-Grillet's assertion) as a result of the magical gloss applied to it through the process of creation.

But this supplementary act also reveals an implicit despair, a collective lament about the problems involved in using language to convey reality, especially through the delusion of realism.[25] In other words, through the use of magical supplements, the linguistically determined text seems to span the chasm between signifier and signified. But it cannot. "Reality is too subtle for realism to catch it," Robert Scholes maintains. "It cannot be transcribed directly. But by invention, by fabulation, we may open a way toward reality that will come as close to it as human ingenuity may come."[26] Scholes' claim, however, betrays that very element which undermines such an assertion: attempts to signify can never overcome the deficiencies which any sign system presupposes. This is not to say that magical texts do not have any champions, however; Jameson, through a Heideggerian formula, observes that a magical supplement may allow the *worldness* of the *world* to show itself.[27]

The magic realist's predilection toward the unreal may also reveal an awareness of the impossibility of successful signification — complete information transference — as magic is used to flaunt these same limitations. "You who read me, are You sure of understanding my language?" asks Borges' narrator in "The Library of Babel."[28] Magic realism courts the inevitable problem of signification by offering the impression of success, a supplemental diversion which appears to bypass the limitations of the realistic text, evading its failures through the incorporation of imagination.

Still, as neat as this sounds, perhaps it doesn't work. Although Jameson, while referring specifically to magic in the genre of romance, may be overstating the situation when he asserts that "the fate of romance as a form is dependent on the availability of elements more acceptable to the reader than those older magical categories for which some adequate substitute must be invented," he is also at least partially correct, for there is undoubtedly something unsatisfactory about the strategy of magic realism.[29] Even the naive inhabitants of García Márquez's Macondo eventually become indifferent to flying carpets.

Plato contends in *Phaedrus* that the ideal language to use in any discourse is inescapably just that — ideal. In his Second Speech, Socrates says: "As for the soul's immortality, enough has been said. But about its form, the following must be stated: To tell what it *really is* would be a theme for a divine and a very long discourse; what it *resembles*, however, may be expressed more briefly and in human language."[30] Socrates' assertion also unveils a major dilemma of magic realism: the divine language needed to bring about complete signification (what *it* "really is") can never transcend its illusory status. Supplementation (magic, in this instance) only adds another layer to the significative deception. The *thing itself* always slips away.

The textual economy that magic realism creates for itself undoubtedly introduces several problems. Angel Flores suggests that the desire to maintain some semblance of reality as a textual ground engenders an indeterminate element which further decreases what could be called reader comprehension. To Flores, supplementation of realism is far less preferable than working from an entirely fantastic base. After all, it is possible that the purely magical mode more closely approaches Socrates' "divine language" than does realism heightened by magic. In addition to the previously mentioned linguistic drawback that magic realism faces, the concern for the limits of partial magic adds another difficulty to the act of textual transmission, for—as Coleridge noted—the reader's doubt carries a great deal of weight.[31] Yet Tzvetan Todorov offers an interesting counterassertion: " '*I nearly reach the point of believing*': that is the formula which sums up the spirit of the fantastic. Either total faith or total incredulity would lead us beyond the fantastic: it is hesitation which sustains its life." [32] It is unlikely, however, that a reader would have any reason to "believe" what is said in a text; the question of doubt always lurks (or should always lurk, anyway) between the lines because the physical presence of the text ceaselessly calls attention to its inherent falseness as a construct.[33]

This stifling predicament may, in fact, explain why Borges and García Márquez themselves became disenchanted with magic and moved on to other concerns. In an interview Borges remarked:

> I feel that the kind of stories you get in *El Aleph* and in *Ficciones*
> are becoming rather mechanical, and that people expect that kind
> of thing from me. So that I feel as if I were a kind of high fidelity,
> a kind of gadget, no? A kind of factory producing stories about mis
> taken identity, about mazes, about tigers, about mirrors, about people
> being somebody else, or about all men being the same man or one
> man being his own mortal foe.[34]

As Borges observes, the magical text cannot maintain its illusion under close scrutiny. García Márquez reveals a similar disquietude in this exchange with interviewer Plinio Apuleyo Mendoza:

> A.M.: Is it that you feel the success of *One Hundred Years of Solitude*
> is unfair to the rest of your work?
> G.M.: Yes, it's unfair. *The Autumn of the Patriarch* is a much more im
> portant literary achievement. But whereas it is about the solitude of
> power *One Hundred Years of Solitude* is about the solitude of every
> day life. It's everybody's life story. Also, it's written in a simple, flow
> ing, linear and . . . superficial way.
> A.M.: You seem to despise it.

G.M.: No, but since I knew it was written with all the tricks and artifices under the sun, I knew I could do better even before I wrote it.

A.M.: That you could beat it.

G.M.: Yes, that I could beat it.[35]

The underlying desire for rhetorical strategies which may increase the possibility of successful signification seems to be an optimistic semiotic gesture. Discontent with the strictures of realism, magic realists such as Borges and García Márquez construct elaborate magical supplements which imply a purifying concern for textual generation. "Fantasy has always articulated a longing for imaginary unity, for unity in the realm of the imaginary," Rosemary Jackson suggests. "In this sense, it is inherently idealistic. It expresses a desire for an absolute, an absolute signified, an absolute meaning."[36] Still, as García Márquez and Borges demonstrate, the use of magic is a self-conscious (perhaps painfully so) attempt to overcome significative loss, to bridge that space between the ideal and the achievable (or, semiotically—to remove the bar between signifier and signified). And in this regard, magical texts necessarily reveal their limits in the course of their operation.[37] But the magical text almost triumphs over its otherwise crippling imperfections by commenting on its own questionable condition while simultaneously presenting itself. In this manner, magical texts reflect upon their own blind spots, generating a metacritical discourse about their own indeterminate modality.

Such is the case of *One Hundred Years of Solitude*, which questions and answers this situation by creating itself through the very workings of the novel it conceals itself within. Accordingly, *One Hundred Years of Solitude* is "about" a book titled *One Hundred Years of Solitude*. García Márquez's novel becomes and betrays itself at the same time, playing upon the problematic textuality that can be granted only conditionally to any text, even one which tries to transcend this representational trap through magical supplementation.

García Márquez achieves—or attempts to achieve—this magical effect by having one character (Melquíades) write the novel, and another (Aureliano) decipher it from an unknown "code" (which is actually Sanskrit). The novel ends as Aureliano comes to the close of Melquíades' manuscript, and by manipulating the unavoidable conclusion that any text presupposes by beginning (perhaps with the exception of such arguably cyclical texts as *Finnegans Wake* and Julio Cortázar's *Hopscotch*), García Márquez correlates the two events as though it were a textual possibility—which ultimately it may be. By doing this, he manages to go beyond the bounds of realistic texts (mentioned earlier: "However good or bad they may be, they are books which finish on the last page") as his text ends both literally and magically within itself. The text virtually supplements itself out of its textual plane through a magical dodge which appears to prevent its conclusion (i.e., the physical end of the book). Yet, within the drive behind the magical supplement, a maneuver constantly out-maneuvering itself like a dog chasing its tail, the text always disappears into itself, an envelope of infinite beginnings forever grounded by the medium it employs to escape the textual dead end.

Notes

1 See, for example, Emir Rodríguez Monegal, "Realismo mágico versus literatura fantástica: un diálogo de sordos," in *Otros mundos otros fuegos: Fantasía y realismo mágico en Iberoamérica*, ed. Donald Yates (East Lansing, Mich.: Latin American Studies Center, 1975), pp. 25–37; and Roberto González Echevarría, *Alejo Carpentier: The Pilgrim at Home* (Ithaca: Cornell University Press, 1977). Both discuss Borges in relation to magic realism.

2 Robert Scholes, *Fabulation and Metafiction* (Urbana: University of Illinois Press, 1979), p. 9.

3 Franz Roh, *German Art in the Twentieth Century* (Greenwich, Conn.: New York Graphic Society, 1968), p. 70.

4 González Echevarría develops this assertion at length in *Alejo Carpentier*, pp. 107–29.

5 Angel Flores, "Magical Realism In Spanish American Fiction," *Hispania* 38 (1955): 187–92, reprinted in this volume.

6 Luis Leal, "Magical Realism in Spanish American Literature," p. 121 in this volume.

7 Rodríguez Monegal, p. 26.

8 Fredric Jameson, "On Magic Realism in Film," *Critical Inquiry* 12 (1986): 302.

9 González Echevarría, *Alejo Carpentier*, p. 116.

10 Emir Rodríguez Monegal, "Lo real y lo maravilloso en *El reino de este mundo*," *Revista Iberoamericana* 37 (1971): 619–49.

11 Thus Jackson was probably off base when she concluded in 1981:

The text has not yet become non-referential, as it is in modernist fiction and recent linguistic fantasies (such as some of Borges's stories) which do not question the crucial relation between language and the "real" world outside the text which the text constructs, so much as move towards another kind of fictional autonomy. (36)

12 Plinio Apuleyo Mendoza and Gabriel García Márquez, *The Fragrance of Guava*, trans. Ann Wright (London: Verso, 1983), p. 56.

13 Jameson, "On Magic Realism in Film," p. 311.

14 George R. McMurray, *Gabriel García Márquez* (New York: Frederick Ungar Publishing, 1977), p. 86.

15 Alejo Carpentier concludes his famous essay "De lo real maravilloso americano," translated in this volume, by asking, "After all, what is the entire history of America if not a chronicle of the marvelous real?" See p. 88 in this volume.

16 Gabriel García Márquez, *One Hundred Years of Solitude*, trans. Gregory Rabassa (New York: Avon Books, 1971), p. 22. Subsequent quotations from this text will be cited parenthetically.

17 Jorge Luis Borges, *Labyrinths: Selected Stories and Other Writings*, ed. Donald A. Yates and James E. Irby (New York: New Directions Publishing, 1964), p. 20.

18 See Harold Bloom, *The Anxiety of Influence: A Theory of Poetry* (New York: Oxford University Press, 1973).

19 Christine Brooke-Rose, *A Rhetoric of the Unreal: Studies in Narrative and Structure, Especially of the Fantastic* (Cambridge: Cambridge University Press, 1981), p. 9.

20 Scholes, *Fabulation*, p. 10.

21 Borges, "The South," in *Ficciones*, ed. and trans. Anthony Kerrigan (New York: Grove Press, 1962), p. 170. Subsequent quotations from this text will be cited parenthetically.

22 Borges, *Labyrinths*, p. 92.

23 Brooke-Rose, *A Rhetoric of the Unreal*, p. 4.

24 Alain Robbe-Grillet, "From Realism to Reality," in *For A New Novel: Essays on Fiction*, trans. Richard Howard (New York: Grove Press, 1965), pp. 161–62.

25 This is reflected by a comment about a later Aureliano in *One Hundred Years of Solitude* who abandons worldly pleasures for a lesser "written reality." This Aureliano and his friend Gabriel suggest that texts verify reality when they settle a debate about the reality of an alleged event by asserting that "after all, everything had been set forth in judicial documents and in primary-school textbooks." Writing is therefore granted the capacity to confirm reality. But the narrator points out this semiotic dilemma by noting that the two "were linked by a kind of complicity based on real facts that no one believed in" (pp. 357, 359).

26 Scholes, *Fabulation*, p. 13.

27 Jameson, "Magical Narratives: Romance as Genre," *New Literary History* 7 (1975): 142.

28 Borges, *Labyrinths*, p. 58.

29 Jameson, "Magical Narratives," p. 143.

30 Plato, *Phaedrus*, trans. W. C. Helmbold and W. G. Rabinowitz (Indianapolis: Bobbs-Merrill, 1956), p. 28, emphasis added.

31 Magic realism presupposes a certain amount of doubt from the reader who can never escape that element of make-believe which pervades magic. The reader, like José Arcadio, faces "the torment of fantasy" (p. 45).

32 Tzvetan Todorov, *The Fantastic: A Structural Approach To A Literary Genre*, trans. Richard Howard (Cleveland/London: Press of Case Western Reserve University, 1973), p. 31.

33 Even those texts which question the notion of truth/fiction—such as the nonfiction novel, the new journalism—or even those forms of the media which present daily *versions* of current events, exhibit nothing more, in the long run, than a purely provisional status, a status forever shifting under the influence of relative values and acts (perception, interpretation, analysis, and so on).

34 Richard Burgin, *Conversations With Jorge Luis Borges* (New York: Holt, Rinehart and Winston, 1969), p. 130.

35 Mendoza and García Márquez, *The Fragrance*, p. 63.

36 Rosemary Jackson, *Fantasy: The Literature of Subversion* (New York: Methuen, 1981), p. 179.

37 Borges' narrator in "The Secret Miracle" comments: "Hladik felt the verse [drama] form to be essential because it makes it impossible for the spectators to lose sight of irreality, one of art's requisites" (*Labyrinths*, pp. 90–91).

PART II

Theory

WENDY B. FARIS

Scheherazade's Children: Magical Realism
and Postmodern Fiction

In 1980 John Barth rejected membership in any imaginary writer's club that did not include Gabriel García Márquez.[1] That statement, an homage directed from North to South, marks an important shift in literary relations and can serve to signal an increased worldwide recognition of magical realism—"a now widely available elixir," according to John Updike, and, as I wish to suggest here, an important component of postmodernism.[2] Very briefly, magical realism combines realism and the fantastic in such a way that magical elements grow organically out of the reality portrayed.

I invoke Scheherazade's children as its standard bearers because they might be imagined as "replenished" postmodern narrators, born of the often death-charged atmosphere of high modernist fiction, but able somehow to pass beyond it. These narrative youths herald, perhaps, a new youth of narrative—Witold Gombrowicz proposes the slogan of "man wants to be young" to counter what he believes is the foundational nostalgia of existentialism, "man wants to be God"—and with that youth a desire for an accessibility that contrasts with the hermeticism of many modernist texts.[3] Magical realist fictions do seem more youthful and popular than their modernist predecessors, in that they often (though not always) cater with unidirectional story lines to our basic desire to hear what happens next. Thus they may be more clearly designed for the entertainment of readers. (Compare, for example, the great modernists Proust, Joyce, and Faulkner with the postmodern magical realists Günter Grass, García Márquez, and Salman Rushdie.) That the genre has been extending—often via novels—into film, including mainstream American film (*The Witches of Eastwick, Ironweed, Field of Dreams, Ghost*) confirms my sense of this accessibility. But what about the magic? These postmodern storytellers may need magic to battle death, a death more depersonalized even than the one their

mother faced from King Shariyar; they inherit the literary memory, if not
the actual experience, of death camps and totalitarian regimes, as well
as the proverbial death of fiction itself. My invocation of Scheherazade's
children also echoes the title of Rushdie's *Midnight's Children*, the novel
that exemplifies the mode of magical realism best for my purposes here—
among other reasons because it is quite real, quite magical, and not from
Latin America, where the genre is usually imagined to reside. And Rushdie
clearly had Scheherazade in mind in *Midnight's Children*; allusions to *The
Thousand and One Nights* proliferate.

Scheherazade herself is a popular paradigm of the high modernist narrator—exhausted and threatened by death, but still inventing.[4] Scehera-
zade, as everyone knows, has taken up the cause of the virgins whom her
father had to find for King Shariyar to sleep with every night and put to
death every morning (in order to assuage his disillusionment at his wife's
infidelity). Her father is in danger of being beheaded because the supply
of women is running out. Scheherazade volunteers, and begins to tell the
king stories embedded in each other: he must wait until the next night to
hear the end of a tale, by which time Scheherazade has embedded it in
yet another. The king can't bear to kill her, and so she survives in this way
for a thousand and one nights. By this time she has given birth to three
children, at which point she confronts the king with the situation and he
relents, giving up his disillusionment and its attendant punishments. In
their embedded structure, one growing out of the other, and continuing
for 1001 nights, Scheherazade's tales point up the autogenerative nature
of fictions, indeed of language itself, a characteristic made more and more
explicit in our post-Joycean age. In Scheherazade's tales, as in *Finnegans
Wake*, language takes on magical properties to light up the nights verging on nightmares in which they are told. This generativity operates at all
levels in the fictions that I am identifying as Scheherazade's children: on
the structural plane with stories that grow out of other stories; on the mimetic front with characters who duplicate themselves in miraculous feats
of doubling; in the metaphorical register with images that take on lives of
their own and engender others beyond themselves, independent of their
referential worlds.

Like many postmodern texts, these children of Scheherazade have a
powerful precursor to overcome. In the case of the Latin American fiction to which the label of magical realism has most frequently been applied, that precursor is European realism—a tradition that dominated

Latin American letters until mid-century and remains strong in modern and contemporary fiction. Indeed, this magical supplement to realism may have flourished in Latin America not only because it suits the climate there, as Alejo Carpentier has argued in his well-known essay on *lo real maravilloso*,[5] but also because in dismantling the imported code of realism "proper" it enabled a broader transculturation process to take place, a process within which postcolonial Latin American literature established its identity.[6] The postcolonial nature of magical realism I leave for another time, but in any case, the category of magical realism can be profitably extended to characterize a significant body of contemporary narrative in the West, to constitute, as I've suggested, a strong current in the stream of postmodernism.[7] Most importantly, it seems to provide one source of the replenishment that Barth sees in contemporary fiction, a revitalizing force that comes often from the "peripheral" regions of Western culture — Latin America and the Caribbean, India, Eastern Europe, but in literary terms a periphery that has quickly become central and yet still retained the intriguing distance of that periphery. Like the frontier, like primitivism, the lure of peripheralism (more recently called by other names like the subaltern, the liminal, the marginal) dies hard, because the idea is so appealing and so central to the center's self-definition.

Geographical stylistics are problematic, but one might speculate about the existence of a tropical lush and a northerly spare variety of this plant. In the latter cases, there is less magic and its range is more circumscribed: the programmatic magic of smell in Patrick Suskind's *Perfume*, for example, contrasts with the pervasive magic in García Márquez and Rushdie; the occasional magic of Toni Morrison's *Beloved* is somewhere in between the two.[8] Jean Weisgerber makes a similar distinction between two types of magical realism: the "scholarly" type, which "loses itself in art and conjecture to illuminate or construct a speculative universe" and which is mainly the province of European writers, and the mythic or folkloric type, mainly found in Latin America. These two strains coincide to some extent with the two types of magical realism that Roberto González Echevarría distinguishes: the epistemological, in which the marvels stem from an observer's vision, and the ontological, in which America is considered to be itself marvelous (Carpentier's *lo real maravilloso*).[9] The trouble is that it is often difficult to distinguish between the two strains. We can attempt it with reference to two of Cortázar's stories, otherwise quite similar. "Axolotl" is set in Paris, in the aquarium section of the Jardin des Plantes zoo, but the Axolotl itself is an American organism with a Nahua (Aztec) name, and so categories begin to crumble — just as I was about to put this story nearer the European, epistemological branch of the genre. Following my initial impulse, however, we can note that it is the narrator's identity with the amphibian that begins the magic. In "The Night Face Up," on the other hand, we might say that it is the extraordinarily strong presence of the indigenous past in modern Mexico — a more specifically American cultural phenomenon, like the atmosphere of belief in Haiti in Carpentier's *The Kingdom of this World* — that motivates the narrator's magical trip back into that past, or forward from it into the modern present. And so these categories of European versus American have a certain validity even though they are far from absolute.

In arguing that magical realism, wherever it may flourish and in whatever style, contributes significantly to postmodernism, it is useful to consider Brian McHale's idea that modernism is epistemological, concerned with questions of knowledge, while postmodernism is ontological, concerned with questions of being. (In the one we ask how we know something and in the other we ask what it is.) McHale cleverly locates a point in Faulkner's *Absalom, Absalom!* where this line is crossed. It is the moment when Quentin and Schreve leave off their attempts to remember and reconstruct, and begin self-consciously to invent. At this point they may have moved, with Barth, from exhausted to replenished fiction. That moment of invention, the realization of an imaginary realm, can also be seen to distinguish magical realism from realism. In the former, it happens not provisionally in the voices of narrators, but concretely in the reality depicted. Returning to Scheherazade and her children for a moment, we might say that though Scheherazade prefigures an ontological mode (her *being* is at stake, in her role as narrator), she is primarily concerned with epistemological questions, with figuring out how to extend her store of knowledge to stave off her death. Her children, on the other hand (whom we must imagine, as Quentin and Shreve imagine Sutpen and his offspring, since they have no substantial part in the frame of the tales), have to contend with their own narrative existence. They owe that existence to the fertility of their mother's mind (as well as to that of her body), but now they must invent their fictional identities for themselves. They come into being first as a function of Scheherazade's need to narrate, hence almost as epistemological objects, but then they must go forward as subjects, crossing into the ontological domain. And they no longer feel, as did their immediate modernist predecessors, so crushed by the narrative burden of the past; somehow—and we don't quite know how—they manage to invent beyond it; the difficulty of that task is perhaps another reason why they need magic to perform it. For this literature often plays tricks; it is eminently performative.

The group of novels I had in mind most constantly as I formulated my ideas includes Gabriel García Márquez, *One Hundred Years of Solitude* (1967), Milan Kundera, *The Book of Laughter and Forgetting* (1979), Salman Rushdie, *Midnight's Children* (1980), Robert Pinget, *That Voice* (1980), Carlos Fuentes, *Distant Relations* (1980), D. M. Thomas, *The White Hotel* (1981), William Kennedy, *Ironweed* (1983), Patrick Suskind, *Perfume* (1985), Toni Morrison, *Beloved* (1987), Laura Esquivel, *Like Water for Chocolate* (1990), and Ana Castillo, *So Far from God* (1993). Other eminent precursors and contemporaries whom I recall more peripherally are Gogol, James, Kafka, Borges, Carpentier, Paz, Cortázar, Grass, Calvino, Wilson Harris, Allende, and Ben Okri. And there are many more; the list is constantly growing. Latin American practitioners may head it—or have in the recent past—but my aim here is to extend the mode beyond that region, beyond *el boom*, which put magical realism on the map of world literature, and to keep to very recent fiction, and so I include only a few Latin American works.[10] (*One Hundred Years of Solitude* is no longer "very recent," but it is too seminal to omit.) I include Pinget's *That Voice* here partly for shock value, because it is not ordinarily considered magical realist writing and is not similar to the more canonical texts in that mode. And yet for those very reasons, given its significant points of contact with magical realism via its creation of material metaphors, its use of voices from beyond the grave, and its consequent spiritual aura, it underscores ways in which magical realism is interwoven with many strands of contemporary fiction.[11]

To begin with, it is helpful to list the primary characteristics of magical realist fiction. I suggest five:

(1) The text contains an "irreducible element" of magic, something we cannot explain according to the laws of the universe as we know them.[12] In the terms of the text, magical things "really" do happen: young Victor and André in *Distant Relations* "really" become a twinned fetus floating in a pool; Remedios the Beauty in *One Hundred Years of Solitude* "really" does ascend heavenward; Grenouille in *Perfume* "really" distills a human scent from the bodies of virgins; Francis Phelan's dead enemies in *Ironweed* "really" do hop on the trolley he is riding and speak to him. The

irreducible element says to us, in almost existential fashion, "I EKsist" —
"I stick out." We might even see here the remnants of existential anguish at an un-co-optable world, but tempered by the more playful mood
of surrealism. In *So Far from God*, for example, Ana Castillo specifically
confirms the irreducible nature of a dead person's reappearance by verify-
ing her sighting by several people: "Esperanza was also occasionally seen.
Yes, seen, not only by La Loca, but also by Domingo who saw her from
the front window. . . . And once, although she had thought at first it was a
dream, Esperanza came and lay down next to her mother." [13]

Like the metaphors we shall see in a moment, which repeatedly call
attention to themselves as metaphors, thus remaining partially unassimilated within the texture of the narrative, the magic in these texts refuses
to be assimilated into their realism. Yet it also exists symbiotically in a foreign textual culture—a disturbing element, a grain of sand in the oyster
of that realism.

Irreducible magic often means disruption of the ordinary logic of cause
and effect. Lisa's pains in *The White Hotel* appear *before* she experiences
the atrocities at Babi Yar that cause them and kill her. Saleem's claims
in *Midnight's Children* that he caused this or that historical event—by
singing a song, moving a pepper pot on a dining table—are similar logical reversals. Melquíades' manuscript turns out to be a prediction rather
than just a recording of events in *One Hundred Years of Solitude*, implicitly asking whether he—and we—are the masters or the victims of our
fate. Even though we may remain skeptical in the face of these proposed
sequences, the enormity of the historical events, the human suffering involved in them, and the dissatisfaction we feel at the traditional ways such
phenomena have been integrated into cultural logic, cause us to question
that logic as a result of these new fictional arrangements.

In the light of reversals of logic and irreducible elements of magic, the
real as we know it may be made to seem amazing or even ridiculous. This
is often because the reactions of ordinary people to these magical events
reveal behaviors that we recognize and that disturb us. Grenouille's per-
fuming abilities and the uncannily entrancing scent he manufactures for
himself are magical, but the mass hysteria that they engender and that
tears him literally limb from limb and devours him at the end of the novel
is real, and all-too-familiar as an analogue for the atrocities of persecution
and scapegoating in recent history. Thus magic also serves the cause of
satire and political commentary, as we see less seriously than in *Perfume*

when the magical rebirth of La Loca in *So Far from God* serves to satirize the bureaucratic machinations of organizations. The particular one
in question here is "M.O.M.A.S., Mothers of Martyrs and Saints," and it is
our collective desire to codify the sacred that is satirized: "The decision
as to whether a ''jito' of a M.O.M.A.S. member would be designated as a
saint or a martyr was also very touchy for a lot of people. . . . Saints had
the unquestionable potential of performing miracles while martyrs were
simply revered and considered emissaries to the santos." However, these
bureaucratic problems don't spoil the joy of the organization's annual conventions: "what a beautiful sight it all became at those reunions: 'jitos
from all over the world, some transparent, some looking incarnated but
you knew they weren't if you tested them in some way, like getting them
to take a bite out of a taquito or something when, of course, after going
through all the motions like he was eating it, the taco would still be there.
Although, it really wasn't such a respectable thing to do to test a santo,
even if he had once been your own chiple child!"[14]

(2) Descriptions detail a strong presence of the phenomenal world—
this is the realism in magical realism, distinguishing it from much fantasy
and allegory, and it appears in several ways. Realistic descriptions create a
fictional world that resembles the one we live in, in many instances by extensive use of detail. On the one hand, the attention to the sensory detail
in this transformation represents a continuation, a renewal of the realistic tradition. But on the other hand, since in magical realist fiction, in
addition to magical events (like Beloved's appearances, Frances Phelan's
conversations with the dead) or phenomena (like Melquíades' manuscript,
Saleem's transmitting and receiving radio head, or Grenouille's nose), the
best magical realist fiction entices us with entrancing—magic—details,
the magical nature of those details is a clear departure from realism. The
detail is freed, in a sense, from a traditionally mimetic role to a greater
extent than it has been before. This is still true even when we consider
canonical realist texts from a Barthesian perspective. That perspective
questions their mimetic qualities, endowing details with an "effet de réel,"
which renders them principally markers that tell us not any particular information but simply that this story is real; but magical details can serve
as markers that lead in the opposite direction, signaling that this might
be imaginary.[15]

My second point here has to do not with description but with reference.
In many cases, in magical realist fictions, we witness an idiosyncratic recre-

ation of historical events, but events grounded firmly in historical realities — often alternate versions of officially sanctioned accounts.[16] García
Márquez's rewriting of the history of Latin America in that of Macondo,
for example, including a massacre that has been elided from the public
record, and the opening of *The Book of Laughter and Forgetting*, which
restores a man airbrushed out of history by party doctrine, are elements
distinct from the mythical components of those tales, though related to
them. The combination implies that eternal mythic truths and historical
events are both essential components of our collective memory. Thus these
histories can include magic and folk wisdom — events told from Ursula's
or Melquíades' point of view, in *One Hundred Years of Solitude*, for example, recipes and remedies in *Like Water for Chocolate* and *So Far from
God*. But history is the weight that tethers the balloon of magic, and as if
to warn against too great a lightness of magical being, both Fuentes and
Kundera include dangerous sets of floating angels in their novels; they
represent the lightness of ahistorical irresponsibility. The twin fetus at the
end of *Distant Relations*, the remainder of old Heredia's desire to create
an angel, floats "with a placidity that repudiates all past, all history, all re-
pentance" — a dangerously unanchored position (225). Historical anchor-
ing is well demonstrated in what John Foster calls "felt history," whereby a
character experiences historical forces bodily.[17] This phenomenon is exaggerated and particularized in magical realist fictions. Clear examples are
the coincidence of Saleem's birth with that of the nation of India, Lisa's
pains that anticipate her death at Babi Yar, Grenouille's magical nose born
from the smells of Renaissance Europe, the division of Fuentes' characters between Latin America and Europe.

As I have suggested, the material world is present in all its detailed and
concrete variety as it is in realism — but with several differences, one of
them being that objects may take on lives of their own and become magical in that way. (Here we are proceeding beyond both description and
reference.) The yellow butterflies that appear with Mauricio Babilonia in
One Hundred Years of Solitude and the basket in which Saleem travels
from Bangladesh to Bombay in *Midnight's Children* are good examples, as
are the shiny spherical object young Victor Heredia finds at the ruins of
Xochicalco in *Distant Relations* and the door that opens at Felipe's touch
in Fuentes' *Aura*. This materiality extends to word-objects as metaphors,
and they too take on a special sort of textual life, reappearing over and
over again until the weight of their verbal reality more than equals that of

their referential function. Saleem's spittoon and the sheet through which Aadam Aziz in *Midnight's Children* first examines his future wife Naseem function in this way, as does the tick on the tree branch in *Perfume* or the recurring roses, breasts, hotels, and hair in *The White Hotel*. The part of Surrealism that could be written down, its textual poetics, exploited to the fullest the magic of metaphor, foregrounding the enchanting quality of all poetry as it defies reason and logic. In taking this poetics of defamiliarization to its extreme, magical realism, as is often recognized, is a major legacy of Surrealism. However, in contrast to the magical images constructed by Surrealism out of ordinary objects, which aim to appear virtually unmotivated and thus programmatically resist interpretation, magical realist images, while projecting a similar initial aura of surprising craziness, tend to reveal their motivations — psychological, social, emotional, political — after some scrutiny. Thus Kafka and Gombrowicz, who actualize metaphors by projecting inner states outward, as in the case of Gregor, or public characterizations inward, as in the case of the less well known *Pornografia*, which, as Gombrowicz himself has said (in the preface), "is the grotesque story of a gentleman who becomes a child because other people treat him like one," belong here.

(3) The reader may hesitate (at one point or another) between two contradictory understandings of events — and hence experiences some unsettling doubts. Much of magical realism is thus encompassed by Tzvetan Todorov's well-known formulation of the fantastic as existing during a story when a reader hesitates between the uncanny, where an event is explainable according to the laws of the natural universe as we know it, and the marvelous, which requires some alteration in those laws.[18] But this is a difficult matter because many variations exist; this hesitation disturbs the irreducible element, which is not always so easily perceived as such. And some readers in some cultures will hesitate less than others. The reader's primary doubt in most cases is between understanding an event as a character's hallucination or as a miracle. The mysterious character of Beloved in Morrison's novel of that name slithers provokingly between these two options, playing with our rationalist tendencies to recuperate, to co-opt the marvelous. Women outside of Sethe's house ask themselves, "Was it the dead daughter come back? Or a pretend? Was it whipping Sethe?" A bit farther on "Paul D. knows Beloved is truly gone. Disappeared, some say, exploded right before their eyes. Ella is not so sure. 'Maybe,' she says, 'maybe not. Could be hiding in the trees waiting for another chance.'"

And at the very end of the book, we hear that "They forgot her like a bad dream." (Of course we ask ourselves whether she may have been just that.) "It took longer for those who had spoken to her, lived with her, fallen in love with her, to forget, until they realized they couldn't remember or repeat a single thing she said, and began to believe that, other than what they themselves were thinking, she hadn't said anything at all." [19]

At times like these (other examples are the yellow butterflies or Pilar Ternera's age in *One Hundred Years of Solitude*, the transformation of the pool at the automobile club in Paris into a tropical rainforest in *Distant Relations*, or Saleem's dispersal into the multitudes of India at the end of *Midnight's Children*) we hesitate. At other times we do not; in *One Hundred Years of Solitude* the flying carpets, Remedios' ascension to heaven, José Arcadio's blood traveling across Macondo and finding Ursula are clearly magic, as are the voices of Midnight's children in Saleem's head or Parvati the Witch's spiriting him from Pakistan to India in a basket. But in some cases we get there slowly, as in Felipe Montero's transformation into General Llorente in *Aura*, in the floating twins in the pool at the end of *Distant Relations*, in the growth of Grenouille's extraordinary sense of smell in *Perfume*. Another possibility is to interpret a particular bit of magic in an otherwise realistic fiction as a clear use of allegory. This interpretive strategy is tempting in Kundera's *The Book of Laughter and Forgetting*, when we see people rise above the ground in a charmed circle of ideological bliss—for Kundera an example of the "unbearable lightness" that totalitarian ideologies will tend to engender. Even so, I would argue that since the magic here is presented as such it belongs in the mode of magical realism.

(4.) We experience the closeness or near-merging of two realms, two worlds. [20] We might say, as H. P. Duerr does in his *Dreamtime*, that in many of these texts "perhaps you are aware that *seeing* takes place only if you smuggle yourself in between worlds, the world of ordinary people and that of the witches." [21] The magical realist vision exists at the intersection of two worlds, at an imaginary point inside a double-sided mirror that reflects in both directions. Fluid boundaries between the worlds of the living and the dead are traced only to be crossed in *One Hundred Years of Solitude*, *Midnight's Children*, *That Voice*, *Distant Relations*, *The White Hotel*, and *Ironweed*. If fiction is exhausted in this world, then perhaps these texts create another contiguous one into which it spills over, so that it continues life beyond the grave, so to speak. From the first sentence, *Ironweed* weaves a web of connections between the lands of the living and the dead: "Riding up the winding road of Saint Agnes Cemetery in the back of the rattling old truck, Francis Phelan became aware that the dead, even more than the living, settled down in neighborhoods." Later on, Francis sees in his mind's eye "his mother and father alight from their honeymoon carriage in front of the house and . . . climb . . . the front stairs to the bedroom they would share for all the years of their marriage, the room that now was also their shared grave, a spatial duality as reasonable to Francis as the concurrence of this moment both in the immediate present of his fifty-eighth year of life and in the year before he was born." [22] Conveniently for my purposes, Kennedy has written about *Distant Relations* in terms that join his own novelistic crossing of boundaries to that of Fuentes: in *Distant Relations*, according to Kennedy, Fuentes "asserts that the various cultures are not separate but unified in dream and fantasy through history, populated by ghosts and specters who refuse to die, and who live their afterlives through endless time in ways that reshape the present." [23]

Another related boundary to be blurred is the one between fact and fiction. McHale again confirms that magical realism is central to postmodernism: in a chapter entitled "A World Next Door," he explores the generalized effect of a fantastic " 'charge' [which] seems to be diffused throughout postmodernist writing," though he claims that the hesitation in traditional fantastic writing between this world and the next has been displaced to "the confrontation between different ontological levels in the structure of texts." [24] This formulation thus stresses the magic *of* fiction rather than the magic *in* it.

(5) These fictions question received ideas about time, space, and identity. With "four years, eleven months, and two days" of rain and an insomnia plague that erases the past and hence the meaning of words, a room in which it is "always March and always Monday," José Arcadio who languishes half-dead and half-alive for years under a banana tree in the courtyard of his house, and a final whirlwind that abolishes a race's second opportunity on earth, our sense of time is shaken throughout *One Hundred Years of Solitude*. Our sense of space is similarly undermined when tropical plants grow over the Paris automobile club's pool at the end of *Distant Relations*. As Fredric Jameson sets out the project of realism, one thing it achieves is "the emergence of a new space and a new temporality." Its spatial homogeneity abolishes the older forms of sacred space; likewise the newly measuring clock and measurable routine replace "older forms

of ritual, sacred, or cyclical time."[25] Even as we read Jameson's description, we sense the erosion of this program by magical realist texts — and of course by other modern and postmodern ones as well. Many magical realist fictions (like their nineteenth-century Gothic predecessors) carefully delineate sacred enclosures — Aura's house, Macondo, Saleem's pickle factory and pickle jars, Branly's house (in *Distant Relations*), Baby Suggs' leafy clearing — and then allow these sacred spaces to leak their magical narrative waters over the rest of the text and the world it describes. Magical realism reorients not only our habits of time and space, but our sense of identity as well: with over five hundred children of midnight talking through his head, is Saleem himself anymore? Similarly, we ask ourselves who is the voice in *That Voice*, and who/what are the relations in *Distant Relations*?[26] According to Linda Hutcheon, "In *The White Hotel*, the realist novel's concept of the subject, both in history and in fiction, is openly contested."[27] That contestation is all the more convincing because it comes from within; the magic contests but it contests from within a realistically rendered historical fiction and a realistically conceived character.

As we read magical realist texts, the magic seems to grow almost imperceptibly out of the real, giving us, as Rushdie puts it, a dense "conmingling of the improbable and the mundane" (4). A graphic illustration of this phenomenon, really an extension of the strong mimetic quotient of magical realism, and related to its historical dimension, is the way in which events are usually grounded textually in a traditionally realistic, even an explicitly factual manner. Felipe Montero in *Aura* reads of the magically potent job he will eventually take in a newspaper; we begin *The White Hotel* with fictional letters from Ferenczi and Freud; Rushdie situates his narrative in the events surrounding India's independence and the turmoil that followed it; Remedios the Beauty's levitation begins concretely enough, when Fernanda, as she is hanging out the laundry, feels a "delicate wind of light pull the sheets out of her hand and open them up wide."[28] Remnants of this quality, of magic's gentle blossoming out of reality, persist even when the fantastical element shows its colors quickly and clearly. In *Perfume*, for example, Jean Baptiste Grenouille, with his magically powerful and discriminating sense of smell, is born in geographical space "in Paris under the sway of a particularly fiendish stench," and in a textual time following the opening catalog of stenches "barely conceivable to us modern men and women."[29] Like the perfumers whose ranks he joins, Grenouille is a product of this smelly environment — perhaps even compensating for his mother's "utterly dulled" sense of smell (5).

Another list, of several secondary or accessory specifications, is helpful in building magical realist rooms in the postmodern house of fiction; this one is longer, more provisional, and serves less to distinguish magical realism from the rest of contemporary literature than to situate it within postmodernism and to furnish the rooms we've just constructed.

(1) Metafictional dimensions are common in contemporary magical realism: the texts provide commentaries on themselves, often complete with occasional mises-en-abyme—those miniature emblematic textual self-portraits. Thus the magical power of fiction itself, the capacities of mind that make it possible, and the elements out of which it is made—signs, images, metaphors, narrators, narratees—may be foregrounded. In *Distant Relations*, Fuentes refers again and again to the process of storytelling that goes on between him and the Heredias and Branly as the story of all three gets told. Near the end of the novel, we hear the narrator's anguished cry that "I didn't want to be the one who knew, the last to know, the one who receives the devil's gift and then cannot rid himself of it. I didn't want to be the one who receives and then must spend the rest of his life seeking another victim to whom to give the gift, the knowing. I did not want to be the narrator."[30] And the notion of ghosts *in* the story can be extended to encompass the story itself. Just as Lucie Heredia seems to be Branly's ghost, and "will live the moment my friend Branly dies," so this story we are reading has been the ghost of the stories that were being told within it, and just as it dies off again as we turn the pages, so it lives in our reading of it—until . . . until . . . we kill it with a definitive interpretation (220). In *Midnight's Children*, metaphors for the making of fictions, from the partial view obtained by a Muslim doctor of his patient through a hole in a sheet, to the chutnification of history in jars that equal the novel's chapters, recur with amazing frequency: "To pickle is to give immortality, after all: fish, vegetables, fruit hang embalmed in spice-and-vinegar; a certain alteration, a slight intensification of taste, is a small matter, surely? The art is to change the flavour in degree, but not in kind; and above all (in my thirty jars and a jar) [equalling the thirty one chapters of the novel] to give it shape and form—that is to say, meaning. (I have mentioned my fear of absurdity.)"[31] Beloved also seems to have an almost metafictional dimension to her; she seems to elicit stories at various points: " 'Tell me,' said Beloved, smiling a wide happy smile. 'Tell me your diamonds.' It became a way to feed her. . . . Sethe learned the profound satisfaction Beloved got from storytelling. . . . As she began telling about the earrings, she found herself wanting to, liking it."[32]

In the tradition of the nouveau roman, Pinget's *That Voice* is something of a maverick in this imaginary anthology. There, as in many of Robbe-Grillet's novels, we readers follow a voice as it articulates fragments of a potential story and induces us to participate in its composition. On the one hand, this autogenerative mode enables us to filter out the irreducible element, attributing an apparent reappearance of a dead character, for example, to the process of articulation. On the other hand, the autogenerative mode highlights the fertile magic of language itself, its capacity to create absorbing worlds out of thin event. In a similar way, when the name of Fuentes's character Artemio Cruz appears in *One Hundred Years of Solitude*, or the poet Paul Eluard in *The Book of Laughter and Forgetting*, we experience what seems to be the magical power of literary heritage — ghostly presences of a particular sort. Magical realism is not alone in contemporary literature in foregrounding metafictional concerns; on the contrary, that it does so joins it with other modern and postmodern writing. But it tends to articulate those concerns in a special light, to emphasize the magical capacities of fiction more than its dangers or its inadequacies.

(2) The reader may experience a particular kind of verbal magic — a closing of the gap between words and the world, or a demonstration of what we might call the linguistic nature of experience. This magic happens when a metaphor is made real: we often say that blood is thicker than water, for example, and sure enough, in *One Hundred Years of Solitude*, when José Arcadio Buendía shoots himself, a trickle of his blood "came out under the door, . . . went out into the street, . . . went down steps and climbed over curbs, . . . turned a corner to the right and another to the left," and once inside the Buendía house, hugged the walls "so as not to stain things," and came out in his mother Ursula's kitchen (129–30). When this sort of literalization happens, we may supply the words, as in this case, or the text itself may provide them: shortly before Remedios' levitation we hear that "Remedios the Beauty was not a creature of this world" (188). Similarly, in *Midnight's Children*, we hear that Saleem is "handcuffed to history," and then witness the invasion of his head by the voices of his compatriots. This linguistic magic, which runs through magical realism, thrives on the pervasive intertextual nature of much postmodern writing and the presence of intertextual bricolage. Intertextual magic in which characters from other fictions appear is relatively common, making *Don Quixote* one of our first magical realist novels. All of this celebrates the solidity of invention and takes us beyond representation conceived pri-

marily as mimesis to re-presentation. We are surprised by the literality of the play of language in linguistically motivated fictional moments.

(3) The narrative appears to the late-twentieth-century adult readers to which it is addressed as fresh, childlike, even primitive. Wonders are recounted largely without comment, in a matter-of-fact way, accepted— presumably—as a child would accept them, without undue questioning or reflection; they thus achieve a kind of defamiliarization that appears to be natural or artless. Even *Perfume*, which pursues Grenouille's magical gifts of smell through all their marvelous variety, details them for the most part with a certain air of narrative naïveté. And Grenouille, through whose nose much of the novel is focalized (or should we say olfactorized), mixing perfumes in Baldini's shop, "looks like a child." Baldini thinks he looks "just like one of those . . . willful little prehuman creatures, who in their ostensible innocence think only of themselves" (81). Often we hear descriptions of phenomena experienced for the first time and participate in the fresh wonder of that experience. Such is the case when Grenouille first smells wood, when the Buendías discover ice or a magnifying glass or a train—"something frightful, like a kitchen dragging a village behind it" (210), one of a series of "marvelous inventions" that shook up the Macondoans so that "no one knew for certain where the limits of reality lay" (212). As if in homage to the fresh vision of discovering ice at the start of *One Hundred Years of Solitude*, at the beginning of *Midnight's Children* we hear that as Saleem's grandfather Aadam Aziz begins a day in Kashmir, "the world was new again. After a winter's gestation in its eggshell of ice, the valley had beaked its way out into the open" (4). Kundera and Thomas, of course, present us with a different kind of freshness, the freshness of totalitarian terror—when we follow Tamina onto the dystopian island of children or Lisa into the shocking extermination at Babi Yar.

(4) Repetition as a narrative principle, in conjunction with mirrors or their analogues used symbolically or structurally, creates a magic of shifting references.[33] Saleem's life in *Midnight's Children* mirrors that of the new Indian nation with which he was born. Borges' Aleph reflects all the world and the self. In Cortázar's story "Axolotl" the aquarium wall through which the narrator watches the axolotls and through which he finally passes to become one is a kind of magical spatial mirror. Similarly, the place of Cortázar's narrator in "The Night Face Up," between modern and Aztec worlds, is a temporal double-sided mirror. In *Distant Relations* as well, the doubling of characters and stories that constitutes a

mirror principle of narrative structure is reinforced by reflecting surfaces within the novel — especially windows. A similar kind of narrative mirroring structures *The White Hotel*, where the same story is retold through reflected personalities; like reflections in actual mirrors, the reflected narratives are and are not the same as the "original" ones. Moreover, in such cases, the notion of origin itself is undercut by the repetitions. The same is true of *That Voice*. As I have suggested earlier, even images participate in this process. They return with an unusual and uncanny frequency, confusing further our received notions of similarity and difference. Interestingly enough, ghosts, which figure in many magical realist fictions, or people who seem ghostly, resemble two-sided mirrors, situated between the two worlds of life and death, and hence they serve to enlarge that space of intersection where magically real fictions exist.

A variation on this mirror phenomenon is the occurrence of reversals of various kinds — plot-mirroring, so to speak. This is a common feature in all literature, of course, but in these texts it occurs with particular frequency and highlights the metaphysically revisionist agenda of magical realism. In *The White Hotel*, Freud the analyst is analyzed, in a way, through Lisa's poetic narratives, which include him, and ultimately by historical events themselves, which can be seen to deconstruct his analytical system, because the personal past is ultimately not the origin of Lisa's suffering and hence an awareness of it cannot cure her. In *Distant Relations*, Branly and Lucie Heredia change places as haunter and haunted. And at the end of the novel, the reader hears that "You are Heredia," and inherits the narrative confusion from the character Fuentes in the same way that Fuentes inherited it from Branly. So the roles of narrator and listener are reversed: if Fuentes hands us on the story, he can resume the status of listener and will no longer be condemned, as we have heard him fear above, to be the narrator. The powerfully charismatic perfume in Suskind's novel is manufactured by Grenouille to enhance his life; after doing just that, it causes his death. From the empowered he becomes the overpowered. Such patterns of reversal implicitly figure a lack of human control over events: what you thought you controlled controls you.[34]

(5) Metamorphoses are a relatively common event (though not as common as one might think).[35] They embody in the realm of organisms a collision of two different worlds. In *Distant Relations* young Victor and André Heredia are changed into a sinister twin fetus — really an incomplete metamorphosis, and perhaps on one level a critique of minds that crave perfect

magic. At the end of *The White Hotel* the hellish scene of Babi Yar is metamorphosed into a kind of paradise of earthly delights. In *Midnight's Children*, Parvati the Witch changes Saleem into an invisible entity for a while. In India, of course, beliefs regarding reincarnation make metamorphoses through time particularly ubiquitous, and many of the characters in *Midnight's Children* duplicate a deity, Saleem's much mentioned nose (to cite only one instance) corresponding to Ganesh the elephant-headed god's trunk. Saleem's "chutnification of history"—his art of transforming and preserving the chaotic passage of time and event—is more metaphorical in nature than these other examples, but similarly metamorphic in spirit.

(6) Many of these texts take a position that is antibureaucratic, and so they often use their magic against the established social order. Saleem's midnight congress is a clear alternative to the Congress Party, which the narrator seems to believe maintains a death grip on Indian political life; his magic is explicitly used against the "black widow" Gandhi's magic. The univocal authority of one voice from above is questioned by the cacophony of many voices from all over. That the rather lovable Francis Phelan in *Ironweed* is a bum, not well integrated into the capitalist system, is no accident. In *The Book of Laughter and Forgetting*, it's a bit more indirect. "Circle dancing is magic," we hear.[36] The magical levitation of party members as they dance in a ring, like the chorus of girls who agree with their teacher, has a sinister air; the magic signals the danger of conformism, of rising on the unbearably light wings of coherent doctrine rather than being grounded in incoherent reality. As we learn in Kundera's next novel, being is unbearably light enough by nature; if we unground ourselves still further with doctrines and theories, then we float dangerously far from reality. Kundera and Rushdie, especially, create a poetics of subversion, of the non-co-optability of people, events, laughter, love, objects, even images. And with this we are back at number two on this list of secondary features, with the materiality of metaphor—with language that asserts its rights of opacity, of resistance to referentiality. Like the hat in *The Book of Laughter and Forgetting*, which floats inappropriately off a mourner's head to rest in an open grave, or Sabina's hat in *The Unbearable Lightness of Being*, which signals the nonconforming nature of Sabina's desire, this kind of language is linguistically unruly, whatever its political thematics.

Turning to that thematics for a moment, in several instances, magical realist texts are written in reaction to totalitarian regimes. Günter Grass publishes *The Tin Drum* and Suskind *Perfume* after World War II (in both cases quite a long time after, it is true, but partly in response to it and to the Nazi period in Germany); Latin American writers of magical realism criticize North American hegemony in their hemisphere; Kundera is opposed to the power of Soviet Communism; Rushdie writes *Midnight's Children* in opposition to Mrs. Gandhi's autocratic rule. Toni Morrison writes *Beloved* in direct response to the atrocities of slavery and its aftermath, and Isabel Allende builds *The House of the Spirits* in part to critique the barbarity of Pinochet's Chilean regime. These texts, which are receptive in particular ways to more than one point of view, to realistic *and* magical ways of seeing, and which open the door to other worlds, respond to a desire for narrative freedom from realism, and from a univocal narrative stance; they implicitly correspond textually in a new way to a critique of totalitarian discourses of all kinds. Scheherazade's story is relevant again here, for even though she narrated for her own life, she had the eventual welfare of her state on her shoulders as well, and her efforts liberated her country from the tyranny of King Shariyar's rule.

That realism has been a European, or first world, export, in conjunction with its mimetic program, its claim to fashioning an accurate portrait of the world, has in some instances tended to ally it with imperialism — Spanish, English, French, Russian, U.S. — endowing it with an implicitly authoritarian aura for writers in colonial situations. Taking all of this into account, we can see that magical realism does continue in the critical vein of realism, but it achieves its critical aims with different, postsurrealistic, resources and questions homogeneous systems in the name of plurality.

Jameson's discussion of realism and romance in the nineteenth century is helpful here. Jameson argues that "it is in the context of the gradual reification of realism in late capitalism that romance once again comes to be felt as the place of narrative heterogeneity and of freedom from that reality principle to which a now oppressive realistic representation is the hostage."[37] It is that "now oppressive realistic representation" that some of magical realism as an inheritor of romance disturbs. Jameson claims that in the nineteenth century, for the most part, the reinvention of romance substitutes "new positivities" like theology and psychology for the older magical content and that modernism likewise substitutes a kind of vacant expectancy (usually of city streets). Thus he believes that this new romance's "ultimate condition of figuration" is a transitional moment when two different modes of production, or of socioeconomic development, coexist.[38] Since their conflict is not yet socially manifest as such, its resolution is projected as a nostalgic or a utopian harmony and hence is ultimately not politically progressive.

This is where magical realism may differ, because since we are situated clearly in reality, that harmonic world, either in the past, or the future, is not constituted, and the conflicts of political systems are more in evidence. According to Jameson, romance can make class conflict fade into bad dreams or fantastic scenarios. The irreducible element in magical realism, in conjunction with its documentary elements, may work against such fading, or cooption. Lisa's pains in *The White Hotel,* for example, are not just a bad dream but the magical premonition of a terrible, but an unmistakably real, historical nightmare. Likewise with the magical and not magical atrocities of the aftermath of partition in *Midnight's Children* or the banana company massacre in *One Hundred Years of Solitude* or the mass hysteria that devours Grenouille at the end of *Perfume.* Through that combination of history and selective magical detail (as opposed to the creation of a separate imaginary realm), magical realism moves beyond the way in which, as Jameson formulates it, in high realism and naturalism, time seems sealed off in its "perfected narrative apparatus." And, as we have been seeing, the techniques of that apparatus, "the threefold imperatives of authorial depersonalization, unity of point of view, and restriction to scenic representation" are also often disrupted by the postmodern fictional strategies of magical realist texts.[39]

As it has with other historically relevant fictions, the cultural and psychological pluralism which has inspired much magical realism can prove politically problematic. When I was working on this essay in London, the controversy over Rushdie's *Satanic Verses* was unfolding — a grisly manifestation of the collapse of a distinction between words and the world, as well as of the political and social realities Rushdie's books describe. The Rushdie-like character of the poet in *Iranian Nights* (the short drama presented at the Royal Court Theatre in London in response to the crisis) laments, "What madness have my verses unleashed? A fiction greater than any poet's imagination. Now jokes become daggers and rhymes become bullets."[40] Like their mother before them, these children of Scheherazade fear for their lives, and the linguistic magic we have been describing expands to alarming proportions. As Howard Brenton (one of the authors of the piece) puts it in an afterward, "Reality, as we know, is stranger than most fiction. The scenes we are observing could easily be excerpts from a Rushdie novel." What's more, the particular strange terror of the reality we witnessed in the Rushdie affair is precisely that it was partially engendered by a fiction.

Jean-Francois Lyotard ends his book on *The Postmodern Condition* by responding to critiques of postmodern culture which advocate a return to referentiality, a rejection of self-referential discourses, such as those we have been discussing. Lyotard argues against our expecting a reconciliation among different language games, against hoping that a transcendental illusion will "totalize them into a real unity," because for him, "the price to pay for such an illusion is terror." [41] As I have suggested, several of these novels, most notably *The Book of Laughter and Forgetting, Midnight's Children, The White Hotel*, and *Distant Relations*, imply that the price to pay for a comforting textual univocality may be terror.

(7) In magical realist narrative, ancient systems of belief and local lore often underlie the text (more ghosts here). In the superstitious atmosphere of *Perfume* we hear that the inhabitants of the Grasse region believed that their "only possible refuge from this monster . . . was under the . . . gaze of the Madonna"; "other, quicker wits banded together in occult groups" and hired "at great expense a certified witch from Gourdon"; "still others . . . put their money on the most modern scientific methods, magnetizing their houses, hypnotizing their daughters, gathering in their salons for secret fluidal meetings, and employing telepathy to drive off the murderer's spirit with communal thought emissions" (223). Similarly, while not specifically allied to any particular doctrine, this numinous moment in *Ironweed* occurs in the context of the provincial American Catholicism that pervades the story: Francis at one point "felt blessed. He stared at the bathroom sink, which now had an aura of sanctity about it, its faucets sacred, its drainpipe holy, and he wondered whether everything was blessed at some point in its existence, and he concluded yes." [42] Even *That Voice* is set not in an urban area, but in the countryside of France, very much within the ancient magic circle of country village lore and belief, akin in this to *The House of the Spirits, Beloved, Like Water for Chocolate*, and *So Far from God*.

Magical realism has tended to concentrate on rural settings and to rely on rural inspiration — almost a postmodern pastoralism — though *Midnight's Children* and *Distant Relations* are powerful exceptions. A character in *So Far from God*, for example, embodies a latter-day Saint Francis in the Southwest countryside. As the appropriately named Francisco secretly hides out among the agaves and hedgehog cactus to keep watch on his beloved Caridad's trailer, the narrator notes that "anyone looking up at a row of crows puffing away at cigarette butts would only be inclined to look down to see who was supplying them."[43] But this may be changing. For example, *Bigfoot Dreams* by Francine Prose is set in the city and uses the linguistic magic of materialized metaphor I have been describing. From the reappearance of "bigfoot" once a week in the tabloid she works for, comes bigfoot's presence in Vera's mind, on the pages of her own stories, and in her world. Her writing takes the bigfoot theme a step farther than her predecessors did: she tells us that her story " 'I MARRIED BIGFOOT' was a kind of landmark in Bigfoot literature, changing the focus, bringing Bigfoot home."[44] The fantastical "bigfoot" impulse comes home with a vengeance when a story Vera makes up turns out to be real — and she has to deal with the unsettling consequences. The kind of tabloid writing Vera does and her credulous city audiences seem likely sources for recent magical realism; they are urban, "first world," mass cultural analogues of the primitive belief systems that underlie earlier Latin American examples of magical realism.

(8) As Seymour Menton has pointed out, a Jungian rather than a Freudian perspective is common in magical realist texts; that is, the magic may be attributed to a mysterious sense of collective relatedness rather than to individual memories or dreams or visions.[45] The communal magic of storytelling figures prominently in *That Voice, Midnight's Children, Distant Relations, The House of the Spirits, Beloved,* and *So Far from God.* Furthermore, the magic in magical realism is unrepentant, unrecuperable, and thus may point toward the spiritual realms to which Jungian psychology is receptive; as we have seen, the magic cannot usually be explained away as individual or even as collective hallucination or invention. *Beloved* takes an unusual turn here, because, as we have noted, right at the end we get what could be interpreted as a disclaimer concerning her magical existence. The people who had seen her "forgot her like a bad dream," and finally "realized they couldn't remember or repeat a single thing she said, and began to believe that, other than what they themselves were thinking, she hadn't said anything at all." In the final analysis, though, her existence remains shadowy, for we can — and perhaps should — discount this disclaimer, this after-the-fact rejection of her magic, and consider that just because the people "began to believe" this, it is only part of the whole story.

The White Hotel is particularly relevant in regard to Freud and Jung, for there, we seem at first to have the ever more analyzable dreams and hallucinations of a patient—Freud's patient no less—but we discover in the end that her fears have magically proven to prefigure her historical circumstances, which in turn may reactivate universal archetypes. What's more, the book also seems to demonstrate in the psychological realm Gerald Graff's formulation about postmodern literature: "Whereas modernists turned to art, defined as the imposition of human order upon inhuman chaos, . . . postmodernists conclude that, under such conceptions of art and history, art provides no more consolation than any other discredited cultural institution. Postmodernism signifies that the nightmare of history, as modernist esthetic and philosophical traditions have defined history, has overtaken modernism itself."[46] In Thomas' novel, the art of psychoanalysis cannot help us with the nightmare of history.

(9) A carnivalesque spirit is common in this group of novels. Language is used extravagantly, expending its resources beyond its referential needs. These textual communities reveal economies of potlatch rather than ones characterized by a hoarding of resources. Either on the level of plot or of language—or both—they are linguistic analogues for the kinds of primitive fiestas celebrated by Mauss, Bataille, and Paz, antitheses to the more utilitarian modes of most Western capitalist enterprises, whose linguistic economies might be represented by Flaubert's notion of the *mot juste:* the one exact, economically efficient, word for a particular thing.

This is Flaubert's idea, of course, not always his practice, and as Dominick LaCapra has shown, it is possible to align Flaubert's style with a carnivalesque spirit, which is embodied, among other elements, in his problematized ideal of pure art. Even so, whether or not one accepts that view of Flaubert, and taking into account LaCapra's warning about delineations of recent forms "providing an unjustified sense of originality in the present," I think we can still argue that the texts I am examining here go rather farther in the carnivalesque direction than Flaubert does.[47] Their use of magical details, especially, details which are often not allegorically significant or clearly referential at first glance (even if they become so on reflection), celebrate invention moving beyond realistic representation. I am speaking comparatively here, and while Flaubert has recently been shown to be more postmodern than we might think, his texts less univocal, there are differences. Flaubert does not, for example, tell us the same story twice, from two different worlds, as does Cortázar in "The Night Face Up" (although the two views of the *commices agricoles* in *Madame Bovary* may lead to that); he does not tell us the same story from an embedded set of narrators as D. M. Thomas does in *The White Hotel* (though the shift of narrator in the first chapter of *Madame Bovary* might be seen to pave the way for such shifts); nor does he give us a vertiginous array of tenuously connected details and versions as does Pinget in *That Voice* or Fuentes in *Distant Relations*, or use the same exact image over and over again as Rushdie does with the hole in the sheet or the spittoon in *Midnight's Children* (although Emma's black wings of hair and black eyes once again can lead us toward those techniques, as can the bovine elements in *Madame Bovary* or the parrotic ones Jonathan Culler discovers in "A Simple Heart").[48]

Corresponding in the conceptual domain to what, even with all these qualifications, I believe is a generally extravagant, carnivalesque style, we can move from the grand and extravagant passions of the Buendias in *One Hundred Years of Solitude* to the love of Pedro and Tita extending over their entire lives in *Like Water for Chocolate*; these passions probably kill the characters in the end, but for the most part we feel a certain elation at their outrageousness (though that's not all we feel). The same for Tamina's nearly ludicrous (though moving) and highly romantic fidelity to her husband in *The Book of Laughter and Forgetting*; she spends more than he may have been worth, but we're glad. *Midnight's Children* is perhaps the most carnivalesque of all, in its conscious adoption of the style of a Bombay Talkie—a cast of thousands, songs, dances, exaggeratedly sumptuous scenarios, horrifying blood and gore. (Carlos Fuentes' recent *Christopher Unborn* follows this same vein.) This, then, is often a baroque mode of overextension. It is appropriate here at the end of the list to invoke Scheherazade again, with her number of 1001—a numeral of excess, emblematic of the notion that there is always *one more*.

In conclusion, I again cite Lyotard, who characterizes the postmodern as "that which searches for new presentations . . . in order to impart a stronger sense of the unpresentable." Magical realism exemplifies this notion, first of all in its paradoxical name. Part of its attraction for postmodern writers may be its willfully oxymoronic nature, its exposing of the unpresentable, its activation of differences. *Like Water for Chocolate*, for example, ends not with the magical event of Tita and Pedro's passionate combustion, although that scene is the culmination of their love and the novel that chronicles it, but with the practical detail concerning the passing on of Tita's recipes, affirming the combination of the magical and the real in the text. Lyotard could almost be imagined to have the oppositional terms of magical realism in mind when he calls for resistance to retrogressive desires for "the realization of the fantasy to seize reality" — desires which might dissolve the delicate compound of magical realism. Using Lyotard's terms, we might say that in magical realist texts, "the answer is" to "wage a war on totality," to "be witnesses to the unpresentable" — and the irreducible; in sum, to affirm the magic of the storyteller's art, to invite Scheherazade's children over to play, whatever their ignorance of the rules of our games, and however fantastically they may be dressed.[49]

Notes

1 John Barth, "The Literature of Replenishment," *Atlantic Monthly* (January 1980): 65.

2 John Updike, "Chronicles and Processions" (review of Ismail Kadare's *Chronicle in Stone* and José Saramago's *Baltasar and Blimunda*), *The New Yorker* (March 14, 1988): 113.

3 Witold Gombrowicz, preface to *Pornografia*, in *Ferdydurke, Pornografia, Cosmos: Three Novels by Witold Gombrowicz* (New York: Grove, 1978), p. 6.

4 See my article, "1001 Words: Fiction Against Death," *Georgia Review* 36, 14 (1982): 811–30.

5 The essay formed the prologue to Carpentier's novel *El reino de este mundo*, and is included in this volume.

6 In his discussion of the transculturation process in Latin American narrative, Angel Rama cites the example of García Márquez, who, according to Rama, solves the problem of joining historical realities and fantastic perspectives by recourse to oral and popular narrative structures; *Transculturación narrativa en América latina* (Mexico City: Siglo Veintiuno, 1982), pp. 44–45. Magical realism has been instrumental in providing an impulse in Latin American literature that contrasts with the one Roberto González Echevarría has discussed recently as the archival; *Myth and Archive: A Theory of Latin American Narrative* (Cambridge: Cambridge University Press, 1990). That mode is concerned with *writing down*, this one with *rising up*. Book-length studies on magical realism in Latin American fiction are José Antonio Bravo, *Lo real maravilloso en la narrativa latinoamericana actual* (Lima: Ediciones Unife, 1984); Irlemar Chiampi, *El realismo maravilloso* (Caracas: Monte Avila, 1983); Graciela N. Ricci Della Grisa, *Realismo mágico y conciencia mítica en América Latina* (Buenos Aires, Fernando García Cambeiro, 1985). Articles on the topic are too numerous to list; helpful essays, besides those already mentioned, include Amaryll Chanady, "The Origins and Development of Magic Realism in Latin American Fiction" in *Magic Realism and Canadian Literature*, ed. Peter

Hinchcliffe and Ed Jewinski (Waterloo: University of Waterloo Press, 1986), and a series of articles in the collection *Otros mundos, otros fuegos,* ed. Donald Yates (East Lansing, Mich.: Congreso Internacional de literatura Iberoamericana, 1975). There is a bibliography in the article by Antonio Planells, "El realismo mágico ante la crítica," *Chasqui* 17, 1 (1988): 9–23, but there exists quite a lot of recent work in this area. After formulating this notion of the magical supplement to realism, I came on Scott Simpkins' article, "Magical Strategies: The Supplement of Realism," *Twentieth Century Literature* 34, 11 (1988): 140–54 (reprinted in modified form in this volume), which uses the same term.

7 There are, of course, essential connections to be made between these magical realist texts and the particular cultural traditions and historical circumstances that produced them. Articles that describe magical realism in particular areas (besides the ones on Latin America listed above) include several chapters in the collection *Le Réalisme magique: roman, peinture et cinéma,* ed. Jean Weisgerber (Lausanne: L'Age d'Homme, 1987); *Magic Realism and Canadian Literature,* ed. Peter Hinchcliffe and Ed Jewinski (Waterloo: University of Waterloo Press, 1986); J. Michael Dash, "Marvelous Realism—The Way out of Negritude," *Caribbean Studies* 13, 4 (1973): 57–70. I do not intend to devalue such connections, imperialistically subsuming them under one homogeneous discourse. But there is simply not enough space here to encompass them. And my aim at this point is other: to establish that despite such cultural differences and particularities, one can register significant similarities that indicate a worldwide movement of a sort. Cultural imperialisms are to be guarded against, but fear of those specters should not obscure a sense of genuine cultural community, which may eventually help us out of such imperialisms.

8 Several recent efforts to define magical realism have been rather more exclusive than this one, aiming at exactitude. See, for example, the books by Seymour Menton, *Magic Realism Rediscovered, 1918–1981* (Philadelphia: Art Alliance Press, 1983), which concentrates on painting, and by Amaryll Chanady, *Magical Realism and the Fantastic: Resolved Versus Unresolved Antinomy* (New York: Garland Publishing, 1985). The general articles in the Weisgerber volume represent a more inclusive approach. My project here is similarly inclusive, given my wish to argue that magical realism is a central component of contemporary international narrative.

9 Roberto González Echevarría, "Isla a su vuela fugitiva: Carpentier y el realismo mágico," *Revista Iberoamericana* 40, 86 (1974): 35.

10 Cf. Isabel Allende: "What I don't believe is that the literary form often attributed to the works of . . . Latin American writers, that of magic realism, is a uniquely Latin American phenomenon. Magic realism is a literary device or a way of seeing in which there is space for the invisible forces that move the world: dreams, legends, myths, emotion, passion, history. All these forces find

a place in the absurd, unexplainable aspects of magic realism. . . . Magic realism is all over the world. It is the capacity to see and to write about all the dimensions of reality." "The Shaman and the Infidel," interview, *New Perspectives Quarterly* 8, 1 (1991): 54.

11 Another useful resource is the anthology *Magical Realist Fiction* (1984), edited by Robert Young and Keith Hollaman—not only because of the fiction included, but for their introductory discussion as well. *Magical Realist Fiction: An Anthology*, ed. David Young and Keith Hollaman, rpt. (Oberlin, Ohio: Oberlin College Press, 1992).

12 The term "irreducible element" is Young and Hollaman's.

13 Ana Castillo, *So Far from God* (New York: Norton, 1993), p. 163.

14 Ibid., pp. 248, 251.

15 See Roland Barthes, "L'effet de réel," in *Communications* 2 (1968): 19–25.

16 For further discussion of the historical dimensions of magical realism, see Lois Parkinson Zamora, "Magic Realism and Fantastic History: Carlos Fuentes' *Terra Nostra* and Giambattista Vico's *The New Science*," *Review of Contemporary Fiction* 8, 2 (1988): 249–56.

17 See John Burt Foster, "Magic Realism in *The White Hotel:* Compensatory Vision and the Transformation of Classic Realism," *Southern Humanities Review* 20, 3 (1986): 205–19, reprinted in modified form in this volume.

18 See Tzvetan Todorov, *The Fantastic: A Structural Approach to a Literary Genre*, trans. Richard Howard (Ithaca: Cornell University Press, 1974), p. 41. Amaryll Chanady distinguishes magical realism from the fantastic by arguing that in the fantastic, because it encodes hesitation, antinomy, "the simultaneous presence of two conflicting codes in the text," remains unresolved, but that in magical realism, because the narrator's acceptance of the antinomy promotes the same acceptance in the reader, the antinomian conflict is resolved. The reason this distinction seems problematic to me is that we readers' investment in the codes of realism is still so strong that even the narrator's acceptance does not overcome it, and so the hesitation tends to remain, rather than being resolved. See Chanady, *Magical Realism and the Fantastic*, p. 12.

19 Toni Morrison, *Beloved* (New York: Knopf, 1987), pp. 258, 263, 274.

20 Rawdon Wilson, following Lubomir Dolezel's analysis of Kafka's fiction as hybrid, explains how generic characters are born out of this "hybrid" fictional world of two worlds, "bizarre creatures who owe their natures to both worlds at once. . . . At such moments it seems as if two systems of possibility have enfolded each other: two kinds of cause and effect, two kinds of organism, two kinds of consequence." "The Metamorphoses of Space: Magic Realism," in *Magical Realism in Canadian Literature*, Hinchcliffe and Jewinski, ed., p. 75; included in a revised version in this volume.

21 Hans Peter Duerr, *Dreamtime: Concerning the Boundary between Wilderness and Civilization*, trans. Felicitas Goodman (New York: Blackwell, 1987), p. 109.

22 William Kennedy, *Ironweed* (1983; New York: Penguin, 1984), pp. 1, 97–98.

23 William Kennedy, "Carlos Fuentes: Dreaming of History," in *Review of Contemporary Fiction* 8, 2 (1988): 236.

24 Brian McHale, *Postmodernist Fiction* (New York and London: Methuen, 1987), p. 83.

25 Fredric Jameson, "The Realist Floor-Plan," in *On Signs*, Marshall Blonsky, ed. (Baltimore: Johns Hopkins University Press, 1985), p. 374.

26 Dupuis and Mingelgrun also argue that in magical realism "subjectivity always ends up by transforming itself into a kind of objectivity . . . , if only because the latter inevitably opens onto some general truth that transcends the individual circumstances of the hero." "Pour une poétique du réalisme magique," in *Le realisme magique*, Weisgerber, ed., p. 221.

27 As Hutcheon argues with regard to several other notions, the reality of the subject is also reaffirmed; *A Poetics of Postmodernism: History, Theory, Fiction* (New York: Routledge, 1988), p. 173.

28 Gabriel García Márquez, *One Hundred Years of Solitude*, trans. Gregory Rabassa (New York: Avon, 1971), p. 222. Further references are given in the text.

29 Patrick Suskind, *Perfume: The Story of a Murderer*, trans. John E. Woods (New York: Knopf, 1986), p. 3. Further references are given in the text.

30 Carlos Fuentes, *Distant Relations*, trans. Margaret Sayers Peden (New York: Farrar Straus Giroux, 1982), p. 199. Further references are given in the text.

31 Salman Rushdie, *Midnight's Children* (New York: Avon, 1982), pp. 549–50. Further references are given in the text.

32 Morrison, *Beloved*, p. 58.

33 Dupuis and Mingelgrun have also noted this tendency in magical realism: "repetitions, constants, leitmotifs, resemblances, correspondances, conjunctions, mirror effects, symmetries, cyclical structures give the impression of a strange coherence among apparently different elements, spread out horizontally in time and space. Once exploited by the reader, this impression leads him to desubstantiate and to intellectualize the novelistic world to a greater extent, to lift the veil covering the 'other side' of things, in the occurrence of their 'profound reality' "; "Pour une poétique du réalisme magique," p. 226.

34 Isabel Allende sees magical realism as breaking away from a "way of facing reality in which the only thing one dares talk about are those things one can control. What cannot be controlled is denied." "The Shaman and the Infidel," *New Perspectives Quarterly*, p. 55.

35 See Nancy Gray Díaz, *The Radical Self: Metamorphosis from Animal Form in Modern Latin American Literature* (Columbia: University of Missouri Press, 1988).

36 Milan Kundera, *The Book of Laughter and Forgetting*, trans. Michael Henry Heim (New York: Penguin, 1981), p. 63.

37 Fredric Jameson, *The Political Unconscious* (Ithaca: Cornell University Press, 1984), p. 104.

38 Ibid., p. 148.

39 Ibid., p. 104. Once again, Brian McHale's discussion helps place magical realism within the configurations of postmodernism. McHale claims that postmodern historical fictions—examples include Fuentes' *Terra Nostra*, Barth's *Letters* and *The Sot Weed Factor*, Coover's *The Public Burning*—are fantastic, and what's more, they foreground "the seam between historical reality and fiction" by "making the transition from one realm to the other as jarring as possible." McHale, *Postmodern Fiction*, p. 90.

40 Tariq Ali and Howard Brenton, *Iranian Nights* (London: Nick Hern Books, 1989), p. 7.

41 Jean-Francois Lyotard, *The Postmodern Condition: A Report on Knowledge*, trans. Geoff Bennington and Brian Massumi (Minneapolis: University of Minnesota Press, 1984), p. 82.

42 Kennedy, *Ironweed*, pp. 171–72.

43 Castillo, *So Far from God*, p. 199.

44 Francine Prose, *Bigfoot Dreams* (1986; New York: Penguin, 1987), p. 14.

45 See Menton, *Magic Realism Rediscovered*, pp. 13–14.

46 Gerald Graff, *Literature against Itself* (Chicago: University of Chicago Press, 1979), p. 55.

47 See Dominick LaCapra, "Intellectual History and Defining the Present as 'Postmodern,'" in *Innovation/Renovation: New Perspectives on the Humanities*, ed. Ihab and Sally Hassan (Madison: University of Wisconsin Press, 1983), p. 55.

48 See Shoshana Felman, *La Folie et la chose littéraire* (Paris: Seuil, 1978), p. 165, and Jonathan Culler, "The Uses of Madame Bovary," in *Flaubert and Postmodernism*, ed. Naomi Schor and Henry F. Majewski (Lincoln: University of Nebraska Press, 1984), pp. 6–7.

49 Lyotard, *The Postmodern Condition*, p. 81.

THEO L. D'HAEN

Magical Realism and Postmodernism:
Decentering Privileged Centers

Because the term "magic" or "magical realism" has persisted for over half a century but is not yet entirely current, it is useful to trace its origins and use briefly before situating the mode with regard to postmodernism.[1] Most commentators agree that it originated with the German art critic Franz Roh, who in 1925 coined the word to, and here I am quoting the *Oxford Dictionary of Art*, "describe the aspect of Neue Sachlichkeit characterized by sharp-focus detail . . . in later criticism the term has been used to cover various types of painting in which objects are depicted with photographic naturalism but which because of paradoxical elements or strange juxtapositions convey a feeling of unreality, infusing the ordinary with a sense of mystery."[2] *Mutatis mutandis*, I will take the same definition to apply to the literary movement of the same name.[3] From the example the *Oxford Dictionary of Art* offers, namely, the paintings of the Belgian René Magritte, the relevance of the term to surrealism and its environment can be deduced. It is also in this environment, and more specifically with Miguel Angel Asturias and Alejo Carpentier, who both frequented Surrealist circles,[4] that Jean Franco, in her *An Introduction to Spanish-American Literature*,[5] situates the emergence of that particular Latin-American prose most commentators include under the rubric of magic realism. Both Asturias and Carpentier discussed the idea of magic realism in their own works, linking it explicitly to surrealism, Asturias using the very word "réalisme magique" in a 1962 interview in *Les Lettres Françaises*, while Carpentier chose to rechristen it in his influential essay "De lo real maravilloso americano," originally prefacing *El reino de este mundo* and collected in his 1967 volume *Tientos y diferencias*.[6] It should immediately be stated, though, that even before it was generally applied to Latin American literature the term had already been used with regard to

particular tendencies or movements in German-Austrian and Flemish literature.[7] In fact, although Brotherston, referring to earlier publications by
Angel Flores and Luis Leal, noted in 1977 that the term was firmly established well before the 1960s,[8] Franco in her 1969 *Introduction* apparently
found it necessary to apologize for her use of it in a note stating that "this
term has recently been coined to categorise novels which use myth and
legend" (p. 374), and in her slightly earlier *The Modern Culture of Latin
America* (1967), she had not used the term.[9] However, in her 1973 *Spanish American Literature since Independence* she freely and unreservedly
uses Carpentier's "real maravilloso," at least if I am to go by the 1987 edition of the Spanish translation of that book.[10] So does Cedomil Goic in his
1972 *Historia de la novela hispanoamericana*, though he prefers the term
"superrealismo" for the entire tendency of which he sees Carpentier's "real
maravilloso" forming only a part.[11] In the intervening years, of course, the
appearance of Gabriel García Márquez's *Cien años de soledad* (1967) —
and within its wake the worldwide attention given to the so-called Latin-
American *boom*, much of which fits the category we are here concerned
with — had ensured the international literary-critical success of the term
"magic realism" also in non-Spanish critical writing, though still with
almost exclusive reference to contemporary Spanish American fiction.[12]

Like magic realism, the term "postmodernism," though even now it
may seem new to some, goes back several decades, as has been amply illustrated by Michael Köhler and Hans Bertens in their survey articles of 1977
and 1986, respectively.[13] Again like magic realism, the term "postmodernism" has gained wide recognition and acceptance only since the 1960s,
and particularly so in the 80s in which it has come to stand for a general
movement in the arts, and even in forms of behavior and daily life.[14] From a
literary-critical perspective, particularly with regard to prose — the genre
which has figured most prominently in recent literary discussions of postmodernism — the term primarily stands for a combination of those technically innovative qualities most highly regarded by contemporary critical
movements such as poststructuralism. Drawing on discussions by Douwe
Fokkema, Allen Thiher, Linda Hutcheon, Brian McHale, Ihab Hassan,
David Lodge, Alan Wilde, and others, and simplifying matters a great deal,
I would argue that the following features are generally regarded as marking postmodernism: self-reflexiveness, metafiction, eclecticism, redun-
dancy, multiplicity, discontinuity, intertextuality, parody, the dissolution of
character and narrative instance, the erasure of boundaries, and the desta-

bilization of the reader.[15] Most commentators seem to agree that the very term "postmodernism" originated in the 1930s in Latin America, with the critic Federico de Onís, and was reinvented or reused, covering different fields and carrying different meanings, throughout the 40s and 50s both in Europe and the United States. Yet, most commentators would also agree that in its present meaning and with its present scope the term gained acceptance primarily with reference to American, that is, U.S., prose fiction.

In the period in which "postmodernism" and "magic realism" gained their present meanings, then, their use was restricted, respectively, to North- and South-American prose developments. Only recently, and primarily since the early 80s, have these terms allowed for spillage into other linguistic or geographical areas. However, I think few would deny that since they have started doing so they have come to divide not just the New, but also the Old World between them. They now seem almost the only shorthands available to categorize contemporary developments in Western fiction. Increasingly, though, it has proved difficult to distinguish the categories covered by these terms clearly. "Postmodernism" has been undeniably the more successful term to cover developments in other technically sophisticated Western literatures. Often, this has not happened without considerable hesitation, as witnessed by the ongoing discussion with regard to the French *nouveau roman* and *nouveau nouveau roman*. Still, Günter Grass, Thomas Bernhard, Peter Handke, Italo Calvino, John Fowles, Angela Carter, John Banville, and Michel Tournier, as well as Dutch authors Willem Brakman and Louis Ferron, all of whom during the 60s and 70s were considered by some as highly idiosyncratic authors, or representatives of purely national movements or tendencies, during the 80s have increasingly come to be annexed by postmodernism.[16] Indeed, on the basis of the catalog of features I listed before, such inclusion seems fully warranted. Yet, judging from the definition I quoted at the beginning of this essay, it would be hard to deny that much of the work of many of these authors might just as easily be categorized as magic realist. This, in fact, is what has been happening. Richard Todd, in an essay called "Convention and Innovation in British Fiction 1981–1984: The Contemporaneity of Magic Realism," discusses Angela Carter's *Nights at the Circus*, Salman Rushdie's *Shame*, and D. M. Thomas' *The White Hotel*.[17] He sees these novels as challenging, in a magic realist way, both the earlier modes of historical and documentary realism prevalent in post-War British fiction and the more conventional forms of romance. At the same time, though, he sees these novels as achieving their magic realist program by way of the very same techniques usually singled out as marking postmodernism. Geert Lernout, in an essay on "Postmodernist Fiction in Canada," claims that "what is postmodern in the rest of the world used to be called magic realist in South America and still goes by that name in Canada."[18] His list of Canadian magic realists includes Robert Kroetsch, Jack Hodgins, Timothy Findley, and Rudy Wiebe, all of whom he considers to be writing in a tradition that would also include Borges, Grass, Nabokov, Rushdie, and Calvino, but that would exclude Beckett, Robbe-Grillet, and Ricardou. All of these authors are postmodernists, he concludes, but "maybe we do need a more specific term for the first kind of postmodernist works than 'metafiction' or 'surfiction,' and 'magic realism' may in the end not be all that bad" (140). It would seem, then, as if in international critical parlance a consensus is emerging in which a hierarchical relation is established between postmodernism and magic realism, whereby the latter comes to denote a particular strain of the contemporary movement covered by the former. Such, for instance, is already the attitude taken by two late 80s survey works on postmodern writing: Brian McHale's *Postmodernist Fiction* (1987) and Linda Hutcheon's *A Poetics of Postmodernism* (1988).

Looking at it from the other side, from that of Spanish American literature, a similar development can be deduced from a recent article by Julio Ortega on "Postmodernism in Latin America," in which he considers the work of a number of authors who until recently would have been discussed almost exclusively within a magic realist framework.[19] Obviously, to anyone even minimally acquainted with the narrative pyrotechnics of a García Márquez, a Cortázar, a Fuentes, a Donoso, or the early Vargas Llosa, this possibility will have suggested itself immediately from the catalog of features I listed earlier as distinguishing postmodernism. If magic realism, then, seems firmly established as part of postmodernism, the question remains as to *what* part it plays in this larger current or movement, and where and why.

Carlos Fuentes, in an article in which he describes how he came to write about Mexico the way he does, says that one of the first things he learned — from Octavio Paz — is that "there were no privileged centers of culture, race, politics."[20] It is precisely the notion of the ex-centric, in the sense of speaking from the margin, from a place "other" than "the" or "a" center, that seems to me an essential feature of that strain of postmodernism we call magic realism. In literary-critical terms, this ex-centricity can in the first instance be described as a voluntary act of breaking away from the discourse perceived as central to the line of technical experimentation starting with realism and running via naturalism and modernism to the kind of postmodernism Lernout assigned to his second group of authors, the "metafictionists" or "surfictionists" *à la* Beckett, Robbe-Grillet or Ricardou. Even though these various movements may have thought of themselves as critical or subversive of one another, and of the respective societies they stemmed from, their issuing from "privileged centers" made their discourse suspect to those marginalized — geographically, socially, economically — by these same societies. To write ex-centrically, then, or from the margin, implies dis-placing this discourse. My argument is that magic realist writing achieves this end by first appropriating the techniques of the "centr"-al line and then using these, not as in the case of these central movements, "realistically," that is, to duplicate existing reality as perceived by the theoretical or philosophical tenets underlying said movements, but rather to create an alternative world *correcting* so-called existing reality, and thus to right the wrongs this "reality" depends upon. Magic realism thus reveals itself as a *ruse* to invade and take over dominant discourse(s). It is a way of access to the main body of "Western" literature for authors not sharing in, or not writing from the perspective of, the privileged centers of this literature for reasons of language, class, race, or gender, and yet avoiding epigonism by avoiding the adoption of views of the hegemonic forces together with their discourse. Alternatively, it is a means for writers coming from the privileged centers of literature to dissociate themselves from their own discourses of power, and to speak on behalf of the ex-centric and un-privileged (with the risk of being judged "patronizing" by those on whose behalf such writers seek to speak).

That magic realism implicitly proposes this decentering, and that it does so also in other literatures than Spanish American ones, I will try and illustrate with regard to some recent English language novels that all single out some "privileged center" as embodied in traditional literary discourse, and then, via postmodernist and magic realist means, "dis-place" it. I will deal in some detail with J. M. Coetzee's *Foe* (1986), and then briefly touch upon John Fowles' *The French Lieutenant's Woman* (1969), Salman Rushdie's *Midnight's Children* (1981), and Angela Carter's *Nights at the Circus* (1984).[21]

Foe, in typical postmodern fashion, is a rewrite of an English "classic": Defoe's *Robinson Crusoe*. In the autobiographical tale of its protagonist,

Robinson Crusoe literally *is* the story of white male Western colonialism, and thus serves an important symbolic function in the West's cultural conception of itself and its world: it is the epic of that hero of middle-class ideology, *homo economicus*.[22] Coetzee's novel is not told from the perspective of Robinson Crusoe but from that of Susan Barton, a woman shipwrecked on Crusoe's island. She tells Crusoe's story to the hack writer and journalist Foe, hoping to sell it. He is only moderately interested in her story of a morose, surly, and inept old man, uneasily and uncomfortably living on his island with an unruly and disgruntled slave. He is more interested in Susan's own past, and especially in her sexual experiences. Of course, we know that Defoe's *Robinson Crusoe* presents us with a totally different Crusoe and Friday, and makes no mention of a woman. As Susan's story, in Coetzee's text, is presented as the authentic or true version of Defoe's subsequent fiction, we are asked to conclude that the English author removed Susan from the story and reimagined Crusoe and Friday for commercial purposes, thus adapting it to his public ideological expectations.

Looking at it from the opposite end, of course, the question is why Coetzee added Susan Barton to the classic story, and why he had her give her view of Crusoe, Friday, and Foe. Here, a passage from the end of part three of *Foe* can prove helpful. Friday is, literally, dumb: his tongue has been cut out. As Susan realizes that Friday's story is central to whatever happened on the island, she agrees to Foe's proposal that she teach Friday to write. Her efforts remain largely unrewarded. Still, at the end of part three Friday is able to write a whole page of "o"s. Foe comments that next day she has to teach him the "a". This passage can be explained in two ways. First, the "o" can be read as zero. Friday is thus made out to be functionally illiterate in eighteenth-century English society. Alternatively, the "o" can be read as the Greek omega, and thus as a very pointed comment on the civilization landed.[23] As far as he is concerned, this civilization is a "reverse" one that approaches things from the wrong end. Wittingly or unwittingly, Friday is condemned to remain outside the pale of white civilization in which, as Michel Foucault has argued, language is power.[24] And *Robinson Crusoe*, as intimated earlier, is a linguistic codification of the complex of metanarratives legitimizing Western middle-class society. Now we can also understand the symbolism of Friday's cut-out tongue: the civilization that Crusoe embodies literally reduces all who do not speak its discourse to silence. To learn to write starting with the "a" or alpha of Foe's alphabet would then mean that Friday should adopt the discourse, and the corresponding worldview, of white colonial civilization. *Mutatis mutandis* the same thing holds for Susan Barton. She, of course, is not illiterate. Both orally and in writing, she can tell her own story, and she does so in *Foe*. Yet, history—in first instance literary history, but by implication also history in general—has written her out of the story. Thus, she fares even worse than Friday who, in the story sanctioned by history, was at least allowed to linger on as a minor character. Consider the title of the book. "Foe" means "adversary," or even "enemy," and it is clear that the implied author of the fiction that will result from Susan Barton's true story (always in the context of *Foe*, of course), namely, *Robinson Crusoe*, is both her and Friday's enemy, according to the dictates of a society that evaluated human beings in terms of their economic value, and for which blacks, Indians, and members of non-European races were useful as slaves, but for which women held no economic interest whatever.

Irony, of course, has it that "Foe" is the name of the author we know as "Defoe," and that he, along with Samuel Richardson, was the first commercial writer in English literary history.[25] If *Robinson Crusoe*, then, turns out to be an ideological rewrite of a very different and much more untractable reality, the name "Defoe" turns out to be fully as much an ideological rewrite, itself an *objective correlative* for the commercial ideology of capitalism. By opting for the real name of the writer of *Robinson Crusoe* as the title for his own rewrite, Coetzee indicates that he is not so much concerned with the figure of "Robinson Crusoe" but rather with the eponymous book as linguistic codification of a particular privileged center's worldview. Obviously, it cannot be a coincidence that it is a white male South African, of Afrikaner stock, that writes both woman and the negro back into this story. His *Foe* is a linguistic reaction to the likewise linguistic codification of an ideology that lies at the very basis of his own country's origins and way of life. From his own wilfully ex-centric vantage point, he invades, subverts, and corrects that codification, and hence its underlying ideology. To now circle back to my original argument: the only way for Coetzee to write woman, and via her the negro, back into the classic story is by means of magic realist devices. Especially the fourth and last section of *Foe* is revealing in this respect: as the privileged center discourse leaves no room for a "realistic" insertion of those that history—always speaking the language of the victors and rulers—has denied a voice, such an act of recuperation can only happen by magic or fantastic or unrealistic means.

Similar arguments could be developed with regard to the other three novels I wish to analyze briefly. *The French Lieutenant's Woman* situates itself in the context of nineteenth-century English realism. As Fowles himself has stated, the novel is a partial rewrite of Hardy's *A Pair of Blue Eyes*, and takes as its starting point what was marginal and ex-centric to the nineteenth-century English novel: sexuality, and particularly female sexuality.[26] The book appeals to the realist tradition in its form, style, and tone, but at the same time undermines that tradition in the way it handles its characters, and by its metafictional use of the narrator's voice. In combination with the multiple endings to the novel, these elements face the reader with his own freedom *as* reader, complementary to the freedom the female protagonist — the "French Lieutenant's Woman" from the title — claims for herself, and which is totally opposite to the determinism implicit in Hardy's already almost naturalistic view.[27] Important to my argument is that the multiple endings, upon which the effect of the book to a large extent hinges, are accounted for in a magic realist way, via the intervention of Fowles' "foppish impresario."[28] This impresario — obviously a double for Fowles himself — is present throughout the novel as observer and metafictional commentator. When in the penultimate chapter the story has reached a "realistic" happy end in line with the meliorative intentions of many English and American (William Dean Howells, for instance) realists, the impresario appears and puts back the hands of his watch, and thereby also the narrative time of the novel. This allows for an alternative ending, highlighting the existentialist freedom-theme of the novel, and forcing the reader to make his own decision as to which ending he prefers, facing him with his own freedom.

Rushdie's *Midnight's Children* both invokes and subverts the typically English tradition of the colonial novel as written by Kipling or Forster (however divergent in other respects these two authors may be). In this tradition the white man's view of the land, and of its inhabitants, holds a central position. Colonial nature and society thus assume the role of the "other," the exotic, the strange. At variance with this tradition, in Rushdie's novel the focus lies with the Indians themselves, and with their views of their country and society. From this perspective, the exotic becomes something the West has projected upon India.[29] Here it is the Westerner who becomes "other." Magic, which in the colonial novel often functions as the sign of the otherness of non-Western society and civilization,[30] with Rushdie becomes daily reality, and hence magic realism in the sense of Carpentier's *lo real maravilloso*: indigenous magic. All together, the children born in India at the very moment the country gained its independence from England, communicating with each other in such a magic realist way, literally give voice to an entire subcontinent; a proper voice this time, as the subjects of their own story and not as the objects of an English colonial novel.

Finally, we notice something similar in Angela Carter's *Nights at the Circus*. In the first few lines of this novel the Greek myth of Leda and the swan is alluded to. Indirectly, the rape of Leda by Zeus engendered the oldest Western work of literature known to us: Homer's *Iliad*. Throughout the book, this myth, in the various guises it received in the course of literary history, is referred to again and again. At the end of *Nights at the Circus*, though, in contrast to the original myth, the woman in the guise of a "swan" will gently—though passionately—make love to the male protagonist. The outcome of this act remains to be seen, but we may speculate that it will be very different from what happened "the other time": whereas Homer founded a male line in Western literature, Carter offers us a rewrite of Homer that redefines the future of humanity from a feminist ideology. And once again, such a rewrite only proves possible with the help of magic realist means: the female protagonist, "Fevvers," *is* a "bird," not just metaphorically but also literally. And the novel is replete with magic realism in its numerous manipulations of time, place, scenery, and character. To give just one example: during a visit to his palace in St. Petersburg, the Grand Duke shows Fevvers his collection of toy eggs containing all sorts of miniatures. Fevvers is invited to choose one egg as a present, obviously in return for sexual favors. She is tempted to choose a miniature train, but the Duke tells her the next egg is meant for her. This egg contains a gilded, but empty cage. Fevvers, who has been trying to keep the Duke from physically engaging her by instead caressing his male member, realizes she is about to be trapped:

> The bitter knowledge she'd been fooled spurred Fevvers into action. She dropped the toy train on the Isfahan runner—mercifully, it landed on its wheels—as, with a grunt and whistle of expelled breath, the Grand Duke ejaculated.
>
> In those few seconds of his lapse of consciousness, Fevvers ran helter-skelter down the platform, opened the door of the first-class compartment and clambered aboard.
>
> "Look what a mess he's made of your dress, the pig," said Lizzie. (192)

Obviously, it is not a coincidence that the three novels I have briefly discussed here argue the emancipation of those categories—women and non-Western peoples—that were also central to *Foe*. It is precisely these categories that were traditionally excluded from the "privileged centers" of culture, race, and gender, and therefore from the operative discourses of power. Not for nothing Carter refers to feminism in terms of "decolonization."

If we account for magic realism's function within postmodernism along these lines, this might also furnish us with a possible explanation for the pioneering role of Spanish American literature in this mode. During the period under consideration Latin America was perhaps the continent most ex-centric to the "privileged centers" of power. At the same time, though, it was nominally independent enough early enough to utter its "other" -ness in the way I have suggested above. Or perhaps it might be more accurate to say that precisely the discrepancy between its nominal independence and its continuing cultural dependence exacerbated the feeling of ex-centricity of many Latin American authors, and thus alerted them to the problematics of centers and margins in literature, and hence to the possibilities of magic realism, at an earlier stage than authors from other continents or countries, or from other groups, races, or genders.[31] Still, these would follow soon enough, as often as not specifically appealing to Latin American examples, as Rushdie does to García Márquez.

This brings me to a final point. García Márquez himself frequently mentioned Faulkner as his example. The Southerner Faulkner is undoubtedly one of the most ex-centric, in the sense we have here given to that word, of American authors. Of late, of course, Faulkner has been claimed for postmodernism. Should we now also start calling him a magic realist? The very fact that this notion probably strikes most of us as extravagant still might well say more about the resistance of American scholarship to applying this particular term to American literature than about that literature itself. And this regardless of the fact that John Barth, many of whose texts would surely qualify as magic realist, has expressed unreserved admiration for Borges, and for a number of Latin American magic realist authors. In "The Literature of Replenishment" he proclaims Gabriel García Márquez's *One Hundred Years of Solitude* his supreme example of postmodernism: "the synthesis of straightforwardness and artifice, realism and magic and myth"; yet this article, and its equally famous predecessor "The Literature of Exhaustion," are invariably only adduced to buttress the use of the term postmodern.[32] The reason why U.S. scholarship seems most resistant to applying the term magic realism to its own literary products is perhaps that the United States has been the most "privileged center" of all in our postwar world. The preference U.S. scholarship shows for the term "postmodernism" emphasizes to an almost extravagant degree the technical side of literary achievements, at the same time often insisting on the play-character of the text. Of course, this is one way of defusing the possible political repercussions or implications of contemporary texts. Ironically, Marxist and neo-humanitarian critics, inside and outside the United States, here find a common ground to decry postmodernism: for its supposed lack of ethical or materialist concern.[33] However, by stubbornly restricting the term to a geographically limited segment of literature and by moreover exclusively fixating upon one aspect of this literature, these critics fail to see that the really significant resistance within the international postmodern movement is being put up by magic realism. In their blindness, in fact, they fall victim to the same kind of "privileged center" ideology that they claim to combat: a rare case of bad faith indeed!

To my mind, then, the cutting edge of postmodernism is magic realism. As Douwe Fokkema remarks, the postmodernist device of "permutation"—which he circumscribes as "permutation of possible and impossible, relevant and irrelevant, true and false, reality and parody, metaphor and literal meaning"—is "probably the most subversive one with regard to earlier conventions."[34] Significantly, it is also this device that is central to the definition of magic realism I quoted at the very beginning of this article. And obviously, I would see the subversion being worked here as not just reflecting upon earlier conventions, but also upon the metanarratives or ideologies these conventions uphold. In this, I feel supported by most of the critics I have hitherto had occasion to mention. Todd sees the three magic realist novels he discusses, *Nights at the Circus*, Rushdie's *Shame*, and D. M. Thomas' *The White Hotel*, as respectively putting forth a feminist program and showing up the ill effects of political and psychological repression. Linda Hutcheon, in her *A Poetics of Postmodernism*, devotes an entire chapter to "Decentering the Postmodern: The Ex-Centric," claiming that "the theory and practice of postmodern art has shown ways of making the different, the off-center, into the vehicle for aesthetic and even political consciousness-raising" (73). And in her more recent *The Canadian Postmodern: A Study of Contemporary English-Canadian Fiction*, she insists at length upon the ex-centricity of Canadian literature, stating that "[Canada's] history is one of defining itself against centres," and linking the Canadian experience to that of repressed "minorities," approvingly quoting Susan Swan's *The Biggest Modern Woman of the World*

(1983) as saying that "to be from the Canadas is to feel as women feel—cut off from the base of power."[35] For her too, "the ex-centrics, be they Canadians, women, or both, . . . subvert the authority of language," and—echoing Angela Carter—"not surprisingly, language has been called the major issue in the general history of colonisation, whether in terms of gender or nationality" (p. 7). Speaking of magic realism as "an internalized challenge to realism offered by Latin American fiction," she argues that "this kind of realism was less a rejection of the realist conventions than a contamination of them with fantasy and with the conventions of an oral story-telling tradition" (208). As Canadian heirs to Gabriel García Márquez she mentions Robert Kroetsch, Susan Swan, Jack Hodgins, and Michael Ondaatje. Elsewhere I have argued a similarly "subversive" case for Timothy Findley,[36] and, shifting from Canada to Europe, and particularly to Ireland, for John Banville and Desmond Hogan.[37] Even earlier, Wendy Faris had linked magical realism, postmodernism, and emergent literatures in a paper she presented at the 1985 ICLA Conference in Paris.[38] Unfortunately, the proceedings of that conference remain unpublished.

Elsewhere too, I have also argued for the aesthetic consciousness-raising function of all of postmodernism;[39] here, obviously, I would specifically argue for the political consciousness-raising powers of magic realism within postmodernism. With Julio Ortega, I discover in the great novels of Rulfo, Arguedas, García Márquez, Cabrera Infante, Fuentes and Lezama Lima, a

> Latin American groundtone reveals itself as an artistic and cultural practice that re-shapes the traditional models and the need for innovation into new, unique, and powerful articulations of historical necessities, into penetrating statements of critical and political convictions. These novels have their roots in the common scene of International Modernism, while at the same time confronting it with its own needs, problematizing it, and parodying it. They likewise go beyond existing definitions and frameworks by giving their postmodernity an even more critical accentuation, voicing yet new aesthetic needs and social revindications.[40]

From the list of authors Ortega offers, and to which many other names could be added, foremost among them that of the Vargas Llosa of *La casa verde* (1965), *Conversación en La Catedral* (1969), and *La guerra del fin del mundo* (1981), it is clear that this Latin American groundtone of an artistic and cultural practice voicing aesthetic needs and social revindications is also a magic realist one. And this groundtone, it seems to me, is also there in magic realist works by non-Latin American writers.

In order to come full circle, to my opening remarks: magic realism, as I have now discussed it, in its artistic and cultural-political practice, is clearly continuing in the tracks of its earliest progenitor, surrealism. As such it also marks the inclusion, in the discussion about postmodernism, of that "half" that Helmut Lethen still relatively recently regretted as having been excluded from earlier theoretical discussions of this phenomenon by Anglo-American critics, namely, the complementary heritage of the continental European avant-garde.[41] The exclusive attention given to Anglo-American modernism is in itself an indication of "privileged center" discourse. In this respect, then, merely to talk of magic realism in relation to postmodernism is to contribute to decentering that privileged discourse.

Notes

1 For what is probably still the most comprehensive survey, see Jean Weisgerber, "La Locution et le concept," in *Le Réalisme magique: roman, peinture et cinéma*, ed. Jean Weisgerber (Lausanne: L'Age d'Homme, 1987), pp. 11–32.

2 *The Oxford Dictionary of Art*, ed. Ian Chivers, Harold Osborne, and Dennis Farr (Oxford and New York: Oxford University Press, 1988), p. 305.

3 The clearest discussion of the precise nature of magic realism in literature is probably to be found in Amaryll Chanady's *Magic Realism and the Fantastic: Resolved versus Unresolved Antinomy* (New York and London: Garland, 1985). See also her essay in this volume.

4 See Joaquín Soler Serrano's interview with Alejo Carpentier in *Escritores a fondo* (Barcelona: Editorial Planeta, 1986), in which the latter (p. 156) remarks upon his friendship with Robert Desnos, the surrealist poet who in his works combined dream and reality, and where he states that (p. 163) "I began to see America via the Surrealist movement. I saw that the Surrealists searched in their daily lives for marvelous things that were very hard for them to find, and that sometimes they used tricks, very often collecting different things in order to create a prefabricated marvelous reality. And there, in Paris, I realized that we really had all those marvelous things in America, and I began to take account of Latin America and of the baroque phenomenon." Finally, Carpentier's *Tientos y diferencias* (Montevideo: Arca, 1967), contains two previously unpublished texts by Desnos in an appendix.

5 Jean Franco, *An Introduction to Spanish American Literature* (Cambridge: Cambridge University Press, 1969), pp. 309–19.

6 See, in this respect, also Donald L. Shaw, *Nueva narrativa hispanoamericana*

(Madrid: Cátedra, 1981), pp. 18–19. Carpentier's essay is translated by Tanya Huntington and Lois Parkinson Zamora in this volume.

7 See Weisgerber, *Le Réalisme magique*, and also Michael Scheffel, *Magischer Realismus: Die Geschichte eines Begriffes und ein Versuch seiner Bestimmung*, Stauffenburg Colloquium Band 16 (Tübingen: Stauffenburg Verlag, 1990).

8 See Gordon Brotherston, *The Emergence of the Latin American Novel* (Cambridge: Cambridge University Press, 1977), p. 15, and the footnote references to essays by Angel Flores and Luis Leal (reprinted in this volume).

9 Jean Franco, *The Modern Culture of Latin America: Society and the Artist* (London: Pall Mall Press, 1967).

10 Jean Franco, *Spanish American Literature since Independence* (London: Ernest Benn, 1973).

11 Cedomil Goic, *Historia de la novela hispanoamaricana* (Valparaiso, Chile: Ediciones Universitarias de Valparaiso, 1972).

12 In this respect the date — 1972 — of José Donoso's *Historia personal del "boom"* (Barcelona: Anagrama) is instructive.

13 Michael Köhler, "'Postmodernismus: Ein begriffsgeschichtlicher' überblick," in *Amerikastudien* 22:8–18; and Hans Bertens, "The Postmodern *Weltanschauung* and its Relation with Modernism: An Introductory Survey," in *Approaching Postmodernism*, ed. Douwe Fokkema and Hans Bertens, Utrecht Publications in General and Comparative Literature, vol. 21 (Amsterdam/Philadephia: John Benjamins, 1986), 9–51.

14 To cite just some of the more recent and ambitious attempts: Steven Connor, *Postmodernist Culture: An Introduction to Theories of the Contemporary* (Oxford: Basil Blackwell, 1989); David Harvey, *The Condition of Postmodernity: An Inquiry into the Origins of Cultural Change* (Oxford: Basil Blackwell, 1989); Scott Lash, *Sociology of Postmodernism* (London: Routledge, 1990); Mike Featherstone, *Consumer Culture & Postmodernism* (London: SAGE, 1991); Barry Smart, *Modern Conditions, Postmodern Controversies* (London: Routledge, 1992); Steven Connor, *Theory and Cultural Value* (Oxford: Basil Blackwell, 1993); and, of course, the many analyses inspired by Fredric Jameson's 1984 essay "Postmodernism, or, The Cultural Logic of Late Capitalism," now collected in the 1991 Duke University Press volume with the same title.

15 Obviously, as the catalog of works on postmodernism is by now almost endless and growing every day, I can list only some of the better known works here: Ihab Hassan, *The Dismemberment of Orpheus: Toward a Postmodern Literature* (1971; New York: Oxford University Press, 1982); *Paracriticisms: Seven Speculations of the Times* (Urbana: University of Illinois Press, 1975); *The Right Promethean Fire: Imagination, Science, and Cultural Change* (Urbana: University of Illinois Press, 1980); *The Postmodern Turn: Essays in Postmodern Theory and Culture* (Ohio State University Press, 1987); David Lodge, *The Modes of Modern*

Writing: Metaphor, Metonymy, and the Typology of Modern Literature (London: Arnold, 1977); Alan Wilde, *Horizons of Assent: Modernism, Postmodernism, and the Ironic Imagination* (Baltimore: Johns Hopkins University Press, 1981); Douwe Fokkema, *Literary History, Modernism, and Postmodernism* (Amsterdam/Philadelphia: John Benjamins, 1984); Allen Thiher, *Words in Reflection: Modern Language Theory and Postmodern Fiction* (Chicago: University of Chicago Press, 1984); Douwe Fokkema and Hans Bertens, eds., *Approaching Postmodernism* (Amsterdam/Philadelphia: John Benjamins, 1986); Brian McHale, *Postmodernist Fiction* (New York: Methuen, 1987); Matei Calinescu and Douwe Fokkema, ed., *Exploring Postmodernism* (Amsterdam/Philadelphia: John Benjamins, 1987); Linda Hutcheon, *A Poetics of Postmodernism: History, Theory, Fiction* (New York: Routledge, 1988); Marguerite Alexander, *Flights from Realism: Themes and Strategies in Postmodernist British and American Fiction* (London: Edward Arnold, 1990); Alison Lee, *Realism and Power: Postmodern British Fiction* (London: Routledge, 1990); Jerry A. Varsava, *Contingent Meanings: Postmodern Fiction, Mimesis, and the Reader* (Tallahassee: Florida State University Press, 1990); Brenda Marshall, *Teaching the Postmodern: Fiction and Theory* (New York: Routledge, 1992).

16 For instance, see Elrud Ibsch, "From Hypothesis to *Korrektur:* Refutation as a Component of Postmodernist Discourse," in *Approaching Postmodernism*, ed. Fokkema and Bertens, pp. 119–33; Ulla Musarra, "Duplication and Multiplication: Postmodernist Devices in the Novels of Italo Calvino," ibid., pp. 135–55; Hans Bertens, "Postmodern Characterization and the Intrusion of Language," in *Exploring Postmodernism*, ed. Matei Calinescu and Douwe Fokkema, pp. 139–59; Jerome Klinkowitz and James Knowlton, *Peter Handke and the Postmodern Transformation: The Goalie's Journey Home* (Columbia, Mo.: University of Missouri Press, 1983); Theo D'haen, *Text to Reader: A Communicative Approach to Fowles, Barth, Cortázar, and Boon* (Amsterdam/Philadelphia: John Benjamins, 1983); Theo D'haen, "Popular Genre Conventions in Postmodern Fiction: The Case of the Western," in *Exploring Postmodernism*, ed. Calinescu and Fokkema, pp. 161–73; Alfred Hornung, "Reading One/Self: Samuel Beckett, Thomas Bernhard, Peter Handke, John Barth, Alain Robbe-Grillet," ibid., pp. 175–97; Hans Bertens and Theo D'haen, *Het postmodernisme in de literatuur* (Amsterdam: De Arbeiderspers, 1988).

17 Richard Todd, "Convention and Innovation in British Literature 1981–84: The Contemporaneity of Magic Realism," *Convention and Innovation in Literature*, ed. Theo D'haen, Rainer Grübel, and Helmut Lethen, Utrecht Publications in General and Comparative Literature 24 (Amsterdam/Philadelphia: John Benjamins, 1989), pp. 361–88.

18 Geert Lernout, "Postmodernist Fiction in Canada," in *Postmodern Studies 1: Postmodern Fiction in Europe and the Americas*, Theo D'haen and Hans Ber-

tens, ed. (Amsterdam: Rodopi, 1988), pp. 127–41. This quote p. 129. Lernout here also draws on an article by Geoff Hancock in *Canadian Forum* 65 (March, 1986): pp. 23–35.

19 Julio Ortega, "Postmodernism in Latin America," in *Postmodern Studies 1: Postmodern Fiction in Europe and the Americas*, ed. D'haen and Bertens, pp. 193–208.

20 Carlos Fuentes, "Discovering Mexico," *Wilson Quarterly* (Autumn 1988): 148–59; this quote p. 157.

21 J. M. Coetzee, *Foe* (London: Jonathan Cape, 1986); John Fowles, *The French Lieutenant's Woman* (London: Jonathan Cape, 1969); Salman Rushdie, *Midnight's Children* (London: Picador, 1981); Angela Carter, *Nights at the Circus* (London: Picador, 1984).

22 For the classic statement of this position, see Ian Watt, *The Rise of the Novel* (1957; London: Penguin, 1963), pp. 65–88.

23 Of course, it can be explained in many more ways — as the editors of the present volume kindly pointed out to me, Susan might here be trying to teach Friday to write the body in a feminine mode. Obviously, the explanations I focus upon are those that fit my line of argument — though I think that to interpret this passage along the lines suggested by Faris and Zamora might well go to strengthen my own conclusions.

24 Michel Foucault, *Les mots et les choses* (Paris: Gallimard, 1966); and *L'archéologie du savoir* (Paris: Gallimard, 1969).

25 See Ian Watt, *The Rise of the Novel*, pp. 54–61.

26 John Fowles, "Notes to an Unfinished Novel," in *The Novel Today: Contemporary Writers on Modern Fiction*, ed. Malcolm Bradbury (1969; Glasgow: Fontana/Collins, 1977), pp. 136–50.

27 See D'haen, *Text to Reader*, pp. 25–42.

28 It would take me too far to argue the point in detail, but the idea of magical manipulation of time and plot is central to all of Fowles' work; see also Malcolm Bradbury, "The Novelist as Impresario: John Fowles and his Magus," in *Possibilities: Essays on the State of the Novel* (London: Oxford University Press, 1973), pp. 256–71.

29 For a comparable approach, but from a scholarly stance, see Edward Said's celebrated, but also much debated, *Orientalism* (New York: Pantheon Books, 1978); for a discussion of Rushdie's work from a "Saidian" perspective, see Aleid Fokkema, "Indianness and Englishness: Aspects of a Literary and Critical Discourse," Master's thesis, University of Utrecht, 1985.

30 And this not just in English literature. See, for example, the Dutch author Louis Couperus' powerful *De stille kracht* (1900), translated by Alexander Teixeira de Mattos as *The Hidden Force* (London: Jonathan Cape, 1922), and re-

cently (1985) reissued, revised, and edited, and with an introduction and notes by E. M. Beekman, in the latter's superb twelve-volume series of Dutch colonial literature classics, the *Library of the Indies*, published by the University of Massachusetts Press, Amherst.

31 Of course, there may have been other reasons as well—such as strong indigenous narrative traditions, next to narratives of discovery and exploration, all of which to a greater or lesser extent stressed the strangeness, the wonder, of the Latin American reality.

32 John Barth, "The Literature of Exhaustion" and "The Literature of Replenishment," both of which appeared originally in the *Atlantic Monthly* (in 1967 and 1980, respectively), have now been collected, together with Barth's other discursive writing, in *The Friday Book: Essays and Other Non-Fiction* (New York: Putnam, 1984), pp. 62–76 and 193–206. This quote p. 204.

33 See, for instance, Charles Newman, *The Post-Modern Aura: The Act of Fiction in an Age of Inflation* (Evanston: Northwestern University Press, 1985); and articles by Fredric Jameson, for example, "Postmodernism and Consumer Society," in *The Anti-Aesthetic: Essays on Postmodern Culture*, ed. Hal Foster (Port Townsend, Wash.: Bay Press, 1983), pp. 1111–25; and, of course, Jameson's "Postmodernism, or the Cultural Logic of Late Capitalism," cited above.

34 Douwe Fokkema, "The Semantic and Syntactic Organization of Postmodernist Texts," *Approaching Postmodernism*, ed. Fokkema and Bertens, p. 95.

35 Linda Hutcheon, *The Canadian Postmodern: A Study of Contemporary English-Canadian Fiction* (New York: Oxford University Press, 1988), pp. 4 and 120, respectively.

36 Theo D'haen, "Timothy Findley, Magic Realism and the Canadian Postmodern," in *Multiple Voices: Recent Canadian Fiction*, Proceedings of the Fourth International Symposium of the Brussels Centre for Canadian Studies, 29 November–1 December 1989 (Sydney/Mundelstrup/Coventry: Dangaroo Press, 1990), pp. 217–33. I have used some paragraphs from the Findley essay in the present article and also in the Irish Regionalism paper mentioned in the next note.

37 Theo D'haen, "Irish Regionalism, Magic Realism and Postmodernism," paper delivered at the 1990 meeting of the International Association for the Study of Anglo-Irish Literature in Kyoto and to be published in the proceedings; also in *British Postmodern Fiction*, ed. Theo D'haen and Hans Bertens, Postmodern Studies, vol. 7 (Amsterdam/Antwerp: Rodopi/Restant, forthcoming).

38 Wendy B. Faris, "Replenishment from the Peripheries: Magical Realism, Emergent Literatures, and Postmodernism"; cf. for instance the following passage: "In any case, a strong replenishing impulse seems to come from the outer edges of Western literature toward the center rather than the other way around. A

postmodern poetics may now demand a geographical as well as a conceptual decentering of literary culture, a recognition of the force of marginality as an ideological and an aesthetic phenomenon" (Unpublished manuscript, p. 3).

39 See Theo D'haen, *Text to Reader.*

40 D'haen and Bertens, eds., *Postmodern Fiction in Europe and the Americas,* p. 206.

41 Helmut Lethen, "Modernism Cut in Half: The Exclusion of the Avant-garde and the Debate on Postmodernism," in *Approaching Postmodernism,* ed. Fokkema and Bertens, pp. 233–38.

RAWDON WILSON

The Metamorphoses of Fictional
Space: Magical Realism

Concerning [parables] a man once said: Why such reluctance? If you only followed
the parables you would become parables and with that rid of all your daily cares.
Another said: I bet that is also a parable. The first said: You have won. The second
said: But unfortunately only in parable. The first said: No, in reality: in parable
you have lost. — Franz Kafka, "On Parables"

Once, when my son was nine years old and my daughter six, I called them
in from play to read them a story I had just discovered. The story was
Gabriel García Márquez's "A Very Old Man with Enormous Wings" which
I read in Gregory Rabassa's translation. Having protested my summons,
my children stood attentively until I was finished, mouths open, eyes fixed
upon my reading mouth, rapt. My voice performing that which García
Márquez had created (and Rabassa had transmuted), held them completely. For the short time of reading, my voice had become a world for
them. They did not even think to sit down. When I finished, they stood for
a few moments, almost as if they had been stunned. It was not like a fairy
tale nor like a myth, they agreed. It was not even like, my son observed,
The Lord of the Rings. But it had brought to mind all those other texts
they had read. My children had come from actual-world play (which, of
course, might have involved make-believe) and entered García Márquez's
split world of enfolded possibilities where they remained a short while
before returning to their world of play. Several different places were implicated in their experience, but they easily navigated them all and were
never lost nor ever unaware of their own position. They crossed from one
conceptual space (play) to another (fiction) through intermediate stages of
actual-world participation, including their father's performing voice. And

that, I shall argue, is what reading magical realism requires: a faculty for boundary-skipping between worlds.[1]

I am interested in fictional space. How, in reading or viewing a fictional world, is space (the sense of direction and distance, the sheer up and downness and back and forthness, the *scale*) to be imagined? Magical realism makes the problem extremely interesting. The copresence of oddities, the interaction of the bizarre with the entirely ordinary, the doubleness of conceptual codes, the irreducibly hybrid nature of experience strikes the mind's eye. Impossible things, Salman Rushdie writes, "happen constantly, and quite plausibly, out in the open under the midday sun."[2] Imagine the space in a "realistic" novel. Think of Conrad. The navigational routes, the lines on a map, the rational cartographical space, unfold lucidly and unmistakably. (It is, of course, the representation of the space that you take for granted, and in which you walk and move about. It is such a familiar space that you can easily see right through it.) Now think of Spenser. Or, if Spenser seems too remote, think of *Star Trek* (any generation) and try to imagine how very different arrangements of things coexist, different sets of possibilities, different spaces. Now imagine the fictional world that Spenser creates. Or think of any such world in which the plasticity of fantasy-space displaces normal expectations and learned behavior and superimpose it upon one of Conrad's fictional worlds. Try to imagine it as if two distinct geometries had been inscribed onto the same space. Think of it as copresence, as duality and mutual tolerance, as different geometries at work constructing a double space. Magical realism focuses the problem of fictional space. It does this by suggesting a model of how different geometries, inscribing boundaries that fold and refold like quicksilver, can superimpose themselves upon one another.[3]

Let me introduce a parable. Once upon a time, not so long ago, nor so far away, in a village on the pampas, on the prairies, along interminable Pacific beaches, there lived two brothers. They were ordinary real-life people who got up each day and did what they were used to doing: eating normally, walking in more or less straight lines, attending to nature's many calls, feeling the winds of air and heat that blew, seeing with the variable translucencies of light, and living in the linear unfolding of time. Then one day they grew tired of this commonplace existence and began to reinvent the world.

The first brother began by asking whether it was truly necessary to walk in straight lines from one point to another. He reasoned that it might make more sense to walk in curved lines, since they might prove to be more interesting, or even (in the long run) quicker. After all, the universe sometimes seems to be composed of chunks of curved space, so curved lines might make more sense than straight ones. He went on to think about other things that he had been taught to accept, all very ordinary matters, but which might be only assumptions that could be changed or exchanged: the notions that planes have surfaces, that one line and only one may pass through a given point, that distances between points remain constant, or that time passes linearly. All these mundane assumptions about human experience could be overturned and strange, but profoundly exciting, propositions would follow. New worlds would emerge, open to exploration yet blankly locked to the commonplace thinking that the rejected assumptions permit.

Meanwhile, the second brother began to weary of the undeviating predictability of ordinary life. He grew tired of the heaviness of gravity, of the solidity of substance, of the boring on-goingness of cause and effect, and of the sensation of heated air that seemed to be the blowing of the wind. He began to imagine a world in which things floated together again, like quicksilver, and in which things called out meaningfully to each other, but did not cause one another. He began to suppose that all human experience could be counterfactual. Suppose (he mused) that the wind were made of light. Suppose that the sky could be made of flowers and that the clouds were bundles of soft petals, then rain might be the perfume of rose or of poppies. Let us suppose that the winds blow (or illumine) the embryos of our desires.

In this way the two brothers began to invent fresh existences. But it is important to observe that they did so in very different ways without paying much attention to others, their precursors, who had tried to perform similar reinventions in the past. The first brother began by assuming a single proposition that was conrary to reason and to the likelihoods of human life. At different times, he invented different propositions (they were like the axioms of unlike geometries) that led around the compass in all, but always different, directions. The propositions that he invented were often antirational and not at all intuitive, like the axioms of differential geometry. Still, he was able to draw from them fascinating consequences. Once he had made them, extraordinary worlds became possible, and narratives about these worlds, before unimaginable, now thundered in his voice. The it-goes-without-sayings of realistic fiction that he had grown up believing began to fade into insignificance (or into the vast volume of literary conventions) to be remembered, but no longer to be assumed, never again to be revered. Thus he was able to assume that a library could be infinite, that a man might lose his ability to forget detail (and hence to make abstractions), that God could suspend time for one person but not for others, that a coin could have only one side, that a book might have an infinite number of pages, not one of which could ever be rediscovered, or that there might be a world somewhere (call it Tlön) in which perception preceded existence. Once he had invented these counterintuitive propositions, they began to function in his fresh accounts like axioms in fantastic geometries. Once you accepted them, you could not escape where they led.

Now the second brother shared the desire to begin freshly and to discard what had become dustily commonplace. He followed a different method of reinvention. He began by imagining spaces in which common and uncommon things existed side by side: men died, grew old, had children, were born, remembered or forgotten; yet flowers rained from the skies, human persons metamorphosed into animals or angels, ghosts and chimeras abounded, and human psychology lent the structures of its obsessions to the world so that it became, in its reinvention, a labyrinth of emblems. In the second brother's narratives there were no single axioms from which everything descended, or from which the world hung, but there were instead two codes that were interwound, twisted in a grip closer than blood and mind, in a tight choreography of antitheses. The one code put things into place quite normally so that men were shot and died, had ambitions, were deserted, became lonely, and sought sublimations like, say, making gold fish. The second code organized events so that any number of strange things might occur: a man might be everywhere followed by butterflies, another might swim to the bottom of the sea and find lost villages where life continued or where ancient turtles lay by the thousands waiting to be eaten, another might sell the sea so that it could be cut into chunks and reassembled elsewhere on land, still another might build a lighthouse out of ice. In the second brother's imagined narratives, the possibilities of the two worlds were always copresent, their codes lovingly interwound, and clung fiercely to each other.

Both brothers learned to tell stories about their reinvented worlds with a straight face, without shrugs, secret winks, or other hints that it was, after all, just a tale. (The world had not been reinvented, only temporarily disguised.) Some people thought that their talent as storytellers was simply this knack of telling about their newly imagined worlds without drawing attention to themes out of the ordinary, of giving their worlds narrators who never raised problems or suggested that readers and hearers should look for explanations. In the second brother's narratives, there never were any explanations because none were ever required. If the first brother gave explanations, they were fantastic yet always rational. Both brothers' worlds easily generated belief.

No doubt there are always people (more than preachers, policemen, politicians, and pedagogues might wish to admit) who would like to re-invent the world. If they cannot do it for themselves, except in sleep or when the fog is thickest, then they beg others to do it for them. So the two brothers quickly gathered disciples, followers like scattered knights, who swore to reinvent their own worlds according to the rules the brothers had created. As their following grew, the number of disciples increased, uncertainties stuck to the brothers' fame, they became associated with strangers, their origins were forgotten and (worst of all) they became confused with one another. There were some adventurers among the new worlds who said that the brothers were actually just one person who possessed a single magic formula; others who made gazetteers of all the real world's invisible cities, supposing that they lived in this place or that; still others who thought that they were imposters, panvestites, masters of bunco and Buncombe. As often happens a myth (a collective network of little myths) sprang up around the brothers, and they became at once more and less than their true disciples knew them to be. They were everywhere, and everyone spoke much of them and of their power and influence, but who were they? Really, people asked, who really are they? Who, really?[4]

Consider next the following anecdote from literary history, which I shall offer complete with scholia but in a much shorter form than my parable. When Don Quijote first erupted upon the horizon of European literature, bearing the dust of Spain upon his body and the golden worlds of chivalric romance in his mind, a cataclysm convulsed literature. An *episteme* had been shattered and a new one (of ambiguous interiors, doubtful validations, and declarified certainties) called for *its* followers. They were not long in appearing: Gil Blas, Parson Adams, Mr. Pickwick, Prince Myshkin, Emma Bovary, Quentin Compson, Meaulnes, Voss, a host of siblings and offspring appeared and, even now, themselves part of a dying *episteme*, continue sporadically to do so.[5] Yet the precursor, the Knight himself, is endlessly instructive and will help, if not to identify, then to grasp the reasons for the misidentification of the two brothers.

In the second part of his adventures (published about ten years after the first part), Don Quijote encounters a character named Don Alvaro Tarfe and converses with him. Now Don Alvaro Tarfe is a character invented by another writer, not Cervantes, and he has ridden out of the pages of another book: indeed, he has arrived at the same inn as Don Quijote from the pages of the False Sequel, a vandalized continuation of the successful first part of Cervantes' novel. In effect, Cervantes has hired him to meet Don Quijote in the true continuation and swear, after their conversation has been concluded, that the Don Quijote with whom he has just enjoyed such a wise discussion was not, and could not be, the Don Quijote whom he had previously met in another place (and book).[6] It is enough, Robert Alter remarks, to give the reader "ontological vertigo."[7] The bizarre encounter exemplifies an important point about fiction: something new may come along, smash common prejudices, show a new path for storytelling, but be extremely difficult to get straight, elusive to its core. (And, as the two brothers have been thought to be panvestites, bunco-artists who have stolen skills from long-dead fantasists, so even Don Quijote has seemed to some only a carryover from the self-parody of the romances, or a fugitive from sixteenth-century comedy.) Don Quijote, the freshest and the most imitated character in European fiction, everywhere displays the difficulties of getting straight his novel mixture of exterior and interior, of dust and golden flecks.

Don Quijote is, Michel Foucault writes, "himself like a sign, a long thin graphism, a letter that has just escaped from the open pages of a book. His whole being is nothing but language, text, printed pages, stories that have already been written down. He is made up of interwoven words; he is writing itself wandering through the world among the resemblances of things."[8] He was new, became a model (acquired his knights), was borrowed, brought European literature into its modern phases. Scholars such as Alter and Marthe Robert delight in demonstrating that he gave, and continues to give, the modern novel its tasks. Composed out of stories himself, a narrative microcosm, Don Quijote ought to have been precisely imitable, a character splendidly reiterative. Yet he was not. The uncertainty of literary history (if there is such a discourse) stems from the playful potential of paradigms. They remain freely elusive, never hinged upon a didactic center. (Some might say that, at its best, literature is always unhinged.)

Literary paradigms possess considerable plasticity. They disregard visas and other credentials when they cross frontiers (like the Petrarchan son-

net or the picaresque novel), but that does not show that they are easily
naturalized. They often remain, like resident aliens, within their host culture, but always unassimilated. Furthermore, old paradigms inspire weary
variants of themselves. New ones evoke doubles, phantasmal figures that
lurk within other figures, like distorted mirror images. Unlike the process
of paradigm shifts that Thomas Kuhn has mapped for science, in which
new paradigms arise out of a genuine need to resolve anomalies and radically displace what had previously been accepted, the paradigm shifts of
literature often seem more like the shifts of dancers within an intricate
choreography: neither lost nor forgotten, old positions may be resumed.[9]
Thus Don Quijote, the most imitated character in European literature,
was already in his conception the most inimitable: netted, enmeshed, re-
enmeshed, trapped innumerable times, but impossible to capture.

Now what of the two brothers who grew tired of ordinary experience
and set out to reinvent the world? Are there actually two brothers? (Or
only two?) The two modes of reinvention are two distinct modes of fantasy,
both of which are relatively common in contemporary literature. Both oppose themselves to canonical realism in literature. They are also opposed
to another contemporary mode, the minimalist writing that is sometimes
called "dirty realism."[10] Fantasy is normally maximalist. Hence the two
brothers' modes of fantasy are easily confused: both transform the world,
both call upon assumptions that are against the world's likelihoods, both
are counterintuitive, but they are also strikingly different. It is possible
to distinguish them. Indeed, whenever ways of writing appear similar and
are difficult to keep separate, then it makes sense to examine them on the
level of common fictional elements. How such fundamental and recurring
concepts as voice, plot, character, time or space function, what assumptions they entail and what definitions they make possible, should tell one
how the uncertain boundaries are to be drawn. Consider space.

Space, understood in its most primitive sense (a distance to be crossed,
an openness between points, one of which is occupied by a perceiving
subject, filled by something, sunlight, moonlight, hot dust, cold mud or
emptiness) seems omnipresent in literature, but rather hard to place. There
doesn't seem to be a vocabulary sufficiently capacious to discuss space.
You may talk about deictics, copresence, coordination, distances, surfaces,
exteriors, interiors, volume and plasticity, but the units of measurement
are lacking: literary space, in being conceptual, cannot be measured, but it
can be experienced. It is this experience that leads me to claim that space

is invariably present in fiction though never precisely so. It is very much an aspect of the experience of reading, and without it a fictional world would be (I think) impossible to imagine.[11] Even unsophisticated readers, do read in images of space, do interpret fiction as having taken place in space, and they do tend to recall what they have read in terms of directions, distances, places, worlds, and other kinds of spatial imagery. (The experiment is openly available: ask a reader, a student or a child, to recall a fiction and then observe the deformations, the condensations, the simplicities that will reconstruct the spatiality of the reading experience.) As Gaston Bachelard observes (and as Proust demonstrates) memory is, in its structures, highly spatial. It seems to work through visual images of place. In specific memories, intricate diachronic complexities may be collapsed into simpler spatial arrangements.[12] Georges Poulet makes a similar point: memories and places, changes in time and changes in space, spatial image and temporal phase, all intersect in Proust such that the recapturing of lost time is possible only under the form of the rediscovery of lost places.[13] Ricardo Gullón puts the problem of fictional space elegantly: the effective test of narrative, he argues, is whether it affects the reader and makes him or her feel and "understand the meaning of space in which the character exists."[14]

The problem of space in literature may be simplified for discussion. Fictional space invokes an experience of place (volume, distance, coordination, interiority, exteriority, and so forth) which may be both, or either, that of characters and that of readers. It is constituted by deictics and descriptive phrases that place characters and things ("existents" to use Seymour Chatman's term) within a fictional world.[15] This "place," a contextual envelope, emerges from the work of fiction, either gradually and by bits or else all at once (which is what readers learn to expect when they read, say, Conrad who likes to establish an initial setting forth of place), but in either way it does emerge. Place is a rudimentary fictional world. It can be imagined as existing somewhere though it is not easy, as Rushdie remarks, "to be precise about the location of the world of the imagination."[16] (Not only do fictional worlds overlap, in some sense, the actual world, but they also overlap each other, each superimposition being radically divergent from the others. A voyageur among fictional worlds must learn to leap, land, and adjust with all the aptitude of the Little Prince.) Of course, there is much more to a world than space. A fictional world may incorporate values, feelings, principles, laws, and (some) coherence, but its space, however sketchily conceived or incoherently presented, is a necessary condition for being imagined. Whether you think of the worlds in fiction as "possible," "alternative," or simply fictional does not matter much for this discussion: what counts is that they are linguistically created, emerge from deictic and descriptive fields, differ from text to text, and can be experienced in reading. James Phelan, in an exemplary move, argues that the fictional worlds of novels, though "created *out of* language," are best thought of as worlds *from* words that "contain the elements of character and action, which are essentially nonlinguistic and which are more central to our experience" than the mere words that make them possible.[17] Given sufficient signifiers (not too many will be necessary) signification follows, the imagination holds its raw materials close, begins to work, and a fictional world emerges. It will have to possess some coherence (meeting the test of "coherence criteria"), but this will not need to be the same kind of coherence that you find in the actual world.[18]

The concept of a fictional world, in which signification generates the experience of bulk, extension, and placing, may then be (roughly) subdivided into three categories: (1) fictional worlds in which all the deictics and descriptions operate as if they were being used in the extratextual world and which, thus, constantly beg comparison to that world; (2) fictional worlds in which all indications of distance, capacity, or arrangement are generated in accordance with self-contained assumptions, gamelike rules that are experienced as axioms; (3) fictional worlds in which the indications of local place are sometimes those of the extratextual world but at other times are those of another place, very different in its assumptions, and which, if it were to exist purely, would be a closed axiomatic world of the second kind. It is obvious that the second and third types of fictional world answer to the principles of world reinvention that the two brothers in my parable discovered.

If, for the sake of contrast, you think briefly about the first kind of fictional world, it should be possible to remember examples from among the canonical texts of European realism. The worlds of those narratives are England, France, Russia, or some familiar elsewhere that can be located on an actual-world map. The realistic text may be said to borrow diverse modes of discourse, including geographical discourse, that belong to the truth claims made in the world outside the text. By and large, this has always been the way of constructing the transparent window through which every reader of realistic fiction is invited to peer. The text begs comparison, and the reader will easily make it: space in this sense (because it is already familiar) can be, without the constructive force of counterintuitive or gamelike axioms, made vivid before the mind's eye.

In fantasy, the second category of fictional world, space may have any imaginable properties that an axiomlike assumption makes possible. Consider the spatial properties of a classic work of fantasy in English literature: Spenser's *The Faerie Queene*. In that fiction, space has several identifiable properties that consistently manifest themselves throughout the narrative. For instance, distance is both uncertain and extremely plastic. Characters traveling between two points will experience dissimilar journeys, long for one character, short for another, empty or full of obstacles, metamorphic in every feature. The plasticity of space in *The Faerie Queene* follows from a text-specific axiom: distance reflects the moral requirements of individual characters. A work of fiction may contain more than one axiomlike assumption (though there are never a great number, it seems); in fantasy, these assumptions do not always need to work harmoniously together. Space may take many unlike shapes at different points in the narrative. Thus, in the world of *The Faerie Queene* it is possible for interiors to be larger than exteriors. The Cave of Mammon contains a labyrinthine interior in which a single chamber, the throne room of Philotime, commodiously holds in(de)finite multitudes of ambitiously striving people; the mouth of the Blatant Beast is said to contain, variously, either hundreds or thousands of rows of teeth. The Blatant Beast's multiplex oral cavity displays more clearly than any other aspect of Spenser's narrative the axiom of interiority: an interior may contain all the space that it requires independently of its exterior parameters. (For students of popular culture, who may not read many Renaissance texts, the phenomenon of anamorphic spatiality, in which interior volume does not correspond to exterior surface, can be observed in the BBC classic, *Dr. Who*, often replayed on American PBS, where the doctor's TARDIS, like the Blatant Beast's mouth, contains more than the geometry of its exterior predicts.) These two text-specific spatial axioms in *The Faerie Queene* indicate how space is constructed in much fantasy. Space in *Star Trek*, either previous or next generation, is also anamorphic because time is described as highly malleable: subject to warp factors, reversibility, and segmentation. One text-specific assumption in *Star Trek* demands that the potential of space (its shapes, its commodiousness, its very navigationality) follow upon, and reflect, the nature of time. In fantasy, one or two counterintuitive axioms can create an imaginable disposition of spatial arrangements that will diverge immensely, even incredibly, from extratextual experience.

The fantastic method might be compared to a geometry or to a game. In either case, the upshot is a cleidoic, self-consistent disposition of spatial existents and relationships that follows from the narrative's initial assumptions.[19] What occurs in fantasy is memorably exemplified in Borges' narrative "Tlön, Uqbar, Orbis Tertius." Tlön is a fictional world created within the literature of the people of Uqbar (itself quite fictional): "the literature of Uqbar was one of fantasy and . . . its epics and legends never referred to the reality, but to the two imaginary regions of Mlejinas and Tlön."[20] The space of Tlön obeys, as its chief and consistent axiom, the epistemological principle of Berkeley that nothing can exist (that is, have a place in space) unless it has been perceived. For the inhabitants of Tlön the problem of what happens to certain copper coins when they are not being observed is considered a paradox equivalent, the narrator observes, to those created by the Eleatic philosophers. "Tlön, Uqbar, Orbis Tertius" might be read as a metanarrative (and as a metaspatial commentary upon the nature of fictional space), and its lessons are to be found in many of Borges' narratives. In "The Garden of Forking Paths," for instance, all directions are bifurcated, all spatial arrangements labyrinthine, not simply because the narrative concerns a mysterious labyrinth and the *mise en abyme* effect is powerful, but because the central narrative concept is that time bifurcates, that time is labyrinthine, not directly linear, and that fictional space mirrors what is true of time. Hence it seems that, considered from the aspect of spatiality, two writers of fantasy as diverse as Spenser and Borges appear to share similar methods for creating space-constructive assumptions. Both write narratives in which space is extremely plastic, given to unpredictable shapes and deformations, and both link this plasticity to the experience of time. Spenser, it is true, employs this method for the purposes of characterization while Borges follows it in order to comment upon the nature of narrative, but the similar method in both writers serves to point out the common resources of fantasy.

The secret of the first brother's reinvention of the world seems to be no more than to extend this common principle to innovative possibilities. For example, in Italo Calvino's wonderfully Borgesian *Invisible Cities,* Marco Polo creates for Kubla Khan an atlas of fictional cities, each one of which is constructed upon the axiom that the spatial dispositions of a human city can follow from, and build upon, a single human quality in a total projection. In a thin city everything must be thin, including aspiration, hope, and desire. In a city of signs not only do all buildings signify, but they do nothing but signify. Kubla Khan's empire, Brian McHale writes, is a *heterotopia:* "Radically discontinuous and inconsistent, it juxtaposes worlds of incompatible structure."[21] *Invisible Cities* magnifies the plural worldhood built into fantasy, but it does not fundamentally alter the (fantastic) principle of the imaginative copresence of worlds.

In narratives that have come to be called magical realist, a third kind of space unfolds. One way to describe this space is to borrow a phrase that Lubomír Doležel uses to characterize the world of Kafka's fiction: in magical realism space is *hybrid* (opposite and conflicting properties coexist).[22] Typically, a magical realist fictional world asserts its connection to an extratextual world (as neither *The Faerie Queene* nor *Invisible Cities* does directly) and may even, in the manner of canonical realism, seem to create a fenestral translucency through which reality flickers. This opening toward an experiential world may be noted in all magical realist narratives. (At least, I cannot think of any exceptions, nor even how there could be an exception that was still an instance of magical realism.) Novels as diverse as Salman Rushdie's *Midnight's Children* and his *The Satanic Verses* or Robert Kroetsch's *What the Crow Said* incorporate the extratextual world even while constructing a textual space that makes unlikelihoods possible. Kroetsch's careful evocation of an Alberta spring in the opening passage of *What the Crow Said* and his painstaking account of rural life in Big Indian, its pretechnological mind-set dominating the technological world that it inhabits, clearly exemplifies the novel's actual-world grasp.[23] Rushdie's colorful descriptions of Bombay, with its clash of races and language groups, and his detailed transcriptions of street talk and Anglo-Indian slang (words that cannot be found even in the pages of *Hobson-Jobson,* but only on the streets of Bombay or London) evoke a world that you might experience outside the novels.[24] The hybrid nature of this space becomes evident when you observe the ease, the purely natural way in which abnormal, experientially impossible (and empirically unverifiable) events take place. It is as if they had always already been there; their abnormality normalized from the moment that their magical realist worlds were imagined. The narrative voice bridges the gap between ordinary and bizarre, smoothing the discrepancies, making everything seem normal. (The narrative voice itself constitutes the "midday sun" of which Rushdie speaks.) In this hybrid space, eruptions occur normally and sudden folds crease the seemingly predictable, the illusive extratextual, surface.

Consider the openings of two magical realist novels. How reducible are they to actual-world accounts? Kroetsch's *What the Crow Said,* in the midst of realistic description, starts from the image of a young woman raped by a swarm of bees: "People, years later, blamed everything on the bees: it was the bees, they said, seducing Vera Lang, that started everything." Rushdie's *The Satanic Verses* begins with two men, both actors, falling from the sky as an Air India flight explodes over the coast of the United Kingdom: "'To be born again,' sang Gibreel Farishta tumbling from the heavens, 'first you have to die. Ho ji! Ho ji! To land upon the bosomy earth, first one needs to fly.'" Such openings raise a large number of textual questions. Kroetsch's novel evokes rural superstition, the irrational pretechnological (weather centered) beliefs of farmers in a technological culture. *The Satanic Verses* opens by pointing toward the abrupt entrance of postcolonial subjects into the former imperial center; an entrance without transition, without preparation. It would be like falling from the sky, since little could prepare the postcolonial subject's divided self for the mixture of similarity and difference, acceptance and rejection, that the experience of the empire's capital will bring. Reversing the significance of the opening, you may also suppose that the image of the two Indian actors falling from the sky reveals the indifference with which postcolonial subjects are received: where did *they* come from? They have no background, no meaningful existence. Both these openings lead into the narratives in extremely precise ways. They are both intricately related to the subsequent action, and both are expressed in a narrative voice that is noteworthy for its calmness, for its attention to facts and its personal lack of division or bifurcation.

Rushdie's novel soon introduces the problem of transformation, of metamorphosis:

> Mutation?
>
> Yessir, but not random. Up there in air-space, in that soft, imperceptible field which had been made possible by the century and which, thereafter, made the century possible, becoming one of its defining locations, the place of movement and of war, the planet-shrinker and power-vacuum, most insecure and transitory of zones, illusory discontinuous, metamorphic . . . under extreme environmental pressure, characteristics were acquired.[25]

How are you to imagine metamorphic characteristics (Gibreel becomes, or may become, the archangel whose name he bears; Saladin seems to become Satan)? These initial mutations cohere with the pattern developed throughout the novel of metamorphoses, of acquiring and losing characteristics. Rushdie's fictional world possesses an actual-world substance that you might almost take for granted, air, but it is a "transitory" zone, subject to "extreme environmental pressure," in which mutations occur. The fictional world of *The Satanic Verses* comprises cities, such as London and Bombay, but it also includes the desert city, Jahila, the city once made of sand, once disordered but now ordered, now the object of Gibreel's vision/dream.[26] There are other zones in Rushdie's narrative. They are all discontinuous, illusory, and metamorphic *places* within which different kinds of experience fold into each other.

The opening passage of *What the Crow Said* illustrates how different spaces can be superimposed upon one another. This textual convention may be called the principle of spatial folding. Kroetsch immediately establishes the common features of springtime in Alberta ("the crocuses bloomed in spring as they had always bloomed, the buffalo beans cracked yellow, the violets and the buttercups and the shooting stars took their turn") and then he creates a magical fold. Vera Lang, asleep in "a swarm of wild flowers," is raped by a swarm of bees. Two distinct kinds of fictional world have been enfolded together. Where the bee swarm comes from, why it chooses Vera as its queen, how her anatomy can conceive a child from such an impregnation, or even how her cry, at once terrified and ecstatic, can reach the town more clearly than a locomotive's whistle, are not questions that are asked. Given the neutral voice of the narrator, they are not even questions that could be asked. The text excludes them.[27] The world of *What the Crow Said*, like that of *The Satanic Verses*, is hybrid. It is as if there are two worlds, distinct and following dissimilar laws, that interpenetrate and interwind, all unpredictably but in a natural fashion.

Although it is unmistakably a textual mode, magical realism has been given powerful contextual accounts. It has sometimes been explained as the representation of primitive, or naive, reality, more likely to be found in South than in North America.[28] (This may seem like a simple geographical fallacy, but one can see the allure, as with a macaw or a toucan, of thinking along this path.) In this way, magical realism has been seen as reflecting naive superstition, left behind in sophisticated industrial societies. Magical realism can be enlisted in the analysis of postcolonial discourse as the mode of a conflicted consciousness, the cognitive map that discloses the antagonism between two views of culture, two views of history (European history being the routinization of the ordinary; aboriginal or primitive history, the celebration of the extraordinary), and two ideologies. Writers like to play this game: Carlos Fuentes claims that García Márquez (comparing him to the Mexican novelist, Juan Rulfo) is the "writer who refines to their essence and converts into literature the traditional themes of the countryside."[29] Alejo Carpentier gives a famous account of the geographical enrootedness of magical realism:

> Our art has always been baroque: from the splendid pre-Columbian sculpture and that of the [Aztec] codices to the best contemporary novels in America and even including the colonial cathedrals and monasteries. Even physical love has become baroque in the tangled obscenity of Peruvian *guaco*. Hence we do not fear the baroque in style, nor in the implications of [aesthetic] contexts, nor in the vision of the human form entwined in verbal and chthonic vines. . . . We do not fear the baroque, our own art, for it is born from trees, from timber, from retables and altars, from decadent carvings and calligraphic portraits and even late neo-Classicisms. It is a baroque created by the necessity *to name things*, although in so doing we distance ourselves from the techniques in vogue.[30]

Although tempting, the geographical fallacy, locating the bizarre unlikelihoods of magical realism in the bizarre landscape of Latin America, collapses many levels of textual evidence and seems, flatly, to deny the parallels between Latin American (or Anglo-Indian or Canadian) magical realism and the tradition of European fantasy exemplified by, say, Kafka or Bulgakov.[31] The analysis of a textual feature such as fictional space reestablishes magical realism's deep linkages both to a shared Euro-American traditions of fantasy and to the transcultural problem of the way(s) of writing.

Magical realism involves, at the very least, Cartesian dualities: antinomies between natural and supernatural, explicable and inexplicable. (It also employs a certain mode of narrative voice, though critics often ignore this when they think about magical realism.) Magical realism can be, and indeed *is*, used to describe virtually any literary text in which binary oppositions, or antinomies, can be discovered. Furthermore, it is often employed so loosely as a historical-geographical term that its textual implications tend to become obscured. The uncertainties of finding the divisions of postcolonial culture in literary texts can be shown by two essays analyzing Kroetsch's exploration of the unlikely in the midst of the all-too-likely. Stephen Slemon invokes textual evidence from *What the Crow Said* to demonstrate the presence of contradictory voices caught in a discursive dance, expression and suppression losing and resuming positions, in which magical realism's opposed codes manifest the interlocked discourses of colonial and postcolonial literatures.[32] The narrative effects of magical realism stem from a "binary opposition within language," he writes, "that has its roots in the process of either transporting a language to a new land or imposing a foreign language on an indigenous population" (411). Magical realism, thus, constitutes a "speaking mirror" of the colonial encounter which always constructs a "condition of being both tyrannized by history yet paradoxically cut off from it, caught between absolute systems of blind cognition and projected realms of imaginative revision in which people have no control" (418). On the other hand, Brian Edwards, an Australian critic writing a year earlier, cites much the same textual evidence along an opposed path.[33] Edwards finds only an intricate play within the "multiple possibilities as the condition of communication in language" that flowers beneath the fissiparous textual surface of *What the Crow Said* (97). "A game is on," he writes, "the play begins" (98). Where Slemon finds only the textual embodiment of the principles of postcolonial discourse, Edwards finds only multiplex cognitive patterns the tracking of which offers a more "exciting prospect than the closure of fixed definition, a contract which limits discourse" (101). Both Slemon and Edwards problematize textual detail (usually the same detail), expose this detail to an array of theoretical concepts, and systematically transform *What the Crow Said* into a thoroughly transnational fiction. Both discover textual fissures and both follow the paths into them, but the upshots are strikingly different. Edwards finds imagination in magical realism; Slemon, history. Edwards locates textual labyrinths; Slemon, mappable context. Magical realism might seem, to the wary reader, to create the nexus for all theoretical problems: a notional *Wunderkammern* of riddles, conundrums, puzzles, and aporia.

In Kafka, one consequence of superimposing distinct worlds is the creation of a number of bizarre creatures that owe their natures both to the natural and to the supernatural worlds. You might see the rapist bee swarm in Kroetsch's novel in this way as a single hybrid creature, human *and* apian, belonging to two distinct worlds, the possibilities of hybridization always present, never explained. The creatures into which characters metamorphose (through the various transitory zones) in *The Satanic Verses* are also hybrid, calling upon more than one world for their identity. (You should also see that this hybridism is unlike the unitarily monstrous chimeras of much traditional fantasy, such as Spenser's Blatant Beast, that belong to one world only.) This hybridism occurs within the folding of worlds when one, bearing its own distinct laws, erupts into the other. At such moments it seems as if two systems of possibility have enfolded each other: two kinds of cause and effect, two kinds of organism, two kinds of consequence (after having been raped, Vera becomes pregnant, neither dead from bee stings nor even ill), and two kinds of space. You might even see in this interfolding two kinds of textuality. One kind of writing writes over, and into, another. Magical realism is a term that describes the fictional space created by the dual inscription of alternative geometries.

Such world interpenetration takes place in a number of ways. It would be feasible, if there were room to institute either taxonomies or gazetteers, to compile an atlas, a fictional geology, of folds. In this essay, it is at least possible to suggest the range of world interpenetration by one distinction and two examples. On the one hand, the hybrid constructions of magical realism ensue, as they do in the opening lines of *What the Crow Said* and *The Satanic Verses*, when something different from, even inconsistent with, clashes hard against ordinary in-the-actual-world experience. It comes from outside an already granted world (crocuses and buffalo beans, say, or Air India flights to London) and informs it. On the other hand, one world may lie hidden within another. In the second case, the hybrid construction emerges from a secret, always already contained within, forming an occulted and latent dimension of the surface world. This, I think, is what often happens in García Márquez's fiction. The pattern may be seen (to take only one example) in his tale *Innocent Eréndira*. In that narrative the principle of hybrid construction manifests itself most clearly in the green blood that lies occulted, but always waiting to be revealed, within the veins of Eréndira's Minotauric grandmother. In the depths of an always reconstructible labyrinth, she lurks; within her, the always natural, yet neither seen nor foreseen, green blood (like the gems that hide within the oranges that Ulisis and his father grow and smuggle) waits. This is the pattern of hybrid construction that seems to be largely dominant in *The Satanic Verses*, where the metamorphoses, though occurring in the "zones," reveal something important about the characterhood of the characters; in *What the Crow Said*, the unexpected folds come exclusively from outside.

The co-presence of distinct fictional worlds that distinguishes magical realism from both traditional fantasy and from canonical realism suggests a model for textuality itself. The magicalness of magical realism lies in the way it makes explicit (that is, unfolds) what seems always to have been present. Thus the world interpenetration, the dual worldhood, the plural worldhood even, of magical realism are no more than an explicit fore-grounding of a kind of fictional space that is perhaps more difficult to sup-press than to express. Canonical realism may be seen as (in some sense) a more difficult mode of fiction because it must run consistently against the grain. Realism's typical limpidity arises from the muscular suppression of narrative potential. This is strikingly evident in narrative minimalism, or dirty realism, in which the clash of disparate semiotic domains is carefully avoided. The actual world's diversity is canceled, cropped, or brushed out in order to create fictional worlds of great intensity, but narrow semiotic potential. Not many different *kinds* of things occur in dirty realism. The possibilities of border-crossing or boundary-skipping between domains are blocked, methodically delimited. The magic in magical realism names the textual conventions that, expanding the potential of storytelling, fore-ground its literariness. Different semiotic domains are allowed to clash (and to interpenetrate) in order to tell richer, more diverse tales. Magi-cal realism, in its maximalist pyrotechnics, follows the path that narrative minimalism closes. In this it seems near to the core of traditional storytell-ing. The brothers in my parable have been successful because they have discovered only what fiction does best: imagine worldhood and explore the possibilities of its variousness.

Roland Barthes refers to "stereographic space": the space of an intertex-tual *enchaînment* in which one text, or sliver of a text, associates itself with, pulls into its own textual space, some other text, or textual shard.[34] In lit-erature (whatever the case elsewhere), one space can contain other spaces. And while this may seem paradoxical in the extreme, it does belong to the experience of reading. Even children are capable of remembering one text in terms of another, or recalling another text even while reading the one before them and of constructing the space (or rudimentary world) of one text in terms of, and even as, the space of another. Stereographic space is the field (or complex place) of textual inscription. In Derrida's analysis of this problem, space is seen as the relational *habitation* of all sign systems, and it is this, the domain of textuality, of inscriptions, that produces the "spatiality of space." In reading, one may see not only a world in words, a world from a text, but also worlds within the textual world. It is a process more intricate than seeing a merely singular world in a grain of sand.

Imagine a place known as QueAng-QueAng. Listen to the voice of a speculative traveler from that antique land describing one of their customs:

> The people of QueAng-QueAng drink the eyeballs of living animals using a slender metal straw. The trick, that only practice can teach, is to pierce the eyeball through the iris to the exact centre and then drink the vitreous gel in many tiny sips. In QueAng-QueAng, they also execute blasphemers in a similar manner. The community kneels and angrily pierces the condemned person's body with its metal straws. When the execution has been finished nothing much is left but skin and bones. These dry in the desert air until, withered and empty, they blow away into the bleached horizon along the world's flat edge. The condemned, like husks, are soon forgotten.

Now imagine that the people of QueAng-QueAng board an Airbus, carrying their metal straws in their flight bags, and fly to London. It doesn't matter why they are making this flight, but perhaps they wish to locate a writer who has asserted, against their doctrine, the world's roundness. They may wish to practice their distinctive mode of punishment upon the streets of London. Once they land and begin to walk along those streets, they will be like an alien world superimposed upon English space, their doctrines and practices folded into the world they have entered. That ordinary space will now contain them, encysted but highly active, and will inevitably make a little room for their cultural practices. However alien, they are present, making a small (but dangerous) part of the English world. In this manner, the plural worldhood of magical realism reflects and exemplifies the textual theory of inscriptibility: one world lies present, though hidden, within the other, just as one text lies latent within another text. It is the possibility of inscriptions being reinscribed upon others, or upon each other (of multiplex inscriptibility) that, in Derrida's view, generates the human notion of space.[35] There seems to be no single, free-standing, uncontaminated pure text, but only the threads, the weaves, the nets, and the labyrinths of textuality. Similarly, there seems to be no pure, single-formed space in fiction unless it has been purposefully constructed, as in much nonmagical realism, to simplify both human experience and human writing. What I have been calling co-presence and textual enfolding may be seen as the model, the metamorphic image, of writing. In magical realism, plural worlds, like distinct kinds of writing, like parabolic trajectories, approach each other, but do not merge. Magical realism lies close to a pure model of textuality, but it is also the fundamental mode of storytelling. It is neither recent nor ancient, but always the present shape of fiction.

Notes

1 A sixteenth-century English writer, Sir Philip Sidney, remarks that stories have the power to keep children from play and old men from the chimney-corner. They penetrate the ears, grip the imagination and build strange worlds within the mind. Stories hold the attention. Anyone may test Sidney's proposition. Take a child, your own or one that you have borrowed for the purpose, and begin to read. Pay some attention to education and intelligence levels, and either avoid or continuously edit difficult vocabulary. An interesting narrative will have a very positive effect upon a child's attention span. Most magical realist narratives are *very* interesting.

2 Salman Rushdie, *Imaginary Homelands: Essays and Criticism 1981–1991* (London: Granta Books in association with Penguin Books, 1991), p. 302.

3 The problem of fictional space is difficult, and it seems necessary to admit that there is no easy agreement available. The MLA bibliography indicates more than 1,500 articles since 1982 that touch in some manner upon the concept of space. One difficulty is that, unlike time, there is no obvious, immediate spatiality to fiction other than the physical space the book occupies on a shelf or a lap. In contrast, there is always the time of reading, the minimal diachronicity of discourse. Fictional space is a pure effort of the imagination. It is probably most adequately thought of as a notation, a cropped representation of the wholeness of space. I discuss various ways of thinking about space throughout *In Palamedes' Shadow: Explorations in Play, Game, and Narrative Theory* (Boston: Northeastern University Press, 1990), esp. pp. 174–93. I also discuss the topic in "The Space of The Untold: Conrad's Allusiveness," *Victorian Review* 16, 1 and 2 (Summer and Winter 1990): 22–47, 24–39, respectively. The bibliography to *Palamedes* indicates many of the theoretical paths that scholars have taken across fictional space.

4 The notion of the second brother's two codes, mutually interwound and clinging fiercely, parabolizes the scholarly analysis in Amaryll Beatrice Chanady's *Magical Realism and the Fantastic: Resolved versus Unresolved Antinomies* (New York: Garland, 1985).

5 For an incomplete, but very instructive, discussion of this genealogy, see Alexander Welsh, *Reflections on the Hero as Quixote* (Princeton: Princeton University Press, 1981).

6 The term "hiring" to describe a transworld borrowing (or pinching) of a character from one book to employ in your own is Flann O'Brien's. See *At Swim-*

Two-Birds (New York: Pantheon, 1939). Cervantes appears to engage in a fundamental metafictional strategy that Robert Alter identifies as an originary constituent in one line of development that the novel has followed. O'Brien merely recycles on the level of "flaunted artifice," as Alter puts it, what Cervantes understood both first and better. See *Partial Magic: The Novel as A Self-Conscious Genre* (Berkeley: University of California Press, 1975), p. 223. However, hiring characters is only one possible convention (among many) of character-creation. Think of all those characters who, having first existed in someone else's fictional world, move comfortably through Shakespeare's. The lesson, though perhaps small, is relevant to the consideration of magical realism since it, too, is a matter of conventions, reemployment, and modification. The apotheosis of the Don Alvaro Tarfe motif in (at least) the English language novel must be Gilbert Sorrentino's Martin Halpin who, hired from a footnote in James Joyce's *Finnegans Wake*, continuously reflects upon his condition, lamenting the much harder conditions of employment he now experiences. "I can't understand how Mr. Joyce allowed him to take me away. Surely, it can't have been for money? Or does Mr. Joyce even know that I have gone?" See Gilbert Sorrentino, *Mulligan Stew* (New York: Grove Press, 1979), p. 26.

7 Alter, p. 6.

8 Michel Foucault, *The Order of Things: An Archaeology of the Human Sciences* (New York: Pantheon Books, 1970), p. 46.

9 Thomas S. Kuhn, *The Structure of Scientific Revolutions*, 2d ed. (Chicago: University of Chicago Press, 1970). In *Beyond Deconstruction: The Uses and Abuses of Literary Theory* (Oxford: Clarendon Press, 1985), Howard Felperin accepts a simplified version of the Kuhnian concept of a paradigm shift. He sees the generalized notion of a paradigm shift as being directly relevant to the study of literature. It seems, however, that, unlike the case in the sciences which Kuhn discusses, "old" paradigms are never wholly replaced in literary studies. They survive in books and articles that are still read and can return at any time. There are still many new critics in American literary studies and, even where there are not, new criticism persists as an aspect of critical practice in many theoretically oriented critics, such as Felperin himself.

10 Narrative minimalism in North American writing has also been called "brand name" and "supermarket" realism. It is associated with the writings of Raymond Carver, Bobbie Ann Mason, Richard Ford, and Diane Schoemperlen, among others. For the student of narrative forms, dirty realism offers a suggestive contrast with magical realism which is, most often, maximalist. For a discussion of dirty realism with a particular emphasis upon the creation of fictional worlds, see Wilson, "Diane Schoemperlen's Fiction: The Clean, Well-Lit Worlds of Dirty Realism," *Essays in Canadian Writing* 40 (Spring 1990): 80–108.

11 Elsewhere I have argued that space is a *function* of the experience of reading

and that it can be indicated by surprisingly few signifiers. Even a few deictics might do the trick. The assumptions about worldlike qualities that a writer makes perform like axioms in the construction of the world. They are *not* axioms, of course, since they could be replaced and their replacement, or deletion, would not destroy the fictional world (only change it) as an analogous manipulation of axioms in any truly axiomatic system, such as a geometry, would necessarily do. But they are experienced as axioms. For that reason, I have called them pseudo-axioms. A pseudo-axiom is experienced, from within the text, as if it were a true axiom (though it is merely a convention). Try the experiment of reading through Italo Calvino's *Invisible Cities* (New York: Harcourt Brace Jovanovitch, 1978) while reflecting upon the spatial qualities of each city. Each city invokes distinct spatial conventions (which you will experience from within as pseudo-axioms) and the perception of fictional space changes accordingly. Calvino's fictional world is space-dependent, but highly metamorphic. See *In Palamedes' Shadow*, pp. 176–81, 246–47.

12 Gaston Bachelard, *The Poetics of Space*, trans. Maria Jolas (Boston: Beacon Press, 1969), pp. 9–10.

13 Georges Poulet, *Proustian Space*, trans. Elliott Coleman (Baltimore: Johns Hopkins University Press, 1977).

14 Ricardo Gullón, "On Space in the Novel," *Critical Inquiry* 2 (Autumn 1975): 11–28.

15 Seymour Chatman, *Story and Discourse: Narrative Structure in Fiction and Film* (Ithaca: Cornell University Press, 1978), pp. 96–145. Existents include all aspects of setting as well as characters and are opposed, in Chatman's analysis, to events.

16 Salman Rushdie, *Imaginary Homelands*, p. 118.

17 James Phelan, *Worlds from Words: A Theory of Language in Fiction* (Chicago: University of Chicago Press, 1981), pp. 115–16; cf. Phelan's *Reading People, Reading Plots: Character, Progression, and the Interpretation of Narrative* (Chicago: University of Chicago Press, 1989), pp. 1–10.

18 On the question of coherence criteria, see Doreen Maitre's brilliant introduction to the problem of possible worlds in fiction. *Literature and Possible Worlds* (London: Middlesex Polytechnic Press, 1983). See also, *In Palamedes' Shadow*, pp. 174–201. The most encompassing account of fictional worldhood yet written is Thomas Pavel's *Fictional Worlds* (Cambridge: Harvard University Press, 1986). Pavel's magisterial bibliography indicates the range of the scholarly response, in both literature and philosophy, to the problem.

19 For a recent analysis of texts as gamelike decision-trees that transcribe moves, see Thomas A. Reisner, "Game Universes and Literary Scenarios," *Recherches sémiotiques/Semiotic Inquiry* 12 (1992): 49–66.

20 Jorge Luis Borges, "Tlön, Uqbar, Orbis Tertius," *Labyrinths: Selected Stories*

& *Other Writings*, trans. James E. Irby, ed. Donald A. Yates and James E. Irby (New York: New Directions, 1964), p. 5.

21 Brian McHale, *Postmodernist Fiction* (London: Methuen, 1987), p. 44.

22 Lubomír Doležel, "Kafka's Fictional World," *Canadian Review of Comparative Literature* 11 (March 1984): 61–83.

23 Robert Kroetsch, *What the Crow Said* (Toronto: General Publishing, 1978).

24 Salman Rushdie, *Midnight's Children* (New York: Knopf, 1981); *The Satanic Verses* (Dover, Del: Consortium, 1992). Rushdie has written acutely on the Anglo-Indian language of *Hobson-Jobson*. See his essay in *Imaginary Homelands*, pp. 81–83.

25 Rushdie, *The Satanic Verses*, p. 5.

26 It is, of course, the writerly creation of this city, and the religious revolution taking place within it, that brought down the Ayatollah Ruhollah Khomeini's *fatwa* upon Rushdie. It would be pointless to argue that the city is a dream, indeed a dream within a fiction. The Ayatollah thought, and knew in advance, what he did not need to learn. It may even be that what most offended him was Rushdie's characterization of a hairy-legged Imam, whose "eyes are white as clouds," who rides Gibreel "like a carpet" to see his own city in the desert, and observes another revolution being fought in his name (211–15). On the inspiration for the *fatwa* and subsequent actions against Rushdie, as well as those taken on his behalf, see Carmel Bedford, "Fiction, Fact and the *Fatwa*," in *The Rushdie Letters: Freedom to Speak, Freedom to Write*, ed. Steve MacDonogh (Lincoln: University of Nebraska Press, 1993), pp. 127–83. For a discussion of *The Rushdie Letters*, see my review, "Supporting Salman Rushdie: The Politics of Counter-Attack," *Mattoid* (Australia) 46/47 (1993): 55–61.

27 The neutrality of the narrative voice seems like a necessary condition (more than being "important") for the creation of magical realist worlds. Kroetsch not only repeats that "people" are recalling the incidents of his narrative, but he employs stylistic moves to create an impression of an oral, or anecdotal, culture. The most noteworthy mannerism in *What the Crow Said* is apposition. For instance: "When it rained they played hearts, the young girls and Old Lady Lang, around the kitchen table" (p. 213). The mechanism of bardic apposition resonates rather loudly in Kroetsch's novel, but it fulfills its function of establishing distance and neutrality. Compare pp. 24, 34, 41, 96, 98, 110, 118, 138, 154, 173, 179, 188, 191, 201–2, 215. Mannerism and primitivism often bear a hand-in-glove relationship in magical realism.

28 García Márquez has stressed the oral qualities of his writing and its basis in the common anecdotes of Colombian peasant life. His grandmother, he remarks, "used to tell me things and my grandfather took me to see things," both of which experiences inform the governing image of *One Hundred Years of Solitude:* the grown man's memory of the small boy being led by his father to

discover ice. He also notes that his mother remembers the origins of many of the episodes in that novel and "naturally describes them more faithfully than I do because she hasn't elaborated them into literature." See Rita Guibert *Seven Voices: Seven Latin American Writers Talk to Rita Guibert* (New York: Vintage Books, 1972), pp. 23, 317. In one form or another, this has long been a common account of magical realism. It serves the interest of writers and (some) critics alike. Rushdie, oddly, also takes this position. See *Imaginary Homelands*, pp. 300–302.

Accusations of simplification run in both directions when discussing magical realism. Brian Conniff instructively discusses the history of labor relations and the railway in Colombia. Conniff thinks that textual accounts simplify, as ideological stratagems, in order to collapse distinctions (p. 168). See "Apocalypse in *One Hundred Years of Solitude*," *Modern Fiction Studies* 36 (Summer 1990): 167–79. Still, it seems equally simplifying to base an account of a fictional railway upon a historical one. Contextual accounts are, I think, usually always more popular, and more simple, than textual.

29 Carlos Fuentes, "La nueva novela latinoamericana," in *La novela hispanoamericana*, ed. Juan Loveluck (Santiago: Editorial Universitaria, 1969), p. 172. (My translation.)

30 Alejo Carpentier, "Problemática de la actual novela latinoamericana," in *Tientos y diferencias* (Mexico City: Universidad Nacional Autónoma de México, 1964), pp. 42–43 (my translation). He first uses this expression in the prologue to the first edition of *The Kingdom of this World*. See "De lo real maravillos americano," in *Tientos y diferencias* (pp. 96–112); and Tanya Huntington and Lois Parkinson Zamora's translation in this volume. In Carpentier's later writing, "baroque" comes to stand for the phenomena earlier indicated by his expression *lo real maravilloso americano*. For a study of Carpentier's theory of the marvellous American real, see Gonzalo Celorio, *El surrealismo y lo real-maravilloso americano* (Mexico City: Sep/Setentas, 1976). See also Elizabeth Kranz Pérez-Reilly, *"Lo real maravilloso* in the Prose Fiction of Alejo Carpentier: A Critical Study" (Ph.D. diss., Vanderbilt University, 1975), pp. 1–35, and Roberto González Echevarría, *Alejo Carpentier: The Pilgrim at Home* (Ithaca: Cornell University Press, 1977), pp. 107–29.

31 This constitutes one of Chanady's major points in *Magical Realism and the Fantastic* (see note 4 above). She observes that in *One Hundred Years of Solitude*, "there are many supernatural motifs such as flying carpets and levitation that have no more connection with an indigenous world-view than the transformation of Gregor Samsa into an insect in Kafka's *Metamorphosis*." See Amaryll Chanady, "The Origins and Development of Magic Realism in Latin American Fiction," *Magic Realism and Canadian Literature: Essays and Stories*, ed. Peter Hinchcliffe and Ed Jewinski (Waterloo, Ont.: University of Waterloo Press,

1986), p. 50. See also her essay in this volume. Lois Parkinson Zamora, in exploring similarities and lines of influence between Latin American and U.S. fiction, discusses the uncertainties involved in assuming that the former constitutes a single "cultural unit." See *Writing the Apocalypse: Historical Vision in Contemporary U.S. and Latin American Fiction* (Cambridge: Cambridge University Press, 1989), pp. 19–24.

32 Stephen Slemon, "Magic Realism as Post-Colonial Discourse," *Canadian Literature* 116 (Spring 1988): 9–24. (Subsequent page references are to Slemon's modified essay, reprinted in this volume.)

33 Brian Edwards, "Novelist as Trickster: The Magical Presence of Gabriel García Márquez in Robert Kroetsch's *What the Crow Said*," *Essays on Canadian Writing* (Spring 1987): 92–110.

34 Roland Barthes, *S/Z: An Essay*, trans. Richard Howard (New York: Hill and Wang, 1974), pp. 15, 21.

35 Jacques Derrida, *Of Grammatology*, trans. Gayatri Chakravorty Spivak (Baltimore: Johns Hopkins University Press, 1974), p. 290.

JON THIEM

The Textualization of the Reader
in Magical Realist Fiction

Among the mysteries of reading, the greatest is certainly its power to absorb the reader completely. — Victor Nell, *Lost in a Book*

According to Bloy, we are the versicles or words or letters of a magic book, and that incessant book is the only thing in the world; or rather it is the world. — Jorge Luis Borges "On the Cult of Books"

If we can treat the world as a text, as Leon Bloy did, does it follow that we can treat texts as worlds? An even bolder question. If we can literally read the text of the world, can we also enter, literally, the world of a text? An affirmative answer to the second question, which is based on the postmodern assumption that text and world are synonymous, seems preposterous. The idea that a person in the world outside of a text might literally enter the world of, let us say, a fictional text is counterintuitive. Yet this very idea lies behind a distinctive magical realist topos, which I will call a "texualization."

A textualization usually occurs in one of two ways. First, a reader or sometimes an author, or even a nonreader, will be literally, and therefore magically, transported into the world of a text.[1] Here are some literary examples. In Julio Cortázar's story "The Continuity of Parks" the reader of a mystery novel is, or becomes, a character, in fact the victim, in the novel he is reading. Michael Ende's novel *The Neverending Story* has as protagonist a boy who becomes so absorbed in reading a Tolkien-like fantasy novel that he enters its world and becomes its hero. In Woody Allen's story "The Kugelmass Episode" a professor of humanities at CCNY enters the fictional world of *Madame Bovary* and has an affair with Emma. It is, of course, a comparatist who first recognizes the unusual presence of Kugelmass in Flaubert's text.

A second type of textualization takes place when the world of a text literally intrudes into the extratextual or reader's world. In Calvino's *If on a Winter's Night a Traveler*, the first line of the eponymous inset story is a wonderful example of the second type: "The novel begins in a railway station, a locomotive huffs, steam from a piston covers the opening of the chapter, a cloud of smoke hides part of the first paragraph." Or in the same author's *Invisible Cities*, the city of Theodora, having exterminated all species of animal life, is invaded by the multitude of imaginary creatures found in the books of its library, by griffons, sphinxes, chimeras, hydras, harpies, etc.[2] In Borges' "Tlön, Uqbar, Orbis Tertius" the imaginary world of Tlön, about which the narrator has read so much, begins to invade and supplant the world of the narrator. And in Allen's story, Emma Bovary visits Kugelmass in New York City. A more elusive example of this type emerges in the last three pages of García Márquez's *One Hundred Years of Solitude*. There, Aureliano Babilonia, the last Buendía, reads about his own life and his family's history, in a manuscript written, before the events took place, by the magician Melquíades. The world of the manuscript he reads is indistinguishable from his world, the world of Macondo.

Before the twentieth century, textualization fables of either type are rare, and even in the postmodern era, that is the postwar period, when there appears to be a spate of them, such stories are, in fact, not very frequent. Yet two of them, Allen's and Cortázar's, have achieved a kind of canonical status.[3] The purpose, though, of this essay is not so much to catalog or to explicate in detail textualization stories as to explore some of the psychological, cultural, and philosophical implications of this magical motif.

As the preceding examples suggest, this essay will focus less on the textualization of real readers (if such a thing exists) or of fictive readers (ideal, implied, etc.) than on the textualization of fictional readers, that is, readers who are already characters in the fictional world of some text and who themselves get literally absorbed into the world of fictional stories at the hypodiegetic level. Furthermore, our attention will focus primarily on the *lector in fabula*. We will pay little heed to textualizations into nonfictional texts, such as happens to Woody Allen's Kugelmass, whom we last see, alas, in a textbook of Remedial Spanish, "running for his life over a barren, rocky terrain as the word *"tener"* ("to have") — a large and hairy irregular verb — raced after him on its spindly legs."[4]

I

The seeming impossibility of a textualization occurring in the world of the real reader signals the magical realist nature of this topos. To enter the world of a text literally, and not just literarily, is on the same order of impossibility as entering into the world *inside* a mirror or a painting.[5] At best you might break the mirror or poke a hole through the canvas with your finger, but with a text the very means of literal entry seem especially elusive. How *do* you get in? The mind has little other recourse than to the proverbial "black box," and indeed Kugelmass enters *Madame Bovary* through some such thing: a plywood cabinet in the office of the magician Persky.

Few writers have discussed even the possibility of a textualization, but those who have, even the most imaginative, treat such "events" as scandalous, extraordinary, unbelievable. Thus Proust in *Swann's Way* uses textualization as a metaphor to describe the astonishment of Marcel's aunt had she known Swann's true social status, namely, as a guest in the drawing rooms of counts and princes. She would, says Proust, "have found this as extraordinary as having had Ali-Baba to dinner, who, once alone, would re-enter his cave resplendent with unimaginable treasures."[6] Or consider Roland Barthes on a textualization of the second type: "suffice it to imagine the disorder the most orderly narrative would create were its descriptions . . . converted into operative programs and simply *executed*. . . . [T]he novelistic real is not operable."[7]

The wondrous passage from one world to another, the interpenetration of irreconcilable worlds: such phenomena seem incredible. They also partake of a dreamlike quality which aligns them with a host of other magical realist devices and motifs. Again Proust serves us as a valuable witness. On the first page of *Swann's Way*, Marcel describes how as a child he would put down his bedtime book and enter the dreamlike state between sleep and waking. At that point he would experience the dissolution of the boundary between the self and the world of the text: "it seemed to me that it was myself the text spoke of" ("il me semblait que j'étais moi-même ce dont parlait l'ouvrage," 9). Another indication of the oneiric resonance of textualization is the fact that, like so many other dream occurrences, it arises out of the literalization of a common metaphor. In English I can say, and I often do, that I have "lost myself" in a story, or that I am "totally absorbed" by a novel. Other Indo-European languages have similar idioms:

"mi perdo in un libro" or "il libro mi ha preso" an Italian will say, and a German might say "dieses Buch hält mich gefangen." In a textualization the reader is literally "absorbed by" or "lost in" a fiction.

The wide diffusion of these metaphors reflects, of course, an interesting and puzzling psychological phenomenon that often occurs in the reading of fiction. To read a "gripping" story is to feel transported into its fictional world. The intensity of my identification with hero or heroine, the depth of my desire or pity or fear, the keenness of my longing to visit Middleearth or Middlemarch impart, however briefly, the illusion that I am no longer reading, but that I am actually in the story. In "Continuity of Parks" Cortázar memorably evokes this experience of total immersion in a fictional text. His description serves as the psychological basis for the surprising textualization that concludes the story. Cortázar's reader reads a novel that spreads "its glamour over him almost at once." As he reads he tastes "the almost perverse pleasure of disengaging himself line by line from the things around him." Then comes the immersion: "Word by word, licked up by the sordid dilemma of the hero and heroine, letting himself be absorbed to the point where the images settled down and took on color and movement, he was witness to the final encounter in the mountain cabin."[8] Similarly, the author of *The Neverending Story* describes young Bastian Balthasar Bux's gradual immersion in the story, before the actual textualization occurs. The young protagonist finds it very difficult to return to reality after reading the story; he identifies strongly with Atréju the story's hero; and he both longs and fears to enter the imaginary realm of Phantásien.

In Victor Nell's important study of the psychology of pleasure reading, *Lost in a Book*, these fictional views of reader immersion are corroborated.[9] Not only does Nell find reader "trances" similar to dream states, he also describes reader immersion in terms that could also apply to textualization. This serves to confirm the notion that textualizations dramatize an interesting psychological puzzle arising from many readers' experience: the state of being in two worlds at once, in the book and outside of the book. Nell observes that "like dreaming, reading performs the prodigious task of carrying us off to other worlds" (2), and that when a person comes out of a reading trance, he or she seems to be "returning from another place" (1–2).

Nell sees reader trance as a result of pleasure reading, which he calls ludic reading. Let us say, then, that the trance of the ludic reader is the subjective mode or condition of textualization. The ludic reader longs to escape from the extratextual world into the text. Hence the pejorative expression "escapist reading." Or the ludic reader would like to have the world of the text cast its aura over the actual world, enlivening and enriching it. Textualizations in recent fiction do in fact draw on the kinds of texts that are most often the object of ludic reading: Cortázar's protagonist reads a conventional crime novel, Ende's a fantasy novel, and the Pink Panther in Kenneth Graham's textualization fable for children reads a ghost story. Kugelmass, though a professor of humanities, treats *Madame Bovary* as a cross between soft porn and soap opera. Ludic reading in particular seems to open readers to the pleasures and perils of textualization.

But the textualization of the ludic or naive reader is paradoxical. For it is as much the reader's detachment from, as his or her involvement in, the world of the text that enables the feeling of pleasure. Not being literally in the text permits the reader to enjoy the exciting and dangerous fictional world without having to suffer the consequences of living in this world. Upon this delicate balance between detachment and identification rests the traditional apologia for fiction reading: through it we gain experience without having to undergo the suffering and anxiety that actual experience in the extratextual world entails. In a textualization this balance is upset. The world of the text loses its literal impenetrability. The reader loses that minimal detachment that keeps him or her out of the world of the text. The reader, in short, ceases to be reader, ceases to be invulnerable, comfortable in his or her armchair, and safely detached, and becomes instead an actor, an agent in the fictional world. As our fables of textualization show, this condition poses a serious threat not only to the reader's pleasure and the integrity of the text read, but also to the reader himself.

II

Here I sit in my armchair, a comparatist, reading Cortázar's "Continuity of Parks." I read the first sentence: "He had begun to read the novel a few days before." A few sentences later I read that the reader is "sprawled in his favorite armchair." Reading the last sentence of the story I learn that a murderer is sneaking up behind the man in the armchair who is reading a novel in which, at that point, a murderer is sneaking up behind a man in an armchair reading a novel. I become keenly conscious of the fact that I too am sitting in an armchair reading a story about a man in an armchair reading, who is about to be murdered. Involuntarily I turn my head and

look behind me. Safe. But I have been reading a story about a man reading a story. The first man becomes, or is, the man in the story he is reading.
Am I, or could I become, the man reading the story about the other man
reading a story? Are we all in the same story? Are we all the same reader?

Textualization fables tend to make readers more conscious of the act
of reading itself.[10] Thus a textualization is a magical realist topos which
includes a pronounced metafictional dimension. As such, textualizations
explicitly raise in the reader's mind the following questions: what is the
ontological basis, if any, of a fictional world? What is the fictional basis
of the extratextual world? What is the reader's role in *constituting* both
worlds? The magical realist dimension of our motif transforms such questions into powerful fables. In Borges' "Tlön, Uqbar, Orbis Tertius," for example, the narrator reads about the imaginary country of Tlön. The intensity of his attention has the effect of causing the fictional world, literally,
to intrude into his own. Conversely, when Bastian Balthasar Bux returns
from his adventures in the fictional world of Phantásien, he has become
a different person. Fiction has remade him. As these examples show, textualization fables take seriously, and literally, questions of how far readers
may constitute fictional texts, or may be constituted by them.

We may find it helpful to consider this magical realist topos as one of the
most important narrative expressions of postmodern literary theory. Both
focus on the reader. As Jonathan Culler has written, contemporary critics
"have concurred in casting the reader in a central role, both in theoretical discussions of literature and criticism and in interpretations of literary
works."[11] With the disappearance of the author à la Barthes and with the
fall of the determinate text à la Fish, it seems that criticism now is making
its last stand with the reader. More than ever before, literary studies are
concerned with the transformative powers of the consciousness of readers
and of communities of readers, and with the bearing these powers have on
defining, evaluating, misreading, and interpreting texts. From Wolfgang
Iser through the whole spectrum of reader response criticism to Sandra
Gilbert and Susan Gubar, theorists have taught us to be more aware of
how the reader constitutes or activates the literary text.

A textualization is, in a sense, a magical literalization of a common
metaphor used to describe one effect of reading, that is, "total absorption"
in the story. If we move up to the level of professional literary discourse,
we find that this principle of literalization still holds true. It is as if magical realist authors read and take literally the metaphors used by literary

theorists. Here, for instance, is a sentence from Wolfgang Iser describing Roman Ingarden's influential theory of reading: "The literary work is more than the text, for the text only *takes on life* when it is *realized,* and furthermore the realization is by no means independent of the individual disposition of the reader." Iser goes on to say that the reader "sets the work in motion" and "animates" elements of the text.[12] None of these metaphors should be taken literally. The processes of activation and animation that Ingarden and Iser so colorfully describe take place in the reader's mind, not in the external world. Their essential point is that readers mentally fill in gaps in texts, give affect and excitement to elements of the story. In this sense, readers have to be considered producers, not just receivers, of texts.

Yet theories such as these do raise interesting questions about the extreme limits of textual activation. To what extent can a reader bring the world of a text into being? What role does reader identification or misreading play in animating texts? At one point Iser himself seems to approach the borders of magical realism when he asserts, without qualification, that "reading removes the subject-object division that constitutes all perception" (67). Fables of textualization explore the most extreme answers to such questions.

If we look, then, at these magical realist works as allegories of literary theory, what do they tell us about the nature of reader response? Or, to put the question another way, what else do they reveal about the interpretative preoccupations and anxieties of our time?

Most textualizations concern characters who are engaged in reading. Postmodern theorists and writers also focus on the reader, but there is another, little acknowledged, reason that writers in particular do so. They tend to identify with the reader. This strong identification arises out of the fact that postmodern writers and readers in general share the same condition. This is the condition of belatedness. A sharp, sometimes painful feeling of belatedness is one of the defining features of the postmodern outlook, as the term "postmodern" itself suggests. The postmodern writer is acutely aware of the great achievements of his or her precursors and is an avid reader of these precursors. Often, the postmodern writer is haunted by the feeling that if something has not already been written, then it is probably not worth writing. Many of the characteristic features and strategies of postmodern writing—such as the preoccupation with the past and historical representation and the reliance on quotation, pastiche, and parody—arise out of the feeling of being late and derivative.

Like the postmodern writer, the reader is also an epigone, a latecomer. Both seem to be on the receiving end of long, drawn-out developments. Both seem to occupy essentially passive positions. Both tend to see themselves as gleaners, rather than sowers or reapers. In the temporal sequence of author-text-reader, the reader comes last. The reader is thus positioned in relation to author and text as the postmodern writer is to his or her precursors and their texts. Hence the lavish attention given to the reader by such quintessential postmodern writers as Jorge Luis Borges, Umberto Eco, and Italo Calvino. Borges, perhaps the paradigmatic postmodernist, is a good case in point. His various authorial personae, his narrators, and his protagonists are usually inveterate readers. Borges himself seems to write little, and the things he writes tend to be glosses on his reading or stories about his or his avatars' reading. Borges is, however, famous for glorifying in his belatedness, in his derivativeness.

The great tradition of past writing puts the postmodern writer into the position of a reader, who may be thrilled by the riches of the past or feel overwhelmed by their authority. In the reader, the postmodern writer has found an ideal figure through which to explore the splendors and miseries of belatedness.

The real task of the postmodern writer is to transcend the readerly condition, to transform his or her belatedness into something original and interesting. The magical realist textualization of the reader is in fact a figuration and parody of this writerly process. Through a textualization, the fictional reader ceases to be a reader and becomes a character in the text. The reader magically transcends his or her status as passive epigone, breaking the iron law of temporal succession. Hence the wonderful anachronism of Kugelmass popping up in Emma Bovary's bedroom. In the sequence author-text-reader, the textualized reader leaps back to the prior, more powerful, and less belated textual position. Furthermore, by thus changing the text the author has produced, the textualized reader encroaches on the authorial position and assumes to some extent the authorial function of producer of texts. The simplest way in which the reader changes the text is by appearing in it. Like the successful postmodern writer, the textualized reader transcends the readerly condition.

But in doing so the reader becomes a rival and antagonist of the author. The textualized reader seems to represent a significant threat to the already tenuous authority of the postmodern writer. Ludic or otherwise, the *lector in fabula* may do to the postmodern text what the postmodern writer does to the texts he or she has read and rewritten.

This struggle or contest between author and reader, with the text as arena, may help explain the sad fate of so many textualized readers, who become victims, if not tragic figures. Kugelmass is last seen running for his life, chased by a "large, hairy irregular verb." Cortázar's reader in "Continuity of Parks" is about to become the murder victim in the world of the crime novel he reads. Borges in "Tlön, Uqbar, Orbis Tertius" laments the irrevocable destruction of the real world by the intrusive fictional world of Orbis Tertius. And the reader-author in Duranti's *The House on Moon Lake* becomes a wraith, imprisoned in the fictional story he invented. These textualized readers never return, it seems, to the extratextual world. If textualizations are closely related to dreams, then their specific type is usually the nightmare.[13]

The authors of textualization fables usually invent readers of the ludic type. The sort of fiction these readers consume is mostly escapist, and so it seems appropriate that such readers should literally escape into the world of the text. Yet the fact that these readers' intrusions are mostly disastrous suggests that the authors of textualization fables reject naive or escapist reading as an acceptable mode of reader response. Indeed, they seem to be saying that escapist reading in this form may be hazardous to your health. Escape into the world of the text is truly the ultimate reader response: it is the most extreme one but also the final one. Allegorically, these fables tell us that ludic reading distorts the text, if only by admitting some goofy reader into it. The strong emotional identifications that lie at the heart of escapist reading bring about a false, warped understanding of the story. True, all readers are to some extent producers of texts, but ludic readers tend to be incompetent producers. Their sudden appearance in the world of the text, which is their mode of production, establishes beyond a doubt their lack of discrimination.

Postmodern writers above all need to be concerned about the effects of ludic reading. This is because so much postmodern writing is attractive to the escapist reader. One of the most controversial aspects of postmodern fiction is its commercial viability. An astonishing number of postmodern works have become bestsellers in America—one thinks of fiction by John Fowles, Umberto Eco, García Márquez, and Milan Kundera—and this usually means that such works have succeeded in drawing large numbers of escapist readers. Many postmodern works are "double-coded."[14] One code, usually imitative of the forms of popular fiction, contributes to a wide readership and commercial success.[15] The second code, incorporating a whole range of experimental techniques and postmodern philosophical issues, is less popular and more adapted to serious readers, other writers, and those we might call the cognoscenti. Ideally, readers would relate to both code levels, but there is always the fear that the mass public will apprehend only the popular code and therefore read the work in a distortive, reductive way. The treatment of the escapist reader in textualization fables thus seems to be both an expression and an exorcism of this anxiety. The ludic reader, merrily misreading, lands in the world of the text, and, his or her status as reader having thereby been eliminated, the malefactor is summarily punished.

III

The magic in magical realism emerges from the interpenetration of irreconcilable worlds. Textualization is arguably the paradigmatic topos of magical realism because of the way in which it showcases this mystifying phenomenon. Texts may encompass worlds and worlds may be texts, but the way they come together, clash, and fuse in a textualization violates our usual sense of what is possible.

One more point before closing. Textualizations are a specific expression of the postmodern fascination with ontology, that is, the study of possible worlds. As used by Brian McHale and Thomas Pavel, the term ontology refers to the "theoretical description of a universe."[16] One of the central tasks of ontology in this sense is to explain how a world, such as that found in a fictional text, is constituted. Another task is, in McHale's words, the exploration of what happens when "different kinds of worlds are placed in confrontation or when boundaries between worlds are violated" (60). The violation of the boundary between the world of a fictional text and the extratextual world in textualization fables has many ramifications for inquiries into the relationships that are possible between possible worlds.[17]

As this study suggests, one of the main advantages of magical realism as a literary mode lies in its extraordinary flexibility, in its capacity to delineate, explore, and transgress boundaries. More than other modes, magical realism facilitates the fusion of possible but irreconcilable worlds. As the exemplary locus of such fusions, textualization fables will remain important sources for the study not only of postmodern poetics, but also of magical realism itself.

Notes

1 How literally should we take the textualization of a real, as opposed to a fictional, author? John Barth, for instance, intrudes as a character in his "Dunyazadiad," and John Fowles does the same in *The French Lieutenant's Woman*. Cf. Francesca Duranti's *The House on Moon Lake*, where the novel's protagonist, an author-translator, gets textualized into a story of his own invention. Before the twentieth-century, *Don Quixote* is perhaps the best-known locus of the textualization topos, a fact which helps explain, I think, the great appeal of this work for postmoderns. At one point Don Quixote meets Don Alvaro Tarfe, a fictional character from Avellaneda's spurious Second Part, which Don Quixote has read (see Cervantes, part 2, ch. 72).

2 Italo Calvino, *If on a Winter's Night a Traveler*, trans. William Weaver (New York: Harcourt Brace Jovanovich, 1982); Italo Calvino, *Invisible Cities*, trans. William Weaver (New York: Harcourt Brace Jovanovich, 1974), p. 10.

3 Allen's story has, for instance, been anthologized in the *Norton Anthology of Contemporary Fiction* and in the *Norton Introduction to Fiction*. It has also been widely discussed in recent criticism, by Jonathan Culler in *On Deconstruction* and by Brian McHale in *Postmodernist Fiction*, among others. Cortázar's "Continuity of Parks" is anthologized and discussed in Brooks and Warren's influential *Understanding Fiction* and has also received a good deal of critical attention.

4 Nor will we be able to deal with the "textualization" of spectators in dramas, as occurs in Tom Stoppard's play *The Real Inspector Hound* (1969) and in the plays of Pirandello. Woody Allen, "The Kugelmass Episode," in *The Norton Introduction to Fiction* (New York: W. W. Norton, 1985), p. 512.

5 Besides *Don Quixote*, the most important antecedent of textualization is to be found in the illusions of Baroque art, where an aggressive pictorial naturalism endeavors to obliterate the barriers separating spectator space and pictorial space, that is, the world outside of the painting and that within it. Just as a textualization eliminates the reader by absorbing him or her into the text, so Baroque illusionism works to do away with the spectator, who is compelled to become a part of, if not an actor in, the world inside the painting. The trompe l'oeil doors, the thumbs of subjects hooked around the frames of paintings, the protrusion of objects from the pictorial world into ours, the painted subjects who consciously observe the spectator—all contribute to the destruction of aesthetic distance and engender a mystique of participation.

Pictorial illusionism remains a force in the eighteenth and nineteenth centuries and contributes to the rise of the haunted portrait motif in Gothic fiction. In this early magical realist genre illusionism is taken literally: the subjects of paintings or sculptures come to life and enter the spectator's world. In this way, Baroque illusionism served to sustain the fantasy, so compelling in the nineteenth century, that just as the artist can give his deceased subjects a kind of immortality, so can the spectator in the grip of illusion activate the artistic representation and call it back to life. The indispensable guide to this literature is Theodore Ziolkowski's *Disenchanted Images: A Literary Iconology* (Princeton: Princeton University Press, 1977).

6 Marcel Proust, *Du côté de chez Swann* (Paris: Gallimard, 1954), pp. 26–27.

7 Roland Barthes, *S/Z*, trans. R. Miller (New York: Hill and Wang, 1974), p. 80.

8 Julio Cortázar, "Continuity of Parks," trans. P. Blackburn, in *Understanding Fiction*, Cleanth Brooks and Robert Penn Warren, ed. (Englewood Cliffs, N.J.: Prentice Hall, 1979), pp. 241–48.

9 Victor Nell, *Lost in a Book: The Psychology of Reading for Pleasure* (New Haven and London: Yale University Press, 1988), p. 73.

10 Theoretically, the awareness that we are reading should cause us to withdraw from reader trance, for one of the conditions of this state seems to be a momentary loss of consciousness that we are reading, that the fictional world is merely part of a book and therefore impenetrable. But then, with Cortázar's story at least, there is the trancelike impulse to look behind one's armchair. As if textualization had really occurred!

11 Jonathan Culler, *On Deconstruction* (Ithaca: Cornell University Press, 1982), p. 31.

12 Wolfgang Iser, "The Reading Process," in Jane Tompkins, ed., *Reader Response Criticism* (Baltimore: Johns Hopkins University Press, 1981), pp. 50–51.

13 The main exception to this pattern is Bastian Balthasar Bux, who does return to the extratextual world. For him textualization is a means of self-knowledge and self-realization. Cf. also the Pink Panther in Kenneth Graham's storybook for children. The Pink Panther makes friends with the ghost in the story into which he gets literally absorbed. It is perhaps significant that the main audience for both of these stories is juvenile.

14 See Matei Calinescu, *Five Faces of Modernity: Modernism, Avant-garde, Decadence, Kitsch, Postmodernism* (Durham, N.C.: Duke University Press, 1987), pp. 284–85.

15 The most explicit instance of a textualization as punishment for involvement in the popular code is found in Duranti's novel. The protagonist is a writer-translator who, in order to satisfy the mass reading public, fabricates an entire episode in his biography of a major fin de siècle author. The world of this fictional episode invades the translator's world and he proceeds to become a prisoner of the fictional world. Biography, like much postmodern fiction, is regarded by many as suspect, first because of serious doubts about its claims to accurate representation and secondly because of its propensity to be a popular genre.

Consider also the leftist critique of the double-coding of postmodern fiction. The argument runs that the writers of such fiction have sold out, that they have popularized and trivialized modernism for the sake of commercial success. Because such works are not sufficiently different from, or critical of, the late consumer capitalism out of which they arise, their value and their cultural usefulness are negligible.

16 Brian McHale, *Postmodernist Fiction* (New York: Methuen, 1987), p. 75.

17 For further discussion of ontology, or "possible worlds" theory, see Christine Brooke-Rose, *A Rhetoric of the Unreal* (Cambridge: Cambridge University Press, 1981); McHale, *Postmodernist Fiction;* and Thomas G. Pavel, *Fictional Worlds* (Cambridge: Harvard University Press, 1986). McHale discusses a number of textualization fables, including Cortázar's and Allen's (pp. 120–23).

JEANNE DELBAERE-GARANT

Psychic Realism, Mythic Realism, Grotesque Realism:
Variations on Magic Realism in Contemporary
Literature in English

Since the early 1980s when I was asked by my colleague Jean Weisgerber to contribute a chapter on magic realism in the literatures in English to a book which would cover different geographical areas and different fields,[1] I have been interested in the concept itself, but also increasingly dissatisfied with the way in which it is being used and misused. There has been a tendency in recent debates, especially after Stephen Slemon's influential article (which appeared in *Canadian Literature* a few years ago and is included here in revised form), to systematically consider the concept of magical realism "in its specific engagement with postcoloniality."[2] Slemon has had the indisputable merit of breaking new ground and of encouraging comparative analyses across postcolonial cultures including, in his own country, between English Canada and Québec. However, magic realism is not exclusively a postcolonial phenomenon, but a much older one whose various offshoots require more precise and specific definitions.

I would like to point out at the outset that one should perhaps refrain, at least when referring to contemporary works in English, from speaking of "magic realist writers," for magic realism is often used only sporadically in an author's oeuvre, and sporadically even in those of his or her texts commonly regarded as "magic realist." With a view to making the concept a little less confused and certainly more teachable, I have looked in detail at three novels — *The Infernal Desire Machines of Doctor Hoffman*[3] by the British novelist Angela Carter, *The Invention of the World*[4] by the Canadian Jack Hodgins, and *The Carpathians*[5] by the New Zealand poet and novelist Janet Frame — which at first sight have little in common apart from the famous label. The first can be read as a Gothic fantasy, the second as a regional and mythic novel, the third, clearly more experimental, as metafiction. All three are at the crossroads between novel and romance, all three contain a quest or an initiation journey as well as passages that, to a lesser or greater degree, depart from ordinary realism.

Faced with such a dead end, it occurred to me that it was becoming urgent to think out new categories that would leave more room for border-cases and help to situate any contemporary magic realist text, or part of a text, more accurately in a larger conceptual and terminological constellation. A close examination of the three novels led me to coin three additional concepts—psychic, mythic, and grotesque realism—that could eventually be applied to other magic realist works of fiction as well.

Angela Carter's *The Infernal Desire Machines of Doctor Hoffman* is the first-person story of Desiderio, an old and famous politician, who records the events of fifty years before when he became a national hero by ridding his country of Doctor Hoffman, thereby putting an end to the "Great War." That war had started when the Doctor's "infernal" experiments, which consisted in liberating the subconscious by making people's most secret desires materialize, opened a fracture in the real that promptly turned the city into phantasmagoric chaos. Nothing in it was what it seemed and "everything that could possibly exist, did so" (11). As a result of Hoffman's magic tricks with mirrors and clocks, it also became the "kingdom of the instantaneous" (18) as the usual notions of time and space were subverted, and images began to proliferate "along the obscure and controversial borderline between the thinkable and the unthinkable" (22). It was a battle between "an encyclopedist and a poet": the Doctor, "scientist as he was, utilized his formidable knowledge to render the invisible visible" (24), whereas his greatest enemy, the Minister of Determination, saw the city as "an existential crossword puzzle that might one day be solved" (25).

Desiderio, an out-and-out rationalist, was chosen by the Minister to find and assassinate the Doctor. Yet, as his name makes clear, he was not himself immune to desire and had unwisely fallen in love with the Doctor's beautiful daughter Albertina, to whom he dedicates the book we are reading. The pseudo-allegorical story of his obstacle-ridden mission parodies the romance convention. The freaks, grotesques, marginals, disguised or imaginary creatures who force their way into Carter's narrative clearly have a parodic function: they are meant to comment on the ways in which we construct our personal and cultural notions of identity, sexuality, and gender. Desiderio's selfhood, which should normally be central in a quest novel, is constantly subverted by the fact that, everything in the outside world being the projection of someone's desires, there is no way of demarcating his or her consciousness from that of others. Even good and evil are indeterminate. To Desiderio's question whether he casts Doctor Hoffman as God or Satan, the Minister of Determination replies: "As my parable suggests, the roles are interchangeable" (39). The liberated subconscious can itself become a new tyranny when it is no longer opposed by reason.

The book depicts in a parodic way the war (the American title is *The War of Dreams*, 1974) between reason and the irrational that has dominated European thought ever since the Enlightenment. Carter's models — de Sade, Swift and, of course, E.T.A. Hoffmann (like the Doctor, a great admirer of Mozart) — offered, in their own way and in their respective literatures, more or less shocking alternatives to bourgeois realism. In English fiction the war against reason was waged in the gothic novels and later in the "fantastic" reaction against canonical realism with such writers as Poe in America or Carroll, Stevenson, and Wilde in England. Late-twentieth-century English texts labeled "magic realist" reintegrate, as it were, into the realistic mode "fantastic" elements that have been excluded from the mainstream. They usually center on an individual whose fissured self renders him or her particularly sensitive to the manifestations of an otherwise invisible reality and whose visionary power can be induced by drugs, love, religious faith or, as is the case in Carter's novel, erotic desire. The "magic" is almost always a reification of the hero's inner conflicts, hence the vagueness of the spatial setting — Carter's novel is allegedly taking place in an unnamed South American country — and the thematic recurrence of elements linked with the initiation journey. *The Infernal Desire Machines of Doctor Hoffman* is an extreme form, almost a caricature of this type of novel.

For this particular sort of magic realism generated from inside the psyche — and sometimes referred to as "psychomachie" — I would like to suggest the term "psychic realism." It goes back to the earlier, European variety and can be found in the works of, among others, Massimo Bontempelli in Italy, Ernst Jünger in Germany, Johan Daisne and Hubert Lampo in Belgium, Julien Green and Julien Gracq in France. In contemporary literature in English there are examples of psychic realism in little Simon's confrontation with the "Lord of the Flies" in William Golding's novel, a curious fracture in the fabric of an otherwise entirely realistic novel; in the heightened visions of Gibreel (induced by religious fervor) and the hallucinations of Rosa Diamond (induced by loneliness) in Salman Rushdie's *The Satanic Verses*; in the maze in which the protagonist is lost in John

Fowles' *The Magus*, though here, as in Carter's novel, the magic is master-minded by a godlike impresario behind the scenes.

In Europe, magic realism has been more successful on the Continent than in Britain. "I think the main problem with magical realism in this country is a moral, or puritanical one," John Fowles writes; "what the British will not accept is that magic realists can have their cake and eat it — both 'bend' reality *and* be really serious." [6] Comparing it with its South American manifestations, Angela Carter remarked that British magic real-ism "has to draw on a much more *literary* and attenuated folkloristic tra-dition." [7] On the other side of the Atlantic, Alejo Carpentier had already sensed something similar in 1943 when, visiting Haiti after having lived for over a decade in Paris, he was struck by the contrast between the "mar-velous reality" of the Caribbean and the artificial way of "provoking the marvelous" in the Old World. [8] This led him to coin the term *lo real mara-villoso americano* to describe a "magic" reality not created by the imagi-nation or projected from the subconscious but inherent in the myths and superstitions of non-European populations and in the very topography of the Americas.

In the New World, where the climate is often less temperate and the landscapes more dramatic than in Britain, magic realism does indeed often display a deep connectedness between character and place. The Canadian Jack Hodgins' second novel opens with a tidal wave that washes over the little pulp-mill town of Port Annie on Vancouver Island and ends with a landslide that destroys the place; in Robert Kroetsch's *What the Crow Said,* a drunken farmer, caught in a blizzard on his way home from the tavern, tries to mount an imaginary horse and is found frozen, "plow-ing the snow," the next morning; [9] in Michael Ondaatje's *Running in the Family,* the grandmother Lalla, snatched away by the swollen river, dies in the flooded "blue arms of a jacaranda tree." [10] The interpenetration of the magic and the real is no longer metaphorical but literal; the landscape is no longer passive but active — invading, trapping, dragging away, etc. In his afterword to O'Hagan's *Tay John*, Ondaatje notes that in this and other prairie novels, "the landscape . . . is not a landscape that just sits back and damns the characters with droughts. It is quicksilver, changeable, human — and we are no longer part of the realistic novel, and no longer part of the European tradition." [11] "Mythic realism," Ondaatje suggests, would be a more apt way of portraying the west than "magic realism."

I would like to adopt the term "mythic realism" and apply it not just to the Canadian West but to all the countries that still possess "unconsumed space,"[12] where "magic" images are borrowed from the physical environment itself, instead of being projected from the characters' psyches. It seems to me that Ondaatje's term is a suitable one for Second World countries[13] from which indigenous cultures have largely vanished, even though they remain hauntingly present in the place itself.

At the crossroads between Carpentier and Ondaatje, the Guyanese Wilson Harris asserts like the latter that "landscape is not a passive creature."[14] In the story of one of his expeditions as a land surveyor he offers a good illustration of the magic sparking out of the physical environment. While he was gauging the Potaro river for hydroelectric power about a mile or so from the Tumatumari rapids, one of his anchors gripped the bed of the stream and could not be dislodged. Two years later, on another similar expedition, the anchor got caught again at exactly the same place, but this time the situation was more desperate, and the man ordered to sever the anchor rope was so frightened that he could not manage to do so. They joined efforts to pull, and out came not just one anchor but two, the second hooked into the one that had been lost there two years before. For Harris the atmosphere became at once magically crowded with all sorts of echoes and presences:

> It is impossible to describe the kind of energy that rushed out of that constellation of images. I felt as if a canvas around my head was crowded with phantoms and figures. I had forgotten some of my own antecedents—the Amerindian/Arawak ones—but now their faces were on the canvas. One could see them in the long march into the twentieth century out of the pre-Columbian mists of time. One could also sense the lost expeditions, the people who had gone down in these South American rivers. One could sense a whole range of things, all sorts of faces—angelic, terrifying, daemonic—all sorts of contrasting faces, all sorts of figures. *There was a sudden eruption of consciousness, and what is fantastic is that it all came out of a constellation of two ordinary objects, two anchors.*[15]

Later in *Palace of the Peacock*, the concrete anchors are translated into what he calls "a narrative fiction of juxtapositions" or "an architecture of consciousness."

Like Wilson Harris, Michael Ondaatje, and Alejo Carpentier, Jack Hodgins is very much aware of uncanny correspondences between character and place.[16] From Vancouver Island, and proud of sharing the same coastline as Gabriel García Márquez, Hodgins has never made a secret of his admiration for the Latin American novelists; he humorously acknowledges his debt to them by making the giant wave that invades Vancouver Island in *The Resurrection of Joseph Bourne* leave all sorts of Peruvian marvels behind. These include a godlike Peruvian sailor thrown naked on the soaked yellow daisies of Angela Turner's sheets and the beautiful Raimey, the "walking miracle" who turns the little town upside down. By having one of the Islanders refer to her as "that cormorant with the cheeky behind," Hodgins stresses the real-enough physicality of that magic visitant from another world, endowed by the earth-bound people of Port Annie with supernatural powers and indeed capable of bringing one of them literally back to life.

The obvious echoes of *One Hundred Years of Solitude* and *The Autumn of the Patriarch* throughout Hodgins' novel *The Invention of the World* probably explain why this novel was hailed as magic realist in the first place. There are, to mention only a few examples, the parallel between José Arcadio's foundation of Macondo and Keneally's foundation of the Revelation Colony of Truth on Vancouver Island, both at the end of a journey in search of, respectively, the sea and the promised land; Keneally's machine supposed to represent God and devised to impress the Irish peasants much as Melquíades' contraptions impressed the inhabitants of Macondo; the Year of Mist reminiscent of the four years of rain in Macondo; the mode of narration itself, at least in some of its sections, where the record of past events, in a plurality of voices, often begins with the now-famous "many years later" opening of García Márquez's novel, almost a trademark of magic realist narrative style.

Interestingly, these deliberate imitations of *One Hundred Years of Solitude* refer only to Keneally and serve to denounce the immorality of this bad "magician," who resorts to trickery only to exploit or manipulate his too credulous followers. They are part of the "invented" world that Hodgins opposes to the "created" one in the novel.[17] A close look at the different treatment of his two "ghosts"—Horseman, the better side of Wade, and Brendan, Keneally's *invented* twin—throws light on this distinction between the "creation" of the self, rendered through what I have called "psychic realism," and mere "invention," rendered through magic tricks. Keneally and his twin Brendan are very similar to the patriarch and his impostor-doppelgänger Patricio Aragonés in García Márquez's *The*

Autumn of the Patriarch. Horseman and Wade, on the other hand, are, like Dr. Jekyll and Mr. Hyde, two opposed and complementary facets of one character. Horseman is Wade's better self, his "exact duplicate" (152). His unexpected arrival at the wedding feast where he is reunited with his other half clearly signals Wade's "second growth," the fact that he has finally become whole, the "new man" worthy of the "new woman" he has just married. The change in this character who, throughout the book, has been pictured as a good-for-nothing and, indeed, as a small-scale re-incarnation of Keneally, is so literally *extra-ordinary* for the onlookers that only an intrusion of the supernatural can account for it. And for that mat-ter, only a supernatural apparition can turn the cacophonous brawl into such an immediate and "total silence" (353). This is a typical example of what I have called "psychic" realism, that is, a physical manifestation of what takes place inside the psyche. Only through an attentive sorting out of these different kinds of magic realism can one avoid such misinterpre-tations as Robert Kroetsch's, who misconstrues Horseman as death,[18] or Stephen Slemon's, who sees him as the ghost of Keneally.[19]

When it came to creating his unintellectual new Eve, Hodgins tapped the mythic potential of the still uncharted (at least on the literary maps) and largely "unconsumed space" of his native Vancouver Island. Like Wil-son Harris' concrete anchors, it provided him with his "narrative fiction of juxtapositions": Maggie's commune does indeed occupy the same space as Keneally's "Revelation Colony of Truth," itself created on the same physical space as the fake religious commune in which a historical Van-couver Island figure, the notorious Brother XII, enslaved his followers back in the 1920s. The configuration of the landscape also helped Hod-gins to give Maggie's experience a mythic dimension: a marginal from the start like Vancouver Island on which she lives and like Ireland where she has her personal "revelation of truth" (two green and rainy islands of ap-proximately the same size on the edge of a continent), Maggie becomes the "new woman" precisely because of her trans-island, that is, trans-individual quest. She dramatizes a central preoccupation in Jack Hodgins' fiction, the exploration of the mysterious region where two lives "overlap." This "overlapping" occurs at the very moment when Maggie gets rid of fabricated myths to accept the reality of Wade. In that epiphanic moment the magic realist collision of Wade's shoe on Maggie's map subtly shifts into hyperrealism as the shoe becomes flooded with the light of love: "this was like a child's shoe, plain and worn-over and scuffed, with water stains soaked into the sides, a white line like the edge of an alkali lake, like a child who has walked through puddles, playing. For a moment she wanted to touch it, to put her face down, to feel the childlike shape of it with her hands. She was tempted to brush the mud away, with her fingertips" (316–17). We are back momentarily to Franz Roh's rather indiscriminate use of "*magischer Realismus*," and "*neue Sachlichkeit*" (new objectivity). Nothing indeed is more "*sachlich*" than a shoe, but because it is illumined from inside ("*aus unsrem Innern*") in a particularly intense manner, this ordinary object acquires a heightened reality verging on weirdness. Personally, I see here a case of hyperrealism not unlike some passages in Canadian writer Alice Munro's stories or the technique of a Canadian magic realist painter like Alex Colville.

The magic realism of Hodgins' *The Invention of the World* combines "magic" occurrences à la García Márquez with psychic and mythic elements such as I have mentioned above. And it is complemented by what I propose to call "grotesque realism," a combination of North American tall tale, Latin American baroque, and Bakhtinian "carnivalesque." Grotesque elements are used to convey the anarchic eccentricity of popular tellers who tend to amplify and distort reality to make it more credible. Hodgins resorts to it in his use of the local voices that recount the most memorable events of the past. Thus the story of the bailiff of Carrigdhoun who, after receiving his mortal wound in the fight with Keneally, staggers down the mountains, leaving behind him a trail of blood "that scorched the grass and melted stones." Later "these stones formed a paved red trail from field to field the women would use whenever they went out to gather furze" (88). Magnified in each new retelling, such events come to assume epic proportions.

I would suggest, further, that "grotesque realism" be used not just for popular oral discourse but also for any sort of hyperbolic distortion that creates a sense of strangeness through the confusion or interpenetration of different realms like animate/inanimate or human/animal. Examples are the two vehicles crashing into each other like two prehistoric beasts at the beginning of Hodgins' novel, or the confusion between puppet and human figure in the central episode of Michael Ondaatje's *In the Skin of a Lion*. Hodgins' *The Invention of the World* ends with the "grotesque realist" lists of guests and gifts at the wedding of Maggie and Wade. In this particular context, the term "grotesque realism" recalls Bakhtin's carnival body, and beautifully conveys Hodgins' intention. This last section, entitled "Second

Growth," does indeed, like Bakhtin's carnivalesque, emphasize the regenerative power of a new communal and popular consciousness in a selfish and materialist world. At the same time the grotesque is for Hodgins a way of avoiding pomposity when he makes serious points, as he clearly does in the unfashionable happy ending of his novel.

To analyze Hodgins' novel along these lines reveals a much greater complexity and originality than merely placing it in a postcolonial context that fails to distinguish among different varieties of magic realism and thus reduces the scope of Hodgins' central metaphor. The "Colony" represents, in fact, the colonization and exploitation of others in all possible forms, from the unregenerate Wade's exploitation of naive tourists to all the false prophets who, like Keneally, claim to have had a revelation on a mountain top (91). Maggie's own revelation on the same mountain top is one of love, selflessness, and solidarity. Like another fictional Maggie — Ethel Wilson's in *Swamp Angel* — who immediately preceded her in the same "unconsumed space" of British Columbia (itself a magic juxtaposition!), Maggie Kyle manages to set up a generous and decentralized grotesque commune of "Krazies," the closest, Hodgins seems to say with tongue in cheek, one can ever hope to approach utopia.

Janet Frame, another "postcolonial" writer at the remotest edge of Empire, New Zealand, is more "literary" in her use of magic realism than Jack Hodgins. Her fascination with words and word games, her jumbling of different levels of reality, her relish for paradoxes and all manner of trickeries of language are quite unlike the folkloristic and popular magic realism of a Carpentier, closer to the playful erudition of a Borges or a Cortázar.[20] There is, however, no evidence that she has read, let alone been influenced by, these writers. Her very idiosyncratic language games convey a unique and intensely poetic vision of (post)modern culture. From her earliest works Frame has explored the interface between realms usually regarded as antagonistic: sanity and madness, life and death, language and silence. In her latest novel *The Carpathians*, the mimetic coherence of the text is constantly shattered by shifts of ontological levels and, twice, by magic realist occurrences that are actually epiphanic moments of heightened consciousness.

For years the protagonist Mattina Brecon, a well-off New Yorker, has literally "consumed" space by buying real estate all over the world; her latest whim is a place called Puamahara in New Zealand to which she feels attracted because of the Maori legend attached to its beautiful orchards.

The story goes that a young woman, chosen by the gods to retrieve the memory of the land, metamorphosed at her death into a tree on which the "Memory Flower" continues to blossom. Mattina settles in one of the detached houses of Kowhai Street, an epitome of modern New Zealand, planning to collect facts on its residents as raw material for her husband, a novelist suffering from a pathological writer's block.

The first fracture in the realistic surface of the narration occurs when Mattina's point of view is appropriated by her novelist-neighbor Dinny Wheatstone, who thus turns her against her will into a character in her typescript. At this juncture her thus far literal and jet lag-induced disorientation begins to affect her overall perception of reality as she is made to share Dinny's compressed vision of time and place. She begins to sense a mysterious presence in her room at night, "an animal of long ago and far away breathing near her in the dark" (79). Breaking all conventional rules of logic and physics, this magic invasion into her room hints at the existence, at another level of perception, of what Wilson Harris has called "some occult dimension" of the past.[21] We could, then, see here an extreme form of "mythic realism," a synecdoche for any possible encounter between Self and Other. What Mattina is experiencing is not just the "dreamtime" of the land's first people but, more generally, the poet's capacity to abolish distance and time and to identify with any other living creature for, as Dinny "Wheatstone Imposter" puts it, "in an imposter, all points of view are burgled because the imposter has no point of view" (51).

A second, even more disturbing occurrence takes place one night when Mattina witnesses the lethal effect of a phenomenon called "the Gravity Star" on Kowhai Street. As is generally the case in magic realism we are offered no explanation of events, and the calm distancing of the narrative voice makes us forget the implausibility of the strange happenings: "It was midnight when Mattina was awakened by the cries" (125)—the cries are those of her neighbors, but they sound like primitive wails or grunts, their eyes gleam in the dark like animal eyes, their clothes are in shreds and they seem to have forgotten human speech altogether. What falls on them from the sky looks like rain, yet is no real rain but a shower of linguistic particles, "apostrophes, notes of music, letters of the alphabets of all languages" (127). The next morning the empty street is impeccably clean, with no trace left of its residents; only a few minute letters on Mattina's tablecloth remain as evidence that she has not dreamed the nightmarish event. She herself, we are told, has escaped the midnight holocaust by "simply clinging like an insect at the point of destruction to the Memory Flower" (151).

These two magic realist episodes articulate Janet Frame's central opposition in the book between what she calls poetically the "Memory Flower" and the "Gravity Star." They are two key moments in a novel concerned with the clash, beyond all posts and all colonialisms, between two "global" views of reality, identical on the surface though in fact completely antagonistic: one is that of the poets, whose virtual creations ("orchards in the sky") are meant to enhance the natural organic connections between all living creatures, between past and present, between the living and the dead. The other is that of the electronic media whose technologically controlled world of all-at-onceness likewise abolishes distance and time but also obliterates the link with the past and the loving connection between people. Because they are steeped in the electronic culture of global communication, dominated, as Baudrillard has argued, by simulations and discourses with "no firm origin, no referent, no ground or foundation,"[22] the Kowhai Street residents are as ephemeral as the commodities so easily disposed of in their consumer society. Thus they disappear, without leaving a trace.

What is at stake in *The Carpathians* is nothing less than the survival of mankind. Janet Frame, with the hyperlucidity characteristic of her work, prophesies the apocalyptic end of an electronic culture that has penetrated the most remote places of the earth but is totally disconnected from organic reality. The last stage of Mattina's initiation takes place on a Maori farm or "marae" where an old woman answers her inquiry about weaving flax by saying that first she must "*know* flax," for flax is alive: "it *knows* about you. . . . [Y]ou must have a special feeling about flax to be able to grow it, cut it without making it bleed, scrape it without hurting it, and weave it without going against its wishes" (86). Beyond all the cleavages of cultures there remains a common language of nature (flax) and love ("a special feeling"), and the language of the poets ("Housekeepers of Ancient Springtime") which alone can counterbalance the semiotic babble of contemporary electronic culture and, ultimately, as the novel itself testifies, ensure survival. At the end of *The Carpathians* we learn that Mattina has never had any objective existence but is the verbal creation of her son John Henry, a novelist who wrote the book as a tribute to the parents he lost when he was seven years old. By the combined power of love and meaningful poetic language he has brought them back to life, just as

Mattina herself had been able, in her own small way, to re-member the dis-membered residents of Kowhai Street.

Like Dinny Wheatstone in the novel, Janet Frame is herself an "imposter" who handles paradox with playful dexterity. She humorously resorts to self-conscious artifice and to all the devices of postmodernist discourse to express her anti-postmodern stance. She debunks the postcolonial paradigm by blurring the center-margin distinction: what Mattina finds at the furthest antipodean remove from the center (New York) is not the "new" exotic world she had hoped, but rather an intensified version of her own, with which Kowhai Street Maoris and Pakehas alike are even more familiar than she is herself. By means of magic realist strategies, Janet Frame paradoxically manages to create a poetical superrealist vision of our Western culture in which the two worlds she opposed at the beginning of her literary career—"this world" and "that world"—are held in antagonistic balance.[23]

Compare, then, the variations on magical realism in the authors whom I have discussed. Angela Carter resorts to a parodic "psychic realism" to destabilize culturally constructed notions of identity and gender by showing that, like all human constructs, they are, in fact, projections of individual fantasies. Jack Hodgins experiments with a variety of magic realisms to stress the distinction between trickery and reality, invention and creation, and to reinscribe his protagonists' personal quests in a specific physical and cultural landscape of their own. Janet Frame, in one instance, carries "mythic realism" to its antipodean extreme to hint at the poet's all-encompassing vision of life and death. In the other instance, she carries magic realism to the border of fantasy and science fiction, where language (of both the Gutenberg and the Marconi galaxies) loses its roots in the human and disintegrates in a mere collection of unconnected particles. Significantly, the linguistic apocalypse cannot be fully placed in any of the categories discussed in this essay. Both "psychic" and "mythic" realism posit, for their projections from inside and invasions from outside, a link between human beings and the world, a backward and forward movement between the individual psyche and the psyche of nature. But in global electronic culture, the distinction between subject and object has been neutralized or turned into interchangeable equivalence. "Grotesque" realism, too, proves unsuited to Frame's vision, for it requires a sense of corporeality and community that has also been canceled in the electronic culture she describes.

The tidal wave of magic realism that invaded the novel in English at a time when some of its practitioners were speaking of its "exhaustion"[24] has undoubtedly led to a revitalization of the genre, pushing the limits of realism and displacing established relations of power in such a way that British literature has now lost its leading position while other literatures in English, breaking new ground and offering new paradigms, are coming to the foreground. It may seem strange, in a discussion of magic realism, that I have dropped the first term of the oxymoron and replaced it by alternative adjectives that in fact qualify the real. This is perfectly legitimate, however, for the magic and the real do not have equal weight in First and Second World fiction in English. All the texts I have discussed or alluded to devise ways of heightening the real, rather than doing away with it. Their authors often slip into the various modes of magic realism that I have elaborated here just at the point when they have something particularly significant to say, magic realism being thus, as it were, a post-modernist equivalent to the epiphanic moments of the modernists. Their fiction remains strongly anchored in the real and the moral—a far cry from a novel like *One Hundred Years of Solitude*. Even the few deliberate echoes of García Márquez's fiction in Hodgins' *The Invention of the World* are indirectly at the service of a moral vision.

Much as the Anglophone world wants to challenge traditional realism, it is not the Hispanic world. The pragmatic and puritanical Crusoe, not the well-balanced magic realist couple Sancho/Quixote, stands at the front door of its house of fiction. As for Friday, he has gone his own way, back to the "marvelous" reality of his native Africa, where novels like Ben Okri's *The Famished Road* clearly pull the balance in the opposite direction.

Notes

1 Jean Weisgerber, ed., *Le Réalisme magique: roman, peinture et cinéma* (Lausanne: L' Age d'Homme, 1987).

2 Stephen Slemon, "Magic Realism as Post-Colonial Discourse," *Canadian Literature* 116 (1988): 10 (p. 407 of the revised essay in this volume).

3 Angela Carter, *The Infernal Desire Machines of Doctor Hoffman* (1972; Harmondsworth: Penguin, 1982). Page references are cited parenthetically in the text.

4 Jack Hodgins, *The Invention of the World* (1977; Toronto: Macmillan Paperbacks, 1986). Page references are cited parenthetically in the text.

5 Janet Frame, *The Carpathians* (Auckland: Century Hutchinson, 1988). Page references are cited parenthetically in the text.

6 John Fowles, unpublished letter to Jeanne Delbaere, March 10, 1980.

7 John Haffenden, *Novelists in Interview* (London: Methuen, 1985), p. 79.

8 Alejo Carpentier, prologue to *El reino de este mundo* (*The Kingdom of this World*, 1949), published in amplified form in *Tientos y diferencias* (Montevideo: Arca, 1967), pp. 96–112, and translated in full in this collection by Tanya Huntington and Lois Parkinson Zamora.

9 Robert Kroetsch, *What the Crow Said* (Toronto: General Paperbacks, 1983), p. 31.

10 Michael Ondaatje, *Running in the Family* (1982; Toronto: General Paperbacks, 1984), p. 113. The landscape here is of course that of Sri Lanka.

11 Michael Ondaatje, Afterword to O'Hagan's *Tay John* (Toronto: McClelland and Stewart, 1989), pp. 271–72.

12 The European space can indeed, with very few exceptions, be regarded as "consumed" in the sense that technology has so completely invaded it that its mythic charge has been reduced to practically nothing; even the Greek island of *The Magus* has to be reenergized by Conchis' imagination. There remain a few spots of unconsumed space in remote places like Wales or Cornwall where the ancient myths still break through, as does, for instance, the Grail legend in the Glastonbury of John Cowper Powys. In general, however, the myths have to be projected from inside.

13 The term is used by some critics like Lawson, Slemon, and Maes-Jelinek to distinguish the former settler colonies like English Canada, Australia, and New Zealand from the Third World.

14 Wilson Harris, "The Fabric of Imagination" (1973) in *The Radical Imagination*, ed. Alan Riach and Mark Williams (Liège: Language and Literature, 1992), p. 76. Further page references are noted parenthetically in the text.

15 Wilson Harris, "A Talk on the Subjective Imagination," *New Letters* 40 (October 1973): 40–41, italics mine.

16 In "Separating," the first story in Jack Hodgins' *Spit Delaney's Island*, the magic derives from the uncanny correspondence between Spit's personal situation (his simultaneous divorce and retirement) and the strange question "where is the dividing line?" that he hears on a Pacific beach, not far from the rifted submarine ridge separating the continents. Like Harris' anchors, Hodgins' "dividing line" is a powerful concrete image borrowed from his own physical environment.

17 In an interview with Geoff Hancock, Hodgins opposes "Reality with a capital 'R' " to "this imitation that we are too often contented with. The created rather than the invented world. I didn't call my novel *The Invention of the World* because it is an arresting title. It is a story about counterfeits." *Canadian Fiction Magazine* 32/33 (1979): 47.

   One may wonder to what extent Hodgins himself was aware that his own "imitation" of García Márquez was used to characterize a shameless "imitator."

18 Robert Kroetsch, *The Lovely Treachery of Words: Essays Selected and New* (Toronto: Oxford University Press, 1989), p. 70.

19 Stephen Slemon, "Magical Realism," p. 412 in this volume.

20 This does not mean that other magic realist writers do not present reality as a construct. One has only to remember that *One Hundred Years of Solitude* is the dream of the first Buendía or the manuscript written by Melquíades and that Macondo ends when the last Buendía reaches the last page, or that during the amnesia plague the real world is replaced by a world of words.

21 Wilson Harris, *The Radical Imagination*, p. 87.

22 Jean Baudrillard, *Selected Writings*, ed. Mark Poster (Cambridge: Polity Press, 1988), pp. 6–7.

23 Marc Delrez has argued that the midnight holocaust is not magic realism but "superrealism," "an exacerbation in plastic terms of a change all too real in the modern world, but too insidious perhaps to be normally noticed." Though this may be the ultimate effect of the passage, the style and images in which it is couched are clearly not realistic. See Marc Delrez, " 'Boundaries and Beyond': Memory as Quest in *The Carpathians*," in *The Ring of Fire: Essays on Janet Frame*, ed. Jeanne Delbaere (Aarhus: Dangaroo Press, 1992), p. 214.

24 See John Barth, "The Literature of Exhaustion," *Atlantic*, August 1967: 29–34. Reprinted in *The American Novel since World War II*, ed. Marcus Klein (New York: Fawcett Publications, 1969), pp. 267–79.

PART III

History

JOHN BURT FOSTER JR.

Magical Realism, Compensatory Vision, and
Felt History: Classical Realism Transformed
in The White Hotel

The title of Seymour Menton's book on magical realism in painting reads like an urgent appeal to students of twentieth-century culture. As we look back over the wildly jumbled terrain left by all the modern movements in literature and art, suddenly Menton sends the message, *Magic Realism Rediscovered.*[1] To judge from the book's discussion of painting, this concept deserves a place of its own in the historical-typological vocabulary with which we isolate distinctive trends and try to emphasize their main defining features.[2] Because magical realism refers to an international cultural tendency, it is broader than any single group of writers and/or painters, such as English Vorticism, Russian Acmeism, or Dutch De Stijl. At the same time, it lacks the all-encompassing cultural scope of categories like modernism, the avant-garde, or postmodernism. Magical realism seems ultimately to belong with such intermediate terms as surrealism, expressionism, and futurism, all of which designate movements with a significant presence in several national cultures but with no pretension to characterize an entire epoch.

In a broader sense, students of culture in all periods should welcome magical realism as a rediscovery. As a term originally developed in painting and then extended to writing, it epitomizes one major approach to an international view of literature—the art historical model. This approach had come under serious attack in the early 1980s when Menton published his book; but now, after the emergence of the new historicism and cultural studies, it has once again become an important option. Just as art historians, freed by the nature of their subject from the constraint of linguistic boundaries, could identify and define international period styles in art, so comparatists and other critics seeking to transcend single national literatures might hope to correlate different traditions and arrive at overarching historical categories. Not poststructuralist theory and the linguistic model, which dominated efforts to define literature when *Magic Realism Rediscovered* was published, but a more empirical approach, through stylistic and cultural periodization, provides a key for general accounts of the literary. This approach originally looked to Heinrich Wölfflin's *Principles of Art History* as its single greatest prototype.[3] And here is where magical realism assumes a special symptomatic importance: as a critical term, it dates back to this very intellectual milieu. Faced in the 1920s with the cooler, more objective art that emerged after expressionism, the German art historian Franz Roh characterized this new kind of painting by using the dialectical method of opposing criteria which Wölfflin had originally applied to the shift from Renaissance to Baroque.[4] For literary and cultural historians, therefore, the present interest in magical realism gives a new currency to problems of historical thought and periodization that are deeply embedded in their disciplines.

The issue of magical realism thus takes us back to the recurrent dilemma of history versus theory. Debate would probably show that the dilemma is a false one, that theoretical positions and historical insights coexist in a complex state of mutual interdependence, but such a debate is not my purpose in this essay. Instead, I propose to examine the implications of one specific case. I will assume that cultural history on an international scale is both possible and necessary despite its difficulty; that it cannot dispense with periods and movements; and, more specifically, that it is useful to have a historical label like magical realism. In that case, new critical tasks come to the fore: as part of defining what the label means, we need to test its applicability in widely varied cultural contexts and to try to grasp its relation to other historical terms.

In both of these areas my choice of a specific case, the British novelist D. M. Thomas' *The White Hotel* (1981), provides special insight. We shall see later the important ways in which the main character's psychological illness illuminates the relation between magical realism and the classic realism of the nineteenth-century novel. This relation is crucial, for critics have sometimes tried to align magical realism with postmodernism, as a particular movement within a larger epoch. But the two terms are semantically quite different: whereas "postmodern" fuses a critique of early twentieth-century modernist literature with broader questions about modern Western history since the Renaissance, "magical realism" embodies a certain polemical stance toward realism. But before we can pursue this issue, we must first consider how *The White Hotel* relates to magical realism itself. Instead of being a typical example like paintings by Henri Rousseau (see Menton, 57) or de Chirico (45), or novels such as García Márquez's *One Hundred Years of Solitude* (22), Thomas' novel is eccentric. It stands at one extreme limit of the movement, and thus sharpens critical understanding by forcing us to reexamine conceptual boundaries and assumptions.

I

If we review the unusually varied array of cultural signposts with which *The White Hotel* greets its readers, none of them has much to do with magical realism. In the epigraph, which quotes some lines about the Irish Civil War by the later, more modernist Yeats, Thomas presents himself as a British man of letters. By referring to Yeats' evocation of bitter political hatred, he sets the stage for the harsh events of modern European history to be treated in *The White Hotel*.[5] Meanwhile, at the back of the title page, Thomas includes a special note of acknowledgment which recalls his position as an admirer and translator of Russian literature. In the scene which presents an episode from the Jewish Holocaust, he has drawn on the documentary realism of Kuznetsov's *Babi Yar* (1970), especially on Dina Pronicheva's eyewitness account of mass executions in the Babi Yar ravine of Kiev (vi). But Thomas' self-proclaimed affinities with poetic modernism and documentary realism do not add up to magical realism, and it is hard to square the British Isles and Russia with a movement that has flourished on the European continent, in Latin America, and in the United States.

Even more problematic is Thomas' emphasis on Freud. Sandwiched between the acknowledgment of Kuznetsov and the Yeatsian epigraph, a special "Author's Note" draws attention to the role that "the great and beautiful modern myth of psychoanalysis" plays in *The White Hotel* (vii–viii). And Thomas begins the novel itself with a prologue consisting of fictitious letters by and about Freud (3–12), conceives of part three as a Freudian case history of the heroine Frau Lisa (89–144), and eventually has her refer to the Wolf Man as "a kind of Christ figure of our age" (193). These attitudes place Thomas and the magical realists on opposite sides of a major divide in twentieth-century speculative psychology. As Menton explains, "The juxtaposition of magic and realism is clearly an artistic reflection of the psychological-philosophical ideas of Carl Jung" (13), and of course Jung became a major critic and opponent of Freud's. By contrast, an interest in "individual Freudian case-studies" is "more typical of surrealism" (35) and thus represents another modern movement entirely. No meaningful direct connection, either artistic or intellectual, seems to join *The White Hotel* with magical realism.

This impression changes, however, if we turn from the novel's cultural affiliations to its historical subject matter. Unlike the epigraph from Yeats, which views recent European history through the lens of immediate national experience, Thomas chooses a story that is not British but Russian and Central European. His heroine, Frau Lisa, whose mother is a Polish Catholic and whose father is a Russian Jew, grows up in Odessa, then spends some years in St. Petersburg, and finally moves to Vienna where she marries an Austrian German just before World War I. This marriage soon breaks up, and she is suffering from a severe case of hysteria by the time Freud treats her in 1919 and 1920. Frau Lisa then pursues a musical career until she returns to the Soviet Union in the 1930s, when she marries and settles in Kiev.

Missing from this summary is the changing tempo of the narrative, which leads to a reshaping of Thomas' historical material. If some episodes are treated at great length, others are drastically abridged, with the result that *The White Hotel* tends to focus on key events in the German-speaking world. For example, the Russian Revolution of 1905 is not described directly or in any detail, since it figures in the story only as the source of a heavily censored trauma in the heroine's memory. On the other hand, as the setting for Frau Lisa's breakdown and Freud's cure, the Austrian experience of World War I and its aftermath receives full attention during several sections of the novel. Later on, the rise of Stalin remains in the background, told not shown, though its effects on Kiev in the 1930s are readily apparent. After Hitler's invasion, by contrast, the arrival of German occupying troops is a dramatic event, and then the final solution begins, as rendered in searingly direct narration. Frau Lisa dies in the ravine of Babi Yar, the victim of a mass execution organized by a Nazi *Einsatzgruppe*.

Thomas' decision to highlight the Central European experience is significant, because in doing so he has recreated the distinctive historical conditions which originally led to the emergence of magical realism. As Menton suggestively argues, magical realism grew out of the "tremendous despair" and the "crushing defeats" that, in different ways obviously with different groups, molded the lives of people in and around the German-

speaking countries during the two world wars (10). These special conditions have since been greatly broadened. The origins of magical realism
in an intractable and agonizing historical situation help account for the
movement's vitality after mid-century, at least in painting, which Menton
interprets as a response to the Cold War and the continuous threat of an
atomic holocaust (14, 86).[6] In other words, magical realism has as an unspoken historical premise the same or similar experiences of extremity—
of random victimization, of powerlessness, of hysteria and panic before
unmanageable events—as the ones Thomas so emphatically foregrounds
in the German sections of *The White Hotel.*

Even more important than these historical parallels, Thomas and the
magical realists both reacted in the same way to extremity. As Menton explains, the magical realists characteristically responded to the harshness
of modern history by developing a compensatory vision. They sought to
create in their art a "peace and tranquillity" that had been destroyed by
events (10). This aim closely mirrors Jung's doctrine of the collective unconscious, which works through artists and other spiritual leaders at any
given period in an effort to heal "its bias, its particular prejudice, and its
psychic ailment." Or, in Northrop Frye's restatement of the Jungian position, literature and art have the psychic function of "driving toward a
renewing transformation in the teeth of all probability."[7]

A similar improbable effort to rectify the irremediable characterizes the
controversial final section of *The White Hotel.* At the end of the previous
section, following a bleak recital of the horrors of Babi Yar, an omniscient
voice has broken in, invoking psychological and spiritual values reminiscent of Jung: "But all this had nothing to do with the guest, the soul,
the lovesick bride, the daughter of Jerusalem" (253). Then, in the final
section, in a realm of dream or afterlife that stands beyond history, the
murdered victims of Babi Yar do take the ardently desired train trip which
the Nazis had falsely promised them as a way of assembling them for execution. Moreover, though the section is called "The Camp" and initially
seems to evoke later stages of the Jewish Holocaust, their destination is
a genuine place of healing. At last, in the midst of this Jungian compensatory vision, Freud reappears. But now his authority is greatly reduced:
his diagnosis of Frau Lisa's hysteria no longer seems valid, and he himself looks "dreadfully ill and unhappy" (260–61). Here, though the final
effect of "The Camp" is too fantastic to qualify as magical realism in Menton's terms,[8] Thomas has at least adopted a basic premise of Jung and the

magical realists. And, in showing that he is not a Freudian on all points, he has resolved the question left hanging in the prologue to *The White Hotel.* For, despite the Freudian "Author's Note," Thomas began the novel by raising the issue of Jung's challenge to Freud, by including a curiously noncommittal letter that described tensions between the two psychologists on their American trip of 1909.[9]

On balance, therefore, *The White Hotel* does have one important point of contact with magical realism. To be sure, the novel's position with respect to this broad tendency in twentieth-century culture is basically eccentric: too many of Thomas' main affiliations, and especially his dominant psychological outlook, lie elsewhere. Still, when the book moves in the last section toward a compensatory response to the harshness of Central European history, it has reenacted both the original experience that produced magical realism and the characteristic gesture with which magical realists confronted that experience.

II

Within the overarching compensatory vision that aligns *The White Hotel* with magical realism, one prominent and even startling motif permits a further sharpening of critical understanding. I am referring to Thomas' depiction of Frau Lisa's psychological illness, which comes to suggest crucial historical meanings as her story unfolds. These historical meanings give a sharp new twist to an important strategy in the nineteenth-century realistic novel. This transformation of earlier fiction will illuminate the process of cultural change and will clarify the distinction between the elements of magical realism in *The White Hotel* and some basic assumptions of classic realists like Stendhal and Tolstoy.

Frau Lisa originally came to Freud with hysterical symptoms that included sharp pains in her left breast and near her pelvis. In the two sections of the novel that record her fantasies — the poetic "Don Giovanni" and her reworking and expansion of the same material in prose for "The Gastein Journal" — these symptoms express themselves in various ways, as grotesque images of breasts and wombs or as secondary characters with injuries to these organs. Even more prominent among her fantasies are accidents involving falls from a great height or live burial in avalanches. But Freud's analysis of Frau Lisa in "Frau Anna G.," though helpful to her in many ways, fails to explain either these catastrophes or her hysterical symptoms. His method as an interpreter is etiological, and because he searches for an original trauma from which all else developed, he does not consider the future. This future-oriented meaning for Frau Lisa's symptoms and fantasies is, of course, her death at Babi Yar. While lined up with other victims on a narrow ledge, she first avoids being shot by jumping into the ravine. Then, as she lies injured from the fall, a robber kicks her violently in the breast and pelvis; finally, just before her death, she faces being buried alive. Her hysteria turns out to include a subliminal foreknowledge of her fate, and so the symptoms she asked Freud to treat actually represent physiological clairvoyance. Appropriately enough, as the novel closes with the compensatory vision of the camp, we learn that her sojourn there has succeeded in healing the sharp pains that marked her encounter with modern history.

This motif of Frau Lisa's physiological clairvoyance is Thomas' version of "felt history," a term I use to designate one powerful way that literature can depict history. Felt history must be distinguished from official history with its attention to leaders, its overview of events, or its analysis of underlying trends. And it should also be distinguished from emotions or feelings, since history's psychological effects are usually less dramatic and revealing than its immediate feel, its physical impact on the body and the senses. In essence, then, felt history refers to the eloquent gestures and images with which a character or lyric persona registers the direct pressure of events, whether enlarging and buoyant or limiting and harsh. In this broad sense, of course, any critic who is sufficiently judicious in defining the historical context of a work could interpret most literature as felt history. But the term has special relevance for nineteenth-century realism and its successors. Because this fiction has such strong historicizing ambitions of its own, it refers explicitly to various social, political, and economic issues which, taken together, build up an elaborate historical context within the work itself. Then, as this context reacts directly on the characters in the novel, history and literature have an opportunity to come together with unique specificity and force. In nineteenth-century realism, felt history can be more than an interpretive construct by the critic; it becomes an integral part of one's reading experience.

Brief discussion of several realist works whose characters undergo harsh historical experiences will at once illustrate this concept and provide parallels with which to gauge Thomas' achievement in *The White Hotel*. Among the early models for realism, certainly Stendhal's *Red and Black* succeeds brilliantly in realizing the possibilities of felt history. This "Chronicle of 1830," as Stendhal calls it in the subtitle, gives a reasonably full picture of a specific historical milieu: from the provinces in Part I to Paris in Part II, we see Restoration France, with its uneasy aristocrats, its reactionary cabals, and its massive repression of the revolutionary and Napoleonic past. But a panoramic view of this kind does not capture the feel of history. The full moral squalor of the Restoration only becomes explicit in the scene where Mathilde de la Mole, the cynosure and apex of the whole society, catches sight of the Count Altamira at a magnificent ball. He is a political exile from Naples, condemned for his role in a liberal conspiracy, and Mathilde reflects sardonically that at least his death sentence, unlike the honors of Restoration France, was a distinction that could not be bought.[10]

As the novel ends and Stendhal's hero Julien Sorel is beheaded, this witty sally by a bored and impertinent young noblewoman has become prophetic. To be sure, Stendhal describes the execution itself in an understated, summarizing phrase: "Everything proceeded simply, decently, and without the slightest affectation on his part."[11] But the abrupt turn in Julien's fortunes, from general acknowledgment as a nobleman himself to an accusation of murder, has produced an equivalent feeling of violent termination at the level of narrative tempo. So sudden a plot reversal can be as shocking as the most graphic description, and not surprisingly the end of *Red and Black* has generated much controversy. From our perspective, however, Stendhal's narrative technique has brilliantly captured the feel of the descending blade of the guillotine, which itself serves to reveal the pressure of the times on Julien Sorel. For during his trial Julien's open references to Restoration anxieties about the social order have driven home the point that his death bears witness to a fearful and repressive epoch.

Like Stendhal, whom he admired, Tolstoy creates a broad historical picture of the contemporary world in *Anna Karenina*. He portrays a society in transition: in the wake of Tsar Alexander's great reforms of the 1860s, Russia is being Westernized and modernized. As in the older Russia of Tolstoy's previous novel *War and Peace*, the upper classes imitate European models in everything from food and their notions of marriage to the use of foreign languages in conversation and the importation of intellectual fashions from abroad. But in *Anna Karenina*, following the liberation of the serfs and other reforms, the European influences now include such fundamental changes as modern Western notions of citizenship, legal procedure, and ownership. At the same time, economic development is creating new industries and entrepreneurs and covering the country with railroads, leading to a decline of the landed gentry, the class to which Tolstoy's main characters belong.

Though explicit, all of these historical factors remain in the background of *Anna Karenina.* Throughout *War and Peace* Tolstoy had fought a running battle with official history, and in the famous opening to this novel — "All happy families are alike but each unhappy family is unhappy in its own way" — he announces his intention of focusing on private life. Nevertheless, the historical situation does break into the family sphere. This is especially true with Anna, whose terrifying nightmares express more than submerged guilt and anguish at her tangled commitments to the two Alexeis, one her husband Karenin, the other her lover Vronsky. Thus, in her recurrent dream of a Russian peasant who bends over some iron and mumbles in French, the obscurely menacing images correlate with issues presented elsewhere in the novel, most notably the accounts of agricultural problems after the liberation of the serfs, the references to new industrial ventures, and the scenes portraying Russian dependence on European models.[12] The result is an imaginatively powerful but ominous vision of the large transitions that frame the various family dramas.

Anna's nightmares qualify as felt history because, by translating Westernization into vivid images, they dramatize the psychic costs of social change. The final scene of her suicide (an anecdote of a similar death had given Tolstoy the original idea for the novel) is even more graphic. Though Tolstoy refuses to linger over the details, he does succeed in showing the crude impact of historical forces as they overwhelm the personality. First he emphasizes that Anna crosses herself before throwing herself beneath a passing train, a gesture that momentarily restores her sense of the richness of life. But her eyes remain fixed on the wheels of the passing cars, whose hypnotic effect stifles this new openness to life. So she jumps anyway, and as she dies her psychic inertia reappears as a physical presence, in the "huge and relentless" force of the train that crushes her.[13] To the extent that railroads have come to epitomize the new Russia in the world of this novel, Anna's suicide is thus the culminating and decisive expression of felt history. Of course, her death is above all a moving human tragedy, and also suggests more than Tolstoy probably intended about the situation of women in Western culture. Even on the historical plane, Anna's fate does not exhaust the range of responses shown in the novel, which also tells the story of Anna's brother Stiva Oblonsky, with his easy ability to move with the flow of events, and of the hero Konstantin Levin, who manages to stand against the current. But because Anna has been swept away, she is the character who reveals the pressure of the times the most directly.

For another example of felt history we should turn to Thomas Mann. Mann, of course, is a pivotal figure in the history of the novel, for he is a twentieth-century innovator often linked with modernists like Joyce and Proust, but he is also closely tied to nineteenth-century realism and to Tolstoy in particular. For our purposes he is especially important because his historical subject matter closely parallels *The White Hotel*. Just as Frau Lisa foresuffers the Holocaust, so several of Mann's stories and novels convey his sense of possible disaster in Germany and Central Europe.

Death in Venice is the key work. Though published in 1912, this story begins prophetically by alluding to diplomatic crises that threaten a European war and ends by depicting an utterly demoralized society. City officials in Venice have decided to cover up a cholera epidemic that would hurt the tourist trade, but their lowered public standards spread through the city, resulting in increased crime, debauchery, and murder. And Mann's hero Aschenbach, the descendant of officials himself and an honored representative of modern Germany, condones and, in his dreams at least, participates in the sinister Saturnalia. This premonition of social crisis becomes direct experience in the scene where a Neapolitan street-singer, insolent and vaguely criminal, performs before Aschenbach and other tourists at the Grand Hotel. As a finale he sings a laughing song that aggressively mocks the audience yet sweeps it along with him, dissolving all social and moral distinctions to produce a nihilistic mood that Mann calls "an unfounded mirth . . . feeding on nothing but itself."[14] The street-singer's infectious yet destructive laughter has translated the cholera epidemic and its implications of social collapse into a vivid psychic-physiological experience. This emphasis on eloquent bodily sensation, though less immediately life-threatening than Julien's decapitation or Anna's suicide beneath the train, has continued the tradition of felt history.

Thirty-five years later, in his novel *Doctor Faustus*, Mann himself confirmed the prophetic implications of this scene. The novel tells the story of the fictitious German composer Adrian Leverkühn, who lives through the years of crisis during and after World War I but goes insane before the rise of the Nazis. These later events do enter the book, however, through the narrator, a close friend of Leverkühn's who decides to write his biography during World War II and who comments freely on his own situation. In the novel Mann presents the inner meaning of recent German history as demonic, particularly when he focuses on Leverkühn's imagined interview with the devil, which occurs at the very middle of *Doctor Faustus*.[15] The devil appears to Leverkühn in three shapes, the first one being a pimp, whose insolent and vaguely criminal manner recalls the street-singer in *Death in Venice*. But in the end he takes the form of a theologian, whose discourse on the tortures of hell correlates with historical material presented elsewhere in the novel to evoke the worst features of the Nazi regime: "Every compassion, every grace, every sparing, every last trace of consideration for the incredulous, imploring objection that you verily cannot do so unto a soul: it is done, it happens."[16] Only the sufferings of the damned can capture the feel of this epoch of extremity. The theologian has proclaimed the fulfillment of that dissolution of traditional restraints and that advent of nihilism so vividly bodied forth by the street-singer's aggressive laughter.

In its relation to nineteenth-century realism, Flaubert's *Madame Bovary* is just as problematic as Mann's work. But felt history does figure prominently in a famous realistic reading of the novel, written by a critic who, like Mann, became an exile from Nazi Germany. I am referring to Erich Auerbach, whose classic study *Mimesis* does not actually use the phrase "felt history" but nonetheless illustrates the concept very well. Auerbach's discussion of *Madame Bovary* focuses on a paragraph at the end of Part I where Emma's dissatisfaction with her marriage seems to crystallize. She is at the dinner table, and direct sense impressions abound — a smoking stove, a creaking door, the oozing walls, the damp floor tiles. These impressions then coalesce to reveal a special psychological state in which vague lethargy passes over into definite repulsion: "with the steam from the boiled beef, there rose from the depths of her soul other exhalations as it were of disgust."[17] Having shown the close connection between Emma's mood and the images around her, Auerbach then goes on to argue that even though Flaubert is less explicit than other realists in referring to official history, still he does register the pressure of his times. His novels provide real "insight into the problematic nature and the hollowness of nineteenth-century bourgeois culture" (490), for they portray a "political, economic, and social subsoil" that "appears comparatively stable and at the same time intolerably charged with tension" (491). Auerbach concludes that Flaubert's power as a realist lies in his ability to communicate the "concealed threat" on two levels at once, "both in the individual occurrence and in his total picture of the times" (491). In short, Auerbach has linked Emma's incipient feelings of disgust, as expressed most vividly by the images at the dinner table, with the inner picture of her epoch as portrayed throughout *Madame Bovary*. It is precisely this interaction of specific sense impressions with a broad historical context that defines the tradition of felt history.

III

These memorable instances of felt history in realistic fiction immediately raise questions about Thomas' achievement. Despite his success in conveying the intense horror of the Holocaust, largely through a skillful use of Dina Pronicheva's experiences as conveyed by Kuznetsov's *Babi Yar*, Thomas' portrayal of Frau Lisa's death can seem overly crude and strident as an image for the pressures of history. In part, simple differences in historical vision or knowledge help account for the distinctive tone of this scene. Flaubert's epoch of boredom has to appear subtle and low key alongside an epoch of extremity, while Mann's forebodings about the German future in *Death in Venice* are necessarily less graphic than Thomas' certainty after the fact. And yet, because Auerbach and Mann themselves lived through the success of the Nazis, their insights into the sources of extremity are more detailed and provocative. Thus Auerbach can present Flaubert as the diagnostician of middle-class boredom charged with threatening possibilities, while in *Doctor Faustus* Mann acknowledges the relevance of his earlier picture of demoralization and nihilism spreading infectiously through an entire society. Both of these writers maintain a sense of historical process, while Thomas risks overawing the reader with the horrifying result.

Moreover, Thomas' description of the violence inflicted on Frau Lisa at Babi Yar—which includes not only the blows to her body already mentioned but also a gruesome bayonet rape—is brutally explicit. He has deliberately chosen this approach, for comparison with the documentary material in Kuznetsov shows that Dina Pronicheva experienced no such rape.[18] Here a contrast with Stendhal and Tolstoy is illuminating. Though Anna's and Julien's deaths are equally painful to imagine, the details are left to the reader, whose strong sense of shock springs rather from abrupt reversals of mood or expectation: that last ineffective flash of love for life before Anna dies and that sudden change in the plot of *Red and Black*. Defenders of Thomas' method might argue that Frau Lisa's encounter with history has to be brutal if it is to represent a scene of mass execution like Babi Yar, or even the Holocaust as a whole. And it is also true that such violence against a woman connects meaningfully and ingeniously with the Jungian and Yeatsian affiliations of *The White Hotel*. Thus the bayonet rape suggests a psyche at sharp variance with Jung's androgynous ideal and recalls his view of contemporary history as the product of radical dislocations in the spirit.[19] At the same time, the rape also fits with Yeats' schematization of history in terms of annunciations made to women, with Frau Lisa replacing Leda and Mary as the harbinger of a harsh new epoch that particularizes the "rough beast" of "The Second Coming."[20] Despite these arguments in Thomas' favor, however, doubts persist about his handling of felt history. Tolstoy and Stendhal were able to communicate an irremediable harshness in historical experience without having to resort to raw sex and violence.

In several other respects, however, the juxtaposition of *The White Hotel* with classic realism is less problematic, for it suggests a line of descent leading from nineteenth-century fiction to the magical realists. This line of descent demonstrates the relevance of a Nietzschean or Foucauldian cultural genealogy, with its successive reinterpretations and transformations.[21] For, whatever Thomas' conscious intentions, when he appropriates the tradition of felt history, he radically alters the basic assumptions on which it rests. Thus Frau Lisa's physiological clairvoyance is essentially occult, in that it represents a way of perceiving history that claims to reveal an otherwise hidden future. Here Auerbach provides a telling counter example, for during his analysis of *Madame Bovary* he goes out of his way to deny the apparent mysticism of felt history in that novel. When Flaubert links Emma's sensations at the dining table with the hollowness and tension of her epoch, Auerbach insists that his approach — "like all true mysticism, based upon reason, experience, and discipline" — depends on "a self-forgetful absorption in the subjects of reality which transforms them" (486). In other words, for Auerbach Flaubert's historical insight did not derive from special prophetic powers but from the lucidity and fullness with which he apprehended the contemporary world. Emma's feelings in that oppressive dining room are both a product and an index of current conditions, so that, through her, readers can discover something crucial about the basic mood of mid-nineteenth-century France. Similarly,

Mathilde de la Mole's fascination with death sentences, Mann's intuitions of social disaster, and even Anna's ominous nightmares begin as projections of contemporary social experience as rendered in their novels. They only become prophetic by virtue of their immersion in the present. By contrast, Thomas' story hinges on Frau Lisa's symptoms being a detailed and explicit premonition of Babi Yar but does not show with equal detail how this outcome was conditioned by the contemporary world in which her symptoms first appeared. Appropriately enough, in the move from realism to *The White Hotel*, the epistemological assumptions of felt history have indeed become magical.

In the last section of the novel, where Thomas adopts the compensatory vision which parallels a basic impulse of the magical realists, he again transforms realism. As a realm beyond death, the camp differs strikingly from the final responses to felt history presented in realist novels. Thus *Madame Bovary* ends with the sardonic vision of a world where nothing has changed; Homais triumphs, the very character who epitomized the provincial milieu Emma found so stifling. Or, when Aschenbach dies on the beach in Venice, shattered by his riotous dreams and infected with cholera, Mann cuts the story off as abruptly as Stendhal. And Aschenbach's last vision of Tadzio as "a pale and lovely summoner" leaves only the most ambiguous hints of some other reality. Even in *Anna Karenina*, where Levin continues his quest for spiritual meaning after Anna's suicide, his search remains rooted in this world. The novel closes with his decision to pursue an ethical struggle that depends on his own efforts: "My life, my whole life . . . has an unquestionable meaning of goodness with which I have the power to invest it."[22] Among the great classic realists, with their focus on secular experience, there can be no miraculous cures like Frau Lisa's for the wounds of felt history.

Thus, whatever the reader's doubts about the full artistic success of *The White Hotel*, it does provide historical insight on several levels. As a boundary work, Thomas' novel cannot possibly suggest the whole sweep and richness of magical realism; there is nothing quintessential about it. But it does illuminate how this artistic tendency relates to the general history of its time, to Freud's split with Jung as a major issue in intellectual history and to the motif of "felt history" within the tradition of literary realism. Thus, in its reliance on compensatory vision as a basic narrative strategy, the ending of *The White Hotel* closely parallels the response of magical realists to the extremities of modern history in central Europe. In intellectual terms, meanwhile, the turn to compensatory vision qualifies

Thomas' normally Freudian outlook and, at least on this issue, aligns him with the Jungian affinities of the magical realists.

Most important, however, Frau Lisa's physiological clairvoyance pinpoints a major shift from nineteenth-century classic realism to magical realism, as new attitudes toward epistemology and historical experience transform the author's handling of felt history. It thus illustrates the semantic bias of magical realism as a cultural term, which includes a certain tendency to spotlight differences (but also affiliations) with nineteenth-century fiction. Postmodernism, by contrast, focuses attention on the early twentieth century, at times from a perspective where modernism and realism can seem essentially indistinguishable. In analyzing cultural changes of this kind, moreover, critics must often rely on telltale swerves in a single motif like felt history to identify the values and presuppositions at stake. Comparative analyses of specific instances, therefore, can be just as productive as more speculative approaches, though in the end, of course, neither history nor theory exists in isolation. Instead, each necessarily complements the other, often in unacknowledged ways, in any critic's effort to study cultural transformation.

Notes

1 Seymour Menton, *Magic Realism Rediscovered, 1918–1981* (Philadelphia: Art Alliance Press, 1983). Menton is a professor of Spanish and comparative literature who conceives of his book as an indispensable first step in establishing magical realism as a general cultural term. Thus, though he focuses on magical realism in painting, he also mentions writers like Kafka, Borges, Robbe-Grillet, and García Márquez.

2 For a theoretical discussion of the historical-typological method, see Claudio Guillén, *Literature as System: Essays Toward the Theory of Literary History* (Princeton N.J.: Princeton University Press, 1971), esp. section 5. Guillén places period and movement terms "somewhere between the order of chronology and that of an atemporal typology" (437–38) and emphasizes "the elucidation of structures in history (375). For several quite different applications of this approach to twentieth-century culture, see Matei Calinescu, *Five Faces of Modernity: Modernism, Avant-Garde, Decadence, Kitsch, Postmodernism* (Durham N.C.: Duke University Press, 1987); Marjorie Perloff, *The Futurist Moment: Avant-Garde, Avant Guerre, and the Language of Rupture* (Chicago: University of Chicago Press, 1986); and Fredric Jameson, *Postmodernism, or, The Cultural Logic of Late Capitalism* (Durham N.C.: Duke University Press, 1991).

3 For the classic statement, see René Wellek and Austin Warren, *Theory of Lit-*

erature (New York: Harcourt Brace and World, 1948), pp. 120–23. Marshall Brown reassesses *Principles of Art History* and its approach to periodization in "The Classic is the Baroque: On the Principle of Wölfflin's Art History," *Critical Inquiry* 9, 2 (1983): 379–404. For current cross-cultural and transnational approaches to literary history, see *Comparative Literary History as Discourse: In Honor of Anna Balakian,* ed. Mario J. Valdés, Daniel Javitch, and A. Owen Aldridge (Bern: Peter Lang, 1992).

4 Menton, *Magical Realism Rediscovered,* pp. 9, 17–19. Examples of Roh's criteria would be contrasts between dynamic and static, thick color texture and thin paint surface, or ecstatic and sober subjects. His efforts to distinguish magical realism from expressionism are highlighted by the title of his 1925 book, *Nachexpressionismus, magischer Realismus: Probleme der neuesten europäischer Malerei* (Leipzig: Klinkhardt and Biermann, 1925). Later in his career Roh would also stress the differences between magical realism and surrealism.

5 D. M. Thomas, *The White Hotel* (New York: Viking, 1981), p. xi. Thomas quotes the lines "We had fed the heart on fantasies, / The heart's grown brutal from the fare; / More substance in our enmities / Than in our love" from "Meditations in Time of Civil War," which Yeats wrote in 1921–22. Given Thomas' emphasis on compensation outside of history, as discussed below, he significantly omits Yeats' last lines from his epigraph. These lines pray for an end to political bitterness, taking a viewpoint *within* history: "O honey-bees, / Come build in the empty house of the stare."

6 Although he is a Hispanist, Menton does not discuss the historical context of Latin American fiction in *Magic Realism Rediscovered.*

7 Similar ideas may be found throughout Jung and Frye. For the passages quoted here, see Carl Jung, "Psychology and Literature," in his *Modern Man in Search of a Soul,* reprinted in *Modern Literary Criticism, 1900–1970,* ed. Lawrence J. Lipking and A. Walton Litz (New York: Atheneum, 1972), p. 428; and Northrop Frye, "The Return from the Sea," in his *A Natural Perspective,* reprinted in Lipking and Litz, eds., p. 243.

8 For Menton (p. 13), magical realism focuses on "the strange, the uncanny, the eerie, and the dreamlike—but not the fantastic."

9 The letter includes the explicit statement, by Jung, that "Freud had *lost* his authority as far as he was concerned" (Thomas, p. 6). For other interpretations of the Freud-Jung tension throughout the novel, see Marsha Kinder, "The Spirit of *The White Hotel,*" *Humanities in Society* 4 (Spring–Summer 1981): 143–70, esp. 147–50; and Krin Gabbard, "*The White Hotel* and the Traditions of Ring Composition," *Comparative Literature Studies* 27, 3 (1990): 230–48, esp. 237–38, 242–45.

10 Stendhal, *Red and Black,* trans. and ed. Robert M. Adams (New York: Norton, 1969), p. 230 (part 2, chap. 8).

11 Stendhal, p. 407 (part 2, chap. 45).

12 Leo Tolstoy, *Anna Karenina*, ed. George Gibian, trans. Louise and Aylmer Maude (New York: Norton, 1970), p. 329 (part 4, chap. 3). This is the fullest account of the dream, which is also mentioned elsewhere in the novel.

13 Tolstoy, p. 695 (part 7, chap. 31).

14 Thomas Mann, *Death in Venice*, trans. and ed. Clayton Koelb (New York: Norton, 1994), p. 52 (chap. 5).

15 Mann, *Doctor Faustus*, trans. H. T. Lowe-Porter (New York: Modern Library, 1966), chap. 25. If we count the three parts of chapter 34 as separate chapters, this chapter comes at the middle of a 49-chapter novel.

16 *Doctor Faustus*, p. 245 (chap. 25).

17 Erich Auerbach, *Mimesis: The Representation of Reality in Western Literature*, trans. Willard R. Trask (Princeton, N.J.: Princeton University Press, 1953), p. 483. Compare Gustave Flaubert, *Madame Bovary*, ed. and trans. Paul de Man (New York: Norton, 1965), p. 47 (part 1, chap. 9).

18 A. Anatoli (Kuznetsov), *Babi Yar: A Document in the Form of a Novel*, trans. David Floyd (New York: Farrar, Strauss, and Giroux, 1970), pp. 109–11.

19 On the Jungian notion of androgyny in magical realism, compare Menton, p. 35, where he analyzes the paintings of Anton Räderscheidt in terms of the effort to overcome dislocation.

20. For Yeats' conception of historical epochs based on annunciations to women, see William Butler Yeats, *A Vision* (New York: Macmillan, 1937), especially Book V, "Dove or Swan," pp. 267–302. For the place of "The Second Coming" in this scheme, see pp. 262–63.

21. For an especially pointed expression of Nietzsche's method, which holds that "whatever exists, having somehow come into being, is again and again reinterpreted to new ends, taken over, transformed and redirected," see Friedrich Nietzsche, *Genealogy of Morals*, in *Basic Writings of Nietzsche* trans. and ed. Walter Kaufmann (New York: Modern Library, 1968), p. 513 (Essay II, section 12). For a Foucauldian commentary on this method, see Michel Foucault, "Nietzsche, Genealogy, History," *Language, Counter-Memory, Practice*, ed. David F. Bouchard (Ithaca, N.Y.: Cornell Univ. Press, 1977), pp. 139–64.

22 *Anna Karenina*, p. 740 (part 8, chap. 19).

P. GABRIELLE FOREMAN

Past-On Stories: History and the Magically Real,
Morrison and Allende on Call

The storyteller takes what [s/he] tells from experience — [her] own or that reported
by others. And [s/he] in turn makes it the experience of those who are listening to [the] tale. . . . In every case the storyteller is a [wo]man who has counsel
for [his or her] reader. . . . Today having counsel is beginning to have an old-
fashioned ring . . . because the communicability of experience is decreasing. —
Walter Benjamin, "The Storyteller," in *Illuminations*[1]

In the postmodern world of dead authors and destabilized subjects, "experience" sounds like something embarrassingly antiquated. Nonetheless,
repossessing historical experience is Isabel Allende's work, as it is Toni
Morrison's. In *The House of the Spirits* Allende writes to "keep alive the
memory" of her country Chile. Similarly, in *Song of Solomon*, Morrison is
explicitly concerned with the process of "rememory," as she will be later
in *Beloved*. "Somewhere," she often says, "someone forgot to tell somebody something."[2] Morrison states: "We don't live in places where we can
hear those stories anymore; parents don't sit around and tell their children those classical, mythological, archetypal stories that we heard years
ago. But new information has to get out, and there are several ways to do
it. One is the novel."[3] For these authors, memory is grounded in the recuperation of the historical. Allende and Morrison, like the storytelling
women protagonists they create, are animated by the desire to preserve
pasts too often trivialized, built over or erased, and to pass them on.

The interrelation of history, ontology, and the magically real — and how
these authors' interventions posit women as both the site of and link between these categories — will be the subject of this essay. The relation between ontology and naming is explicitly figured in both *The House of the
Spirits* and *Song of Solomon*. Morrison locates defining power in speech

and listening, survival skills quite distinct from mere mimetic talking and passive hearing. Allende subverts the Adamic power of literal naming and so posits a new genesis, one in which woman challenges her always-already fallenness. Instead, as in Morrison, women become the site of a history that survives and so nurtures the present.

It is in the revelation of family histories that the worlds of *The House of the Spirits* and *Song of Solomon* are constituted: worlds full of walking, talking ghosts, women with green hair and no navels, marvelous worlds. Magic realism, unlike the fantastic or the surreal, presumes that the individual requires a bond with the traditions and the faith of the community, that s/he is historically constructed and connected. Echoing Alejo Carpentier, who first named the phenomenon, critic Marguerite Suárez-Murias contends that "the marvelous [*lo real maravilloso*] presupposes an element of faith on the part of the author or the audience."[4] She argues further that both the fantastic and the surrealistic require "the total negation of faith and tradition. It is here where magic realism splits away" (103). Unlike magical realism, the fantastic and the uncanny posit an individual who experiences a world beyond the community's parameters.

Although the term magic realism has been used primarily to categorize a Latin American literary practice, I assume its relevance in examining an aspect of African American literature. Gabriel García Márquez, whose *One Hundred Years of Solitude* is the most famous example of the mode, often cites the African Caribbean coast of Colombia as the source of his magically real. And Isabel Allende has asserted that magic realism "relies on a South American reality: the confluence of races and cultures of the whole world superimposed on the indigenous culture, in a violent climate."[5] These, too, are the dynamics of Africans in the Americas; they are inscribed, though differently, in both Allende and Morrison's texts. Ultimately, I will argue that Allende revises García Márquez's master text by positing women as the site of the magical. Additionally, in contradistinction to García Márquez, Allende's magical realism gives way in the end to political realism. Yet, despite critical valorization of her use of the magical, I will eventually contend that Allende does not fit comfortably into Suárez-Murias' paradigm. Instead, she feminizes generic codes to employ magic realism as a bridge to a history recoverable in the political realm, a history that she will ultimately constitute in her text as distinct from the magical.

I

The fathers may soar
And the children may know their names.
— Toni Morrison, *Song of Solomon*, epigraph

In Toni Morrison's *Song of Solomon*, women are simultaneously the site of the historical and the magical. Although Morrison uses a male character, Milkman Dead, as the principle narrating character, his Aunt Pilate performs the role that Walter Benjamin names: she is the giver of stories, of counsel, the link to a precarious but necessary past. Though we hear the stories told by Macon and Ruth, Milkman's parents, these tellers do not communicate the past freely, but only when they feel coerced. The first time Milkman hears of his father's childhood is when Macon is forbidding his son to go to his Aunt Pilate's. Milkman challenges his father:

> "You keep saying you don't have to explain nothing to me. How do you think that makes me feel? Like a baby, that's what. Like a twelve-year-old baby!!"
>
> "Don't you raise your voice to me. . . . Watch you mouth!" Macon roared.[6]

As a result of this confrontation Macon decides to relate his own version of Lincoln's Heaven, the farm where he and Pilate grew up, and of how his father got his name. Yet he ends by saying, "I haven't changed my mind, I don't want you over there." "Why? You still haven't said why," his son pleads. And Macon doesn't. At the end of the conversation, "his father had explained nothing to him" (54–55).

Far from the ostensible complicity Billie Holiday expresses in "Hush Now, Don't Explain," Milkman's insistence that the past be related to him provokes both his father's personal and projected censorship. Not only does Macon refuse to "tell things" but he also insists that his son watch his own mouth. The power of the oral, as in Shahrazad Ali's hysteric bestseller on the dangerous black woman, is marked as potentially out of control, a darkened "wild zone" to be feared and controlled.[7]

Pilate, unlike her brother, tells stories spontaneously and continually. She is a symbol of kinetic orality,[8] a Shahrazad Ali-an nightmare: "when she was neither singing nor talking, her face was animated by her constantly moving lips. She chewed things. As a baby, as a very young girl, she kept things in her mouth — straw from brooms, gristle, buttons, seeds, leaves, string. . . . Her lips were alive with small movements" (30). Pilate is also the symbol of aurality. She takes the only word her father ever wrote, her name which he copied from the Bible, puts it in her mother's snuff box and strings it to her ear to give it meaning. Morrison inverts the black tradition of recording family names in the Bible. Pilate takes the word out of the Bible and puts it in her ear to symbolize her belief that the value of the word is in the hearing, in the telling, that the living tradition is an oral/aural one, rather than a written one.

Pilate the counselor, the storyteller, teaches Milkman to value these traditions. She begins, as critic Joseph Skerret points out, by teaching the teenaged Milkman and his best friend how to talk properly:[9]

> "Who's you little friend? . . . Do he talk?"
> "Yeah. He talk. Say something." Guitar shoved an elbow at Milkman without taking his eyes off Pilate.
> Milkman took a breath, held it, and said, "Hi."
> Pilate laughed. "You all must be the dumbest unhung Negroes on earth. What they telling you in them schools? You say "Hi" to pigs and sheep when you want 'em to move. When you tell a human being "Hi," he ought to get up and knock you down." (37)

Their manhood, Pilate schools them, has more to do with their speech than their sexuality; it is contingent on their no longer being "dumb," on their mastering speech. Her admonishment, "You all must be the dumbest unhung Negros on earth," appropriates into her own educational discourse fetishized phallic myths about the black male. The power to subvert myths of phallic symbolism, change their locus, and avoid their violent translation, their hanging, is situated in the power of speech.

Pilate also teaches them how to listen, a survival strategy not taught, she points out, at the schools they attend. Hearing her speak, they must also learn to respect the storyteller. When Pilate starts out, Guitar interrupts her to ask about her father's death:

> "Who shot your daddy? Did you say somebody shot him?" Guitar was fascinated. . . .
> "Five feet into the air. . . ."
> "Who?"
> "I don't know who and I don't know why. I just know what I'm tellin you: what, when, and where."
> "You didn't say where." He was insistent.

"I did too. Off a fence."

"Where was the fence?"

"On our farm."

. . . He gave up on "where." "Well, when then?"

"When he sat there — on the fence."

Guitar felt like a frustrated detective. "What year?"

"The year they shot them Irish people down in the streets. Was a good year for guns and gravediggers I know that." (41–42)

By the end of their visit the boys learn to value the interaction between Pilate and themselves, as well as the information, double entendres, and coding of the tales; they absorb the lessons barnacled to the undersides of speech and meaning, without imposing their own demands on the story. They "watched, afraid to say anything lest they ruin the next part of her story, and afraid to remain silent lest she not go on with its telling" (43). They must learn to occupy the space between speech and silence, between stories to pass on and not to pass on, between being hung and unhung; they must learn to acquire and define their "manhood" and also to stay alive.

Listening, not only to what he wants to hear but to what is being said, becomes central in Milkman's quest for life. These values are learned but not yet incorporated by a twelve-year-old on an afternoon visit. Years later in Shalimar he finally realizes that the commodities in which his father has invested are not, ultimately, of value. There, on a midnight hunt, "there was nothing . . . to help him — not his money, his car, his father's reputation, his suit, or his shoes. In fact they hampered him" (280). Realizing this, Milkman begins to rely upon the values that Pilate has taught him, how to talk, be silent, and listen: "Feeling both tense and relaxed, he sank his fingers into the grass. He tried to listen with his fingertips, to hear what, if anything, the earth had to say, and it told him quickly that someone was standing behind him and he had just enough time to raise one hand to his neck and catch the wire that fastened around his throat" (282). The power of listening allows Milkman both to save his own life and to figure out what it is, who he is, that he is saving. Listening also allows him to puzzle out the pieces of Pilate's song and recognize in it his family history. And again that which he had relied upon in the past proves useless. On a sleepy Shalimar morning, Milkman is pulled out of his own thoughts by the children playing a game, singing Pilate's song: "Milkman took out his wallet and pulled from it his airplane ticket stub, but he had no pencil to write with, and his pen was in his suit. He would just have to listen and

memorize it. He closed his eyes and concentrated while the children . . .
performed the round over and over again. And Milkman memorized all of
what they sang" (306). In Milkman's search, Pilate's values again triumph
over his father's censorship and constraint. There is nothing in Milkman's
wallet that will help him; he must rely upon the skills he has learned in
listening to the children. Stripped of pencils and pens, Milkman abandons
his status as observer and becomes a participant in his own history.

In African American culture, naming is often a creative and subversive practice in a country that has historically denied, manipulated, and
mangled black names. Reappropriation, in other words, leads to agency,
to the power to redefine white declaratives. The community in *Song of
Solomon* renames Mercy Hospital "No Mercy Hospital." The street they
call "Doctor Street" city officials insist is not "Doctor Street." Fine, they
nod, "Not Doctor St." On Pilate's porch, during that first storytelling session, Milkman first feels that his identity is connected somehow to his
name:

> Again Guitar spoke up. "You his daddy sister?"
>
> "The only one he got. Ain't but three Deads alive."
>
> Milkman, who had been unable to get one word out of his mouth
> after the foolish "Hi," heard himself shout: "I'm a Dead! My mother's
> a Dead! My sisters. You and him ain't the only ones!"
>
> . . . He wondered why he was suddenly so defensive—so posses-
> sive about his name. He had always hated that name. . . . Now he was
> behaving with this strange woman as though having the name was a
> matter of deep personal pride, as though she had tried to expel him
> from a very special group. (38)

Names, Milkman finally realizes, bear witness, bear witness to "yearnings,
gestures, flaws, events, mistakes, weaknesses" (333) and resistance. Morrison herself contends that "each thing is separate and different; once you
have named it, you have power."[10] Drunk one night, trying to sort out
all his father has loaded on him in exchange for the blow Milkman had
dealt him at the dinner table, Milkman and Guitar again end up ponder-
ing names:

> "What's your trouble? You don't like your name?"
>
> "No. . . . No, I don't like my name."
>
> ". . . Sweet Hagar. Wonder what her name is."

". . . Ask Pilate."

"Yeah. I'll ask Pilate. Pilate knows. It's in that dumb-ass box hanging from her ear. Her own name and everybody else's. Bet mine's in there too. I'm gonna ask her what my name is." (88–89)

Although he doesn't know it, Pilate has already taught him that simple explanations aren't there for the asking. Names are historically embedded, and their recovery involves a certain kind of responsibility to them, a responsibility that Milkman isn't yet ready to accept. The always-already absence in the history of black naming in the United States emerges in Milkman's exchange; he doesn't like a name he doesn't, he says lines later, even know. Pilate replaces that absence with collective naming: Milkman's, her own, and "everybody else's." Only after Milkman acknowledges this nexus can he connect himself in history.

II

Whatever the man called each living
creature, that would be its name.
—Genesis 2:19

Pilate's biblical name also signifies its homonym, pilot, one who leads the way; Allende gives her character, Clara del Valle, a name that literally means light, brightness, lucidity—one who lights the way. *The House of the Spirits* revolves around Clara's family: her husband, Esteban Trueba, a conservative senator, patron, and patriarchal "head" of family; Blanca, their daughter; and Alba, their granddaughter. Allende plays on Clara's name, having Trueba call out to "Clara, the clearest" [Clara, claríssima],[11] writing of her death that "she seemed to be detaching herself from the world, growing ever lighter [más clara], more transparent [aún más clara], more winged," (289) and at his death, murmuring, "Clara, clearest, clairvoyant" (431). Clara's female offspring are christened with seried synonyms: Blanca means white, Alba means dawn, the beginning of light, "Clara" both diffused and renewed.

Like Morrison with Pilate, Allende locates Clara as the site of naming; and this wrests Adamic power from her husband, Trueba. When she is pregnant, he starts:

"I hope this time it will be a boy so we can give him my name," I [Trueba] joked.

"It's not one, it's two," Clara replied. "The twins will be called Jaime and Nicolás, respectively," she added.

. . . I got furious, arguing that those were names for foreign merchants, that no one in my family or hers had ever had such names, that at least one of them should be called Esteban, like myself and my father, but Clara explained that repeating the same name just caused confusion in her notebooks that bore witness to life. Her decision was inflexible. (115)

Despite Trueba's temporary first person narrative "control" in this section of the novel, Clara's appropriation of his rights of naming displays Allende's irony, for Trueba delimits his expansive use of the *droit du seigneur* precisely on the basis of maintaining a economically "pure" and patriarchal familial structure:

Whenever a woman showed up at his door with a newborn baby in her arms asking for his surname . . . he would send her away. . . . He figured that when he was ready to have children he would find a woman of his own class, with the blessings of the Church, because the only ones who really counted were the ones who bore their father's surname; the others might just as well not have been born. (66)

Yet ultimately his family also rejects his surname and the values it signifies.

Along with her power of naming, Clara's clairvoyance, like Pilate's magic storytelling, is a commodity that men wish to privatize and control. Trueba believes that Blanca will benefit from limited exposure to her mother's magic. He thinks, with absolute confidence, that her "destiny was marriage and a brilliant life in society, where the ability to converse with the dead, if kept on a frivolous level, could be an asset. He maintained that magic, like cooking . . . was a particularly feminine affair" (136). Trueba's trivialization of his wife's and daughter's magical inclinations confirms his fear of the public, the feminized political, and the power of the magical — for to what, by the end of this novel, will Chile's dead be testifying? Trueba responds to the power of the magical by moving from the familial to the protected political. When Clara's mother, Nivea, worries that "people are going to start lining up and looking at [Clara] as if she were a monster," her father anticipates "the damage to his political career that could be caused by having a bewitched child in the family" (9). Women's power, even when obscured by the prepubescent gender neutrality of a child, is tolerated by men if it does not impinge on the masculinist world of public affairs.

Ultimately, it is Blanca's political and sexual displays rather than her magical ones that cause her father displeasure. The conflict between women's desires, expressions, and the expectations of their decorum within the established social order is at issue when Trueba responds to Blanca's love for (and lovemaking with) the peasant and political singer Pedro Tercero. As he wishes to domesticate her magical power, he also wishes to delimit any step outside of the paternally protected domestic world, particularly one that in his sexual/political economy signals a "fall." After discovering her affair, Trueba beats Blanca and then vents his anger on Clara, accusing her of raising her daughter "without morals, without religion, without principles, like a libertine atheist, even worse, without a sense of her own class."

> "Pedro Tercero hasn't done a thing you haven't done yourself," Clara said when she could interrupt him. "You also slept with unmarried women not of your own class. The only difference is that he did it for love. And so did Blanca."
> Trueba stared at her [and then] he lost control and struck her in the face, knocking her against the wall. (200)

In his consideration of the affair, Trueba erases his daughter's displayed agency and, instead of assuming his own, insists on his wife's responsibility. By denying his role in the upbringing for which he upbraids Clara, he implies that the mother, Woman, Eve is responsible for her "fall." While Clara is implicated in this fall, she herself has not forsaken the privileges she enjoys as a yet nonfallen woman. When Clara responds by naming Trueba's behavior, however, she too, oversteps the line. It is Clara's bringing Trueba's past from the unspoken to the articulated private that precipitates his striking her. This defining act symbolizes Clara's step beyond the slash separating the fallen/nonfallen opposition, for the violence he had directed at other women and from which he had refrained with Clara is what had marked her "privileged" and contained status.

Clara, like Pilate, and like Ursula in *One Hundred Years of Solitude*, appropriates naming power, that is, ontological power. Critic Gordon Brotherston asserts about *One Hundred Years of Solitude* that: "the [Buendía] family . . . owes its existence and its coherence to Ursula, their guardian. Her insight alone can detect the "real" motives behind her offspring's actions; her memory alone can retain their history."[12] Similarly, Pilate is responsible for Milkman's conception and birth. She gives her sister-in-law Ruth a potion to add to Macon's food in order to bring him back, if temporarily, to their unshared bed. And the Trueba family owes its existence to Clara, who seems to attract Trueba magically to marry her.

Clara and Pilate pass this defining power on to their descendants. Alba "writes" the text that becomes the novel that we read with the help of Clara's notebooks, which name and "bear witness to life." When Alba is being tortured under Esteban García's direction, "her Grandmother Clara, whom she had invoked so many times to help her die, appeared with the novel idea that the point was not to die since death came anyway, but to survive, which would be a miracle. Clara also brought the saving idea of writing in her mind, without paper or pencil, to keep her thoughts occupied and to escape the doghouse and live" (414).[13] As Pilate teaches Milkman the skills that save him the night of the hunt, and that allow him to memorize the song of Solomon when he had neither pencil nor pen, so through Clara's teaching Alba lives. And as Milkman sings to the dying Pilate the song she sang as he was being born, so Alba lives to take on Clara's task of recording family history and politicizing it.

Aware of the separation of the magical and the historical in *One Hundred Years of Solitude*, Allende subverts the potential apoliticism of magic realism. At the end of *The House of the Spirits*, she eclipses magic with political realities, foregrounding the historical legacy preserved and handed down, as magic was earlier, by her women characters. Mario Rojas argues that "*The House of the Spirits* is a femino-centric novel in that the female characters here are not in the traditional roles found in masculine writing, but rather are force fields that challenge patriarchal despotism, social-sexual prejudices, dictatorship and political repression."[14] Another critic argues that the feminist perspective Allende brings to her novel "surely prevents it from being categorized as a mere reworking of *One Hundred Years of Solitude*."[15] The critic's choice of "mere" expresses the dynamics of reception with a novel that so heavily reworks a (male) master.[16] In other words, Allende's allusions in this first novel, for some who have read García Márquez's earlier masterpiece of magic realism, work too loudly. But rather than being simply mimetic, they often create textual ruptures, spaces through which she both feminizes and politicizes the magical mode.

Allende's ultimate allegiance to the political and historical marks her text's difference from García Márquez's. Referring to *One Hundred Years of Solitude*, Brotherston states that "the greater the danger that a given event may seem to be historical, the stronger is García Márquez's mythical antidote: the banana company's massacre of thousands of strikers, for example is followed by endless rain . . . which washes away precise memory."[17] Allende inverts this technique — the stronger the historical moment, the more distant the magical — as if to counter the threat of history becoming "merely" enchanted and so subsumed. The historical references in Allende's novel are explicit: though she never mentions Chile, several of her characters obviously represent Chilean political figures. Blanca's lover, Pedro Tercero embodies the famous political poet/singer Victor Jara, whose hands were also mutilated. The Poet, with his ship figure collection and his death soon after that of the President, is obviously Pablo Neruda. The Candidate/President is, of course, Allende's uncle, Salvador Allende. These characters are firmly rooted in their historical context: in them we find no traces of the earlier domestic magic of Clara and her female offspring.

In the beginning of *The House of the Spirits* Allende seems to employ a feminized magic realism as a technique to pull the reader into a political-historical novel. If, as Suárez-Murias suggests, "myths and historical references coexist; they nurture each other" (100), in *The House of the Spirits*, they most often do so only in the isolated domestic spaces that Clara's family inhabits. In *Narrative Magic in the Fiction of Isabel Allende*, Patricia Hart goes even further, suggesting that there is a "continuous campaign during the novel . . . to place magical realism in trivial settings."[18] With the exception of the limited town reactions to Rosa the Beautiful and the interaction of the Mora sisters and their séanced entourage, the magical world of Clara and her family is theirs alone; or, at least, we have little indication of how their magic interacts with the rest of the community, as Suárez-Murias' analysis would posit it must. As a result, the immediacy of this world fades after Nana, Nivea, and Clara die. Alba attests to this, saying: "It is a delight for me to read [Clara's] notebooks from those years, which describe a magic world that *no longer exists* . . . where the prosaic truth of material objects mingled with the tumultuous reality of dreams and the laws of physics and logic did not always apply" (82, emphasis mine). By the novel's close, Alba has little *living* access to her magical matrilineage. Only the memory of the magical survives, but this memory helps Alba to survive the penetration of the patrilinear political sphere. In contrast to Morrison, where myths and historical references do coexist throughout the novel, the magic in Allende's world is swept away by the political cataclysm she describes.

It is a critical commonplace to note that marginalized authors code their texts when they have reason to anticipate that their perspectives will threaten an audience's assumptions and challenge hegemonies that have the power to silence their voicing.[19] For U.S. readers, explicit politics in the novel may suggest "gauche" reenactments of the protest novel, the potential compromising of aesthetics for "mere" polemics. U.S. critics still speak of Allende's (and others') ability to "transcend" the political.[20] Allende seems to have realized that the literary market of readers and critics expects Latin American novels to follow the pattern of a family chronicle in a magical world. And it is exactly this stereotypical vision of Latin American fiction on which many reviewers have myopically focused. Many Latin American male authors enjoy avid international audiences; Allende has been one of a few post-Boom Latin American woman novelists who does. She makes a conscious and politically astute gesture, I would argue, to maneuver within the realms of politics and magic to create the wedge that gained her book crossover status. Robert Antoni suggests that "there is a gradual shift in the focalization . . . as the book shifts . . . from family saga (fantasy), to love story, to political history."[21] She uses magic to engage her reader; this is hardly an "alluring, sometimes magical tale [and] tumultuous story of love among three generations,"[22] but rather a powerful fictive intervention in the historical construction of the Chilean coup.

III

Where there is a woman there is magic. . . .
This woman is a consort of the spirits.
—Ntozake Shange, *Sassafras, Cypress and Indigo*

The mythical and magical do not fade in Morrison's narrative but rather become sharper, more immediate as Milkman's story unfolds. Guided by Pilate, Milkman travels from his father's world, in which there is no room for spirits or spirituality, to his own where he absorbs his history, and like his grandfather, learns to fly. Morrison says that in *Song of Solomon*, she blends "the acceptance of the supernatural and a profound rootedness in the real world at the same time, without one taking precedence over the other."[23] Suárez-Murias suggests that central to magic realism is "the validity of interior worlds of faith which blossom in everyday realities and coexist with other available realities" (105). Morrison's novel is an example of a work where the mythical and the historical coexist and, indeed, nurture each other.

As Clara is the principal vessel of magic in *The House of the Spirits*, Pilate functions as its center in *Song of Solomon*. Milkman confirms this when he thinks to himself: "Here he was walking around in the middle of the twentieth century trying to explain what a ghost had done. But why not? . . . One fact was certain: Pilate did not have a navel and if that was true anything could be" (298). Pilate's perfectly smooth belly acts as Milkman's confirming referent: he measures the limits of "reality" against that which he knows. He knows that Pilate has no navel, and so he reasons, "why can't ghosts exist?"

Milkman's beliefs are not confined to domestic realities; rather, they are shared with and by the community. Pilate's daughter Reba's fight with her most recent man illustrates the community's collective acceptance:

> A few neighbors who had heard Reba's screams had gathered in Pilate's backyard. They knew right away that the man was a newcomer to the city. Otherwise he would have known . . . not to fool with anything that belonged to Pilate, who never bothered anybody, was helpful to everybody, but who also was believed to have the power to step outside of her skin, set a bush afire from fifty yards, and turn a man into a ripe rutabaga — all on account of the fact that she had no navel. (94)

Pilate reads her neighbor's respect differently; she feels that her having no navel isolates her from her people, "for, except for the relative bliss on the island [where no one knew her secret], every other resource was denied her: partnership in marriage, confessional friendship, and communal religion. Men frowned, women whispered and shoved their children behind them" (148). Yet in truth the community of the Southside accepts her; theirs is a relationship of dynamic resource. Rather than isolating Pilate, they build their own intricate sets of beliefs around her difference; and once they have defined it and its limitations, they play by the rules they have established. When Reba's man beats her, the community feels that he should have known not to mess with "anything that belonged to Pilate. . . . So they didn't have much sympathy for him. They just craned their necks to hear better what Pilate was telling him" (94). Milkman is not Pilate's sole listener; as she does with her nephew, Pilate tells the community a story. Once the story is over, and Reba's man has run off down the road, "a neighbor offered to drive them [to the hospital] and off they went" (95). So the broader community supports her, if sometimes grudgingly. Marcelline accepts Reba's Hagar rushing into *The Shoppe* at closing time, expecting somebody to do her hair, because she's Pilate's: "Pilate know I turned her down she wouldn't like it" (316). As Guitar and Milkman have learned, the community knows that difference must be respected and learned from.

What is commonly regarded as lying outside the parameters of "reality" in the Western world is accepted and confirmed by the community in *Song of Solomon*. Suárez-Murias argues that this faith differentiates magic realism from fantastic or surrealistic literature. Morrison approaches the magical in *Song of Solomon* through the everyday, placing it within her cultural context. African Americans "are a very practical people," she tells us: "but within that practicality we also accept what I suppose could be called superstition and magic. Which is another way of knowing things. . . . To blend those two worlds together at the same time is enhancing."[24] It is this cosmology that Alejo Carpentier speaks of in his 1949 essay of definition, "Lo real maravilloso americano," translated in this volume. Here, for the first time, he distinguishes surrealism and the fantastic from *lo real maravilloso* on the ground that it does not explore another or second reality, but rather amplifies the parameters of our present reality. Critic Darwin Turner asserts that Morrison, too, amplifies that reality. She "commands the storyteller's skill to persuade a reader to suspend disbelief by discovering the credibility in the magic of the tale"[25] and thus brings her or him into this world of amplified realities. Moreover, she often does this through the storytelling itself. The reader has no privileged relation with an omniscient narrator but learns at the same time and in the same way as, for example, Ruth, Milkman's mother, does. Through this storytelling strategy, as Pilate unfolds the tale to Ruth, we first discover that Pilate has seen her father: "Macon seen him too. After we buried him, after he was blown off that fence. We both seen him. I see him still. He's helpful to me, real helpful. Tells me things I need to know" (141). The audience become "participatory readers,"[26] extended listeners of the tale and thus inclined, by extension, to imbibe the cosmology of the community.

In contrast to the Del Valle world, characters who are *not* Pilate's family members may also experience this world of talking ghosts and strange premonitions. Furthermore, Pilate is not the only storyteller from whom we hear these events. Macon's workman, Freddie, tells Milkman stories of *his* family: "Ghosts killed my mother," he explains: "She was walking cross the yard with this neighbor friend [and there was] a woman comin down the road. . . . When the woman got near, the neighbor called out howdy and soon's she said the word, the woman turned into a white bull. Right before their eyes" (110). Nor is the belief in the magical confined to the community of the Bloodbank and stories of their ancestors. During Milkman and Guitar's first storytelling session on Pilate's porch, she tells them of the man she worked for whom she tried to save from falling off a cliff one day as he stood in the kitchen asking her for some coffee:

> He said he couldn't figure it out, but he felt like he was about to fall off a cliff. Standing right there on that yellow and white and red linoleum, as level as a flatiron. . . . So I told the man did he want me to hold on to him so he couldn't fall. He looked at me with the most grateful look in the world. "Would you?" . . . But as soon's I let go he fell dead-weight to the floor. . . . And you know what? He went down so slow. I swear it took three minutes." (41)

It is not the reality of the cliff we are convinced of; rather, it is the experience that Pilate and this man share and the intensity of his faith that we are expected to believe. Interestingly, the two — the reality of the cliff and the man's belief in it — are equally "magical," as are their consequences. They aptly demonstrate the Carpentier's amplification of the categories of the real.

Morrison pulls readers into her own amplified reality — a reality solidly rooted in the world of African Americans, in black cultural traditions. The faith that is a necessary component of magic realism is organic to the cosmology upon which Morrison draws. For this reason, magic is clearly present throughout Morrison's fiction: in *Sula,* most notably in the Deweys and the plague of birds that precede Sula's return; in *Tar Baby,* in the blind horsemen that inhabit Isle de Chevaliers and the breathtaking scene of the African woman in the yellow dress who spits at Jadine while balancing an egg on her shoulder. *Beloved*'s most basic premise lies in the magical: it is the community's shared belief in magic that enables them to save Sethe from its negative effects.

This cosmology has complicated the reception of Morrison's novels, for readers are drawn into a space that seems to suspend their usual connections to the "logical" and the "real." Yet Morrison's world is not a fantastic one cut off from cultural and communal traditions, but rather it is closely tied to them. The magic in her fiction functions to bring readers into a space that is clearly African American and is so without pretense or explanation.

In an interview, Morrison asserts of the flying myth in *Song of Solomon:* "If it means Icarus to some readers, fine; I want to take credit for that. But my meaning is specific: it is about Black people who could fly. That was always part of the folklore in my life; flying was one of our gifts. I don't care how silly it may seem. . . . it's in the spirituals and gospels. Perhaps it was wishful thinking . . . but suppose it wasn't?"[27] Solomon, the flying African, is not simply a fantastic figment of a single author's imagination; rather, he springs from her imagination *and* black cultural traditions. That he is presented in her novel without explanation — his "gift" is simply assumed, as is all of the magic in the novel — demonstrates the element of faith in magic and represents a break with the explanatory mode of African American literature.[28] "I don't know why I should be asked to explain,"[29] Morrison asserts. She does not write to offer legitimation for her culture, her traditions, her words. In many ways though, Morrison's role is explanatory, for she recovers history for her people, using her language on her own terms.

IV

While we remained silenced it was as if nothing ever happened;
that which isn't named, almost doesn't exist.
—Isabel Allende, *Eva Luna*

Allende and Morrison use magical realism differently: Allende to bridge the powerful story of a troubled political era and Morrison to strengthen generational ties to African American cosmologies and thus offer to a deracinated generation strategies for survival. Yet, they assume similar responsibilities. Clara, Alba, and Pilate are the storytellers; they are women recording history. Her novels, Morrison tells us, "should clarify the roles that have become obscured; they ought to identify those things in the past that are useful and those things that are not; and they ought to give nourishment."[30] This, too, is Allende's goal: "In *The House of the Spirits,* in some sense I recuperated the world that I had lost, that was taken from me. I feel as if *The House of the Spirits* is the size and form of a brick to show the world what was my house."[31] Each vision reacquaints us with a history that has been erased or that has written women out of it; each works to keep memories alive so that we can learn from past mistakes, so that we can take a brick and use it in the foundations of what we build.

Yet neither Allende nor Morrison attempts to offer definitive explanations. Walter Benjamin suggests that the storyteller's counsel "is less an answer to a question than a proposal concerning the continuation of a story which is unfolding."[32] Both *The House of the Spirits* and *Song of Solomon* resist linearity and closure. Morrison incorporates material that "suggests what the conflicts are, what the problems are. But it need not solve those problems because it is not a case study, it is not a recipe."[33] Both novels work richly with the task Morrison suggests. Both are "beautiful and powerful, but . . . also work to record and reclaim their histories,"[34] histories that, like Clara's name, enlighten, and like Pilate's, point the way to an understanding of the past and thus to a more fruitful reckoning with the present and future.

Notes

1 Walter Benjamin, "The Storyteller," *Illuminations*, trans. Harry Zohn (New York: Schocken Books, 1969), pp. 86–87.

2 Taped interview with Ntozake Shange. Critic Barbara Christian also often quotes this phrase.

3 Toni Morrison, "Rootedness: The Ancestor as Foundation," in *Black Women Writers*, ed. Mari Evans (New York: Anchor Books, 1984), p. 340.

4 Marguerite C. Suárez-Murias, "El realismo mágico: Una definición étnica," in her *Essays on Hispanic Literature/Ensayos de literatura hispana: A Bilingual Anthology* (Washington, D.C.: University Press of America, 1982), p. 100, my translation. Subsequent references are cited parenthetically in the text.

Carpentier often speaks of the responsibility of the writer to name and describe the unnamed American realms — *lo real maravilloso americano*. See, for example, his prologue to his 1949 novel, *The Kingdom of this World* (*El reino de este mundo*), translated in this volume.

5 Isabel Allende in "Ventana: Barricada Cultural," *La Barricada* (Nicaragua) no. 323 (23 Jan. 1988): 7.

6 Toni Morrison, *Song of Solomon* (New York: Signet Press, 1977), p. 50. Subsequent references are cited parenthetically in the text.

7 Shahrazad Ali, *The Black Man's Guide to Understanding the Black Woman* (Philadelphia: Civilized Publications, 1989).

8 Cornel West defines "kinetic orality" as "dynamic repetitive and energetic rhetorical styles that form communities." My usage refers more specifically to the literal meaning of kinetic. See Cornel West, "Black Culture and Postmodernism," in *Remaking History*, ed. Barbara Kruger and Phil Mariani (Seattle: Bay Press, 1989), p. 93.

9 See Joseph T. Skerret's "Recitation to the Griot: Storytelling and Learning in Toni Morrison's *Song of Solomon*," in *Conjuring: Black Women, Fiction, and Literary Tradition*, ed. Marjorie Pryse and Hortense J. Spillers (Bloomington: Indiana University Press, 1985), for an excellent discussion of this theme.

10 Toni Morrison, quoted in Thomas LeClair, "The Language Must Not Sweat," *The New Republic* (21 Mar. 1981): 25.

11 Isabel Allende, *The House of the Spirits*, trans. Magda Bogin (1982; New York: Bantam, 1986), p. 295. Subsequent references to this novel are cited parenthetically in the text. The repeated plays on Clara's name are lost in the English translation.

12 Gordon Brotherston, *The Emergence of the Latin American Novel* (Cambridge: Cambridge University Press, 1977), p. 128.

13 This conflicts with Alba's later contention that it is Trueba who suggests that they write this story. At the end of the novel, Alba suggests that Clara was a "helper" but did not precipitate the writing (430–31).

14 Mario Rojas, "Un caleidoscopio de espejos desordenados," *Revista Iberoamericana* 132–33 (1985): 919.

15 Sharon Magnarelli, review of *The House of the Spirits*, *Latin American Literary Review* 14, 28 (1986): 102.

16 For a discussion of the similarities between these novels, see Robert Antoni "Parody or Piracy: The Relationship of *The House of the Spirits* to *One Hundred Years of Solitude*," *Latin American Literary Review* 16, 32 (1988): 16–28.

17 Brotherston, p. 127. Here García Márquez inverts the classic definition of magical realism in having the marvelous of this incident hinge upon the community's *disbelief* of a historical moment, rather than its belief in a magical one.

18 Patricia Hart, *Narrative Magic in the Fiction of Isabel Allende* (London: Associated University Presses, 1989), 39. Hart, too, suggests that Allende uses "magical realism to make a feminist point." Yet, she argues forcefully that the magical in *House* is a metaphor for female passivity and so Alba must break from it in order "to accept responsibility for the world in which they live." She counters my argument that magic is used "to get our attention" and then abandoned with the suggestion that if clairvoyance (which she comes close to conflating with magic realism) is a trope for bourgeois passivity, it *must* be abandoned in order to preserve the feminist strength of *House*. Her reading, then, radically alters the way Allende's magical realism is usually discussed and instead posits the writer as generically and generically oppositional. See Hart's chapter "Clara/Clarividente."

19 Nineteenth-century conventions of the sentimental novel are a case in point. Both African American and white authors manipulated the genre, encoding challenges to gender and racial expectations. See Valerie Smith, "Loopholes of Retreat: Architecture and Ideology in Harriet Jacob's *Incidents in the Life of*

a Slave Girl," in *Reading Black, Reading Feminist,* ed. Henry Louis Gates Jr. (New York: Penguin Books, 1990), pp. 212–26; and Susan Harris, "'But Is It Any *Good?*': Evaluating Nineteenth-Century American Women's Fiction," *American Literature* 63, 1 (1991): 43–61.

20 See Jonathan Yardly's *Washington Post* review excerpt in the opening quotations of the Bantam paperback edition cited above.

21 Antoni, "Parody or Piracy," p. 22.

22 See the opening blurb of the paperback edition of *The House of the Spirits* (Bantam, 1986).

23 Morrison, "Rootedness," p. 342.

24 Ibid.

25 Darwin Turner, "Theme, Characterization, and Style in the Works of Toni Morrison," in *Black Women Writers,* p. 361.

26 Morrison tells us, "My writing expects, demands participatory reading. . . . It's not just about telling the story; it's about involving the reader." Quoted in Claudia Tate, *Black Women Writers at Work* (New York: Continuum Publishing, 1983), p. 125.

27 Toni Morrison, quoted in LeClair, "The Language Must Not Sweat," pp. 26–27.

28 One can trace the trajectory of this explanatory writing from the beginning of Afro-American fiction writing, where men and women like William Wells Brown and Frances E. W. Harper attempted to draw counterstereotypes to the existing negative depictions of black people in both the media and literature. This continued through the Harlem Renaissance, and one can still see novelists, critics, and community struggling with this issue — the responsibility of authors to provide "positive" characterization of their own people in a society that constantly sketches us in the most negative light. The debate over *The Color Purple* and other recent novels and theater pieces by Afro-American women clearly demonstrates this point.

29 Morrison, quoted in LeClair, "The Language Must Not Sweat," p. 28.

30 Ibid., p. 26.

31 Verónica Cortínez, "Polifonía: Entrevista a Isabel Allende y Antonio Skármeta," *Plaza* (Spring–Fall 1988): 77 (my translation).

32 Benjamin, "The Storyteller," in *Illuminations,* p. 87.

33 Morrison, "Rootedness," p. 340.

34 Ibid., p. 341.

RICHARD TODD

Narrative Trickery and Performative
Historiography: Fictional Representation of National
Identity in Graham Swift, Peter Carey,
and Mordecai Richler

Narrators of magic realism play confidence tricks on their readers, disavowing the more straightforward claim of the mimetic naturalist realist that what she or he is narrating actually happened in a heterocosmic world related to the one we know by analogy. Instead the magic realist narrator distorts the very idea of analogy and operates syncretically, asking the reader to believe, for instance, that the natural order of things can be subverted in the world of her or his fiction: hence the emphasis on extraordinary longevity or on the performance of bodily functions such as excessive urination or multiple motherhood, events that are not to be met with in the natural world.

An exemplary expression of the confidence trick leading to the subversion of the natural order of things is to be found in the alternative historiography that in various ways outrageously transgresses the "given facts" of history: Carlos Fuentes, Salman Rushdie, and Toni Morrison spring to mind as various practitioners of the transgressive historiography, and their work has received considerable attention. Of the three writers mentioned, however, it is Rushdie's form of magic realism that differs from the others in the way the narrator's voice, in texts such as *Midnight's Children* (1981) or *Shame* (1983), connives in the unfolding of the tale.

I want here to examine the work performed by the narrator's voice in the subversive unfolding of distinct national historiographies by three white male novelists not usually privileged in discussions of magic realism. This terrain is still actually rather unexplored, and I shall be considering instances of self-consciously performed trickery in the narration of national fictions of historiography. The fictional historiographies may not themselves be as transgressive as, for example, Fuentes' *Terra Nostra* (1975), in which sixteenth-century Iberian colonial history is actually rewritten, nor as culturally "different" as, for example, Morrison's *Beloved* (1988), in which the presence of ghosts and the community of mothers are more central features than they would be in a white European male magic realist fiction. But my justification for grouping together all three texts discussed here is that they are united by their status as *performance*. That status in turn justifies these texts' inclusion in a volume devoted to various aspects of history and community in magic realist fiction.

My case studies are these: Graham Swift's *Waterland* (1983), whose narrator's professional function as a teacher of history allows him to manipulate the chronology of his narrative, bringing it into confrontation with his own personal dynastic history, is the most diffident of all three narrators; Peter Carey's *Illywhacker* (1985), whose narrator performs the most ostensibly linear execution of his national historiography but is quite explicitly the least trustworthy of all three; and Mordecai Richler's *Solomon Gursky Was Here* (1989, 1990), whose narrative unfolds in such a way as to challenge his own existential presence in that narrative, a narrative whose form is the most fragmented of all three and comes to reflect the historiographical quest of all three.[1] The respective historiographies are those of (fenland) England, Australia, and Canada: I shall treat each case study in chronological order of publication.

Graham Swift: Waterland *(1983)*

Although the order of presentation of my three studies accords with the chronology of their publication, I regard it as particularly significant that a white male English writer has produced a fiction that can be claimed as magic realist; he has done so by turning to the regional historiography of a distinctive part of the British Isles and juxtaposing it against a more national historiography of England. This aspect of Swift's achievement distinguishes it from the European canvas delineated by his compatriot D. M. Thomas, whose *The White Hotel* is discussed elsewhere in this volume. Swift's strategy in *Waterland* is to posit alternatively performed historiographies to the publicly available regional and national historiographic narrative. It can be claimed that five kinds of historiography are performed in this novel. The list may well not be exhaustive but it does give an indication of the polyphony of Swift's performative historiographic art. Furthermore it allows us to see an osmotic relationship between these five kinds and to highlight the striking feature of the tone of the narrator, the history teacher Tom Crick.

Publicly available documented political historiography, events such as the French Revolution and Napoleonic conquests (1789–1815), the coronation of George V (1911), and the 1914–18 and 1939–45 world wars, run alongside the dynastic history of the narrator Tom Crick's own family. We shall see that only intermittently can public history be said actually to "make sense" of, or offer an explanation for, the private dynastic history: Tom's shell-shocked father is nursed back to health by his future bride; the teenage Crick himself enters a relationship with the equally youthful Mary Metcalf the course of which is certainly affected, though in no way decisively, by his being posted to Germany in the mid-1940s. What does affect the course of that relationship will be seen to belong to another historiographic realm altogether.

Running beside these two historiographies, the publicly national and the privately dynastic, is a third kind. This is a fantasy historiography tinted by the historical period to which it relates. It includes the description of the events leading up to the catatonia of Sarah Atkinson, her living death—following an assault by her husband—covering the period 1820 to 1874, her portentous cries of "Smoke!" "Fire!" "Burning!", the ghostly apparitions allegedly seen after her flood-ridden funeral in October 1874, and the fire that consumes the Atkinson brewery after an almost frenzied communal celebration by the town of Gildsey of the coronation of George V in 1911. All this belongs to a recognizable tradition of English Gothic.

A fourth kind is the topographical historiography of a unique area of the British Isles: the fen landscape of East Anglia. Such a historiography involves understanding how that landscape has shifted, advanced, and retreated over the years; how rivers alter their courses and coastlines change; how man-made engineering skills attempt to control the landscape. (It is not surprising that *Waterland* was a best-seller in the Netherlands.) An important figure is that of drainage, and it is preposterously brought into confrontation with aspects of other historiographies, notably bloodshed (that of a manslaughter victim in civilian life, those of the victims of the French Revolution).[2] Christopher Driver, reviewing *Waterland* when it first appeared, related this aspect of the novel to its narrative mode most felicitously: "[Swift's] very narrative method [is] preoccupied with ebbs and flows, backings and fillings. It floats hither and thither, and under critical pressure floods at an irresistible pace, but it avoids any sense of steady current. Crick's story is an apologia for history."[3]

A fifth kind of historiography is found in a life cycle whose mysterious-

ness seems incommensurate with or disproportionate to the seemingly atavistic nature of the animal, the eel, that undergoes it. A chapter is devoted
to the patient quest of the Danish ichthyologist Johannes Schmidt, who
from 1904 until the 1920s traced the increasingly small larvae of *Anguilla
anguilla* to the Sargasso Sea. At the same time, Europe is documented as
teetering toward, then collapsing into, cataclysm ("this four-year intermis-
sion").[4] Indeed, the concurrence of public and private historiographies is
held before us as other kinds than this fifth category are related. During
the catatonia of Sarah Atkinson, for instance, her absence is nevertheless
significantly *present* on the various civic and national occasions for celebration with the increasingly potent, even potional, Atkinson beer that
mark these years: the openings of water transportation facilities in 1833
and railroad transportation facilities in 1839; the Great Exhibition of 1851;
Sarah's son George's election as mayor of Gildsey in 1864, to name but
a few.

Early on in the fiction, we are given instances of fenland superstition:
"When you see the new moon, turn your money in your pocket; help someone to salt and help them to sorrow; never put new shoes on a table or
cut your nails on a Sunday. An eel-skin cures rheumatism; a roast mouse
cures whooping cough; and a live fish in a woman's lap will make her
barren" (15–16). These superstitions coexist arbitrarily for a while until
during an adolescent game of sexual daring, the future manslaughter victim, sixteen-year-old Freddie Parr, drops a live eel, a "good three-quarter
pounder" into Mary Metcalf's "school-regulation knickers" (166). It is as a
result of a botched abortion carried out by the village wise-woman Martha
Clay, or possibly also of Mary's prior attempts to effect the abortion herself, that irreversible physical damage occurs, leading to infertility. That
fact is to affect the postmenopausal Mary's sanity, so that she snatches
a child from a supermarket;[5] this episode threatens to terminate Crick's
career, jeopardized as it is already by a combination of his own subversive
history classes and the headmaster Lewis Scott's desire for retrenchment.
Fenland folklore — or one aspect of it — comes disastrously yet ludicrously
true, and we have here perhaps the most outrageous instance in *Waterland*
of osmosis between rival historiographies as they bleed into each other.[6]

For that botched abortion cannot be isolated from the private historiographies that surround it, and indeed the reader must wonder at Swift's
superb structural control of the multiple interrelated strands of the narrative Tom Crick relates. The adolescent Mary Metcalf and Tom Crick have

embarked on a sexual relationship; but Mary has also experimented sexually with Tom's mentally handicapped elder brother, aptly named Dick, and flirted with Freddie. Dick is the product of an incestuous union between Tom's mother, Helen Atkinson, and her own father, Ernest. Ernest has been born, portentously, during the 1874 floods that coincide with the funeral ceremony for his grandmother, the ninety-two-year-old Sarah Atkinson. Although possessing the mental age of a young child, Dick is endowed with extraordinary physical strength and legendary genitalia: he wins a swimming contest that is the pretext for the game of sexual bravado and is thus entitled to a "show" from Mary. He desists, but Mary keeps both Tom and Freddie Parr on a string by intimating that she has tried to have sex with Dick but that the latter is "too big." Dick knows, obscurely, that he himself is "a bungle . . . [s]omething that shouldn't be" (279), the result of a union that in the human world is socially taboo and that he must not attempt to reproduce himself. The counterpoint between Dick and *Anguilla anguilla* is maintained to the end, with Dick's apparent suicide by drowning, or rather, perhaps, his affirmative reception into his true element, the real event to which his entire life has led up and for which his winning achievement in front of Mary and his rivals has been a mere rehearsal:

> He turns. . . . He clambers on to the rail, shoeless, upon it, disdaining the handhold of the adjacent derrick stanchions. Stretches to full height. For a moment he perches, poises, teeters on the rail, the dull glow of the western sky behind him. And then he plunges. In a long, reaching, powerful arc. Sufficiently long and reaching to quite discount the later theory that he must have become entangled in the anchor-chain or the sling-lines; sufficiently reaching and powerful for us to observe his body, in its flight through the air, form a single, taut and seemingly limbless continuum, so that an expert on diving might have judged that here indeed was a natural, here indeed was a fish of a man. (309)

The almost Shakespearean cadence, with its finely judged play on "natural,"[7] suggests that Dick has been appropriated away from any naturalist historiography into the magically realist world that has always been as it were waiting in the wings of Crick's naturalist narrative. This naturalist narrative moves forward very little in time to culminate bathetically in the child-snatching episode (another "miscarriage") involving the increasingly deranged Mary Crick. The narrative does not return, after Dick's suicide, to the naturalist mode, yet the full unfolding of the pretext for Dick's amphibious apotheosis is contained in an episode that belongs fully to the naturalist mimetic world. Tom Crick the narrator discovers that Freddie Parr has been killed by Dick, owing to Dick's confusion concerning the paternity of Mary's child. Mary has told Dick the child is Dick's; yet even she seems uncertain which of the Crick brothers is actually the father. The possibility that the father might, after all, be Dick, perhaps at one level motivates Mary's inducing the abortion that Martha Clay, "the witch," performs. Tom must discard the fetus into the Ouse without looking (since that is supposed to be unlucky), but he does so all the same. Is this another instance of fenland superstition only engaging occasionally and by pure chance with the reality it purports to predict? The text gives no decisive answer.

The autopsy has shown Freddie's blood-alcohol to be of a level consistent with death by drowning while in a stupor (his father has been bootlegging whisky from the American air force pilots stationed in the area in the early 1940s); we have learnt from the narrative that Freddie cannot swim; in trying to fish Freddie's corpse out of the river (the episode with which Tom Crick's narrative begins), Tom's lockkeeper father Henry damages it with a hook. In so doing, Henry Crick obscures what turns out to be the mark inflicted by his "half-son" Dick, who has struck Freddie with a beer bottle from a collection totemically bequeathed to him by his (and Tom's) late mother. Dick, having once tried this potent and potional beer and having suffered the consequences unusually severely, has superstitiously hoarded the rest. Now, prepared for his apotheosis, he swallows a final bottle (one liquid element comprising his and Tom's dynastic historiographical identity) and commits himself to the Ouse (another liquid element comprising his and Tom's regional historiographical identity). The novel ends on the arresting image of a human, who has never been in his true element, instinctively and atavistically finding his natural one, as do the eels with which this extraordinary narrative wriggles and threshes.

Peter Carey: Illywhacker (1985)

If *Waterland* is suffused with instances of regional and national historiography constantly being elbowed out of center stage by an obsessive dynastic preoccupation with pedigree, the national historiography running alongside Herbert Badgery's performance as the narrator of *Illywhacker* is constantly upstaged, or artfully finessed, by scrutiny of the diaspora that has brought about twentieth-century Australian society, a dynamic stirring up or displacement within the national gene pool. This vision of Australian society in search of a self is, as elsewhere in Carey's work, counterpointed by the belief that Australia consistently presents herself as an exploited colony. As her history has progressed, the colonizing power has changed: from the British through the nineteenth century, the colonial reins pass to American hands in the period through World War II, before finally being surrendered to Japan, as the Pacific rim is constructed to conform to its late twentieth-century postindustrial contours.[8] The particularity of this aspect of Australian historiography, and the way in which it will be seen to differ from Richler's text's perception of Canadian historiography, need stressing. At the same time it must be allowed that both cultures — although in different ways — present themselves defensively in regard to the United States.

I have already suggested that *Illywhacker* is the most linearly presented narrative of the three under discussion here, but I need to qualify this suggestion in two ways. The entire six hundred-page novel is, to be sure, one enormous flashback from the point at which the bandy-legged Herbert Badgery claims to be 139 years old, and apparently in some way an exhibit. But there are, firstly, smaller movements back and forth within the larger framework of the flashback. Secondly, and more significantly, despite Badgery's admission that he is a "terrible liar," his age, he tells us, is:

> the one fact you can rely on, and not because I say so, but because it has been publicly authenticated. Independent experts have poked me and prodded me and scraped around my foul-smelling mouth. They have measured my ankles and looked at my legs. . . . When they photographed me I did not care that my dick looked as scabby and scaly as a horse's, even though there was a time when I was a vain man and would not have permitted the type of photographs they chose to take.[9]

The linear execution of Badgery's mode of flashback presentation affects a trustworthiness that is free of the evasions and chronological manipulations of Swift's and Richler's texts. Yet there is a problem at the outset. It is not simply that Badgery's longevity challenges straightforward realist assumptions in the way any such challenge can be mounted in a historical narrative. Carey flaunts the ontological dubiousness of his whole enterprise from the very start: the flashbacks are episodic, but Badgery (who has promised that he is not lying about his age even though he may lie about anything else) begins with an episode that takes place in 1919 when he is himself thirty-three. If this is so, we must accept that he was born in 1886 and has reached the age of 139 in 2025.[10] Whereas the reader's initial accommodation to the magic realist convention of excessive longevity is a strategy that may be enacted from the book's opening page, it is almost immediately made to submit to the need to accommodate to the ontological status of a magic realist fiction narrated, apparently, some forty years in advance of the novel's historical publication in 1985. Even by magic realist criteria this opening presents the reader with an unusually sharply focused need to confront the confidence trickery of the narrator of *Illywhacker*, especially as the novel's second epigraph is one of philological pedantry: it uses a dictionary of Australian colloquialisms to trace the term "Illywhacker" as "A professional trickster, esp. operating at country shows" (9; the first epigraph cites Mark Twain on the lying truthfulness of Australian history). Later, Leah Goldstein will curtly echo the dictionary: "A spieler. . . . A trickster. A quandong. A ripperty man. A con-man" (246). A little later still, Badgery is required to sell a client a car: "Of course I liked Miss Adamson. I was about to sell her a car. I would have loved her if I had needed to" (267). In such ways does trickery direct the course of Badgery's narrative.

Having urged that the ontological dubiousness of the entire narrative is made to coexist with its linear execution, I should now single out the three major periods in Badgery's life, conforming to the text's division into three sections (Books), through which *Illywhacker* contrives to convey the larger historiographical narrative of twentieth-century Australia: not simply through diaspora leading to a cultural mosaic, but by genetic and marital displacement leading to subversion of pedigree; not simply through colonization by greater powers, but by cultural pluriformity (here understood in a profoundly dynastic sense) as well. Pluriformity extends into a community peopled by machines and animals in abundance, one indeed whose human inhabitants have extraordinary affinities with these manifestations of pluriformity. So strong are these affinities that human experience can be and frequently is actually displaced by the mechanical or the animal: it is as such totalizing phenomena that diaspora and colonialism are to be understood in the historiographical community of *Illywhacker*. What emerges from the narrative is that the magic realist fiction can present genetics and heredity that operate at both literal and figurative levels syncretically, as the straightforward realist fiction cannot. The literal and the figurative coexist, in this particular magic realist fiction, through the displacing agency of trickery.

Reducing the countless riches of Badgery's narrative flashback to barest essentials for the purposes of sketching out patterns of dynastic displacement, then, we observe that the novel's first book opens in 1919. Badgery, a Model T Ford sales agent and amateur air pilot, encounters the McGrath family: Jack (who suffers from deafness), Molly (née Rourke, who may have inherited a trait of insanity from her own mother), and their daughter Phoebe, whom he will marry. Phoebe gives her (or a) reason for being attracted to Badgery: "You have invented yourself, Mr. Badgery, and that is why I like you. . . . You can be anything you want" (91). Not until toward the end of the book do we discover that the marriage is (on Badgery's part) bigamous: indeed Badgery has not only suppressed his first wife from his story, but largely written his own parents out of it as well. Jack and Molly McGrath thus come, to a certain extent, to fulfill the parental roles, giving the illicit relationship with the bisexual Phoebe a further, quasi-incestuous, twist.[11] (If we are to believe Badgery later on, who recalls the episode for a purpose of his own while admitting most of it was lies, he and his mother-in-law Molly have a year-long affair after Jack's death and Phoebe's defection.) There are two children of his marriage to Phoebe, Charles and Sonia. The elder, Charles, apparently conceived on Phoebe's and Badgery's wedding night, survives Phoebe's attempt to abort him after she has fallen in love with an epileptic poet named Horace Dunlop. Here the text explicitly poses the question of agency and (implicitly) additional questions of legitimacy and heredity: "So while we all made decisions, thinking it up to God, or the doctor, my willpower or Phoebe's connivance, it was none of our doing at all, and it was Charles who fought and won the battle against the cloudy liquid [procured for the attempted abortion]" (181). For a while before Charles' birth Badgery repeatedly sees a ghost he takes to be that of Jack (who has been bitten to death by one of Badgery's snakes) and begins obsessively to connect this ghost, writhing with snakes, to the impending event.

The second book advances Badgery's narrative to 1931 and beyond. In this most picaresque section of *Illywhacker*, Badgery and his two children encounter the dancer Leah Goldstein, whose relationship with her estranged husband Izzie Kaletsky and his charismatically politicized parents Rosa and Lenny (who can bend iron bars between his teeth) is presented as not wholly dissimilar to that between Badgery and the McGrath household in the first book. Badgery and Leah set up a peripatetic circus act (Badgery & Goldstein) that is constantly being harassed and made to move on for politically institutionalized anticommunist and anti-Semitic reasons. Badgery's contribution to the act was intended to be his ability to make himself disappear, which he has been taught as a child in 1897 by the "Chinaman" Goon Tse Ying but is only once more ever in his life able to repeat. A precondition is fear, and in metafictional terms it could be argued that Badgery is too confidently in control of his narrative to submit to this emotion. Badgery & Goldstein is rescued by Charles' emerging affinity for snakes, which become a part of the act.

It is Leah who reminds Badgery of what she at any rate sees as the reason for their picaresque lifestyle:

> "The matter is obvious. The land is stolen. The whole country is stolen. The whole nation is based on a lie which is that it was not already occupied when the British came here. If it is anybody's place it is the blacks'. Does it look like your place? Does it feel like your place? Can't you see, even the trees have nothing to do with you." (307)

And later:

> "[This] is not a country where you can rest. It is a black man's country, sharp stones, rocks, sticks, bull ants, flies. We can only move around it like tourists. The blackfeller can rest but we must keep moving. That is why I can't return with my husband as he wishes," she announced, seeking rest in a simple theory, "because I am selfish, addicted to movement." (323)[12]

The second book is terminated by two tragedies. Leah returns to Izzie after he has lost both legs under a train while trying to escape from police thugs. In addition the train, "like some Corsican bandit who wishes to leave a sign, cut[s] the top of an index finger with a neat razor slice" (362). Charles and Sonia have both been intrigued by the possibility of the disappearing trick, and each has tried it, repeatedly and unsuccessfully. For each it represents something different: for the physically gauche and unprepossessing Charles, truly his father's son, it is an escape from a hostile world that he is fortunately too doggedly unself-conscious to see as such (in this sense, if no other, he can make himself disappear). Sonia, perhaps spoiled by her father after Phoebe's desertion (so, at any rate, Leah sees things) and certainly her mother's daughter, develops into an eclectically pious little girl who has herself confirmed five times in various churches. She dreams of a Blessed Assumption and performs the disappearing trick conclusively and spectacularly when she vanishes down a disused mine shaft. Badgery, blaming Charles for the accident, hits him so hard over the head as to deafen him. Subsequently Badgery reencounters a by now completely anglicized Goon Tse Ying, no longer a "Chinaman" but the Australian "Charlie" Goon. Badgery's recall of events in 1897 is destabilized by Goon's alternative version ("I remember you. . . . You made up stories all the time. . . . Hing said you were a sorcerer. Mrs. Wong was frightened of you. You made her frightened with a story about a snake" [369]). Badgery, blaming Goon for Sonia's disappearance, sees Goon's answer as a betrayal, but to the reader he and Goon are seen—literally—to be talking two different languages. To Goon's mother (we learn) to make a "dragon" is both to tell a frightening story and to lie. Badgery resolves to steal Goon's accounts book, the cover of which is adorned with dragons. He is successful and in addition acquires Goon's bleeding index finger in the scuffle. By the third book, dismembered extremities as displaced talismans will come to accumulate, functioning as a cluster of magic signifiers.[13]

By now we have established, among much else, that Charles Badgery has come displacedly, through *both* Badgery's narrative sleight of hand *and* his bizarre stirring up of the national gene pool, to "inherit" from his grandfather Jack McGrath his deafness and his affinity for snakes. Charles has also inherited his bandy legs from Badgery himself. Manipulation of his hearing aid will enhance Charles' ability to "disappear." Badgery serves a prison sentence for theft and assault: the third book finds Charles in 1938—having missed an opportunity to fight against Franco in Spain and having left what he sees as the threatening sophistication of Sydney (where he has been briefly reconciled with Phoebe)—riding his motorbike into the Victorian outback to cure a mouse plague with his bag of pythons. This book will take us up to the "present"—whenever that is—from which Badgery is relating his flashback. Meanwhile the sadistic police sergeant "Moth" ("if there's a light on, he'll turn up" [458]) has Goon's finger preserved in formaldehyde and sells it to Badgery in prison, reminding him how things change shape in dreams. Accordingly Goon's finger grows a wart that increases in size, before "chang[ing] like a face in a dream": "I will not upset myself by describing the slimy monsters that tried to free themselves from that bottle, but rather tell you about the morning I woke early and found it filled with bright blue creatures that darted in and out of delicate filigree forests, like tropical fish feeding among the coral" (415). Stranded near Jeparit, Victoria — when, the mouse plague in the Chaffey household having been eradicated, his host Les Chaffey obsessively dismembers Charles' motorbike and procrastinates its reassembly — Charles begins to amass the fauna that will form the basis for the "Best Pet Shop in the World." He makes his mark on the community of Jeparit when he rescues the young schoolteacher Emma Underhill, whom a six-foot goanna has mounted thinking her to be a tree. Only Charles has sufficient affinity with the animal kingdom to capture the goanna and free Emma, whom he subsequently marries.

In gaol Badgery is visited by Moth's brother, Fr. Moran, who, apparently attempting to exorcise what is in the formaldehyde jar, accidentally drops it. It would appear later, however, that the jar does not break, as Badgery has it with him on his release from gaol. Fr. Moran's accident is juxtaposed with the outbreak of World War II and Australia's mobilization on September 11, 1939, on which day the goanna, attacked by a fox terrier it then manages to disembowel, nonetheless parts with a foreleg. Emma loses her reason (much as Molly McGrath née Rourke had earlier lost hers — another instance of genetic displacement) and intermittently but increasingly imprisons herself and her baby Henry in a cage. Emma has two more children, George (a little younger than Henry) and Hissao (much younger, whom Charles had thought to be named Michael). The paternity of Hissao, whose looks are Japanese, is left uncertain even though among the visitors to Emma's cage is a Mr. Lo, apparently Chinese, a "marine architect, illegal immigrant" (499). By the time Badgery arrives on the scene (and from this point, time becomes gradually less specific), Mr. Lo has confined himself to, or been granted asylum in, a neighboring cage, and Emma "[has given] him a job" (500). Badgery sees his lost daughter Sonia in Hissao. Mr. Lo increasingly comes to seem a red herring the more we learn about Hissao: nonetheless Hissao has displacedly inherited architectural skills. In a marvelously ironic passage Badgery tells us that Hissao:

> had somehow slipped through the genetic minefields his progenitors had laid for him. Not only were his legs straight but he avoided the lonely excesses of masculinity represented by his bull-necked, jutjawed Easter Island father. He had curling black hair, smooth olive

skin, and red cherubic lips which suggested, strongly at some times, weakly at others, an oriental parent who did not exist. (557)

Not only is Hissao bisexual, apparently losing his virginity in both orientations on consecutive days at the age of eighteen: he is capable of appearing feminine rather than masculine, Italian rather than Japanese according to the beholder and/or the circumstances.

It is Hissao who is especially fascinated by the goanna's double penis, and Charles who is revolted by the way Emma likes to stroke it (or them) into arousal. Eventually Emma discloses that the contents of the formaldehyde jar have turned into a half-human, half-goanna fetus, claiming this to be Hissao's half-brother; perhaps the goanna's mistaking Emma for a tree is to be regarded, quite implausibly, as some kind of delayed reptilian impregnation. Charles has Hissao take him and the by now twenty-four-year-old goanna to a patch of wasteland and shoots it before turning his rifle on himself. Later, back in Badgery's possession, the contents of the formaldehyde bottle reveal themselves to him as "a dragon, a solid being, two inches tall. . . . It reared up on its hind legs and scratched at the glass with its long black claws while its whole body pulsed with rage, changing from a deep black green to a bloated pearlescent grey" (579).

Charles' suicide occurs on the day the Best Pet Shop in the World comes under American management. Hissao comes to represent the ultimate in genetic displacement: his fascination with the goanna's double penis is mysteriously though inexplicitly connected with the wanton puzzles Badgery proffers and withholds concerning what Emma may or may not have known about his parentage. In this way the genetic pool is stirred still further. Eventually Hissao secures a deal from the Mitsubishi company that enables a Japanese takeover of the Best Pet Shop in the World, and Badgery the *Illywhacker* and Leah Goldstein (advertised as "Melbourne Jew") are revealed to be among the exhibits.

One final little emblem may be cited to conclude this exploration of the way *Illywhacker*'s narrative trickery works. The emblem serves to show how a given reality may, through an act of sleight of hand (or what, in this particular case, is specifically termed "counterfeit"), come to comprise an allotrope or constitute a heterocosmic world. As such it forms one of the many building bricks out of which the displaced genealogical historiography of Australia is fashioned and shows how that historiography has constructed itself. Leah's father, Sid Goldstein, has a physically pitiful doctor friend known as "Poor Wysbraum" with whom he has shared a suit of clothes. Their fortunes improve, and Sid gives the suit away to a shoelace seller whose need is greater than theirs. The solitary Wysbraum is aghast ("You have given away my history"), and Sid undertakes to repair the damage done. This means nothing less than reconstructing the suit in its existential entirety, "lovingly counterfeit[ing] the tear Wysbraum had made falling off the cable car twenty years before," for instance, and replacing all the olfactory richness and squalor of years of split meals, so that when Sid returns the suit Wysbraum is able to accept it emotionally as "a perfect copy" (240–42).

Mordecai Richler: Solomon Gursky Was Here *(1989)*

The three communities that my reading of *Illywhacker* has served to highlight in its portrayal of Australian national historiography are profiled more sharply still in Mordecai Richler's chronologically chaotic portrayal of the Canadian cultural mosaic.[14] In *Solomon Gurksy Was Here*, communal myths are examined quite explicitly as they come into conflict with each other, dissolving at the novel's end into a profoundly unanswerable icon: the black raven comes to represent some kind of statement as to where Canada's cultural identity can be said to lie. Again, in the space available here I can only select some of the many ways in which Eskimo myths of creation, Judaic myths of diaspora, and WASP (here, Scottish Presbyterian) myths of colonization combine and intermingle to place legitimacy and bastardy in a delicate balance. In such a selection, regretfully, many of the novel's resonances must remain undiscussed. Here there is no "either/or" between dynastic claims made through close blood relations (as in *Waterland*); neither are there dynamic stirrings-up of the national gene pool (as in *Illywhacker*). What faces the reader of *Gursky* before the narrative even begins is a genealogical tree (complete with a list of "begats") asserting the centrality of the hot-eyed Ephraim Gursky (1817–1910), the sage whose "anointed one"[15] is his second grandson Solomon (1899–1934 [*sic*]). The perception of Solomon's special status is that of the eldest grandson Bernard (1898–1973). Yet the text does not hide their grandfather Ephraim's promiscuousness: indeed it explicitly records the fact or legend that Ephraim "never . . . laid eyes on his son [by a Mrs. Nicholson in the early 1830s], the first of what would become twenty-seven unacknowledged offspring, not all of them the same color" (220). Gursky confronts the Canadian community with various forms of inheritance that range from the tangibly financial to the intangibly numinous.

At the most factually realist level, the narrative relates the rise of the whisky empire headed by Bernard Gursky, a character so skillfully created as constantly to avoid deterioration into cliché and stereotype. Bernard Gursky seems to be modeled on the historical Samuel Bronfman of Seagrams, at once God in his own empire yet powerless to break into Canada's WASP establishment. As with the historical Bronfman, Bernard Gursky's greatest yearning is for public acclaim expressed in terms of a Senate seat and as an officer of the Order of the British Empire, and these things are denied him. It later transpires as a matter of some significance that Canadian citizens, though subjects of the same head of state as the United Kingdom, are ineligible for British knighthoods. Having received a send-off to eternity about as hagiographic as that accorded the late Robert Maxwell, Bernard and his conduct in extremis are more phlegmatically recalled by the cryptic youngest brother Morrie (b. 1901):

> Mr. Bernard tried to scratch [his wife Libby], intent on drawing blood, but he no longer had the strength. "No, no" was all he could manage.
>
> "Bernie, Bernie," she sobbed, "do you believe in God?"
>
> "How can you talk such crap at a time like this?"
>
> "It's not crap, sweetie pie."
>
> "It's not crap, she says. Don't you understand? Don't you understand anything? If God exists, I'm fucked."
>
> And then, Mr. Morrie said, he was gone. (496)

This episode is related to Morris Berger, himself caught in a variety of ways in the Gursky web. Moses' father, L.B., an intense but quixotic literary hack, finally begins to achieve some worldly success, and in consequence finds himself first losing touch with the Jewish bohemians of his younger days before being actually lionized by gentile Canadian high society.

> Then came the summons from Sinai. L.B. was invited to an audience at Mr. Bernard's opulent redoubt cut high into the Montreal mountainside and he descended from those heights, his head spinning, pledged to unheard-of abundance, an annual retainer of ten thousand dollars to serve as speech writer and cultural adviser to the legendary liquor baron.

"And this," Mr. Bernard had said, leading him into a long room with empty oak shelves running from ceiling to floor, "will be my library. Furnish it with the best. I want first editions. The finest morocco bindings. You have a blank check, L.B."

Then Libby was heard from. "But nothing secondhand."

"I beg your pardon, Mrs. Gursky?"

"Germs. That's all I need. We have three children, God bless them." (18)

Characteristically, Richler has the hitherto taciturn but exotic Shloime Bishnisky speak out, in a way Moses will later recall more than once:

"What I am trying to say, forgive me, is that such princes in America are entitled to their mansions, a Rolls-Royce, chinchilla coats, yachts, young cuties out of burlesque shows. But a poet they should never be able to afford. It has to do with what? Human dignity. The sanctity of the word. I'm explaining it badly. But the man I took you for, L.B., you are not. Forgive me, Bessie, but I can't come here anymore." (19)

This reproach exercises Moses in profoundly complex, even obsessive, ways. It begins to alienate him from his father and leads him to seek identification with another such figure. Moses becomes drawn into the Gursky family, particularly into Solomon's mysterious disappearance during the 1934 prosecution brought by the Royal Canadian Mounted Police for tax evasion consequent on the family's pursuing a lucrative bootlegging trade during the United States Prohibition years (1919–33). It is on this trade that the bulk of the Gursky fortune has been built, although it should be pointed out that the initial capital is actually raised by Solomon's spectacularly successful poker gamble with the minute Gursky holdings as they had been in 1916. Like the historical Bronfman, who was tried under similar circumstances, the surviving Gursky brothers are acquitted. A later encounter with an anglicized European exile, Sir Hyman Kaplansky, appears finally to result in Moses having once more found his lost father figure. Not only does L.B.'s becoming lapdog to Bernard Gursky result in Moses' first encountering Lionel, the outrageous Gursky heir-presumptive; Moses also meets Lionel's cousins, the late Solomon's children Henry and Lucy, both severely disturbed psychologically and emotionally. Moses keeps up with both into later life: with Lucy as she declines into an eccentric and increasingly drug-ridden existence as a theatrical impresario; with Henry as he grows into even more eccentric retreat into the Arctic north (from where Ephraim first appears in the narrative's opening in 1851) and into marriage with the Eskimo Canadian Nialie, who bears the first *legitimate* son to a Gursky by a member of the local ethnic community.[16] This son, Isaac, is paradoxically (in view of his maternal inheritance) brought up into orthodox Jewry at Henry's behest and with Nialie's compliance. Henry's childhood stammer and enuresis disappear, and he becomes as adept as his father and great-grandfather at survival north of "sixty degrees." Moses becomes additionally intertwined in the Gursky history through his alcoholism: he is seriously addicted to the spirituous liquid through which the grandsons of Ephraim Gursky have made their millions. In this way, incidentally, the entire narrative defies a stereotype of Judaism and alcoholic temperance. It is perhaps helpful to relate this subversion to the way in which Moses' own Judaic inheritance is something he comes to feel deeply ambivalent about: indeed in this respect his plight illustrates the dilemma of any member of the Canadian mosaic, which is a community unlike any other. What happens to one's identity when once accepts institutional subsidies to preserve that identity within a multicultural community? Is to accept such subsidy an affirmative gesture, or is it to permit oneself to become marginalized or even ghettoized? This dilemma, which Moses never manages to solve, both gives the narrative great poignancy and at the same time motivates his quest for what really happened to Solomon Gursky when he took off into a whiteout in his Gypsy Moth during the 1934 tax evasion proceedings.

That disappearance is the mirror image of Ephraim Gursky's irruption into the narrative, a narrative whose authorship remains unclear but at any rate changes irreversibly on a second and subsequent reading. Much but by no means all of what appears omniscience from a voice outside the story turns out on a second or subsequent reading to be Moses' reconstruction and rewriting of Solomon's diaries, which come into Moses' hands thanks to Sir Hyman Kaplansky.[17] The chaotic nature of the entire narrative serves simultaneously to refract Moses' alcoholism, which takes the form of binge alternating with clinic treatment, and the extended mirror relationship binding Ephraim and Solomon Gursky. For, just as the factual realist aspect of the story is constituted out of the narrative of the Gursky whisky empire, so the magic realist aspect is compounded of the events preceding Ephraim Gursky's appearance in southern Quebec in the record cold winter of 1851 and those subsequent to Solomon Gursky's disappearance in 1934.

Ephraim's arrival in Canada itself is presented as a piece of transgressive historiography. *Gursky*'s reader is invited to believe that Ephraim is the illegitimate progeny of an affair between his father Gideon (1773–1828) and an opera singer that brings Gideon's career as cantor in a Minsk synagogue to an end. The Gurskys relocate to Liverpool, and when orphaned at the age of eleven, Ephraim makes his picaresque way to London. During the course of this journey Ephraim learns Latin and penmanship from the pederastic schoolteacher Mr. Nicholson, a training that enables Ephraim to forge documents. After a brief exotic youth of crime, Ephraim is sentenced to transportation to Van Diemen's Land in 1835 on forgery charges. He manages to escape this fate, and he and his companion Izzy Garber set up as bonesetters. In the Orkneys they illicitly join the doomed Franklin expedition in search of the Northwest Passage in 1845, with Ephraim as surgeon to HMS *Erebus*. History tells us that there were no survivors of this expedition: the novel tells us otherwise. Izzy Garber apparently dies shortly after the pair's arrival in Canada in 1846. Meanwhile Ephraim sets himself up as a shamanic rabbi and brings his bizarre Judaeo-Eskimo millenarianism to the local population, contriving to discredit the local shaman by trickery. Included in the millenarian credo is a version of Yom Kippur, a law "laid down [by Ephraim] in a foolish and absentminded moment, overlooking the fact that his faith provided for all contingencies save that of the Arctic adherent" (403). (It is characteristic of Richler's densely textured narrative that Ephraim's great-grandson, the Dostoevskian holy fool, Henry, takes it on himself to ensure no errant members of the sect be consigned to spend Yom Kippur in the four-month Arctic night.)

One indication of the complexity with which the magic realist elements intermingle with the factually realist family chronicle of the Gursky whisky empire may be briefly given here. In one of his aliases, that of the Reverend Isaac Horn, it can be said to be Ephraim Gursky who actually sows the seeds of the 1934 prosecution. Horn charismatically engineers a fraudulent campaign of disaffected English emigrants in 1901, offering them the Promised Land in northern Saskatchewan. After a nightmare voyage, the emigrants arrive to discover the ghastly truth of their barren destination. A descriptive sample of the surreal nature of that voyage will show how skillfully Richler can control the tone of the various forms of realism he employs:

> In two weeks at sea the Reverend Horn, secure in his cabin, was seen below decks only twice. On the fourth day out a miner had his arm broken in a drunken brawl, and it was the Reverend Horn who set the bone and fixed it with a splint. He was seen again after another fight, this one with knives, come to stitch the men's wounds. But a certain Mrs. Bishop swore she had seen him striding up and down the bridge the night of the gale, the puny *Excelsior* scaling twenty-foot waves before plunging into a trough, sliding trunks smashing into walls, splinters flying, the ship's fracturing surely imminent. Bare-chested he was, drunken, howling into the lashing wind and rain. "Face-to-face. I want to see you face-to-face just once." (77)

Among the ship's emigrants are a hapless couple named Archie and Nancy Smith. Their son Bert, born in 1903, receives a strictly fundamentalist upbringing, emerging as a character virtually as repellent as Bernard Gursky himself. It is Smith's persistent halitotic snaggle-toothed obduracy that finally secures, against the better judgment of establishment parties with vested interests, the 1934 prosecution.

The "elusive, obscenely rich" (457) Sir Hyman Kaplansky emerges in wartime London as a philanthropist, receiving his knighthood for services to the Conservative party. He too transgresses authorized historiography: in his iconic guise as an elderly man sitting with his chin propped on his malacca cane, he is seen in a July 1962 photograph in Moses' possession of John F. Kennedy and Marilyn Monroe.[18] Among his Monroe autopsy material Moses also possesses an unsigned telegram sent from Madrid: "I KNOW WHAT YOU ARE THINKING BUT THE LAST PHONE CALL WAS NOT FROM ME" (71). At the novel's denouement Moses discovers in Kaplansky's possession in England the striking portrait of Solomon Gursky's abandoned femme fatale Diana McClure, one eye blue and one eye brown, a portrait that had disappeared from the Gursky mansion shortly after Solomon himself did.[19] Kaplansky deftly rescues the occasion by pointing to another picture:

> A raven perched on a half-open sea-shell, human beings struggling to emerge from it.
> "This is the raven that stole the light of the world from an old

man and then scattered it throughout the skies. After the great flood had receded, he flew to a beach to gorge himself on the delicacies left behind by the water. However, he wasn't hungry for once." Looking directly at Moses, a stricken Moses, [Kaplansky] went on to say, "But his other appetites—lust, curiosity, and the unquenchable itch to meddle and provoke things, to play tricks on the world and its creatures—these remained unsatisfied." (455)

Kaplansky then sends Moses on a wild-goose chase to Paris, and while Moses is away he learns that Kaplansky has "apparently drowned in stormy seas" (456) while taking his prebreakfast swim despite warnings about the weather. Opening the package with which he has been entrusted, Moses not only finds three more volumes of Solomon Gursky's journals but discovers that his further investigations into the Gursky myth will be financed by Corvus Investment Trust, Zurich. This is the legacy of which at various points earlier in *Gursky* Moses has been unwilling to speak. Perusal of earlier installments of Solomon's journals has confirmed Moses' belief, against all probability, that the 1934 disappearance was faked: there is, for instance, an account of Mao's Long March of 1935, with Solomon and the remnants he accompanies being saved after the mysterious appearance of a raven Solomon has apparently summoned, as both Ephraim and Solomon have done elsewhere. Later, Kaplansky resurfaces in various increasingly preposterous guises, as Mr. Cuervo, Mr. Corbeau, or retrospectively in wartime aliases such as the Swiss financier Herr Dr. Otto Raven. The etymologies supply the links at which the narrative hints.[20]

Both Ephraim and Solomon are linked by their multiple aliases, protean identities, and by their transgressive presence in authorized historical events. They are also linked by such things as the social poise and sexual charisma that exercise universal appeal and destabilize the social and sexual identities of those around them; astonishing powers of survival in hostile environments whether air, land, or water; and the ability constantly to finesse and wrong-foot their opponents. Is all this merely the raven's "unquenchable itch to meddle and provoke things"? Not entirely: Solomon's disappearance is linked with the quarrel among the Gursky brothers at the time of the 1934 prosecution as to whether or not Bernard should be the majority shareholder. Solomon threatens to return from the grave if necessary to prevent his own children Henry and Lucy from being disadvantaged—a feat he manages to achieve, perhaps even desecrating the tomb of Bernard *Gursky* with "[a] raven skewered and harpooned to the grave" (234). Is the mark on the harpoon a Gimel, the third letter of the Hebrew alphabet, or the "maker's sign" (236)? In any event, the Gursky empire is inherited by Isaac and Barney (son to Mr. Morrie) and Bernard is cut out. Isaac has been rehabilitated by the family following the accident in which Henry had been killed on his last Arctic journey and Isaac had had to cannibalize his father's corpse to survive, just as Ephraim and Izzy had survived by cannibalism in 1846. Mr. Bernard's portrait is removed from the Fifth Avenue office in New York and replaced by that of Ephraim. The inheritance has been reclaimed. Solomon, who has been quoted in the novel's epigraph as saying "Living twice, three times maybe, is the best revenge," has sent Moses a perplexing note that voices a doubt the reader must feel too: "I once told you that you were no more than a figment of my imagination. Therefore, if you continued to exist, so must I" (507).

Conclusion

In *Waterland* Graham Swift presents us with a magic realist fiction embedded within the recall that constitutes the subversive history lessons of Tom Crick. Crick's own contemporaneous narrative is impoverished, sterile, and reduced. What gives Swift's text the magic it possesses is the way in which Crick's alternative historiographies, Gothic, topographical, and atavistic, performatively osmose or bleed into each other through various kinds of rhetorical trickery, suffused as they are with a claustrally intense feeling for region, pedigree, dynasty, legitimacy, and its opposite. In *Illywhacker* Peter Carey allows Herbert Badgery's narrated genealogies to exercise a displacing effect so that genetic transfer can actually be figured metaphorically as well (as in the narrative trickery whereby deafness and madness pass down the generations). Herein lies the magic of this text. The alternative historiographies of *Illywhacker* are displacedly dynastic and the national gene pool is stirred up in such a way that the national historiography provides individual dynastic subversions with a vast dusty backdrop. Communal historiography becomes in *Illywhacker* something utterly "unclaustral": it is made up of unbelonging, it is nomadic and picaresque; and it is so strongly counterpointed by illicitness and collusion in performance that in the end the text gives no distinct answer as to whether finally Badgery is indeed to be seen as the trickster or the tricked. In *Solomon Gursky Was Here*, the trickery of Solomon increases in the magically realist sections of the narrative posterior to his disappearance from Canada in 1934 and in so doing mirrors that of his grandfather Ephraim prior to the latter's mythical arrival in southern Quebec in 1851. Moses Berger, the assembler and chronicler of these lives, is magically animated as he performs his discovery of how Ephraim's heritage is passed on through the trickery of his "anointed one," Solomon. For Moses to apprehend this magic dimension to Canadian historiography requires that a failed myth of Canada (as represented in the sheer materialism of the Bernard Gursky family) be discarded: here is that myth, as drunkenly expounded to Solomon by Tim Callaghan, a former bootlegging confederate of Solomon's:

> Let me put it this way. Canada is not so much a country as a holding tank filled with the disgruntled progeny of defeated peoples. French Canadians consumed by self-pity; the descendants of Scots who fled the Duke of Cumberland; Irish the famine; and Jews the Black Hundreds. Then there are the peasants from the Ukraine, Poland, Italy, and Greece, convenient to grow wheat and dig the ore and swing the hammers and run the restaurants, but otherwise to be kept in their place. Most of us are still huddled tight to the border, looking into the candy-store window, scared by the Americans on one side and the bush on the other. And now that we are here, prospering, we do our damn best to exclude more ill-bred newcomers, because they remind us of our own mean origins in the draper's shop in Inverness or the *shtetl* or the bog. What was I talking about? (367)

Perhaps nothing in all three novels discussed in this paper puts the sense of the here and now so uncompromisingly drably. What the narrative trickery of Tom Crick, Herbert Badgery, and Moses Berger seems paradoxically to have achieved, an achievement that differs only in degree in each case, is that their existential selves are upstaged by the historiographies they perform. For those performances have such power that the drab failed myths of the here and now are themselves upstaged and the realism transcends individual experience to cross all kinds of boundaries into a magic domain in which communal past, present, and future are united in singular and exciting ways.

Notes

1 Although Richler's novel first appeared in 1989, it was not published in the United Kingdom until 1990. This enabled it to be shortlisted for that year's Booker Prize.

2 This aspect of *Waterland* is reminiscent of parts of Rushdie's *Midnight's Children*.

3 Christopher Driver, "Floating," in *London Review of Books* October 6–19, 1983: 20.

4 Graham Swift, *Waterland* (London: Heinemann, 1983), p. 174. All other page references will be to this edition and will be given in the text itself.

5 Where the outcome here is a happy one for the child and its parents, the more gruesome possibilities of this contemporary urban phenomenon from the donnée for another recent English novel with distinctly magic realist elements, Ian McEwan's *The Child in Time* (1987).

6 Alan Hollinghurst, "Of Time and the River," *Times Literary Supplement*, October 7, 1983: 1073, plausibly saw an intertextual relationship with George Eliot's *The Mill on the Floss* (1860).

7 In addition to the primary sense of "one in or returning to his natural element," we may cite *OED* 14a: "one who is by nature deficient in intelligence."

8 Carey addresses the nineteenth-century period in his subsequent novel *Oscar and Lucinda* (1988), which won Britain's Booker Prize that year.

9 Peter Carey, *Illywhacker* (1985; London & Boston: Faber & Faber, 1986), p. 11. All other page references will be to this edition and will be given in the text itself.

10 The point is noticed but not developed in Nicholas Spice's perceptive review, "Phattbookia Stupenda," *London Review of Books*, April 18, 1985: 20. Luc Herman has put the paradox well: Badgery "is evidently lying when he goes on to say that his age is the one thing the reader can rely on. If so, this means that he is lying about everything, including the lying itself, so that as a confidence man, he is beaten at his own game." *Post-war Literatures in English: A Lexicon of Contemporary Authors* 14 (December 1991): 6. While recognizing the paradox I prefer to express it differently. Herman usefully points out that the Australian historian M. V. Anderson, whom the gaoled Badgery cites ("Our forefathers were all great liars" [456]) is or was himself fictitious. In this context it is worth recalling that on his release from gaol in 1949, Badgery undergoes a "transformation . . . model[ling him]self on M. V. Anderson" (488). If space permitted, I should want to pay more attention to the (in this light) fascinating status of purloined letters, and notebooks commented on by others, in this novel.

11 In this way, Carey echoes a theme from his earliest novel, *Bliss* (1981).

12 The late Bruce Chatwin's extraordinary novel *The Songlines* (1987) explores this aspect of the Australian outback.

13 There is insufficient space here to elaborate this point as fully as I should like. In addition to Izzie's severed legs and the top of his index finger, there is a more specific proleptic intimation in the lie (as it then was) that Badgery tells the Geelong draughtsman about his having torn a finger off Mr. Regan, town clerk of Grafton (cf. pp. 120 and 375: "so it was, at a time when it seemed too late, that I began to have some understanding of the power of lies"). Analogously we may cite the parrot Badgery tears the head off when it refuses to leave its cage (331) and the goanna's missing foreleg, adumbrated at the beginning of the second Book (209) to make its full narrative appearance in the third. There are many other such instances, both more and less closely integrated into the swirling narrative matrix.

14 See Peter Hinchcliffe and Ed Jewinski, eds., *Magic Realism and Canadian Literature: Essays and Stories* (Waterloo, Ont.: University of Waterloo Press, 1985).

15 Mordecai Richler, *Solomon Gursky Was Here* (London: Vintage, 1990), p. 422. All other page references will be to this edition and will be given in the text itself.

16 Cf. the way in which "a roving band of natives out of King William Island," granted last names instead of numbered identification disks by the Ottawa government in 1969 along with the rest of the Eskimo community, chose "Gursky or variations thereof, including Gor-ski, Girskee, Gur-ski, and Goorsky" (55).

17 Some of the sexism in the narrative voice may be attributed to Moses' wistful and hopeless melancholy, addicted as he is to the trickster who is the object of his quest.

18 Other photos picture Solomon with George Bernard Shaw and H. L. Mencken.

19 In a way Diana McClure functions in Solomon's life much as the "raven-haired beauty [Beatrice Wade], with breasts too rudely full for such a trim figure and coal-black eyes that shone with too much appetite" (49) does in Moses'. Both relationships with the cultural other are doomed, if not for the same reasons.

20 The forms "Gor-ski" and "Goorski" are particularly interesting in that they suggest not a Russian but a Germanic etymology: a "gorcrow" is an English dialect form referring both to the raven and to its greed. *Gursky* is filled with episodes of gastronomic and sexual excess of which the most memorable is probably Kaplansky's revenge on the anti-Semitic elements in the British establishment in the "infamous dinner party in his Cumberland Terrace flat [, a] Passover seder, of all things" (458). The Eskimos called Ephraim "Tulugaq, which means raven in their lingo" (176). The "lingo" is elsewhere (45) identified as Inuktikuk.

PATRICIA MERIVALE

Saleem Fathered by Oskar: Midnight's Children, Magic Realism, and The Tin Drum

Salman Rushdie's *Midnight's Children* (1981) is characterized throughout by a translation, as flamboyant as it is skillful, of themes, topoi, events, characters, images, and above all rhetorical and metaphorical strategies, from western fictions,[1] of which Gabriel García Márquez's *One Hundred Years of Solitude* (1967) and Günter Grass' *The Tin Drum* (1959)[2] are the two most significant, into the Indian terms of Rushdie's own narrative. Magic realism is, among other things, a shorthand term for many of these strategies: *Midnight's Children* owes its "magic," one could say, to García Márquez and its "realism" to Günter Grass, even though such a formulation smacks of that somewhat primitive version of intertextuality employed by Grass' hero, Oskar, when he "shuffle[s] the loose leaves of *Rasputin* and [Goethe's] *Elective Affinities* like playing cards, so creating a new book" (*G* 86).[3]

Midnight's Children asks to be categorized as magic realism, if only because of its obvious and often-noted indebtedness to García Márquez, the *fons et origo* of magic realism for the present generation. In its multiplied fantasies, its introductions of the supernatural into the everyday, its hauntings and its "traffic of the dead" (*GM* 378), its characters fatally crushed by their obsessions, and above all in its apocalyptic vision of the extinction of a family from the earth, standing synecdochically, at its conclusion, for a more general apocalypse, it is indeed a most "Márquezan" book, and its magic is largely a "Márquezan" magic. But insofar as *Midnight's Children* can be seen for the most part as an imitation of history, it is chiefly indebted to *The Tin Drum*. In books where ambiguous paternity forms a large part of the search for origins (and in a metafiction where "origins" must also be metatextual ones), the putative father of Rushdie's hero-narrator, Saleem Sinai, must be (by a somewhat subtler *genealogical* model of intertextuality) Grass' dwarf, Oskar, even though, metaphorically speaking, Saleem thinks of himself as "fathered by history" (*R* 118).

Both Grass' and Rushdie's heroes are "handcuffed to history" (*R* 420), obliged to bear witness to their times, with "no getting away from the date" (*R* 9) for either of them. Year by year, event by event, the times build up their selves as well as their stories; "myself, in my historical role" (*R* 86) links self and story through comic zeugmas of synchronicity, like Oskar's observation that "Kurt's whooping cough, simultaneously with the Afrika Korps, came to an end" (306), and hyperbolic assertions of responsibility, like Saleem's comment that "Nehru's death . . . too, was all my fault" (279).

This is a completely different notion of the historical from that found in García Márquez, where time is measured not by dates but by generations of unlikely length; cyclical time is at odds with linear time; the connections to key elements of Latin American history in general or to Colombian history in particular are deliberately stylized and abstracted; the book is more about History than it is about the history of Colombia. Indeed, Colonel Aureliano Buendía, who is García Márquez's nearest approach to a historical character, either extrinsically (being, it seems, modeled on an actual historical character) or intrinsically (being Macondo's chief link to the rest of the world in historical, political, and military terms), has a historical status explicitly deconstructed within the text: "the proprietress argued . . . that Colonel Aureliano Buendía, of whom she had indeed heard speak at some time, was a figure invented by the government as a pretext for killing Liberals" (359). "Real facts that no one believed in" jostle "the false [versions] that historians had created" (322) to deconstruct, indeed, the very notion of history.[4]

Saleem and Oskar share grotesque physical deformities: by the end of the book they are both impotent and suffering the excruciating pains of physical dissolution. Indeed, Saleem has become, in his own eyes, "a big-headed, top-heavy dwarf" (*R* 447). They share, further, an alienated perspective on their world, and a picaresque life journey appropriate to a trickster/artist-hero with a thousand-and-one faces and several names; but, above all, they share an artistic compulsion to seek their own identity through, in Stephen Kellman's phrase, a "self-begetting novel,"[5] one which will also account for the history of their time and place. Saleem's face is "the whole map of *India*" (231) and his thirty years of life are a microcosm of India's thirty-year course from Independence through Emergency (1947–78). Like Oskar, "the real lead [who] had been cast in

the role of an extra" (*G* 276), Saleem, this "perennial victim [of history],
persists in seeing himself as [its] protagonist" (*R* 237).

At the very beginning of his story, Rushdie pays conspicuous though
oblique tribute to Grass in his account of the German connections of
Saleem's supposed grandfather, Aadam Aziz. Aziz spent five years in Germany; his nose yields three drops of blood (*R* 10) in seeming echo of the
three Parsifalian drops on the snow to which Oskar alludes (*G* 459); his
German anarchist friends, Oskar (who, incidentally, "died . . . like a come-
dian" [*R* 29]) and Ilse, unsettle his Muslim and Indian presuppositions,
yet at the same time distance him with their "Orientalist" notion "that
India—like radium—had been 'discovered' by the Europeans . . . that he
[Aziz] was somehow the invention of their ancestors" (*R* 11). Thus Rushdie,
although he valorizes many of Grass' literary strategies throughout, makes
clear that he will transpose or translate them on his own terms. Since (in
his review of García Márquez's *Chronicle of a Death Foretold*) Rushdie
sees "*El realismo magical,* magic realism, at least as practiced by [García]
Márquez, [as] a development out of Surrealism that expresses *a genuinely
'Third World' consciousness,*"[6] it is not surprising that he finds its techniques helpful in making such transpositions. Rushdie might well agree
with Stephen Slemon that "Read as post-colonial discourse . . . magic realism can be seen to provide a positive and liberating response to the codes of
imperial history and its legacy of fragmentation and discontinuity" (21). As
Aruna Srivastava has pointed out (66–72), Rushdie poses an ideological,
postcolonial opposition to that linear, imperialist version of history which
represses and distorts India's own sense of its history. In her terms, Saleem
both suffers from and reports on a "disease of history" in need of Nietzschean, Foucauldian, perhaps especially (Mahatma) Gandhian, medicines.

"To understand just one life, you have to swallow the world" (*R* 109).
It is legitimate to see this—as Srivastava does (65)—as a specifically
Indian urge to encapsulate the whole of reality. And I have not forgotten
that Ganesh, the elephant-headed Indian "patron deity of literature,"[7] is
the patron deity of *Midnight's Children,* that Saleem has one Indian parent (H. Hatterr of G. V. Desani's wonderful novel "all about" him, perhaps?) and that *Midnight's Children* as metafiction is, among other things,
as Timothy Brennan tells us, a specifically *postcolonial* metafiction, "[a]
novel . . . *about* Third-World novels" (85; my emphasis). But for my immediate purpose I need to stress that Rushdie, like Grass and García
Márquez, is writing an "encyclopedic" fiction, and to do so he is deploy-

ing strategies adapted largely from these two major Western models. This adaptation Brennan describes accurately (albeit somewhat pejoratively) as Rushdie's "overt cosmopolitanism—[his] Third-World thematics as seen through the elaborate fictional architecture of European high art" (27).

Each of the three books is shaped encyclopedically, in the first instance, as the family chronicle of an extended, claustrophobic, ingrown, quasi-incestuous, matriarchal, and doomed family. But Grass and Rushdie, un-like García Márquez, want us, having swallowed the world and the family, to go on to "understand one life." *The Tin Drum* and *Midnight's Children* are, of course, both Bildungsromans—indeed *Künstlerromans*—as well as genealogical allegorizings of historical and metatextual particularities. Both autobiographies start, Shandeanly,[8] well in advance of the hero's birth. Saleem's listener fears, indeed, that he will never reach it: "You better get a move on or you'll die before you get yourself born" (38). Both are much concerned with tracing origins, and particularly with establish-ing paternity, for the Name of the Father is multiple in each. Oskar is sure, at least, who his mother is, but has a choice of two fathers; Saleem col-lects fathers throughout the book (though his biological or "true" father turns out, significantly for the intertextual allegory, to be an Englishman) and has at least three mothers. They pass their ambiguity of origins on to the next generation: Kurt (he of the whooping cough) is (probably) the son of Oskar's (probable) father rather than Oskar's own son; Kurt, the black marketeer, the quintessence of the normal and ordinary in post-war Germany, inevitably and from the beginning rejects Oskar's paternal claim upon him—a taste for drumming, Oskar has to admit, is not inheri-table. Aadam Sinai, on the other hand, although certainly *not* Saleem's son, has the elephant ears that go with Saleem's elephant nose to assert a clear affinity of Ganesh-like temperament. It seems likely that Aadam *will* acknowledge Saleem's paternal claim upon him.

Oskar and Saleem are both "thirty-year-old heroes," in Theodore Ziol-kowski's sense of the term.[9] They retreat, at thirty, to "the fringes" of life (*G* 138), an insane asylum and a pickle factory, respectively, to reckon up the moral debts of an individual as well as a collective past and to come to grips with their own share of collective responsibility and guilt for "those who had come to grief on the shoal of [our] existence" (*G* 569). Then, facing the indestructible principles of evil in their lives, Oskar's "Wicked Witch/ Black as pitch!" and Saleem's Widow (a "Black Angel" whose his-torical manifestation was Indira Gandhi), and having written these books as testaments, they turn toward death. They are "human being[s] to whom history could do no more" (*R* 447).

These two heroes are both freaks who, for much of their lives, possess a pair of uncanny powers: Saleem's telepathy and sense of smell; Oskar's impossibly expressive drumming and glass-shattering voice. They are both clairaudient from birth: "I lay in my crib and listened, and everything that happened, happened because of me" (*R* 133; cf. *G* 40). Born under strange circumstances, surrounded by omens and prophecies, endowed with ambiguous talents, these child-voyeurs learn too much, for "the grownups lived their lives in [their] presence without fear of being observed" (*R* 129).

"I was linked to history both literally and metaphorically, both actively and passively," says Saleem (238). His and Oskar's passive roles as witnesses and their magical capacities for witnessing provide a pseudo-realistic rationale for their accounts of both private and public history, in which their more active role usually takes the form of strange influences over crowds and individuals. Furthermore, they both play at being messianic. Oskar becomes the leader of the gang of Dusters, for whom his glass-shattering voice makes him a mock-Christ; Saleem becomes the leader of the Pakistani army tracking team, for whom the guiding power of his remarkable nose makes him a mock-Buddha. They are also for a while part of small collectives of similar freaks. Oskar's friendship with his fellow-dwarfs anticipates both Saleem's uneasy fellowship, by way of the telepathic linking between him as human radio receiver and the 'gang' of Midnight's Children (the thousand and one children born at the midnight of India's independence), and his later and easier one with his fellow-entertainers, the magicians of the New Delhi ghetto. Both heroes lose their primary powers under similarly dramatic circumstances. First a misguided sinus operation on Saleem's titanically overstuffed nose deprives him of the apparent source of his telepathic powers, and then the blow of a "silver spittoon" at his "parents' funeral pyre" (343) deprives him of his magic sense of smell. Oskar starts to grow again after being struck by a stone at his putative father's funeral, which blow (echoing his original fall downstairs as Saleem's loss echoes his original nasal episode and his concussion) prompts Oskar, like a tiny Prospero, to bury his drum and return, part-way, to normal life. Note that here, as often, Rushdie *multiplies* episodes from Grass; in this case he is doubling the events which first provide and then take away their special magic powers.

Saleem and Oskar are witnesses to their places as well as to their times.

García Márquez's Macondo is a landscape of the soul, one shifting phantasmagorically over time in size, status, and culture, while Rushdie's Bombay and Grass' Danzig are utterly specific, time-bound, mappable urban topographies, to which we are given city guides, as well as bird's-eye views with both spatial and temporal perspective: "Our Bombay, Padma! . . . grew at breakneck speed, acquiring a cathedral and an equestrian statue of the Mahratta warrior-king Sivaji which (we used to think) came to life at night and galloped awesomely through the city streets — right along Marine Drive! On Chowpatty sands!" (93). Saleem can never be as inward as this with the places of his exile, in Pakistan ("I won't deny it: I never forgave Karachi for not being Bombay" [*R* 307]), any more than Oskar can render the specific actuality of Düsseldorf with the same passionate attention which has been squandered on every stone and corner of Danzig. Their visions of their respective cities are small-scale versions of their synoptic visions of Europe, India, and the world:

> I have made the Vistula and the Seine flow and set the waves of the Baltic and Atlantic dashing against coasts of pure disembodied string . . . the resulting landscape . . . I call Europe for short. (*G* 408; cf. 373, 378, 384)

> The world as discovered [telepathically] from a broken-down clocktower [like Oskar's view of Danzig from the Stockturm, *G* 96]: . . . in Calcutta I slept rough in a section of drainpipe. By now thoroughly bitten by the travel bug, I zipped down to Cape Comorin and became a fisherwoman . . . standing on red sands washed by three seas. (*R* 173)

Oskar's vision of the world is also a vision of world war: "[A]t my feet I saw not only Europe but the whole world. Americans and Japanese were doing a torch-dance on the island of Luzon . . . Mountbatten was feeding Burmese elephants shells of every caliber . . . while rain fell in Ireland, [Koniev and Zhukov] broke through on the Vistula" (373).

The thirty years of history to which (and for which) these heroes feel responsible include partitions, shifting of boundaries, transfers of population, "ten million refugees" (*R* 357), racism, atrocity, war. German currency reform, leading to the "economic miracle" for the sole benefit of the "bourgeois-smug," has its analogies in the years of the great land reclamations which gave Bombay its hollow golden age. These two postwar prosperities are sharply satirized for their frauds, fakes, and complacencies.

Youth gangs (similarly nicknamed) are proleptic for adult gangs in each book, as the child-hero falls victim to his contemporaries. A certain Mian Abdullah, Oskar-like, shatters glass by his high-pitched humming, but for once Rushdie miniaturizes a point from Grass, for Abdullah smashes only a single glass eye, and one (key) window (*R* 48). Small- and large-scale firebugs destroy godowns and mills, synagogues and cities: Oskar's catalog of Danzig's millennium-long history of arson suitably culminates with the Russian invasion (*G* 378). The dictatorship of Indira Gandhi, who bull-dozes slums and ensures, with vasectomies and castrations, that India's hope, the Midnight's Children, will have neither progeny nor future, is a historical climax of equivalent status, for Rushdie's fiction, to the perse-cutions of Jews in Danzig and other, remoter, horrors of the Third Reich, as Oskar perceives them. "Fascinated by an immediate reality that came to be more fantastic than the vast universe of [their] imagination," as García Márquez puts it (44), Oskar and Saleem find the historical actuali-ties "fantastic" to the point of horror, and often past the point of endur-ance. They are indeed human beings "to whom history could do no more." But they are not deconstructing the historical in favor of the mythical, as García Márquez usually does, finding, because of the falsity of history, that atrocities can only be *truly* remembered in legend. Rather, for Grass and Rushdie, the historical has a clear ontological status, but it may be perceived, described, and interpreted in such a way as to show the mar-velously grotesque inherent in the actual.

The events of history and the nature of history coalesce in that region where both are made of words. Choice and change of nationality go with the juggling of boundaries; so do choice and change of language. "The old folks had been turned into Germans. They were Poles no longer and spoke Kashubian only in their dreams" (*G* 289). The consequences of the Indian language riots, triggered in the story by Saleem's inadvertently mocking Gujarati jingle, are as inflammatory as are many of Oskar's drumming ex-ploits: "But the boundaries of these states were not formed by rivers, or mountains . . . they were instead, walls of words. Language divided us. . . . I am warming over all this cold history, these old dead struggles between the barren angularity of Marathi . . . and Gujarati's boggy, Kathiawari soft-ness" (*R* 189). These riots "ended," as it happened, "with the partition of the state of Bombay" (192), a major historical event clearly (*post hoc ergo propter hoc*) brought about by Saleem's seemingly trifling intervention.

The linguistic causes and consequences of history, which are given such emphasis in these accounts, may serve to remind us that magic realism is not only, as it is so often described, out of partial tribute to the painterly origins of the term,[10] a way of *seeing*—"reality is a question of perspective," says Saleem (165)—but also a way of *saying*. On a larger scale it is a way of telling a story. On a smaller scale, it is a way of showing reality more truly with the aid of the various magics of metaphor.

Both Rushdie and Grass (unlike García Márquez) tell a first-person, seemingly episodic story in a sequence of chapters, grouped in each case into three books: of eight, fifteen, and seven chapters respectively in *Midnight's Children*, of sixteen, eighteen, and twelve chapters respectively in *The Tin Drum*. In Rushdie the chapters, which correspond to pickle jars (of which, as Saleem would say, more later), explicitly add up to Saleem's age as he ends the book: thirty. In Grass the last of his forty-six chapters is called "Thirty," for the same reason. Each chapter in both books has a title which captures pithily and emblematically a key object or situation, and many of Rushdie's titles are sufficiently similar to Grass' to remind us of some thematic resemblances. (I give the Rushdie title first in each pair.) Titles like "The Perforated Sheet" and "The Wide Skirt," "Accident in a Washing Chest" and "In the Clothes Cupboard," "Under the Carpet" and "Under the Raft," suggest, among other similarities of plot, the womb-like retreats suited to the voyeurism and escapism of these largely passive heroes. "All-India Radio" and "Special Communiqués" suggest the metaphor of telecommunications as the means by which "news" makes itself known, available for turning into "history." "Mercurochrome" and "Disinfectant" suggest the key role of hospitals in each hero's life, and Oskar subtitles his penultimate chapter "Adoration of a Preserving Jar."

Saleem and Oskar are writing, telling, or reading out their stories within a frame narrative, to a clearly delineated listener, a "narratee," who is a stand-in for the implied reader and a perpetual reminder of the present tense of narrating time. Bruno, Oskar's warder in the insane asylum, and Padma, Saleem's fellow-pickler in the pickle factory, eventually his fiancée, but chiefly his "necessary ear" (149), are both permitted to interrupt and even to contribute short sections of their own. Both provide—Padma through her "paradoxical earthiness of spirit" (150)—some Sancho-like, that is, "Panzaic," realism, some reader-responsiveness from within the text, to keep the narrator's tale on track and his quixotic feet on the ground.[11]

Critics have praised Grass for his "sensitivity to the magic qualities of things" and for his "realistic precision [in the] pursuit of fantasy as part of reality." They are already rightly praising Rushdie for the same qualities. But further keys to mimesis in Grass and Rushdie may also be found in their (largely epic) figures of speech.

The two authors share an encyclopedic taste (like that of García Márquez) for "swallowing the world" through inclusiveness and exactness of description, especially in the form of lists—the tables of contents are the first lists in each book to establish a sense of "the supremacy of the inanimate."[12] Sometimes such lists provide cryptic anticipations of the story to come, as in the prophetic verses uttered just before Saleem's birth: "Washing will hide him—voices will guide him/ . . . Spittoons will brain him—doctors will drain him" (87). Often they serve as a recapitulation of the plot thus far, as in Oskar's Hamlet-like rumination in the graveyard— "My grandmother's four skirts . . . the maze of scars on Herbert Truczinski's back, the blood-absorbing mail baskets at the Polish Post Office, America—but what is America compared to Streetcar Number 9 that went to Brösen?" (444)—or in his final peroration to the shadow of the Black Witch—"The Witch, black as pitch, . . . had always been there, [in] all words . . . and all stones . . . and all the shattered glass . . . and all the groceries, all the flour and sugar in blue pound and half-pound bags . . . cemeteries I stood in, flags I knelt on, coconut fiber I lay on" (571). Such Rabelaisian catalogs mimic all-inclusiveness by a canny selection of apparently random items. They are largely made up of talismanic objects, like Saleem's spittoon or Oskar's drum, which are, in both their descriptive roles and their symbolic references, constantly recurring leitmotifs.

The telepathic catalog of Saleem's vision from the Bombay clocktower (*R* 173) becomes an olfactory catalog of his experience of Karachi (*R* 317– 18): "Formlessly . . . the fragrances poured into me: the pustular body odours of young men in loose pajamas holding hands in Sadar evenings . . . the aroma of contraband cigarettes and 'black-money' . . . Mosques poured over me the itr of devotion." Then his "overpowering desire for form assert[s] itself." Synesthetically, Saleem classifies the scents by color, then shapes them into a "general theory of smell," and then into a "science of nasal ethics" (*R* 318), a key set of Rushdie's rhetorical strategies for making the moral/emotional concrete. Saleem's marvelous nose can identify "the nauseating odour of defeat" (317) and "the old aroma of failure"

(202) or detect that "unfairness smelled like onions" (370). "Smells assail [Oskar]" throughout as well (568). Again Rushdie *multiplies* a Grassian trope.

All three authors are linked through such figures of speech as the hyperboles of amnesia, or of Rushdie's charming variation on a theme by García Márquez: "for forty days, we were besieged by the dust" (*R* 271). Such characteristic exaggerations testify to an aesthetic of abundance, the feature which most clearly distinguishes their work from the sparer imaginings of Kafka and Borges, their immediate predecessors in the interweaving of the tangible and the marvelous. One of Rushdie's minor characters encapsulates this aesthetic destiny: "a painter whose paintings had grown larger and larger as he tried to get the whole of life into his art . . . wanted to be a miniaturist and . . . got elephantiasis instead!" (*R* 48). Perhaps the most concentratedly magical of such metaphors are those of abstractions reified. The infectious weeping in Oskar's Onion Cellar, the objective correlative of the collective pseudo-remorse (following the collective amnesia) of the Germans, is like the "pigmentation disorder" (*R* 179) which occurs among those prosperous Indians who turn white upon inheriting colonial prerogatives from the departing British. Each ailment serves as a compact moral allegory for a collective historical phase.

Oskar's "carnival make-believe" (452), the telepathic connections among the Midnight's Children, the games that the Delhi magicians play with illusion, all suggest in context that "Reality can have metaphorical content; that does not make it less real" (*R* 200), but rather, in terms of magic realism, more real: "[T]he magicians were people whose hold on reality was absolute; they gripped it so powerfully that they could bend it every which way in the service of their arts, but they never forgot what it was" (*R* 399). Saleem seems to contrast an Indian magic realism, like that exemplified by these magicians, with a Pakistani fantasy, denigrating the latter: "[In my Indian childhood] I was beset by an infinity of alternative realities, while in [my Pakistani adolescence] I was adrift, disorientated, amid an equally infinite number of falsenesses, unrealities, and lies" (*R* 326). Such an attitude has political consequences: "Karachiites had only the slipperiest of grasps on reality, and were therefore willing to turn to their leaders for advice on what was real and what was not. [They were] beset by illusionary sand-dunes and the ghosts of ancient kings" (*R* 308).

What seems to be Saleem's description of his own style likewise suggests a commitment to magic realism: "Matter of fact descriptions of the outré and bizarre, and their reverse, namely heightened, stylized versions of the everyday—these techniques . . . are also attitudes of mind" (*R* 218). "Heightened, stylized" descriptions can be found, for example, in insertions of refrain-structured prose poems (very similar in form to some of Oskar's incantatory flights) into Saleem's first-person narration, already crammed with "matter of fact descriptions of the outré and bizarre."

The magicians, like Saleem, bend reality without ever forgetting what it is. They, too, are magic realists and thus evidently artists. But so, in a humbler way, is Saleem's foster mother, Mary Pereira: " 'nobody makes achar-chutney like our Mary . . . because she puts her feelings inside [it]! '" And the feelings of others as well: very early in his life "she stirred [Saleem's] guilt into green chutney" too (458). She resembles in this respect Oskar's supposed father, Matzerath, whose epitaph is that "he, an impassioned cook, had a knack for metamorphosing feelings into soup" (*G* 36). These several parent figures supply our artist-heroes with a method for metaphor based on the emotional significance of material things, on food as art, the homeliest yet the most pervasive of the innumerable metaphors in these books for the operations of the creative imagination.[13]

The primary self-reflexive image for the creative imagination in *Midnight's Children* seems to be Saleem's eponymously telepathic powers, but it is quickly replaced by the more widely diffused olfactory image, which, in turn, modulates into the gastronomic images of his jars of chutney (he is following in Mary's footsteps). Lined up, they constitute the chapters of the book itself. Similarly, Oskar, who can create an art work simply by coughing and sneezing (349), is chiefly known for his drumming. This audible art form is (synesthetically) mirrored in Herbert Truczinski's historical back scars (a tip of the hat to Kafka's "In the Penal Colony"?), which are, in turn, reproduced in Bruno's string constructions, a *mise en abyme*, like Oskar's "ever so fragile house of cards" (*G* 232), literally exchangeable with Oskar's own storytelling. "Every time I tell [Bruno] some fairy tale, he shows his gratitude by bringing out his latest knot construction" (9).

Speaking more abstractly than usual, Oskar says, "inevitably the thread of events wound itself into loops and knots which became known as the fabric of History" (373). Evidently Bruno can, with his string art, reify the metaphoric "fabric of history" into the concrete loops and knots of "a figure, which in accordance with Mr. Matzerath's [Oskar's] story, I [Bruno] shall call 'Refugee from the East'" (408). And there follows a recapitulation of Oskar's adventures in the familiar catalog form—all turned into string, that is, History. It climaxes in Bruno's attempt to delineate, in the form of "a single [string] figure which, moreover, should present a *striking resemblance to himself*" (Oskar, my emphasis), that Goethe-Rasputin dialectic—"how many miles of string I have tied into knots, trying to create a valid synthesis of the two extremes" (412), Bruno complains—which has shaped Oskar's artistic life. Bruno has thus made a *mise en abyme* in string (cf. Eddie Amsel, in Grass' *Dog Years*, who turned History into scarecrows) of Oskar's "new book," *The Tin Drum*, itself the synthesis of Oskar's two sacred texts. And Rushdie has multiplied, and complicated, like so much else in the patterns adapted from Grass, such allegories of intertextual origins.[14]

The two chief avatars of the artist in these books are those of the artist-as-entertainer—their chief role within the *action* of each book—and of the artist-as-historian—their chief role in the *narration* of each book. The two roles overlap in, for instance, Oskar's "paint[ing] the blockade of Berlin on the table-top with champagne" (454). Both heroes are aware of themselves in motley, as court jesters, as fools in the carnival tradition (see, e.g., *G* 452). Their most direct influence upon history is in such scenes as the incitements of the Language Riots in Rushdie and the Pied Piping of the Onion Cellar in Grass, where their enacting of their "historical role" (*R* 86) is chiefly manifested in their role as entertainers. "Entertainers would orchestrate my life" (101), says Saleem. Bebra, the master-entertainer of the troupe of dwarfs with whom Oskar is briefly affiliated, likewise orchestrates Oskar's. Both heroes make their living largely as entertainers, though again art and history overlap in Oskar's employment as a carver of epitaphs upon gravestones. As narrators they are also entertainers; they are very conscious of the need to hold their audience, which consists, in the first instance, of their reader-surrogates, Bruno and Padma. Saleem, as Nancy Batty has emphasized, is particularly struck (as is García Márquez) by the analogy of his role as storyteller to that of Scheherazade and of his story to the frame narrative of *The Thousand and One Nights*.

The literal connections between the heroes and history are deliberately strained; it is a necessary fiction for both narrators to see themselves as "protagonists," yet, paradoxically, also as "victims." But however remote or indirect Saleem's and Oskar's "attempt[s] at rearranging history" (*R* 260), or however strained their metaphoric grounds for supposing that they *are* acting upon history (while being, at the same time, its central victims), their self-delusion is most appropriate to magic realism, for it empowers those subjective distortions and those grotesque shifts of perspective that touch the historical with the marvelous. These are key metaphoric strategies in magic realism as a whole, perhaps, insofar as it constitutes a critique of history.

"My [glass-shattering] number was conceived along historical lines," says Oskar (*G* 318). Oskar's and Saleem's obligations as historians override in the end their obligations as entertainers. The gastronomic metaphors for art become metaphors for history, as Saleem finally puts *his* whole "number" together. "Pickle-fumes . . . stimulate the juices of memory" (166), and it is an almost Proustian taste of chutney that brings Saleem back to his Bombay heritage, very much as Oskar, in the asylum, must recollect his life, through the process of redrumming its events, in order to compose his story. "It happened that way because that's how it happened" (461) is Saleem's final, historian's, justification for whatever most strains credulity in his account. The making of art or story is thus a perfect image of the operations of magic realism, for what is true is *also* "what the author can manage to persuade his audience to believe" (*R* 270–71). Thus, if you are skilled at incorporating "memories, dreams, ideas" into your chutney, and possess "above all a nose capable of discerning the hidden languages of what-must-be-pickled," you may, like Saleem, create magic *through* the mimetic, in a "chutnification of history; the grand hope of the pickling of time!" (459–60).

In this essay I have only touched on the variety of Rushdie's intertextual strategies and merely suggested the astonishing density of allusions to and echoes of *The Tin Drum* in *Midnight's Children*. Nor have I more than hinted at Rushdie's bricolage of other texts, both Western and Indian. To what purpose or effect is his voraciously appropriative pastiche (I adapt Jean Franco's terms here) of Günter Grass, amounting to, in Bader's pithy, nonjudgmental formulation, "an Indian *Tin Drum*"? Given that, as Franco puts it, "there is no innocent relationship between discourses" (105),[15] what are we to make of Rushdie's totalizing intertextuality? There is no evidence of a satire or critique of Grass.

Is Rushdie, as Srivastava would have it, inverting the processes of "colonial" domination, or is he displaying the "overt cosmopolitanism" of which Brennan, more judgmentally, speaks? His mimicry of Grass seems to me to be, rather, a celebration, in the mode of magic realism, of "people who had been translated, who had . . . entered the condition of metaphor," and of "writing ... at the frontier between ... cultures" (Rushdie, *Voices*, 63, 59).

With the help of Rushdie's recent critical collection, *Imaginary Home-lands*, we can now piece together the views that underlie his magic realism, expressive as it is not only of a specifically "third-world consciousness" but also of the more generally "international" and "migrant" status that he claims to share with, among many others, Günter Grass. Such a writer is free, he says, "to choose his parents ... [from] a polyglot family tree" (20–21): in this way, I suggest, Saleem's intertextual relationship to Oskar is a genealogical allegory of Rushdie's 'choosing' of Grass. And for the "migrant" writer, magic realism *is* the appropriate mode, for it provides the "stereoscopic vision" with which he can "see things plainly" enough to "invent the earth beneath his feet" (19, 125, 149). Thus Rushdie finds the marvelous in what, like Macondo, is magic precisely *because* it is real (302), "imbuing the ... world [and the world of the text] with ... radiance and meaning" (251) by means of his "translation" of Grass.

"It is normally supposed," says Rushdie, "that something always gets lost in translation," but he clings, "obstinately, to the notion that something can also be gained" (17).

Notes

1 A brief version of this paper was read at the MLA section, chaired by Wendy B. Faris, on "The Mimetic Quotient of Magic Realism" (1983); it was adapted for publication as "Saleem Fathered by Oskar: Intertextual Strategies in *Midnight's Children* and *The Tin Drum*," *Ariel* 21, 3 (July 1990): 5–21. It appears here, somewhat altered and updated, by kind permission of the editors of *Ariel*.

2 *One Hundred Years of Solitude* (1967), trans. Gregory Rabassa (New York: Avon, 1971). *The Tin Drum* (1959), trans. Ralph Manheim (New York: Fawcett, 1966). *Midnight's Children* (1981) (London: Picador, 1983). Page references to these works will be given in the text, using the abbreviations *GM*, *G*, and *R*, respectively.

3 Rushdie has acknowledged and developed his deep interest in Grass in "Salman Rushdie on Günter Grass," *Granta* 15 (1985): 179–85, which constitutes an introduction to Grass' own essay, "*The Tin Drum* in Retrospect," pp. 187–93. I use the Manheim translation of Grass, because Rushdie (knowing no German, see *Granta*, p. 182) used it: "In the summer of 1967 ... when I was twenty years old, I bought from a bookshop in Cambridge a paperback copy of Ralph Manheim's English translation of *The Tin Drum*. . . . there are books which

give [writers] permission to become the sort of writers they have it in themselves to be" (*Granta* p. 180; see also Rushdie's *Imaginary Homelands: Essays
and Criticism 1981–1991* [London: Granta/Viking, 1991], p. 278). Rushdie's
Granta introduction also appears in Grass' *On Writing and Politics: 1967–1983*
(tr. Manheim, 1985). Rushdie and Grass amiably discuss politics and writing,
from clearly similar perspectives, in the Channel 4 television series, "Voices."
Rushdie and Grass, "Writing for a Future," *Voices: Writers and Politics*, ed.
Bill Bourne, Udi Eichler, and David Herman (Nottingham: Spokesman, 1987).
The Grass-Rushdie connection has been briefly noted by several reviewers, by
James Lasdun ("Life's Victims: Recent Fiction," *Encounter* 62, 1 [1984]: 69–
73, esp. 72), and by Keith Wilson ("*Midnight's Children* and Reader Responsibility," *Critical Quarterly* 26, 3 [1984]: 23–37, esp. 23), and more extensively,
but from a more thematic perspective, by Rudolf Bader, "Indian Tin Drum,"
International Fiction Review 11 (1984): 75–83, who provides many additional
points of similarity. Kenneth R. Ireland's "Doing Very Dangerous Things: *Die
Blechtrommel* and *Midnight's Children*," *Comparative Literature* 42, 4 (Fall
1990): 335–61, makes many additional points, and with welcome collaboration
of much of my evidence; it reaches, however, an almost opposite conclusion.
Only Timothy Brennan, in *Salman Rushdie and the Third World: Myths of the
Nation* (Basingstoke and London: Macmillan, 1989), has grappled with any
subtlety with this relationship—though briefly, and from an explicitly "postcolonial" perspective (27, 39, 66, 81); he also points to the "direct influence"
of *One Hundred Years of Solitude*.

4 "If history is composed of fictions, then fiction can be composed of history,"
says Nancy Batty pithily. "The Art of Suspense: Rushdie's 1001 (Mid)Nights,"
Ariel 18, 3 (1987): 49–65, esp. 64. Roberto González Echevarría develops, with
much subtlety and detail, similar propositions on the relationship of myth, history, and literature in Latin America as a whole and in *Cien años de soledad*
in particular. "*Cien años de soledad*: The Novel as Myth and Archive," *Modern Language Notes* 99, 2 (1984): 358–80. *One Hundred Years of Solitude*
is, clearly, another book that gave Rushdie "permission to become [his own]
sort of writer." Allusions to both its rhetorical strategies ("Many years later,
when . . ." [*R* 11]) and to details and incidents from it ("the magicians . . . having
forgotten everything to which they could compare anything that happened . . ."
[*R* 444]) occur throughout *Midnight's Children*.

5 Stephen G. Kellman, *The Self-Begetting Novel* (New York: Columbia University Press, 1980).

6 Rushdie, "Angel Gabriel," *London Review of Books* Sept. 16–Oct. 6, 1982: 3,
my emphasis. See also Rushdie's *Imaginary Homelands*, p. 301; Stephen Slemon, "Magic Realism as Post-Colonial Discourse," *Canadian Literature* 116

(1988): 9–24 (modified version is included in this volume); Aruna Srivastava, "'The Empire Writes Back': Language and History in *Shame* and *Midnight's Children*," *Ariel* 20, 4 (1989): 62–78.

7 See Chelva Kanaganayakam on Ganesh and on Rushdie's many comic inversions and variations of Indian mythic intertexts, as well as on Rushdie's position among Indo-Anglian authors generally. "Myth and Fabulosity in *Midnight's Children*," *Dalhousie Review* 67, 1 (1987): 86–98. G. M. Desani's *All About H. Hatterr* (1948; New York: Lancer, 1972) seems a particularly promising analogue, as well as an influence Rushdie acknowledges. (See also Maria Couto, "*Midnight's Children* and Parents: The Search for Indo-British Identity," *Encounter* 58, 2 [1982]: 61–66). Again Brennan gives the strongest and fullest account of Rushdie's crucial (yet "critical") relationship to the "Indo-Anglian" tradition.

8 Wilson (23 ff.) establishes numerous parallels between *Midnight's Children* and *Tristram Shandy*, one of Rushdie's most commented-upon intertexts. Rushdie (*Voices*, 59) "found, in novels like *Tristram Shandy* . . . a very similar spirit" to that of his own work. However, Keith Miles (*Günter Grass* [London: Vision, 1975], p. 51) emphasizes *Grass*' debt to Sterne; intertextuality is multifoliate.

9 Theodore Ziolkowski, "The Novel of the Thirty-Year-Old," *Dimensions of the Modern Novel* (Princeton: Princeton University Press, 1969), pp. 258–88.

10 See Seymour Menton, *Magic Realism Rediscovered: 1918–1981* (Philadelphia: Art Alliance, 1983) on the history of the term, making a strong yet rather static case for its visual and painterly connotations, of no material assistance to the critic attempting to use the term to categorize narrative and action. His earlier paper on Borges and magic realism ("Jorge Luis Borges, Magic Realist," *Hispanic Review* 50 [1982]: 411–26), however, adapts the painterly context to a more narrative one. See also Slemon's bibliography, pp. 21–24.

11 Wilson (p. 25) makes the case for Padma's strengths and limitations as a reader-surrogate; he employs the useful formula that Rushdie is to Saleem as the reader is to Padma. Batty privileges Padma even further in her narratological analysis of Rushdie's Scheherazadean strategies, which, in her view, make *Midnight's Children* an act of sedition against (Indira Gandhi's) Indian state, with Gandhi herself as the ultimate "implied reader" of the book. This distinctly appealing interpretation is indeed corroborated to a degree by Gandhi's considerable annoyance with both the book and its author. She was, however, notably less vengeful than the Islamic Republic has been in respect to Rushdie's recent, and more explicit, alleged blasphemy against the (Muslim) faith.

12 R. Hinton Thomas, in Thomas and Wilfried van der Will, *The German Novel and the Affluent Society* (Manchester: Manchester University Press, 1968), p. 80, is translating from Günter Böcker's review of *Hundejahre* (1963); Miles (49) quotes Grass himself ("Interview," *Encounter* 35, 3 [1970]: 26–29, esp. 29), who

is specifying the influence on his work of Melville's *Moby Dick*. "Like all fabulists, Calvino loves lists," says Rushdie (*Imaginary Homelands*, 257), and "the fable is now the central, the most vital form in Western literature" (*Imaginary Homelands*, 287). One could add that "fable" is also perhaps the most suitable *generic* term for such magically realistic fictions as *Midnight's Children*.

13 See Batty on Rushdean metaphors for narrative: "narrative is a perforated sheet, concealing the whole while revealing a part" (p. 61); it can also be an episodic cinema, a symphony, a labyrinth.

14 Such allegories are developed more explicitly and at greater length in Rushdie's children's-book-for-grownups, *Haroun and the Sea of Stories* (London: Granta, 1990), a book whose polysemous intertextual allegory could be read in toto as the text of a magic realism self-reflexively considering its own nature:

> the Plentimaw Fishes were . . . "hunger artists" — Because when they are hungry they swallow stories through every mouth, and in their innards miracles occur; a little bit of one story joins on to an idea from another, and hey presto, when they spew the stories out they are not old tales but new ones . . . no story comes from nowhere; new stories are born from old — it is the new combinations that make them new. (85–86)

Note that "history" (i.e., that part of Rushdie's autobiography that has now, all-too-tangibly, become "history") is presented obliquely, almost covertly, in *Haroun*. "History," on the other hand, is front-and-center in *Midnight's Children*, while, in a chiasmic reversal, it is intertextual allegory that is covert.

15 Jean Franco, "Pastiche in Contemporary Latin-American Literature," *Studies in Twentieth-Century Literature* 14, 1 (1989): 95–107.

STEVEN F. WALKER

Magical Archetypes: Midlife Miracles in
The Satanic Verses

Jungian psychology, with its interest in the occult, with its high regard for primitive cultures and their mythological worldviews, and with its relentless search for mythological parallels in the dreams of modern men and women, has the potential to inspire fresh psychological perspectives on magical realism, which has often been analyzed in terms of purely formalistic or political and cultural concerns. Although the Flemish novelist Hubert Lampo may take credit for first sensing the affinity of the Jungian interest in archetypal images and myths deriving from the experience of the collective unconscious, and the phantasmagorical and mythological motifs of magical realism in his 1967 essay *De ring van Möbius*,[1] his intuition has not yet inspired a broadly based study of the Jungian context for magical realism in literature that Seymour Menton's 1983 study *Magic Realism Rediscovered, 1918–1981*[2] makes the case for privileging in the study of the visual arts. As things stand, literary critics still need convincing that archetypal criticism and magical realism are made for each other.

This essay's aims are more modest, however. It will attempt to demonstrate—with the hope that such a demonstration will inspire further and more comprehensive studies—that a Jungian psychoanalytic approach to magical realist texts can be of value in disengaging *symbolic meaning*. Symbolic meaning is the bridging concept that links the study of psychology and literature. All narrative texts—even texts like *Madame Bovary* that function mainly within the charmed circle of realism, even *romans d'analyse* that come with their own internal analysis of motivation, character, etc.—are vehicles for latent symbolic meaning, in spite of themselves, so to speak. But magical realist texts, with their inspiredly absurd supernaturalism that vigorously resists analysis, psychological or otherwise, are prime candidates for the hermeneutics of symbolic meaning. There is in such texts a hermeneutical blank, a *terra incognita* marked "here live monsters." Such magical realist monsters should be the quarry of a hermeneutics of symbolic meaning that, when successful, will find in symbols not only meaning but a "surplus of meaning," to borrow Paul Ricoeur's formulation.

The test case for this essay will be Salman Rushdie's *The Satanic Verses* (1988),[3] a text most widely known for its sensational role in the "Rushdie Affair," which has now overshadowed the censorship of Joyce's *Ulysses* as the twentieth century's most significant challenge to free artistic expression. It deserves, however, to be equally well known as a masterful evocation of a male midlife crisis in magical realist symbolic terms. To do justice to the novel, this psychological theme must be seen as important as Rushdie's controversial revisioning of the foundation myth of Islam. The midlife phantasmagoria surrounding the fall of Saladin Chamcha and Gibreel Farishta is peopled with monsters, symbols that point to intrapsychic processes and transformations.[4] Eventually, the novelist's imagination shows the way out of the midlife labyrinth into a new life — at least, for Saladin Chamcha, one of several bewitched, bothered, and bewildered forty-year-olds in *The Satanic Verses*.

Myths and dreams are often full of incongruous and unlikely happenings, and so are magical realist texts. A Jungian approach to such a text has the advantage of recognizing in these sensational incongruities the mythological motifs that are keys to the interpretation of dreams. This essay will proceed in three related directions in analyzing the mythopoetic world of *The Satanic Verses*. First of all, in the theme of flight and magical descent through the air it will discover a symbol of the Eternal Youth's fortunate fall into life as discussed in Marie-Louise von Franz's now classic study of that archetype, *Puer Aeternus: A Psychological Study of the Adult Struggle with the Paradise of Childhood* (1970).[5] As regards the typically magical realist theme of metamorphosis (in this case primarily Saladin Chamcha's metamorphosis into a pop mythology devil, complete with hooves and horns), the Jungian concept of the *shadow* will allow a discussion of political and cultural issues to feed into psychological issues, a discussion that does not reduce one set of concerns to another. Finally, the key archetypal image of the Eternal Youth in *The Satanic Verses* (the boy on the bicycle) will establish the psychological context of another major magical realist theme, the theme of dream becoming reality, in an episode that is crucial for understanding the resolution at the end of the novel of the issues regarding midlife crisis raised at the outset.

In spite of its alleged "difficulty" (early defenses of the novel sometimes seemed to imply that, since it was tedious and unreadable, it was presumably incapable of causing any serious damage to Islamic sensibilities), *The Satanic Verses* belongs to a kind of postmodern fiction that, as Wendy B. Faris says in her essay in this volume, seems "clearly designed for the entertainment of readers" in a way that contrasts with the deliberate hermeticism of many modernist texts. Although it has achieved notoriety as the occasion for a bitter confrontation between Islamic fundamentalism and Western secularism, *The Satanic Verses* really deserves to be read as a serio-comic "entertainment" (to use Graham Greene's modest generic tag) — a masterpiece of the genre, one should add. It is, as Rushdie has said more than once, a funny novel. And it is worth taking seriously.

My basic question would be, as regards *The Satanic Verses* as a magical realist text: can Jungian psychology provide a context that enables the reader to detect unconscious symbolism and to assign symbolic meaning without disregarding the text's own symbolic constructs and self-interpretations? Consider, for example, the problems involved with assigning meaning to the following hallucination of Gibreel Farishta (having miraculously survived a fall from an exploding jetliner earlier in the day, he and Saladin have been taken in by Rosa Diamond, an elderly English-woman whose house overlooks the English Channel):

> Running along the midnight beach in the direction of the Martello tower and the holiday camp, — running along the water's edge so that the incoming tide washed away its footprints, — swerving and feinting, running for its life, there came a full-grown, large-as-life ostrich. Down the beach it fled, and Gibreel's eyes followed it in wonder, until he could no longer make it out in the dark. (148)

The ostrich (presumably a three-toed South American ostrich, that is, a rhea, not a true ostrich) is clearly a reminder of Rosa Diamond's affair in the Argentine pampas with a man whom she feels Gibreel mysteriously resembles.[6] Gibreel's synchronistic hallucination can be assigned meaning through juxtaposition with the Argentinian idyll of Rosa Diamond alone. But it also marks the beginning of Gibreel's involuntary visions, which are a major structural element of the novel. The presence of the

Martello tower refers the reader back to the opening of Joyce's *Ulysses* as a subtext—but to what purpose? Is Rushdie presenting Gibreel as another Stephen Dedalus? It seems unlikely, but it is just possible; if so, are his later (re)visions of the foundation myth of Islam to be taken as similar to Stephen's ambitions to forge in the smithy of his soul the uncreated conscience of his race? In the end, the ostrich hallucination resists interpretation; it has the playful opacity of a magical realist representation of an intrapsychic event, not the relative transparency of an allegory or of a soon-to-be-interpreted dream text.

By way of comparison, here is Christopher Isherwood's nonfictional account of an intrapsychic event in a diary entry for November 12, 1940:

> Sitting with closed eyes in the darkness, I suddenly "saw" a strip of carpet. . . . As I watched, I "saw," in the middle of the carpet, a small dirty-white bird, something like a parrot. After a moment, it began to move, with its quick stiff walk, and went under the bed. This wasn't a dream. I was normally conscious, aware of what I saw and anxious to miss no detail of it. As I sat there, I felt all around me a curiously intense silence, like the silence of deep snow. The only sinister thing about the bird was its air of utter aloofness and *intention*. I had caught it going about its business—very definite business—as one glimpses a mouse disappearing into its hole.[7]

What does this vision of the "dirty-white bird" "going about its business" signify? A playful allusion to the white rabbit in *Alice in Wonderland*, with Isherwood as Alice? An allegory of the state of his soul ("dirty-white")? An encounter with a shamanistic power animal or guardian spirit? An epiphany of Flaubert's famous parrot, and hence a reproof of Isherwood's decision to abandon his career as a writer in order to become a Vedantic monk? Isherwood says nothing, interprets nothing. Like Gibreel's ostrich, Isherwood's parrot ultimately *means* nothing, although it certainly *is* something—but what? To return to Todorov's distinction between the marvelous and the fantastic and to elaborate: the marvelous leads us not to ask: can this be possible? what could this mean? but rather: what *is* this?

Thus the question of meaning is apparently neither here nor there, when magical realism seems bent on following Cocteau's injunction "astonish me!" No doubt, political and social allegory is present in many magical realist texts, but the search for allegorical meaning is not the only option we have when dealing with magical realism's marvelous tricks: meaning may be *symbolic* as well as allegorical. Allegory is quickly decoded, and once decoded, is of no further interest. C. G. Jung's theory of the symbol (a symbol has no preassigned meaning, but rather a latent potential for generating meaning) is useful in that it leaves a space for astonishment as well as for the *eventual* discovery of meaning. A perspective informed by the procedures of the Jungian analysis and interpretation of dream images and symbols can add a dimension of symbolic meaning to magical realist ostriches. Just as the apparently meaningless dream text slowly yields meaning under the pressure of analysis, so a Jungian psychoanalytical approach may create a context in which intriguing but to all appearances purely sensationalistic procedures of magical realism become meaningful as strategies of symbolization. And not only in terms of psychological meaning: Jungian psychological perspectives enrich the discussion of political issues as well.

It is true that *The Satanic Verses'* own internal commentary is more political and social than psychological. For instance, one reference point that the novel makes explicit for its use of magical realist symbolic strategies, especially metamorphosis, is the power of racist definitions of the Other, as experienced by the Third World immigrant community in the United Kingdom. Magical realist metamorphosis is self-interpreted, for instance, in a strange dialogue between Saladin Chamcha, who has been partially metamorphosed into a goatlike devil figure, and a former male model now changed into a manticore (man-tiger) in the hospital ward in which Chamcha is recovering from a racially motivated police beating:

> "The point is," it said fiercely, "some of us aren't going to stand for it. We're going to bust out of here before they turn us into anything worse...." "But how do they do it?" Chamcha wanted to know. "They describe us," the other whispered solemnly. "That's all. They have the power of description, and we succumb to the pictures they construct." (168)

The Immigrant as Other, defined and described in terms of degrading and animalistic racist stereotypes, undergoes, in the world of magical realist procedures, an actual metamorphosis into manticore, devil, or other fantasmagorical figures. In magical realist terms, metamorphosis is as common an event as racist stereotyping is in terms of traditional social realism. Chamcha's own metamorphosis into a pop mythology devil (horns, cloven hooves, and enlarged phallus) is not seen by the police who are carting him off as anything extraordinary; the event "was being treated by the others as if it were the most banal and familiar matter they could imagine" (158), because their image of the Third World immigrant as sexually potent devil was the "picture" their racist imaginations had already "constructed" and superimposed on him.

Behind other strange events that might seem to represent a somewhat gratuitous use of magical realist supernaturalism lies a forceful presentation of images of the daily racial harassment inflicted on London's immigrant community, as in this Bangladeshi housewife's interior monologue:

> Plus also: they had come into a demon city in which anything could happen, your windows shattered in the middle of the night without any cause, you were knocked over in the middle of the street by invisible hands, in the shops you heard such abuse you felt your ears would drop off but when you turned in the direction of the words you saw only empty air and smiling faces, and every day you heard about this boy, that girl, beaten up by ghosts. — Yes, a land of phantom imps, how to explain. (250)

Magical realism in Rushdie's hands becomes a way of rendering her experience of a world in which all usual expectations of happiness and security are undermined by disguised threats and hidden dangers, the result of racist hostility and violence. For this aging and disoriented Bangladeshi housewife, "the arrival of a fully developed devil, a horned goat-man, was . . . something very like the last, or at any rate the penultimate, straw" (251). But young people, including her own two daughters, react differently. For them, Chamcha as devil is the hero of their wildest dreams, and his popularity creates a fad for wearing rubber devil horns.

The Satanic Verses, however much it has fallen into the vortex of tendentious journalistic commentary after the sentence of death imposed on the author on February 14, 1989, by the Ayatollah Khomeini (an unspeakably sadistic magical realist Valentine, so to speak), deserves to have the brilliance of its conjoining of the political and the psychological celebrated. The two natives of Bombay who fall from the jetliner onto a Channel beach are, we find out soon, just forty years old, and this symbolic age sets them up for a shared midlife crisis in which cultural confusion and stage-of-life disorientation are both to play important roles. Saladin Chamcha and Gibreel Farishta are as helplessly embroiled in psychological complexities as they are in the net of postcolonialist racial oppression. In particular, the

two major magical realist themes of metamorphosis and of miraculous flying and falling—themes that derive from what Todorov called "the psychological marvelous," a subcategory that encourages symbolic interpretation
—turn out to have significant psychological as well as social relevance.

Symbolic interpretation is ultimately the study of intertextuality—in the
case of psychoanalytical approaches to literature, of studying the relationship between literary and psychoanalytical texts. The text that I intend
to juxtapose with *The Satanic Verses* is a major work by a major Jungian
analyst. Marie-Louise von Franz was trained both as classical philologist
and (under Jung's personal direction) as a psychotherapist; her literary
sense is unusually acute for a nonspecialist. Her book *Puer Aeternus* includes an exemplary psychological reading of Saint-Exupery's *The Little
Prince*, whose vision she criticizes for its immature attitude toward life
and its overreliance on youthful values. Her anatomy of the *puer aeternus*
archetype (the archetype of the "Eternal Youth") and of the *puer* personality of the man who has fallen under its archetypal sway, seems especially
enlightening for a study of *The Satanic Verses*, in that it provides a psycho-
mythological context that enhances one's appreciation of the novel as a
magical realist performance with great depth of symbolic meaning.

In *Beyond Good and Evil* Nietzsche speculated on the way dreams can
enter reality and gave as an example dreams of flying, whose impact on the
waking life manifests itself as *das Gefühl einer gewissen göttlichen Leicht-
fertigkeit* ("the feeling of a kind of godlike lightness").[8] For those blessed
with this sense of the lightness of being, flight may come to operate as
a central metaphor for life. In *Puer Aeternus*, however, von Franz problematizes this happy metaphor, since she considers it to be indicative of
the *puer's* too angelic distance from life. For the man with a *puer* personality, high flying and youthful irresponsibility and freedom may come to
an abrupt end through a fall into life, which may turn out to be a fortunate fall or a tragic crash, depending on how the crisis is resolved.

With von Franz's interpretive framework in mind, the opening scene of
The Satanic Verses may be read as a magical realist symbolic representation of the *puer's* fall into life. The angelically named Bombay film star
Gibreel (=Gabriel) Farishta (=Angel) tumbles from the sky, singing a song,
the burden of which (based on Gramsci's saying) is that "to be born again,
first you have to die" (3). Appropriately enough for the theme of death and
rebirth, the time is "just before dawn one winter's morning, New Year's
Day or thereabouts" (3). Falling along with Gibreel is the mock-heroically

named Saladin Chamcha (alias "Spoono," from *chamcha*, spoon or—metaphorically—toady or sycophant),[9] a long since transplanted native of Bombay who identifies passionately with English culture, has married an English aristocrat by the name of Pamela, and works in London as a radio actor. Both have survived the terrorist explosion that has destroyed minutes earlier the Air India Jumbo jet *Bostan*, whose name, appropriately enough for the adumbration of the Jungian mythopoetic theme of "the adult struggle with the paradise of childhood" (the subtitle of von Franz's *Puer Aeternus*), designates one of the gardens of paradise in Islam. They fall "from a great height, twenty-nine thousand and two feet"—the earlier estimate of the height of Mount Everest, India's and the world's highest mountain. The two are now plummeting "like bundles dropped by some carelessly open-beaked stork" (4), a simile that underscores the theme of fall as a prelude to rebirth—in this instance, rebirth at midlife, since we learn that Gibreel is "within a week of his fortieth birthday" (11) and that Chamcha is the same age.

In her analysis of the aviator-author Saint-Exupéry's fairy tale *The Little Prince*, Marie-Louise von Franz characterizes the *puer*'s "fascination for dangerous sports, particularly flying and mountaineering" as an expression of a desire "to get as high as possible, the symbolism of which is to get away from the mother, i.e. from the earth, from ordinary life" (2–3). Thus "to come down to earth" (9) means for von Franz "to come down into life" (136), and this fall can result in a "crash landing" (129, 138) for someone whose life is run by the energies of the unconscious archetype of the Eternal Youth. Such a fall is a liminal situation fraught with peril; at the same time, it extends the opportunity of rebirth and renewal.

If Farishta is—literally—a high flyer, his female counterpart and eventual nemesis, the angelically named Alleluia ("Allie") Cone, female mountaineer and conqueror of Everest, is waiting for him in London. In spite of the fallen arches that seem to condemn her from now on to a limping life on earth (this is the physical sign of her metaphorical status as a fallen *puella*, the female counterpart of the *puer*), she is haunted by a *puella's* dream of attaining the greatest possible symbolic distance from life, which for her is concretized in the ambition of realizing a solitary ascent of Mount Everest. Allie's sudden appearance in Gibreel's life at the moment when he had lost his faith in Islam and was gobbling down vast amounts of forbidden pork in a Bombay restaurant as a sign of his apostasy, had seemed to signal the beginning of a new life for him: at "that moment when his life had been in pieces at his feet," "she had become its meaning" (85).

But this "climber of mountains, vanquisher of Everest" compounds through her high altitude *puella* characteristics Gibreel's own midlife *puer* problems. Near the end of the novel, when she has arrived in Bombay on the first leg of her project of a solitary ascent of Everest, Gibreel kills her and her suspected lover in a fit of jealous rage; shortly afterward, he puts a pistol in his mouth and kills himself in the presence of his erstwhile chum Saladin Chamcha. Gibreel's suicide may be seen retrospectively as the death by fire(arm) of a modern Icarus, a mythological parallel brought up earlier in another context, when Allie is shown reflecting on "the dangers of attempting to *fly:* what flaming falls, what macabre hells were reserved for such Icarus types" (307). Behind Gibreel Farishta's tragedy lies the mythological paradigm of what happens when — in von Franz's words — "Icarus loses his wings and falls" (165) — for Gibreel, not rebirth, but insanity, murder and suicide.

Von Franz's description of the man whose life is dominated by the archetype of the Eternal Youth/*Puer Aeternus* sheds some additional light on Gibreel Farishta's psychological makeup. First of all, the *puer* suffers from a *mother complex* that keeps him from maturing: "in general, the man who is identified with the archetype of the *puer aeternus* remains too long in adolescent psychology; that is, all those characteristics that are normal in a youth of seventeen or eighteen are continued into later life, coupled in most cases with too great a dependence on the mother" (1). Gibreel Farishta's original name, Ismail (Ishmael), already suggested the drama of the Biblical and Koranic Abraham's/Ibrahim's illegitimate son sent out into the desert with only his mother Hagar to protect him. His stage name Farishta (Angel) also suggests this dependence, since it derives from his mother's term of endearment:

> Gibreel confided to Saladin Chamcha that his choice of pseudonym had been his way of making a homage to the memory of his dead mother, "my mummyji, Spoono, my one and only Mamo, because who else was it who started the whole angel business, her personal angel, she called me, *farishta,* because apparently I was too damn sweet, believe it or not, I was good as goddamn gold." (17)

Next, the *savior or Messiah complex* that von Franz finds characteristic of the *puer* (2) is represented in Gibreel's insane delusion that he has actually become his namesake the archangel Gabriel.[10] This form of megalomania begins to haunt him in a series of dreams that make up the even-numbered chapters of *The Satanic Verses.* (These are the chapters that deal with a revisioning of the foundation myth of Islam and that some Moslems have found offensive.)[11] Eventually dream becomes reality, and Gibreel Farishta believes that he has become the archangel Gabriel in order to save London from apocalyptic destruction. In the tragedy of his life, this Messianic delusion constitutes a "fatal flaw" (315), since one reason for his suicide is his fear that this delusion (labeled "paranoid schizophrenia" in the novel, p. 429)—which has already turned him into a homeless lunatic muttering in the streets of London—will never cease to plague him. Nevertheless, all is not delusional with Gibreel: if he fails to realize his fantasy of becoming the archangel Gabriel, at least he saves the life of Saladin Chamcha, whom he pulls from a burning building. In that sense—as Saladin's angel—he deserves his name.

Don Juanism is another characteristic of von Franz's *puer* that finds a parallel in Gibreel, who as a Bombay film star "had so many sexual partners that it was not uncommon for him to forget their names even before they had left his room" (25). Another characteristic, that of having a *rich fantasy life*, turns out to be an understatement when applied to Gibreel, whose fantasies concerning the foundation myth of Islam make up almost half the novel. Finally, von Franz considers that *work* is of great therapeutic value for the recovering *puer*, whose initial reluctance to settle down to a task and to stick with it constitutes "one of the many self-delusions . . . by which he keeps within the mother and [maintains] his megalomaniac identification with the god [the archetype]" (157). It is important to stress that it was precisely at the moment when Gibreel stopped working in the film studios of Bombay that his megalomanic identification with the angel of the apocalypse began.

At this point where political and psychological commentaries begin to overlap, it is possible to interpret in two ways Gibreel's tragic failure to make good on his expectations of a new life. On the one hand, Gibreel's hallucinatory self-delusion is a rendition of Franz Fanon's insight, quoted in *The Satanic Verses*, that "the native is an oppressed person whose permanent *dream* [my emphasis] is to become the persecutor." The paragraph in which this quotation is embedded shows Gibreel Farishta/Archangel Gabriel overwhelmed by just such an apocalyptic dream of persecutory power: "He would show them—yes!—his *power.*—These powerless English!—Did they not think their history would return to haunt them? . . . Then away with all fogs. He would make this land anew. He was the Archangel, Gibreel" (353). But the insane nature of Farishta's identification with the Archangel Gabriel must derive partly from the fact that, as a Bombay film star, citizen of India and lover of the English-woman Alleluia Cone, he is precisely *not* in the situation of Fanon's colonial native, but rather in a more complex postcolonial situation, to which the native's dream of becoming the persecutor no longer exactly corresponds. For Farishta, Fanon's native's dream has become an insane delusion, which, rather than expressing a genuinely revolutionary impulse, expresses mainly a *puer's* savior complex, equally ill adapted to his personal life as it is to social reality. And to bring matters to the point where the accumulating allusions to Shakespeare's Othello find their tragic correspondence, Gibreel's jealous murder of Alleluia Cone and her alleged lover can be accounted for partially as the result of an outbreak of what von Franz has called the *puer's* "dark gangster-shadow" (141) — the especially vicious underside of the charming youth.

Von Franz views the *puer's* fall into the complications of adult life as the precondition for renewal and maturation: "if you have succeeded in falling down, you are not at the end of the story; you just have to climb up again. Falling down is only one rhythm in life. The glorious spark is like a star plunging from heaven that must fall into the mud. But then it has to rise out of the mud again" (142). Gibreel's tragedy is that his fall leads to no renewal of life, but rather to life complications that he is completely unable to handle.

For Saladin Chamcha, however, the midlife crisis will turn out differently — although he will pull through only by the skin of his teeth, saved from the fire by Gibreel and later by Gibreel's suicide from Gibreel's rage over "the little satanic verses" with which Saladin, Iago-like, has driven him mad. The two form an odd couple, one destined to live, the other to kill himself. The sadism that presides over their relationship is not the least puzzling and disconcerting aspect of the novel.

Like Gibreel, Saladin is age forty[12] when he falls with Gibreel from the jumbo jet *Bostan* — a paradise that had changed into a hell thanks to a terrorist hijacking. His magical realist midlife fall into life leads directly to his metamorphosis into a goatish, horned, and cleft-footed devil, in which shape he is as distressingly grotesque as Kafka's homologous hero as *ungeheueres Ungeziefer* in *The Metamorphosis*, Gregor Samsa, the sound of whose family name may well be deliberately echoed in "Chamcha." But, unlike Gregor Samsa and unlike his companion Gibreel Farishta, Saladin Chamcha seems by the end of *The Satanic Verses*, especially after his reconciliation with his dying father, to have made a successful transition to a new life — a new start symbolized more than anything else by the new love of his life, the irrepressible, dark-skinned, life-affirming Zeeny from Bombay. Saladin Chamcha, after all, is more than Chamcha/Spoono/"Toady"/Samsa. He is also named after the great Islamic hero Saladin who fought the Crusaders — one expects something heroic of him in the end, if only a victory over his own (that is, Spoono/Chamcha's) toadying to the English.

Saladin Chamcha's life is thus linked with a more hopeful presentation of the theme of metamorphosis. Somewhat paradoxically, his magical realist metamorphosis into a pop mythology devil proves in the long run to be therapeutic in a way that Farishta's angelic halo and messianic pronouncements do not. One might detect the hidden hand of William Blake in this transvaluation of good and evil. Or is it because, as Nancy Gray Diaz has speculated, that "metamorphoses like that of Gregor Samsa seem to enhance the character's self-awareness"?[13] The psychological paradox remains: the angel Gibreel succumbs to his delusions, the devil Saladin becomes in the end saner than ever. As we have seen, on the societal level Chamcha's metamorphosis has a positive valence: the Badness of the immigrant Other revindicated as the power to resist racist violence and oppression by the Good, that is, by the proper English. But his metamorphosis changes sign on the personal level, for Saladin's conduct toward Gibreel, whom he drives mad with his voice actor's talent by making phone calls impersonating Allie's alleged lovers, is truly devilish; it is a manifestation of pure evil, inexcusable and unredeemable. Or is it? In an interview given the day before the publication of *The Satanic Verses*, Rushdie spoke as follows: "I had thought that the devil-angel relationship would be straightforward. What I found was that my view of them changed radically. And it was when I came to see how the emotional lives of these two characters connected that I began to know how to write the book. But it took ages."[14] The reader may also need time to come to terms with the enigma.

From a Jungian perspective, Saladin Chamcha's diabolical metamorphosis can be taken as a symbol of his coming to awareness of his *shadow*, that is, of the repressed side of his otherwise respectable personality: the Mr. devilish Hyde of his Dr. proper Jekyll. The theme of the return of the shadow at midlife is a commonplace of Jungian discussions of the midlife crisis, where what has long been repressed finds an opportunity to emerge in the midst of the feelings of stagnation and disorientation that characterize the crisis. In Saladin's case, the repressed side of his prim and toadyish personality *becomes him* (as Mr. Hyde took over Dr. Jekyll); the grotesque devil Saladin Chamcha is the embodiment of his repressed vitality, social rebellion, hatred, and rage, along with some oedipally sadistic impulses which link him more specifically to "the enigma of Iago" (424). While Saladin is trapped in his devil shape, he flies into "the vilest rage" (273); later he will sum up his devil experience as having "learned the power of hatred" (401).

In fact, the rage that fuels his persecution of Gibreel and Allie, while apparently inexplicable and unexplained in the novel's internal commentary (unlike modernist hermetic texts, *The Satanic Verses* usually winds up providing the key to paradoxes and obscure allusions), is perhaps best explained as an acting out of oedipal rage against the father. Saladin's earlier problematic relationship with his bullying father Changez has turned into what seems to be a permanent estrangement. But by the end of the novel Saladin has tormented Gibreel (played Iago to his Othello, as the text makes explicit, through his impersonation of the voices of Allie's supposed lovers), narrowly escaped being murdered by Gibreel, and has had a deathbed reconciliation with his father. One must presume some symbolic cause and effect in all this brutal psychological mess, and one plausible explanation is that by acting out oedipal rage against Gibreel, Saladin has vented enough of his oedipal hatred of his father to enable him — at the last minute and with the help of Zeeny — to love his father before Changez dies. But this type of "acting out" — however therapeutic and liberating it may have proved to be for Saladin — is clearly, from an ethical perspective, quite devilish.

For Jung, the encounter with one's own personal devil, the shadow, is of the greatest psychological importance for the individual. Coming to terms with the shadow is a necessary step on the individual's path to self-knowledge and individuation. "*One cannot avoid the shadow* [Jung's emphasis] unless one remains neurotic, and as long as one is neurotic one has omitted the shadow."[15] Jung preferred personification over abstraction in his description of unconscious structures — another point where magical realism and the Jungian mythopoetic imagination coincide. In descriptions of the shadow ("the imperfect being in you that follows after you and does everything you are loath to do, all the things you are too cowardly or too decent to do,")[16] Jung personifies it much as the shadow appears personified in dreams. Through the common trope of personification, the link between dream text, narrative text, and psychoanalytic text is clearer in Jungian depth psychology than in other schools of psychoanalysis. The figures of Robert Louis Stevenson's Mr. Hyde, often cited by Jungians as a stock example of literary representation of the shadow, and of Salman Rushdie's Saladin Chamcha as pop mythology devil, are the results of a similar strategy: the magical realist personification of an unconscious dimension of the psyche.

To take Saladin's devil metamorphosis as a symbolic representation of his shadow is not, however, to deprive it of potential for positive meaning. Jung adopted toward the shadow a vitalist as well as an ethical attitude. In terms that could readily characterize Saladin as devil, Jung stated that: "the shadow is merely somewhat inferior, primitive, unadapted and awkward; not wholly bad. It even contains childish or primitive qualities which would in a way vitalize and embellish human existence, but convention forbids!"[17] Saladin Chamcha's personal evil is no doubt shocking, since his "little satanic verses"—the jealousy-and-madness-inducing phone calls he makes to Gibreel—are partly responsible for Gibreel's Othello-like murder of Allie and self-destruction. But the symbolic teleology of his devilish action, in which the acting out of unconscious oedipal hatred eventually releases him from its grip, puts it perhaps in Jung's category of the "not wholly bad." This partial redemption of the shadow, however, is not fully realized as a theme in *The Satanic Verses*, and this significant silence may indicate a certain oedipal blindness in the text itself.

Although Rushdie uses the word "shadow" at two significant junctures early in the novel ("Watch out, Chamcha, look out for your shadow. That black fellow creeping up behind" [p. 53] and "his old self . . . a dead self, a shadow" [p. 58]), there is no clear indication that he intended it to be taken in the Jungian sense of the term, just as there is no sign that Rushdie writes from a consciously Jungian perspective anywhere in *The Satanic Verses*. In both cases, the word "shadow" refers to Chamcha's rejected Indian identity—the identity he has spurned in order to become a proper Englishman, but which haunts him and trails after him like a shadow.

However, as is frequently the case in *The Satanic Verses*, a magical realist strategy of personification branches out from the sociopolitical to the psychological. Behind the theme of Saladin Chamcha's social and cultural alienation may be discerned the theme of the *puer's* shadow, as described by von Franz: the "cold, brutal man somewhere in the background, which compensates the too idealistic attitude of consciousness and which the *puer aeternus* cannot voluntarily assimilate" (8). The most puzzling aspect of the novel—the "enigma of Iago," "the little satanic verses"—, Saladin's cold-blooded plot to drive Gibreel mad with jealousy, however explicated as ordinary oedipal acting out, is sinister and diabolical. Identifying with his brutal *puer* shadow, both in terms of magical realist metamorphosis (as devil Saladin has *become* his shadow) and realist acting out of shadow impulses against Gibreel, proves to be life-enhancing for Saladin. Rushdie seems to ignore the ethical dimension of "the enigma of Iago" in favor of a vitalist, psychological validation of it that coincides partially with Jung's vitalist approach toward the shadow; Jung, however, did not circumvent ethical considerations as Rushdie seems to be doing. In all events, by the end of *The Satanic Verses*, Saladin Chamcha appears, not as a Raskolnikov in need of confession, penitence, punishment, and forgiveness, but rather as an ethically enigmatic figure who seems to have benefited from the evil he has done to Gibreel. His return to India, his happiness with Zeeny, and his reconciliation with his father—all these are the indirect results of act-ing like a devil. Ethically suspect, his actions call for a different context, which one might constitute along the lines of Jung's assertion that "no-one stands beyond good and evil, otherwise he would be out of this world. Life is a continual balancing of opposites, like any other energic process. The abolition of opposites would be equivalent to death." [18]

Still, it is hard to dismiss the ethical dimension completely. On the next to the last page of the novel, in a tense scene where it is still unclear whether Gibreel is going to shoot Saladin or himself, Saladin was thinking "about how he was going to die for his verses ["the little satanic verses" of his jealousy inducing phone calls], but could not find it in himself to call the death-sentence unjust" (546). Although he considers himself de-serving of death, Saladin lives on; Gibreel dies instead. The angel is dead, long live the devil! And with the reconciliation scene with his father and visions of a future life with Zeeny, the novel ends on such a cheerfully amoral note that, given the near total ethical confusion of the ending, one is forced to consider a symbolic interpretation. In such an ethical aporia the theme of the integration of particularly brutal *puer* shadow contents makes welcome symbolic psychological sense.

So Saladin as magically real devil may be seen as having evolved, once he has learned "the power of hatred" and regained his human shape, into the hero of a symbolic oedipal victory over a father figure—over Gibreel as the boastful lover of Allie. This victory enables him to bond with his actual father. In symbolic terms, Saladin's Dr. Jekyll and Mr. Hyde have merged into one figure, a new Saladin who is capable of both good *and* evil. In persecuting Gibreel, Saladin has punished his father to the point where he can forgive him. Seen from this perspective, the ethically untenable situation at the end of the novel can be more appropriately termed a representation of the integration of brutal shadow contents and the resolution of oedipal rage.

As we have been seeing, *The Satanic Verses* provides examples of how magical realist and Jungian strategies coincide in the choice of key metaphors and images. Magical realist author and Jungian psychoanalyst intuitively use similar symbolic images in order to express similar psychological insights. We will examine briefly two of them: the *puer* as *actor* and as someone separated by some *odd barrier* from life.

Like Gibreel Farishta, Saladin Chamcha represents the *puer* at midlife. He is a "fortyish fellow," and again like Gibreel, he is an *actor*. In *Puer Aeternus* von Franz employs the metaphor of acting in order to symbolize the *puer's* distance from life; *puers* "act to themselves to convince themselves that they are living"; they "do not feel alive," but rather "describe it as being as though they were acting, acting to themselves" (151).

It is the *puer's* mother complex that separates him from life. As von Franz describes it, the mother complex keeps him "away from life under a *plastic cover*" [my emphasis] (129). Rushdie uses a similar metaphor, literalized of course in magical realist fashion, of *glass skin*. The potential for symbolic meaning is stressed in the text by the fact that it occurs in one of Saladin's dreams. On his return flight to Bombay after years of playing the proper Englishman in London, Saladin dreams of "a bizarre stranger, a man with a glass skin, who rapped his knuckles mournfully against the thin, brittle membrane covering his entire body and begged Saladin to help him, to release him from the prison of his skin" (33–34). After waking from this dream, Saladin "found his speech unaccountably metamorphosed into the Bombay lilt he had so diligently (and so long ago!) unmade" (34).

The most obvious interpretation of this dream is cultural and political: imprisoned as though by a glass skin in his postcolonial anglophilia, Saladin needs to regain contact with native culture, to free his Indian self from the proper English persona in which he has enclosed himself, English accent and all. This at least is the interpretation of his sassy Bombay lover Zeeny, who sees Saladin as a silly "salad" or mixture of cultural traits:

" '[L]isten,' Zeeny put her arm through his. 'Listen to my Salad. Suddenly he wants to be Indian after spending his life trying to turn white. All is not lost, you see. Something in there still alive' " (54).

But there is also in the image of the man with a glass skin the psychological representation of von Franz's *puer* who grows up by falling into life. The literary text implicitly confirms this particular perspective through a variation on the glass skin image: the *ice skin*. After Saladin has been "reborn" after his fall from the jumbo jet onto a Channel beach ("Saladin Chamcha coughed, spluttered, opened his eyes, and, as befitted a newborn babe, burst into foolish tears" [10]), the man with the glass skin is *him;* although there is no indication that the connection with the glass skin dream and this ice skin fantasy is apparent to him, the text makes the connection:

> Saladin: was not dead, but weeping. The tears of shock freezing on his face. And all his body cased in a fine skin of ice, smooth as glass, *like a bad dream come true* [my emphasis]. In the miasmic semiconsciousness induced by his low body temperature he was possessed by the nightmare-fear of cracking, of seeing his blood bubbling up from the ice-breaks, of his flesh coming away with the shards. (131)

Von Franz's "plastic envelope" and Rushdie's "ice skin" and "glass skin" can be taken as symbolic images of the *puer's* separation from life; for Saladin the image of the breaking of the ice can be taken as a symbolic foreshadowing of psychic renewal.

But being reborn into a "new life" (141) is going to mean coming to terms with his shadow—with himself as devil. It is this devil metamorphosis to which we now turn in order to clarify once more the affinity of magical realism with Jungian psychology.

Saladin's shadow contains, first of all, what von Franz designates as a major component of the *puer's* shadow: "shut-off masculinity" (128). His incarnation as pop mythology devil makes this clear: Saladin is "taken aback by the sight of his phallus, greatly enlarged and embarrassingly erect, an organ that he had the greatest difficulty in acknowledging as his own" (157). Coming to terms with his sexual shadow proves to be no easy matter; the sexual repressions of his "Englished soul" (439) do not pass off quickly. When, for instance, "thoughts of Zeeny Vakil welled up, guiltily, nervously, he forced them down again" (257).

Conscious as he is now of what he has missed, he is devoured with envy for Gibreel Farishta's easy, complacent, and confident Don Juanism. He "longs to stand in Farishta's shoes" (426); Farishta, "the embodiment of all the good fortune that the Fury-haunted Chamcha so signally lacked," quickly becomes "his hated Other" (429). As the magically real lover of Rosa Diamond, the elderly woman/mother figure/archetypal image of the feminine (cf. rose) who took them both in after their fall, Gibreel has already played the role of oedipal rival, reinforced when he does nothing to stop the police from arresting Saladin as an illegal alien in Rosa's own home. Gibreel's later lavishly detailed accounts of his and Allie's lovemaking only reinforce Saladin's own sexual repressions: "he [Saladin] could almost feel her [Allie's] coolness, her responses, almost hear her cries. — He controlled himself. His desire disgusted him" (438). In hounding Gibreel into insane jealousy by a series of phone calls that purport to be from Allie's numerous lovers, Saladin is persecuting his hated Other, driven by shadow projection, which leads him to hate and persecute the one on whom he has projected the most troublesome aspect of his own psychology.

Rushdie's spectacular development of magical realism's potential for symbolic meaning in *The Satanic Verses* creates a version of the psychological marvelous that seems eminently explicable in Jungian terms. The masterstroke of this strategy is found in a mysterious scene that purports to explain how it was that Saladin decided to play Iago to Gibreel's Othello, to commit himself to a course of action he will later characterize as "infernal, *childlike* [my emphasis] evil" (445). Over the years Saladin had had a recurring dream about "a small boy of about five," "his imagined son" (400), whom he was teaching to ride a bicycle in a city park; "balance came like a gift of flight," and both the boy and Saladin are delighted with how quickly the boy learned to ride. Later, walking with Gibreel in a London park, Saladin is startled to recognize the scene of his recurring dream. As in the dream, a young boy (this time age six or seven) is riding a bicycle. Saladin gives great significance to this synchronous coincidence of a real scene and a dream scene, although a boy riding on a bicycle in an English park can hardly be an uncommon occurrence. But in Jungian terms, Saladin is right, not only because of the synchronicity — that is, the juxtaposition of events related meaningfully but not causally — but also because of the archetypal dimension of the experience: the "boy," as we shall see, may be taken as an archetypal image of the *Puer Aeternus*.

For Saladin, this scene in the park becomes the fateful "moment before evil" (438). Yet there is no obvious reason why seeing a boy riding a bicycle in a park, even if it reminds him of the boy in his recurring dream who is "his imagined son," should trigger the evil of "the little, satanic verses" — should lead to his devilish persecution of Gibreel Farishta. The paradox that Rushdie's text presents, without internal commentary, can perhaps be translated into von Franz's terms of the bipolarity of *puer* innocence (cf. "childlike") and *puer* shadow brutality (cf. "infernal"), that presides over an "infernal, childlike evil." The "boy" in Saladin's dream would then correspond to an archetypal image of the *puer aeternus* — a dream image, that is, of the hidden power, the patron deity, that presides over Saladin's spirit of youthfulness prolonged into midlife. Riding a bicycle, a "gift of flight," would represent symbolically that high-flying distance from life that characterizes Saladin's psychologically and culturally ungrounded existence. As in Günter Grass' *The Tin Drum*, where this figure is foregrounded to a greater extent, an archetypal childlike *puer aeternus* is given a paradoxical affinity with evil.

That magical proof that Saladin's dream has a more than personal (i.e., archetypal and collective) reference is the fact that his friend Jumpy Joshi, who is sleeping with Saladin's wife Pamela after Saladin's disappearance, has had exactly the same dream (411). Such a synchronistically shared dream may be said to be archetypal, that is, to derive its significance from the collective unconscious, not the personal unconscious. No doubt Saladin interprets his dream as a simple wish fulfillment for a son he never had in his childless marriage with Pamela. But why then does the dream open the door to his persecution of Gibreel? The paradox of evil affiliated with innocence is better explicated by von Franz's *innocent-puer-with-brutal-shadow* paradigm. Furthermore, as Jung pointed out in his essay "The Psychology of the Child Archetype," the child motif appears frequently during the midlife maturation process, during which time "in dreams it often appears as the dreamer's son."[19] Saladin's dream and later experience of dream-becoming-reality represent a spontaneous coming to consciousness of an archetypal image, whose affinity with evil is linked with Saladin's need to come to terms with his shadow, and whose imaginary resemblance to the son he never had is a token of his readiness to be a father and not just his own father's son.

As we have seen, the polarization of *puer* personality and *puer* shadow is extreme: "innocent" boy counterpoised with "satanic" gangster shadow. Saladin's devil metamorphosis represents symbolically a stage at which his shadow side can no longer be ignored; in Jungian terms, he is in a state of *inflation*, that is, of identification with unconscious contents of the shadow: he has *become* a devil. But this is only a stage: Saladin is soon brought back to his old human shape. Rushdie represents this de-metamorphosis in an intriguing way: it is the result of decreased emotional repression, especially of anger, hatred, and rage. For instance, "during Chamcha's brief but violent outburst against Gibreel, the horns on his head . . . definitely, unmistakeably, — by about three-quarters of an inch, — *diminished* (273). This scene of magical de-metamorphosis represents symbolically a moment during which Saladin is able to integrate some of his aggressive shadow's emotional charge — if only briefly, for soon afterward he becomes more devilish than ever. For under the renewed pressure of repressed rage he grows "to a height of over eight feet, and from his nostrils there emerged smoke of two different colours . . . his tail was swishing angrily, his eyes were a pale but luminous red" (291). But as time goes on Saladin returns to his human form, "*humanized*," as Rushdie emphasizes, "by the fearsome concentration of his hate" (294). The magic of the scene stresses the humanizing effect of integrating shadow contents into his conscious personality: Saladin has "learned the power of hatred and regained human shape" (401).

Jungian psychology has reached far beyond the narrow circle of Jungian analysts and analysands in recent years and is rapidly becoming part of the mainstream intellectual culture of our times. The eminent American poet Robert Bly, a great admirer of "Marie-Louise" [von Franz], recently published a quasi-Jungian analysis of a Grimm fairy tale; his book *Iron John* (1990)[20] was on the *New York Times* best-seller list for over a year. In an earlier Jung-inspired essay *A Little Book on the Human Shadow* (1988) Bly described a Zen Buddhist method of integrating shadow anger that may shed light on Chamcha's devil metamorphosis and on how he was "*humanized* . . . by the fearsome concentration of his hate*." Bly describes how

> in meditation one might allow the anger to come in, so that the whole body burns with anger. The anger is not repressed; your whole body *is* anger. One may want to feel that anger for three or four hours. During this time one is neither expressing it nor repressing it. Then, when the meditation ends, one has the choice to express the anger or not. The ego or personality can make the choice later, to express it or not.[21]

The "whole body as anger" might be the psychological state that in Jungian terms would be equivalent to a controlled identification with the shadow, and in the magical realist strategy of *The Satanic Verses* Saladin Chamcha as pop mythology devil. Once again, magical realism's pop mythological extravagance is a strategy that reintegrates the psychological marvelous into the postmodern narrative. Saladin Chamcha has become his hatred—literally, bodily. After that, he is free to make choices.

Unfortunately, the choice he will make is an evil one: to vent his hatred onto Gibreel Farishta and drive him mad with his "little, satanic verses." After his de-metamorphosis from his pop mythology devil shape, he becomes even more of a devil in human form. We are back to "the enigma of Iago."

Saladin Chamcha's encounter with his devil shadow, with what von Franz has called the *puer's* "dark gangster shadow" (141), sets up an ethical quandary which, as we have seen, is only partially resolved in the text. To the extent that Saladin's angry shadow is associated with the anger that immigrants feel when subjected to racist violence (cf. his own change of shape as he was being carried away by abusive police as an illegal alien), it seems justified. But it is difficult to find anything righteous in his persecution of Gibreel Farishta, even if we consider it to be a somewhat inevitable symbolic acting out of oedipal rage.

But through this acting out, however evil it may be, Saladin has freed himself to some degree from the compulsive hold oedipal rage has had over his life. Partial integration of shadow oedipal rage may be said to have liberated Saladin's capacity to love his bullying father Changez (named appropriately in the novel after the old tyrant Genghiz Khan). He had defined his earlier sexually repressed, anglophilic self in opposition to this sensual Bombay merchant whom he had judged and dismissed as "domineering, tyrannical and cruel." But now that he sees his dying father as having been also "mischievous, loving and brilliant" (524), he is able to reconcile himself with him: "to fall in love with one's father after the long angry decades was a serene and beautiful feeling: a renewing, life-giving thing" (523). Reconciliation with his father leads to reconciliation with his once despised and rejected Indian self; Saladin Chamcha now calls himself by his original unanglicized name, Salahuddin Chamchawala, and begins "to find the sound of his full, un-Englished name pleasing for the first time in twenty years" (524).

A narrative of midlife crisis that began with the *puer's* fall concludes with Saladin's entering a new stage of life. His return to his Bombay lover Zeeny marks a return to his cultural roots and a willingness to reestablish contact with Indian sensuality. Zeeny's remark "now you can stop acting at last" triggers Saladin's perception that a new life had begun for him: "yes, this looked like the start of a new phase, in which the world would be solid and real" (534). Magical metamorphoses can now cease, after having accomplished their psychic goals of growth and integration. The last scene of *The Satanic Verses* shows him looking out from his childhood home onto the Arabian Sea and suggests that his infantile illusions and *puer* innocence are over and that (in Robert Bly's playful terminology) he is now a "recovering *puer*":

> The moon was almost full; moonlight, stretching from the rocks of Scandal Point out to the far horizon, created the illusion of a silver pathway, like a parting in the water's shining hair, like a road to miraculous lands. He shook his head; could no longer believe in fairy-tales. Childhood was over, and the view from this window was no more than an old and sentimental echo. (546–47)

Notes

1 See Jean Weisgerber, "La locution et le concept," in *Le Réalisme magique: roman, peinture et cinéma*, ed. Jean Weisgerber (Paris: L'Age d'Homme, 1987), pp. 11–32, esp. pp. 17–18.

2 Seymour Menton, *Magic Realism Rediscovered* (Philadelphia: Art Alliance Press, 1983).

3 Salman Rushdie, *The Satanic Verses* (New York: Viking, 1988).

4 The phantasmagorical magic of the male midlife crisis was not Rushdie's particular discovery: Joyce Carol Oates had already shown herself to be an admirable magician in evoking the terrors of this specifically Jungian life crisis in her unjustly neglected novella *Cybele* (Santa Barbara: Black Sparrow Press, 1979), in which poor Edwin Locke embraces the goddess of his worst dreams and dies a miserable death, much like Gibreel Farishta. Written just after the author had turned forty, the text was inspired partly by the spectacle of some of her male acquaintances going through what by then was becoming commonly termed the "midlife crisis" (conversation with the author, Feb. 7, 1994). The year before the publication of *The Satanic Verses* Wim Wender's and Peter Handke's film *Wings of Desire/Der Himmel über Berlin* (1987) represented symbolically a middle-aged *puer's* fall into life as the fall to earth of an amiable angel played by Peter Falk; the film may well have von Franz's treatise as a subtext.

5 *Marie-Louise* von Franz, *Puer Aeternus: A Psychological Study of the Adult Struggle with the Paradise of Childhood*, 2d. ed. (Santa Monica, California: Sigo Press, 1981).

6 Throughout this episode one senses the presence of Carlos Fuentes' magical realist novella *Aura* (1962) as a subtext.

7 Christopher Isherwood, *My Guru and His Disciple* (New York: Farrar, Straus, Giroux, 1980), pp. 70–71.

8 Friedrich Nietzsche, *Jenseits von Gut und Böse*, section 193, *Samtliche Werke*, vol. 5, Giorgio Colli and Mazzino Montinari, eds. (Berlin and New York: De Gruyter, 1980), p. 114.

9 Like most points that a Western reader (but not a Bombay reader) would fail to understand immediately, this bit of Bombay slang is eventually explained in the novel's own internal commentary (see p. 54). My thanks to my friend Cyrus Mehta, who originally explained the expression to me.

10 See John Weir Perry, "The Messianic Hero," *Journal of Analytical Psychology* 17, 2 (July 1972): 184–98 for a Jungian approach.

11 The Islamic tradition is rich in heterodox perspectives; Islamic fundamentalism ignores this fact. See Saadi A. Simawe, "Rushdie's *The Satanic Verses* and Heretical Literature in Islam," *Iowa Review* 20, 1 (1990): 185–98.

12 Cf. p. 69: the walnut tree his father planted at his birth is now forty years old.

13 Nancy Gray Diaz, *The Radical Self: Metamorphoses to Animal Form in Modern Latin American Narrative* (Columbia: University of Missouri Press, 1988), p. 5.

14 Salman Rushdie, interview with Sean French in *The Observer* (London), Sept. 25, 1988. Reprinted in *The Rushdie File*, ed. Lisa Appignanesi and Sara Maitland (Syracuse, New York: Syracuse University Press, 1990), pp. 6–8.

15 C. G. Jung, *Letters*, vol. 2, ed. Gerhard Adler (Princeton: Princeton University Press, 1973), p. 545.

16 C. G. Jung, *Dream Analysis: Notes of the Seminar Given in 1928–1930*, ed. William McGuire (Princeton: Princeton University Press, 1973), p. 76.

17 C. G. Jung, *Collected Works*, ed. William McGuire (Princeton: Princeton University Press, 1958), vol. 11, paragraph 134.

18 C. G. Jung, 1949 preface (tr. R. F. C. Hull) to Erich Neumann, *Depth Psychology and a New Ethic*, tr. Eugene Rolfe (New York: Harper and Row, 1973), p. 16.

19 C. G. Jung and C. Kerényi, *Essays on a Science of Mythology: The Myth of the Divine Child and the Mysteries of Eleusis*, tr. R. F. C. Hull (Princeton: Princeton University Press, 1969), p. 78.

20 Robert Bly, *Iron John: A Book About Men* (New York: Addison-Wesley, 1990). In the preface Bly writes "My first teacher in unfolding the fairy story was Marie-Louise von Franz, and I tried to be as true to the masculine stories as she has been to the feminine in her many books" (p. xi).

21 Robert Bly, *A Little Book on the Human Shadow* (San Francisco: Harper and Row, 1988), pp. 56–57.

DAVID MIKICS

Derek Walcott and Alejo Carpentier: Nature, History, and the Caribbean Writer

The lexicographer's lizard eyes are curled in sleep.
The Amazonian Indian enters them.

Between the Rupununi and Borges,
between the fallen pen tip and the spearhead
thunders, thickens, and shimmers the one age of the world.
—Derek Walcott, "Guyana"

The classics can console. But not enough.
—Derek Walcott, "Sea Grapes"[1]

The choice to center a study of magical realism in Caribbean literature around the works of Derek Walcott may at first glance seem surprising.[2] Walcott, the Caribbean's greatest Anglophone poet, and its second Nobel laureate in literature (after Francophone poet St. John Perse), does make use of magical realist techniques, notably in the 1970 play *Dream on Monkey Mountain;* but he tends to shy away from the more flamboyant juxtapositions of fantasy and reality exploited by Alejo Carpentier, García Márquez, Wilson Harris, Carlos Fuentes, and others. Though not a full-blown magical realist, Walcott has frequently noted the importance to his work of writers like Carpentier and García Márquez. Among others, these two magical realists, Walcott has claimed, exemplify a prevailing regional aesthetic rooted in the cultural and historical reality of the Caribbean.[3]

Walcott's claim for magical realism as the authoritative aesthetic response to the Caribbean cultural context that defines his own work, as well as that of the Hispanophone writers, combined with his own occasional use of magical realist technique, makes him a pivotal figure for an attempt to define magical realism in a regional setting. Rather than claiming Walcott as a magical realist, I plan to demonstrate a family resemblance between Walcott and magical realist writers, notably Carpentier, and by doing so, to illuminate the picture of New World culture that is common to Walcott and his magical realist cousins. Specifically, I will argue that in Walcott magical realism forms one aspect of a much larger strategy of cultural mixing — a creolizing or transculturation — that is central to much of what Vera Kutzinski has called "New World writing."

Magic and reality may sound like a contradictory pairing. In literary history, however, the two terms seem to exist in oxymoronic or paradoxical cohesion, rather than antithesis. Magical realism finds itself especially at home in the novel, a form that claims realist authority through its grounding in ordinary life. Magical realists assert that the realist impulse, in order to fulfill itself, may require what seems at first glance to be a violation of everyday appearances by the rich and strange world of dreams. But this transgression presents itself as a neighboring of or intimacy between fantasy and empirical sobriety. Magical realism turns out to be part of a twentieth-century preoccupation with how our ways of being in the world resist capture by the traditional logic of the waking mind's reason — an interest that Heidegger, Freud, and Wittgenstein share with literary and artistic modernism.

The magical realists' project to reveal the intimate interdependence between reality and fantasy is shared by the modernists, but magical realism and modernism proceed by very different means. Modernism tampered with the representational function of language, questioning the rightness of mimesis as such, because representation had obscured the reality of the writer's object. As Woolf, for example, argues in a polemic like "Mr. Bennett and Mrs. Brown," nineteenth-century realism obstructs the world that a truer, more accurately perceptive modernist writing must dedicate itself to revealing. Magical realism, unlike Woolf's modernism but like the uncanny, wills a transformation of the object of representation, rather than the means of representation.

Magical realism, like the uncanny, a mode with which it has strong affinities, projects a mesmerizing uncertainty suggesting that ordinary life may also be the scene of the extraordinary. Such dreamlike suspension on the border between the fantastic and the mundane offers a utopian, if evanescent, promise of transfigured perception, the hypnotic renewing of everyday existence.[4] Both the uncanny and magical realism narrate fantastic events not merely alongside real ones, but as if they were real. What seems most strange turns out to be secretly familiar. What is the difference, then, between the uncanny and magical realism itself? I will argue that magical realism is a mode or subset of the uncanny in which the uncanny exposes itself as a historical and cultural phenomenon. Magical realism realizes the conjunction of ordinary and fantastic by focusing on a particular historical moment afflicted or graced by this doubleness. Since magical realism surrounds with its fabulous aura a particular, historically resonant time and place, the theory of magical realism must supply an approach to history, not merely literary genre. The lucid fantasia that the magical realist mode offers is not an aesthete's intoxicant: magical realism appeals to Caribbean writers because it addresses the weight of historical memory that survives in the day to day life of the West Indies.

This idea of magical realism as a self-consciously historical form is suggested by Alejo Carpentier's influential discussion of *lo real maravilloso,* or marvelous reality. Carpentier gives birth to magical realism as a concept special to or necessarily implied by New World history. According to Carpentier's seminal formulation in his prologue to *The Kingdom of this World* (*El reino de este mundo,* 1949), the utopian imaginative freedom only dreamt of by the Old World surrealist becomes flesh in the New World, and especially in its Caribbean margin. Both Anglophone and Hispanophone Caribbean writers have followed Carpentier by asserting that the New World possesses an original aesthetic virtually embedded in its social and natural landscapes, a magical reality unavailable to the European artist or writer. Not the writer's style, but the historical scene that his or her writing reveals, provides the magic.

Fredric Jameson more explicitly formulates the historical basis of the magical realist aesthetic implicit in Carpentier's definition. For Jameson, magical realism relies on disjunctions among differing cultures and social formations, which coexist in the same space and time in the New World as they usually do not in Western Europe.[5] Jameson suggests that magical realist writing often stems from a place and time in which different cultures or historical periods inhabit a single cultural space (contemporary Eastern Europe and the South of Faulkner are Jameson's other examples).

Carpentier's prologue, like his novels, gives evidence for Jameson's reading by juxtaposing the relics of European conquest with the practices of Amerindian and African cultures. We might infer that the uniqueness of the New World and its aesthetics derives from the dynamism of such cultural combinations: in the Haiti described in *Kingdom*'s prologue, for example, the palace of Pauline Bonaparte appears along with the drums of *vodoun*. The cultural conflicts visible in such a mixture, the result of European imperialism, can also result in future-oriented macaronic fantasies of the kind that appear in Wilson Harris and Edward Kamau Brathwaite as well as in Carpentier. Walcott, like these writers, draws on the New World's meddling or mediation among cultures in conflict to turn a pessimism derived from historical violence into an optimistic hope for imaginative rebirth.

The Caribbean and Latin America mixing of cultures (African, European, Amerindian) can, then, become a source of invention whose energy derives from the conjunctions and cross-influences of radically different modes of thought and life. An example is the St. Nevis "tea meeting" described by folklorist Roger Abrahams, a rite that relies on the Africa-derived communal aesthetics of contributive interruption to provide a parody of cosmopolitan or overly Europe-centered rhetoric.[6] Participants in a tea meeting undergo elaborate coaching and preparation in order to deliver speeches in ornately literate style; yet each speaker's attempt at high propriety must yield to the continual freewheeling interruption of audience heckling and commentary. It is important to note that the parody involved in a tea meeting is ambivalent or dialogic in Bakhtin's sense and that the participants are seriously invested in the ideal of an eloquent, well-traveled sophistication even as they spoof it.

In the literary sphere, examples of creolization or cultural mixing analogous to the tea meeting appear in the works of the Barbadian poet Edward Kamau Brathwaite and the Trinidadian novelist Samuel Selvon. Both make expert use of dialect and folk culture within genres that obey the standards of a literary tradition derived from Europe. Walcott's own brilliant use of dialect in "high" literary forms equals Selvon's and surpasses Brathwaite's. Such mixing of cultures, I will suggest, also surfaces in the magical realist moments in Walcott's, and others', work.

The symbiosis of folk and high culture, along with the mixing of African, European Asian, and Native American strains forms a central part of the magical realist aesthetic, as Carpentier suggests in his essays. The magical realist novel of exploration, Carpentier's *The Lost Steps* (*Los pasos perdidos*, 1953) or Harris' *Palace of the Peacock* (1960), relies on such a geographical and historical fact of coexistence: South America sets alongside one another the prefeudal jungle, the modern capitalist city, and the feudal countryside. In *One Hundred Years of Solitude*, too, the magical

realist compression of fantasy and mimetic narrative in which, for example, ghosts are a low-key realist feature of the Buendía household, finds
its basis, particularly in the novel's early chapters, in the coincidence of
two drastically different cultures that most readers would expect to belong
to different eras: a folkloric magic with, as García Márquez has acknowledged, African roots,[7] and rationalist scientific investigation. Similarly, the
involuted, often incestuously repetitive character of the Buendía generations in *Solitude* finds its basis in a simultaneity of historical and social
epochs.[8] Gypsies, necromancers, and the relics of Francis Drake take their
place alongside United Fruit; and even Macondo's priest resorts to the
pagan magic of levitation.

A juxtaposition of fantasy and reality akin to the instances I have cited
from García Márquez provides the foundation for the central magical
realist episode in Walcott's autobiographical epic *Another Life* (1973). In
this scene Auguste Manoir, a merchant and "pillar of the Church" (168) in
Walcott's native island, St. Lucia, is transformed into his dog, a snarling
beast "more wolf than dog." Up to this point, the poem has been realistic in its narrative; the Manoir episode represents a sudden outbreak of
the supernatural in a verisimilar context. Jameson's thesis of a cultural
disjunction (in this case, that of Europe and Africa) as the foundation of
magical realism seems to be borne out here, since Walcott's shift toward
a magical realist mode occurs as a reaction to the European aspirations
represented by characters like Manoir.

Let us take a closer look at the Manoir episode. Walcott has just been
describing the Methodist church in St. Lucia. The Methodists' "Jacobean
English" offers the poem's narrator a dialect associated with the figures
of "Arnold, staid melancholy of those Sabbath dusks" and "those rigorous teachers of our youth, / Victorian gravures of the Holy Land" (166).
The narrator then juxtaposes to this high-toned European belief a depiction of the African tribal religion that is the source of the werewolf myth,
"an atavism stronger than their Mass." As Edward Baugh notes, Walcott's
werewolf myth is related to the *jâ-gajé* (*gens engagés*) of St. Lucian folklore described by Daniel Crowley—humans who sell their services to the
devil. "One step beyond the city was the bush" and its "obeah-man"; "One
step beyond the church door stood the devil" (167).[9] Manoir's werewolf
metamorphosis represents the revenge of Africa on Manoir. Manoir, in
guarding his status as a pillar of the Christian church, has repressed the
presence of Africa-derived magic in the West Indies.[10] Manoir's attempt to

disguise the African roots of West Indian society is frustrated by the magical realist assertion of Africa's place beside Europe's in the New World.

Another Life at first glance seems to indulge in what I will call a classicizing strategy, an attachment to Europe similar to the one it attributes to Manoir. But the poem actually transforms classicizing into something wholly new and different from Manoir's mode, as Walcott sets his own use of classical and European tradition against the official or imperial exploitation of tradition that he associates with characters like Manoir. As it draws on classical motifs, *Another Life*'s style itself becomes an arena for the debate over the renewal of culture in the New World.

Yet Walcott's approach to classicizing style is still more complicated or mixed than I have indicated, since he can detect no clear or reliable distinction between an oppressive and a promising cultural inheritance. An example will illustrate. In lines like "The moon maintained her station, / her fingers stroked a chiton-fluted sea" (147), Walcott moves from a view of the empire as mundane or routinized ("maintained her station") to a classical ennobling of the colonial setting signaled by the adjective "chiton-fluted." As in the Manoir episode, such classicizing description—here of Castries, St. Lucia's port town, and Walcott's home—presents first of all an attempt to cover or disguise the reality of the New World with a European veneer:

> The moon maintained her station,
> her fingers stroked a chiton-fluted sea,
> her disc whitewashed the shells
> of gutted offices barnacling the wharves
> of the burnt town, her lamp
> baring the ovals of toothless facades,
> along the Roman arches . . .
> her alternating ivories lay untuned,
> her age was dead, her sheet
> shrouded the antique furniture, the mantel
> with its plaster-of-Paris Venus, which
> his yearning had made marble, half-cracked
> unsilvering mirror of black servants,
> like the painter's kerchiefed, ear-ringed portrait: Albertina. (147)

The poet's elegantly poised description of the moon "strok[ing]" a "chiton-fluted sea" hints at a disharmony with its setting. The comparison of the sea to the ancient Greek chiton or tunic, familiar from classical painting and sculpture, offers a "whitewash[ing]" of the devastated landscape that it frames, as the rather jarring succession of images that follows indicates: the "gutted offices" and "toothless facades" present a discordant and grotesque, an "untuned," accompaniment for Hellenic grace. As the passage continues, it becomes clear that the classical images—the Roman arches, the cracked plaster-of-Paris Venus—are actually crumbling to ruins. The Europe-fixated aspiring of the young protagonist's imagination has denied this reality, transforming it to a marble worthy of his poetic heritage. But perhaps, as in the youthful Milton's tribute to Shakespeare, the authority of his precursors has immobilized the nascent poet and trapped him, for all his prodigious yearnings, in a place of poverty and loss. Fixed in a paralysis like that of his decrepit surroundings, the poet has been (in Milton's words) "made marble with too much conceiving." The chiton with which we began has waned, dwindling to a brilliant facade that conceals—but for only a moment—the disjunction between European tradition and Caribbean reality, as well as the gap between past and present.

Yet we can also find, in this same passage from *Another Life*, a hint of Walcott's inclination toward the West Indies' mixing of traditions, despite his yearning for a classicism that remains estranged, haughtily resisting a Caribbean translation. In this vein, Walcott suggests a likeness between the Venus and the portrait by his painting tutor, Harry Simmons, of the servant Albertina, which echoes a Delacroix portrait. Yet the comparison to the Greek goddess looks "half-cracked." Albertina, unlike Venus, here appears in traditional costume, kerchiefed and ear-ringed—that is, Africa-derived. But she also, of course, stems from Delacroix; and her very double-sidedness images a rough and equitable coherence of Europe and Africa, in contrast to the usual attempt to deny or restrict the African element. Simmons' portrait of Albertina therefore figures a more honest or answerable, a more indigenous, way of negotiating between Europe and the New World than the repressive sophistication of Manoir or the official classicism institutionalized in West Indian schools. The discord of traditions she represents is not so out of tune as the strained, and ultimately false, attempt to ignore such discord represented by the plaster-of-Paris Venus, which holds up an "unsilvering"—that is, false or foilless—mirror of its Caribbean setting. Walcott notes in his early manuscript that Albertina's "heroic," Europeanized features were combined in Simmons' portrait with her "honest" (i.e., realistically West Indian) costume, and that the young Walcott thus "saw that black woman could be beautiful as art." [11]

But the effort at an indigenous cultural syncretism figured in Simmons' Albertina, a reconciliation between old and new worlds that would avoid overreliance on the old, is not so easily achieved. Walcott in his notebook for *Another Life* reveals that the Europeanized aesthetic represented by Manoir, and by his own early identification with the British empire, remained a temptation for him in his writing of the poem: "I have not eradicated my hatred and longing for Europe." [12] At one point Walcott writes that in the West Indies "our values remain Victorian, protective" — the values of a vanished colonial world. "We seem to remember an imitative 'classic' landscape. Legacies of a marble museum, of Vergilian Latin and Athenian dialectic." Even the "Marxist-colonial" C. L. R. James, next to Frantz Fanon the most famous West Indian intellectual rebel, was, Walcott muses, "indoctrinated with the Graeco-Hellenic values of Arnold." "Our colonial adolescence even in the wrong climate and history was nourished like any young European's on bare ruined choirs, broken moonlit castles, on the inaccessible princess and the early death. Our spirits, if not our complexions, loitered palely around sunsets, darkening beaches and dramatic promontories looking seaward." [13]

Even as he indulges the memory of an adolescence steeped in lush, Victorian melancholy, Walcott in this notebook passage asserts the "wrong"ness of Victorian imagination and its cherished "Graeco-Hellenic" aura. Such fond European decadence seems incongruous with any potentially indigenous New World aesthetic. Yet Walcott's ambivalence about classical and late-Romantic tradition, his continued investment in the wispy Victorian plangency whose inappropriateness he derides, remains apparent in his notebook as he attempts, and then suddenly calls off, a classical invocation filtered through the English nineteenth century: "smoke: the leisure and frailty of recollection. I have an astigmatic memory. Assist me, mother of the Muses. Seaspray, noon-haze, the smoke of a green brush fire. Christ! No one needs that Denton Welch melody, that Palinuran-Tibullan languor, all elastic hexameters, the prose of convalesence [*sic*], the pallid, fevered hand." [14]

Walcott cannot, does not want to, entirely disdain the pale brow and hand of Victorian classicism, as *Another Life* will show. He will, instead, search for a way of using the classics that is sharply different from the colonial nostalgia he resists. Walcott's classicizing habit, in its aspiration to become native West Indian expression, follows Simmons' method in adapting Delacroix, rather than Manoir's loyalty to an essentially foreign Arnoldian piety.

Before discussing further Walcott's revisionary New World use of the classics in *Another Life*, I will mention one more colonial or official use of them. The invocation of the classical as a desperate attempt at the cosmopolitan status provided by Europe occurs in St. Lucia's Virgilian motto, "statio haud malefida carinis." In a memorable scene, Walcott depicts the line being drummed into the heads of St. Lucia schoolboys who, "solemn Afro-Greeks eager for grades,"[15] recite their rote responses in an accent influenced by the island patois. Interestingly, the motto, which means "a safe harbor for sheeps [ships]" (as the students answer, sheeplike), offers a negation—actually an unintentionally ironic reversal—of the *Aeneid*'s description of the harbor at Tenedos, where the Greek navy hides while their horse is offered to the Trojans. The original line as it appears in Virgil, "statio male fida carinis" (untrustworthy harbor for ships), signifies not safety but trickery. In this imperial context, which relies on classical culture for ideological indoctrination, Walcott makes sure to amplify the phrase's original connotation of *male fida*, bad faith. The British empire, like the Trojans with their horse, connives at destruction, concealing its threat by distorting a Virgilian warning into a praise of safety and non-deception. Britain's addition of a *haud* ("not at all") in inventing the motto for its colony cannot mask the deceit necessary to Europeanize or classicize a culture like that of St. Lucia, which remains predominantly African in character.

Walcott responds to such manipulative uses of classical tradition in the official schoolroom context by imaginatively recasting the classics in the West Indies. In an early chapter of the poem, the young narrator, preparing for bed at dusk, remembers a classroom order from earlier in the day: "Boy! Who was Ajax?" (158). Already half asleep, he responds with a dreamlike catalog of St. Lucia characters, recalling Helen's catalog of warriors in the *Iliad*'s book 3. This fantasy about the Homeric identities of contemporary Caribbean lives comprises the first crossing of dream and reality in the poem, a blurring of realms that will in a few pages generate the outright magical realism of the Manoir episode. Among Walcott's characters here is one Emanuel Auguste:

> Emanuel Auguste, out in the harbour, lone Odysseus,
> tattooed ex-merchant sailor, rows alone

through the rosebloom of dawn to chuckling oars
measured, dip, pentametrical. (160)[16]

In his notebook version of *Another Life* Walcott dwells at much greater length on the character of Emanuel Auguste, whom he remembers as a merchant seaman who "would quote his Shakespeare at length." Auguste remains both critical of his surrounding culture and faithful to his self-definition as a West Indian. "No one had a more painful love for his people," Walcott writes, "but he was experienced enough to let them know who they were. He never flattered or abused them," in spite of their abuse of him (he is jeered and interrupted on a feast day during his recital of Robert Service's "The Lifeboat").

Walcott, in his notebook, presents Auguste as a kind of model for the citation of European tradition. Auguste transforms this tradition, reinventing it as native performance. As a result of Auguste's recitals, Walcott writes, "I was drawn to grandeur, to a Shakespearean glory, to declamatory verse. I believed that these actors had inherited, in fact owned the literature which they recited. I never saw them as black or brown men trying to be English."[17] This notebook meditation on Auguste's character is important for our understanding of what Walcott is trying to accomplish when he depicts Auguste and others in the final published version of *Another Life* as analogous to characters in a European (Homeric) tradition. Through cross-cultural analogy, the poet tries to make Homer West Indian, just as Auguste made Shakespeare West Indian for the young Walcott: by appropriating and transforming the West Indies' European inheritance, rather than assuming it as debt or burden.

Anachronistic identification or analogy thus becomes one of Walcott's crucial ways of transfiguring a potential burden into an appropriated vision. The poet, in this choice of method, has a polemical axe to grind. Walcott's identification of St. Lucia's inhabitants with Homeric characters (a horse as Ajax, the "town's one clear-complexioned whore" as Helen, the "ex-merchant sailor" as a "lone Odysseus") represents an unofficial or private linking of the Caribbean with the ancient past, a way of bypassing the imprisoning choice between eager acceptance and contemptuous rejection of Europe—the opposites exemplified, respectively, by conservative and radical islanders. Walcott in *Another Life* speaks against those Caribbean rightists who affiliate themselves with Euroclassicism and "gild cruelty" by seeing "the colors of Hispanic glory/greater than Greece, /

greater than Rome" in the conquest of the Aztecs. But he also condemns their leftist opponents, who reject the cruel oppression of tradition while staying frozen in its spell. Fixated on colonial injustice, the leftists "remain fascinated, / in attitudes of prayer, / by the festering roses made from their fathers' manacles" (286).

Walcott sees a dire inadequacy in the choice he is offered between the rebellious, bitter Caliban and the suffering, loyal Ariel as alternative role models for the New World.[18] As Walcott describes it, the New World exists in a fractured or mediated relation to the European tradition's Prosperos, rather than the direct relation that both Ariel and Caliban claim. As Walcott notes in an interview, Eliot's idea of the "unbroken arc" of tradition looks strangely inapplicable to "the education of the black in the Western world," in which "a sensibility . . . has been broken and recreated."[19] The discontinuity of European empire with the African and Amerindian cultures that it has conquered reveals a historical violence that the Eliotic notion of tradition cannot smooth over. The European tradition in the New World shows signs of, not a continuous inheritance, but a turbulent persistence within revolutionary change. As the Guyanese novelist Wilson Harris writes, considering "the divide pre-Columbian/post-Columbian," "The question is—how can one begin to reconcile the broken parts of such an enormous heritage, especially when those broken parts appear very often like a grotesque series of adventures, volcanic in its precipitate effects as well as human in its vulnerable settlement?" Yet the very vulnerability inflicted by historical oppression, Harris continues, also leads to a "charg[ing]" of the New World landscape "with the openness of imagination," and thus a potential freedom from the past.[20]

In his effort to avoid the sterile, confining alternative between affiliating himself to and reacting against European tradition, Walcott in an important essay, "The Muse of History," identifies Whitman, Neruda, Borges, and St. John Perse as New World writers who overcome this restrictive dualism. These figures prove their difference, not by a Caliban-like cursing of the European past, but by a renewal of certain classical European themes as "instant archaism": "So [in Borges' 'Streetcorner Man'] the death of a gaucho does not merely repeat, but is, the death of Caesar. Fact evaporates into myth."[21] (Similarly, in *Another Life*, the merchant seaman Emanuel Auguste *is* Odysseus.) Exploiting anachronism to generate an "Adamic" vision of the New World, Walcott goes on, causes a primitive "wonder" (similar to Carpentier's *lo real maravilloso*), "an elation which sees everything as renewed," liberated from the oppression of the past, and yet which also sees the past that remains visible within the present, "the ruins of great civilizations."

New World ruins offer an ancient magic in the form of a wild, new freedom. The genuine difference of the New World situation — as Walcott expresses it in terms that ally him to Carpentier, Harris, and García Márquez — argues against the use of European or classical tradition as a means of either loyal affiliation or formative antagonism, since both loyalty and rebellion would imply the conservative, unbroken authority of European tradition. Instead, Walcott's tale of his "black Greek[s]" (294) in *Another Life*, as in his major epic *Omeros* (1990), acknowledges the fragmented afterlife of European tradition in the New World by inventing freely revisionary parallels between Homeric instances and the modern Caribbean.[22]

The release from a burdensome colonial inheritance by means of fantastic analogies between the present and the past, like Walcott's connection between the Homeric world and the contemporary West Indies, is only one way for New World writing to respond to the risks of history. Another way is that of Carpentier, who makes the magical realist mode a key strategy in his New World project of transculturation (that is, creolizing, or cultural mixing). To clarify the similarity between magical realism and other ways of transculturation in West Indian discourse, I will describe some specific affinities between Walcott and Carpentier.

As I have suggested, magical realism may transfigure a historical account *via* phantasmagorical narrative excess. The effect is to liberate history's destructive aspect into an imaginative sense of future. In such magical realist reinterpretation, the evidence of imperialist oppression remains visible in the forms of ruins whose decrepit appearance signals the pastness, as well as the persistence of imperialist power. The writer domesticates the memory of European rule, transforming it into a fantastically fertile subject for creative imagination. For example, the Spanish galleon in García Márquez's *One Hundred Years of Solitude*, its hallucinatory repose offering occasion for both the writer's and Macondo's fantasies, produces an imaginative freedom from the real cruelty of colonial history.

Yet, in the writers I have mentioned, and most notably in Walcott, the New World's colonial past is not always a magical ruin tamed by authorial fantasy. History may prove to be very much alive in its tenacious hold over both colonial masters and victims. Carpentier's narrative of the Haitian revolution, *The Kingdom of this World* (1949), provides an important case in point. In Carpentier's novel, fantastic Afro-Caribbean myth and natural landscape join forces in a battle against a cyclical, inevitably recurring historical violence that binds its victims to the colonial past even after the revolutionary achievement of independence. The malevolent power of history looks even more threatening as a result of the analogy between history and nature in *The Kingdom of this World.*

In *The Kingdom of this World,* Carpentier resists the demonic alliance that he has constructed between historical and natural forces. Walcott in *Another Life,* bearing the influence of his Caribbean precursor Carpentier, echoes Carpentier's doubleness by both grimly proclaiming a catastrophic bondage to the past and hopefully offering a natural wilderness as recourse against that past. Nature, for Walcott, figures a magically Edenic future that can stand against history. Yet such magic, in Walcott as in Carpentier, finally proves transient and powerless, forcing us to return to culture as the necessary site of poetic making.

In his notebook drafts of *Another Life,* Walcott develops his Edenic vision by drawing on Carpentier's idea of an aesthetic indigenous to the Caribbean setting,[23] as well as the notion, reminiscent of García Márquez's Macondo in its early days, that in the New World "nothing [was] so old it could not be repeated."[24] (In the final version of *Another Life* this is transformed into the even more Macondoesque image of a world "with nothing so old / that it could not be invented" [294].) In this fantasy of the New World as paradise, social life matches a voluptuous, Edenic nature in its freshness and possibility—a dream that the later history of Macondo reveals as a delusion.[25]

Walcott's separation of history from natural landscape shows him to be an inheritor of Carpentier's anxious imaginative stance. For both Carpentier and Walcott, the turn from history and toward a wild, self-renewing nature seems a possible way to free the imagination from the oppressive nearness of the past. However, the nature that the protagonist quests after proves to be, in both *Another Life* and *The Lost Steps,* a solipsistic and oddly sterile solution to the question of New World writing. As both Carpentier and Walcott realize, an Edenic image of nature, though at first a deeply attractive prospect, proves futile exactly because it means denying the cultural complexities that make up the New World. In the next section of this essay, I explore further the attraction and the risk, for both Walcott and Carpentier, of the flight into nature conceived as an alien and incorruptible source.

> First, there was the heaving oil,
> heavy as chaos;
> then, like a light at the end of a tunnel,
>
> the lantern of a caravel,
> and that was Genesis.
> Then there were the packed cries,
> the shit, the moaning:
>
> Exodus.
> Bone soldered by coral to bone,
> mosaics
> mantled by the benediction of the shark's shadow,
>
> that was the Ark of the Covenant.
> —Derek Walcott, "The Sea is History"

Carpentier's novels, like Walcott's poetry, demonstrate a creative unease with the confluence of history and nature in the New World. Such discomfort can culminate, in both writers, in a desire to escape history and to exalt instead the fierce power of a natural landscape that overshadows and shows up all human projects. This celebration of a sublime, apocalyptic nature occurs in Carpentier as a reaction against a history that claims omnipotence for itself. Thunder accompanies the propitiatory rituals announcing the Haitian slave revolt that provides Carpentier's historical subject matter, and nature itself seems complicit in the upheaval that, in Carpentier's words, "would bring the thunder and lightning and unleash the cyclone that would round out the work of men's hands."[26] The novel's conclusion, in which the ex-slave Ti-Noël is reduced once again to servitude under the new black masters of Haiti, drives home Carpentier's grim, implacable vision of history. For Carpentier, history offers a cycle of punishment as repetitive and irresistible as nature itself. But at the same time the novel's end teases us with the possibility of an apocalyptic release from repetition, the liberation that Ti-Noël might manage by mastering nature: "The old man hurled his declaration of war against the new masters. . . . At that moment a great green wind, blowing from the ocean, swept the

Plaine du Nord, spreading through the Dondon valley with a loud roar."[27] Ti-Noël, in the novel's final pages, displays his conjuring power not only by raising a storm, but also by metamorphosing into a creature of nature, the man-bird of African-American folklore.[28]

The ending of Carpentier's *Kingdom*, then, suggests the possibility that an African magic associated with nature might escape colonial history. In fact, though, Ti-Noël's magic, like that of the arch-rebel Mackandal earlier in the novel, offers liberation only on the fictive level. The black man's real, historical status as victim will continue. Carpentier keeps in deliberate irresolution the distance between imagination and the historical facts that resist imagination's transformative magic. The magical realist technique of treating the fantastic as if it were real suggests a tempting, but too hopeful, promise of imaginative liberation: Ti-Noël as airborne saviour, a soaring half-god, half-beast bringing black freedom.

History and nature, joined through most of *Kingdom*, are uncertainly and hopefully disjoined at its conclusion. *The Kingdom of this World* finds the source of its marvelous, hallucinatory quality as narrative not only in the cycles of history, the terrible return of imperial oppression in the shape of Henri-Christophe and his successors, but also in the tantalizing and unrealizable project of a flight into nature as escape from history. The hope for escape is, I suggest, an important aspect of magical realist narrative, existing in tension with the historical basis of the mode itself as Jameson describes it.

The fragile wish for a separation of nature and history initiated in *The Kingdom of this World* continues in Carpentier's next novel, *The Lost Steps* (1953). Early on in the novel, the narrator stumbles into a stereotypical scene of revolution in the South American country he is visiting in his search for the origin of musical instruments. Carpentier's hero responds to the revolution by turning from history in order to pursue a reassuringly prehistorical prospect: the primal relation between humanity and music. He ignores the political uproar, the "magic situation" of violent disorder, and follows his scientific quest to the heart of the jungle.[29] As at the end of *The Kingdom of this World*, Carpentier's protagonist wishes for an imaginative empowerment, a magic, associated with the secrets of a nature that predates historical oppression. Tellingly, he wants to find the origin of music in human imitation of a natural phenomenon, the cries of animals.

The Lost Steps bears particular significance for a reading of Walcott because it focuses, like *Another Life*, on the predicament of a narrator whose

writing stems from a personal history intimately bound up with his artistic capacity. (This emphasis on the autobiographical nature of creativity
is shared by *The Lost Steps* and Wordsworth's *Prelude*, the most obvious
poetic model for *Another Life*.) The narrator's journey in *The Lost Steps*
is not just a scientific project; increasingly, it becomes a personal one, an
effort to find a properly familial origin. In South America, he returns to
the Hispanophone context of his infancy as well as to the maternal security provided by his girlfriend Rosario. The narrator, who feels that his life
has turned stale and repetitious, believes that he can find the ideal ther-
apy for his anomie in a landscape that transcends history, the supposed
permanence or eternality of the New World wilderness. The wilderness
will enable him to regain his creative powers as a composer as well: it
presents a virtual blank slate for the artist as explorer. Motivated, then, by
both artistic ambition and personal neurosis, Carpentier's hero proposes
to himself the "Adam's task" of naming the New World in words and music.

Yet the wilderness that the narrator discovers in *The Lost Steps* fails to
offer the hoped-for empty canvas or blank page ready for Adamic telling.
This nature recalls a history: most significantly, the chronicle of European explorers who, traveling long before Carpentier's narrator, confirm
his most amazing perceptions:

> I turned toward the river. So vast was its stream that the torrents, the
> whirlpools, the falls that perturbed its relentless descent were fused
> in the unity of a pulse that had throbbed, from dry season through
> rainy season, with the same rests and beats since before man was in-
> vented. We were embarking that morning, at dawn, and I had spent
> long hours looking at the banks, without taking my eyes for too long
> from the narration of Fray Servando de Castillejos, who had brought
> his sandals here three centuries ago. His quaint prose was still valid.
> Where the author mentioned a rock with the profile of an alligator
> high on the right bank, there it was, high on the right bank.[30]

Throughout the narrator's journey into the jungle, he finds his point of
view already inscribed in the landscape by travelers like Fray Servando,
his precursor.[31] Such historical precedent presents both a comfort and a
frustration: a comfort because it seems to prove the permanence of the
explorer's vision, its duration over the course of centuries; a frustration
because it unavoidably places the narrator in the position of the belated
outsider, despite his longing to discard his Western cosmopolitan perspec-

tive, to become one with the wilderness and its inhabitants. In *The Lost Steps*, only an alienated character like the narrator can rightly perceive the indigenous or native quality of the wondrous American real.[32] So it is for Carpentier's readers: we sense the auratic thrill of magical realism as, wary of its spell, we approach it from outside—from the cold realm of realist expectation.

Nor does the wilderness, finally, provide the unmarred, unchanging stability that Carpentier's protagonist desires: at the end of the novel, he makes a second trip into the South American jungle, and finds himself unable to locate and return to the sights he encountered on his previous journey. As Carpentier remarks in his essay "Conciencia e identidad en América" ("Conscience and Identity in America"), describing the journey up the Orinoco that provided the autobiographical basis for his novel, the river stays "immutable" and yet paradoxically ever-changing, in Heraclitean fashion.[33] The fact that the Orinoco does change, despite its appearance of eternality, indicates the elusiveness and, finally, the futility of the narrator's hope for a secure and permanent origin. As Roberto González Echevarría writes, "The attempt to return to th[e] source shows in *The Lost Steps* that no such unity exists, that writing unveils not the truth, nor the true origins, but a series of repeated gestures and ever-renewed beginnings."[34]

The Lost Steps, then, by eliciting the reader's intimate identification with Carpentier's first-person protagonist, makes the reader participate in a search for origins that Carpentier then ironizes by submitting it to the presence of colonial history. Not only does the protagonist repeat the postures of the European explorers, he also stumbles on the absence of the meaningful identity or grounded truth that outsiders always, and always vainly, hope to find in the wilderness. Carpentier's irony is shared by Walcott, who, at the end of *Another Life*, first seeks nature as such a ground, as a possible way to overcome colonial history, and then shows what motivates this search: a desperate need to deny social and historical fact.

Walcott's most important theoretical statement, the "overture" to his 1970 volume *Dream on Monkey Mountain and Other Plays*, centers on a similar paradox, one clearly indebted to the shaky Heraclitean quality of Carpentier's marvelous real. In this overture, which bears the Nietzschean/Eliotic title "What the Twilight Said," Walcott, like Carpentier in *The Lost Steps*, asks if it is possible to see the New World through new, rather than old (whether European or African) eyes. Given his title, Wal-

cott is perhaps reflecting here on the alternative between Nietzsche's affirmation, his desire for a dawn that would follow the twilight of European
ressentiment, and the early Eliot's nocturnal despair over cultural decline.
In fact, a Janus-faced reaction to the project of transfiguring culture, suggesting both Nietzsche's hope and Eliot's pessimism, becomes visible in
the course of Walcott's essay. Poised between home and exile, Walcott reflects in "What the Twilight Said" on his ambiguous position as a black
West Indian drawn toward Europe, a character allied to, yet distant from
Caribbean culture.

In "What the Twilight Said," Walcott largely occupies himself with his
experience as director of the Little Carib/Trinidad Theatre Workshop from
1959–76, a time during which he confronted both the facts of West Indian
society and the temptation to aestheticize these facts by turning the social
into a kind of folkloric Eden. Significantly for my theme, Walcott expresses
this temptation as an inclination toward magical realism. Walcott begins
the essay by reflecting on his own aestheticized perception of the West
Indies' endemic poverty as a magic reality, ripe for cinematic or theatrical
rendering in the Vincente Minnelli colors of the gorgeous tropics: "One
walks past the gilded hallucinations of poverty with a corrupt resignation
touched by details, as if the destitute . . . were all natural scene-designers
and poverty were not a condition but an art. . . . In the tropics nothing
is lovelier than the allotments of the poor, no theatre is as vivid, voluble
and cheap." [35]

Despite the essay's epigraph, a quotation from Beckett's *Waiting for
Godot* in which Pozzo speaks to the foreigners Vladimir and Estragon of
"what *our* twilights can do" (emphasis mine), Walcott begins "What the
Twilight Said" from the point of view of a traveler or distant observer
alienated from the West Indian scene.[36] The traveler occupies a fortunate
position, since the West Indian setting, like Carpentier's marvelous real,
reveals its magic only to the stranger. As the essay continues, Walcott considers and rejects a possible (and highly popular) alternative to the role
of distant, abstracted stranger encountering a foreign magic. Instead of
choosing exile, one might proudly accept Caribbean culture, including its
deprivations, as one's own. In Caribbean drama, writes Walcott, this embrace of the popular means "the cult of nakedness in underground theatre, of tribal rock, of poverty, of rite." One problem with such a primitivist
solution, according to Walcott, is that it remains tied to the past. The claim
for an impoverished native culture as properly West Indian remains "an

enactment of remorse for the genocides of civilization." Resentful leftism portrays Afro-Caribbean culture as the victim and avenger, and therefore the antagonistic mirror, European civilization.[37] At its grimmest, Walcott's essay meditates on what he sees as the inevitable fact that any "authentic" expression of Caribbean folk culture cannot be self-directed, but must instead react to a European perspective. Before anything else, the islands' authenticity is a consumer item for the neo-imperialist powers that economically dominate the region.

Walcott presents a second, related argument in "What the Twilight Said" against the primitive-folklorist approach to Caribbean culture, the simplistic proclaiming of African origins touted by the "witchdoctors of the new left with imported totems" (35).[38] The New World has permanently transformed Africa, as it has Europe and Asia; the syncretism of these new conditions displays itself in Walcott's own "generation," which "had looked at life with black skins and blue eyes." "We are all strangers here" (9–10), in the rich and strange Caribbean, and this setting's newness demands, not an impossible return to the African roots that have been irrevocably changed, nor a continuing protest against the slavemaster that can only perpetuate the old roles, but a future-directed artistry, "a new theatre . . . with a delight that comes in roundly naming its object" (26). The imagery that Walcott uses to describe his goal of an innovative, future-directed theater in the Caribbean suggests, once again, an Edenic picture of nature. In order for this theater to "Roundly name its object" — like Adam in the garden — "for imagination and body to move with original instinct, we must begin again from the bush" (25–26). Ironically, of course, the image of the bush suggests Africa, the origin that in Walcott's argument hampers originality. Walcott's irony hints that the idea of a newly Edenic beginning must prove deceptive since, despite the author's wishes, it allows the past to have its voice.

Since "we ha[ve] no language for the bush" (37), no means to recapture the positive value of "the African experience" (37), Walcott in his career as a theatrical director and playwright struggles against the poisonous contagion of mythical African origins: "The myth of the organic, ineradicable tsetse, the numbing fly in the mythically different blood, the myth of the uncreative, parasitic, malarial nigger, the marsh-numbed imagination that is happiest in mud. . . . After a time invisible lianas strangle our will." During the work of preparing a stage production, "every night some area in the rapidly breeding bush of the mind would be cleared, an area where one could plan every inch of advance by firelight" (33–34). The irony is pungent: the director, after militantly clearing the bush for his theatrical project, renders the landscape barren. His artistic purism in Crusoe-like isolation, "wrecked on a rock while hoping that his whirlpool was the navel of the world" (36).[39] As we shall see, Walcott writes into the conclusion of *Another Life* a similarly strong implication of the alienated solipsism hidden within the desire for Edenic artistry.[40]

"What the Twilight Said" finally recovers from the implications of such authorial isolation, which were themselves earlier defined as a temptation toward an Edenic-solipsistic New World vision, through its display of socially concerned ironies. Walcott depicts a scene in which the playwright/director and his actors climb upward to see themselves in the landscape of Walcott's youth, the famous promontory of St. Lucia called the Morne:

> A band of travellers, in their dim outlines like explorers who arrived at the crest of a dry, grassy ridge . . . with the view hidden, then levelling off to the tin-roofed, toy town of his childhood. The sense of hallucination increased with the actuality of every detail, from the chill, mildly shivering blades of hill-grass, from their voices abrupted by the wind, the duality of time, past and present piercingly fixed as if the voluble puppets of his childhood were now frighteningly alive. . . . [S]ome turned towards the lush, dark-pocketed valleys of banana with their ochre tracks and canted wooden huts from whose kitchens, at firelight, the poetry which they spoke had come, and further on, the wild, white-lined Atlantic coast with an Africa that was no longer home, and the dark, oracular mountain dying into mythology. . . . It was as if they had arrived at a view of their own bodies walking up the crest, their bodies tilted slightly forward, a few survivors. (38)

This passage noticeably allies itself to a central aspect of magical realist and uncanny aesthetics, the sense of a world that looks all the more fantastic because of its extreme or hyperreal "actuality." The *unheimlich* landscape at once both invites and alienates: "The sense of hallucination increased with the actuality of every detail." This double vision of the self, a Pisgah sight of both past (Walcott's personal history) and future (his artistic goals), goes beyond self-concern to suggest a tableau of the New World as visionary frontier.

But the communal character of this vision does not alleviate the artist-observer's estrangement from his native landscape and its population: "Knowing the place could not tell me what it meant," Walcott writes, "I watched them but was not among them." Finally, he adds that "we would have to descend again" from this inspired "achievement" (38) to more mundane difficulties. And it is important to note that the retrospective author describes the vision itself as a "dying into mythology," not a living future. The theater company's ascent of the Morne, then, may be no closer to a dawn of living creation than the earlier solipsistic picture of a search for the individual "body['s]" "original instinct" and for an Edenic landscape, vacant of the social, to surround it. In both cases, the artist's isolation seems built into the structure of his perception, and his ambition to "roundly name [his] object" by demonstrating his native relation to it therefore appears enmeshed in a vicious circularity.

The descent or "dying," the sense of a culture of tragic "survivors," that occurs at the end of Walcott's "What the Twilight Said" stands in ironic counterpoint to the conclusion of the play that this "overture" introduces, *Dream on Monkey Mountain* (1970). The hero of *Dream*, Makak, climbs back to his mythical home at the play's end after beheading the white goddess who has imprisoned him in his role as a black messiah. Now, after violently freeing himself from an oppressive past, Makak returns, Noah-like, to "walk with God" back to the mountain of his origins: "Now this old hermit is going back home," he proclaims, "back to the beginning, to the green beginning of this world" (326).

The exalted conclusion of *Dream on Monkey Mountain*, replete with Christological significance, provides an obvious contrast to the sad decline of Walcott's own darkening vision at the end of "What the Twilight Said." *Dream*'s notion of a "green beginning," an origin that liberates the hero by freeing him from the cultural symbolism of master and slave, oppressor and oppressed, proves impossible in the autobiographical world depicted in "What the Twilight Said," which like *The Lost Steps* implies that every "new" beginning conceals an obsessively self-conscious return to the past. The liberating potential of magical vision, then, seems to decrease for Walcott as it becomes subject to the artist-observer's consciousness of the central role that his own alienated perspective plays in this magic. Such self-consciousness remains largely absent from *Dream on Monkey Mountain*, but it is prominent in "What the Twilight Said" and *Another Life*.

Walcott's search for Edenic origin as escape takes an even more compromised or ambivalent form in *Another Life* than it does in "What the

Twilight Said." At the end of *Dream*, Makak's beginning is "green" because
it remains at one with the natural landscape of his island, the mountain;
it is a beginning because he has divested himself of the weight of the imperialist past. Similarly, in *Another Life* Walcott the poet-narrator begs to

> begin again,
> from what we have always known, nothing,
> from that carnal slime of the garden . . .
>
> by this augury of ibises
> flying at evening from the melting trees,
> while the silver-hammered charger of the marsh light
> brings toward us, again and again, in beaten scrolls,
> nothing, then nothing,
> and then nothing. (286–87)

    The beginning that Walcott vaguely, if resonantly, suggests at the end
of *Dream on Monkey Mountain* becomes explicit in *Another Life*. But this
flight into nature, repeatedly promised in *Another Life*, is just as repeatedly withdrawn. In the passage cited above, Caribbean nature, by giving
the poet a life and a writing all its own (the "beaten scrolls"), offers an
alternative to those "who remain fascinated . . . /by the festering roses
made from their fathers' manacles,/ . . . /who see a golden, cruel, hawk-
bright glory/ in the conquistador's malarial eye" (286) — that is, those who
fetishize historical oppression as the product of either heroic mastery or
wretched vulnerability. Nature instead offers a blankness or innocence, a
"nothing," ready for the Adamic mission of the writer: naming.
    Tellingly, Walcott gives as one of his epigraphs to *Another Life* the
passage from *The Lost Steps* in which the narrator endows himself with
"Adam's task" of name-giving (188). Yet, also tellingly for Walcott's purposes, the Carpentier passage reveals what we have already seen: the difficulty, really the futility, of this Edenic task, as Carpentier's narrator likens
himself in this same passage to the Europe-obsessed South American artists who will not even attempt to describe their native environment.[41] Indeed, there is something empty in the "nothing" that remains after the
New World landscape has been denuded of its cruel and complex history.
It presents an ironic vacuity, as hopeless as the "vacant eyes" of the artists who, in the Carpentier passage, turn away from America and toward
Europe. Carpentier's magical America is not just the outcome of a mixing

of cultures. In a passage like this one, the New World's auratic charm also conveys the writer's effort to evade the fact of such mixing and come out into a pure landscape, cleared of history.

Walcott shares with Carpentier the impulse to purge his writing of historical *conciencia* by identifying it with an Edenic New World landscape. Early in *Another Life*, however, Walcott takes a different daring turn. He asserts the implication of the Caribbean landscape in the historical events that took place in it, rather than separating out the natural scene as he will later on. After evoking the history of European empire taught him by his "choleric, ginger-haired headmaster" in St. Lucia ("a lonely Englishman who loved parades,/sailing, and Conrad's prose"), Walcott suddenly describes the most famous incident associated with St. Lucia's major landmark, the Morne:

> The leaping Caribs whiten,
> in one flash, the instant
> the race leapt at Sauteurs,
> a cataract! One scream of bounding lace (213)

In 1651 the Carib Indians of Grenada, surrounded and outnumbered by the British, leapt off a steep hill that later became known as the "Morne des Sauteurs" (Leapers' Hill).[42] Walcott follows his description of the Caribs' leap with breathless, relentlessly enjambed lines depicting a kind of poetic self-annihilation to match the Caribs' suicidal charge: he presses Pegasus' hoof back into the earth whence it sprouted.

> I am pounding the faces of gods back into the red clay they
> leapt from the mattock of heel after heel . . .
> and I have wept less for them dead than I did
> when they leapt from my thumbs into birth, than my
> heels which have never hurt horses that now pound them
> back into what they should never have sprung from,
> staying un-named where I found them —
> in the god-breeding, god-devouring earth! (213)

As Walcott sees it here, the return to mute nature figured in the Caribs' leap surpasses the artist's effort to represent this mass suicide. The Indian warriors transcend the aesthetic by jumping back into the unrepresentable. Their action overwhelms the poetic artistry that would depict it as history because it digs deeper than history, literally embedding culture in the natural fact of landscape. In the face of this desperate indigenous intensity, poetry yields.

Walcott's surrendering of poetic artifice to nature seeks to establish a presence still marked in the landscape: the miraculous yet historically genuine event of the Caribs' self-sacrifice. Strong and enraptured, the writer submerges his word in the rushing vocables of the self-naming, suicidal *sauteurs:*

> yet who am I, under
> such thunder, dear gods, under the heels of the thousand
> racing towards the exclamation of their single name,
> Sauteurs!
>
> . . . I am one
> with the thousand runners who will break on loud sand
> at Thermopylae, one wave that now cresting must bear
> down the torch of this race, I am all, I am one
> who feels as he falls with the thousand now his tendons harden
> and the wind god, Hourucan, combing his hair. (214)

The mass of warriors are a breaking wave. This moment of oneness, the immersion of the poetic self in the currents of a history seen with and as nature, points toward a Whitmanian general embrace. With his cross-referencing of the New and the Old World in the passage I have just cited, Walcott erases the divisions among American, African, and European ancestry that have been a constant theme in his work.[43] The advancing Caribs look like the runners at Thermopylae, and the entire passage ends with a mixing of European and American — the mention of the Amerindian god Hourucan in the context of ancient Greece. As with Borges' identification of the gaucho as Caesar, or Walcott's of Emanuel Auguste as Odysseus, a fabulous historical analogy here obscures the actual history of colonial conquest, beginning a luminous, revisionary reworking of the cultural energy that passes from the classical to the contemporary. Along with the transfiguring of history into natural landscape — also a trick of magical realism in its lush, paradisal moments — comes the disappearance of the poet's alienated point of view, his prison of colonial inheritance. With the *sauteurs'* flight, the oppression of the past lifts and frees us into imagination.

Walcott's claim in this passage that "I am all, I am one" with a mass of historical individuals looks back to Whitman, as I have suggested, but also to one of Whitman's descendents, Pablo Neruda. In his exalted and tremendous poem *The Heights of Machu Picchu* (*Las alturas de Machu Picchu*), Neruda prophetically invokes the monumental relics of the Inca site Machu Picchu, identifying himself with the oppressed masses who survive within or below its ruined scene.[44] The poet's self-identification with a past people—Walcott with the Caribs, Neruda with the Incas—demands the finding of a historically resonant and indestructible place (the Morne, Machu Picchu). In both cases, culture lives on as nature. As González-Echevarría notes, Neruda's *Canto general,* the longer poem that enfolds *The Heights of Machu Picchu,* begins by conflating human history and natural landscape.[45] Walcott's passage, with its Genesis-inflected mention of the Caribs as "red clay" being "pounded" back into earth by the poet-potter as he searches after the power of origins, echoes this opening moment of *Canto general.* Neruda, like Walcott and like Carpentier's narrator in *The Lost Steps,* seeks the birth of humanness out of natural fact: "Man was earth, a vessel, the eyelid/ Of the quivering clay, a shape of potter's earth,/ Carib spout, Chibcha stone."[46]

Yet if Walcott, like Neruda, plays a prophetic role by assuming the bardic voice of creation, he also backs away, later on in *Another Life,* from Neruda's overwhelming descent toward excruciating empathy with an ancestral people ("Tell me everything, chain by chain,/ Link by link, and step by step,/ File the knives you kept by you,/ Drive them into my chest and my hand").[47] Like Carpentier, Walcott turns from Neruda's impulse toward incarnate solidarity with the primitive or ancient. The final two sections of Walcott's poem attempt to focus the diffident, nervous consciousness of a narrator not sure how to identify, much less identify with, the history that surrounds him, yet who responds to it with an attentive care. In the penultimate section of *Another Life,* Walcott invokes the Wordsworthian "child" who

> puts the shell's howl to his ear,
> hears nothing, hears everything
> that the historian cannot hear, the howls
> of all the races that crossed the water,
> the howls of grandfathers drowned
> in that intricately swivelled Babel,
> hears the fellaheen, the Madrasi, the Mandingo, the Ashanti,

> yes, and hears also the echoing green fissures of Canton,
> and thousands without longing for this other shore
> by the mud tablets of the Indian provinces . . .
>
> see, in the evening light by the saffron, sacred Benares,
> how they are lifting like herons,
> robed ghostly white and brown,
> and the crossing of water has erased their memories.
> And the sea, which is always the same,
> accepts them. (285)

Walcott's beautiful recollection of the African and Asiatic voices driven to the new shores of the Caribbean [48] does not, this time, give us a rough courage that runs with the masses toward historical suffering and glory, but instead a subtle persistence allied to the nature imaged in the seashell and "the sea, which is always the same." Nature effortlessly assimilates, and erases, its crowds of human inhabitants, soothing them into oblivion. Here, then, a fluid, all-forgiving cosmos distances the poet from Caribbean history, rather than stamping it into place as a monumental memory, as in the *sauteurs* passage. One central subtext for Walcott is Wordsworth's celebration, in the *Prelude*, of the infant memories borne by a maternal nature that persists beneath the strata of revolutionary violence and biographical trauma.[49]

Like Whitman more than Wordsworth, Walcott uses nature to welcome the human masses into a healing depth of unborn process: "The crossing of water has erased their memories./ And the sea, which is always the same,/ accepts them." Walcott, in an interview with Edward Hirsch, speaks of "the erasure of the idea of history" in Caribbean nature, "in the surf which continually wipes the sand clean, in the fact that those huge clouds change so quickly."[50] This therapeutic forgetting, nature's promise of healing human history through obliteration and mutability, makes Walcott want "to teach [him]self the poetry of natural science."[51]

In the notebooks for *Another Life*, Walcott presents his wish for a poetics of nature devoid of the human by championing a fellow solitary, "the figure of Crusoe" (a favorite Walcott character in other poems as well). Walcott invokes a Crusoe who has become "tired of the gift," the quintessentially human capacity of being "articulate." "He has learnt the indifference of his dog, but their separate emptinesses are terrible. Empty his mind as monotonously as he wants he cannot become a dog since he has more than a dog's desires."

Walcott presents Crusoe's impulse toward a doglike state of inarticulate emptiness as an alluring ascetic project, a Stevensian pursuit of poverty that aims to empty out the self's intellective wiles. When Friday arrives, Crusoe loses his mission, returning to human language and to the "commonplace sanity" and "self-righteous" -ness that accompanies it. For Walcott, the Crusoe we see with Friday has been infected by "a puritanism that has learnt something from experience, when, unlike most men, he once really understood nothing."[52] With Friday's appearance, then, Crusoe loses the crude, reductive stability of his earlier devotion to "nothing."

For Walcott's Crusoe, nature promises a potential solace or refuge from humanity. But the final pages of *Another Life* question the viability of this refuge more radically than elsewhere in Walcott, by way of the solitary figure of the poet. In *Another Life* the poet wishes for himself the inhuman "nothing" that he grants the lone Crusoe in his notebook. Near the end of the poem, Walcott wants only the inarticulate, pure "nothing" of a nature devoid of human culture, "the real/rock I make real." Here the isolated self alone within stony, unyielding landscape represents an escape from the master-slave conversation of Crusoe and Friday, whose relation seems an infernal model for the whole of colonial history:

> Inured. Inward. As rock,
> I wish, as the real
>
> rock I make real,
> to have burnt out desire,
> lust, except for the sun
>
> with her corona of fire.
> Anna, I wanted to grow white-haired
> as the wave, with a wrinkled
> brown rock's face, salted,
> seamed, an old poet,
> facing the wind
>
> and nothing, which is,
> the loud world in his mind. (290)

Like Oedipus or Lear, the poet is supported by his daughters: "balanced . . . by the weight of two dear daughters."[53] Walcott calls on the aged, self-imposed isolation of these two tragic heroes, both hoping for the peace that might come about through a quieting of the destruction that their own stubborn wills have brought about. In addition to Shake-speare and Sophocles, in this densely allusive section of the poem we can hear the voices of at least four other texts that convey, in varying tones, the desire for peace, for a respite from the cruelty of will: Ginsberg's *Howl,* Eliot's *Ash Wednesday,* and Stevens' "The Snow Man" and "The Rock."

A reduction of Edenic possibility to the aridity of bare rock, Walcott's nature remains a strenuously deliberate projection. The poet hopes that "inured" will rhyme with "inward," that his "tireless hoarse anger" will be ossified, as rock, into impermeable Stoic stasis. But as Walcott well knows, such a wish to mimic the assurance of the rock's solidity marks a neces-sary falling short, a hopeless effort to evade the contingency and confusion of human culture. (The immediately preceding section on imperialist his-tory has raised the stakes beyond the personal by reminding us that, for Walcott, the will has a malignant historical form.)

Walcott's evacuation of cultural and historical subject matter, his strategy for securing the self by shoring it up alone with nature, will not last. In the final section of *Another Life,* he returns to his autobiographi-cal story, and with it to the people of St. Lucia. Now, in an abrupt reversal, the social seems "stronger" than nature. Suddenly, the wave is no longer a phenomenon that can transcend, save, or provide escape from the human, as it has been throughout the poem. Instead, it represents the writer's "de-sertion" of his "folk"'s culture:

> Forgive me, you folk,
> who exercise a patience
> subtler, stronger than the muscles
> in the wave's wrist . . .
>
> forgive our desertions. (293)

The embrace of the popular culture of St. Lucia aims at a "patience" that, the poet hopes, will succeed where a rigid, Stoic self-torment has failed. The acceptance of the folk marks out a third way, beyond both the isolation of the solitary Crusoe and the torment that occurs between Crusoe and Friday. But Walcott shifts his ground yet again when he fol-lows his celebration of the people's strength with a vision of the artist's autonomous mastery: as godlike creator, he fashions his own world, inde-pendent of any popular basis. The invocation of Walcott's painter friend Gregorias (Dunstan St. Omer) here removes the presence of the island's culture entirely in the interest of quasi-Edenic artistic freedom:

> We were blest with a virginal, unpainted world
> with Adam's task of giving things their names
> with the smooth white walls of clouds and villages
> where you devised your inexhaustible,
> impossible Renaissance. (294)

The dissonance between this dream of the artist "devising" in an un-populated, paradisal wilderness and the embrace of the "folk" that directly precedes it forces us to juxtapose the conclusion of *Another Life* to more pessimistic versions of the same theme, like the guilty aestheticizing of island poverty in "What the Twilight Said" or the passage from the note-book for *Another Life* in which Walcott writes that he sought out the poor "not only to depict and record, but to be like them": "Yet the more he learnt, the wider the crack between them grew." [54] The palinodic accep-tance of the "folk" near the end of *Another Life,* in its sentimental need for "forgive[ness]," is less assured as poetry than the earlier and later images of artistic isolation that surround it. There seems to be an insurmount-able division between the artist, who lives within the European tradition, and the folk culture that supplies the object of his depiction and that he also, in his peculiar way, inhabits. The permanent fact of such divisions, as I have argued, provides the foundation of Walcott's art and unites him with Carpentier and other New World magical realists. Like Borges' hero in "The South," he stands aloof, frightened and entranced by his image of the folkloric powers that surround him. Walcott's work, like Carpentier's and García Márquez's, conjures with an elusive grammar that at once joins and disjoins realism and fantasy, Europe and Africa, high and low culture, traveling artist and indigenous folk.[55]

Notes

1 All citations of Walcott's poetry refer to his *Collected Poems 1948–1984* (New York: Farrar, Straus and Giroux, 1986).

2 A case for the kinship between the English-speaking Caribbean and the phan-tasmagoric world of the Latin American novel could perhaps best be made with reference to the novels of the Guyanese writer Wilson Harris, whose hal-lucinatory narratives are contemporary with García Márquez's. For a treatment of Harris in terms of magical or marvelous realism, see Selwyn Cudjoe, *Resis-tance and Caribbean Literature* (Athens, Ohio: Ohio University Press, 1980), pp. 255–57. Walcott's "Guyana," from which I draw an epigraph for this essay, joins Harris to Borges as "the surveyor" and "the lexicographer," respectively

(Harris worked as a surveyor in Guyana). The point of the conjunction is Walcott's frequently voiced desire for an indigenous New World style of writing, one suited to its unique geographical and cultural landscape. On the question of "New World writing" I have been influenced by Vera Kutzinski's admirable *Against the American Grain* (Baltimore: Johns Hopkins University Press, 1987), though I hope to show in Walcott's work some of the tensions and resistances to cross-cultural juxtaposition that Kutzinski tends to play down. So far the most advanced study of Walcott's work is Rei Terada's *Derek Walcott's Poetry: American Mimicry* (Boston: Northeastern University Press, 1992).

3 See the interview with Sharon Ciccarelli, in *Chant of Saints,* ed. Michael Harper and Robert Stepto (Urbana: University of Illinois Press, 1979), in which he states the similarity he perceives between himself and "Spanish-American poets" on the basis of a shared regional culture (306), noting that "I probably am a total stranger to the African, whereas I am not a stranger to [García] Márquez, or Fuentes, or Paz" (307). Walcott also notes that he is "interested in writers like [García] Márquez who have an instinctive way of handling the natural and the legendary in close proximity" (307).

4 Compare what Rosalind Krauss, paraphrasing Fredric Jameson, calls the utopianism of "Van Gogh's clothing of the drab peasant world around him in an hallucinatory surface of color." Krauss, "The Cultural Logic of the Late Capitalist Museum," *October* 54 (1990): 11, and Jameson, "Postmodernism, or the Cultural Logic of Late Capitalism," *New Left Review* 146 (1984): 59.

5 See Fredric Jameson, "On Magic Realism in Film," *Critical Inquiry* 12, 2 (Winter 1986): 301–25. In addition to Jameson, I am also relying for my version of the aesthetics of magical realism on its closeness to the category of the "marvellous," defined by Tzvetan Todorov in *The Fantastic* (1970; Columbus: Ohio State University Press, 1973) as the rendition of exotic or supernatural events as if they were real.

6 See Roger Abrahams, *The Man-of-Words in the West Indies* (Baltimore: Johns Hopkins University Press, 1983).

7 See Vera Kutzinski, "The Logic of Wings: Gabriel García Márquez and Afro-American Literature," *Latin American Literary Review* 13 (January–June 1985): 133–46. For example, the flight of Remedios the Beauty (*One Hundred Years of Solitude* [1967; New York: Bard/Avon, 1970], pp. 22–23) stems from African folklore. See also Rosa Valdés-Cruz, "El realismo mágico en los cuentos negros de Lydia Cabrera," in *Otros mundos, otros fuegos* (East Lansing: Michigan State University Press, 1975), pp. 206–9, and Mireya Camurati, "Fantasía folklórica y ficción literaria," in the same collection, pp. 287–91.

8 For the incest theme as a return of the past, see, for example, *Solitude,* pp. 145, 217; for the themes of hereditary memory and the sense of a continual degeneration combined with continual repetition, pp. 166–67 and 177. For Father Nicanor's levitation, see pp. 84–86.

9 Crowley's article "Les êtres surnaturels à Ste. Lucie," *Le Caraibe* 8 (June–July 1955), is cited in Edward Baugh, *Derek Walcott, Memory as Vision: Another Life* (London: Longman, 1978), p. 11. It is, I believe, significant in this context that Carpentier in his Prologue to *The Kingdom of this World* dwells on lycanthropy and that Mackandal and Ti-Noël undergo animal metamorphoses in the novel.

10 Interestingly, in the early manuscript versions of *Another Life* (1964–65), which is largely in prose, Walcott presents the werewolf story as a mere fable that he refused to believe even in his youth. Further references to the two notebook manuscripts, now in the collection of the University of the West Indies in Mona, Jamaica, will be designated as Notebook 1 and Notebook 2.

11 Notebook 1 (September 11, 1965): 38. Compare Simmons' reading of George Campbell's poem on the black child that occurs near the beginning of the poem (149).

12 Notebook 1 (September 30, 1965): 10. Critics have sometimes accused Walcott of an excessive attachment to, and too-perfect mastery of, European poetic tradition; see especially Helen Vendler's review of *The Fortunate Traveller* in the *New York Review of Books*, March 4, 1982: 23–27.

13 Notebook 1 (September 30, 1965): 4.

14 Ibid., 8.

15 Cited from "Homecoming: Anse La Raye," in *Collected Poems*, p. 127. Walcott frequently makes use of Odyssean images and even Homeric epithets in his poetry; see, for example, the title poem of *Sea Grapes* (in *Collected Poems*, pp. 297–98).

16 In this section of the poem Walcott succeeds admirably in his adaptation of Robert Lowell's manner. For a sharp assessment of the Lowell-Walcott connection, see Calvin Bedient's valuable "Derek Walcott, Contemporary," *Parnassus* (Fall–Winter 1981): 31–44.

17 Notebook 2 (November 12, 1965): 76–78. Walcott (76) implicitly contrasts Auguste's mode with the elevation of an "embalmed yet corruptible tradition," as if it were the Host or the fragments of the true cross — an image that carries over into the final poem (183–84).

18 The use of the Ariel and Caliban figures as emblems of the colonial's relation to the colonizing Prospero has a long history including the works of José Enrique Rodó (most famously), O. Mannoni, Aimé Césaire, Roberto Fernández Retamar, and others. The related issue of the ritual posing of white against black as rival and independent essences, a strategy that ties both white and black to an oppressive past, is discussed in Frantz Fanon's *Black Skins, White Masks*, trans. Charles Lam Markmann (1952; New York: Grove Press, 1967) and developed in Abdul janMohamed's *Manichaean Aesthetics* (Amherst: University of Massachusetts Press, 1983).

19 See Sharon Ciccarelli's interview with Walcott in *Chant of Saints*, p. 303.

20 Harris' 1964 address, "Tradition and the West Indian Novel," is cited in Cudjoe, pp. 255–56.

21 Walcott, "The Muse of History," in *Is Massa Day Dead?*, ed. Orde Coombs (Garden City, N.Y.: Anchor/Doubleday, 1974), p. 2.

22 The practice of introducing the classical as analogous to the modern finds its most influential modern instance in the practice of Pound, Joyce, and Eliot. Interestingly, it appears as willful failure in one of the magical realist texts that Walcott cites in *Another Life*, Carpentier's *Lost Steps*, Harriet de Onís (1953; New York: Bard/Avon, 1979). In Carpentier, the narrator's chimerical attempt to identify the Greek Yannos as an Odyssean character signals the overextended and obsessive aspect of his personal quest for primitive origins (the origin of music and his own discontent). In Carpentier's novel, classical parallelism represents just another version of the ironic and futile search for origins.

23 "We have still not invented a language natural to our landscape, for fear of irregular syntax and bad pronunciation" (Notebook 2: 82, December 20, 1965 entry).

24 Notebook 2: 110, June 10, 1966 entry.

25 For the distinction between the earlier Edenic and the later decadent Macondo, see Lois Parkinson Zamora, *Writing the Apocalypse* (Cambridge: Cambridge University Press, 1989), pp. 25–32.

26 Cited in Roberto González Echevarría, *Alejo Carpentier: The Pilgrim at Home* (Ithaca: Cornell University Press, 1977), p. 136. González Echevarría's consideration of nature and history in Carpentier prompts my (rather divergent) reflection on the same issue here.

27 Alejo Carpentier, *The Kingdom of this World* (*El reino de este mundo*), tr. Harriet de Onís (1949; Harmondsworth: Penguin, 1980), p. 112.

28 See ibid., pp. 26–27, 108–12.

29 See *The Lost Steps*, pp. 55, 88–91.

30 Alejo Carpentier, *The Lost Steps*, p. 102. In his essay "Conciencia e identidad en América" ["Conscience and Identity in America"], Carpentier, in a similar vein, writes that "the conquistadors saw very clearly the aspect of marvelous reality [*el aspecto real maravilloso*] in American things." Here Carpentier alludes to Bernal Díaz's mention of Amadís de Gaula as a precursor text for his own vision of America. In *La novela latinoamericana en vísperas de un nuevo siglo y otros ensayos* (Mexico City: Siglo XXI Editores, 1981), pp. 130–31, my translation.

31 See González Echevarría, "Carpentier y el realismo mágico," in *Otros mundos, otros fuegos*, pp. 221–31.

32 Rosario, for example, remains too immediately or emotionally present, too natively allied to the context of the jungle, to feel its magic. See *The Lost Steps*, pp. 99, 104.

33 "For me, the Orinoco started to become the water of Heraclitus, unchanging, present, always renewed, and it harmonized with the saying of Heraclitus that 'you can bathe in the same river, but never twice in the same water,'" "Conciencia e identidad," in *La novela latinoamericana*, p. 106.

34 González Echevarría, *The Pilgrim at Home*, p. 212.

35 Derek Walcott, *Dream on Monkey Mountain and Other Plays* (New York: Farrar, Straus and Giroux, 1970), pp. 3–4.

36 Samuel Beckett, *Waiting for Godot* (New York: Grove, 1954), p. 24. Walcott is attentive to the irony that Vladimir and Estragon are more "native" to the scene of *Godot* than is Pozzo; Beckett's play profoundly questions the idea of a native landscape or home. In more general terms, Beckett's exile from Ireland is not unlike Walcott's from St. Lucia.

37 Walcott's notion of the danger involved in bondage to the past, specifically to the history of colonial oppression, is indebted to Fanon, but divorced from Fanon's revolutionary optimism; it will play an important role, as I will argue, in his response to Neruda in *Another Life*.

38 See also p. 27, with its reference to "reactionaries in dashikis" who "screamed for the pastoral vision, for a return to nature over the loudspeakers." Walcott's hostile relation to the 1970 Black Power revolt in Trinidad is very noticeable in "What the Twilight Said"; his 1982 play *The Last Carnival*, by contrast, sees the revolt as a tragedy rather than a misguided farce.

39 Walcott has often used the Crusoe image in his poems: see, for an early example, "Crusoe's Island."

40 Bedient, p. 34, wonderfully describes Walcott's tendency in his poems to wish for disconnection and isolation. See also Vendler, p. 26.

41 "That night," Carpentier writes shortly after the lines that Walcott cites, "as I looked at them [the artists] I could see the harm my uprooting from this environment, which had been mine until adolescence, had done me" (71).

42 See Baugh, p. 45.

43 For an early example, see the well-known "A Far Cry from Africa."

44 See the final section of Neruda's poem, along with Emir Rodriguez-Monegal's essay on the Whitmanesque and the prophetic (rather than materialist) quality of *Las alturas de Macchu Picchu:* "El sistema del poeta," in *Pablo Neruda*, ed. Rodríguez Monegal and Enrico Mario Santi (Madrid: Taurus, 1980), pp. 63–91.

45 See González Echevarría, *The Pilgrim at Home*, pp. 160–61.

46 The translation of the Neruda passage is by Anthony Kerrigan (from Pablo Neruda, *Selected Poems* [New York: Delta, 1970]).

47 Translation by John Felstiner from his *Translating Neruda: The Way to Macchu Picchu* (Stanford: Stanford University Press, 1980), p. 239.

48 Many Indian laborers were imported into the West Indies, mostly as cane-

cutters, by Great Britain in the later nineteenth century to make up for the loss of slave labor; and Chinese merchants and workers are also common in the islands.

49 The other major echo in the passage I have just cited is Walcott's heartbreaking variation on a line of the *Aeneid*'s book 6, which portrays the dead souls reaching out in "longing for the farther shore" of Elysium (Aen. 6.314: "tendebantque manus ripae ulterioris amore"). In general, Virgil represents *imperium* in the poem; Homer's *Odyssey*, here as in other Caribbean works, represents the promise of freedom offered by the New World voyage. Walcott's interest in the Odyssean analogy for New World experience is evident in his work; I have already pointed to one salient example, the title poem of *Sea Grapes* (in *Collected Poems*, pp. 297–298).

50 Edward Hirsch, "The Art of Poetry XXXVII: Derek Walcott" (interview), *The Paris Review* 101 (1986), p. 214. I am indebted to Edward Hirsch for additional information concerning his conversations with Walcott.

51 Notebook 1 (August 4, 1965): 20.

52 Notebook 1 (August 7, 1965): 23.

53 Walcott here recalls the late Wordsworth poem that begins with the poet leaning on his daughter and citing *Samson Agonistes:* "A LITTLE onward lend thy guiding hand . . . ."

54 Notebook 1 (August 4, 1965): 21.

55 I would like to thank the University of Houston for a Research Initiation Grant enabling me to do much of the research for this piece, and the University of the West Indies (Mona, Jamaica) for their assistance. Lois Parkinson Zamora and Elizabeth Gregory offered helpful editorial guidance. Finally, Derek Walcott graciously gave me permission to quote from his manuscripts.

PART IV

Community

STEPHEN SLEMON
Magic Realism as Postcolonial
Discourse

The concept of magic realism is a troubled one for literary theory.[1] Since Franz Roh first coined the term in 1925 in connection with postexpressionist art, it has been most closely associated, at least in terms of literary practice, with two major periods in Latin-American and Caribbean culture: the 1940s and 1950s, in which the concept was closely aligned with that of the "marvelous" as something ontologically necessary to the regional population's "vision of everyday reality,"[2] and the "boom" period of the Latin-American novel in the late 1950s and 1960s, where the term was applied to works varying widely in genre and discursive strategy. In none of its applications to literature has the concept of magic realism ever successfully differentiated between itself and neighboring genres such as fabulation, metafiction, the baroque, the fantastic, the uncanny, or the marvelous,[3] and consequently it is not surprising that some critics have chosen to abandon the term altogether.

But the term retains enough of what Fredric Jameson calls a "strange seductiveness"[4] to keep it in critical currency, despite the "theoretical vacuum"[5] in which it lies. In Latin America, the badge of magical realism has signified a kind of uniqueness or difference from mainstream culture—what in another context Alejo Carpentier has called *lo real maravilloso Americano* or "marvellous American reality"[6]—and this gives the concept the stamp of cultural authority, if not theoretical soundness. And recently, the locus for critical studies on magic realism has been broadened from Latin America and the Caribbean to include speculations on its place in the literatures of India, Nigeria, and English Canada,[7] this last being perhaps the most startling development for magic realism in recent years, since Canada, unlike these other regions, is not part of the Third World, a condition long thought necessary to the currency of the term in regard to literature, though not to art. Further, critics until very recently have been singularly uninterested in applying the concept of magic realism to texts written in English.[8]

The incompatibility of magic realism with the more "established" genre systems becomes itself interesting, itself a focus for critical attention, when one considers the fact that magic realism, at least in a literary context, seems most visibly operative in cultures situated at the fringes of mainstream literary traditions. As Robert Kroetsch and Linda Kenyon observe, magic realism as a literary practice seems to be closely linked with a perception of "living on the margins."[9] This doesn't mean that magic realism somehow worms its way into all, or even most, literary texts written from marginal cultures, or that it is somehow absent from the literary archives of the imperial center, or that the emergence of what seem to be magic realist literary texts at a given moment in a given literary culture can be explained by any single, causal relation that ranges across literary cultures, independent of historically specific accounts of agency or of literary circulation. It does mean, however, that a structure of perception — if only in literary critical registers — dogs the practice of magical realist writing, that is, the perception that magic realism, as a socially symbolic contract,[10] carries a residuum of resistance toward the imperial center and to its totalizing systems of generic classification. This structure of perception, of course, is a controversial one for studies in magic realism — especially under this present moment of "globalized postcolonialism," as mainstream writers find a ready market for the recirculation of what the imperial center takes to comprise the "characteristic" literary and cultural forms of formerly colonized cultures. But it does help to underscore the fact that the established systems of generic classification are complicit with a centralizing impulse in imperial culture. Their incompatibility with the practice of magic realism — that which makes magic realism a problem case for the understanding of genre — rests on their history of construction: the reading of literary texts of almost exclusively European or United States provenance. The critical use of the concept of magic realism can therefore signify resistance to monumental theories of literary practice — a way of suggesting there is something going on in certain forms of literary writing, and in the modalities of cultural experience that underlie those forms, that confounds the capacities of the major genre systems to come to terms with them. At the same time, of course, the concept of magic realism itself threatens to become a monumentalizing category for literary practice and to offer to centralizing genre systems a single locus upon which the massive problem of *difference* in literary expression can be managed into recognizable meaning in one swift pass.

What I want to do in this essay is employ a little of the liberty provided by magic realism's lack of theoretical specificity and, rather than attempt to define the concept in terms of genre, attempt instead to place the concept within the context of English-Canadian literary culture in *its* specific engagement with postcoloniality. To this end, I plan to focus on two magic realist texts from English Canada and attempt to show the ways in which these texts recapitulate a postcolonial account of the social and historical relations of the culture in which they are set. I have chosen to work with Jack Hodgins' *The Invention of the World* and Robert Kroetsch's *What the Crow Said*, but I should add that other texts set in English Canada could also carry the argument, Susan Kerslake's *Middlewatch*, for example, or Keith Maillard's *Two-Strand River*. My focus will be on elements in these texts that help us work toward a clearer concept of magic realism in a postcolonial context, and so I will be concentrating on aspects of these two novels that at some level correspond to prevalent concerns in other postcolonial literary practices. Behind this project is the belief that the concept of magic realism can provide us with a way of effecting important *comparative* analyses between separate postcolonial literatures, and the belief that magic realism can enable us to recognize continuities within literary cultures that the established genre systems might blind us to: continuities, that is, between present-day magic realist texts and apparently very different texts written at earlier stages of a culture's literary history.

The term "magic realism" is an oxymoron, one that suggests a binary opposition between the representational code of realism and that, roughly, of fantasy. In the language of narration in a magic realist text, a battle between two oppositional systems takes place, each working toward the creation of a different kind of fictional world from the other. Since the ground rules of these two worlds are incompatible, neither one can fully come into being, and each remains suspended, locked in a continuous dialectic with the "other," a situation which creates disjunction within each of the separate discursive systems, rending them with gaps, absences, and silences.[11]

In *The Invention of the World*, Hodgins achieves this effect through a process of undercutting. His formal beginning to the novel (following a brief prologue) declares the work to be clearly within the conventions of realism: "On the day of the Loggers' Sports, on that day in July, a mighty uproar broke out in the beer parlour of the Coal-Tyee Hotel, which is an old but respectable five-story building directly above the harbour and only a block or two from the main shopping area of town."[12] But soon a fantastic element enters the text, appearing first in the second-degree or intradiegetic level of narration told by Strabo Becker, the historian/taleteller figure, and soon beginning to appear in the extradiegetic narration—Horseman's miraculous escape from Wade's fort, for example (162). As the novel progresses toward the status of a twice-told tale, the motif with which it ends, the reader is pulled away from a tendency to neutralize the fantastic elements of the story within the general code of narrative realism and begins to read the work as being more closely aligned with the fantastic. Yet a complete transference from one mode to the other never takes place, and the novel remains suspended between the two.

The process of narration in *What the Crow Said* is the opposite of that in Hodgins' book. Kroetsch's novel opens in pure fantasy or myth: a description of the impregnation of Vera Lang on a spring afternoon by a swarm of bees. But at the close of the novel, the past-tense narration that has prevailed throughout the work is replaced by a present-tense realism describing Tiddy Lang and Liebhaber rising from their bed into a new morning; and here, for the first time in the novel, the crow will caw, not speak. The fantastic element in the novel never quite manages to dominate an undercurrent of realism; as Kroetsch says elsewhere, we are "always in the world,"[13] despite the lighthouse made of ice, the war with the sky, and the ghostly image of dead Martin Lang perpetually present, ploughing the snow.

Although most works of fiction are generically mixed in mode,[14] the characteristic maneuver of magic realist fiction is that its two separate narrative modes never manage to arrange themselves into any kind of hierarchy. In Mikhail Bakhtin's formulation, the novel is the site of a "diversity of social speech types"[15] in which a battle takes place "in discourse and among discourses to become 'the language of truth,' a battle for what Foucault has called power knowledge."[16] In magic realism this battle is represented in the language of narration by the foregrounding of two opposing discursive systems, with neither managing to subordinate or contain the other. This sustained opposition forestalls the possibility of interpretive closure through any act of naturalizing the text to an established system of representation.

In the context of a comparative, postcolonial literary criticism, this use of language has important consequences. Here, the argument is often made that colonization, whatever its precise form, initiates a kind of double vision or "metaphysical clash"[17] into colonial culture, a binary opposition within language that has its roots in the process of either transporting a language to a new land or imposing a foreign language on an indigenous population. "Our way of seeing," as Coral Ann Howells puts it, "is structured by the forms in which our language enables us to 'see',"[18] and so for some, the dream of historical process is that over time a process of transmutation will occur which will enable this language, and the cognitive system it carries, to articulate the local within a "realist" representational contract. In a postcolonial context, then, the magic realist narrative recapitulates a dialectical struggle within language, a dialectic between "codes of recognition"[19] inherent within the inherited language and those imagined, utopian, and future-oriented codes that aspire toward a language of expressive, local realism, and a set of "original relations"[20] with the world. In this context, the magic realist text can be read as reflecting in its language of narration real conditions of speech and cognition within the social relations of a postcolonial culture, a reflection García Márquez thematizes in *One Hundred Years of Solitude* as a "speaking mirror."[21]

The "speaking mirror" of the language of narration in magic realist texts, however, does not only reflect in an outward direction toward postcolonial social relations. It also sustains an inward reflection into the work's thematic content, initiating a fascinating interplay between language and thematic network similar to that which Michael Holquist, in another context, describes as a "templating of what is enunciated with the act of enunciation."[22] The representation of social relations, in other words, can be seen to be templated into the text's language of narration *and* into the text's thematic structure, and in magic realism these social relations tend to be thematized in three separate but related ways. The first involves the representation of a kind of transformational regionalism[23] so that the site of the text, though described in familiar and local terms, is metonymic of the postcolonial culture as a whole. The second is the foreshortening of history so that the time scheme of the novel metaphorically contains the long process of colonization and its aftermath. And the third involves the thematic foregrounding of those gaps, absences, and silences produced by the colonial encounter and reflected in the text's disjunctive language of narration. On this third level, the magic realist texts tend to display a pre-occupation with images of both borders and centers and to work toward destabilizing their fixity.[24]

In *The Invention of the World*, Hodgins' portrayal of the Vancouver Island community, and especially the Revelations Colony of Truth, now renamed the Revelations Trailer Park, always remains grounded in the real world of known and familiar space. The realism of the site is desta-bilized, however, by the condensed historical reenactment that transpires within it,[25] a metaphorical representation of the process of colonization which serves to transform the novel's regional setting into a metonymic focal point for English-Canadian culture as a whole.[26] This historical re-enactment reaches back from the present-tense setting to the near-mythic, and now vanished, Irish village of Carrigdhoun, the point of origin for the Revelation colonists' flight from history[27] to the New World. Even before Donal Keneally arrives in Carrigdhoun and brings to the isolated villagers their first experience of fear, the village is already the emblem of colonized space. An English bailiff owns all property, and his dogs are the agents of his administration of law. Keneally delivers the villagers from the first phase of colonialism only to initiate a second phase in which he employs the authority of Celtic legend and Prospero magic to establish a system of absolute patriarchal domination over them. Still "slaves of history" (99), the villagers are brought to the New World and another kind of isolation in the Revelations Colony of Truth where, in what Cecilia Coulas Fink calls a "replay of history,"[28] Keneally becomes the figure who releases his dogs on them. As the agent of a neo-colonial mode of domination, Keneally "represents what most of the world believed anyhow" (257) and when he dies, he never quite disappears: he is buried underground in a collapsed tunnel whose entrance is never found, and his ghost appears at the close of the novel at Maggie and Wade's carnivalesque wedding celebration. The legacy he leaves is a paralysis in regard to history and a preference for fabricated historical monuments such as Wade's phony Hudson's Bay Company fort, a dysfunctional "umbilical chord to the past" (223) except to the U.S.-American tourists who can't tell the difference between it and the real thing, anyway. Given the very unappealing nature of real history, this preference for fabrication is entirely understandable. But it is an eva-sion, not a creative response, and at the end of the novel, Maggie, the symbolic heiress of the process of colonization, achieves her longed-for liberation from colonialism's foreclosure of the imagination precisely by going back into history to where the Keneally legend and the process of New World domination began: a mountain top in Ireland upon which a circle of standing stones exercises "dominion" (315) over the landscape.

The novel recapitulates a process, then, of psychic liberation from Old World domination and its cognitive codes. But a fascinating aspect of Hodgins' treatment of this theme is that this reenactment process seems to energize a release from historical domination that those who do not undergo do not achieve. Nowhere in the novel is the colonial encounter depicted more violently than in the Revelations Colony of Truth, and those characters who come later to inhabit its site eventually attain new conditions of liberation and community. But those not in or heir to this community, those who have historically opposed its presence among them, remain caught in inherited ways of seeing that blind them to new imaginative possibilities and seal them off from significant communal participation. The statement of Coleman Steele, one of the excluded, and now living on Hospital Road, makes this clear:

This is an English town, mister. Or was. The people who settled here knew what kind of life they were building, they had fine models at Home they could follow. But do you think *that* bunch paid any attention? The Indians went along with it. Why shouldn't they? And all those Chinamen they brought over to work in the mines went with it, some of them turned into the best Englishmen of all. And there were other Irishmen who came over and weren't afraid to fit in with the scheme of things, doing the things that Irishmen are meant to do. But not old Whozzit, Keneally! He comes over here with his pack of sheep-people and sets up his own world like the rest of us don't exist, see, like the world stopped and started at the edge of his property. He was a King in there, like something out of the Dark Ages, and the fact that the rest of us out here were busy building a modern *civilized* society with decent values never occurred to him. And you may not agree with me on this, but I'm entitled to my opinion as they say, I think that's when everything started to go wrong. First thing we knew you have people pouring in from all over the world, your Belgiums and your Italians and your Ukrainians, pouring in from all the place, which is just fine with me, but when they get here do they fit themselves in? No sir. They look around and they see this one bunch that isn't paying any attention to the rest of us and so they think it's all right for them to do what they want, too. So I blame him for *that*, mister, and it's no small matter. I blame that Keneally for throwing it all off the track. Just look around at what's happened to this town and blame him for that. Drugs and sex and socialism. None of it would've happened. You can't tell me they have things like that in England. (174–75)

What we have at the thematic level of Hodgins' magic realist text, then, is a fairly direct portrayal of the process of colonization, one that recapitulates a problem in historical consciousness in postcolonial English Canadian culture. This focus on the problem of history is shared by that body of criticism in postcolonial cultural studies which argues that people in postcolonial cultures engage in a special "dialogue with history."[29] In this account, "double vision" or "metaphysical clash" emerges in the space of incommensurability between inherited notions of imperial history as "the few privileged monuments"[30] of achievement and a cluster of opposing views that tend to see history more as a kind of alchemical process, somewhat analogous to a way of seeing, in which the silenced, marginalized, or dispossessed voices within the colonial encounter themselves form the record of "true" history. The "re-visioning" of history, then, takes place when the voices or visions—what J. Michael Dash calls "the counterculture of the imagination"[31]—come into dialectical play with the inherited, dominant modes of discourse and cognition in colonialism's "phenomenal legacy"[32] and work toward transmuting perception into new "codes of recognition."

This framework provides a way of reading the means by which *What the Crow Said* functions at the thematic level as a "speaking mirror" of postcolonial, English-Canadian culture. Kroetsch's novel is set in a region lying "ambiguously on the border between the provinces of Alberta and Saskatchewan,"[33] and in it people enjoy absolute control over the horizontal dimension. The "vertical world" is "all a mystery" (158) to them, however, and in a series of motifs such as the stranding of the dying Martin Lang "between sky and earth" (26), JG's fatal fall from the tree, Jerry Lapanne's, or Joe Lightning's, fall from the sky, or the townsfolk's war against the sky, Kroetsch establishes that human control in this second dimension represents an impossible goal. This constriction within distorted binary oppositions such as that between horizontal control and vertical incompetence is a constraining one, as is shown by Isadore Heck's trans-

ference, in pure either/or fashion, from the relative security of believing
in nothing that can't be seen, to the opposite position of believing that
everything that can be imagined exists. This second position eventually
kills him, for it lies behind his decision to shoot himself out of a cannon
into the air in a futile attempt to end the war with the sky.

The text also presents a range of similar binary constrictions in parallel to this spatial one—two conflicting time schemes, for example, so that
the passage of only a few seasons contains several years of calendar time,
and all of colonial history from the horse-and-buggy period to the appearance of oil derricks on the Canadian prairies. Binary constriction, in fact,
represents a key principle in the book, and it provides the vehicle for reading the site of the novel as a metonym for postcolonial space. In *What the
Crow Said*, the binary opposition between control in one dimension and
incompetence or bewilderment in the other reflects the dialectic operative
in postcolonial cultures between inherited, sure, and constraining codes of
imperial order and the imagined, precarious, and liberating codes of postcolonial "original relations." At the close of his novel, Kroetsch employs
the image of Tiddy and Liebhaber coming together in the "naked circle
of everything" (215) to posit a point beyond binary constriction. In postcolonial terms, this represents an imaginative projection into the future,
where the fractures of colonialism heal in the "re-visioning" process that
produces a "positive imaginative reconstruction of reality."[34]

This imaginative reconstruction has echoes in those forms of postcolonial
thought which seek to recuperate the lost voices and discarded fragments
that imperialist cognitive structures push to the margins of critical consciousness, and both Hodgins and Kroetsch share an interest in thematically decentering images of fixity while at the same time foregrounding the
gaps and absences those fixed and monumental structures produce.[35] In
The Invention of the World, Hodgins raises images of fixity and center in "a
certain piece of this world" (viii)—"certain" here carrying a dual meaning
—only to work toward undermining them. The central house of Keneally's
Revelations Colony conceals a subterranean tunnel whose entrance is
never found, an absence in the monolith of his legend evocative of his
mother's loss of all memory at the time of his conception and of the Carrigdhoun villagers' absence of fear. In Keneally's death, absences become
ghostly presences, as Strabo Becker begins to sift through the "shreds and
fragments" (69) of events and to comb the beaches for "the debris of his-

tory" (viii) that will form the base elements for his story. Through Becker's tape recorder, a plurality of voices joins in the narration; and through the ruminations of the characters, history's dispossessed "voices" are drawn into the novel. Julius Champney's reflections on landscape, for example, conjure the presence of two "Indians" from the early colonial period who were tried and subsequently hanged for a murder they did not commit:

> *The trial is in English. Though an attempt is made to provide an adequate translation, the long exchange of foreign mouth-sounds could be the yattering of squirrels to the ears of Siam-a-sit. . . .*
>
> *On the platform, beneath the nooses, the flat chocolate eyes shift to the hangman, whose hands could be made of old rope. Throats, dry with fear, can only whisper. Cannot refuse to whisper.*
>
> *You could tell us, first, what we done.*
>
> There was no record, anywhere that he had seen, which ever hinted that the two condemned men, or one of them, said those words before the ropes snapped their necks. Nor was there anything in official records or in the newspaper reports to indicate that they said anything at all, or if they did, anything that could be understood by the white men who were witnesses. . . .
>
> And the voices existed out of time, anyway." (240–41)

These official records, like all monuments to fixity, omit what they cannot hear. Hodgins likens them to maps, projections of line and order that do not correspond to the "real island," which defies geometry (229) and whose landscape is "ungovernable" (223). Keneally's life, symbol of high colonialism, is planned at birth like a "map of roads" (90); but for Maggie, his symbolic heir, maps only block the guiding capacities of her instinct and memory, and they can't help her find her way home. But for her to realize this, to finally discard them, she has to encounter directly the fixed spaces of alien order, and this process is an important one in *The Invention of the World*. Seen from within new "codes of recognition," fixed systems betray the presence of their own "otherness" hidden within them, as is symbolized by Donal Keneally's brief fragmentation into identical twins, one of them the opposite of the tyrannical self that will finally own him. The absence of this missing self in the New World is his legacy to Wade, who sees himself mirrored in Horseman only to be told that he has buried his own hidden twin within him (307). Through images such as these,

Hodgins' text conveys that the silencing of otherness is inscribed into the colonial encounter. But it also suggests that awareness of this can provoke the imagination into recovering lost aspects of self, habitual absences in the postcolonial consciousness.

It is obsession with fixity that betrays, then, and Hodgins' most sustained approach to undermining it is his destabilization of the fixity of origins. Critics of the novel have noted the astonishing number of mythic and historical origins upon which the imagery of the text seems to be based.[36] These range through classical origins (Taurus-Europa, Lycaon, Charon), Celtic origins (the *Táin bó Cúailnge*, the war between the Fomorians and the Tuatha de Dannan), Christian origins (Genesis, Exodus), and historical origins (the Aquarian Foundation of Brother XII). This wide pluralizing of origins annihilates the privileging or monumentalizing of any one of them and suggests that the "shreds and fragments" that come down from them in distorted form, in time, themselves comprise the "real" historical legacy of postcolonial space. Madmother Thomas, a direct victim of colonialism's violence through her childhood trauma under Keneally's patriarchal order, must learn this. For most of the novel, she wanders in the margins of the text, searching obsessively for her birthplace, but finally, she relinquishes her need for fixed and known origins and returns to the uncertain center of the Revelations Trailer Park, thus becoming at last a sustaining presence in the community. The operative process of cognition here is one of *imaginative*, not factual, recovery, and at the novel's close Hodgins releases it into full play on the metafictional level in the parodic carnivalization of the wedding ceremony, where he summons into presence all those figures made absent from the text by the formal system of writing itself:

> The mayors of several towns on the island, with their wives, and more than one elected MLA and several judges, lawyers, doctors, and businessmen had come. . . . Mainlanders had come across, and sat silently along the wall benches, wondering what to expect. Victoria people had driven up, and sat together near the punch bowl, with their backs to everyone else. The premier of the province, who was unable to attend, sent a representative, a little freckle-faced man who shook hands, before the evening was through, with every person in the hall, including the lieutenant-governor of an eastern province who had flown in at the last minute and had to leave for his plane as soon as the cake was cut. The Prime Minister of Canada was rumoured to be

in the crowd somewhere, but the Queen of England had disappointed everyone by accepting an invitation elsewhere. (346)

Kroetsch's technique for foregrounding the gaps and silences of the dispossessed in *What the Crow Said* differs from Hodgins' in that Kroetsch works less with the material of history in this thematic level and more with the portrayal of constricting binaries, a thematic equivalent to the dialectic operative in the language of narration. From a postcolonial critical perspective, these binaries can be read as legacies of the colonial encounter: a condition of being both tyrannized by history yet paradoxically cut off from it, caught between absolute systems of blind cognition and projected realms of imaginative revision in which people have no control. In Kroetsch's handling, these binary constrictions undergo a process of dialectical interplay between opposing terms which undermines the fixity of borders between them. Each term invades the other, eroding its absolute nature and addressing the gaps or absences, the distanced elements of "otherness," that fixed systems inevitably create.

Liebhaber, for example, editor and printer of the local newspaper in the town of Big Indian, has forgotten the past but three times in the course of the novel remembers the future. At the root of this loss of memory is an obsession with print: Gutenberg, he feels, has "made all memory of the past irrelevant" and "only the future" is free from his "vast design" (116). Print, in obliterating the need for memory, inevitably contains and fixes the past as dead record of the monuments of achievement, but it also creates marginal spaces in which the silenced voices of totalizing system can speak. The prisoner Jerry Lapanne, an emblem of incarcerated desire, is one of Kroetsch's images of such a voice. He repeatedly tries to escape *into* the site of the text toward Rita Lang, sender of erotic love notes to prisoners all over the country. It is print, then, that motivates him, and his movement is always toward it, his action one of struggle to inhabit the locus of textuality. But the police are always there on the borders of municipality to stop him; and his one breakthrough results in his death. Through this image, Kroetsch foregrounds the absence on the other side of writing, a human equivalent to suppressed memory that Gutenberg's print seemingly makes obsolete. A corresponding image is that of the cattle buyer who makes a brief appearance in the text to court Tiddy Lang and then vanishes "like a character gently removed from the vast novel that all the printers in the world were gallantly writing for Gutenberg's ghost" (73). In thematizing print in this manner, Kroetsch portrays the process by which a totalizing system can initiate its own dialectic with its "other." Print excludes, but it also energizes. It is like the "phenomenal legacy" of postcolonial history: it silences, but within it lies the possibility of voice, a dialectic that can produce a "positive imaginative reconstruction of reality."

Binary constriction is also thematized in the novel's representation of race and gender. Both are seriously imbalanced, dominated by one pole of the binary in such a way as to produce a paralyzing separation between terms. For example, the name of the town of Big Indian resonates against the almost complete absence of native peoples from its site. The only exception is Joe Lightning, and he lives in a car, not a house. The "Indian list" (115), a racist term for the list of those proscribed from being served alcohol, contains the complete register of "every white male over the age of twenty in the Municipality of Bigknife" (114), but no Indian names appear on it. These patterns of exclusion seem to be intricately tied to the process of language, where "Gutenberg's curse" (163) links the presence of print to the condition of becoming "anonymous, almost not invented in (one's) own story" (73). Being caught between presence and absence, however, is also a way of mediating between binary terms, of crossing the borders between them and thus beginning the process of breaking them down. Except for Liebhaber, Joe is the only adult male in the district who is *not* at war with the sky, and thus his ambiguous status in one binary constriction enables him to mediate in another: that of the division of male and female modes of activity.

An interesting thematization of the way in which binary terms themselves energize a crossing over between poles, and the creation of gaps within each of them, lies in Kroetsch's presentation of the black crow and the character JG. The crow, whose gender is ambiguous (97) and who thus mediates in another context the polarization in male and female power relations, speaks on JG's behalf in the human world. JG, on the other hand, is for most of the novel silent, "forever innocent" (62), and able to walk only in a figure-eight, the symbol of infinity. John Thieme writes of the way animals in some Canadian texts stand for "a world which may exist before Western rationalist thought imposes dualistic modes of description. They represent life before discourse, before history, and before gender stereotyping."[37] Something of the same process of signification is operative in this text, but it requires both terms of the JG-black crow binary to produce it. The crow's ambiguous gender combines with JG's silence, innocence, and association with infinity to suggest all that is opposed to Liebhaber's word-centered rationality. But at the same time, the JG-black crow binary works toward deconstruction of this prerational signification when JG begins to speak pig-Latin, and we recognize that what the crow usually says are judgmental, arbitrary pronouncements on human behavior that seem to issue from the parodic mask of an omniscient, patriarchal God.

The novel closes on an image of resolution in binary separation, a symbolic drawing together of the oppositions of male and female, past and present, absence and presence, and silence and voice in a suspended moment that requires both terms of the text's narrational mode—realism and fantasy—to sustain it. Throughout the novel, Liebhaber and Tiddy Lang, opposite poles in a binary system, have been held apart, the dead Martin Lang, who represents absence to Liebhaber but presence to Tiddy, throwing up an uncrossable barrier between them. But at the novel's close, Liebhaber, whose obsession with words has been at the root of his loss of memory, and Tiddy, who had "meant to make a few notes, but hadn't," and who now "remember(s) everything" (214), are brought together, he "the first and final male" and she the world-dreamer, "dreaming the world" and unable to "tell her memory from the moment" (214, 216). As each of them embraces otherness, the crows, outside, "are cawing" (218) in the infinitely suspended moment that fuses the real with the numinous in the actuating imagination.

Both *The Invention of the World* and *What the Crow Said*, then, thematize a *kind* of postcolonial discourse: one involving the recuperation of silenced voices as axial to a "positive imagined reconstruction of reality."[38] Both texts foreground plurality and gaps—those produced by the colonial encounter and those produced by the system of writing itself; and in both texts, marginalized presences press in toward the center. The site of each text is a localized region that is metonymic of English-Canadian postcolonial culture as a whole. And in each text, history is foreshortened so that the forces operating in the culture's social relations are brought metaphorically into play. The metaphysical clash or double vision inherent in colonial history and language is recapitulated in transmuted form in the text's oppositional language of narration and mirrored in its thematic level. This mode of narration requires the reader to read the novel in a dialectical manner, forestalling the collapse of either one of the two narrational modes into the other, but recognizing the erosion in massive and totalizing system that the dialectic effects in each. The texts thus demand a kind of reading process in which the imagination becomes stimulated into summoning into being new and liberating "codes of recognition." These elements, I believe, are characteristic of many postcolonial magic realist texts.

If certain forms of magic realist expression are read in this way as comprising a kind of postcolonial discourse, a framework for reading texts across postcolonial cultures might possibly be established not reductively, on the basis of shared conditions of marginality in relation to metropolitan cultures, but productively, on the basis of their sustained dialogic engagement with the cognitive legacies of colonialist language and history. This may correspond to what E. D. Blodgett has in mind when he speculates on the possibility that given the right kind of reading strategy, Spanish-American literature might provide a matrix for "dialogue between deaf Canadians," [39] English and French — García Márquez mediating, as it were, between Aquin and Miron, on the one hand, and Hodgins, Kroetsch, Kerslake, and Ondaatje on the other. Such a framework could provide a basis for comparing works differing widely in genre and provenance, and within it a comparative reading of Salman Rushdie's work with that of the Australian writer Rodney Hall, for example, might prove fruitful, though at first sight odd. Radical modes of reading postcolonial texts are constantly coming into being, challenging the fixed certainty of traditional generic systems, so that when Wilson Harris, in his groundbreaking critical work *The Womb of Space*, notes that within the "so-called realism" of Patrick White's *Voss* there exists a "curiously subversive fantasy," he proposes not just a new strategy of interpretation for the text itself, but also a way of reading the text back into the cross-cultural imagination that many forms of postcolonial critical studies actively seek to promote. The text of *Voss*, he argues, can allow us "to perceive realism and fantasy as a threshold into evolution and alchemy. That threshold is a component of the "mental bridge" within and across cultures." [40]

Within the separate postcolonial cultures themselves, this approach to magic realism could operate in such a way that this seemingly new mode of fiction is recognized as continuous with apparently dissimilar works of fiction in which an oppositional and dialogic style or narration also echoes against the postcolonial legacy, but in different ways: Ethel Wilson's *Swamp Angel* is one example in the English-Canadian context; Sheila Watson's *The Double Hook* is another. As W. H. New notes in *Articulating West*, an opposition between a need to formalize experience and a realization that the Canadian wilderness is "formless" creates "a tension at the heart of the Canadian experience," [41] and a structurally similar kind of tension occupies the language of narration in many present-day magic realist texts. This suggests that the critical position that would see the English Canadian, or for that matter any postcolonial culture's, literary tradition as "discontinuous," one in which writers find no "usable past" [42] in the apparently colonized literary productions of earlier times, may itself be blind to modes of continuity that can prevail beneath the surface of established generic classifications.

Read as a form of postcolonial discourse, the magic realist texts I have engaged with here comprise a positive and liberating engagement with the codes of imperial history and its legacy of fragmentation and discontinuity. By embedding the binary oppositions of past and present social relations into the "speaking mirror" of their literary language, these texts implicitly suggest that enabling strategies for the future require revisioning the seemingly tyrannical units of the past in a complex and imaginative double-think of "remembering the future." This process, they tell us, can transmute the "shreds and fragments" of colonial violence and otherness into new "codes of recognition" in which the dispossessed, the silenced, and the marginalized of our own dominating systems can again find voice and enter into the dialogic continuity of community and place. This capacity for transmutation, they imply, is itself part of the "phenomenal legacy" that comprises at least a part of the "real" for postcolonial places and postcolonial times.

Notes

This paper had its beginnings in a conference talk I gave in May 1986 at the biennial meeting of the Association for Canadian Studies in Australia and New Zealand and was subsequently published in *Canadian Literature* 116 (Spring 1988): 9–24. I have revised this paper slightly, but nonetheless the paper's enabling assumptions remain those of almost a decade ago, and in terms of postcolonial critical theory this decade can look like a lifetime. Since that time, too, the critical production of "magic realist" writing as what Peter Hulme has described as "a hyper reality of international proportions" has become one of the paradigmatic critical tropes for justifying an ignorance of the local histories behind specific textual practices and for securing first-world postmodernism's naturalization of—again Peter Hulme's words—that "casual, unmoored international audience" which claims everything in the wide world as somehow its own (Introduction, *Colonial Discourse/Postcolonial Theory*, ed. Francis Barker, Peter Hulme, and Margaret Iversen (Manchester: Manchester Univ. Press, forthcoming), p. 14. This is a development that this present article, I think, fails to anticipate. I welcome, however, this chance to put two English-Canadian—two postcolonial—literary texts before what will be in the main non-English-Canadian readers, and I want to thank Wendy Faris and Lois Zamora for the opportunity. Thanks also to Helen Tiffin and Bill New for their sustained assistance with this project, and to the Social Sciences and Research Council of Canada for its doctoral funding from 1985 to 1988.

1 Surveys of the critical use of the term appear in Armaryll Chanady, "The Origins and Development of Magic Realism in Latin American Fiction," in *Magic Realism and Canadian Literature*, ed. Peter Hinchcliffe and Ed Jewinski (Waterloo: Univ. of Waterloo Press, 1986), pp. 49–60; Roberto González Echevarría, *Alejo Carpentier: The Pilgrim at Home* (Ithaca: Cornell Univ. Press, 1977), pp. 108–29; Fredric Jameson, "On Magic Realism in Film," *Critical Inquiry* 12 (1986): 301–3; Jean Weisgerber, "Le Réalisme magique: La locution et le concept," *Rivista di letterature moderne e comparate* 35, fasc. 1 (1982): 27–53; and Robert Wilson, review of Geoff Hancock, ed. *Magic Realism*, in *Quarry* 32, 2 (Spring 1983): 84–91. Important distinctions in the term's use are also pointed out by Susan Beckmann, "The Place of Experiment," *Canadian Literature* 89 (Summer 1981): 152–55; Enrique Anderson Imbert, " 'Magical Realism' in Spanish-American Fiction," *International Fiction Review* 2, 1 (Jan. 1975): 1–8; James Irish, "Magical Realism: A Search for Caribbean and Latin-American Roots," *Literary Half-Yearly* 11, 2 (July 1970): 127–39; and Seymour Menton, "Jorge Luis Borges, Magic Realist," *Hispanic Review* 50 (1982): 411–26.

2 Jacques Stéphen Aléxis, "Of the Marvellous Realism of the Haitians," *Présence Africaine* 8–10 (June–Nov. 1956): 269. For discussions of the "marvelous," see also M. Ian Adams, *Three Authors of Alienation: Bomba, Onetti, Carpentier* (Austin and London: Univ. of Texas Press, 1975), p. 82; and J. Michael Dash, "Marvellous Realism—The Way Out of Negritude," *Caribbean Studies* 13, 4 (1973): 57–70, and *Literature and Ideology in Haiti: 1915–1961* (London: Macmillan, 1981), pp. 190–202.

3 The term, writes González Echevarría, pp. 111–12, 116, has "neither the specificity nor the theoretical foundation to be convincing or useful," since "the relationship between the three moments when magical realism appears are not continuous enough for it to be considered a literary or even a critical concept with historical validity." In regards to the novels of the Latin-American "boom," critical use of the concept has "rarely gone beyond 'discovering' the most salient characteristics of avant-garde literature in general."

4 Jameson, "On Magic Realism in Film," p. 302.

5 González Echevarría, p. 108.

6 Ibid., p. 110.

7 Jean-Pierre Durix, in "Magic Realism in *Midnight's Children*," *Commonwealth* 8, 1 (Autumn 1985): 57–63, applies the concept to Salman Rushdie's work, while Jameson, p. 302, mentions it in reference to Amos Tutuola. The discussion of magic realism in the context of English-Canadian fiction was initiated by Geoff Hancock in "Magic Realism, or, the Future of Fiction," *Canadian Fiction Magazine* 24–25 (Spring/Summer 1977): 4–6, and followed up in his introduction to his anthology *Magic Realism* (Toronto: Aya Press, 1980), pp. 7–15. Since then, numerous critical works have continued this trend. See, for example, Beckmann, pp. 152–55; Cecelia Coulas Fink, "'If Words Won't Do, and Symbols Fail': Hodgins' Magic Reality," *Journal of Canadian Studies* 20, 2 (Summer 1985): 118–31; Geoff Hancock, "Magic of Realism: The Marvellous in Canadian Fiction," *Canadian Forum* (March 1986): 23–35; Keith Maillard, "'Middlewatch' as Magic Realism," *Canadian Literature* 92 (Spring 1982): 10–21; Shirley Neuman and Robert Wilson, *Labyrinths of Voice: Conversations with Robert Kroetsch* (Edmonton: NeWest Press, 1982); Uma Parameswaran and G. Sekhar, "Canadian Gothic," *CRNLE Reviews Journal* (May 1982): 65–67; and Robert Wilson, Review of Hancock, ed., *Magic Realism*, pp. 84–91, and "On the Boundary of the Magic and the Real: Notes on Inter-American Fiction," *The Compass* 6 (1979): 37–53.

8 See Weisgerber, p. 45.

9 Linda Kenyon, "A Conversation with Robert Kroetsch," *New Quarterly* 5, 1 (Spring 1985): 15. See also Stanley McMullin, "'Adam's Mad in Eden': Magic Realism as Hinterland Experience" (in Hinchcliffe, pp. 13–22), who reads magic realism as implicitly "ex-centric."

10 See Fredric Jameson, *The Political Unconscious: Narrative as a Socially Symbolic Act* (1981; London: Methuen, 1983).

11 This reading of magic realism's mode of narration takes issue with those approaches that suggest a seamless interweaving of, or synthesis between, the magic and the real: see, for example, Maillard, p. 12, and Fink, p. 119.

12 Jack Hodgins, *The Invention of the World* (1977; rpt. Scarborough: Signet, 1978), p. 3. Further references are to this edition and appear in the text.

13 Robert Kroetsch, *The Crow Journals* (Edmonton: NeWest Press, 1980), p. 23.

14 See Alastair Fowler, *Kinds of Literature: An Introduction to the Theory of Genres and Modes* (Oxford: Clarendon Press, 1982), p. 108.

15 M. M. Bakhtin, *The Dialogic Imagination*, trans. Caryl Emerson and Michael Holquist, ed. Michael Holquist (Austin and London: Univ. of Texas Press, 1981), p. 263.

16 David Carroll, "The Alterity of Discourse: Form, History, and the Question of the Political in M. M. Bakhtin," *Diacritics* 13, 2 (Summer 1983): 77.

17 Helen Tiffin, "Commonwealth Literature: Comparison and Judgement," in *The History and Historiography of Commonwealth Literature*, ed. Dieter Riemenschneider (Tübingen: Gunter Narr, 1983), p. 32.

18 Coral Ann Howells, "Re-visions of Prairie Indian History in Rudy Wiebe's *The Temptations of Big Bear* and *My Lovely Enemy*," in *Revisions of Canadian Literature*, ed. Shirley Chew (Leeds: Univ. of Leeds, Institute of Bibliography and Textual Criticism, 1984), p. 61. For detailed discussions of this process within the languages of postcolonial cultures, see David T. Haberly, "The Search for a National Language: A Problem in the Comparative History of Post-Colonial Literatures," *Studies in Comparative Literature* 11, 1 (1974): 85–97; D. E. S. Maxwell, "Landscape and Theme," *Commonwealth Literature*, ed. John Press (London: Heinemann, 1965), pp. 82–89; W. H. New, "New Language, New World," in *Awakened Conscience: Studies in Commonwealth Literature*, ed. C. D. Narasimhaiah (New Delhi: Sterling, 1978), pp. 360–77; Uma Parameswaran, "Amid the Alien Corn: Biculturalism and the Challenge of Commonwealth Literary Criticism," *WLWE* 21, 1 (Spring 1982): 240–53; and Helen Tiffin, "Commonwealth Literature: Comparison and Judgement," pp. 19–35, and "Commonwealth Literature and Comparative Methodology," *WLWE* 23, 1 (Winter 1984): 26–30.

19 Howells, p. 62.

20 See R. E. Watters, "Original Relations," *Canadian Literature* 7 (Winter 1961): 6–17.

21 Gabriel García Márquez, *One Hundred Years of Solitude*, trans. Gregory Rabassa (1967; New York: Avon, 1971), p. 383.

22 Michael Holquist, Introduction to Bakhtin, *The Dialogic Imagination*, p. 28.

23 John S. Brushwood, *The Spanish American Novel: A Twentieth-Century Survey* (Austin and London: Univ. of Texas Press, 1975), pp. 282–84, notes a link between a "telescoping of time" and the use of "transcendent regionalism" in novels that employ abstract narrative techniques in depicting seemingly "real" people attached to a familiar world. W. H. New's observation in "Beyond Nationalism: On Regionalism," *WLWE* 23, 1 (Winter 1984): 17, that the region in postcolonial cultures can stand for the "social variations within the society" suggests that this approach to regionalism is not restricted to works of magic realism in the "new" literatures.

24 Robert R. Wilson, in "The Metamorphoses of Space: Magic Realism" (in Hinchcliffe, pp. 61–74), conceives of magic realism as a "fictional space created by the dual inscription of incompatible geometries." Wilson's "principle of spatial folding" could provide yet another means of envisioning magic realism's thematic level as a "template" of what I read as the oppositional system of incompatible discursive modes in magic realism's language of narration.

25 See David L. Jeffrey, "Jack Hodgins and the Island Mind," *Book Forum* 4, 1 (1978): 72.

26 In an interview with Alan Twigg in *For Openers* (Madeira Park: Harbour Publishing, 1981), p. 192, Hodgins notes: "It's possible to see the history of Vancouver Island as the history of failed colonies. So I chose (the title) *The Invention*

of the World because it implies that the different levels of the novel are allegorical."

27 See Jeffrey, p. 75.

28 Fink, p. 125.

29 Dash, "Marvellous Realism—The Way Out of Negritude," p. 65.

30 González Echevarría, p. 259.

31 Dash, "Marvellous Realism—The Way Out of Negritude," p. 66.

32 See Wilson Harris, "The Phenomenal Legacy," *The Literary Half-Yearly* 11, 2 (July 1970): 1–6.

33 Robert Kroetsch, *What the Crow Said* (Don Mills: General Publishing, 1978), p. 36. Further references are to this edition and appear in the text.

34 Dash, "Marvellous Realism—The Way Out of Negritude," p. 66.

35 Jameson, "On Magic Realism in Film," pp. 303, 311, notes that Latin American magic realist films depict history as "history with holes, perforated history," and he advances "the very provisional hypothesis that the possibility of magic realism as a formal mode is constitutively dependent on a type of historical raw material in which disjunction is structurally present." This observation helps explain why magic realism may be especially viable as a mode of discourse in postcolonial cultures.

36 See Fink, p. 122; Jan C. Horner, "Irish and Biblical Myth in Jack Hodgins' 'The Invention of the World'," *Canadian Literature* 99 (Winter 1983): 11; Jeffrey, p. 75; Robert Lecker, "Haunted by a Glut of Ghosts: Jack Hodgins' *The Invention of the World*," *Essays in Canadian Writing* 20 (Winter 1980–81): 85, 95; and Joann McCaig, "Brother XII and *The Invention of the World*," *Essays in Canadian Writing* 28 (Spring 1984): 128–40.

37 John Thieme, "Beyond History: Margaret Atwood's *Surfacing* and Robert Kroetsch's *Badlands*," in *Re-visions of Canadian Literature*, p. 74.

38 This specific postcolonial discourse is by no means coterminous with *all* post-colonial discourse, and in fact the dominant register in postcolonial critical theory at present works *against* recuperation as a modality of empowerment and against expressivist notions of cultural or national resistances in literature or language. Needless to say, this debate within postcolonial theory is a hot one: see Gayatri Chakravorty Spivak's critique of nostalgic recuperation of subaltern voices in "Can the Subaltern Speak," *Wedge* 7 (1985): 120–30; and Benita Parry's spirited defense of recuperative readings in "Problems in Current Theories of Colonial Discourse," *Oxford Literary Review* 9, 1–2 (1987): pp. 27–52.

39 E. D. Blodgett, *Configuration: Essays on the Canadian Literatures* (Downsview: ECW Press, 1982), p. 34.

40 Wilson Harris, *The Womb of Space* (Westport, Conn.: Greenwood, 1983), pp. 69–70.

41 W. H. New, *Articulating West* (Toronto: New Press, 1972), p. 25.

42 Diane Bessai, "Counterfeiting Hindsight," *WLWE* 23, 2 (Spring 1984): 359.

Metoikoi *and Magical Realism*
in the Maghrebian Narratives of Tahar ben Jelloun
and Abdelkebir Khatibi

Métèque. *n.m.* (1743, *mestèque* au sens 1; empr. du gr. *metoikos*, de *meta*, et *oikos*, "maison", propremt. "qui change de maison").
1. *Antiq. gr.* Etranger domicilé en Grèce, qui n'avait pas droit de cité. (*Le Robert* dictionary)

Metic. *n.*-s (1743, *mestic* first meaning, borrowed from Gk *metoikos*, fr. *meta* + *oikos*, "house," *lit* "he who changes houses").
1. *Ancient Gr.* Foreigner domiciled in Greece, who was without civil rights.

The term magical realism, coined by Franz Roh in 1925 as a descriptive category for German art, referred to the depiction of the supernatural in a realistic setting. Alejo Carpentier, in his prologue to the narrative *The Kingdom of this World* (*El reino de este mundo*) in 1949, used the term to describe inherent qualities of the lush, tropical landscape of Latin America. Others applied it to themes of Amerindian myth and superstition. It has since come to refer widely to narratives by contemporary Latin American writers that blur "the traditional realist distinction between fantasy and reality."[1] Valbueno Briones argues that magical realism, far from being a phenomenon confined to Latin American narratives, is "a universal tendency, which, it may be added, is inherent in human existence."[2] Gregson Davis turns to non-Hispanic Caribbean writing in applying the term to the work of Aimé Césaire, while various critics have used it to characterize texts of other so-called emergent cultures beyond the Hispanic and Antillean worlds, as well as texts of migrant literature by writers such as Salman Rushdie.[3]

Most commentators of magical realism have underscored its function as a differential mode of literary expression that valorizes a discourse whose perceptual orientation is essentially non-Western, or that at least diverges from the logocentric tradition of mainstream Western thought and literature. By viewing the North African narrative of French expression in terms of magical realism, I seek to discern the form that divergence takes in certain Maghrebian texts written in a language of Western provenance. I seek, moreover, an understanding of how their tactics of opposition counter the ideological restrictions informing that language in order to speak to the concerns and perceptions of the North African. I hope, finally, that we may come to appreciate their remarkable affinities with postcolonialist discourses from other non-Western cultures in Africa and other areas of the world.[4]

The term magical realism must be defined with care, for critics have used it indiscriminately, often confounding it with the marvelous or the fantastic.[5] The "marvelous" narrative depicts a fictitious world totally removed from conventional reality, while the "fantastic" narrative heralds the sudden apparition of the supernatural in the midst of the everyday world. In the former, the supernatural fails to surprise the character; in the latter, it elicits an affective reaction from the character, for the intrusion of the supernatural, as Roger Caillois describes it, results in "a scandal, a laceration, a strange and almost unbearable irruption in the real world."[6] The fantastic narrative turns on the resolution of the supernatural through rational explanation.

In narratives marked by magical realism, to the contrary, two diametrically opposed ontologies coexist on equal terms: the empirical world of reason and logic and the supernatural world of unreason. In such narratives the supernatural serves to rupture the "coherence" of the systematized empirical world by revealing it to be, not a universally true or absolute representation of external reality, but only one of several possible representations. As Caillois says about the effect of the fantastic: "the regularity, the world order so painfully established and proved by the methodical investigation of experimental science, [cedes] to the assault of irreconcilable, nocturnal, demonic forces" (23). But, as differentiated from the fantastic, rather than the displacement of one by the other, in magical realism the "real" and the "magical" realms exist side by side on equal terms.

Confronted by the irruption of the fantastic in the workaday world, the reader may, on the one hand, be able to resolve the indeterminacy of the events if s/he can perceive them as dream-inspired or hallucinatory (as in the first version of Maupassant's "The Horla"), that is, to explain them in rational terms, such that the laws of the world go unthreatened—in which case we remain in the realm of the fantastic. On the other hand, s/he may be forced to accept the strange events as arising without apparent cause, in which case s/he encounters an alternate reality ruled by unknown laws. The fantastic for Tzvetan Todorov exists in the reader's hesitation between these possibilities.[7]

Chanady suggests replacing the term "hesitation" by antinomy, a fortunate term that calls to mind sophist antilogic by suggesting the coexistence in the self-same text of two conflicting predicates ("codes," she calls them) of apparently equal validity, neither of which "can be accepted in the presence of the other" (12). Chanady cites Irène Bessière who, in speaking of Jacques Cazotte's *The Devil in Love* (*Le Diable amoureux*) — a text that challenges conventional narrative — says, "the text seeks to present from the outset the natural order and the supernatural order . . . so as to deconstruct them simultaneously and call into question all signs, before reconstructing in fine the complementary existence of these orders."[8]

I examine a similar process of magical realism occurring in the postcolonialist narratives of two Moroccan writers: *Love in Two Languages* (*Amour bilingue*, 1983), by Abdelkebir Khatibi, and *The Sand Child* (*L'Enfant de sable*, 1985), by Tahar ben Jelloun. In these narratives, the coexistence of mutually incompatible predicates (natural/supernatural) results in a deconstructive movement that throws doubt on the certainty of the representation itself (the "sign"). Such postcolonialist discourse introduces a process that puts into play a set of antiprogrammatic imperatives challenging authoritarian discourses of power by rejecting binary either/or reasoning, whether Western or indigenous. It affirms that which is and is not, that is not either/or but both and neither. It entertains affinities with the Sophist strategy of antilogic and with Jean-François Lyotard's concept of paralogism (which reintroduces sophistic rhetorical tactics into contemporary theory). Abdelkebir Khatibi develops the metaphor of the "bilangue," literally a bilingual person, metaphorically a language and speaker who refuse to conform either to a Western or an indigenous idiom.[9] In the narratives of both Khatibi and ben Jelloun, particularly that of the latter, the resulting process pushes narrative form and language itself to the edge of indeterminacy.

"The story fell joyously that autumn: the leaves, the leaves of paper, that very real enchantment of my summer"[10] — so in the epilogue to *Love in Two Languages* (115), Khatibi describes the interpenetration of the supernatural and the real in his story, as well as their metaphoric exchange.

The novel begins with a brief epigraph (from the Greek, *epigraphe,* which derives from the suffix *epi-* plus the root verb to write, *graphein*). Curiously, the opening paragraph is enclosed between parentheses, as if to insist on closure of the speech act within a circumscribed space. Indeed, the first sentence seems to say as much: "He [the narrator] left, he came back, he left again. He decided to leave for good." There is a beginning and an end, past definite verbs in French that convey the sense of a completed action, or an action frozen in repetitiveness, and an allusion (in the original) to the *definitive* character of that action. The very next sentence, however, still within parentheses, spills over boundaries, undercuts the implied containment — "The story should stop here, the book close upon itself" — by introducing the element of uncertainty with the verb "should" (*devrait*) that suggests deviation from the expected. Customarily, the use of an epigraph signals the theme or spirit of the work. Based on the title and first paragraph of *Love in Two Languages,* the spirit is one of deviation in the frame of writing and language. That deviation will extend as well to story: for example, the narrator-protagonist describes the movement of the woman he loves as "an infinite digression, wrapped in landscapes, signs, and emblems" (26).

Digression, deviation, difference — characterize Khatibi's narrative. In usage, the prefix *epi-* denotes several relationships: besides, near to, over, outer (*epidermis*), anterior, prior to, and even after. In all cases it imparts the sense of otherness, something apart from the text or extratextual. In specific relation to what occurs in Khatibi's narrative, it suggests thematically the act of writing-apart that characterizes not only the metatexts (epigraph/epilogue) but the author's entire discourse of the non-Western other and the introduction of the other-than-natural (supernatural) into the natural (conventional narrative) on equal footing, which marks the text as magical realist.

As the epigraph indicates, the narrative does not stop; language continues on its own ("Sentence that composed itself unaided," p. 3) and the narrator-protagonist voices the sensation of being written by his surroundings (3). Allusions to the madness of language — reminiscent of Rimbaud's *dérèglement de tous les sens* (derangement of all the senses) — will occur throughout the narrative. The supernatural that erupts in the middle of the ordinary arises in fact from language run riot. The narrator, an Arab writing in French, reflects that the foreignness of a language makes it more beautiful, more terrible for a non-native. Words detach themselves from their conventional context and interrelate within the same language and between languages. Everywhere in his speech the narrator engages in a cabalistic, glossophilic verbal play: the French noun *mot* (word) calls forth *mort* (death), the French past definite *calma* (he calmed down) establishes a cratylusian-like[11] *correspondance* with the Arabic word *kalma* (word), which then emits a chain of associated words. Words observe words within the narrator, "preceding what had now become the rapid emergence of memories, fragments of words, onomatopoeias, garlands of phrases, intertwined to the death: undecipherable" (4).

In reflecting on the words for sun and moon whose genders in French become reversed in Arabic, the narrator believes that in this inversion he has found the explanation for his obsession with androgyny. In inhabiting a "midground between two languages" (4), he speaks a bilanguage (*bilangue*) that is not two languages as the English translation implies (*Love in Two Languages*) but superimposed languages, languages overlaid one on the other, that emerge from a linguistic space "at the threshold of the untranslatable" (5). His madness (the division of his being between two languages), "which denies as it affirms itself in a double foundation which is itself transitory keeps me," he says, "in good health" (5). He equates not only health but truth with madness. The narrator describes the *bilangue* in this way:

> If I happened to substitute one word for another . . . , I didn't have the impression that I was making a mistake or breaking a law but rather that I was speaking two words simultaneously: one which reached her hearing [that of his beloved] . . . and a second word, an other, which was there and yet was far away, a vagabond, turned in upon itself.
>
> Difference which exalted me. My objective was also to maintain myself in this gap, carrying it into a listening where all opposition between dead language and living language would be forbidden, where everything that unites through separation and everything that separates by continually translating itself would be affirmed. (28)

This gap or midground (*écart*) where mutually canceling oppositions and the contradictory terms of the oxymoron coexist constitutes the same space of writing Khatibi refers to in *Multiple Maghreb* (*Maghreb pluriel*), that interval in the text between identity and difference, in which the postcolonial writer radically inscribes himself. "That interval is the scene of the text, what it puts into play. In Maghrebian literature, such an interval—when it becomes text and poem—imposes itself through its radical strangeness, that is, through writing that seeks its roots in another language, in an absolute outsidedness" (141, my translation; cf. *Love in Two Languages*, 40).[12]

The word *écart* connotes gap or interval, but it means more than simply the space of separation. The first meaning glossed by *Le Robert* dictionary is the "distance that separates two things that one moves apart or that move apart from each other," while its second meaning is the "difference between two magnitudes or values (of which one in particular is a mean or a scale of reference)." Still another meaning is the act of "deviating from a moral rule, social etiquette," etc. Thus *écart* connotes the separation of two things, which may be magnitudes or values, or separation from an established frame of reference.

One cannot help but think of Michel Serre's use of the word/concept *écart* in *The Parasite* (*Le Parasite*). Using the example of La Fontaine's fable of "Le rat de ville et le rat des champs" ("The City Mouse and the Country Mouse"), Serre points to the flaws inherent in the phenomenon of system that allow the writer to counter it. No system functions to perfection, he states, "without loss, without leakage, without erosion, without slips, without irregularities, without opacity."[13] He consequently reconceptualizes system as integrally bound to its own *écarts* (lapses, slips, gaps). "The book of slips [*écarts*]," he says, "of [strange] noise and of disorder would be the book of distress only for those who would defend a God who has calculatedly authored an incorruptibly dependable world. That's not the way things are. The slip is part of the thing itself," he concludes, "and perhaps produces it" (22–23). This idea accords with Derrida's assertion that "Law implies a counter-law . . . lodged at the very heart of the law, a law of impurity or a principle of contamination."[14] The *bilangue* operates as a disordering noise, a counterdiscourse, at the heart of the ruling linguistic/cultural systems/discourses of the West and East, the corrosion within the engine of system that admits the exceptional, the supernatural, as a coexistent entity alongside the natural or "real."

One observes two faces of Khatibi's *bilangue:* the face of the double that analogizes the writing space of the postcolonial author forging a parallel or alternate language within (in this instance) French[15] and the closely related face of oppositionality. The *bilangue* operates under the sign of the androgyne, that sex, described by Aristophanes in Plato's *Symposium,* which "was a distinct sex in form as well as in name, with the characteristics of male and female." The androgyne was sprung from the moon, which partakes equally of the sun (the male) and the earth (the female). The strength of the androgynes was prodigious, Aristophanes relates, and they challenged the very gods. To weaken them, Zeus cleaved them into two parts, female and male, which ever after have sought out of desire to find the other half and embrace it. Aristophanes draws a moral in saying that "love is simply the name for the desire and pursuit of the whole."[16]

In conjunction with his discussion of "impure purity" (his demand for pure love but fascination with prostitutes), Khatibi's narrator speaks of his obsession with the androgyne as coming from his bewitchment since childhood with "this duplicity of body and language" (23). "To translate impurity into purity, prostitution into androgyny" guided his travels throughout the world (23). His obsession with the *bilangue* parallels, moreover, his fascination with ventriloquists, albinos, cripples, "all these bizarre types which swarm through my very real phantasmagorias" (24).

At one point the narrator speaks (in the third person) of his fleeting dreams, comprised of fragments, "Devastated memory, words smashed up, torn apart, flying off in pieces . . . thought which was being built according to an order with no foundation. Marvelous thought, vigil of the unsaid, thought of the void which kept him awake in the midst of sleep" (9). The state he describes evokes Hermagoras' rhetorical category of *adoxis* that exists without relation to the ruling doctrine (*doxa*). It is a state ruled by the non-said, by processes and figures like synesthesia ("unheard-of thought," 22) and the oxymoron: "Ritual wandering" (30); by the indeterminate: "Sleeping but not sleeping, dreaming and not dreaming, in order to get nearer to the unsayable" (9–10). The unsayable—approached in the *bilangue*, which is neither one nor the other of his two languages but in between—becomes his proper language. Providing the atmosphere for the unsayable is the description of time and place "with no set limits" (10). The French language undergoes transformation. For the narrator, it is "this passion for the untranslatable" (65).

The androgyne in *Love in Two Languages*, more specifically, the cleaved state of the androgyne, figures the double in postcolonial writing and the phenomenon of magical realism itself, a state in which two diametrically opposed ontologies—the supernatural world of unreason and the natural world of reason and logic—cohabit, a multipartite space of oppositionality that repositions everything by giving the lie to binary either/or reasoning ruled by universal absolutes. The deconstructive movement of Khatibi's text that gives rise to this state throws into doubt the certainty of the sign, of identity and origin. The magical realist aspect of Khatibi's *bilangue* lies in its replay of the desire and pursuit of the whole by the two sexes once making up the androgyne, through the search for the complementary existence of antinomical orders — supernatural/natural — that constitute the whole. Just as language (the *bilangue*) spills over the boundaries of the real, so events and objects transgress/transcend the boundaries of conventional representation. Natural objects become animate in Khatibi's world — the night writes the narrator and watches him dozing (3); the sea becomes language ("The scansion, the cadence from wave to wave" [7]); "flowers, trees, and crystals love me enough to take my hand," and the narrator is "meditated by the flowers in the garden" (55). He communes with the elements as he swims in the sea.

> His eyes half shut, he swam into the night. He needed even more stars around him, more of their astral flash and brilliance, he needed the power of the night and the breath of the stars. Drunk on this outrageous sight, he gave himself utterly to the Ocean, offering up his thoughts to the night's very substance. Transfigured, he broke through into the unknown. Superabundant joy! His visions were radiant: he saw himself astride a solar horse, flying above the water. The visions brought him gently back to earth, to light, to the beloved night. (8)

The natural becomes a mode of transfiguration and the external is confounded with the beloved. He is moved by desire and ejaculates into the ocean. This interaction (intercourse) between the sensate and the nonsensate, the animate and the inanimate, results in an interpenetration of orders, the intrusion of the supernatural into the natural, that marks Khatibi's narrative.

The narrative frequently turns hallucinatory:

> It was just such a call [from the archangel — "an angel . . . winged and androgynous," 36] which, early on, had brought him face to face with the question of where his name fit in the hierarchy of angels and praying men. Later on, he became drunk with the divinity of what he read. One evening, he went into a trance. He climbed the steps of the Book, spelling it one word at a time; separating heaven from earth, good from evil, and woman from man, he ascended to heaven. Then

he threw wide the invisible doors. He turned over every page in the Book, devouring each one with his eyes. All at once, he saw God. At that moment, he became the Book. (37)

Such hallucinatory images often derive, as here, from an involved play on words that calls forth a chain of associations—allusion to the Book, for example, which at the same time alludes to the Qur'an and turns on an autobiographical allusion to Khatibi's own name (from *kateb,* book).

But the fantastic that erupts into the midst of the real is attributable not only to hallucination. The layering of events renders a similar effect. The narrator in guise of the third-person protagonist ("he") loses control of his car, skids off the road, and falls asleep next to it, only to awaken in the middle of a wheat field. This event is fused with a car accident in which the narrator ("I") is involved and ends up in a field of wildflowers. And in still a third version intertwined with these, the narrator has no accident but continues to drive to the sea where he takes a night swim. Upon this latter version the narrator overtly layers another story of a visit to Caracas: "Right in the middle of the sea is where I want to tell you another beach story—wet your fingers to turn the page—that happened one evening in Caracas" (72).

In Caracas he "did the town" with a lame companion who taught him "to walk on one leg and to dance on one foot. A drunken dance, of course, a dance of poetry and of revolution that was sweeping the whole continent" (72–73). He laments the death of his companion and plunges into a Joycean rush of description that ends with a song he heard in Caracas entitled "Punto y raya":

> Entre tu pueblo y el mío
> hay un punto y una raya
> La raya dice: no hay paso
> El punto, vía cerrada.
> Y así entre todo los pueblos,
> raya y punto, punto y raya
> Con tantas rayas y puntos
> el mapa es un telegrama.
>
> [Between your town and mine
> there is a dot and a dash
> The dash says do not enter

> The dot says road closed.
>   And thus between all towns
>   dash, dot, dot, dash
>   With so many dashes and dots
>   The map is a telegram.]

The layering of episodes or planes of existence is much like the dance of his own narrative; it is the dance of the *bilangue*. Points and dashes, that, while both offering closure, suggest diacritical orders based on difference (like the components of Morse code)—are these not further suggestive of the two types of order that are brought into contiguity in the *bilangue:* the systematized order of convention (dot), the open-ended order of the supernatural or nonconventional (dash)?

The protagonist learns, we are told, that all languages are bilingual, "oscillating between the spoken portion and another, which both affirms and destroys itself in the incommunicable" (20). Khatibi bases his creation of a postcolonial language expressive of his desires and concerns on this midground, on the paradox of a language balanced between the communicable and the incommunicable. Like the Beckettian narrator who experiences failure in face of the language, the postcolonial writer makes of that failure the basis for a new idiom.[17] Except that, contrary to Beckett, namelessness (the impossibility of a name) is not solely the source of pain but fascination and salvation as well—"What fascinated him [the narrator-protagonist], attracted as he was by the no-name, was this utopia and this void which, erasing their sources, wanted to be this grace of the unnameable, this charm of forgetting. He admired this stupifying illusion that battled reality" (27). Elsewhere he says, "I name myself in two languages in unnaming myself; I unname myself in telling my story. Speaking in this no-name sense, the body experiences pleasure in outbursts of rage, in breakup" (79). The process of "unnaming" is valorized: "She appeared, on her part, to savor that loss of name, to draw new strength from it" (omitted from the English translation, 25; cf. 42).

The fact that the love object, the woman, is often confounded with language, makes us acutely aware of the processes by which the *bilangue* functions. The narrator says that "that which I desired in her was reversed in me: love's mirror, so they say" (64), leaving us to scan this thought in terms of language and its reversal, its transformation into a discourse of the other. Mere reversal is not the technique utilized by Khatibi and ben Jelloun, however, but rather a depositioning of discourse whereby all discourses lose position, are put on the same level. Khatibi's narrator says, "I'm aiming at something else in the incalculable, this ordeal of the unthought-of, which accepts and refuses all categories of thought, without either nullifying or uniting them, and which ceases transmitting anything at all" (108). He seeks a *pensée-autre*, an other-thought, by which equalities, equivalences, and dialectical pairs (beloved/lover, angel/demon, 108) become unclassifiable. "Yes, the end of any hierarchy like this was the resolve of this other-thought, naked and explosive" (108–9).

The creation of a *pensée-autre* has been a strong concern of Khatibi. In a chapter on that subject in *Multiple Maghreb* (*Maghreb pluriel*, 11–39), he proposes a rethinking, a decentering, a subversion of the *dehors* (the "outside")—Europe and the West—to turn it from its dominating determinations, in order to develop a linguistic, cultural and political pluralism that is non-Western. The *pensée-autre* he proposes would build on its very marginality and poverty because "a thought that is not inspired by its own poverty is always elaborated with the purpose of dominating and humiliating; a thought that is not of the minority, marginal, fragmented and unfinished, is always a thought of ethnocide" (18). Khatibi argues for "a pluralistic thought that does not reduce others (societies and individuals) to the sphere of its own sufficiency" (18).

The *pensée-autre* presents the basis for a new literature. At one point the narrator-protagonist of *Love in Two Languages* asks, "Literature? Why not? Let's agree, nothing is to be condemned! An other-literature according to thinking that is no less other, right up to the end of time" (the English translation leaves out the phrase "rien n'est condamnable, voyons!" 118).

In a postface written for Khatibi's *Tatooed Memory* (*La Mémoire tatouée*), Roland Barthes speaks of the interest he shared with Khatibi in images, signs, traces, letters, and marks. "And at the same time, because he shifts these categories as I conceive them, because he carries me to his realm, away from myself, to my very limits, Khatibi teaches me something new, shakes me up in my own knowledge." Barthes acknowledges the former's contribution to his awareness of the degree to which the Western semiotic enterprise "has remained the prisoner of the categories of the Universal that regulate, in the West, since Aristotle, every method." And he tells how he formerly believed that he was postulating a general truth, a universal human identity, whereas it was a truth applying only to the cultural identity of his own country—not a "popular" culture, but a culture "fashioned by successive waves of rationalism, democracy, mass communication" (214).

Khatibi's originality, according to Barthes, lies in the fact that he proposes to "rediscover at the same time identity and difference: an identity of such a pure metal, so incandescent that it obliges us to read it as difference." [18] The narrative of Khatibi's fellow countryman, ben Jelloun, turns as well on the inseparability of identity and difference, a mark of postcoloniality, of the magical real that characterizes the discourse of certain African authors.

Tahar ben Jelloun's narrative interweaves two non-Western intertexts: the writings of Jorge Luis Borges and the Persian *Alf Layla wa Layla* or *A Thousand and One Nights*.[19] Borges' fictional embodiment appearing in *The Sand Child* in the character of the Blind Troubadour, a blindman who "sees," and *A Thousand and One Nights* with its storyteller who does not finish, exemplify in turn the silenced voices of the non-Western other (the non-Greek, the *metoikoi*) that "speak" and the discourse or narrative without end. These intertexts will serve as touchstones to discuss how the magical realist discourse of ben Jelloun counters the system of traditional Western narrative by rejecting the reductive ideology underlying it and speaks essentially to non-Western concerns.[20]

One of a procession of storytellers in *The Sand Child*, the Blind Troubadour (BT) relates in chapter 17 how he has set out in search of an Arab woman of mysterious origin who visited him in his library in Buenos Aires. His narration begins fairly straightforwardly but soon undergoes permutations and shifts that make it difficult to identify the speaker, becoming at times so entangled that it is nearly impossible to decipher. In chapter 18, for example, we encounter a confusing, discontinuous narrative that appears to be a dream narrative, whose central character is a male (masculine agreements in French). Interpretations proliferate as we try to locate the source of the dream: the possibility arises that (1) the BT relates the dream of the mysterious woman in which he is dreamt by the character, that (2) the dream related is a direct retelling by the BT of his own dream, that (3) he and the mysterious woman are indistinguishable, that (4) the narrative alludes to more than one dream (perhaps to both his and hers), that (5) the narrative relates her dream of herself, that (6) everything is encompassed within a dream in which the BT dreams of her and her recitation of a dream, that (7) the dream is by neither him nor her but yet a third person, etc.

The narrative here as elsewhere conjoins the threads of all these possibilities, resulting in an antilogical discourse in the sense G. B. Kerford gives to it, as consisting "in causing the same thing to be seen by the same people now as possessing one predicate and now as possessing the opposite or contradictory predicate." [21] Its structure resembles that of the medina described in the dream itself: "The medina presented itself to my eyes as an entanglement of places — streets and squares — where all miracles were possible" (192). Like the air space Rushdie describes in *The Satanic Verses* as a "defining location" where anything is possible, the medina serves ben Jelloun as a metaphor for the magical space of postcolonial narrative.

The BT's tale reflects two processes integral to the narrative of ben Jelloun: (1) the interpenetration of characters/narrators/authors and (2) the folding into itself of the narrative, whereby the external becomes internal, the outside/inside become reversed.

In regard to the first process, numerous instances of the interpenetration of separate narrative realms occur in *The Sand Child*, such as the declaration of the storyteller Fatouma that she lost the "great notebook," tried vainly to reconstruct it, and set forth in search of the narrative of her former life, which she found being told by the principal storyteller, called the *conteur*, in the great square. The revelation of Fatouma's identity as the central character Ahmed/Zahra introduces the anomaly of a second-level (intradiegetic) narrator simultaneously fulfilling the role of a third-level (metadiegetic) character.

It is with the appearance of the BT, however, whose intrusion in the tale takes up some twenty pages, that the most curious instances of interpenetration of narrative levels come to light. From the outset the text signals our initiation into a quixotic game by the words of the stranger (the BT) who joins the storytellers Ahmed and Salem: "The Secret is Sacred but is always somewhat ridiculous" (171), for the stranger draws this sentence word for word from Borges' short story, "The Sect of the Phoenix," and studiously encloses it in quotation marks. [22] Several allusions in the pages that follow link the BT to the historical Borges: his blindness and vocation as a writer, his life in Buenos Aires, knowledge of Spanish, livelihood as a librarian, his mention of the character Stephen Albert in Borges' "The Garden of Forking Paths" as being one of his characters (181), his allusion to an unnamed story from which he cites a passage (Borges' "The Circular Ruins"), references to the zahir, a coin that gives its name to one of Borges' stories, and his preponderant interest in esoterica. Yet, in ben Jelloun's anomalistic presentation, nothing is ever certain, for it concurrently offers many allusions that problematize the BT's identity.

In addressing the storytellers Amar and Salem, the BT speaks of being in their "story," of coming from afar, "from another century, poured into one tale by another tale" (172), of having been "expulsed" from other stories (172). He describes himself as passing between dreams. Places, like dreams, become not only interchangeable but exist simultaneously and within each other just as the tales within tales. He speaks of their frequenting a cafe in Marrakech while at the same time finding themselves in the heart of Buenos Aires! During the visit of the mysterious woman to his library in the latter city, he tells of having had the sensation of being a character in a book, even of being a book (177–78). The woman presents a letter of introduction from one of his (Borges') own characters, Stephen Albert. Her voice recalls to him a voice he had previously heard in a book he had read—the voice of Tawaddud in *A Thousand and One Nights.*

The BT operates on multiple levels: a fictional replication of the historical author Jorge Luis Borges, he functions as one of the second-level (intradiegetic) narrators and is in that role a character in the tale of the first-level (extradiegetic) narrator; he functions also on various metadiegetic levels in his direct interaction with the character of the mysterious woman who visits him and his participation as character in other stories (including his own and *A Thousand and One Nights*). The pivotal figure of the mysterious woman visitor, while on the same narrative level as the BT, bears strong resemblances to the principal character Zahra, raised in male disguise under the name of Ahmed. The BT describes her as "a character or rather an enigma, two faces of a selfsame being" (178). He refers to her as being from Morocco (184). We learn at the end of the narrative, taken up again and ended by the *conteur* [storyteller], however, that Ahmed/Zahra is a fictional representation invented by the storyteller and adapted to a Moroccan setting to tell the story of an Alexandrian woman's uncle, Bey Ahmed, who had undergone similar experiences (207–8).

The BT, who brings outside inside, is also the device whereby outside/ inside (Bey Ahmed-Ahmed/Zahra) displaces levels of discourse, whereby characters are put on the same level as their creators and vice versa. The most extreme instance of movement from one narrative level to another occurs when the BT speaks of himself as coming from and having lived a story whose concluding words he cites—it is a Borges story entitled "The Circular Ruins." Those words, which he says may help to unravel the enigma that unites him with the other narrators, describe a character, a magician awaiting death, who, desiring to dream into being a man, comes to understand that "he too was a mere appearance, dreamt by another" (BJ 173; Borges 50). The dream related in chapter 18 leaves us to speculate that the BT also may be dreamt by another, by Zahra, the character of another storyteller, and that he might consequently inhabit a still more remote level—a meta-meta-metadiegetic level![23]

What purpose does this interpenetration of narrative levels serve? It pushes illogic and contradiction to the limit and throws into doubt the certainty of the representation itself. It refuses the reader the possibility of getting a fix on the narrators and characters, of making the story intelligible with relation to fixed reference points. The BT—referred to repeatedly as the "stranger," of foreign origin, whose tale turns on encounter, loss, and unending quest for a mysterious woman of Arabic origin—is homologous with the North African, at once subject of his or her proper narratives and object-Other (shadow without substance) of the narratives of Western society, recounting his/her "tale" in the language of another, menaced with the loss of his/her own culture and existence.

The description by the *conteur* [storyteller] in the opening paragraph of *The Sand Child* of "the veil of flesh that maintained between him [Ahmed/Zahra] and others the necessary distance" adumbrates the movement of the narrative and articulates the development of narrators and characters. It valorizes, moreover, the positive potential of alterity with regard to the Maghrebian writers themselves. The distancing veil of flesh symbolizes a protective covering that allows them to lead their own existence equidistant from sameness (assimilation) and otherness (alienation), to exist in the face of the power play of Western culture as well as traditional Islamic culture.

Rather than action in *The Sand Child* becoming in Jamesian terms an illustration of character, ben Jelloun's narrators/characters may be viewed as subserving the action, such that we encounter what Tzvetan Todorov has called an a-psychological narrative.[24] Considered grammatologically, by valorizing the predicate rather than the subject of the verb, by emphasizing intransitive action—even to the extent of threatening a loss of the psychological coherence of character—a-psychological narrative throws into relief the *event itself.* Historical process is replaced by a sequence of events. The character becomes thereby "a virtual (potential) story that is the story of his life. Every new character signifies a new story. We are in the realm of narrative-men" (Todorov 82). In *The Sand Child*, a story of a woman masquerading as a man, we encounter narrative-(wo)men whose loss of psychological coherence is vital to the reversal of roles or rather the leveling of sexual differences. The story of Ahmed/Zahra told by ben Jelloun's succession of characters/narrators exhibits a variable relationship with preceding stories, which are always under revision, just as on the discursive level we observe a plan of unending revision.

The second process integral to *The Sand Child*, the folding into itself of the narrative, results from the type of operation described by Todorov. This process resembles the device of *enchâssement* or embedding found in *A Thousand and One Nights*, where the narrative, passing through several degrees of embedding, ends by the embedding story (Scheherazade) embedding itself. As Borges points out,

> None [no interpolation in *A Thousand and One Nights*] is more perturbing than that of the six hundred and second night, magical among all the nights. On that night, the king hears from the queen his own story. He hears the beginning of the story, which comprises all the others and also — monstrously — itself. Does the reader clearly grasp the vast possibility of this interpolation, the curious danger? That the queen may persist and the motionless king hear forever the truncated story of the *Thousand and One Nights*, now infinite and circular.[25]

Ben Jelloun carries narrative enclosure to its remotest reaches by embedding stories within stories to such a degree that levels meld, barriers separating characters and creators/storytellers are breached and become traversable, fused, confused, narrators/characters pass freely from one level to another, move in and out of stories without impingement, just as we move in and out of dreams and in and out of the characters themselves. As the storyteller says: "it is useful to know that in every story there exist entryways and exits" (49). In fact, openings abound in *The Sand Child*: doors, gates, entryways, exits, windows, shutters — openings that may become closings; just as other objects serve dually to protect or enclose: walls, rooms, hedges, etc. On one level, they signify the disparity between the male and female condition: Ahmed tells her father that her condition (of male) opens up doors for her (50), for in Islamic society the male can move freely, whereas the movement of women is sharply circumscribed by walls and closed doors. Even on the level of storytelling, a narrator such as ben Jelloun's can move malelike in and out of stories, while women such as Zahra or Scheherazade must create stratagems to preserve themselves while making use of the sole (male) narrative available to them.

The Sand Child is a discourse or narrative without end, that folds into itself. The secret of the subject's identity posed at the beginning of the narrative was said to be found in the "great notebook" possessed by the storyteller — "there, in these pages, woven out of syllables and images" (12). We should indeed have been forewarned, for the secret was after all purely one of language: Ahmed at one point reveals his paper identity as he speaks of himself as being enclosed in an image (54); another time the storyteller speaks of the story as a blindman's dance in which one could fall at any moment, held up only by a few commas inserted by God (ostensibly the author) (65); finally, the storyteller describes his story in theatrical terms — "Companions! The stage set is made out of paper! The story I recount to you is old wrapping paper" (126). The narrative is indeed susceptible to all the vagaries of language under the pen of the author, whom one of his own narrators (the BT) calls "a contrebandist, a trafficker in words" (173; the BT designates himself as "a falsifier . . . the biographer of error and falsehood"). At its end, the instability of the narrative that has all along haunted us leaves its final mark: we are told that "the book was emptied of its writings by the full moon" (208–9), washed clean, ready to be written over and over, endlessly. (A cluster of such metaphors of erasure or illegibility appears: the great notebook made undecipherable by tears shed on it [54]; letters whose signature is unreadable [59]; Ahmed's "petits billets" that are illegible or "strange" [89]; the crossed-out words in the anonymous correspondent's notes [96]; the carrying off of words and images by insects from the manuscript in disintegration, a process hastened by the stream that runs through its pages [107–9]; the mirror of Zahra that fogs over [115]; etc.).

In her notebook, Ahmed/Zahra describes her visit as a small child with her mother to the women's *hammam* (public bath). In a passage reminiscent of Rabelais' thawing words in *The Fourth Book* (*Le Quart Livre*), she describes the words of the women rising to the ceiling of the *hammam* and dripping on her, like drops of water — disincarnated speech, creating "a strange discourse": "The ceiling was like a slate or a writing board. Everything that was drawn on it was not necessarily intelligible" (33–36). The description recalls the electronic writing machine described by a character in *The Time of Tamango* (*Le Temps de Tamango*, 1981) by the Senegalese novelist Boubacar Boris Diop, programmed to erase the cries of revolt and hate of the populace. Just as Diop (whose own magical realism is consciously inspired by Gabriel García Márquez) transforms this totalitarian machine into a metaphor for oppositional narrative that itself transforms the Master's speech, so the motifs of the *hammam* ceiling and writing over reflect the postcolonialist author's store of magic that converts the resources of the oppressor's language into devices for linguistic liberation. The BT, as spokesman for the latter, says that he has spent all his life in opposing "the force of the real and imaginary, the visible and hidden world" by the power of words: "I have to say that I took greater pleasure in adventuring into dream and the invisible than in that which appeared to me violent, physical, limited" (181).

Such motifs, along with the inevitable destabilizing of personages and objects, of temporal and spatial demarcations, the unhinging of the narrative from sequential progression, the digressions and series of metamorphoses that blur distinctions and transform things, the strings of surreal images — often bathe ben Jelloun's narrative in a hallucinatory light. Ben Jelloun's is a world in which fantasy and reality, the supernatural and the empirical, coexist in an antinomical interfacing that marks his special brand of magical realism and, more generally, the alternative postcolonial discourse of the "non-Greeks," the *metoikos*, the *métèques*.

The structure of ben Jelloun's narrative, an avatar of that of *A Thousand and One Nights*, resembles the invaginated structure of which Derrida speaks in regard to Blanchot's *The Madness of the Day* (*La Folie du jour*)[26] — a structure to which I prefer to give the term involuted, which recalls its Latin root *involvere*, implying not solely hidden involvement but being rolled inward at the edges, like a conch in which the whorls are wound tightly around an axis that is concealed. The pauses between different storytellers (second-level narrators), which indicates a provisional end and a provisionally new beginning, may be seen as inner whorls or folds of this structure (see Derrida 114).

By the reversible inside/outside maneuvers of his writing, ben Jelloun literally and literarily turns inside out the traditional Western narrative and, by extension, the relation of power between the West and the so-called Third World. Through just such devices as the interpenetration of narrative levels and the transformation of the tale into an event without end, which plunge us into a realm of magical realism where the skin of empirical reality is perforated by supernatural eruptions, the discrete elements of the traditional narrative disintegrate; it is reconfigured from a contiguous structure into a magical narrative of substitution, reconstituted out of the very flaws and imperfections that exist in the systems it counters. This tactic of ben Jelloun, to which I have elsewhere given the name leveling, deprives the discourse of power of its positional value, exposes the arbitrary nature of the underlying philosophical precepts that legitimate it, and reveals it as just one discourse among many.[27]

Derrida's description of a text applies admirably well to the type of text we encounter in *The Sand Child:*

> what I still call a "text," for strategic reasons . . . —a "text" that is henceforth no longer a finished corpus of writing, some content enclosed in a book or its margins, but a differential network, a fabric of traces referring endlessly to something other than itself, to other differential traces. Thus the text overruns all the limits assigned to it so far, . . . everything that was to be set up in opposition to writing (speech, life, the world, the real, history, and what not, every field of reference—to body or mind, conscious or unconscious, politics, economics, and so forth). (Derrida 84)

The inside/outside text of *The Sand Child* is indeed constructed around a network of differential traces. Each story or narrative segment contains traces of that which has preceded as well as of that to come, such that no story or segment is identical to itself but always somewhere else, present and absent simultaneously, never where or what it appears to be. The result is a narrative that teeters on that edge of indeterminacy to which I alluded earlier. The spillover of ben Jelloun's narrative discourse holds no respect for margins, frames, or partitions, as it sets about to break down the "structures of resistance" of ideological and literary systems that attempt to assign limits to our thought. It represents a challenge to the reader to follow—a narrative whose very losses are its gains. Indeed, by virtue of these bizarre tactics, it stands as an example of writing in the magical realist framework of the so-called emergent cultures that succeeds in creating an effective narrative to counter the ideological forces at work in the European idiom in which it is cast.

The discursive operation of *The Sand Child* has strong affinities with the work of certain experimental novelists in France, such as Claude Simon, as well as with the work of other postcolonialist authors from Africa and the Caribbean. One calls to mind such narratives as the Tunisian Abdel-wahab Meddeb's *Phantasia* (1986), the Congolese Tchicaya U Tam'Si's *The Madman and the Medusa* (*Les Méduses, ou les orties de la mer,* 1982), the Guadeloupian Daniel Maximim's *Lone Sun* (*L'Isolé soleil,* 1979), or the Martinican Edouard Glissant's *Mahogony* (*Mahagany,* 1987). It calls to mind as well the works of several other postcolonial authors writing in languages of European origin, such as Salman Rushdie, Gabriel García Márquez, Julio Cortázar, and Carlos Fuentes. Of particular note among similar narrative projects is, as we have seen, the work of ben Jelloun's countryman Abdelkebir Khatibi.

In sum, Khatibi's and ben Jelloun's magical narrative structures and their manner of elaboration reflect the goal of the postcolonial African writer to rewrite the language of the oppressor by effacing all metanarratives and beginning again and to replace the pseudo-African (neocolonialist) discourse of the African leaders with an African discourse. African post-colonialist writing, north and south of the Sahara, through the type of leveling discourse we have seen, through the thinking of the "unthought-of" that rejects categories of Western thought "without either nullifying or uniting them," from a Western perspective ceasing to transmit anything at all, as Khatibi says, is in the process of constituting an other-literature out of the shards and laminae of colonialist and neocolonialist discourse. One form of narrative renewal has been the introduction of the sort of magical realism we have observed in Tahar ben Jelloun's *The Sand Child* and Abdelkebir Khatibi's *Love in Two Languages.* In the byzantine world of those narratives contradictory predicates (not necessarily opposites) co-habit, without being nullified or united, in an antinomical, magical reality standing outside of or apart from and rejecting categories of binary reasoning and rhetoric that inhere in Western thought. "I must definitely have my story translated into Braille," Khatibi's narrator tells us, "before the computer has swept up everything into the communicable" (24). We re-call the translation machine to which he sarcastically alludes (49). These machines approximate the totalitarian machines of Huxley, Orwell, and Gilliam's *Brazil,* or Diop's electronic machine—all instruments of reduction by either/or categories. Such machines are but avatars of the magisterial language itself, which must be turned against itself.

The late Tchicaya U Tam'Si, novelist and poet from the People's Republic of the Congo, expressed in an interview his desire to pursue in his writings the operation of what he called the Manichean and the unreality (*irréel*) he saw as underlying African culture.[28] The Tunisian Abdelwahab Meddeb, in *Phantasia*, speaks of his own brand of magical realism, like Khatibi's obsessed with "images, signs, traces, letters, and marks," which incessantly short circuits the logic of the Master's discourse: "I construct figures and exile them from the events which they have brought about. And I put them on stage in the capacity of signs. I subvert history as chronicle and I rather propose clairvoyance."[29] He adds, "We stride in ancient footsteps. The earth resonates beneath our feet. We move toward uncharted realms. On the dunes or at sea, the footsteps disappear as soon as they are made."

The phenomenon of making the incommunicable, the unthought-of, the unfinished, the basis of a new discourse, I see as a special version of an African magical realism observable in varying measure in postcolonial African authors like Meddeb, Diop, and Tchicaya. This phenomenon links their discourse, along with that of ben Jelloun and Khatibi, to postcolonial discourse of writers from other non-Western cultures, striving to create a discourse in which, as Barthes says of Khatibi, identity is read as difference.

Notes

1 Edwin Williamson, "Magical Realism and the Theme of Incest in *One Hundred Years of Solitude*," in *Gabriel García Márquez, New Readings*, ed. Bernard McGuirk and Richard Cardwell (Cambridge: Cambridge University Press, 1987), p. 45.

2 A. Valbueno Briones, "Una cala en el realismo mágico," *Cuadernos Americanos* 166, 5 (Sept.–Oct. 1969): 236.

3 Gregson Davis, trans. and intro., *Non-Vicious Circle: Twenty Poems of Aimé Césaire* (Stanford: Stanford University Press, 1984). Critics have also seen the phenomenon of magical realism in Western authors such as Kafka and Proust. See, for instance, Angel Flores, "Magical Realism in Spanish American Fiction," *Hispania* 38, 2 (May 1955): 187–92, reprinted in this volume.

4 I apply the term postcolonial in contradistinction to colonial and neocolonial. It is perhaps the least value-laden term, unlike the terms "Third-World," "emergent," or "Francophone," as applied to culture/literature, terms all defining a hierarchy in which the metropole occupies a privileged position. For

me, the term postcolonial will denote a cultural counterdiscourse expressive of a struggle consciously undertaken by the writer against the controlling norms of the dominant culture/discourse, whether indigenous or Western.

5 To distinguish among these terms and to define magical realism, I have found useful the work of Amaryll Beatrice Chanady, *Magical Realism and the Fantastic: Resolved Versus Unresolved Antimony* (New York & London: Garland Publishing, 1985).

6 Roger Caillois, *Anthologie du fantastique* (Paris: Gallimard, 1966), 1: 8.

7 Tzvetan Todorov, *Introduction à la littérature fantastique* (Paris: Editions du Seuil, 1970), p. 29. (*The Fantastic: A Structural Approach to a Literary Genre,* tr. Richard Howard [Cornell University Press, 1975]).

8 Irène Bessière, *Le Récit fantastique: La poétique de l'incertain* (Paris: Librairie Larousse, 1974), p. 57.

9 Lyotard's concept of paralogism is expressed throughout his work. Khatibi's notion of the "bilangue" is perhaps best exemplified in *Maghreb pluriel* (Paris: Denoël, 1983) and in his novel *Amour bilingue* (n.p. [Montpelier]: Fata Morgana, 1983). Translations from the former work of Khatibi are mine. Translations from the latter are drawn from the English translation of Richard Howard, *Love in Two Languages* (Minneapolis: University of Minnesota Press, 1990).

10 I have changed the translator's "extravaganza" to "enchantment," which more closely renders the meaning of the original: "toute cette féerie très réelle."

11 See Plato, *Cratylus,* in *The Works of Plato* (London: Henry G. Bohn, 1850), 3: 283–395. Cratylus, who maintains that names derive from the inherent characteristics of a person or object, sustains his naturalist theory against his opponent Hermogenes who argues that names derive from a conventionally agreed upon nomination (the conventionalist theory). Genette proposes yet a third position, held by Socrates and located somewhere between the two latter. See Gérard Genette, "L'éponymie du nom," in *Mimologiques: Voyage en Cratylie* (Paris: Seuil, 1976).

12 In *La Mémoire tatouée,* Khatibi says, "In rereading myself, I discover that my most finished (French) sentence is a calling to mind. The calling to mind of an unpronounceable entity, neither Arab nor French, neither dead nor living, neither man nor woman: generation of the text. Wandering topology, schizoidal state, androgynous dream, loss of identity—on the threshold of madness." (Paris: Union Générale d'Editions, 1979 [ed. Denoël, 1972], p. 207, my translation.)

13 Michel Serres, *Le Parasite* (Paris: Grasset, 1980), p. 22. My translation.

14 Jacques Derrida, "La loi du genre," *Glyph* 7 (1980): 178 [176–210]. My translation.

15 Mallarmé spoke of "alternate languages, purer, more rigorous, [that] flourish at increasing distances from or below the surface of common discourse." Cited

by George Steiner, *After Babel: Aspects of Language and Translation* (New York & London: Oxford University Press, 1975), p. 181.

16 Plato, *The Symposium*, trans. W. Hamilton (1951; Harmondsworth, Middlesex: Penguin Books, 1962), pp. 59–65.

17 Samuel Beckett stated to Georges Duthuit that it is the very absence of relation "between the artist and the occasion" that he wished to make the subject of his art. It is up to the modern artist "to make of this submission, this fidelity to failure, a new occasion, a new term of relation, and of the act which, unable to act, obliged to act, he makes an expressive act, even if only of itself, of its impossibility, of its obligation." Samuel Beckett and Georges Duthuit, *Three Dialogues*, vol. 3, "Bram Van Velde," *Transition forty-nine* 5 (Dec. 1949). Rpt. in *Samuel Beckett: A Collection of Critical Essays*, ed. Martin Esslin (Englewood Cliffs, N.J.: Prentice-Hall, 1965). *Transition*, p. 103; Esslin, p. 21.

18 Roland Barthes, Postface, "Ce que je dois à Khatibi" (What I owe to Khatibi), Khatibi, *La Mémoire tatouée*, pp. 213–14. The translation of the first sentence in these two paragraphs is taken from the back cover of *Love in Two Languages*.

19 Tahar ben Jelloun, *L'Enfant de sable* (Paris: Seuil, 1985). An English translation by Alan Sheridan, *The Sand Child*, is available (New York: Harcourt Brace Jovanovich, 1987), but I choose to use my own.

20 For an extended discussion of the role of the Blind Troubadour in *The Sand Child* in terms of political narrative, see my article, "Writing Double: Politics and the African Narrative of French Expression," *Studies in 20th Century Literature* 15, 1 (Winter 1991): 101–22.

21 G. B. Kerford, "Dialectic, Antilogic and Eristic," in *The Sophist Movement* (Cambridge: Cambridge University Press, 1981), p. 61.

22 Jorge Luis Borges, "The Sect of the Phoenix," in *Labyrinths, Selected Stories & Other Writings* (New York: New Directions, 1964), p. 103. This volume contains as well the other stories on which ben Jelloun draws: "The Garden of Forking Paths," "The Circular Ruins," and "The Zahir." English translations in my text, of phrases rummaged by ben Jelloun from Borges' stories, come from the New Directions volume.

23 "I had frequented her [the unknown woman] in books and dream. . . . I was no longer the same. I had just engaged my entire being in a system [*un engrenage*]. . . . That's how I am closed up in this room [his library] with a character or rather an enigma. . . . I was that old man, prisoner of a character whom I would have been able to create." *L'Enfant de sable*, pp. 178–79, my translation.

For the terminology describing the operation of this interpenetration or movement from one level of narrative to another, see Genette's description of *metalepses*, particularly the *metalepse de l'auteur* (authorial metalepsis) where we see an "intrusion of the extradiegetic narrator or narrataire into the diegetic universe (or of the diegetic person into a metadiegetic universe, etc.) or, inversely, as in the case of Cortázar." Gérard Genette, *Figures III* (Paris: Seuil, 1972), p. 244. (*Figures 3: Figures of Literary Discourse*, vols. 1–3 [New York: Columbia University Press, 1982]).

24 Tzvetan Todorov, "Les hommes récits," in *Poétique de la prose* (Paris: Seuil, 1971), pp. 78–79. My translation. (*The Poetics of Prose*, trans. Richard Howard [Cornell University Press, 1977]).

25 Cited by Todorov, p. 84. The English translation in my text is that of James E. Irby, from "Partial Magic in the *Quixote*" in Jorge Luis Borges, *Labyrinths*, p. 195.

26 Jacques Derrida, "Living On: *Border Lines*," trans. James Hulbert, in Harold Bloom et al., *Deconstruction and Criticism* (New York: Seabury Press, 1979), p. 97.

27 Cf. Jean-François Lyotard, "Sur la Force des faibles," *L'Arc* 64 (1976): 6. "Now the eccentricities of these mad Cynics, of these wild Megarites, of these Sophist clowns, will constitute no school . . . : they are exteriorized like slaves, like women, like barbarians, like children who are excluded from the citizenry, from Hellenity, from viril homosexuality. But for them this outside is not an outside, because the last place, the last word, the ultimate referent, the absolute — have, to be sure, no positional value. For them, there is no outside, because there is no inside, no *en-soi:* the *en-soi* as pretended interiority immediately falls into exteriority. There is only exteriority. Or better, there is exteriority."

28 Interview with Eric Sellin, quoted in Preface to Tchicaya's *The Madman and the Medusa* (Charlottesville: University Press of Virginia, 1989), p. xli.

29 Abdelwahab Meddeb, *Phantasia* (Paris: Editions Sindbad, 1986), p. 45. I have used the translation of Eric Sellin in his relevant and stimulating essay, "Obsession with the White Page, the Inability to Communicate, and Surface Aesthetics in the Development of Contemporary Maghrebian Fiction: The *mal de la page blanche* in Khatibi, Farès, and Meddeb," *International Journal of Middle East Studies* 20 (1988): 171.

SUSAN J. NAPIER

The Magic of Identity: Magic Realism
in Modern Japanese Fiction

Akutagawa Ryunosuke's 1920 short story "The Nose" (*Hana*) concerns
an old priest in ancient Japan with an embarrassing problem: his nose is
ridiculously, unbelievably, long. Although he realizes that he should be
above such mundane matters, the priest feels humiliated by the mockery
of others and tries a variety of remedies, eventually succeeding in shrinking his nose down to normal size. Surprisingly, the priest soon finds himself wishing for his old nose again, as everyone mocks him all the more in
his new improved condition. One day he wakes up to find a miracle has
occurred: his nose has returned to its old larger shape. Satisfied, he whispers to himself "Now no one will laugh at me any more," his nose blowing
softly in the breeze.

"The Nose" is an early but classic story by Akutagawa, one of the most
brilliant and versatile of Japan's fantasy writers: it delivers a matter-of-
factly surreal world in compact form with a distinctive twist that turns our
expectations upside down at the end. Also typical of Akutagawa's work, it
is closely based on an old tale, in this case from the tenth-century collection, the *Konjaku monogatari*. In fact, Akutagawa changes relatively little
of the original text. His greatest alteration is simply to allow the reader to
see the tale through a modern sensibility, as Borges' Pierre Menard is said
to do with *Don Quixote*.

It is this implicit modern sensibility, on the part of both writer and
reader, that makes the story a key example for the purpose of this chapter, making it possible to include it under the category of "magic realism."
Rather than dwelling on the fantastic quality of the nose or its miraculous recovery, Akutagawa's text takes the supernatural for granted and
spends more of its space exploring the gamut of human reactions, from
the mockery of those around the priest, to the priest's own unexpected

disappointment in his newly normal nose. The use of the supernatural and the story's basis in an old tale is also typical of Akutagawa. But it is the variety and often contradictory quality of human emotions explored by the narrative that makes the story both memorable and modern. The story's ending, what might be called the Akutagawan twist, is also "modern," with its ironic focus that is ultimately realistic rather than escapist.

"The Nose" also exemplifies more general aspects of Japanese fantastic fiction and, indeed, of Japanese fiction overall. As in Gogol's "The Nose," from which to some extent it derives, the priest's nose is linked to his identity.[1] (In fact, when referring to themselves, Japanese people tend to point to the nose.) In Akutagawa's story this nose/identity is not so much lost as radically changed, forced to be something that it is not. The priest's unease is hardly surprising, therefore: not only he, but everyone else, is aware that the normal nose is not his "real" nose.

Allied with this theme of an uneasy new identity is the nose's changing shape, a metamorphosis from grotesque to normal to grotesque again. This negative and in some ways meaningless (as in having no overtly teleological or allegorical function) metamorphosis is, as Rosemary Jackson points out, a process peculiar to modern fantasy, where "there are no delightful transformations . . . changes are without meaning and progressively without will or desire of the subject."[2] Ironically, it is the priest's pathetic attempt to "will" transformation to normality that ends badly. Only when he accepts his passive state in relation to the forces outside him does the nose miraculously return.

This theme of a constantly and negatively shifting form of identity is a fundamental one in modern Japanese literature, and one that is particularly suited to the genre of the fantastic. What the writer Natsume Soseki described as essentially a "national nervous breakdown" is perhaps an extreme metaphor, but it gives some indication of the enormity and suddenness of the changes since the Meiji Restoration in 1868 opened Japan to the West. Needless to say, Japan's "identity crisis" vis-à-vis the West and modernity is hardly unique among non-Western nations. What is unique, however, is that Japan, unlike virtually any other non-Western nation, was never colonized by Europe. Its development of a new, "modern" identity was implemented by its own leaders under the slogan "Civilization and Enlightenment."

The motivations behind this government-sponsored development program are complex. They range from an eminently rational fear of Western domination, based on the tragic example of Western imperialism in China, to what might be called an inferiority/superiority complex that led to an obsessive desire to beat the West at its own game by transforming Japan into a first rate capitalist power. Modern Japan has undeniably accomplished that goal but, at least in the eyes of many of its intellectuals, only at the cost of transforming itself into a country where outside harmony hides a variety of interior grotesques. To many writers and intellectuals, modern Japanese culture is a culture whose identity has been warped and transmogrified, not by outside pressures so much as by its own response to outside pressures.[3]

Nowhere is this problematic process of transformation more clearly etched than in the fantasy literature of modern Japan, not only in its content but in the formal history of its existence over the last hundred years. This is a period in which fantasy went from a genre that at the turn of the century was ignored or made light of as being old fashioned, even embarrassing, to the post-war years where some of the best of contemporary Japan's writers routinely create their own form of magic realism to describe a Japan that mimetic fiction can no longer encapsulate.

To trace the history of magic realism in Japan is thus to comment both on the development of Japanese fiction in general and on the changing notions of the Japanese identity over the last century. In their introduction to *Magic Realist Fiction*, Hollaman and Young suggest that one of magic realism's "crucial features" is its duality, the provocative and unsettling tension between real and unreal.[4] The history of Japanese fiction since the Meiji Restoration in 1868 has also been based on a duality—a conflict between the Western-inspired dominant literary current of naturalism and the various fictional reactions against it. This duality can be read initially in terms of "modern" vs. "traditional," as we will see in our discussion of turn-of-the-century writer Izumi Kyoka, whose fantastic fiction was disparaged as old fashioned by naturalist writers. As time went on, however, this tension was complicated by both the Japanese version of naturalism and the reactions against it.

Naturalism's doctrine of a brutally objective, "scientific" analysis initially seemed to liberate Japanese writers from the baroquely fantastic melodramas that had characterized literature before the Restoration. In the long run, however, naturalism created its own stranglehold on Japanese fiction, especially in the peculiarly Japanese form of the *shishosetsu* or "I novel," a confessional work where literary merit was usually subordinated to the perceived "truthfulness" of the often minute details of the protagonist's life.[5] Such a claustrophobic form of literature inevitably spawned reactions against it, ranging over a considerable amount of literary territory, from proletarian novels to neoromantic works.

It is increasingly being recognized, however, that some of the most intriguing and significant literary reactions against naturalism have been in the realm of fantastic literature. Indeed, a surprising number of Japan's greatest writers, including those famous for their powerful mimetic portrayals of modernizing Japan, also used the genre of the fantastic to create visions of a chaotic, fascinating, occasionally marvelous, but more frequently uncanny, fictional world. Such works were even more memorable than their mimetic fictions.

Not all of the fantastic literature written since Japan's opening to the West can be encompassed under the term "magic realism," but enough of it plays on the intersection between the magic and the real to make it a meaningful category. This essay examines some of the most important of Japan's "magical realist" writers, from the early twentieth century to the present. Although the writers' approaches and results differ considerably, certain key elements remain in common.

One of the most important is also the most general: the fact that the use of the fantastic implies, at some level, the rejection of the real, or at least the rejection of the discourse of realism as the only way of depicting the world. Sometimes this rejection can be overt within the narrative, as when Izumi Kyoka's fantastic characters avenge themselves on the unbelieving modern philistines who have abandoned them. In more recent fiction the rejection may be buried within the surrealist confines of the text itself, as in Abe Kobo's despairing vision of a world so bizarre that it can no longer be apprehended through realistic means or the decision of one of Murakami Haruki's protagonists to live in the "unreal world" created by his own mind rather than return to a dismal reality.

As with the magic realism of Latin America, this Japanese rejection of realism has political overtones, and these overtones are perhaps even more complex than with Latin America, especially for contemporary Japanese. Precisely because the dynamic of modernization has been played out apparently so successfully in Japan, the tension between what is Western/modern and what is Japanese is not necessarily expressed in terms of the duality of real vs. unreal. The problem is not only that the West has access to the language of the real, but that the Japanese themselves are participating in the creation of a new language of modernity.[6]

The history of fantasy and magic realism in Japan thus becomes almost a mirror image of Japan's relation with the West. In the period shortly after the opening of Japan to the West, the thorough identification of realism with Western culture meant that at the turn of the century a rejection of naturalism and realism in general could be a reactionary or at least conservative gesture, an affirmation of old values at the expense of the new imported ones. During the twenties and thirties, however, it could be argued that the use of fantasy was an escapist one, either to ignore or hide from the ominous political realities of the present. Since the war, the use of fantasy has clearly become a radical one, indicating a rejection, not necessarily of reality per se, but of the government and media-controlled vision of a rosy, harmonious society.

Overall, the most pervasive use of magic realism in modern Japanese literature has been as a means to search for Japanese identity, often through the process of recovering history by resuscitating myth (Oe Kenzaburo, Izumi Kyoka, Inoue Hisashi) or in the image of a mysterious, marvelous woman who may represent old Japan as a maternal figure, forgiving those who have abandoned her (Kyoka) or of a virginal girl (Kawabata) whose purity suggests a lost innocence that can be restored only for a fleeting moment. Writers such as Abe Kobo and, more subtly, Murakami Haruki show this search for identity only to underline its ultimate futility in visions of a grotesque and anonymous modern world.

Given this emphasis on identity or lack of it, it is not surprising that many of these fictions contain variations of metamorphosis. Usually these are negative transformations, as characters degenerate into beasts or grotesques but one also finds what might be termed "blocked metamorphosis" as a major theme, as when a protagonist desperately wants, but cannot ultimately achieve, the desired change (or, as in "The Nose," when the transformation is a disappointing one).

Natsume Soseki and the Magic of the Past

The theme of metamorphosis, often combined with a problematic past, is an important one in the fiction of Natsume Soseki (1867–1916), considered by many Japanese to be the greatest of modern Japanese writers for his portrayals of agonized intellectuals. In recent years, however, critics have begun turning to Soseki's previously neglected fantasy works — in particular a unique piece of writing called *Ten Nights of Dream* (*Yumejuya*, 1908). This is a short collection of ten purported dreams that are evocatively and believably dreamlike and yet at the same time obviously works of art, products of a superior creative mind. Although short, each eerie dream creates a small, dense world, often more nightmarish than dreamlike, a world that encapsulates a variety of fears, anxieties, and longings in a peculiarly effective fashion. Perhaps because of their concentrated form, the dreams come across as intensely personal and yet remarkably universal, surreal explorations of the problems of being a modern human being.

Metamorphosis is important in a number of the dream narratives. "The First Night" relates a more traditional, apparently positive form of transformation in which a beautiful woman dies and returns to a faithfully waiting man in the form of a lily. This dream encapsulates a favorite search of many Soseki protagonists for a mysterious ideal woman, often associated with flowers. The transformation into a beautiful flower suggests both purification and aestheticization, a means of turning the woman into a nonthreatening, asexual object that offers a kind of aesthetic relief to many of Soseki's agonized male characters.

Other dreams deal with metamorphoses that are far less positive or, worse, frustrated. In "The Second Night," for example, a samurai attempts to will himself into enlightenment, a state that he calls "Nothingness." The more he tries, however, the more "Nothingness" eludes him, leaving him with no alternative but to kill himself.

"The Sixth Night" offers a more overtly fantastic example of this "blocked metamorphosis" in which the dreaming "I" finds himself in a contemporary crowd, watching a thirteenth-century sculptor carving "guardian gods" out of wood. None of the rather vulgar crowd, which consists largely of rickshaw drivers, appear particularly surprised by the sculptor's medieval appearance, preferring to restrict their comments to his skill. One of the rickshaw men explains to the "I" that the sculptor is not so much carving as *discovering* gods already in the wood. Inspired by this, the "I" returns and assiduously attempts to carve his own gods, only to fail repeatedly. Finally he gives up, realizing that "there were no guardian gods in the wood of today."[7]

The dream of the guardian gods is clearer than most of the dreams in its obvious indictment of modernity and its longing for the past. Its final disappointed statement is poignant rather than strident. By placing the longing for the past first in a dream context, and then contrasting this emotion with the everyday commentary of the rickshaw men, Soseki emphasizes the distinction between modern and traditional without extraneous moralizing. This comparatively subtle approach makes the impossibility of ever rediscovering the guardian gods of the past both more understandable and more painful. In this dream the metamorphosis from tree into god can never occur. The time of "delightful" transformations, typical of premodern fantasy, is over.

"The Sixth Night"'s vision of a man who cannot recreate the past is one side of modern Japan's tragedy. "The Third Night," perhaps the most famous of the dreams, represents the other side, the inability to escape the past. In this dream a man walks through a dark forest carrying a heavy, blind child on his back. The man hopes to find a place to get rid of his burden, but the child seems to understand his thoughts and jeers at him, telling him that he will be even heavier soon. They walk on into a dark forest, the child "shining like a mirror; like a mirror that revealed my past, my present and my future." Finally they arrive in the heart of the forest in front of a cedar tree, and the child informs him that it was here "exactly one hundred years ago that you murdered me." The story ends with the I's despairing realization that he had indeed killed a blind man at the root of this cedar tree one hundred years before: "And at that moment, when I knew that I had murdered, the child on my back became as heavy as a god of stone." [8]

The metamorphosis in this story is not a blocked one but a negative one, the child who becomes as heavy as "a god of stone" (*Jizo* in the original), and who can never be escaped. The burden of the past is the real weight that rests on the man's shoulders, some of it relating to Soseki's own miserable childhood and feelings of guilt toward his family. But the stone god on the dreamer's shoulders also suggests both Buddhist Karma and a collective past that cannot be escaped. Where the sculptor of "The Sixth Night" tries to take control of the present and carve out new guardian gods, the actor in "The Third Night" can only move passively, forced (by memory, guilt?) to repeat an experience that he wishes to forget. Caught between a desire to recover the past and a desire to escape it, it is no wonder that so many of Soseki's characters, like the samurai in "The Second Night," long for Nothingness, either through enlightenment or death.

Izumi Kyoka and the Magic of the Old

While Soseki's *Ten Nights of Dream* seems remarkably modern in the compactness and surreality of its imagery, the works of Izumi Kyoka (1873–

1939), Soseki's contemporary and one of Japan's greatest fantasists, hark back to premodern traditions in both subject matter and style. Indeed, some of Kyoka's works are obvious descendants of classical kabuki melodrama such as his "The Tale of the Castle Tower" (*Tenshu monogatari*), a play full of ghosts, sorcerers, and severed heads, where any trace of realism is completely subordinate to "magic."

Even such a traditional piece as "The Castle Tower" was not written in a vacuum, however. Kyoka was very much aware of the Japan of Civilization and Enlightenment around him, and of his own contemporaries' preference for naturalism. His determination to write romantic fantasy must, therefore, be seen as a conscious rejection both of the naturalist prose style and the modernity it represented. In some of his most interesting works this rejection took narrative form, involving fantasies where modernity and tradition, in the form of realism and magic, confront each other within the confines of the narrative. This confrontation is most notable in Kyoka's 1900 masterpiece *The Monk of Mount Koya* (*Koya Hijiri*), where it is the tension between magic and real that makes the story a particularly powerful work, not only in the text's extraordinary imagery but in its overall vision of a Japan where the old lies in wait to revenge itself on the new.

The Monk of Mount Koya is a variation on the Japanese version of an archetypal quest narrative, *kishu ryuritan*, the so-called "exile of the young noble," about a youth who is subjected to various forms of trials and temptations but emerges stronger as a result.[9] In this case, however, the youth is a young monk and the country of his exile is really old Japan, the Japan before modernization, a place that is both dangerous and alluring.

The narrative within the narrative begins as the monk reminisces about a youthful journey into the mountains of Shinshu in central Japan. Like many fairy tales, the story is completely realistic until he turns off onto an "old road" in order to warn a medicine peddler whom he had met earlier that the road is in danger of flooding. The monk does not find the peddler, which is actually a relief since he disliked the man's crudeness, but he discovers too late that the road is wild and lonely, leading him into a forest consisting largely of mud, rain, and leeches. In an extraordinary scene, which the monk himself links to a vision of apocalypse, he is attacked by the leeches and loses consciousness in a welter of mud and blood.

When he finally revives and escapes the forest, the monk is only too willing to yield to the ministrations of a beautiful woman who lives in a lonely house near the forest, even though at first glance she appears to have scales and a tail. In an obvious temptation scene the woman takes him bathing in a forest pool but the monk (barely) resists her charms and returns to the house for a night's sleep, although troubled by the noises of a variety of animals that seem to be surrounding the house. The next morning he discovers from the woman's old retainer that she is actually an enchantress who turns men who attempt to seduce her into animals. In fact, the medicine peddler of the previous day has been turned into a horse. The monk has been saved by the woman's compassion for his purity but ironically, he has already fallen in love with her and wishes he could stay with her forever. The story ends on a note of nostalgia as the monk, now grown old, finishes his story in a sentimental fashion making it clear that at some level he is still in love with her.

In certain ways *The Monk of Mount Koya* may be almost too much like a fairy tale to fit into the category of magic realism. What makes it worthy of inclusion here is the strange intrusion of the highly realistic medicine peddler and his many anonymous forbears, the men who have all been turned into beasts. Although the basic theme of forced metamorphosis by an enchantress is a traditional, indeed, archetypal one, the difference here is that these victims are not simply fairy tale villains but realistic modern men while, in contrast, the woman has many explicit associations with traditional Japan. The men's attempts to take advantage of the woman can, therefore, be read symbolically as the raping of old Japan by the new vulgar men of Meiji who can no longer appreciate her. Their enforced transformation may also be read both as Buddhist allegory—the underlying affinity of Man with the rest of nature—and as a subtle slap at the Darwinist doctrine of evolution and survival of the fittest that had taken Japan of that period by storm.

The double-edged character of the woman is interesting as well. The monk's initial vision of her as a snake places her in a long line of demonic serpentine female figures in premodern Japanese literature, usually women driven by jealousy to revenge and magic. But in *The Monk of Mount Koya* the woman's motivations are both more vague and more complicated than those of her classical ancestresses. The fact that she lives at the end of the "old road" strongly associates her with a hidden, old Japan; but this is a Japan that fights back. Obviously, she enjoys having power over men, as is clear when she speaks commandingly to some of the men-beasts around her, but the young monk's innocence brings out the motherly side of her, and she is content simply to bathe him.

This motherliness also associates her with traditional Japan. Maternality has long been considered an essential characteristic of Japanese womanhood, tying in with a distinctive psychology of dependence (*amae*) in which the Japanese state is seen as playing a kind of maternal role. Kyoka seems to be suggesting that old Japan can still forgive and nurture her citizens, if approached in the right spirit.

What can happen if "she" is not approached correctly is shown in Kyoka's play *Demon Pond* (*Yashagaike*), where the spirit-princess of a mountain pond takes revenge on a group of villagers who refuse to believe in magic. In this case she unleashes a flood on the village, killing them all, including a young writer and his wife who have fled Tokyo to become closer to old Japan. Like *The Monk of Mount Hijiri* this play is more "magic" than "real," but the characters of the villagers and the young writer are realistic portraits of contemporary Japanese people. The apocalyptic ending is reminiscent of the monk's vision of destruction in the forest. In *Demon Pond*, however, no one is saved, except perhaps the young writer and his wife who are allowed the dubious distinction of apparently being transformed into the new rulers of Demon Pond. This "backward" metamorphosis is intriguing, another suggestion that the only way to deal with modernity is to escape it, often through violent means.

The savagery of the magic/traditional characters is a notable aspect of Kyoka's work, perhaps an unconscious manifestation of Kyoka's own sense of humiliation and resentment toward the naturalist writers, many of whom dismissed his work as old fashioned. Where Soseki's works both mourn and rage against the past, Kyoka's writings attempt through fantasy to re-empower the past, the "old road" that can lead to both birth and death. It is interesting to note that it has been only in the last decade or so that the magnitude of Kyoka's brilliance has been rediscovered by contemporary Japanese critics, suggesting a former critical unwillingness to see either fantasy or traditional forms in a serious light.

Of course, not all of Kyoka's contemporaries were always so disparaging. Some were able to perceive a certain realism beneath Kyoka's romantic gloom. Indeed, one critic, Masamune Hakucho, emphasized the realism in Kyoka's ghost stories when he pointed out that the reader is made to feel "a sense of rationality within the basic irrationality."[10]

Akutagawa Ryunosuke and the Magic of Art

In contrast, the stories of our next writer to be considered, the previously mentioned Akutagawa Ryunosuke (1892–1927) essentially stand Hakucho's description on its head, discovering the irrational within what appears to be, or is hoped to be, a rational world. The works of Akutagawa encompass both the surrealism of Soseki's *Ten Nights of Dream* and the extravagant imagery of Kyoka's works, while at the same time adding a new dimension. This dimension may be described as a fascination with uncertainty, and a concomitant rejection of a knowable "real," underlined by Akutagawa's brilliant use of the comic and the grotesque.

A superb stylist who wrote short stories almost exclusively, Akutagawa is particularly known in the West for his work "Rashomon" (1915, actually two short stories, the other called "In a Grove" [*Yabu no naka*], 1922), which was made into the 1950 Kurosawa film of the same name. "In a Grove" illustrates one of Akutagawa's primary techniques, the use of the fantastic to inject a further note of uncertainty into an already unknowable world. In this work, Akutagawa uses a mystery story format, particularly a trial scene, in which victims and perpetrators of a crime are gathered together to ascertain the actual truth of a rape-murder of an aristocratic woman and her husband. Each of the participants left alive gives startlingly different accounts of the incident until finally the woman's murdered husband is summoned from the dead. In a traditional ghost/mystery story, this introduction of the supernatural would lead to the final unraveling of the mystery. In "In a Grove," however, Akutagawa's fantastic twist is simply one more turn of the screw: the ghost gives a completely different, but obviously prejudiced, version of the events and the final truth is never discovered.

Akutagawa's use of the fantastic as a means to a final awareness of unknowability rather than to a final truth is modern, perhaps even postmodern, in a way that neither Kyoka nor even Soseki could ever be. At the same time, more than any other Japanese writer before or since, Akutagawa made thorough use of ancient Japanese stories, many of them fantastic. Sometimes he changed these stories considerably; at other times, as in "The Nose," he kept to a reasonably accurate retelling, but simply by recounting them in the modern context with a different emphasis changed their final effect considerably.

At first glance, Akutagawa's works seem far less concerned with the problems of indigenous tradition versus modernity and the West than does either Kyoka's or Soseki's fiction, but in fact they emblematize that tension on a less obvious, perhaps more encompassing level. Akutagawa's fictional influences were not only premodern Japanese literature but also the latest European writers such as Maupassant and Baudelaire. The kind of stories he wrote also varied widely, from mysteries to ghost stories to the satirical novella *Kappa* (1927), a fantastic, dystopic vision of modern Japan in which the protagonist's final refuge is madness, the insane creation of another world. As in *Kappa*, many of his works play on the excitement and danger of the creative process. Akutagawa saw himself as an artist first and Japanese second, and tried to believe that the Olympian identity of an artist would raise him above the chaos of the world around him, although his fiction itself sometimes shows the undermining of that desire.

In "The Dragon" (*Tatsu*), for example, an old priest makes up a story about a dragon rising up from a pond near his temple on a forthcoming date. The entire countryside is taken in and, much to the priest's embarrassment, thousands of people assemble on the appointed day to watch the miraculous event. Bored with waiting, the priest too is beginning to wonder if just possibly something might happen, when a thunderstorm opens up above the pond and he sees a "blurred vision of a black dragon more than one hundred feet long ascending straight into the sky."[11] Others see it too, and the event becomes a well-known miracle. Years later the priest confesses to having made up the story, but no one believes him.

In "The Dragon" Akutagawa plays not only with the pleasures of uncertainty but with the pleasures and powers of fiction. The priest, initially unconscious of his own artistry, is able to create a tale that is ultimately as true and powerful as anything in real life.

"The Dragon" is a lighthearted look at the powers of the imagination but the 1918 "Hell Screen" (*Jigokuhen*) is a terrifying look at the same subject. "Hell Screen" concerns a brilliant painter whose increasing arrogance leads him to burn to death his young daughter for the sake of the perfect picture of hell. The story is a tour de force of horror leading to a vision of art as the final danger, no longer a refuge from the problems of reality.

Akutagawa's later fiction turns increasingly dark as his protagonists are unable to control their fantastic visions. One of his last stories, the autobiographical "Cogwheels" (*Haguruma*, 1927), in which the main character is haunted by visions of a man in a raincoat and hallucinations of swirling cogwheels, takes on a hallucinatory and traumatic intensity, somewhere on the boundaries between realism and fantasy. Increasingly, Akutagawa's sense of the unknowability of life led to despair; Akutagawa killed himself at the age of thirty-three. It is not a surprise to find that Akutagawa's suicide note mentions "a vague anxiety about the future" as one of his reasons for killing himself. On a literary level, Akutagawa's "anxiety" was a fruitful one, but on the psychological level he paid a heavy price.

Kawabata Yasunari and the Magic of Escape

The works of Japan's first Nobel Prize winner, Kawabata Yasunari (1899–1972), are perhaps best known in the West for portraying an almost stereotypical notion of old Japan, revolving around the tea ceremony, ikebana, and geishas. Although primarily realistic, these works can also be seen as a kind of fantasy of escape, on the part of both protagonists and Kawabata himself, from an increasingly unappealing modern world. Kawabata's sense of a lost Japan resembles Kyoka's or Soseki's feeling, though the tone of his work is more elegaic and resigned than that of the earlier writers. It is also interesting to note that, like Kyoka and Soseki, Kawabata's fiction also often revolves around a quest for an ideal woman, although this woman is usually a combination of virgin and temptress rather than Kyoka's mother-temptress or Soseki's asexual flower woman.

Kawabata never completely rejected the West or modernity, however. He despised much that was modern in Japan, but at the same time he was in many ways an experimental writer whose celebrated "haiku" style owes as much to European literature of the twenties as it does to traditional Japan. His fantasy literature too, although certain aspects of it are uniquely Japanese, owes perhaps more to European Surrealism than it does to any specific Japanese motif.

Limited in output, his fantastic literature is peculiarly memorable, encapsulating two of Kawabata's most basic themes, the search for love and the desire for escape. One of the most distinctive of these fantasies is the story "One Arm" (*Kataude*, 1961), a classic piece of magic realism in which a young girl calmly lends the story's narrator her arm for the night. The intersection of magic and real is seamless: the narrator is pleased rather than shocked at her gift and happily takes the arm home with him, examining it tenderly and admiring its rosy pinkness. He takes off his own arm and attaches the girl's arm to himself, going tranquilly to sleep with it. The next morning, however, he wakes up screaming and tears the arm off.

The story ends with a paean to an ideal of perfect femininity that is also a resigned acknowledgment of the fundamental impossibility of connection between the sexes: "If the dew of woman would but come from between the long nails and the fingertips." [12]

"One Arm" makes an interesting comparison with Alfonso Reyes' "Major Aranda's Hand," because the basic narrative conceit, a severed hand with a life of its own, is the same in both stories. [13] However, while Reyes' hand, true to its military heritage, is aggressive and violent before finally "committing suicide" in a case full of army heirlooms, Kawabata's hand remains passive and delicate, an erotic symbol that evokes not only sexuality but love as well. The transitoriness of the loan underlines Kawabata's theme of the inevitability of human loneliness, while the yearning for the perfect woman is also typical of many of his protagonist's quests for an elusive feminine ideal.

"One Arm" also brings up the problem of fragmentation, a subtheme of the idea of blocked metamorphosis. The narrator in his loneliness tries to unite with the arm, but is only able to do so while asleep. Awakening, he realizes its alienness (and his essential solitude) and screams. While Kyoka's monk was able to relax into infantilism while being bathed by the woman, Kawabata's protagonist tries for another type of asexual union but is ultimately frustrated by his own fears.

Other fantasies of Kawabata also explore the temptation and the transience of escape. In "Snow" (*Yuki*, 1964) an elderly man checks himself in year after year to the same hotel room to lie in bed and see certain nostalgic fantasies connected with childhood and love. "Snow" is an example of Todorov's definition of the fantastic as based on reader hesitation, [14] because the reader is never given the chance to decide whether these fantasies actually materialize or whether they are simply an old man's hallucinations. But the images — a father and son lost in an immense snowy landscape like that of a screen painting, a cloud of women arriving on white wings — are marvelous in both senses of the word.

Kawabata also indulged in overt fantasy, as in the 1963 story "Immortality" (*Fushi*), about a young girl who commits suicide over the loss of her lover, but who faithfully returns to collect him when he himself dies (perhaps by suicide) many years later. This story's rather sentimental happy ending may be due to the fact that the appealing idea of a magical love beyond death overwhelms the tawdry reality of the girl's suicide.

In Kawabata's final unfinished novel *Tampopo*, magic and reality are once again poised in creative confrontation in a tale of a young girl with a mysterious disease that causes parts of her body to seem to disappear. Although this fragmentation through sickness has echoes of "One Arm," the emphasis is on psychology rather than the surreal, and both she and the people around her, her mother and her fiancé, are worried rather than delighted. No longer enchanting, this metamorphosis is disturbing, suggesting a world in which reality can no longer be held onto and in which magic cannot be controlled. This sense of being out of synch with the world was undoubtedly personal to Kawabata, who committed suicide in 1972, but it also may represent an implicit criticism of his country, whose people were rushing to remake themselves in ways that were not always healthy, at least in his eyes.

Abe Kobo and the Loss of Identity

The illustration of modern alienation through fragmentation and metamorphosis achieves its greatest range in the works of Abe Kobo (1925–93). Abe is perhaps the most internationally recognized of the writers mentioned here, probably because of the relentlessly anonymous style he uses to explore modern alienation, a style that owes more to Kafka and Sartre than to any native Japanese writer. Characters and places rarely have names, while the imagery, usually monochromatic or grotesque, is almost the antithesis of Kawabata's determined "Japaneseness" (although, at the same time, much of Abe's work is a brilliant black-humored satire on modern Japan).

Part of the reason for this anonymity may be Abe's unusual background. Growing up in Japanese occupied Manchuria, he made his way through the war torn continent in time to return to Japan to study medicine. The themes of rootlessness, loss, and anonymity in his stories are frequently associated with labyrinthine hospitals or laboratories, nonplaces where the protagonists often end by losing each other or themselves through some grotesque transformation.

Other works simply dwell on the process of transformation itself. One of Abe's most famous early stories, "The Stick" (*Bo*), features a typical suburban father who leans over a department store roof to get away from his nagging children and falls off. By the time he reaches the ground he finds that he has become a stick. Like Kafka's Gregor Samsa, the stick passively accepts his new state, ultimately enduring the humiliation of being picked up and analyzed by a strange trio, a pair of students and their professor who conclude that the stick is "absolutely banal"[15] and who, as punishment, leave it behind to remain forever a stick. The story ends with the stick hearing what might be his children's voices calling, "Daddy, Daddy," but knowing there is nothing it can do.

"The Stick"'s surreal sense of entrapment and immobility may recall Soseki's *Ten Nights of Dream*, but it also suggests the rigid world of the postwar Japanese white collar worker, caught in a network of obligations and unable to move freely. Many of Abe's other works deal with this theme of imprisonment in varied and imaginative ways, usually employing the primary technique of a single fantastic twist to be followed by more or less realistic events. Thus, in his 1967 play "Friends" (*Tomodachi*), a young man is visited by a family who then refuse to leave. The family seem perfectly normal except for their refusal to leave, and their very surface normality makes it impossible for the young man to get either the police or his fiancée to believe that they have trapped him. Eventually, the "friends" put him in a cage and kill him with poisoned milk, insisting all the time that he brought it on himself. The situation "Friends" describes could happen in any country, but its satirization of collective harmony and the importance of the group has particular relevance to some of the most important of Japanese ideals.

In perhaps his most fully realized vision of entrapment, *Woman in the Dunes* (*Suna no onna*, 1960), Abe posits a man forced to live in a sandpit at the bottom of a dune village from which it is impossible to escape. This reworking of the myth of Sisyphus is achieved with surprising realism, although once again with a sharp satiric swipe at another of Japan's myths, the happy village. In *Woman in the Dunes* it is the bestial villagers themselves who have trapped the man in order to get help to sweep out the sand. At the novel's end, the man finally discovers the chance to escape, a rope ladder accidentally left behind, but he is by now inured to his existence in the pit and doesn't climb out, rationalizing that he can escape some other time.

Ultimately, it is of course oneself that one cannot escape, no matter how fantastic a device one invents. This is clear in Abe's novel *The Face of Another* (*Tanin no kao*, 1964), where a badly disfigured scientist, his face covered with keloid scars (the same scars as the victims of Hiroshima, incidentally), creates an incredibly realistic face mask. The scientist is disappointed in his primary goal for the mask's creation, which was to allow him to live out a fantasy seduction of his wife. Thinking he has accomplished this, he is horrified when she reveals that she has known his real identity all along. Unwilling to accept his own failure to forge a new identity, the frustrated scientist decides instead to kill his wife.

The violence implicit at the end of *Face* became increasingly explicit in subsequent works as Abe became more overtly fantastic, with the initial fantasy incident leading to more and more complex and grotesque fantastic events. Perhaps his darkest vision is the 1977 *Secret Rendezvous* (*Mikai*), in which a man's wife is kidnapped by an ambulance in the middle of the night. Searching for her at the hospital where he believes she has been taken, the man encounters a grotesque and horrifying array of doctors and patients, including one doctor who dreams of recreating himself as half-horse, half-man in order to restore his sexual potency. This theme of unnatural sexuality, aligned with uncontrollable technology to create bizarre new identities, is intensified in an extraordinary scene toward the end of the novel. In this scene the hospital holds a festival that turns out to be a kind of high-tech Walpurgisnacht where a woman, who may or may not be the narrator's wife, is strapped to a machine that measures orgasms and offers to service any man who is willing.

The narrator never does discover the identity of the woman, and at the novel's end he himself is clearly losing his own identity. In the reader's last vision of him he has retreated into the labyrinthine depths of the hospital with his only friend, a girl patient whose shrinking disease has liquified her bones to the point where she "seem(s) to recede farther and farther from human shape."[16] Embracing what is left of the girl while licking water from the hospital walls in order to survive, the man waits patiently for death, a "tender, secret rendezvous for one."

Abe's vision is thus increasingly anarchic and despairing. His characters are trapped in worlds of supposed harmony (the village, the family) or healing (the hospital) whose inner core is something dark and horrible. Willed metamorphosis either cannot work or else ends up creating something grotesque, like the half-man, half-horse. Identity is ever more easily lost, either through the machinations of evil others or simple fate, as exemplified by the young girl's wasting disease, similar to that of the sick girl in Kawabata's *Tampopo*.

Although Abe's early work often had a clear political subtext as in his "Song of a Dead Girl" (*Shinda musume no uta*), where the ghost of a factory worker forced to turn prostitute comes back to haunt the work site, his later work seems to despair of doing anything more than fantastically illustrating the horrors of a repressive social system. Where Kyoka's forest still held the potential for salvation at its heart, Abe's world leads into labyrinths which only get darker and darker.

Oe, Inoue, and the Magic of Nostalgia

One writer who still uses fantasy as part of an overt political agenda is the 1994 Nobel Prize Winner Oe Kenzaburo (1935–), some of whose works are comparable to those of Gabriel García Márquez. More than any of the other writers mentioned here, Oe, like García Márquez, attempts through his fiction to portray the sweep of modern Japanese history in all its contradictions and complexities. In recent years he has increasingly turned down two literary avenues in order to do this: history, in terms of his own version of the "historical novel," and the fantastic, often combined with the grotesque and even, in his most recent work, science fiction.

Oe's primary fictional country has tended to be a mythicized version of the place where he grew up, the island of Shikoku, the smallest and still most rural of the four large islands that make up the Japanese archipelago. Compared to centers such as Tokyo or Osaka, Shikoku is "marginal," and Oe exploits this marginality, in terms of both space and character, to limn a world that is a mirror image of the stereotypical picture of Japan as Number One. Oe's fictional Japan is a place marked by confrontation rather than harmony, violence rather than peace, and repression rather than freedom.

His most complex and controversial expression of this vision to date is his 1979 novel *The Game of Contemporaneity* (*Dojidai gemu*). *The Game of Contemporaneity* attempts, like García Márquez's *One Hundred Years of Solitude*, to tell Japanese history from the periphery, in this case through a remote unnamed Shikoku village, founded by a group of samurai escaping from the Tokugawa shogunate. While García Márquez's text implicitly equates the founders of Macondo with Adam and Eve, *The Game of Contemporaneity* explicitly positions the founders of the village in opposition to the ruling Japanese mythology of the Sun Goddess by suggesting that they are descendants of the "dark gods," gods expelled from heaven by Ameterasu, the sun goddess and progenitrix of the Japanese imperial house.

Thus, even more obviously than Macondo, Oe's village is in direct confrontation with the established order, an order whose mythology, centering around the Imperial house, Oe excoriates. *The Game of Contemporaneity* creates an entire countermythology complete with a foundation myth involving a shadowy figure known as the Destroyer, so called because he demolishes a huge mass of rock that was blocking the voyage upstream as the founders of the village fled the shogunate.

The Destroyer appears in and out of the village's history, sometimes in tales and sometimes in dreams, an obviously supernatural figure who is said to die, but then returns, often at a particularly momentous period in the village's history. For example, he helps command, through magic, the village's defense when they go to war in an attempt to secede from Japan. The Destroyer is not always positive, however. At one point forces unleashed by him and his last wife create an enormous upheaval, causing the village to change its social hierarchy completely (an oblique reference to the turmoil of the 1960s). After this, the villagers take revenge on the Destroyer, cut up his body into three hundred parts, and eat him. At the novel's end, however, the narrator believes that the Destroyer has returned to life, although he is still only "the size of a dog" and that he is being cared for by the narrator's twin sister, the shamaness of the village shrine.

The character of the Destroyer is an interesting one, since he is both savior and trickster figure and therefore not a purely positive messiah. Indeed, his very amorphousness may remind us of the figure he is supposed to replace, the Japanese emperor, not to mention the shadowy manipulators behind Japanese factional politics. But, unlike recent emperors or prime ministers, the Destroyer does save his people on various occasions, and the hope of his rebirth, albeit metamorphosed in size, is regarded within the novel as a positive event. The village is in need of this new possibility because it has been on the point of losing its identity under the increasing pressure from what the narrator calls the "Great Japanese Empire," despite the range of stratagems, some realistic, some fantastic, that the villagers have employed to hide themselves from the central authorities.

One of these strategies is interesting in light of Oe's fictional technique itself. During a period known as the Fifty Day War the village children attempt to fend off the Greater Japanese Empire by creating mazes in the forest into which they lead and lose the empire's armies. Although successful, the scheme has a cost: the children themselves are lost. The narrator, however, refuses to see this as tragic, commenting, instead that: "From the instant the children had entered the closed circle of the maze they had escaped the influence of time and would remain eternally children, walking forever through the primeval forest."[17]

The maze in the forest is a reminder of the literary text itself. Oe weaves words to create a fantastic labyrinth against the demands and strictures of the central culture. Unlike Abe's mazelike hospitals and cityscapes, the forest labyrinth remains as a reminder that artifice can be salvation in an increasingly absurd world. The appearance and reappearance of the Destroyer in a variety of forms also suggests the hope of a positive metamorphosis. The village identity may yet remain intact.

Oe's work is less despairing than Abe's in other ways as well. Much of his fiction is saturated by a feeling known in Japanese as "*natsukashisa*" or nostalgia. The Shikoku village that Oe's fiction repeatedly returns to illustrates both the allure and the danger of *natsukashisa*. In *The Game of Contemporaneity* these aspects are concretized in the incestuous longings of the narrator for his twin sister, whom he finally seems resigned to giving up to her more important role as shamaness to the Destroyer. Unlike *One Hundred Years of Solitude*, where incest eventually produces the child with the tail of a pig who is then devoured, incest/nostalgia are finally displaced by the potential for genuine rebirth on the part of the village, as symbolized by the grotesquely metamorphosed figure of the Destroyer. In fact, throughout much of Oe's work, metamorphosis and the grotesque are seen as hopeful symbols of change and vitality, a concept that owes much to Oe's reading of Bakhtin.

The Game of Contemporaneity lacks the color and enchantment of *One Hundred Years of Solitude*, or many of Oe's own novels for that matter, perhaps because its anti-emperor ideological agenda is so strident. It remains a landmark in Japanese literature, however, an attempt to retell Japanese history "from the ground up" by emphasizing the energy and potentiality of the people, encapsulated in the protean figure of the Destroyer. *The Game of Contemporaneity* has also lead to a whole generation of so-called "new political novels" some of which, such as Inoue Hisashi's monumental *The People of Kirikiri* (*Kirikirijin*, 1980), are also characterized by the use of the fantastic.

Inoue's *The People of Kirikiri* can be seen as another magical realist vision of a country village although, in this case, the magic is kept to the peripheries in the form of a super high-tech hospital, rather like a more benign version of Abe's hospitals. The people are not magical, being remarkably believable modern farmers, but the village itself has fantastic aspects, symbolized by the fact that it is built with buried treasure, an appropriately fairy-tale touch in what is basically a modern novel.

Inoue's and Oe's use of the fantastic village, at a time when Japanese culture has rapidly grown more urban, suggests not only the strength of nostalgia still remaining in the Japanese world but also the increasing need for fantasy through which to express it. Their use of the fantastic to suggest possibilities of Otherness still remaining within their own culture is both highly contemporary, even political, and highly traditional, leading back all the way to Kyoka, who also used the traditional to confront the modern. Other contemporary writers such as Oba Minako (b. 1930) and Nakagami Kenji (1946–1992) have similarly gone back to traditional magic for empowerment. Oba's "Smiles of the Mountain Witch" (*Yamauba no bisho*) is a brilliant satire on women's place in society, made darker by her heroine's longing to become a mountain witch (a traditional folkloric figure) and retreat from society. Nakagami's violent and provocative "The Immortal" (*Fushi*, 1984) also uses traditional magical creatures, once powerful but now impotent, to suggest the loss and emptiness endemic to modern society.

The work of these writers is in contrast to certain aspects of Akutagawa and Kawabata's use of the fantastic, which, although implicitly critical of society, is essentially escapist, and also to Abe Kobo's fantasies, which have become less and less political, now seeming only to emphasize the grimness of reality with increasing despair. Oba, Kyoka, Oe, and Inoue share a belief that the Other can be more than a refuge, that it can also be an alternative, and they leave us with a vision of remote villages and valleys where fantasy and a better, stronger Japanese identity are linked forever.

Murakami Haruki and the International Identity

The questions of identity and history, both personal and national, are important themes in the works of our last writer to be considered, Murakami Haruki (1949–). Perhaps the most popular writer of the current younger generation, Murakami's works are particularly good examples of contemporary Japanese magic realism. Set in clearly modern and largely urban settings containing recognizably contemporary characters, and told in an ironic and detached style, Murakami's novels and stories are at the same time permeated with the presence of the marvelous and uncanny. His short story "TV People" (1989) describes a man lounging in his apartment on an ordinary Sunday afternoon when three silent miniaturized people walk in through the front door, set up a television set and silently depart. The protagonist sees them again the next day at his company but in neither case does anyone else seem to see them. The "TV People" come back to him one last time to make an oddly shaped airplane and to tell him that his wife has left him for good. The story ends on a note of resigned despair with the narrator standing helplessly by the telephone thinking: "Maybe somewhere, at some terminal of that awesome megacircuit is my wife. Far, far away, out of my reach. . . . *Which way is front, which way is back?* I stand up and try to say something, but no sooner have I got to my feet than the words slip away."[18]

"TV People" may usefully be compared to Abe Kobo's previously mentioned play, "Friends." In both cases the protagonist's apartment is invaded by a group of unearthly Others whose strangeness is apparent only to the protagonist. Both works also satirize the group or corporate identity of the modern Japanese by implicitly setting their protagonist in opposition to the group mentality. The important difference between the two works lies in the protagonist's reactions. In Abe's play the protagonist strives mightily, although futilely, to rid himself of the invaders and to convince his peers of their threatening presence. Although his continued confrontation with the "Friends" ultimately leads to his death, he has at least made a genuine and serious effort to maintain his identity and integrity within an increasingly surreal and sinister world. The main reaction of the protagonist in "TV People," on the other hand, seems to be largely one of amiable bemusement. When neither his wife nor his colleagues react to the "TV People," he simply accepts the situation with affable passivity.

Although Abe is usually described as bleakly nihilistic, the final impression given by Murakami's "TV People" may actually be a more despairing one. Murakami's protagonist accepts that his identity is determined by outside forces who tell him what to think and how to react, and he makes no effort to oppose the situation. Like Akutagawa's bemused protagonist in "The Nose," the protagonist seems to have learned that we have no control over the bizarre manifestations of fate, and he no longer cares "which way is front" or "which way is back."

The passivity of Murakami's characters has alarmed some older Japanese critics and scholars who see his characters' passive reactions to an increasingly bizarre world as a disturbing reflection of the younger generation's unwillingness to assert themselves, and their concomitant rejection or ignoring of history. Thus, in Murakami's surreal novel *Hard Boiled Wonderland and the End of the World* (*Sekai no owari to hado boirudo wandarando*, 1985), the protagonist chooses at the novel's end to remain in a static unreal world known as the Town, the inhabitants of which possess as their main characteristic a willingness to relinquish their "shadows" or memories.

Murakami's attitude toward history is not always negative, however. His novel *A Wild Sheep Chase* (*Hitsuji o meguru boken*, 1982) is a work that may fruitfully be compared to Oe's *The Game of Contemporaneity* and Inoue's *The People of Kirikiri*. Like both these novels, *A Wild Sheep Chase* privileges a rural and marginalized Japanese past, in this case a tiny Hokkaido village established by dispossessed farmers. Unlike the other two works, however, *A Wild Sheep Chase* also deals at length with another, less romantic, aspect of the Japanese past, the colonization of Manchuria by Japan in the 1920s and the rise to power of right-wing militarists.

The key to both of these pasts is contained in the elusive form of a magic sheep, last seen on a remote farm in Hokkaido, but actually a phantom inhabitant of the brain of a shadowy right-wing power broker. The sheep itself is an amusing but sinister image, reminiscent of the stone child in Soseki's "Third Night," a burden of the past that is impossible to escape. Through the protagonist's increasingly surreal quest for the phantom sheep, the reader is led to confront previously unacknowledged or downplayed aspects of Japanese history in a manner that is both original and provocative. Murakami's use of the fantastic brings a fresh perspective to many of the problems of urban modernity, most of which are not restricted to Japan. It is perhaps not surprising that his works are popular in the United States as well. The surreal and absurd world of Murakami's characters is a universal one, suggesting that the problems of identity for contemporary Japan are ones shared throughout the modern world.

Notes

1 See Beongcheon Yu's discussion of "The Nose," in Yu, *Akutagawa: An Introduction* (Detroit: Wayne State University Press, 1972), pp. 15–17.

2 Rosemary Jackson, *Fantasy: The Literature of Subversion* (London: Methuen, 1981), p. 81.

3 One fascinating example of this kind of intellectual concern is the spectacu-

lar suicide of the writer Mishima Yukio in 1970 and subsequent reactions to it. Mishima's suicide, calling for a restoration of traditional Japanese values, led many Japanese to question or at least problematize the notion of the postwar Japanese success story. Perhaps even more revealing is the continued interest, usually of a negative sort, of Japanese intellectuals in Mishima's death. In a discussion of Mishima's continuing influence after his death, two major Japanese men of letters, Shimada Masahiko and Asada Akira, refer to Mishima variously as a "zombie," an "android," and a "monster." (Shimada Masahiko and Asada Akira, "Mishima: Mozo o mozo suru" [Mishima: Counterfeiting the Counterfeit] in Shimada and Asada, *Tenshi ga toru* [Tokyo: Shinchosha, 1988], p. 249.) The use of such grotesque and horrific imagery in a discussion of an essentially literary matter evidences the depth of unease with which even contemporary intellectuals confront their historical situation.

4 David Young and Keith Hollaman, eds., "Introduction" to *Magic Realism: An Anthology* (New York: Longman, 1984), p. 2.

5 For a detailed discussion of the *watakushishosetsu* and the conception of the "real" in Japanese literature, see Edward Fowler, *The Rhetoric of Confession: Shishosetsu in Early Twentieth Century Japanese Fiction* (Berkeley: University of California Press, 1988).

6 This complex attitude vis-à-vis modernity is also exemplified in Japan's increasingly ambivalent relationship with technology. As Tetsuo Najita describes it, throughout most of the twentieth century technology was seen as an imported Other and, as such, was paradoxically more containable than it now seems in contemporary Japan, where it is viewed as highly problematic. (Tetsuo Najita, "Culture and Technology," in *Postmodernism and Japan*, ed. Masao Miyoshi and H. D. Harootunian [Duke University Press, 1989], pp. 3–20. Perhaps for this reason, science fiction and fantasy views of technology are extremely bleak, as is evidenced in Abe Kobo's *Secret Rendezvous* or Murakami Haruki's *Hard Boiled Wonderland and the End of the World*.

7 Natsume Soseki, *Ten Nights of Dream* (*Yumejuya*), trans. Aiko Ito and Graeme Wilson (Tokyo: Charles E. Tuttle, 1980), p. 49.

8 Soseki, pp. 37–38.

9 For a discussion of this paradigm, see Norma Field, *The Splendour of Longing in the Tale of Genji* (Princeton: Princeton University Press, 1987), pp. 33–35.

10 Masamune Hakucho, quoted in Donald Keene, *Dawn to the West* (New York: Holt, Rinehart and Winston, 1984), p. 216.

11 Akutagawa Ryunosuke, *Rashomon and Other Stories*, trans. Takashi Kojima (Tokyo: Charles E. Tuttle, 1975), p. 100.

12 Kawabata Yasunari, *House of the Sleeping Beauties and Other Stories* (*Nemureru bijo*), trans. Edward Seidensticker (Tokyo: Kodansha, 1969).

13 Alfonso Reyes, "Major Aranda's Hand," in *Magic Realism: An Anthology*, ed.

David Young and Keith Hollaman (New York: Longman, 1984), pp. 347–51.

14 Tzvetan Todorov, *The Fantastic: A Structural Approach to a Literary Genre*, trans. Richard Howard (Ithaca: Cornell University Press, 1974), p. 41.

15 Abe Kobo, "The Stick" (*Bo*), in *A Late Chrysanthemum: Twenty-one Stories from the Japanese*, trans. Lane Dunlop (San Francisco: North Point Press, 1986), p. 172.

16 Abe Kobo, *Secret Rendezvous* (*Mikai*), trans. Juliet Winters Carpenter (Tokyo: Charles E. Tuttle, 1981), p. 178.

17 Oe Kenzaburo, *Dojidai gemu* (Tokyo: Shinchosha, 1979), p. 385, my translation.

18 Murakami Haruki, *The Elephant Vanishes*, trans. Alfred Birnbaum and Jay Robin (New York: Alfred Knopf, 1993), p. 216.

MELISSA STEWART

Roads of "Exquisite Mysterious Muck":
The Magical Journey through the City in William Kennedy's
Ironweed, *John Cheever's "The Enormous Radio," and*
Donald Barthelme's "City Life"

In order to define magical realism, it seems necessary to identify the nature
of the relationship between the magical and the rational, and indeed, several descriptions of this relationship have been offered. Some of these descriptions evoke an "antagonistic struggle":[1] the magical "collides" with
the rational, as David Young and Keith Hollaman state,[2] or "another world
[intrudes] into this one," according to Brian McHale (borrowing a phrase
from Thomas Pynchon's *The Crying of Lot 49*).[3] Other descriptions suggest
a more harmonious combination: the "two realms" of the magical and the
rational "merge"[4] or "intersect."[5] A third group proposes that the magical is part of the rational or, as Robert Gibb states, "in magical realism,
the real isn't abandoned; it is extended."[6] Similarly, George McMurray believes that magical realism presents "an expanded sense of reality,"[7] and
Wendy B. Faris speaks of magic that "grows almost imperceptibly out of
the real."[8] The validity of all these descriptions indicates, I believe, that
the potency of magical realism lies in its capacity to explore the protean
relationship between what we consider rational (what is knowable, predictable, and controllable) and irrational (what is beyond our complete
understanding and control).

This interaction of the rational and irrational lies at the heart of one
of the most powerful conceptions of the city: the city as "a paradox verging on oxymoron."[9] Mircea Eliade has theorized that primitive societies
established their communities by imitating, in the form of rituals, their
gods' creation of the universe.[10] Because the city was seen as an image of
the universe, it was thought to exist at the center of the universe (the location of the first creation) and to be the "meeting point of heaven, earth,
and hell."[11] The city, perceived in this way, evidenced the human capacity
to direct the powerful forces of nature and to achieve mastery over our

physical and mental energies. Thus, it reminded its citizens that human beings are unique among living things in their capacity to emulate the gods. Yet the city remained a human realm, encompassing human frailties and vices along with human achievements. Encroaching upon the city was the underworld, which consisted of variously conceived chaotic realms inhabited by demons who commanded terrifying forces of destruction and death. This paradoxical conception of the city as the site of controllable and uncontrollable energies has retained its relevance throughout the succeeding centuries: the city as civilization, the city as wasteland.

In our own cities, we see this paradox of order and disorder, creation and destruction, power and vulnerability manifested in an immense variety of forms. The city is arguably the greatest achievement of the rational mind, with its complex systems of communication, transportation, and commerce. However, because the city also harbors ignorance, disease, poverty, and violence, it may stand as the epitome of human fallibility and malevolence. Compounding this paradox is the potential of our urban systems to generate conditions that elude or destroy the order we seek to establish. Systems deteriorate, break down, become outdated; or, they may be designed to benefit one group of individuals at the expense of another, or others. Thus, failed or flawed or biased systems may create unemployment, homelessness, crime.

Even though we usually perceive what we cannot order or control as a threat to our existence and well-being, we may also find that some irrational aspects of the city delight and intrigue us. In his *City: Rediscovering the Center*, William Whyte meticulously documents activities that are often regarded as disconcerting urban events: furtive pedestrians maneuvering on crowded sidewalks; streets jammed with merchants and street vendors competing for shoppers; unusual, eccentric, and sometimes antagonistic "undesirables" (street people, street musicians, small-time con artists) practicing their self-appointed occupations.[12] But Whyte's interpretation of these activities implies that there is a type of order in this disorder — not an order created by conscious intention, but an order resembling that of an intricate dance, evolving naturally out of the brief yet constant interactions of city dwellers. Whyte's impressions stem from the same awareness that compelled Baudelaire to attribute his fascination with the city to the "beauty of the horrible,"[13] and Theodore Dreiser to observe that "the drama of the city lies in its extremes."[14] The city arises as a collective work from the rational and irrational energies of its creators.

The literature I have selected for this study—William Kennedy's *Iron-weed*, John Cheever's "The Enormous Radio," and Donald Barthelme's "City Life"—are united by a cluster of interrelated issues that can be expressed in this way: human beings create the city, yet they cannot completely control their creation. This paradox is also inherent in magical realism. Kennedy, Cheever, and Barthelme use magical beings, events, and forces to explore what we might call the "urban irrational," and how the individual and the community may accept the irrational without denying or surrendering responsibility for their actions. These authors' magical realism can be considered in terms of their conceptions of the city.

Drawing upon the work of many urban historians, William Sharpe and Leonard Wallock have proposed that since the beginning of the nineteenth century, cities have evolved in three overlapping phases, the "concentrated settlement," the "center city with suburban ring," and the "decentered urban field."[15] The first phase refers to cities in the nineteenth century, generated primarily by industrial capitalism that drew people from rural areas and thus caused a rapid population growth along with greatly increased urban congestion. The second phase, the "center city with suburban ring"—or, as I prefer to call it, the "separated city"—overlaps with the first phase and continues into the first several decades of the twentieth century. Many members of the middle and working classes could afford to move to the suburbs, while poor, unskilled individuals remained in the city. Several factors contributed to this separation: a desire for space and greenery; middle-class prejudice and suspicion directed toward individuals of different race, ethnic origin, class, income; the availability of the automobile; and the migration of businesses to the suburbs (for reasons both economic and social). The third phase, the "decentered urban field," begins in the 1970s. It is characterized by " 'defensible,' low density, residential spaces" connected by "superhighways and freeways" and interspersed with "metrocenters" consisting primarily of businesses and services clustered together and excluding residential occupation.[16] Because these phases define the city in terms of the formation and disintegration of a center, it would seem that they extend the ancient concept of the city as universal center—as the intersection of rational and irrational energies—into the twentieth century.

Kennedy's *Ironweed* (1983) describes a period of time from 1879 to 1938, and we may view it as reflecting the first phase of urban evolution named by Sharpe and Wallock. Cheever's "The Enormous Radio" (1947) describes a post-World War II urban experience and reflects the second phase. Barthelme's postmodern city in "City Life" (1969) reflects the third phase. By identifying these phases, we will recognize each author's portrayal of the city as a "state of mind."[17] More than a physical or historical backdrop for the characters' actions, each urban phase, as conveyed by these authors, dramatizes city life in order to suggest their characters' commerce with the irrational. And they use magical realist devices to do so.

The trajectory of Francis Phelan, the protagonist of *Ironweed*, is deeply associated with Albany, New York. Born in 1879 to Irish Catholic working-class parents, Francis grows up in Albany, becomes the city's most celebrated baseball player, meets his wife Annie, and raises his children there. Yet, the very talent that brings him so much admiration from his community is also the agent of his destruction. During a trolley car strike in 1901, Francis used his skill in throwing a baseball to hurl a stone at a scab trolley car driver and kills the man. Other grievous actions are instigated by Francis' talented hands, his "messengers from some outlaw corner of his psyche."[18] The worst occurs in 1916, when he accidently lets his infant son Gerald fall to his death. Consumed by guilt, Francis abandons Albany and his family for the brutal, chaotic life of an alcoholic bum, traveling from town to town on boxcars, fighting, maiming, and sometimes killing other men in order to survive. Francis' immense burden of worthlessness and self-castigation increases the longer he stays away from Albany. But "reducing [himself] to the level of social maggot, streetside slug" (160) is easier than asking for his family's forgiveness.

Remembering all the men he has killed and injured, Francis asks, "How could a man's hands betray him?" (143). If hands usually signify human industry and creativity—by virtue of their capacity to grasp a hammer, brush, or pen and thus to manifest the visions of the creative, ordering mind—then Francis' question can be interpreted as follows: Why is his capacity for order inseparable from his capacity for disorder? How can a talented and loving man also be capable of such hatred and violence? After Gerald's death, Francis finds these contradictions impossible to reconcile, and because every aspect of himself, destructive as well as creative, is associated with his memories of Albany, the "city once his" becomes "a city lost" (64). His internal fragmentation overwhelms the psychological integration that the city once gave to him.

We recognize three characteristic aspects of the "concentrated settlement" phase of the city's development in Kennedy's depiction of Albany:

the time period of the novel (from the year of Francis' birth in 1879 to the three days in 1938 when he returns to Albany), the physical closeness of the city's structures (almost all of the locations are within walking distance from one another), and the rich physicality of Kennedy's description of the city, its history, and people. What further identifies Albany as a concentrated settlement are Francis' "concentrated" memories. The stadium built on the pasture where Francis played ball, the bus that follows the same route as the old trolley car line, the cemetery where his father, mother, and Gerald are buried—for Francis, these places in Albany are figuratively (and, as we will see, literally) inhabited by ghosts.[19] Just as the ancient city was the mythic site of the gods' interactions with humans, for good and evil, so Albany contains Francis' personal hell, inextricably intertwined with his sources of happiness.[20]

Francis has returned to Albany many times, but has never felt worthy to contact his wife Annie or his adult children. When the novel opens, Francis has returned to Albany once again, and finally learns from his son that, until the previous week, Annie had never revealed to him or his sister that Francis had dropped the baby (19). This knowledge of Annie's apparent lack of animosity seems to give Francis the courage to visit Gerald's grave, which he had never done. With "memory . . . as vivid as eyesight," Francis "reconstructed the moment when the child was slipping through his fingers into death" (18). For the first time, Francis allows himself to remember everything that happened on the day his son died. As he does so, Gerald speaks to him from his grave:

> through an act of silent will, [Gerald] imposed on his father the pressing obligation to perform his final acts of expiation for abandoning the family. You will not know, the child silently said, what these acts are until you have performed them all. And after you have performed them you will not understand that they were expiatory any more than you have understood all the other expiation that has kept you in such prolonged humiliation. Then, when the final acts are complete, you will stop trying to die because of me. (19)

As Kennedy's description of St. Agnes cemetery reveals, and as the succeeding events indicate, Gerald belongs to an extensive magical community of the dead who inhabit the cemetery, as well as to a larger community of the dead that encompasses all of Albany. In addition, Kennedy's description of Gerald suggests that he holds a unique position within these related communities: "Denied speech in life, having died with only monosyllabic goos and gaahs in his vocabulary, Gerald possessed the gift of tongues in death. His ability to communicate and to understand was at the genius level among the dead" (17). Gerald, "an ineffably fabulous presence whose like was not to be found anywhere in the cemetery" (18), is the only member of the dead who is capable of granting Francis' expiation, as Teiresias is the only shade who can foresee Odysseus' return to Ithaka. By blending together a rich array of allusions to Dante's *Purgatorio*, Homer's *Odyssey*, and Roman Catholic doctrine, Kennedy presents Albany as a magical cosmos through which Francis, as a hero/wanderer, must journey.[21]

Francis' Catholic upbringing and Kennedy's use of the language of Catholic doctrine allow us to interpret the process that Gerald initiates in terms of the Catholic sacrament of penance. Because Gerald is endowed with special powers, he appropriately fulfills the function of the priest in this magical expiation by recognizing Francis' feelings of contrition, listening to his confession, and deciding what acts of atonement are appropriate for the type and degree of sin. Francis reveals that he is contrite when he "prayed for a repeal of time so that he might hang himself in the coal bin before picking up the child to change his diaper" (18). His ability to "see, hear, and feel every detail" (18) of the day Gerald died serves as his confession. For the first time since he dropped Gerald twenty-two years ago, Francis accepts the depth of his grief and regret, an indication to Gerald that his father is now ready to complete the process that will finally free him from his guilt.

Albany is the only place where Francis can achieve his expiation, for he must journey through the concentration of memories that Albany holds for him. Magical beings, their power released by Gerald's agency, aid Francis by emerging as embodied extensions of his memories, compelling him to undertake the excruciating process of piecing together the dispersed fragments of his self. As Francis travels through Albany, he encounters the ghosts of six men: each has died violently, and Francis has been involved in each man's death.

Francis leaves Gerald and St. Agnes cemetery and takes a bus downtown. As he rides the "red-and-cream window box on wheels" (21), he remembers nostalgically the Albany trolleys that the buses have replaced. He associates the trolleys with two positive aspects of himself: his love for his father and desire to emulate him and his satisfying skill in repairing the machines. As the bus follows the old trolley route and Francis passes the carbarns that used to house the trolleys, he remembers the trolley car strike of 1901, when he "let fly that smooth round stone the weight of a baseball, and brained the scab working as the trolley conductor" (25). A passenger boards the bus: he is the dead trolley conductor, Harold Allen, and he demands to know why Francis killed him. Francis replies, "You bastards takin' our jobs, what kind of man is that, keeps a man from feedin' his family." The ghost counters that Francis' response is "[o]dd logic coming from a man who abandoned his own family" (26). This meeting with Harold Allen's ghost leaves Francis torn between acknowledging the justness of his motivations and their fatal consequence. Allen's response also revives Francis' bewilderment over the paradoxical effects of his baseball talent.

Francis must once again confront his participation in the strike of 1901 while he is working in Rosskam's junkyard, where he encounters the ghost of Fiddler Quain. Francis' "firebrand style . . . had seduced" (141) Fiddler into joining the strike, and he had helped Francis light the sheets that trapped the trolley driven by Allen. In the violent confusion, Fiddler's head was struck by a soldier's blow; he lived out the rest of his life as a "heroic vegetable" (141). Francis wanted to be a pallbearer at Fiddler's funeral, but his sister denied Francis' request, replying "Your hands have done enough damage. . . . You'll not touch my brother's coffin" (142). Initially, Fiddler's ghost seems to comfort Francis by telling him, "I don't blame you for anything," but Fiddler's final remark mystifies Francis: "It's those traitorous hands of yours you'll have to forgive" (142). Searching for the meaning of Fiddler's message, Francis "sensed for the first time in his life the workings of something other than conscious will within himself: an insight into a pattern, an overview of all the violence in his history, of how many had died or been maimed by his hand, or had died, like that nameless pair of astonished shades, as an indirect result of his violent ways" (145). Francis' intuition turns to despair as he realizes that he harbors forces he will never be able to understand or control.

Francis' sense of hope is restored, however, when he returns to the house where he once lived with Annie and his children and discovers what he believes to be a counterbalance to these forces. He enters and finds himself going through the contents of an old trunk in the attic. There, he discovers a photograph of himself standing in Chadwick Park, surrounded by the citizens of Albany who had gathered to celebrate the victory of their baseball team. Studying the picture, Francis sees his nineteen-year-old self

> tossing a baseball from bare right hand to gloved left hand. The flight of the ball had always made this photo mysterious to Francis, for the camera had caught the ball clutched in one hand and also in flight, arcing in a blur toward the glove. What the camera had caught was two instances in one: time separated and time unified, the ball in two places at once, an eventuation as inexplicable as the Trinity itself. Francis now took the picture to be a Trinitarian talisman (a hand, a glove, a ball) for achieving the impossible: for he had always believed it was impossible for him, ravaged man, failed human, to reenter history under this roof. Yet here he was in this aerie of reconstitutable time, touching untouchable artifacts of a self that did not yet know it was ruined, just as the ball, in its inanimate ignorance, did not know yet that it was going nowhere, was caught. (169)

During his journey through Albany, Francis has perceived individual moments of his history as separate and disconnected, but his guilt prevents him from integrating constructive memories with those that have shattered his identity. These conflicting aspects of himself, all reflected in his memories of the city, have seemed impossible to reconcile. However, Francis' interpretation of the "blur" of the ball's flight suggests that they may somehow be brought together. This "Trinitarian talisman" allows Francis to realize that his positive memories of himself—as a loving father and husband, as Albany's star baseball player—remain an essential part of himself, that their relevance is not negated by his negative actions. Rather than being an obsolete, isolated artifact of Francis' past, the nineteen-year-old baseball player still exists within the fifty-eight-year-old "ravaged man." Gazing at the photograph, Francis muses that "A man can get new teeth, store teeth. Annie got 'em." For the first time in twenty-two years, he feels he can "reenter history under [Annie's] roof" (169).

Encouraged by his interpretation of the photograph, Francis exchanges his rags for the 1916 suit that Annie has saved for him since Gerald's death. As he bathes, he notices a sunburst outside the bathroom window, "as if some angel of beatific lucidity were hovering outside" (172), but when he rises from the tub to look out into the yard, he sees the ghosts of "Aldo Campione, Fiddler Quain, Harold Allen, and Rowdy Dick . . . erecting . . . bleachers" (172). Later, when Francis goes outside, he realizes that the bleachers are occupied by the "forty-three men, four boys, and two mutts" of the talismanic photograph, comprising an audience that unifies the photograph's time, when Francis was accepted and honored by a community, with the many instances when Francis' actions damaged that community. This gathering of ghosts — composed of the celebrants of Francis' talent and the victims of his violence — represents the paradox of Francis' self. Attempting to banish the legacy of his own hands and rid himself of his feelings of guilt, Francis rails against these wraiths who stand between him and a permanent reunion with Annie and his family: "You ain't nothing more than a photograph, you goddamn spooks. You ain't real and I ain't gonna be at your beck and call no more" (177). It is not until Francis sees that each ghost is holding a lighted candle and hears their "antisyllabic lyric" that he realizes "this performance . . . was happening in an area of his existence over which he had less control than he first imagined" (180–81). He becomes frightened when he recognizes the ghosts' words as the "Dies Irae," the sequence of the requiem mass referring to the last day on earth when Christ judges all souls, sending the sinful to hell and the penitent to heaven. Even though his family welcomes Francis' return, Francis returns that evening to the company of bums and begins drinking again: he has been judged by this jury of ghosts, and his penance has been found inadequate.

It is one final encounter with his past that compels Francis to complete his expiation. While talking with a group of bums in the jungle, a makeshift camp for transients located at the edge of Albany, Francis hears that a man has been asking for food for his baby. He immediately seeks the man out and hands him the sandwiches and plum pudding that Annie gave him before he left home. After seeing the baby, Francis returns to the bums and for the first time admits his role in Gerald's death to strangers. When the bums dismiss Francis' story as just another tale of hard luck, Francis feels his confession is "wasted . . . because nobody took it seriously" (215). Disappointed over "yet another wrong decision," Francis recognizes "that he could never arrive at any conclusions about himself that had their origin in reason. But neither did he believe himself incapable of thought. He believed he was a creature of unknown and unknowable qualities, a man in whom there would never be an equanimity of both impulsive and premeditated action" (216). Francis finally comes to terms with the truth he could not face with the gathering of ghosts from the photograph. He acknowledges the existence of "unknowable qualities" within himself that have shaped the course of his life.

The relation between Albany's communities of magical beings and Francis' progression toward integration can be summarized by recalling the function of expiation within the context of Catholic doctrine. The penitent cannot earn God's forgiveness through performing acts of expiation, since divine forgiveness, according to St. Paul, is "a gift of God" not "the outcome of works" (Eph. 2.8–10). Rather, the penitent is given an opportunity to achieve a better understanding of himself and others as he performs these acts. The magical elements of *Ironweed* correspond to this conception of expiation. Gerald, the St. Agnes community of the dead, and the ghosts that Francis encounters are representatives of a suprapersonal power beyond rational comprehension. Gerald compels Francis to perform acts of expiation (acts that, as Gerald predicted, Francis would not understand as expiatory). These acts enable Francis to resume his life in Albany and to accept the central paradox that this urban center holds for him: his simultaneous capacity for rational and irrational actions, both positive and negative.

Francis' integration does not, however, signal the end of his journey through his mythic Albany. In the concluding passage of the novel, he thinks about the paradoxical "artifacts of [his] life"[22] and knows that they will continue to place him in the "intersecting realms" of Albany, the urban site of the center of his self, in which he will discover "all the possibilities that were his" (224). Francis deliberately alienates himself from positive systems of urban order in the "concentrated city," but is ultimately called by the community (past and present) to rejoin that order.

The protagonists of John Cheever's "The Enormous Radio" react to the urban irrational in quite another way: they construct a fortress of order that protects them from external disorder and manifests what they believe to be their harmonious inner state. I propose that their reaction corresponds to the second phase of urban development, the period associated with the dispersion of urban centers and the growth of surrounding suburbs. Although life in suburbia is a future project rather than an actuality for the protagonists of "The Enormous Radio," they share a crucial similarity with Cheever's numerous fictional suburbanites: just as his suburbanites have separated themselves from the chaos of the city through physical distance, the environment Jim and Irene have created within their high-rise apartment is a form of separation. They appear to have achieved what would be for many an enviable state of happiness, unmarred by suffering and conflict:

> Jim and Irene Westcott were the kind of people who seem to strike that satisfactory average of income, endeavor, and respectability that is reached by the statistical reports in college alumni bulletins. They were the parents of two young children, they had been married nine years, they lived on the twelfth floor of an apartment house near Sutton Place, they went to the theatre on an average of 10.3 times a year, and they hoped someday to live in Westchester.[23]

Irene's living room, "its furnishings and colors" chosen "as carefully as she chose her clothes" (314), exemplifies the control that they exert over their lives: nothing exists in their sanctuary that they have not chosen to admit. Like suburbanites, Jim and Irene's capacity to control their environment has been enhanced by technology. In contrast to the urban dwellers of the nineteenth century who often had to venture into the "volatile mixture" of the city[24] to obtain goods and services, the technology of telephones and radios, vacuums and electric blenders have decreased Jim and Irene's need for interaction with the city's turmoil. Machines promote their self-sufficiency and their isolation.

The only way in which the Westcotts "differed from their friends, their classmates and their neighbors" is "an interest they shared in serious music" (313), and while their possession of a radio easily allows them to indulge in their hobby without leaving the security and comfort of their apartment, their desire for music compels them to attend "a great many concerts — although they seldom mentioned this to anyone" (313). They may be reluctant to discuss their concert attendance because it does not readily fit into their preconception of what it means to "strike a satisfactory average." As much as they depend upon technology, their inability to understand "the mechanics of radio — or of any of the other appliances that surrounded them" (313) is another source of uneasiness. Their uneasiness is justified, it seems, when a new radio — an "aggressive intruder" with its "malevolent green light" and its mystifying "dials and switches" (314) — becomes the channel through which the turbulent energies of the outside world invade their protected environment — a crack in the fortress through which the irrational enters.

The radio begins to broadcast conversations that occur in the surrounding apartments, making the Westcotts an audience for marital arguments, family quarrels, the pathos of age, the vulnerability of illness — "demonstrations of indigestion, carnal love, abysmal vanity, faith, and despair" (317). On the night that the magical reception begins, the Westcotts find the radio's broadcasts amusing. While Jim eventually comes to view the continuing radio dramas as an annoying anomaly, Irene becomes more and more distressed by what she hears: "Irene's life was nearly as simple and sheltered as it appeared to be, and the forthright and sometimes brutal language that came from the loudspeaker . . . astonished and troubled her" (317). Her reaction to the radio reaches a climax on the third night when, among other things, she learns that one woman in their building is having an affair with "the hideous handyman," another woman is "a common whore," the elevator operator has tuberculosis, Mrs. Hutchinson's mother is dying of cancer (while Mr. Hutchinson claims they don't have enough money to treat her), and she hears the "screams, obscenities, and thuds" of Mr. Osborne beating his wife (319). Irene becomes hysterical and tearfully entreats Jim to confirm the reality of their own happiness:

> Life is too terrible, too sordid and awful. But we've never been like that, have we, darling? Have we? I mean, we've always been good and decent and loving to one another, haven't we? And we have two children, two beautiful children. Our lives aren't sordid, are they, darling? Are they? . . . We're happy, aren't we, darling? (320)

Inherent in the ancient conception of the city, as I have said, is the human capacity to create order; this capacity to imitate the gods presumably allows human beings to overcome external and internal forces endangering their survival. The Westcotts have taken the capacity to order to its extreme by consciously constructing a refuge from chaos. The radio threatens their order, but the last passage of the story reveals their indelible kinship to the "aggressive intruder." Throughout the story, Jim has seemed relatively nonchalant about the radio, but the pressures of bills coming due, his greying hair, his declining income, Irene's evasiveness about her debts, and his children's future, causes him to abandon the immense effort to maintain his facade of calm. Shaken by his own sense of loss and disillusionment, he confronts Irene with her past: she stands "disgraced and sickened" (321) over the radio. The "aggressive intruder" has, it seems, shared Jim and Irene's sanctuary all along. The broadcasts of the magical radio are an extension of their own human (and here, clearly, their urban) condition. The urge to order that impels them to construct their separated city also impels its destruction, for it precludes the means to integrate the irrational in a productive way.[25]

This irony is also an essential component of the third phase of urban development, the "decentered urban field." If the city represented the center of the universe for some ancient societies, so on a secular level it has continued to be the nucleus of social, commercial, and artistic endeavors. Nonetheless, it has now become necessary to create the oxymoron "decentered urban field" or "decentered city" for, as John Herbers observes, the "once-mighty cities have come apart, and in effect, pieces of them are marching out across the countryside without a center or direction."[26] These "sprawling urban areas with no clearly defined center"[27] raise several interrelated questions. If a city can no longer be defined as a "center," what, then, do we consider a city to be? What new circumstances need to be understood in order to enter the postmodern city? These questions and their ontological analogues are explored by Donald Barthelme in "City Life." As we shall see, Barthelme's story questions the nature of reality in/of the postmodern city, "this exquisite mysterious muck . . . which is itself the creation of the muck of mucks, human consciousness."[28]

The structure and style of "City Life" convey Barthelme's theme: the virtuosity and the fallibility of human consciousness, and the "touch of sublimity" (172) that this paradox confers on city life. His minimalist portrayals of his characters' actions and motivations, and his disjointed presentation of the story's events compel his reader to link the suggestive fragments. Take, for example, Ramona's capture of Charles, Elsa's presumed boyfriend: the very act of kidnapping Charles and the methods that Ramona uses—hiring three men to subdue him and sedate him with a hypodermic needle and then having him chained to a bed—should prompt Charles and Elsa to conclude that Ramona is dangerously psychotic. However, instead of asking Elsa for help when she enters the apartment, Charles is more concerned with chastising her for declaring Ramona's actions against the law, while Elsa finds Ramona's absence from her law classes as troubling as the "extra-legality" of Charles' "sequestration" (158). In addition, the kidnapping seems to have no effect on Elsa's friendship with Ramona since, in the next scene, they are shown placidly watching television together.

More baffling are the circumstances surrounding Elsa's pregnancy at a ceremony of the sun, which Jacques (Elsa's future husband), Charles, Elsa, and Ramona attend:

> The sun dancers were beating the ground with sheaves of wheat.
> —Is that supposed to make the sun shine, or what? Ramona asked.
> —Oh, I think it's just sort of to . . . honor the sun. I don't think it's supposed to make it do anything.
> Elsa stood up.
> —That's against the law!
> —Sit down Elsa.
> Elsa became pregnant. (159)

Elsa's pregnancy is presumably (and hilariously) explained here, for her condition is simply dropped at this point. In the following fragment, we see the outlines of her wedding: "Traffic lights / Pieces of blue cake / Champagne" (160).

The central riddle in Barthelme's decentered city is not Elsa's pregnancy, but Ramona's. The magical conception of Ramona's baby is explored, as Elsa's is not, in a way that questions how we create, collectively and individually, and how we understand our creation(s). The most basic form of creation is the creation of life, and perhaps this is why Barthelme makes the origins of Ramona's pregnancy the story's unsolved mystery. By analyzing Charles' description of a painter's creative powers and processes, we will see why Barthelme invests the conception of Ramona's baby with such mystery. Of course, paintings and babies are of different orders of difficulty, not to mention different ontological orders, but in the fragmented structures of city life/"City Life," the creation of one may reflect the conception of the other.

According to Charles, "every morning [the painter] gets up, brushes his teeth, and stands before the empty canvas. A terrible feeling of being *de trop* comes over him" (170). He may read the newspaper to stimulate his creative powers: "But soon the Times is exhausted. The empty canvas remains" (170). He must do more than just assemble pieces from other realities in order to create his own, and so in desperation he "makes a mark," knowing beforehand that the mark will not be "what he means." Because this mark does not manifest his vision, he is "profoundly depressed." He erases the mark, a gesture that "affords him a measure of satisfaction" (171). He now has to decide "whether or not to venture another mark." The next mark is as "misconceived" as the first, and he erases it too. Although his "anxiety accumulates," the canvas "is now, in and of itself, because of the wrong moves and the painting out, becoming rather interesting-looking." His depression and anxiety begin to lift as he realizes that "a something has been wrested from the nothing." His friends approve: they "drop in and congratulate him on having a not-empty canvas. He begins feeling better" (171). Yet "the quality of the something is still at issue"; the painter "is by no means home free." The painter also acknowledges that "all of the painting—the whole art—has moved on somewhere else, it's not where his head is, and he knows that" (171). The painter is not the sole arbitrator of reality; other realities ("all of painting") exist beyond his own.

Through this parable of the painter, Barthelme gives us the means to enter the mystery of the baby's conception. Ramona arranges the names of possible fathers—Vercingetorix, Moonbelly, and Charles—in patterns of three, concluding that "Upon me, their glance has fallen. The engendering force was, perhaps, the fused glance of all of them" (173). The title of Moonbelly's song, "Cities are Centers of Copulation," (170) emphasizes the urban context of this engendering magic. We may interpret Ramona's act of arranging the three names, and Moonbelly's locating gesture, as corresponding to the painter's process of marking and erasing marks on the space of the canvas. Do Ramona and the painter actually create "a something," or do they invest meaning in "the nothing" because it is "interesting-looking"? As with the painter's canvas, the "quality of the something is still at issue" (171). Has Ramona discovered that the "engendering force" of the city allows "a something" to be created from "the nothing" or from the energies of many?[29] She considers the process of the baby's conception in the passage that concludes the story:

> From the millions of units crawling about on the surface of the city, their wavering desirous eye selected me. The pupil enlarged to admit more light: more me. They began dancing little dances of suggestion and fear. These dances constitute an invitation of unmistakable import—an invitation which, if accepted, leads one down many muddy roads. I accepted. What was the alternative? (173)

Though these muddy roads would seem unrelated to city streets of cement and asphalt, they refer metaphorically, and unmistakably, to urban intercourse. Just before Ramona's final question, she thinks:

I have to admit we are locked in the most exquisite mysterious muck. This muck heaves and palpitates. It is multi-directional and has a mayor. To describe it takes many hundreds of thousands of words. Our muck is only a part of the much greater muck—the nation-state—which is itself the creation of that muck of mucks, human consciousness. Of course all these things also have a touch of sublimity. (172)

Barthelme's touch of sublimity, his muddy roads and mysterious urban muck, lead to magical realism, as they do in the work of William Kennedy and John Cheever. As a mode that emphasizes the variable relationship between the rational and the irrational, magical realism is instrumental in each author's rendering of the paradoxical forces operating in/on the city and its dwellers. Taken together, these works imply that a constant effort must be made to sustain an equilibrium between our rational and irrational energies, in both our surroundings and our psyches. They dramatize how we resist and engage these energies, and how we incorporate them into our experience of the city. We see how urban energies sometimes merge to form a rich collective reality, and how they sometimes clash, causing the whole to be so fragmented that the city's meaning remains confused, elusive. Unlike Jim and Irene in "The Enormous Radio," Francis in *Ironweed* and Ramona in "City Life" accept the "invitation of unmistakable import" to travel down exquisitely mucky city roads on which the rational and irrational intersect, collide, coexist.

Notes

1 Brian McHale, *Postmodernist Fiction* (New York and London: Methuen, 1987), p. 77.

2 David Young and Keith Hollaman, ed., *Magical Realist Fiction: An Anthology* (New York: Longman, 1984), p. 2.

3 McHale, *Postmodernist Fiction*, p. 73.

4 Wendy B. Faris, "Scheherazade's Children: Magical Realism and Postmodern Fiction," p. 172, in this volume.

5 Young and Hollaman, *Magical Realist Fiction*, p. 2.

6 Robert Gibb, *The Life of the Soul: William Kennedy, Magical Realist*, Ph.D. diss., Lehigh University, 1986.

7 George R. McMurray, "Magical Realism in Spanish American Fiction," *Colorado State Review* 8 (1981): 17.

8 Faris, "Scheherazade's Children," p. 245, in this volume.

9 Burton Pike uses this phrase in *The Image of the City in Modern Literature* (Princeton: Princeton University Press, 1981), p. xi.

10 Mircea Eliade, *Patterns In Comparative Religion*, trans. Rosemary Sheed (Cleveland: World Publishing, 1968), pp. 374, 381.

11 Mircea Eliade, *Cosmos and History: The Myth of the Eternal Return*, trans. Willard R. Trask (New York: Harper and Row, 1954), p. 12.

12 William H. Whyte, *City: Rediscovering the Center* (New York: Doubleday, 1988), p. 55.

13 Charles Baudelaire, *My Heart Laid Bare and Other Prose Writings*, ed. Peter Quennell, trans. Norman Cameron (New York: Vanguard Press, 1951), p. 69.

14 Theodore Dreiser, *The Color of a Great City* (New York: Boni and Liverwright, 1923), p. 154.

15 William Sharpe and Leonard Wallock, "From 'Great Town' to 'Nonplace Urban Realm': Reading the Modern City," in *Visions of the Modern City: Essays in History, Art, and Literature*, ed. William Sharpe and Leonard Wallock (Baltimore: Johns Hopkins University Press, 1987), p. 33.

16 Eric Lampard, "The Nature of Urbanization," in *Visions of the Modern City: Essays in History, Art, and Literature*, p. 82.

17 Robert Park, "The City: Suggestions for the Investigation of Human Behavior in the Urban Environment," in *Classic Essays on the Culture of Cities*, ed. Richard Sennett (New York: Meredith Corporation, 1969), p. 91.

18 William Kennedy, *Ironweed* (New York: Penguin Books, 1983), p. 145. Further references will be given in the text.

19 Robert Gibb argues that the dead of *Ironweed*, although not hallucinations, do not have a completely independent existence from Francis' perception. Thus, he rejects the term "ghost" and proposes that the term "shade," derived from Dante's *Purgatorio*, appropriately conveys this intermediary existence. Kennedy himself, however, refers to the dead of the novel as "ghosts." Larry McCaffery and Sinda Gregory, "An Interview with William Kennedy," *Fiction International*, vol. 15 (1984): 169.

In my analysis, I have regarded the dead as representatives of a suprarational level of reality that is not dependent on Francis' perception; I believe that the text provides sufficient indications to support this interpretation.

20 For a more extensive application of Eliade's theories of ancient cosmology to *Ironweed*, see Robert Gibb, *The Life of the Soul: William Kennedy, Magical Realist*. At different points in the novel, "sacred time" (past events of Francis' life) and "sacred space" (places that existed in the city's and Francis' past) exist simultaneously with the events and places Francis experiences as he travels through the "profane" Albany of 1938. Although my interpretation of the rele-

vance of Eliade's theories to *Ironweed* is compatible with Gibb's, my emphasis lies in Eliade's definition of a city as a mythic "center," which I have incorporated into Sharpe and Wallock's description of progressive urban "decentering."

21 Robert Gibb traces Kennedy's allusions to Dante in *The Life of the Soul: William Kennedy, Magical Realist;* for an analysis of Kennedy's allusions to Homer, see Peter Clarke, "Classic Myth in William Kennedy's *Ironweed,*" *Critique* 27 (1986): 167–76, and especially Michael Tierce, "William Kennedy's Odyssey: The Travels of Francis Phelan," *Classical and Modern Literature* 8, 4 (1988): 247–63.

22 "An Interview with William Kennedy," *Fiction International,* p. 164.

23 John Cheever, "The Enormous Radio," in *The Stories of John Cheever* (New York: Knopf, 1947). I cite from the anthologized story, in *Magical Realist Fiction: An Anthology,* ed. David Young and Keith Hollaman, (New York: Longman, 1984), p. 313. Further references are given parenthetically in my text.

24 Marshall Berman, *All That Is Solid Melts Into Air: The Experience of Modernity* (New York: Penguin Books, 1988), p. 168.

25 Burton Kendle compares Jim's and Irene's downfall to Adam's and Eve's expulsion from Eden ("Cheever's Use of Mythology in 'The Enormous Radio'," *Studies in Short Fiction* 4 [1967]: 262–64); Henrietta Ten Harmsel compares their recognition of evil to the protagonist's awakening in Hawthorne's "Young Goodman Brown" ("'Young Goodman Brown' and 'The Enormous Radio'," *Studies in Short Fiction* 9 [1972]: 407–8). Since Jim and Irene construct their "paradise" on the basis of their suppressed knowledge of evil, Cheever's and Hawthorne's stories, Harmsel maintains, share an essential similarity; and as Burton Kendle maintains, Cheever's story portrays not "the fall from good to evil, or from innocence to experience, but the fall from assumed innocence to awareness, specifically self-awareness, and its attendant anguish."

26 John Herbers, "America's Profile Shifts," *New York Times,* Sept. 28, 1986, sec. 6: 64.

27 John Herbers, "Major Cities Ringed by Suburbs Yielding to Sprawl of Small Metropolitan Areas," *New York Times,* July 8, 1983: A9.

28 Donald Barthelme, "City Life," *City Life* (1970; New York: Pocket Books, 1976), p. 172. Further references will be given in the text.

29 Wayne B. Stengel also sees "City Life" as "affirming the urban experience" by emphasizing "the human consciousness that shapes the city and the art that results from the tension between a metropolis and its inhabitants." *The Shape of Art in the Short Stories of Donald Barthelme* (Baton Rouge: Louisiana University Press, 1985), pp. 147–52. While I agree that Ramona can be seen as an artist and heroine, I believe Barthelme is more equivocal about the outcome

of the creative process than Stengel indicates, for the story suggests that the value of "something . . . wrested from nothing" must be conscientiously scrutinized. Stengel does not interpret the baby's conception as a magical event, but a metaphorical one; I see the ambiguity surrounding the baby's conception as reflecting the ambiguity that surrounds the creative process and its results.

LOIS PARKINSON ZAMORA

Magical Romance/Magical Realism: Ghosts in U.S.
and Latin American Fiction

> Ghosts can be very fierce and instructive.
> —Flannery O'Connor, *Mystery and Manners*[1]

In this essay, I will be conjuring a number of literary ghosts and considering how they are embodied (or not) in particular works of prose fiction, whether they are visible (and if so, to whom and why), whether they speak, eat, dream. An investigation of the nature of literary ghosts will tell us a great deal about their authors' metaphysics, politics, and poetics. Some literary ghosts serve their creators as carriers of transcendental truths, as visible or audible signs of Spirit. Other ghosts carry the burden of tradition and collective memory: ancestral apparitions often act as correctives to the insularities of individuality, as links to lost families and communities, or as reminders of communal crimes, crises, cruelties. They may suggest displacement and alienation or, alternatively, reunion and communion. Still other ghosts are agents of aesthetic effect — *el escalofrío, le frisson*, the fantastical release/relief from the constraints of reason. Ghosts of this sort, whose function on first reading seems primarily affective, are not, however, to be taken lightly. They, too, are often bearers of cultural and historical burdens, for they represent the dangers, anxieties, and passional forces that civilization banishes. They may signal primal and primordial experience, the return of the repressed, the externalization of internalized terrors. They are always double (here and not) and often duplicitous (where?). They mirror, complement, recover, supplant, cancel, complete. Which is to say: literary ghosts are deeply metaphoric. They bring absence into presence, maintaining at once the "is" and the "is not" of metaphorical truth.

Ghosts in their many guises abound in magical realist fiction, as we shall see, and they are crucial to any definition of magical realism as a literary mode. Because ghosts make absence present, they foreground magical realism's most basic concern — the nature and limits of the knowable — and they facilitate magical realism's critique of modernity. Their presence in magical realist fiction is inherently oppositional because they represent an assault on the scientific and materialist assumptions of Western modernity: that reality is knowable, predictable, controllable. They dissent, furthermore, from modernity's (and the novel's) psychological assumptions about autonomous consciousness and self-constituted identity and propose instead a model of the self that is collective: subjectivity is not singular but several, not merely individual and existential but mythic, cumulative, participatory. Magical realist apparitions also unsettle modernity's (and the novel's) basis in progressive, linear history: they float free in time, not just here and now but then and there, eternal and everywhere. Ghosts embody the fundamental magical realist sense that reality always exceeds our capacities to describe or understand or prove and that the function of literature is to engage this excessive reality, to honor that which we may grasp intuitively but never fully or finally define. Magical realist texts ask us to look beyond the limits of the knowable, and ghosts are often our guides.

My argument, then, is that magical realism is truly postmodern in its rejection of the binarisms, rationalisms, and reductive materialisms of Western modernity and that its counterrealistic conventions are particularly well suited to enlarging and enriching Western ontological understanding. I will focus on magical realism's opposition to modern ideologies of individualism: magical realist texts universalize the individual self, a strategy that goes a long way in explaining the presence of so many ghosts in magical realist texts. I will be looking at a number of literary ghosts in order to see their creators' postmodern revisions and reunions of the modern divorce between matter and nonmatter, past and present, individual and community. Ghosts are liminal, metamorphic, intermediary: they exist in/between/on modernity's boundaries of physical and spiritual, magical and real, and challenge the lines of demarcation.

Literary ghosts take many forms. For my purposes here, to qualify as a ghost, a literary apparition need not have arms and legs or, for that matter, be limited to two of each. It need only exist as a spiritual force that enters the material world of the fiction and expresses itself as such. The stain on the ceiling in Flannery O'Connor's "Resurrection" is a symbolic repository of religious truth, a holy ghost. Miss Rosa's Sutpen, "man-horse-demon," in William Faulkner's *Absalom, Absalom!* is an archetypal embodiment of cultural memory. The fantastical creatures that haunt Isaac Bashevis Singer's world, the manifestations of ancient gods that irrupt into Carlos Fuentes' fictions—Tezcatlipoca, Huitzilopochtli, Quetzalcóatl, Chac-Mool —are also ghosts in the sense I intend here. Such ghosts, as these examples attest, are culturally specific, behaving according to particular cultural patterns of belief and serving particular cultural (and literary) purposes. Indeed, they may be evoked in order to overcome or escape a particular cultural heritage, that is, evoked in order to exorcise themselves. (Just so, Miss Rosa's paradoxical conjuring of Sutpen's ghost: man-horse-demon.) In Western culture, ghosts have often been cast as dead souls, temporarily returned to, or unable to leave, the living. In their association with death— that most mysterious and extreme condition of the living—ghosts transgress yet other dividing/divisive lines, those between theology, mythology, philosophy, fiction. In this role, they serve their authors to challenge and enlarge the narrative space of each of these forms of ontological inquiry.

As a comparatist interested in U.S. and Latin American fiction, I will be attending to the ghostly presences in works by American writers from a number of countries in the hemisphere. I'll not be able to discuss all of the varieties of ghosts I've just mentioned—that would require a longer study by far than this one—but perhaps my readers will test these types, and others, in their own considerations of magical realism. My essay divides into two distinct parts. I begin by tracing the nineteenth-century U.S. romance tradition with the help of two twentieth-century Latin American magical realists, Gabriel García Márquez and Jorge Luis Borges, in order to show the tendency of both romance and magical realism to archetypalize the self. Whatever the specific political purposes and cultural contexts of romance and magical realism, their characters move toward mythological levels, universal communities, in order to dramatize individual realizations of archetypal human patterns. My first section, then, is primarily concerned with the conditions that favor spectral presences rather than with particular apparitions, though to make my argument I will look through Borges' eyes at one specific example in a story by Nathaniel Hawthorne.

In my second section, I focus on the ghosts who inhabit novels by the Mexican writers, Elena Garro and Juan Rulfo, and the Texas writer, William Goyen. These writers share with Borges and Hawthorne the urge to translate individual into archetype, mimesis into myth. But unlike the ethereal specters of Borges and Hawthorne, the ghosts of Garro, Rulfo, and Goyen live underground, in an earth animated by ancestral inhabitants. Their novels are American books of the dead, necrogeographies of the buried traces of indigenous cultural identity in a shared region of America. My aim in both sections (like the magical realists') is to blur boundaries—in this case, literary and national boundaries—in order to speak of traditions of American counterrealism in a hemispheric sense. To enter this vast territory, it will be useful to survey in a general way some of the ontological and formal issues that make spectral presences so common in magical realist texts.

Magical realist texts, like ghosts, subvert "the commonsense dichotomies of the daylight consciousness," dichotomies upon which modern prose fiction depends, according to Northrop Frye in his seminal discussion of fictional modes in *The Anatomy of Criticism*.[2] The subversions of "commonsense dichotomies" in magical realism are, as I have suggested, both ontological and generic. Magical realist texts question the nature of reality *and* the nature of its representation. In this, then, magical realist texts share (and extend) the tradition of narrative realism: they, too, aim to present a credible version of experienced reality. The crucial difference is that magical realist texts amplify the very conception of "experienced reality" by presenting fictional worlds that are multiple, permeable, transformative, animistic. And (it follows) they create readers whose relations to the fictional world are necessarily ambiguous, unpredictable. Contemporary magical realist narratives remove the ground upon which the reader of conventional novels and short stories expects to stand—the ground of a fictional world that is stable enough to be knowable. In this way, magical realist texts dramatize the process of knowing (and not knowing): the reader is obliged to wonder how we are to locate the "real" in magical realism. This repositioning of the reader with respect to the truth-claims of the narrative further obliges us to recognize our responsibility for the constitution of *all* meanings in the world, to recall our fundamental and necessary implication in the definition of reality as such.

Magical realism's unsettling of generic and ontological assumptions calls new attention to old questions about narrative form and to the fictional worlds that narrative form seeks to create. Whereas conventional narrative realism constructs the illusion of a fictional world that is continuous with the reader's (and whose ontological status is therefore naturalized, transparent), magical realism foregrounds the illusionary status of its fictional world by requiring that the reader follow its dislocations and permutations. So we arrive at an essential paradox: contemporary magical realists write *against* the illusionism of narrative realism by heightening their own narrative investment in illusion. They undermine the credibility of narrative realism by flaunting the relative *in*credibility of their own texts. In short, they point to the literary devices by which "realistic" literary worlds are constructed and constrained, and they dramatize by counterrealistic narrative strategies the ways in which those literary worlds (and their inhabitants) may be liberated. I would, therefore, propose that contemporary magical realism, in flaunting its departures from narrative realism, is self-reflexive and metafictional, even as I recognize that not all self-reflexive fiction is magical realist: Fielding, Sterne, Unamuno, Nabokov, Barth, and many others question the conventions of literary realism without necessarily engaging magical realist modes of narration. My point is that contemporary magical realists are closely allied to writers in other traditions of counterrealism, with whom they share the urge (as Nabokov puts it) to write novels to show that the novel does not exist.[3]

Magical realist texts, in their most distinct departure from the conventions of literary realism, often seem to pulsate with proliferations and conflations of worlds, with appearances and disappearances and multiplications of selves and societies. These magical instabilities depend upon an array of narrative strategies that multiply/blur/superimpose/unify or otherwise transgress the solidity and singularity of realistic fictional events, characters, settings. In magical realist fiction, individuals, times, places, have a tendency to transform magically into other (or all) individuals, times, places. This slippage from the individual to the collective to the cosmic is often signaled by spectral presences. Consider, for example, Toni Morrison's *Beloved*, where Sethe is haunted by her dead daughter, a symbolic and historical embodiment of both her past and her future; Julio Cortázar's stories in *All the Fires the Fire* and *End of the Game*, which shift among times and places and selves, brilliantly subverting our analytic efforts to decide which are dreamed, which not; Isabel Allende's *The House of the Spirits*, where the women characters' domesticity and spirituality are inseparable, a point made literal by the mundanity of the ghosts who rattle the cupboards of the family residence and bring messages that forecast rain.[4] In this novel, as in magical realism generally, the cosmic and quotidian are the ends of a continuum along which both characters and readers move.

The temptation is to multiply examples, so rich and varied are the spectral presences in recent American literature: Fuentes' *Aura*, William

Kennedy's *Ironweed*, Maxine Hong Kingston's *The Woman Warrior*, Leslie Marmon Silko's *Ceremony*, Louise Erdrich's *Tracks*, José Donoso's *A House in the Country*, John Crowley's *Little Big*, Paul Bowles' remarkable short stories set in Mexico and Morocco, "Fernandes/Joyce Carol Oates"' collection of ghostly tales, *The Poisoned Kiss and Other Stories from the Portuguese*. I will resist the temptation to enter all of these haunted worlds now, trusting that my readers will to do so sooner or later (or already have). Here, I want to consider the most influential of recent American magical realists, Gabriel García Márquez and Jorge Luis Borges, and their possible precursor, the U.S. romancer Nathaniel Hawthorne.

I

In *One Hundred Years of Solitude*, Macondo does not pulsate or proliferate into multiple times and spaces, though it does, of course, eventually disappear into thin air. The Buendías are another matter. García Márquez systematically unsettles discrete, stable identity with his familial repetitions and self-reflections and his integrations of the living and the dead. The repeating José Arcadios and Aurelianos are the successive generations of a family, but not in any realistic sense. Rather, we may think of them, paradoxically, as a simultaneous series, an on-going progression of ahistorical archetypes. That *One Hundred Years of Solitude* was originally published in Spanish without a genealogy suggests García Márquez's archetypalizing intent: the Buendías are more significantly connected to prior human patterns than to prior individuals. Only when the novel was translated into English, in deference to the expectation of readers for individualized characters, was the genealogy added. With or without the genealogy, one José Arcadio is in some sense all José Arcadios, one Aureliano all the rest; the Buendía twins, who seem to reverse the archetypal patterns, may, we are told, have been switched at birth. It is, then, as if the José Arcadios and Aurelianos are their own dead precursors, their own ghosts. This shifting relation of individual to archetype often attends the psychology of magical realist characters, making them the offspring of Jung, not Freud.[5] The Buendías are ciphers of a collective unconscious, related to each other less by family history than by mythic paradigm.

The presence of the dead among/in the living in *One Hundred Years of Solitude,* the simultaneity of selves, becomes explicit in the case of the matriarch Ursula:

> "Poor great-great-grandmother," Amaranta Ursula said. "She died of old age."
> Ursula was startled.
> "I'm alive!" she said.
> "You can see," Amaranta Ursula said, suppressing her laughter, "that she's not even breathing."
> "I'm talking!" Ursula shouted.
> "She can't even talk," Aureliano said. "She died like a little cricket."
> Then Ursula gave in to the evidence. "My God," she exclaimed in a low voice. "So this is what it's like to be dead."[6]

Death and the past are present and alive in Macondo (as they are throughout García Márquez's fiction: consider the mythic corpses in *Leaf Storm,* 1955, and "The Handsomest Drown Man," or the mythic almost-corpse in *The General in his Labyrinth,* 1989.) Macondo's timeless paradise ends and its communal history begins when Prudencia Aguilar's ghost arrives. Prudencio brings with him the past and death, that is, time: his apparition incites the clocks to tick in Macondo. Not only the history of Macondo but also its narration depends upon the arrival of a ghost. Melquíades' ghost, returned to Macondo from death by fever on a beach in Singapore, narrates its history and provides a generative instance of the simultaneity of selves and ontological strata characteristic of magical realism.

The Autumn of the Patriarch (1975) also cycles and recycles a character, a nameless dictator who dies and returns from death to impose an endlessly repeating series of political abuses. His status as archetype depends upon this sense of eternal return, as surely as does Melquíades' and the Buendías'. Clearly, García Márquez's phantoms facilitate their creator's account of the vicious circles of Colombian politics. Like Carlos Fuentes' self-replicating characters in *Terra nostra* (1976), García Márquez's characters convey their author's sense that Latin American reality is haunted by what has gone before. History itself is a ghost to be confronted, exorcized, used, overcome.

Jorge Luis Borges' wraiths are situated elsewhere or, as it often seems, nowhere. Whereas Prudencio Aguilar, Melquíades, the simultaneous series of José Arcadios and Aurelianos, the Patriarch, the General are culturally specific ghosts, Borges' wraiths are not. They are embodied ideas, figures of philosophy or dream. The universalizing of the subject in Borges, and in much magical realism, would seem to undercut the possibility of specific political and cultural critique. After all, archetypes often encode dominant cultural stereotypes, rather than contesting them. And yet it is undeniable that magical realist authors have provided some of our most trenchant contemporary political literature, and with ghosts aplenty. That the most counterrealistic contemporary fiction is also the most political results, I think, in large part from the magical realist insistence upon the universality of the subject. By elaborating for the self a transhistorical context, magical realists give added weight to their dramatizations of specific historical abuses. Archetypal conceptions of subjectivity drawn from collective sources provide bases upon which magical realists may construct political positions resistant to the abuses of individualism — exploitative capitalism and messianic nationalism, among others. These authors generalize in order to unsettle absolutes, to clear a space for a larger perspective from which to view the particular histories and cultures they dramatize. Magical realists are what Flannery O'Connor calls "realists of distance."[7]

My argument, then, is that the effectiveness of magical realist political dissent depends upon its prior (unstated, understood) archetypalizing of the subject, and its consequent allegorizing of the human condition. Magical realists recognize both the cost and the appeal of their discourse of universality, and they negotiate the telescopings of generality and particularity, the accordionlike contractions and expansions of perspective, in a number of ways. Borges knew well that all experience is necessarily individual, but he also knew that individuals necessarily generalize in order to make sense of their experience. In his essay on Hawthorne, Borges refers to C. G. Jung, a reference that I cite below. While I do not wish to make Borges (merely) a Jungian, I do think that he shares with Jung the desire to bridge the gap between multifaceted human experience and its symbolic expression in literature. In *Mythical Intentions in Modern Literature*, Eric Gould states that Jung's theory of archetypes aims "to objectify psychological processes, even while it satisfies our need to locate somewhere (however mysteriously) the universalizing function of symbols."[8] This seems to me to be true in Borges' and García Márquez's fiction and in magical realism generally. The universal is indeed located somewhere, but the location is distilled and magically distanced from everyday experience, even as it also refers directly to it.

Ironically, for Borges in the nineteen-twenties, thirties, forties, to write universalizing tales *was* a specifically political act, because it meant opposing the then-current Argentine mode of literary realism, *costumbrismo* ("local color" realism) and its philosophical bases in materialist philosophy and science. In his 1932 essay, "The Argentine Writer and Tradition," Borges argues a point that now—in part because of Borges—seems irrelevant: that the Argentine writer does not have to write about the specific material realities of Argentina in order to represent Argentine reality. Borges describes himself as positioned simultaneously in the mainstream of Western culture and on its colonized margins, arguing that Argentines, like Jews and the Irish, "can handle all European themes, handle them without superstition, with an irreverence which can have, and already does have, fortunate consequences. . . . I repeat that we should not be alarmed and that we should feel that our patrimony is the universe."[9] He describes his early, failed attempts to depict Buenos Aires realistically, and then his inadvertent success:

> about a year ago, I wrote a story called *"La muerte y la brújula"* ("Death and the Compass"), which is a kind of nightmare, a nightmare in which there are elements of Buenos Aires, deformed by the horror of the nightmare. There I think of the Paseo Colón and call it rue de Toulon; I think of the country houses of Adrogué and call them Triste-le-Roy; when this story was published, my friends told me that at last they had found in what I wrote the flavor of the outskirts of Buenos Aires. Precisely because I had not set out to find that flavor, because I had abandoned myself to a dream, I was able to accomplish, after so many years, what I had previously sought in vain. (181–82)

Borges had, by the time he wrote "The Argentine Writer and Tradition," long been "abandoned to dream." Here, it seems to me, Borges elaborates a postmodernist and postcolonialist stance and self-consciously places it in an American cultural context. So he specifically locates the universalizing impulse that makes magic and politics, transcendental myth and everyday social practice, so powerfully synergistic in contemporary American magical realism. It is an impulse that we recognize in the more overtly oppositional work of García Márquez, Allende, Morrison, Rulfo, Garro, Goyen, and many other American magical realists. And in American romance, as we will see in a moment.

In Borges' stories, selves seem to fuse rather than repeat or reappear, as they do in García Márquez's fiction. The cabalistic ideas that one man is all men and, conversely, that the microcosm contains the macrocosm, animates Borges' magical realism, as does the related idea that the self is a dream of God.[10] A preference for archetype over psychology or sociology consistently marks Borges' fictional creatures. There is no need to search for instances: "The Library of Babel" with its "eternal traveler," the "gray man" of "The Circular Ruins," even the stories with seemingly individualized characters and local settings explicitly dramatize the individual's participation in the universal life. "The Other Death" and "The Life of Tadeo Isidoro Cruz (1829–1874)," published in *The Aleph and Other Stories* (1953), begin at specific times and places in Argentine history and with named agents of the action. I will not say "characters" because the trajectory of both narratives is to undo this specificity, to confuse, then fuse individual identity with archetype. The parenthetical dates in the title of "Tadeo Isidoro Cruz" are highly ironic because the singularity of Cruz's life is eventually revoked and a transindividual mythic identity conferred upon him as he is associated with the archetypal gaucho Martín Fierro. "The Other Death" also concludes with the turn from individual to archetype and with a consequent ironic reversal of "fantastic" and "real." Speaking of the "character" Pedro Damián, Borges' narrator says:

> I have guessed at and set down a process beyond man's understanding, a kind of exposure of reason. . . . It is my suspicion that Pedro Damián (if he ever existed) was not called Pedro Damián and that I remember him by that name so as to believe someday that the whole story was suggested to me by Pier Damiani's thesis. . . . A few years from now, I shall believe I made up a fantastic tale, and I will actually have recorded an event that was real, just as some two thousand years ago in all innocence Virgil believed he was setting down the birth of a man and foretold the birth of Christ.[11]

Borges' rejection of unitary, self-constituting consciousness, and his consequent refusal to draw characters according to the conventions of literary realism, may also take the form of an animistic vision of self and world, in which subject and object are mutually generative and reflexive. In his epilogue to *Dreamtigers*, Borges writes: "A man sets himself the task of portraying the world. Through the years he peoples a space with images of provinces, kingdoms, mountains, bays, ships, islands, fishes, rooms, instruments, stars, horses, and people. Shortly before his death, he discovers that that patient labyrinth of lines traces the image of his face."[12] Individuals, nature, culture interpenetrate, overlap, fuse. Borges reverses the Cartesian priority of autonomous consciousness: the self does not create the world but contains it.

This idea also appears in Borges' essays on literature, where the mythic fusion is of authors and literary texts. If García Márquez's replicating characters carry within them the ghosts of their own ancestors, Borges' authors are ghosts of other authors, and their stories the ghosts of other stories, of an archetypal story. So, the narrator of "The Library of Babel" asserts: "The certitude that everything has been written negates us or turns us into phantoms."[13] Here, "phantom" must be understood in the context of Borges' postmodernist subversions of individualism and originality, not (as it is sometimes read) as a statement of literary exhaustion. In his 1945 essay, "The Flower of Coleridge," Borges refers to Valéry's appreciation that the history of literature is the history not of authors but of the Spirit, and to Shelley's opinion the "all the poems of the past, present, and future were episodes of fragments of a single infinite poem, written by all the poets on earth."[14] In this context, Borges also quotes Emerson: "I am very much struck in literature by the appearance that one person wrote all the books; . . . there is such equality and identity both of judgment and point of view in the narrative that it is plainly the work of one all-seeing, all-hearing gentleman."[15]

From a contemporary feminist perspective, Emerson's and Borges' masculinist language seems to undermine their universalizing impulse, apparently excluding women's experience from their generalizations. But we should recall and admit (while also regretting) that in their cultural contexts, "man" — even "gentleman" — *was* a universal category and, therefore, consonant with their transindividualizing intent. And from a comparatist's perspective, their obliviousness to cultural difference would seem to obviate the very possibility of cultural critique. But in magical realist fiction, as I have already argued, the self is first a transcendental category, then a political one. Borges challenges the limits of ideological certainty by refusing the limits of individual identity, both of the self and the literary work. This challenge implies a further challenge: to the ideology of originality. Originality assumes a Hegelian history that is linear, progressive, future-oriented, and made by autonomous egos. Borges posits instead a mythic participation in a "universal history" that is always present, available, communal: "It may be that universal history is the history of a handful of metaphors."[16] The particular is an apparition of the universal; the self contains all others; history is the moving account of timeless moments. As we will see, this characteristic instability of strata — individual, community, cosmos — impels magical realism toward allegory.

In "The Flower of Coleridge," Borges cites Coleridge's statement: "If a man could pass through Paradise in a dream, and have a flower presented to him as a pledge that his soul had really been there, and if he found that flower in his hand when he awoke — Ay! — and what then?"[17] In Borges' reprise of Coleridge's vision, we hear a nostalgic sigh ("Ay!") for the proof ("that flower in his hand") forever lost to the postmodernist magical realist. In the final question ("and what then?") we hear an invitation into his own created world of spectral presences, where proof is moot.

Borges' references to Emerson's Transcendentalism, Coleridge's and Shelley's Romanticism, and Valéry's Symbolism, suggest the confluent sources of his magical realism and link it to the nineteenth-century U.S. romance tradition.[18] In a study of the romantic sources of U.S. romance writers, Leon Chai argues that they were marked by a deepening awareness of the opposition between spiritualism and materialism, and an "increasing subjectivization of . . . consciousness." Chai notes in particular that Hawthorne's literary project was driven by a search for the "magical quality of the actual."[19] No wonder Borges felt an affinity for these romance writers and saw reflections of his own work in theirs.

The hallmark of magical realism that I am tracing here — its rejection of the rugged Cartesian individual — is congruent with romance narrative practice. Northrop Frye's genre and myth criticism is useful in this context. In elaborating his theory of fictional modes in *The Anatomy of Criticism,* he says of romance:

> The essential difference between novel and romance lies in the conception of characterization. The romancer does not attempt to create "real people" so much as stylized figures which expand into psychological archetypes. It is in the romance that we find Jung's libido, anima, and shadow reflected in the hero, heroine, and villain respectively. That is why the romance so often radiates a glow of subjective intensity that the novel lacks, and why a suggestion of allegory is constantly creeping in around its fringes. (304)

Frye's observations implicitly link romance to magical realism, and both to Jungian archetypes and allegory. Allegory, like magical realism and romance, is less concerned with individual psychology than with archetypal patterns. Borges, in his 1949 essay, "From Allegories to Novels," writes: "The allegory is a fable of abstractions, as the novel is a fable of individuals."[20] And in his essay on Nathaniel Hawthorne, also written in 1949, Borges defends Hawthorne against Poe's charge of allegorizing by recurring to his beloved Chesterton, who, he tells us, "implies that various languages can somehow correspond to the ungraspable reality, and among them are allegories and fables."[21]

Borges' defense of Hawthorne attests their shared sensibilities: Hawthorne's compelling intuition, like Borges', was to find some "ungraspable" symbolic significance in ordinary experience. Hawthorne was deeply influenced by the Puritan allegorical understanding of the visible world as an embodiment of God's invisible purpose and also by the transcendentalist view of the interpenetration of nature and divinity. He was, in fact, caught between the Puritan pessimism about fallen nature and the transcendentalist celebration of nature and natural man, and was deeply skeptical of both. But he embraced instinctively (and also self-consciously) the *openness* of both to the presence of mystery in the commonplace. In a deservedly famous passage from "The Custom-House" introduction to *The Scarlet Letter* (1850), Hawthorne writes of a familiar room in moonlight, of its material contents "so spiritualized by the unusual light, that they seem to lose their actual substance . . . [and become] invested with a quality of strangeness and remoteness, though still almost as vividly present as by daylight."[22] The room, writes Hawthorne, becomes

> a neutral territory, somewhere between the real world and fairy-land, where the Actual and the Imaginary may meet, and each imbue itself with the nature of the other. Ghosts might enter here, without affrighting us. It would be too much in keeping with the scene to excite surprise, were we to look about us and discover a form, beloved, but gone hence, now sitting quietly in a streak of this magic moonshine, with an aspect that would make us doubt whether it had returned from afar, or had never once stirred from our fireside. (31)

This "neutral territory" where "ghosts may enter without affrighting us" is, of course, the territory of twentieth-century magical realism as well.

Once again, in romance as in magical realism, the question arises as to the relation of literary abstraction to particular cultural and political conditions. Fredric Jameson's observation that postcolonial literatures allegorize for the purpose of national self-definition is debatable, but I do agree with him that allegory (often in conjunction with magical realism, and sometimes indistinguishable from it) has become a frequent device of postcolonial writers.[23] Paul de Man's discussion of allegory as "immediacy and mediation" is also pertinent to this question, as is his understanding of the tensions created in the dialectical field of allegory.[24] For Hawthorne, as for Borges, to abstract *was* to react specifically to his cultural situation as an American writer. Like Borges, Hawthorne was skeptical about American cultural relations to Europe: like Borges, he was aware of his belated and adoptive status as a New World writer. Because neither Borges nor Hawthorne used indigenous culture to any significant extent in their definitions of America (as do the novelists in the second section of my essay), both felt the lack of a significant American past when compared to Europe's. And both worried about the present. Hawthorne opposed the prevailing mid-nineteenth-century ideologies of individualism and nationalism, as Borges, eight decades later, opposed similar ideologies in Perón's Argentina. Borges (made inspector of chickens by Perón) recognized Hawthorne's feelings of invisibility, speculating that Hawthorne recorded thousands of trivialities in his notebooks "to show himself that he was real, to free himself, somehow, from the impression of unreality, of ghostliness, that usually visited him."[25] Hawthorne, too, found that he could describe his American reality only by abandoning himself to dream.

Hawthorne foregrounds America's colonized relationship to Europe by setting many of his works in the colonial past. *The Scarlet Letter* begins with an ironic reference to the failed utopian projects of the European forefathers in the New World and traces the story of Hester Prynne, doubly marginalized as a sensualist/sinner and a female.[26] In this novel and throughout Hawthorne's work, one senses his anxiety about (and longing for) past and future ideals: his nostalgia for the lost innocence of the New World, his wistful desire for an ideal realm that the New World might yet become. This romantic longing, projected both backward and forward in time and space, is also present in contemporary magical realism. Borges' wistful speculations on impossible orders and García Márquez's descriptions of failed utopias parallel the ambivalent idealism of Hawthorne's romance, though there are, of course, also points of difference to which I'll return in my conclusion.

Hawthorne uses eighteenth-century European Gothic conventions to reflect ironically upon his own idealizations and those of mid-nineteenth-century America. His most brilliant piece of American Gothic is the haunted ancestral home of the Pyncheons in *The House of Seven Gables.* The house of seven gables is an American version of a gothic castle or ruined abbey, a Puritan house of the spirits. In it, gothic ghosts ironize, then undermine, contemporary ideologies of individualism, science, pro gress, perfectability, and above all, the notion of America's historical innocence. Hawthorne's ghosts remind the living that their past is inescapable and their future encumbered.

Because my primary concern here is with generic practice, I am better served for the moment by Northrop Frye's formal analysis of the effects of abstraction in romance than by Jameson's Marxist or de Man's deconstructive analyses. (I will, however, return to Jameson in my second section, where my primary concern is to correlate generic practice with American historical and cultural conditions.) Having noted the archetypal characters in/of romance, Frye observes:

> Certain elements of character are released in the romance which make it naturally a more revolutionary form than the novel. The novelist deals with personality, with characters wearing their *personae* or social masks. He needs the framework of a stable society, and many of our best novelists have been conventional to the verge of fussiness. The romancer deals with individuality, with characters *in vacuo* idealized by revery, and, however conservative he may be, something nihilistic and untamable is likely to keep breaking out of his pages. (304–5)

It is precisely the "idealized" nature of romance, Frye suggests, that admits the political, indeed, the "revolutionary." As in magical realism, the romance conception of archetypal subjectivity carries within it dynamic political potential. In both modes, the self is politically empowered only when it is mythically connected to communal values and traditions, that is, to the collective unconscious of its culture.

Borges' discussion of Hawthorne's fiction and his survey of the nineteenth-century U.S. literary tradition are useful to my comparative purposes here. Besides his many reviews of U.S. literature for the magazine *El hogar* in the thirties,[27] he collected his lectures on North American literature in *An Introduction to American Literature* (1967).[28] Borges is surely the most idiosyncratic of American literary comparatists. To look over his shoulder as he reads U.S. literature is to see a tradition of fantastic literature that U.S. readers scarcely recognize, to find the makings of magical realism everywhere.[28] He was well aware that the fantastic tradition in U.S. literature had been partially obscured by a naturalistic critical practice, and it is almost as if he set out to redress the imbalance.[29] I want to look at some relevant excerpts from his survey of U.S. literature, and then return to Borges' Hawthorne.

About Washington Irving, Borges says, "He thought that his country lacked a romantic past and so he Americanized legends of other times and places."[30] About the historian William Prescott, whose *History of the Conquest of Mexico* he juxtaposes to Irving's *Tales of the Alhambra* and whose theme, he asserts, was furnished by Irving: "like Irving, [Prescott felt] the peculiar enchantment of the Hispanic world" (16). About Whitman, who demonstrates Borges' own practice of archetypalizing and synthesizing the subject: "In previous epics a single hero was dominant: Achilles, Ulysses, Aeneas, Roland, or the Cid. Whitman, for his part, was determined that his hero should be all men" (32). Borges cites the following lines, from section 17 of "Song of Myself," which again demonstrate not only Whitman's philosophy, but also his own:

> These are the thoughts of all men in all ages and lands—they are
>   not original with me;
> If they are not yours as much as mine, they are nothing, or next to
>   nothing;
> If they are not the riddle, and the untying of the riddle, they are
>   nothing,
> If they are not just as close as they are distant, they are
>   nothing. (32)

Elsewhere he says of Whitman that he "wrote his rhapsodies in terms of an imaginary identity, formed partly of himself, partly of each of his readers."[31] Jack London, whom U.S. readers usually consider a naturalist, becomes in Borges' reading a kind of American Ovid, a contributor to the tradition of tales of metamorphosis. About *Call of the Wild* (1903) Borges writes: "It is the story of a dog that has been a wolf and finally becomes one again" (38); Jack London's "style is realistic, but he re-creates and exalts a reality of his own" (39). Borges' final chapter is on the oral poetry of the Plains Indians. He observes this poetry's "contemplative perception of the visual world, its delicacy, its magic" and notes that its images "are like the echo of an absent, a distant and almost dead world" (89–90).

Borges devotes a relatively long chapter (six pages) of *An Introduction to American Literature* to Transcendentalism.[32] As elliptical as it is, his chapter suggests the principal philosophical affinities of nineteenth-century U.S. romance and his own *ficciones*:

> The roots of transcendentalism were multiple: Hindu pantheism, Neoplatonic speculations, the Persian mystics, the visionary theology of Swedenborg, German idealism, and the writing of Coleridge and Carlyle. It also inherited the ethical preoccupations of the Puritans. Edwards had taught that God can infuse the soul of the chosen with a supernatural light; Swedenborg and the cabalists, that the external world is a mirror of the spiritual. Such ideas influenced both the poets and the prose writers of Concord. (24)

Borges continues, listing the shared beliefs of these writers of Concord, which reflect his own: the immanence of God in the universe; the identification of the individual soul with the soul of the world, and the soul of God with both. Borges paraphrases Emerson's Transcendentalist idea: "If God is in every soul, all external authority disappears. All that each man needs is his own profound and secret divinity" (25). So, Borges concludes: "pantheism, which leads the Hindus to inaction, led Emerson to preach that there are no limits to what we can do since divinity is at the center of each of us" (26). In the irony of his cultural comparison, Borges implies the subsequent abuses of "divine individualism" in the history of our own century.

In the paragraph that I have just cited, Borges makes the Calvinist preacher Jonathan Edwards a precursor of the Transcendentalists.[33] His association of Puritanism and Transcendentalism is historically and philosophically accurate, of course. He was well aware that for the Puritans, and then for the Transcendentalists, reality was always symbolic, experience an allegory of invisible presence. But as usual, Borges is revisionary. He refers to a beautiful image in Edwards' hell-fire-and-brimstone sermon, "Sinners in the Hands of an Angry God," and comments: "Metaphors of this sort have led to the supposition that Edwards was fundamentally a poet, frustrated by theology" (8). Borges' Edwards is not a ranting moralist but a mystic. He believed, Borges tells us, "that the material universe is but an idea in the divine mind," and quotes Edwards' poignant description of God: "He is everything and he is alone" (9). Borges' subtle appreciation of Puritan mystical poetics takes us back to Nathaniel Hawthorne, about whom Borges writes, "By his feeling of guilt and his preoccupation with ethics Hawthorne is grounded in Puritanism; by his love of beauty and his fantastic invention he is related to another great writer, Edgar Allan Poe" (20). In his characteristic anachronizing of literary history, Borges also connects the Salem Puritan to a Prague Jew. In Hawthorne's tales, "we have already entered the world . . . of Kafka—a world of enigmatic punishments and indecipherable sins. . . . There is the murky background against which the nightmare is etched. . . . Hawthorne's particular quality has been created, or determined by Kafka. . . . The debt is mutual; a great writer creates his precursors."[34]

Borges' 1949 essay, "Nathaniel Hawthorne," from which I have taken the preceding statement, serves my comparative purposes here. Borges discusses at unwonted length (thirteen pages of small type in my edition) the writer who is for him the beginning, and perhaps the culmination, of U.S. literature.

> If literature is a dream (a controlled and deliberate dream, but fundamentally a dream), then . . . a look at Hawthorne, the dreamer, would be a good beginning. There are other American writers before him—Fenimore Cooper, a sort of Eduardo Gutiérrez infinitely inferior to Eduardo Gutiérrez; Washington Irving, a contriver of pleasant Spanish fantasies—but we can skip over them without any consequence. (217–18)

That Nathaniel Hawthorne inaugurates U.S. literature is a point upon which Borges insists, as he insists upon the fantastical nature of U.S. literature in comparison to the more "rhetorical" nature of Latin American literature. In the course of his discussion of Hawthorne, Borges reverses our usual sense of Latin American literature as more prone to myth and magic than U.S. literature. Borges writes:

> At the beginning of this essay I mentioned the doctrine of the psychologist Jung, who compared literary inventions to oneiric inventions, or literature to dreams. That doctrine does not seem to be applicable to the literatures written in the Spanish language, which deal in dictionaries and rhetoric, not fantasy. On the other hand, it does pertain to the literature of North America, which (like the literatures of England or Germany) tends more toward invention than transcription, more toward creation than observation. Perhaps that is the reason for the curious veneration North Americans render to

realistic works, which induces them to postulate, for example, that Maupassant is more important than Hugo. It is within the power of a North American writer to be Hugo, but not, without violence, Maupassant. In comparison with the literature of the United States, which has produced several men of genius and has had its influence felt in England and France, our Argentine literature may possibly seem somewhat provincial. Nevertheless, in the nineteenth century we produced some admirable works of realism—by Echeverría, Ascasubi, Hernández, and the forgotten Eduardo Gutiérrez—the North Americans have not surpassed (perhaps have not equaled) them to this day. Someone will object that Faulkner is no less brutal than our gaucho writers. True, but his brutality is of the hallucinatory sort—the infernal, not the terrestrial sort of brutality. It is the kind that issues from dreams, the kind inaugurated by Hawthorne. (229)

Literature in the Spanish language "deals in dictionaries and rhetoric, not fantasy": clearly Borges' essay was written before the flowering of magical realism as such in Latin American literature. 1949 was the year in which magical realism was first described as *lo real maravilloso* and designated an indigenous American phenomenon by Alejo Carpentier,[35] and the year that Faulkner (writing in the "hallucinatory" tradition "inaugurated by Hawthorne") won the Nobel prize for fiction. In any case, in 1949, Borges awarded his own private prize for fantastical literature in the Americas to Hawthorne.

According to Borges, it is Hawthorne's tales and sketches that contain his greatest gift, for in them, Borges argues, Hawthorne is able to present a "situation" rather than "the convolutions of the story [or] the psychological portrait of the hero."[36] Borges notes that whereas the novelist must believe in the reality of his characters, Hawthorne "first conceived a situation, or a series of situations, and then elaborated the people his plan required. That method can produce, or tolerate, admirable stories because their brevity makes the plot more visible than the actors, but not admirable novels" (221). The length of the novel requires detailed specifics, whereas the brevity of the sketches and the tales allowed Hawthorne to generalize and thus to create archetypal characters and allegorical plots. Borges admits to disliking Hawthorne's novels, despite some "memorable passages" in *The Scarlet Letter*, and insists upon the sketches: "Hawthorne liked those contacts of the imaginary and the real, those reflections and duplications of art; and in the sketches I have mentioned we observe that he leaned toward the pantheistic notion that one man is the others, that one man is all men" (221). Borges reads Hawthorne's sketches in the same terms he intends his own *ficciones:* as challenges to Cartesian notions of autonomous consciousness, as necessary unsettlings of identity, desirable diffusions of personality.

What Borges celebrates in Hawthorne's sketches as "situation" — what he sees as facilitating "the contact of the imaginary and the real" — is this: an unstable configuration of circumstance, image, character, that leads to a metaphor of being. This configuration contains plot, which Borges tells us is the more visible because of its brevity, but not "the convolutions of story." By plot, Borges means only the barest outlines of action, indeed, action pared back to the point that the "situation" may figure a universal pattern. Character is also required, but certainly not any detailed "psychological portrait of the hero." Again, Borges requires only enough psychology to posit an archetypal subjectivity. As for images, from Hawthorne's vast corpus Borges chooses as an example a sketch whose central image is a ghost.

Predictably idiosyncratic, Borges selects "Wakefield," a little-read (rarely anthologized) sketch published in *New England Magazine* in 1835 and collected in *Twice-Told Tales* in 1837. Hawthorne's narrator tells of a man in London who deserts his wife with no warning or reason, surreptitiously takes a room across the street from his home, and for twenty years observes the life he might have lived. The world considers him dead: Borges explains, "Without having died, he has renounced his place and his privileges among living men" (223). Then, writes Borges, one afternoon, "an afternoon like other afternoons, like the thousands of previous afternoons," Wakefield decides to return home. "He walks up the steps and opens the door. The crafty smile we already know is hovering, ghostlike, on his face. At last Wakefield has returned. Hawthorne does not tell us of his subsequent fate, but lets us guess that he was already dead, in a sense" (223).

"Already dead, in a sense": Borges' phrase betrays his attraction to this obscure work. It is Hawthorne's "ghostlike" character, who exists in between the living and the dead, who is both at once. Wakefield is his own ghost, his own twice-told tale. Like all ghosts, he is metaphoric in his status as simultaneously absent and present, in his movement between worlds. Hawthorne repeatedly emphasizes Wakefield's identity as in-between: "an almost impassable gulf divides his hired apartment from his former home. 'It is but in the next street!' he sometimes says. Fool! it is in another world. . . . The dead have nearly as much chance of revisiting their earthly homes as the self-banished Wakefield."[37] Hawthorne describes Wakefield as "haunting" his home, "vanishing," ceasing to be among the living "without being admitted among the dead" (42). Wakefield is in-between and also double. If García Márquez's characters proliferate and Borges' characters fuse, Hawthorne's character divides. In each case, psychology merges with ontology, and the literary modes most dependent upon individualized psychologies — novel and short story — are altered accordingly.

At the beginning of his story, the narrator of "Wakefield" expresses the hope that "there will be a pervading spirit and a moral, even should we fail to find them, done up neatly, and condensed into the final sentence" (36). Borges criticizes Hawthorne for sometimes overburdening his sketches with a moral, but in "Wakefield," Borges obviously found the "pervading spirit" that Hawthorne wished, unconstrained by the moralizing that Borges disliked. Hawthorne's conclusion is not "done up neatly, and condensed into the final sentence," though the ending is, of course, a calculated climax:

> [Wakefield] has left us much food for thought, a portion of which shall lend its wisdom to moral; and be shaped into a figure. Amid the seeming confusion of our mysterious world, individuals are so nicely adjusted to a system, and systems to one another and to the whole, that, by stepping aside for a moment, a man exposes himself to a fearful risk of losing his place forever. Like Wakefield, he may become, as it were, the Outcast of the Universe. (44)

Wakefield's "situation" does become a metaphor of being. The story remains inconclusive, "ungraspable" to use Chesterton's word, because it reconfirms in these last sentences its status as allegory and Wakefield's status as archetype. Emily Miller Burdick argues Chesterton's point in more contemporary critical terms: romance performs "what we might see as [its] moral function by remaining decentered and continuously deferring restrictive and hence ideologically coercive meaning."[38] Well, yes. Ungraspable. "Wakefield" achieves what Borges most admires: a universal human "situation" unencumbered by specific moral prescription. Kafka is indeed predicted by Hawthorne.

And yet, precisely because "Wakefield" is allegorical, the reader is asked to speculate on its significance, to grasp at the ungraspable. I have said that magical realism heightens the reader's awareness of our intentional relation to the world; the allegorical structure of romance also performs this function. Readers of romance must constitute meaning and at the same time run the risk of arriving at a meaning "done up [too] neatly." So I recognize this responsibility and also run this risk. I would propose that on its most abstract level, Wakefield configures our human condition as living creatures capable of imagining our own death: we are beings capable of imagining non-being. Hawthorne engages this most basic human ambivalence metaphorically and dramatically in the form of the ghostlike Wakefield. And he does so at a distance. Recall my assertion, using Flannery O'Connor's phrase, that magical realists are realists of distance. Borges chooses a story by Hawthorne set in London as a representative example of U.S. romance, when he might have chosen one of Hawthorne's better-known ghost stories explicitly set in New England: "The Minister's Black Veil," "The Prophetic Pictures," "Lady Eleanore's Mantle," "Young Goodman Brown," "The Wives of the Dead." Perhaps Borges feels that the London of "Wakefield" embodies Hawthorne's New England as, he tells us in his essay "The Argentine Writer and Tradition," the French setting of his own story allowed him to capture the reality of Buenos Aires. In that same essay, Borges cites Gibbon's observation that "in the Arabian book *par excellence*, in the Koran, there are no camels" (181). Absence is not the opposite of presence but its necessary condition.

So, then, are magical realism and romance the same fictional mode? Perhaps nineteenth-century U.S. romance is an early and local flowering of twentieth-century magical realism, if I may permit myself this Borgesian anachronism. Their emphases are different, of course, and here I have treated so few texts that any conclusion is premature. If there were space and time, I would extend (as Borges suggests) the discussion of U.S. counterrealism from Hawthorne to Faulkner, add Flannery O'Connor, and compare the grotesque and gothic conventions in their work to analogous conventions in contemporary Latin American magical realism. I would also look at the ghost stories of Ambrose Bierce, a nineteenth-century U.S. writer whom Borges does not mention but whose "Occurrence at Owl Creek Bridge" is strikingly similar to Borges' "The Secret Miracle" in its dramatization of death's extension of living desire. If I pursued these comparisons, I would find fairly consistent differences. In tone, for example, the comic ebullience and sheer inventive energy of Latin American magical realism differs markedly from the darker, even lugubrious tone (the "hallucinatory" quality, as Borges puts it) of U.S. romance. Further differences would be found in the narrative conventions of romance drawn directly from eighteenth-century Gothic fiction; the more explicit political critique of magical realism against the metaphysical categories of romance; the greater emphasis in romance on natural beauty that may seduce and betray; and so on. Some of these comparative generalizations will be tested in the second part of my essay. But Borges' appreciation for Hawthorne points to the similarities of magical realism and romance, rather than their differences, and to their shared project: the expansion and redefinition of our conceptions of subjectivity against the ideological limitations of Cartesian (and Freudian) consciousness, Hegelian historicism, scientific rationalism.

Because my ostensible subject is ghosts, I return to Northrop Frye's theory of fictional modes to see if there are generic grounds on which to differentiate magical realism from romance. Frye, to conclude his discussion of his five categories of narrative realism, proposes: "Let us take, as a random example, the use of ghosts in fiction." Frye is disingenuous. The example is hardly random, and it goes as follows:

In a true myth there can obviously be no consistent distinction between ghosts and living beings. In romance we have real human beings, and consequently ghosts are in a separate category, but in a romance a ghost as a rule is merely one more character: he causes little surprise because his appearance is no more marvellous than many other events. In high mimetic [i.e., the epic; tragedy], where we are within the order of nature, a ghost is relatively easy to introduce because the plane of experience is above our own, but when he appears he is an awful and mysterious being from what is perceptibly another world. In low mimetic [i.e., the novel], ghosts have been, ever since Defoe, almost entirely confined to a separate category of "ghosts stories." In ordinary low mimetic fiction they are inadmissible, "in complaisance to the scepticism of a reader," as Fielding puts it, a skepticism which extends only to low mimetic conventions. The few exceptions, such as *Wuthering Heights*, go a long way to prove the rule — that is, we recognize a strong influence of romance in *Wuther-*

ing Heights. In some forms of ironic fiction, such as the later works of Henry James, the ghost begins to come back as a fragment of a disintegrating personality. (50)

Frye does not mention "magical realism," of course, since the term was not yet current in literary criticism in 1957 when *The Anatomy of Criticism* was published. Nonetheless, we see immediately that what we now call magical realism fits into Frye's second category, romance, where ghosts are expected inhabitants of reality and (as Hawthorne puts it in "The Custom-House") enter without affrighting us. So, I might reverse my earlier Borgesian anachronism and propose, on the contrary, that twentieth-century magical realism is a recent flowering of the more venerable romance tradition that Frye describes. Indeed, some American magical realist texts are also flowerings of other, and older, non-European and non-literary traditions in which Frye has no interest.

But I do. I want now to look at three American novels in which the spirits of ancestors are enlivened by indigenous mythologies of "afterlife" (which is *not* after life but present in life) and by popular ritual practices that still reflect those mythologies. Whereas Borges' and Hawthorne's counterrealism must be situated with respect to European literature and philosophy, the three writers whom I discuss in the next section of my essay engage systems of belief specific to the American cultural territory. William Goyen, Elena Garro, and Juan Rulfo imagine inhabited undergrounds that recall a time when Texas was Tejas, a state of Los Estados Unidos de México rather than of the United States of America, when the Río Grande/Río Bravo was not a drastic demarcation between vastly different cultures but, on the contrary, a connecting link among indigenous groups and later, among the various colonizers of New Spain. Here, I will shift my discussion from the philosophy of magical realist subjectivity to three novelistic embodiments of it and to the indigenous American cultures and histories they reflect. My aim is to leave off theorizing and to test my theories tacitly by allowing these spectral presences to emerge from/in the mythic ground they inhabit. If Borges and Hawthorne are realists of distance, we may think of Goyen, Garro, and Rulfo as realists of depth. So, now, I bring my discussion of ghosts down to earth.

II

William Goyen's *The House of Breath* (1950), Elena Garro's *Recuerdos del porvenir* (translated as *Recollections of Things to Come*, 1963), and Juan Rulfo's *Pedro Páramo* (1955) are comparable in their investigations of the relations of the dead to the living and the relations of the land to both. These writers create fictional communities that dramatize ironically the inevitability of human solitude, but unlike García Márquez's Macondo or Borges' Triste-le-Roy/Buenos Aires or Hawthorne's Salem/London, the people in Goyen's and Garro's and Rulfo's communities are already dead and buried. Goyen's fictional community of Charity, Garro's Ixtepec, and Rulfo's Comala are ghost towns to which narrators make mythic returns to remember, recount, and reconstitute the histories and cultures of their regions. Their theme is our *residencia en la tierra*, a phrase used by Pablo Neruda to title three volumes of his poetry, a phrase whose preposition, *en*, suggests a crucial ambivalence lost in English: our residence *in* and *on* the earth. These writers entertain the possibility of returning home, even though "home" is underground and the land has been sold.

The House of Breath (1950) is a lamentation for the lost. Charity, Texas, is gone and its inhabitants are ghosts, resuscitated by the efforts of a single estranged survivor. The narrator, archetypalized as "Boy," occupies a present time and place from which he is alienated, and he narrates out of an Orphic need to enter the world of the dead. He announces his need at the outset: "to find out what we are, we must enter back into the ideas and the dreams of worlds that bore and dreamt us and there find, waiting within worn mouths, the speech that is ours."[39] He descends into a realm where

> faces are unreal, worn blurred stone faces of ancient metopes of kin, caught in soundless shapes of tumult, wrestling with invasion of some haunted demon race, half-animal, half-angel — O agony of faces without features like faces in fogs of dreams of sorrow and horror, worn holes of mouths opened, calling cries that cannot be heard, saying what words, what choked names of breath that must be heard. (9)

During the course of the narrator's visit to this underworld, faces come into focus, as do the features of the land above ground. In the end, Boy is able, like Orpheus, to return to the surface to sing to the rocks, the trees, and to a human community that includes the reader. A picture of a blind girl with a lyre on the kitchen wall in Charity, along with the map ("the world's body") tacked up beside her, images Boy's Orphic achievement.

So we understand Boy's problem as the disintegration of the self in a modern U.S. city and his narrative project as his reintegration into the vanished community of Charity and into the natural world that contains it. Repeated images of fog and melting and dissolution remind us of the narrator's need to let go his individual ego, to merge with the community of the dead and with the land. By the end of the novel, Boy has spoken and listened to the inhabitants of Charity, as well as to the voices of the town itself, the river, the well, the shutters, the cistern wheel. The town of Charity is a principal narrator, as is the river that runs through it. The narrator's project of reintegration involves, then, not only his family and his regional culture but the natural world as well. Hence the novel's ambiguous subtitle, *Under All the Land Lies the Title:* Goyen's articulate/d earth can and must be repossessed emotionally, despite the bills of sale.

Elena Garro's *Recollections of Things to Come* (1963) is not so sanguine. Her novel contains more of the narrative devices that we associate with magical realism and, predictably for a Latin American writer, more references to specific political events. Garro's story takes place during the Cristero rebellion, a popular uprising against government repression of the Catholic church that occurred in the aftermath of the Mexican Revolution, primarily in the Mexican states of Jalisco, Michoacán, and Colima, during the second half of the 1920s. The story is set in, and narrated by, the town of Ixtepec.[40] Garro devises a dual narrator: a "we" that is the collective voice of the dead town and an "I" that belongs to the stone promontory upon which the town was situated. The novel begins:

> Here I sit on what looks like a stone. Only my memory knows what it holds. I see it and I remember, and as water flows into water, so I, melancholically, come to find myself in its image, covered with dust, surrounded by grass, self-contained and condemned to memory and its variegated mirror. I see it, I see myself, and I am transfigured into a multitude of colors and times. I am and I was in many eyes. I am only memory and the memory that one has of me.[41]

Here, too, the title lies under all the land, and history is grounded in more ways than one: people speak from underground and the earth itself speaks, and the story they tell is of a community that has gone nowhere.

Porfirio Díaz, Francisco Madero, Venustiano Carranza, Emiliano Zapata,

Pancho Villa, Álvaro Obregón—the great actors in Mexico's now mythic Revolutionary drama—provide the backdrop for the fateful occupation of Ixtepec by federal troops, counterrevolutionary ruffians sent to impose the government's ban on Catholic practices. Their commander, General Rosas, has no interest in the liberal reforms that impelled Mexico's postrevolutionary suppression of the Catholic church. His only interest is to impose his personal will, and he instantly becomes absolute dictator in Ixtepec. Rosas brings with him his captive mistress, Julia, a woman set apart by her electrifying beauty and, as Rosa's mistress, her sexual power. She becomes a living legend in the town, an obsessive presence more dangerous to the communal order than General Rosas himself. But such is her mythic energy that she escapes from Ixtepec magically one night, aided by a former lover, a mysterious stranger who arrives to conjure Julia's getaway.

With their disappearance, political realities overwhelm magical resolutions: the mythologized Julia may escape as in a fairytale, but the town cannot. Isabel Moncada, daughter of an upstanding family in Ixtepec, replaces Julia as General Rosas' lover, but her seduction by abusive power turns her, at the end of the novel, into the very stone that has narrated her story. *Recollections of Things to Come* chronicles not the psychological reintegration of an individual, as does *The House of Breath*, but a community's futile attempt to construct an ongoing history in the face of impossible political obstacles. As my summary suggests, not the least of these obstacles is a social order that defines women—Julia, Isabel—solely in terms of the men with whom they sleep.

The third of my American books of the dead, Juan Rulfo's brief masterpiece *Pedro Páramo* (1955), is the most metaphysical. The word *páramo* in Mexican Spanish signifies a high plateau and carries the connotation of bleak, rugged, abandoned terrain; Pedro/Peter is, of course, *piedra*, stone, rock. In an essay called "Landscape and the Novel in Mexico," the Mexican poet and essayist Octavio Paz says that Rulfo's landscape "is a symbol and something more than a symbol: a voice entering into the dialogue, and in the end the principal character in the story. . . . [It] never refers only to itself; it always points to something else, to something beyond itself. It is a metaphysic, a religion, an idea of man and the cosmos." [42] Rulfo's ghost town, Comala, is explicitly located in his native state of Jalisco, but his haunting and poignant images insistently transcend specific location. I will return to this point, but for now I will say only that Comala combines the necrogeographies of both Catholic and indigenous afterworlds. More than

Goyen's Charity or Garro's Ixtepec, Rulfo's Comala is an archetypal enactment of a culture's conception of the place and performance of the dead.

The novel begins with the first-person account of a character, Juan Preciado:

> I came to Comala because I was told that my father, a certain Pedro Páramo, was living here. My mother told me so, and I promised her that I would come to see him as soon as she died. . . .
>
> It was in the dog-days, when the hot August wind is poisoned by the rotten smell of the saponaria, and the road went up and down, up and down. They say a road goes up or down depending on whether you're coming or going. If you're going away it's uphill, but it's downhill if you're coming back.[43]

Downhill, indeed: Juan finds an underground community of ghosts who have died because the town boss, Pedro Páramo, has willed it so.

In the first half of *Pedro Páramo*, Juan Preciado's conversations with the dead are interpolated with third-person sections describing the career of rape, murder, and political cunning that has made Pedro Páramo the absolute owner of Comala. Midway through the novel, Juan seems to join the dead once and for all, to die himself, though his conversations with the dead before this point leave open the possibility that he has been dead all along. Here, as in *The House of Breath*, images of melting and dissolving signal the character's integration into earth. Juan accommodates himself beside a woman who transforms into the very soil in which they are buried:

> The heat made me wake up. It was midnight. The heat and the sweat. Her body was made of earth, was covered with crusts of earth, and now it was melting into a pool of mud. I felt as if I were drowning in the sweat that streamed from her. I couldn't breath. . . .
>
> There wasn't any air. I had to swallow the same air I breathed out, holding it back with my hands so it wouldn't escape. I could feel it coming and going, and each time it was less and less, until it got so thin it slipped through my fingers forever.
>
> Forever.
>
> I remember seeing something like a cloud of foam, and washing myself in the foam, and losing myself in the cloud. That was the last thing I saw. (55–56)

Death is dramatized as a metamorphosis from one state of consciousness to another, rather than a radical interruption or change of form. So Juan joins the faceless chorus of Comala's *calaveras* (skeletons). The text no longer provides his first-person account; rather, the third-person narrator circles back to recount the decline and death of the town that occurred long before the novel begins.

The voices that tell Comala's history are not so much voices as echoes of voices that float free of faces, bodies, individual histories. Goyen's description of the forgotten inhabitants of Charity at the beginning of *The House of Breath*—"faces in fogs of dreams of sorrow and horror, worn holes of mouths opened calling cries that cannot be heard" (9)—perfectly describes Rulfo's dead in *Pedro Páramo*. But the faces never come into focus for Juan Preciado (or the reader) as they do for Boy in *The House of Breath*. In Comala, images of blurred sight and muffled sound are everywhere: "the thin sound of weeping," "the echo of the shadows," "voices worn out with use." Juan says, "those murmurs seemed to come from the walls, to seep out of the cracks and broken spots. They were people's voices but they weren't clear, they were almost secret, as if they were whispering something to me as I passed, or were only a buzzing in my ears." (57) At one point, Juan calls an interlocutor by the name of Doroteo, to which the voice replies, "My name is Dorotea. But it's all the same." Even gender distinctions are blurred, muted, effaced.

Breath, too, is a central image in *Pedro Páramo*. In the passage I cited above, Juan's breath, so thin it slips through his fingers forever, recalls Boy's final sentence in *The House of Breath:* "it seemed that the house was built of the most fragile web of breath and I had blown it—and that with my breath I could blow it all away" (193–94). Whereas Rulfo's image signals the final dissolution of Juan's ego into the community of death and earth, Goyen's image signals Boy's ultimate movement toward individuation. If the voices of the dead in Charity breathe life into those who can hear, Comala's dead sing no such song. "It was the voices that killed me," Juan tells Comala's ghosts, after he has himself become one of them. I will speculate in my conclusion on these differences. Here, my point is to call attention to the fact that though Rulfo's and Garro's characters are not revitalized by the mythic realities they encounter below the surface of the American land, their narratives of communal disintegration depend upon them as clearly as does Goyen's narrative of individual integration.

What are the shared cultural topographies of these American books of the dead? The ancient Egyptian books of the dead were guides to the underworld, containing prayers and spells designed to ward off dangers that the dead were likely to encounter there. Variously called "Book of

Coming Forth By Day," "Book of the Underworld," "Book of Breathings," these texts were at once how-to manuals and maps of metaphysical space. Western classical literature also abounds in books of the dead, narratives of heroes' and gods' negotiations in the underworld. I have already mentioned Orpheus; one also thinks of Odysseus and Aeneas and their offspring in Dante's more elaborate medieval Catholic underworld. The "theme of descent," as Northrop Frye calls this literary archetype, obviously animates the novels of Goyen, Garro, and Rulfo.[44] When, in *The House of Breath*, Boy says, "I will dive down naked and alone into that place and touch what I never had and hold it there" (178–79), he speaks for the narrators of *Pedro Páramo* and *Recollections of Things to Come* as well. The River that runs through Charity acknowledges the universality of Boy's project: "to drop down into any of us, into depths (in river or self or well or cellar) is to lower into sorrow and truth" (28). Boy is an archetypal descender and a descendant, too, of this archetypal Western literary tradition.

But Boy and Juan Preciado and Isabel Moncada also move in other directions, and so will I. Orpheus and Odysseus and Aeneas are far removed in time and space from the American territory I am mapping here. While Goyen's and Garro's and Rulfo's books of the dead are enriched by resonances of these previous European literary descents, their fiction seems to me to create different kinds of underworlds and stress other aspects of the descent. Their emphasis is not on the characters' capacity to *free* themselves from the earthbound dead, but rather their capacity to become permanent *residents* of the ghostly communities they enter. They must become integral elements of earth itself. Orpheus and Aeneas care nothing for the landscape of the underworld—indeed, Orpheus is commanded upon pain of great loss *not* to look back at it. The French painter Jean-Baptiste Camille Corot understood this classical tradition perfectly: in his 1861 masterpiece, "Orpheus Leading Eurydice from the Underworld," he paints the couple leaving a gray landscape peopled with pale, listless figures, Eurydice still veiled though no longer featureless. Our American books of the dead, on the contrary, give us remarkably specific evocations of place. Their underworld settings—Charity, Ixtepec, Comala—are not mere backdrops for the action, but agents of the action; the earth is animate, and natural phenomena are instrumental, generative. Boy, Juan Preciado, Isabel Moncada enter the earth and converse with it and its inhabitants. The "world's body" is alive, and these characters know that they must occupy its body before they can fully occupy their own. As I have said, these are not realists of distance, but of depth.

Goyen, Garro and Rulfo embody earth as a sedimentation of cultures, as a stratification of the living remains of ancient peoples. The "New World" in their novels is not new but old: they incorporate belief systems that reflect Amerindian attitudes and ritual practices involving the land as the habitation of both the living and the dead. Boy, Juan Preciado, and Isabel Moncada look back with regret to a time before the land was exploited by careless commercialism or appropriated by corrupt *caudillos*. They remember a time before the modern Western separation of culture and nature, when the land was not conceived as private property in need of "development." At first glance, these memories seem to contain the "wilderness" or "virgin land" or "paradise lost" or "utopia" motifs so common in American romance literature. But there is something different, something un-Western, about these embodiments of earth.

In fact, Goyen, Garro, and Rulfo reject the Eurocentric conception of the American land as "virgin" in order to dramatize their characters' experience of the earth as alive with ancient peoples and rituals patterns and sacred places. Their characters speak for/from/as the earth: they speak with dirt in their mouths, they eat the earth, they are themselves "figures of dust," a phrase from "The Children of Old Somebody," a story by Goyen to which I will return. Here, we recall García Márquez's character Rebeca, who eats dirt, experiencing "those secret tastes . . . getting back her ancestral appetite, the taste of primary minerals, the unbridled satisfaction of what was the original food . . . with a confused feeling of pleasure and rage."[45] But *One Hundred Years of Solitude* is not a novel of the animate earth such as these.

In Rulfo's *Pedro Páramo*, Juan Preciado suffers the muffled voices of the dead and their ironic descriptions of Comala's bygone beauty, lies with them, and then melts bodily into their earth. Isabel *is* the rock that is Ixtepec in Garro's *Recollections of Things to Come*, a rock that laments the time when its splendor did not fall on ignorance, on "voluntary forgetfulness": "I saw myself as a jewel. The stones acquired different shapes and sizes and I would have been impoverished if a single one had changed its place" (111). In Goyen's *The House of Breath*, Boy's psychic integration depends upon his physical integration into the earth, upon his bodily, sensuous contact with the world, a contact reiterated in his incantatory phrase, "I touch you and name you." Boy makes love to the River, and the River to the land. The River summarizes Boy's erotic engagement of earth: "Everything flows into everything and carries with it and within it all lives of its life and others' life and all is a murmuring and whispering of things changing into each other" (28). Phenomena and consciousness merge: the physical and the metaphysical, body and mind, self and other, life and death intermingle and conjoin.

The perspectives of Rulfo's and Garro's narrators reflect the cosmology of the Nahuatl-speaking peoples of the central and northern highlands of Mexico. The Nahua peoples conceived of five "world-directions": North, South, East, West, and the Center, the direction of up and down. The human figure representing this direction in the pre-Hispanic Borgia Codices is painted as if propelled by centrifugal force, his body spinning, his feet above his head, his arms below and in motion. Earth is above and below and around him: he hovers within it. So also Garro's narrator circles above and around herself, as it were, in the Center: "From this height I contemplate myself: vast, lying in a dry valley. I am surrounded by spiny mountains and yellow plains inhabited by coyotes. . . . I wish I had no memory, or that I could change myself into pious dust to escape the penalty of seeing myself" (3). The "pious dust" is proposed as the earth's antidote to the abuses of human history—too late, it would seem, since the abuses have already occurred, the community is already dead. But the land is still animate, still contains the community, still functions as a psychic component of character and a source of narrative energy.

Nahua culture posits the integral relation of human, natural, and cosmic realms. Garro's characters are repeatedly described in terms of natural phenomena. The eyes of one character, an outsider to the town, are described as "deep and [having] rivers and sheep bleating sadly in their depths." Another is "cut off from my voices, my streets, my people. Her dark eyes showed traces of cities and towers, distant and strange." Yet another is described as wishing to escape "the single, bloody day of Ixtepec" to find "the comings and goings of the stars and the tides, the luminous time that spins around the sun." Topography, climate, the products of the land are registered in/as the characters' psychic terrain. Like Goyen's narrating town, river, wind, Garro's narrative voices become a kind of spirit-field that penetrates the earth and the population of Ixtepec.

Garro refuses the Western hierarchy that places nature at the service of human beings. Rather, she returns mythically to the pre-Hispanic belief that it was humans who served the earth, who nourished it with their blood. Octavio Paz writes about the pre-Hispanic practice of human sacrifice, without which, it was believed, the sun would not rise: "Without human blood, life would cease to flow and the universe would come to a halt. This view of the world and of mankind is the exact opposite of our modern conception, which sees nature as an enormous reservoir of energy and resources that the human race can dominate and exploit with impunity."[46] Beyond practices of human sacrifice, Paz writes that Mesoamerican cultures projected onto the natural world what he calls a "universal sympathy," a "vital fluid that unites all animate beings—humans, animals, plants—with the elements, the planets, and the stars" (20). Garro's narrator would seem to trace what happens when humans upset this universal sympathy, when neither the earth nor the cosmos can redress their violations. This narrative strategy allows her to reaffirm the agrarian, communitarian, mythic underpinnings of Mexico's indigenous heritage even as she describes their unsettling by European attitudes and their ultimate demise.

Juan Rulfo's *Pedro Páramo* engages the indigenous elements of modern Mexican culture particularly, as I have said, in its dramatization of Mexican attitudes toward death. Rulfo's underground community of Comala reflects the Catholic concept of purgatory, as critics have frequently noted. But more importantly (and more subtly) it reflects the complex afterworld of pre-Hispanic Mexico. Hugo G. Nutini, in his remarkable book, *Todos Santos in Rural Tlaxcala*, states that among Nahuatl-speaking peoples there was no fundamental distinction between cosmology and theology:

> the origins of the gods and the world, the provenance of human beings, their trajectory on earth, their relationship to the gods, and their final destination were basically a single normative system. In this conception of the universe, humans were created by the gods, went through life in intimate ritual and ceremonial contact with their creators, and joined them in their final destination. . . . *The structure and social organization of earthly life were mirrored in the afterlife*, where the dead went to serve their creators. As servants of the gods in the afterlife, the dead were at the same time men and gods.[47]

The realms of the dead and the living reflect one another, are penetrable, permeable, mutually knowable. Mictlan, literally "the place of the dead," is not like the Catholic purgatory in that it implies no system of reward or punishment. An individual was accommodated in one of its nine infraworlds or thirteen supraworlds not according to his or her moral behavior but according to the cause or circumstances of his or her death. Thus, someone who had died by drowning or in circumstances associated with water would naturally proceed to the region of Tlaloc, god of water; those who died in battle or in childbirth joined Huitzilopochtli, god of war and the sun; death from natural causes, from disease, death in infancy, also resulted in discrete communities around appropriate deities whom the dead served as intermediaries with the living. Nutini tells us that there were, presumably, "as many celebrations of the dead during the year as there were identifiable ways of dying marked by patron gods" (69). One's place and activity in death follows directly from one's final act or condition in life: death is not a truncation of life but a continuation. If the Christian purgatory separates the dead from the living by a psychological (as well as theological) abyss, the Nahua afterworld is joined to this world and reiterates its structures and concerns, a conception that offers a bridge to the world of the living, not a radical judgment upon it.

Amerindian mythology is not explicit in *Pedro Páramo*, but indigenous attitudes toward death are nonetheless present as they are practiced in Mexico on the Day of the Dead, *Día de Muertos*, also called *Todos Santos*, All Souls Day, November 2. On this day, food is placed on the graves for the spirits of the dead, who return to converse with the living. Candles and flowers are arranged on altars (*ofrendas*) to welcome departed friends and family members into homes, restaurants, markets, as well as to cemeteries and churches. To make the dead feel at home, their favorite foods are placed on the *ofrendas*, along with traditional breads and sweets. Objects that were used by the dead during life in their professions and pastimes are also placed on the altars and graves to make their one-night stay familiar.

The most important symbol of the Day of the Dead celebrations are the toy replicas of skeletons (*calaveras*, literally "skulls"). They are everywhere, made of everything—paper, papier-mâché, wire, wood, sugar—and are associated historically with a satirical verse form also called a *calavera*. *Calaveras* are still published in tabloids sold in the streets at the time of *Todos Santos:* presumably social criticism can be practiced with impunity only from the grave. These satirical verses are, in turn, visually associated with the engravings of the great Mexican printmaker José Guadalupe Posada (1852–1913), who illustrated them in the popular press at the end of the last century and the beginning of this one. In Posada's engravings, *calaveras* form communal scenes representing social classes and political events; on individual graves, miniature *calaveras* reenact the favorite activities of the person buried there. *Calaveras* celebrate the pleasures of the living, mock our follies, and remind us that death is a part of life. They laugh at death, domesticate it, socialize it. Rulfo's characters in *Pedro Páramo* must be thought of as *calaveras* in this popular tradition of the living dead: they are satiric go-betweens for whom life and death are indistinguishable, for whom "underworld" and "afterworld" are meaningless spatial and temporal markers.

It is here that Goyen's fiction most clearly converges with Rulfo's and Garro's: the necrogeography of *The House of Breath* also subverts the Western separation of life and afterlife, body and soul. In a fashion more Mexican than Texan, Goyen privileges the past by honoring the animate earth and the living spirits it contains. The River is, again, the novel's authority: "And we are to keep turning the wheels we turn, we are wind we are water we are yearning; we are to keep rising and falling, hovering at our own marks, then falling, then rising. (Who can set a mark or measure us? They cannot name my tides or measure me by the marks drawn on a wall; I hover)" (28). Goyen, like Garro and Rulfo, challenges the hierarchy upon which Frye's Western "theme of descent" is based, a hierarchy that places earth below heaven, the world of the dead below that of the living. He recognizes that this metaphoric axis does not fully express his narrator's need, that it belies our *residencia en la tierra*, our complex location *in/on* the world's body. Goyen's earth is circumambient and central, and like the turning figure in the Borgia Codices that represents the direction of the Center in the Nahua cosmos, his characters must learn not only to dive, but also to hover.

The photographer Keith Carter records the topography, fauna, and flora of East Texas. *The Blue Man* is Carter's collection of photographic images of this region — William Goyen's region and his own — to which he refers in an interview as Deep East Texas.[48] For Carter, this regional denomination — Deep East Texas — suggests the mythic depths of place, though the term is also used (unmythically) by professional and commercial associations to indicate the fifteen-county area along the Louisiana border between the Trinity and Sabine rivers. Keith Carter reminds us that this part of Texas has little in common with the dry, flat terrain of the rest of the state:

> East Texas is primarily rural and dotted with forests and lakes. It's culturally and ecologically diverse. The Big Thicket is there. Four of the five carnivorous plants found in North America occur in the

thicket. You can find things like orchids growing next to cactus. The last vestiges of the red wolf are thought to be there, and every now and then you hear the sightings of the supposedly extinct ivory bill woodpecker. It's a real peculiar place, a landscape full of baygalls and titi thickets. (124)

The interviewer asks Carter to describe these natural phenomena.

Well, a baygall is a depression that has been cut off from a river or creek at one time. It's a very swamp-like region with tupelo and cypress. Alligators, beavers, deer, otters will make their homes in a baygall. They're very dark, very mysterious places. A titi thicket is made up of the titi vine, which is something like a grapevine. The region is called the Big Thicket because in some areas it's virtually impenetrable. All kinds of buried treasure is in there, legends, Indian ghosts, unexplainable moving lights. Anyway, it's a landscape that knows how to keep a secret. (124)

A landscape that knows how to keep a secret, and Goyen grew up hearing the whispers.

In his introduction to *The Collected Stories* (1975), Goyen insists upon the ancient voices that animate his Deep East Texas earth: "The landscape of my stories, generally East Texas, is pastoral, river-haunted, tree shaded, mysterious and bewitched. Spirits and ghosts inhabit it: the generations have not doubted their presence, their doings."[49] Goyen's reference to "the generations" suggests the rootedness of Deep East Texas, a relatively poor rural population that does not conform to U.S. patterns of mobility. In *The Blue Man*, Keith Carter refers to a family in one of his photographs that has been on the same land since before Texas was a republic. They have no telephone, no television, so he asks them what they do for entertainment. The mother replies:

"We go down to the creek after it rains," she said. "Arrowheads, spearheads, we have mounds all over this land. We have all these animals." She took me into this little room. They live in the house that Mr. Cutler's great-grandfather built, and there's this whole wall of arrowheads and spearheads that I suspect some museum would dearly love to have. (128)

Deep East Texas is spotted with Caddoan burial mounds, testaments to a past that still exists in the present of this region.

I do not know whether Goyen was consciously influenced by Amerindian social structures or cosmogonies, as Rulfo and Garro certainly were. But I do know that Goyen's East Texas retains echoes, subterranean and indistinct, of non-European cultures, both in his own experience of growing up in the region and in the reader's experience of the region that he creates in his fiction. Because my perspecive is comparative, I will again cite Octavio Paz. In a useful essay of cultural comparison, "Mexico and the United States," Paz writes about modern Mexican culture that there is always a part of the culture that is not Western: "Every Mexican carries within him this continuity, which goes back two thousand years. It doesn't matter that this presence is almost always unconscious and assumes naive forms of legend and even superstition. It is not something known but something lived."[50] Deep East Texas resembles Mexico in this way, and Goyen, like Rulfo and Garro, *lives* this knowledge. Goyen dramatizes an indigenous part of the collective unconscious of his region, a part that is intuited, imagined, invented.

My argument will need historical grounding, because it does not generally occur to contemporary residents of the United States that Amerindian culture might be an integral, living presence in our culture. Rather, the "minority" status of Native American cultures is recognized as something that survives separately in New Mexico, Oklahoma, Oregon, Alaska, but that does not affect U.S. culture generally. Goyen's fiction reflects a different attitude. In his fictional construction of the animate earth and its inhabitants, he resists the accepted American ideology that our indigenous past, because it is no longer visible in most parts of the United States, has been totally erased. He refuses to resign himself to such a loss.

Why should Goyen's attitudes seem so Mexican? And why should he hear indigenous ancestral echoes that most U.S. writers do not? I propose that it is because the culture of Deep East Texas, like that of Mexico, is the product of racial and cultural *mestizaje*, the *mixing* of histories and races and cultures. Of course Rulfo and Garro, as contemporary Mexican writers, write in and about a *mestizo* culture, that is, a culture created out of the encounter and mixture of European and indigenous cultures and races in Mesoamerica. Rulfo's state of Jalisco is not as populated by indigenous groups as Garro's state of Puebla; nonetheless, we may easily assume in both novels the active presence of indigenous cultural beliefs and practices alongside those imported from Europe. But what about William Goyen, writing in and about Deep East Texas in the mid-twentieth century?

Again, Octavio Paz's insights will be useful to us. Paz makes a strong distinction between the culturally exclusive model, upon which the United States was founded, and the culturally inclusive model of Mexico. In the essay to which I have referred above, Paz argues that whereas Mexico was settled by Spaniards who justified their military conquest on the grounds of the need (and duty) to convert the conquered, North American Protestant settlers had no such aim. The imperial project of the Spanish Catholics demanded the assimilation of indigenous peoples and their cultures: the idols were baptized and indigenous women impregnated. The Protestant settlers of North America, on the contrary, had little interest in converting Native Americans or intermarrying. Indeed, the early Puritan settlers had a horror of such contact, as their name suggests and their written texts amply confirm. They preferred to ignore the indigenous cultures they encountered in America, and their descendents to annihilate them when they could no longer ignore them.

From our historical position, we deplore the destruction of cultures and lives caused by the imperial ideologies of both Spain and England. Certainly Paz's point is not to vindicate the crimes of either empire, but to show the cultural consequences of these different policies in New Spain and New England. He shows that the Spanish colonizers were culturally centralist and inclusive, whereas the Anglo colonizers were pluralist and exclusive. By this he means that the Spanish included cultural differences within their single ecclesiastical hierarchy, whereas the English did not because they did not need to. In a pluralist culture, differences can be separated out, tolerated, ignored, excluded. If a group or individual in New England differed from one's own, that group or individual simply separated and began another cult or colony. Paz notes that this exclusivity worked well in North America, where indigenous groups were nomadic rather than settled, their cultural economies based on hunting rather than agriculture. English settlers did not need to reckon with great cities such as those in Mesoamerica, with their dense populations and monumental constructions. Thus, unlike modern Mexico, which is a *mestizo* culture resulting from imperial policies that included and assimilated indigenous cultures, modern U.S. culture is the product of a pluralist model that moved indigenous cultures to the margins and then off the edge. Paz concludes:

> In the United States, the Indian element does not appear. This, in my opinion, is the major difference between our two countries. The Indians who were not exterminated were corralled in "reservations." The Christian horror of "fallen nature" extended to the natives of

America: the United States was founded on a land without a past. The historical memory of Americans is European, not American. (362)

Paz's analysis contradicts our national ideology of a great "melting pot," for it implies that the "melting" has corresponded to a national need to homogenize cultural differences, rather than respect and understand them. The English colonizers were largely blind to indigenous cultures, a blindness that has continued to afflict U.S. culture until today.

Paz's argument is historically sound with respect to colonizing patterns, but is geographically limited, for it addresses only the northeastern and central plains regions of North America. Deep East Texas, and William Goyen's fiction, do not conform to Paz's generalizations. After all, Texas was not settled by Anglos until after the first quarter of the nineteenth century and not in significant numbers until after 1848. It was, of course, a part of the Spanish Empire in the New World, explored by Cabeza de Vaca beginning in 1528 and Hernán de Soto in 1541 and subsequently colonized by Spaniards. After Mexico gained its independence from Spain in 1821, Tejas was a state in the Mexican Republic; in 1836, when a group of Anglo settlers declared their independence from Mexico, Mexico sent troops to prevent the secession. Texas' admission to the Union in 1845 was considered by Mexico as an act of war, but by 1848 Mexico was forced to relinquish Texas and more than half of the rest of its territory as well. The Treaty of Guadalupe Hidalgo legitimized the purchase of Mexican land that was not for sale, land usurped by the United States in what Octavio Paz calls "one of the most unjust wars in the history of imperialist expansion" (124). Until 1848, then, Texas was Hispanic, populated by settlers who operated according to the centralist, inclusive cultural model outlined by Paz.

There were a great number of distinct indigenous groups in Tejas/Texas, many of which do correspond to Paz's generalization about North American indigenous groups as nomadic hunters rather than settled cultivators. In the western and northern Tejas plains, there were buffalo-hunting Apaches and Comanches and Kiowas; in South Texas and Northern Mexico, the Coahuiltecas, hunters of small animals and gatherers of wild crops.[51] Again, though, East Texas is an exception. The Caddoan-speaking cultures of East Texas were primarily settled agriculturalists rather than hunters. But before discussing this exception, we should recognize the shared characteristics of the tribal groups in the region.

William W. Newcomb, Jr., points out that all of the groups indigenous to Tejas/Texas were structured according to bonds of kinship rather than occupations or classes or wealth: family relationships extended through-out entire tribal communities.[52] Furthermore, all tribal groups shared a sense of the natural world; they lived in a direct, personal, and intimate relationship with the nature and invested animals and natural phenomena with supernatural powers. Newcomb states:

> Perhaps the most dramatic differences between Anglo-Americans and Indians are found in attitudes about the earth. No Indian people in Texas regarded the varied lands they hunted over or raised corn on as commodities to be bought and sold, or to be held or owned by individuals. The majority, at least implicitly, regarded themselves as belonging to or as part of the natural world. Often the earth was re-garded explicitly as Mother. Many consciously sought to live in har-mony with the earth, with the animals it nurtured, and the forces that created it all. (47–48)

Newcomb mentions especially the Caddoan-speaking groups as believing that the Earth Mother had given birth to everything and that "people lived on her and flourished under her guidance; it was unimaginable that individuals might possess her, inconceivable that they could sell her." (48)

The Caddo confederacies, loosely associated tribal groups sharing a common language, were, as I have said, a settled culture of agricultural-ists. East Texas' climate and topography favors agriculture as the rest of Texas territory does not: it is a subhumid, mild climate, a low-lying land that slopes gently toward the Gulf of Mexico. The name Texas comes from the Hasinai confederation of Caddoes. Pronounced "Tayshas" or "Tay-chas," the word means "allies" or "friends" and refers to the tribes in the confederation. The Caddoes also used "Taychas" to refer to the Spaniards (however mistakenly, we now feel), and the Spaniards in turn used it to refer to the Caddoes and to other friendly indigenous groups.[53]

The abundant food supply of the agricultural Caddoes allowed for a denser population and more complex social institutions than those of the plains hunters. Large ceremonial centers, including burial and temple mounds, formed the nucleus of Caddoan communities, and their burial practices are well documented by the Spanish colonizing clerics. Fray Francisco Casañas described the tribal practices of the Caddoan culture in his record written between 1691 and 1722.[54] For the Caddoes, as for the Nahuatl-speaking cultures of central Mexico, life and death were not separate conditions. The spirit was not thought to leave the body immediately, but needed nourishment for six days after death. Food was brought for the spirit (one thinks of contemporary Mexican practices of placing food on the graves on the Day of the Dead), and personal equipment and artifacts were buried with the body for later use. It was customary for the mourners to touch the corpse and then touch their own bodies in order to send messages with the corpse to dead relatives. Just before burial, a holy man would advise the dead person that he or she must now go to "that other house" to join the dead and take up life there (Newcomb, 1961, 302–3). Caddoan burial mounds began with the subsurface burial of five individuals; over the years, their complex layerings grew to heights of twenty feet and more.[55] There is, in fact, an important Caddoan site near Alto, Texas, about forty miles to the northeast of Goyen's hometown of Trinity. The site was first noted by archeologists in 1919 and excavated systematically during the 1930s. The residents of the region would surely have been aware of the burial mounds and the ancient communities they represented. Despite the virtual disappearance of the Caddoes by the last quarter of the nineteenth century, their traditions continue to be lived, if not known (to use Paz's formulation), in Goyen's Deep East Texas.[56]

Besides the indigenous underpinnings of *The House of Breath*, we may locate explicit traces of Transcendentalism in Goyen's animate earth. Like Borges, Goyen responds to the transcendentalist doctrine of the immanence of Spirit in the universe, the interpenetration of the physical and spiritual. In one italicized passage, Goyen's narrator metaphorically becomes the world: "*O I am leaf and I am wind and I am light. Something in the world links faces and leaves and rivers and woods and wind together and makes them a string of medallions with all our faces on them, worn forever round our necks, kin*" (48). Conversely, as we have seen, nature is humanized, embodied. A voice from the well, a "well-voice," is described "like a speaking mouth filled with wind, opening and closing in the wind" (61). The Emersonian identity of microcosm and macrocosm, individual and archetype, is lyrically presented by (and in) Boy: "Something forms within the world of a tear, shaped by the world that caused it; something takes shape with this uttered breath that builds an image of breath" (43). And Whitman is echoed here, too — not Whitman the bombastic individualist but, on the contrary, Borges' Whitman, the poet whose epic hero is everyman. In a direct allusion to Whitman's "As a Child Went Forth," Boy says, "I melted into the world and changed into everything that had ever been created or constructed, buildings, woods, rivers, pomp, love, history; and everything entered into me, all involved in all" (33). In such images, we sense the complementary conceptions of "universal sympathy" in Transcendentalism and pre-Hispanic Mesoamerican mythology.[57] I do not wish to cast Goyen oversimply as a Texas Transcendentalist, but I do think that he adds the fecundity and agency of romantic nature to the vitality of the spirits of Mesoamerican myth. In *The House of Breath*, the nineteenth-century U.S. romance tradition provides the natural landscape in which Goyen's magical realist ghosts become audible.[58]

It is not just Goyen's first book, *The House of Breath*, that we hear ancestral voices. The stories in his second book, *Ghost and Flesh* (1952), are his most Deep East Texan in their singular focus on kinship in/on/with the animate earth. Like *The House of Breath*, *Ghost and Flesh* is influenced by U.S. romanticism, but there are few literary allusions—only Goyen's sensitivity to his rural, regional culture, to the East Texas earth and its inhabitants. In these stories, Goyen's ear is pressed to the ground.

In "Ghost and Flesh, Water and Dirt," Goyen's narrator is a woman who buries her daughter Chitta after an accident, and her husband two weeks later when he kills himself from grief and guilt. Her husband returns to visit her from the dead, and he seems more an embodied *calavera* in Mexican style than a disembodied wraith. " 'I'm Raymon Emmons,' the steamin voice said, 'and I'm here to stay; putt out my things that you've putt away, putt out my oatmeal bowl and putt hot oatmeal in it get out my rubber-boots when it rains, iron my clothes and fix my supper . . . I never died and I'm here to stay.' "[59] But Raymon Emmons' wife knows he's dead, however hungry and desiring, and she longs to join him underground: "I wish I uz dirt I wish I uz dirt. O I uz vile with grief" (57).

As in Juan Rulfo's Comala, where water is always seeping, steaming, dripping upon the dead who swelter underground, this narrator's "Texis" (as she pronounces it and Goyen writes it) is hot and wet. "I wish I'd melt—and run down the drains. Wish I uz rain, fallin on the dirt of certain graves I know and seeping down into the dirt, could lie in the dirt with Raymon Emmons on one side and Chitta on the other. Wish I uz dirt" (55). She visits the graves "carryin potplants and cryin over the mounds" and lamenting "all my life is dirt I've got a famly of dirt" (53, sic). The story concludes, as does Goyen's fiction so often, by affirming grief and demonstrating the interdependence, the comingling of the realms of the dead and the living. The narrator tells her listener (who is the reader): "there's a time for live things and a time for dead, for ghosts and for flesh 'n bones: all life is just a sharin of ghosts and flesh. Us humans are part ghost and part flesh. . . . there's a world both places, a world where there's ghosts and a world where there's flesh" (58). She concludes that "ghosts can give you over to flesh 'n bones; and that flesh 'n bones, if you go roun when it's time, can send you back to a faithful ghost. One provides the other" (59).

In "The Children of Old Somebody," another of the stories in *Ghost and Flesh*, Goyen again dramatizes the permeability of the worlds of the dead and the living. This time he creates not so much a ghost or *calavera* as a mythological presence, a communal legend called "Old Ancestor" or "Old Somebody."

> he was a shape of dust — and if all things return to dust, fall back into it, dust was his great pile, he the dust grubber, himself formed of the dust of the ground, from which he would find the first things formed out of the ground and bring them to himself and to us all to see what would we call them. Breathed out of dust, he was yet the enemy of dust-eaters; he would save the dust from the appetite, from the blind voracious driving bit of hunger: the grasshopper and the worm. Then, before it all is eaten, he would have his hands in it, on it, to touch it to smut it with his fingermarks — but even more: to shape it, out of its own dust and with the miraculous light of his own dust, and thus set it away, preserved. (76)

Goyen connects the vitalizing activities of eating and touching to the earth and to lying buried in it. The communal narrator of the story insists: "If we build the bridge of flesh we must cross over, over it, into the land of dust, and burn the bridge of burning flesh behind us: *cross over flesh to reach ghost*" (85, Goyen's italics).

This call to heed the voices that inhabit the earth is dramatized in the mythic origins of "Old Somebody." He is the impossible son of Cora and Bright Andrews, an old and barren couple, magically born in the woods and placed in a log, "a little wood animal," "a druid":

> This little tree spirit, could you believe it, lay unmolested by the life of the ground or by gypsies, never an ant stung it or snake bit it, there was no hostility between its world and the creatures' world, that hostility is learnt. . . .
>
> Now in the old histories we can read of such, like of Childe Perci-

val and like of little princes, secret folk, kept in secret woods places by charmers or enchanters. But would you believe it that this child could be put there in our sensible time, so far along later after old fables have faded away into just stories to be told for want of fable, after all the fancies had perished. (82)

The communal narrator laments the loss of mystery "in our sensible time," when all the "fancies" have perished, but he nonetheless insists upon the possibility of recuperation: "See how an old Shape hidden in the depths and folds of the mind can appear, knocked for, when it is time, and show its meaning, salvage the dust of the truth" (85). It is the "old Shape" of buried ancestral cultures that Goyen summons in his fiction, a rescue operation that is more Tejano than Texan.

Goyen's invocation of Childe Percival, charmers and enchanters, leads me to my concluding question, a variant of the question that concluded the first section of my essay. Do romance and magical realism respond to essentially the same cultural conditions and purposes? Clearly, all three novels — Goyen's, Garro's, Rulfo's — correspond to Frye's definition of romance and to my own definition of magical realism, but I will not trace those correspondences here. Rather, I want to speculate on why these writers — indeed, why any contemporary American writer — chooses romance and/or magical realism to express his or her version of reality. Fredric Jameson's materialist critique will be useful to my speculations.

In "Magical Narratives: Romance as Genre," Jameson writes that romance

> expresses a transitional moment, yet one of a very special type: its contemporaries must feel their society torn between past and future in such a way that the alternatives are grasped as hostile but somehow unrelated worlds. . . . [T]his genre expresses a nostalgia for a social order in the process of being undermined and destroyed by nascent capitalism, yet still for the moment coexisting side by side with the latter.[60]

Jameson gives widely separated examples of romance to support his argument. Shakespearean romance, *Wuthering Heights*, the "great art romances of the Romantic period": according to Jameson, all are "only too obviously symbolic attempts to come to terms with the triumph of the bourgeoisie and the new and unglamorous social forms developing out of the market system" (158). This, too, may be said of many contemporary American magical realist texts. In the final passage cited from "Old Somebody," we hear Goyen's narrator "coming to terms" with a culture in which "old fables have faded away into just stories to be told for want of fable." In both form and content, each of the works that I have discussed dramatizes the transition between modernity's failed conceptions of self and society and alternative constructions of community and consciousness. The ghosts of Goyen, Garro, and Rulfo may be thought of as metaphors for the transitional periods these novelists represent: in between, neither here nor there.

These novelists write out of a sense of cultural displacement — displacement of traditional communities, indigenous and rural, and the resulting ruin of the land. Each feels his or her community and countryside torn between past and future, between hostile and unrelated worlds, as Jameson describes the conflict. Their ghosts, themselves in-between beings, dramatize the painful economic and social liminality caused by the obliterating forces of modernization. In *The House of Breath*, Goyen's Charity is destroyed by economic forces (the sawmill closes) and the resulting urbanization (members of the community must exile themselves to Houston to find work). The "world's body" becomes "the bare scalp of earth stretched scabrous and feverish under the metallic light," and the underground community stagnates: "all of bone and rock and metal, we could no longer melt together but stood apart hard as bone and rock. What ruined us?" (38–39). Yet the heard voices of ghosts — dead family and friends and the land itself — rescue the ruins for Boy and allow him to establish a viable community above ground.

Rulfo and Garro also present their transitional dramas metaphorically as the conflict between a buried community and abusive activities above ground. Like Goyen, they participate in an essential romance pattern: the struggle between higher and lower realms and values, with the higher values here paradoxically invested in ghosts underground. In their novels, as I have said, the tension between levels is political rather than personal. The Mexican Revolution is their failed utopian dream, and both project the characteristic ambivalence of traditional romance: nostalgia for a lost innocence and longing for a future ideal. But here, the signs of romance signify differently: "lost innocence" is construed as actual past indigenous cultural coherence, rather than Hawthorne's and the U.S. transcendentalists' Eurocentric longing for a unitary "virgin" realm of moral purity; and "future ideal" is construed as a coherent system of revolutionary political and social justice. I stress the ideal of coherence rather than unity here, for when indigenous myths interact with the structures of romance, the idealized vision that results (whether projected backward or forward in time) is of coherence, not unity. Indeed, coherence is conceivable only when cultural differences are asserted, unity when no "other" is imagined.

In their self-conscious rejection of the binarisms of modern Western culture and their engagement of alternative indigenous cultural models, Rulfo, Garro, and Goyen are magical realists; in their symbolic fusion of the material and the spiritual in a foregrounded natural order, they reflect and amplify the romance tradition. The former category implies a more self-consciously oppositional, postmodernist stance; the latter corresponds to the modernist intuition that there still exists somewhere a center that will hold. Both impulses operate in relative degrees of intensity in all of the U.S. and Latin American literary works that I have discussed, and their differences may be considered in terms of the extent to which the balance ultimately tips toward one impulse or the other. Goyen and Hawthorne still imagine a center that holds, however tenuously — a Texan house of breath, a Salem house of spirits. Even Faulkner, Hawthorne's offspring (according to Borges), declares a potential reconciliation of races and families at the end of *Absalom, Absalom!*

Rulfo and Garro share romance patterns with Goyen, as I have pointed out, but they project a tragic vision as Goyen does not. In Goyen, the U.S. Transcendentalist legacy combines with his sensitivity to indigenous cultural currents, allowing his character to integrate the animate underground with the world's body. Boy is able to unite past with present, unite the ghosts of family and community with the living self as Rulfo's, Garro's, García Márquez's, Borges' characters cannot. Dissolution (Comala), petrification (Ixtepec), apocalypse (Macondo), Borges' "elegant hope" of an undiscovered order in his daunting library of Babel are recognizable conditions of Latin American magical realism. Here, then, I arrive at a crucial difference between U.S. and Latin American traditions of counterrealism.

I would argue that most contemporary U.S. magical realists find a way to bring their ghosts above ground, that is, to integrate them into contemporary U.S. culture in order to enrich or remedy it. Like Goyen, Isaac Bashevis Singer, Leslie Marmon Silko, Maxine Hong Kingston, and Toni Morrison imagine reestablished communities after disruptive cultural transitions and political abuses. How these writers do so, and with what reservations, is the subject of another essay. The specific cultural conflicts they dramatize make their communal resolutions very different from one another, of course, but communal nonetheless. Most contemporary Latin American magical realists, on the contrary, refuse such consolation: magical resolutions are considered, then canceled by crushing political realities. Elena Garro's *Recollections of Things to Come* is a representative example of this trajectory, Isabel Allende's *The House of the Spirits* an exception that proves the rule. Latin American literature has always had a political function, and Latin American writers a dissenting role, that U.S. writers have not.[61] Contemporary Latin American magical realists repeatedly represent the destruction of communities caught between indigenous and Western cultural models of self and society, between solidarity and solitude. Modernist centers have ceased to hold in Latin American magical realism, the better, it would seem, to envision salutary postmodernist decenterings.

The different historical positionings of these contemporary American writers with respect to their branches of the romance tradition may explain in part the greater subversiveness of Latin American magical realism when compared to U.S. counterrealism. Contemporary Latin American magical realism does not look back to a relatively recent local romantic flowering analogous to the nineteenth-century U.S. romance tradition but, as Borges argues in his essay on Hawthorne, to a naturalistic tradition of "dictionaries and rhetoric." Borges' attention to U.S. romance and its Transcendentalist foundations may be taken as evidence of his own argument: there is no Emersonian mainstream in which contemporary Latin Americans must necessarily bathe (or wash their hands of), as there is for U.S. writers. Rather, Latin American writers must recur to more distant Spanish sources, to *Don Quixote* and the *Amadís de Gaula*, for their romance tradition, and to pre-Hispanic indigenous American mythologies for their archetypal patterns—that is, to traditions preceding the disasters of modernity that magical realism opposes. This distance has, I think, liberated contemporary Latin American writers to invent fantastical strategies for political purposes, to expend dazzling narrative energy on political entropy, and to resist the temptations of resolution that narrative conclusions offer.

Still, both U.S. and Latin American writers share the experience that Jameson describes of being torn between incompatible pasts and futures and, as we have seen, between contradictory conceptions of subjectivity.

Traditional (mythic/archetypal) standards of selfhood based on similarity compete with modernity's standards of difference: archetypes have been individualized, ghosts have been buried and silenced. Or almost. The ghosts who still inhabit magical realist fiction contest the annihilation of the traditional self by the modern self: paradoxically, magical realists are most postmodern in their recuperation of premodern conceptions of subjectivity. They refuse to remain locked into modern categories of individual psychology, insisting instead that the self is actualized by participation in communal and cosmic categories. Even when such participation fails—in Macondo, Comala, Ixtepec—magical realism's essential commitment is to universality rather than uniqueness. Not that magical realists avoid engaging specific cultural, racial, gender distinctions: the writers I have discussed and those discussed in the other essays in this collection are ample proof to the contrary. By means of their galleries of ghosts, magical realists may describe the inhabitants of Argentina and Massachusetts, Mexico and Texas, at the same time that they project a universal human condition free of essentializing stereotypes.

In late twentieth-century Western culture, divided as we are by economic self-interest and competition, injustice among races and classes and nations, violence against women, to write universalizing fictions is a revolutionary act. As each of us risks becoming an embattled community of one, the archetypal strategies of magical realism and its confluent romance traditions may yet remind us of our shared humanity. Flannery O'Connor was right. Ghosts *can* be very fierce and instructive.

Notes

1 Flannery O'Connor, "The Grotesque in Southern Fiction," in *Mystery and Manners* (New York: Farrar, Straus, and Giroux, 1961), p. 45.

2 Northrop Frye, *Anatomy of Criticism* (Princeton: Princeton University Press, 1957), p. 314. A gender specific study of "ghost stories" by U.S. women writers is *Haunting the House of Fiction: Feminist Perspectives on Ghost Stories by American Women*, ed. Lynette Carpenter and Wendy K. Kolman (Knoxville: University of Tennessee Press, 1991).

3 Vladimir Nabokov, *Strong Opinions* (New York: Vintage, 1973), p. 115.

4 Isabel Allende, *The House of the Spirits*, trans. Magda Bogin (New York: Knopf, 1985), pp. 108, 218. See my essay on Allende's magical realism: "The Magical Tables of Isabel Allende and Remedios Varo," *Comparative Literature* 44, 2 (1992): 113–43.

5 Seymour Menton elaborates the relation of Jung's theories to magical realism in *Magic Realism Rediscovered: 1918–1981* (East Brunswick, N.J.: Associated University Presses, 1983), passim.

6 Gabriel García Márquez, *One Hundred Years of Solitude,* trans. Gregory Rabassa (New York: Avon, 1970), p. 316.

7 Flannery O'Connor, "The Grotesque in Southern Fiction," in *Mystery and Manners,* p. 44.

8 Eric Gould, *Mythical Intentions in Modern Literature* (Princeton: Princeton University Press, 1981), p. 19.

9 Jorge Luis Borges, "The Argentine Writer and Tradition," in *Labyrinths,* ed. Donald A. Yates and James E. Irby (New York: New Directions, 1962), pp. 184, 85.

10 Jaime Alazraki relates this theme to the Kabbalah, which he convincingly locates as a primary source of Borges' mystical investigations. *Borges and the Kabbalah* (Cambridge: Cambridge University Press, 1988).

11 Jorge Luis Borges, "The Other Death," in *The Aleph and Other Stories,* trans. Norman Thomas di Giovanni (New York: Dutton, 1968), pp. 110–11.

12 Borges, *Dreamtigers,* trans. Mildred Boyer and Harold Morland (Austin: University of Texas Press, 1978), p. 93.

13 Borges, "The Library of Babel," in *Labyrinths,* p. 58.

14 Borges, "The Flower of Coleridge," in *Other Inquisitions: 1937–52,* trans. Ruth L. C. Simms (Austin: University of Texas Press, 1965), p. 10.

15 Emerson, *Essays: Second Series,* "Nominalist and Realist," 1844, cited by Borges in "The Flower of Coleridge," p. 10.

16 Borges, "The Fearful Sphere of Pascal," in *Labyrinths,* p. 189.

For a comparative discussion of American ideologies of history, including the postmodernist position of Borges, see my "The Usable Past: The Idea of History in Modern U.S. and Latin American Fiction," in *Do the Americas Have a Common Literature?,* ed. Gustavo Pérez Firmat (Durham: Duke University Press, 1990), pp. 7–41.

17 Borges, "The Flower of Coleridge," pp. 10–11.

18 Borges' sense of these multiple confluences of Romanticism led him, for example, to link Whitman and Valéry, an unexpected pairing but, as Borges shows, a justifiable one based on their shared impulse (with Borges') to archetypalize the subject: "One of the purposes of Whitman's compositions is to define a possible man — Walt Whitman — of unlimited and negligent felicity; no less hyperbolic, no less illusory, is the man defined by Valéry's compositions." "Valéry as Symbol," in *Labyrinths,* p. 188.

19 Leon Chai, *The Romantic Foundations of the American Renaissance* (Ithaca: Cornell University Press, 1987), pp. 6, 39. For a discussion of the characteristics of the romance genre beginning with medieval romance, see Fredric

Jameson, "Magical Narratives: Romance as Genre," *NLH* 7, 1 (1975): 135–63; and Edgar A. Dryden, *The Form of American Romance* (Baltimore: Johns Hopkins University Press, 1988), who extends the U.S. romance tradition to contemporary writers, from Hawthorne and Faulkner to John Barth.

20 Borges, "From Allegories to Novels," in *Borges: A Reader*, ed. Emir Rodríguez Monegal and Alastair Reid (New York: Dutton, 1981), p. 232.

21 Borges, "Nathaniel Hawthorne," in *Borges: A Reader*, p. 219.

22 Nathaniel Hawthorne, *The Scarlet Letter* (New York: Norton, 1978), p. 31.

23 Fredric Jameson, "Third-World Literature in the Era of Multinational Capitalism," *Social Text* 15 (Fall 1986): 65–88. See also my essay on contemporary political allegory: "Allegories of Power in the Fiction of J. M. Coetzee," *Journal of Literary Studies* (Pretoria) 2, 1 (1986): 1–14.

24 Paul de Man, *Allegories of Reading: Figural Language in Rousseau, Nietzsche, Rilke, and Proust* (New Haven: Yale University Press, 1979), p. 191.

25 Borges, "Nathaniel Hawthorne," in *Borges: A Reader*, p. 228.

26 Larry J. Reynolds places Hawthorne's work in broad political perspective in *European Revolutions and the American Literary Renaissance* (New Haven: Yale University Press, 1988). A more specific study of Hawthorne's political ambiguity is Sacvan Bercovitch, "The A-politics of Ambiguity in *The Scarlet Letter, NLH* 19 (1988): 1–27.

27 Borges, *Textos cautivos: Ensayos y reseñas en* El hogar *(1936–1939)*, ed. Enrique Sacerio-Garí and Emir Rodríguez Monegal (Barcelona: Tusquets Editores, 1986).

Borges also wrote essays on Melville and Whitman and paid homage to Poe's mystery stories in his own. Borges appreciated Poe's sleuth Dupin because Dupin expressed his deep distrust of analytical rationality and his preference instead for the intuitive and metaphoric processes of poetry. See John T. Irwin's essay on Borges and Poe: "Mysteries We Reread, Mysteries of Rereading: Poe, Borges, and the Analytic Detective Story; Also Lacan, Derrida, and Johnson," in *Do the Americas have a Common Literature?*, ed. Gustavo Pérez Firmat (Durham, N.C.: Duke University Press, 1990), pp. 198–242.

Besides Borges' ironic rewritings of Poe's mystery stories, he read Poe's *The Narrative of Arthur Gordon Pym of Nantucket* (1838) for its descriptions of fantastic fauna and flora and includes one of them in his *Manual de zoología fantástica* (*The Book of Imaginary Beings* 1957) under the title, "El animal soñado por Poe" ("The Animal Dreamed by Poe").

28 In discussing Borges' magical realism, critics have uniformly focused on Borges' essay, "Narrative Art and Magic" (1932). While interesting, this essay is less informative about Borges' own literary preferences and practice than *An Introduction to American Literature* (cited below) and his essays on U.S. romance writers.

29 There are, of course, critics who emphasize the counterrealistic aspects of mid-nineteenth-century literature. For a useful summary and critique of the romance theorists, including Lionel Trilling, Richard Chase, Joel Porte, see Russell Reising, *The Unusable Past: Theory and the Study of American Literature* (London and New York: Methuen, 1986). See Emily Miller Budick, "Sacvan Bercovitch, Stanley Cavell, and the Romance Theory of American Fiction," *PMLA* 107, 1 (1992): 78–91.

   In this context, I recommend Allan Gardner Lloyd-Smith's *Uncanny American Fiction* (New York: St. Martin's Press, 1989). Lloyd-Smith discusses the "romantic uncanny" of Poe, the "transcendental uncanny" of Hawthorne, the "psychological uncanny" of Bierce and Jack London, the "symbolic uncanny" of James, in ways that correspond to and complement Borges' understanding of these writers.

30 Borges, *An Introduction to American Literature*, trans. L. Clark Keating and Robert O. Evans (Lexington: University Press of Kentucky, 1971), p. 16.

31 Borges, "Valery as Symbol," in *Labyrinths*, p. 197.

32 My purpose here is not to explore in detail the nature of transcendentalist thought as such—there are many excellent critical studies of this subject—but to trace Borges' understanding of it. More general studies are Roger Asselineau, *The Transcendentalist Constant in American Literature* (New York: New York University Press, 1980), and William Ellis, *The Theory of American Romance: An Ideology in American Intellectual History* (Ann Arbor: UMI Research Press, 1989).

33 Again, this aspect of Transcendentalism has been amply explored: Lawrence Buell calls the Transcendentalists "children of the Puritans." See *Literary Transcendentalism: Style and Vision in the American Renaissance* (Ithaca: Cornell University Press, 1973), pp. 146 ff.

34 Borges, "Nathaniel Hawthorne," in *Borges: A Reader*, pp. 223–24.

   Borges links another nineteenth-century U.S. writer to Kafka: Of Henry James, Borges says, "From the Perplexities of the American in Europe James went on to the theme of the perplexity of man in the universe. He had no faith in an ethical, philosophical, or religious solution to essential problems; his world is already the inexplicable world of Kafka. Despite the scruples and delicate complexities of James, his work suffers from a major defect: the absence of life." *An Introduction to American Literature*, p. 55.

   Given this conclusion, it is no wonder that Borges excludes James altogether from his discussion of literature as dream or hallucination. Still, Borges might have cited James' critical preface to Volume 17 of the New York edition, "The Altar of the Dead," a volume that includes some of James' "ghost" stories. Here, James states that he "is prepared with the confession that the 'ghost-story,' as we for convenience call it, has ever been for me the most possible form of the fairy-tale. It enjoys, to my eyes, this honour by being so much the neatest—neat with that neatness without which *representation*, and therewith beauty, drops." *The Art of the Novel: Critical Prefaces* (Boston: Northeastern University Press, 1984), p. 254.

35 Alejo Carpentier, preface to *El reino de este mundo* (*The Kingdom of this World*) (Mexico City: Fondo de Cultura Económica, 1949); reprinted as part of "De lo real maravilloso americano," in *Tientos y diferencias* (Montevideo: Editorial Arca, 1967), pp. 96–132, and translated in this volume.

36 This phrase is from Borges' introduction to the short fiction of Kafka, in which he again (though here, implicitly) aligns Kafka with Hawthorne by arguing for the centrality of "situation" in Kafka's work as well, and the consequent superiority of his short fiction: "Plot and atmosphere are the essential characteristics of Kafka's work, not the convolutions of the story or the psychological portrait of the hero. This is what makes Kafka's stories superior to his novels." Foreword to *Stories 1904–1924*, trans. J.A. Underwood (New York: Futura, 1981), p. 8.

37 Hawthorne, "Wakefield," in *Hawthorne's Short Stories*, ed. Newton Arvin (New York: Vintage Books, 1946), p. 41.

38 Emily Miller Budick, "Sacvan Bercovitch, Stanley Cavell, and the Romance Theory of American Fiction," *PMLA* 107, 1 (1992): 80.

39 William Goyen, *The House of Breath* (New York: Random House, 1950), p. 9.

40 Ixtepec is the name of a town on the isthmus of Tehuantepec with a long history of popular political resistance. Garro's novel, however, is set in north central Mexico, as is clear from her description of political events and the landscape.

41 Elena Garro, *Recollections of Things to Come*, trans. Ruth L. C. Simms (Austin: University of Texas Press, 1969), p. 3.

42 Octavio Paz, *Alternating Current*, trans. Helen R. Lane (1967; New York: Seaver Books), p. 15.

43 Juan Rulfo, *Pedro Páramo*, trans. Lysander Kemp (New York: Grove Press, 1959), pp. 1–2.

44 Northrop Frye, *The Anatomy of Criticism*, pp. 187–88.

45 Gabriel García Márquez, *One Hundred Years of Solitude*, p. 67.

46 Octavio Paz, "The Power of Ancient Mexican Art," *New York Review of Books*, Dec. 6, 1990: 21.

47 Hugo G. Nutini, *Todos Santos in Rural Tlaxcala: A Syncretic, Expressive, and Symbolic Analysis of the Cult of the Dead* (Princeton: Princeton University Press, 1988), p. 69, my italics.

48 Keith Carter, *The Blue Man* (Houston: Rice University Press, 1990), interview with Anne W. Tucker, p. 124.

49 William Goyen, *The Collected Stories of William Goyen* (Garden City, N.Y.: Doubleday, 1975), p. xi.

50 Octavio Paz, "Mexico and the United States" (1979), included in *The Labyrinth of Solitude* (2d ed. New York: Grove Press, 1985), pp. 362–63.

51 See W. W. Newcomb, Jr., *The Indians of Texas: From Prehistoric to Modern Times* (Austin: University of Texas, 1961).

52 W. W. Newcomb, Jr., "Harmony with Nature, People, and the Supernatural," in *Texas Myths*, ed. Robert F. O'Connor (College Station: Texas A & M University Press, 1986), p. 47.

   Elizabeth York Enstam confirms this point, referring to "a cohesiveness within the villages that went much beyond the support systems provided even by an extended family." She speaks of "a sense of family that was virtually tribal in extent; they knew a kind of community long vanished among peoples of European descent and culture. Of all nineteenth-century inhabitants of Texas, only Afro-Americans had anything like the Indian familial organization." "The Family," in *Texas Myths*, p. 146.

53 Newcomb, *The Indians of Texas*, p. 280.

54 Fray Francisco Casañas, *Description of the Tejas or Asinai Indians, 1691–1722*, trans. Mattie Austin Hatcher, *Southwestern Historical Quarterly* 30 (1927): 206–18, 283–304; cited in Newcomb, *The Indians of Texas*, pp. 303–5. Newcomb also cites from Fray Gaspar José de Solís, "Diary of a Visit of Inspection of the Texas Missions Made by Fray Gaspar José de Solís in the Year 1767–1768," trans. Margaret K. Kress, *Southwestern Historical Quarterly* 35 (1931): 28–76.

   See also J. Alden Mason, "The Place of Texas in Pre-Columbian Relationships between the United States and Mexico." *Texas Archeological and Paleontological Society Bulletin* 7 (1935): 29–46.

55 *Caddoan Mounds: Temples and Tombs of an Ancient People*, Texas Parks and Wildlife Department, May 1984.

56 For further discussion of the thematic treatment of *mestizaje* in Goyen's fiction, see Eleanor Wilner, " 'The Road Runner in Woolworth's': An Appreciation," in the issue devoted to William Goyen of *Mid-American Review* 13, 1 (1992): 55–61. See also my own essay in this issue of *Mid-American Review*, where I trace Goyen's theme of *mestizaje* in more detail than I am able to here. "The Animate Earth," pp. 81–85.

57 Recall Octavio Paz's metaphoric formulation of this "universal sympathy" characteristic of pre-Hispanic Mesoamerican cultures: a "vital fluid that unites all animate beings — humans, animals, plants — with the elements, the planets, and the stars." "The Power of Ancient Mexican Art," *New York Review of Books*, Dec. 6, 1990: 20.

58 Wayne Ude also relates indigenous and romance traditions in "Forging an American Style: The Romance-Novel and Magical Realism as Response to the Frontier and Wilderness Experiences," in *The Frontier Experience and the*

American Dream, ed. David Mogen, Mark Busby, and Paul Bryant (College Station: Texas A & M University Press, 1989), pp. 50–64.

59 William Goyen, *The Collected Stories of William Goyen* (New York: Doubleday, 1975), p. 51.

60 Fredric Jameson, "Magical Narratives: Romance as Genre," *NLH* 7, 1 (1975): 158. Reprinted in slightly different form in *The Political Unconscious: Narrative as a Socially Symbolic Act* (Ithaca: Cornell University Press, 1981), chap. 2, "Magical Narratives: On the Dialectical Use of Genre Criticism," pp. 103–50.

61 I discuss this difference in chap. 8, "Individual and Communal Conclusions," in *Writing the Apocalypse: Historical Vision in Contemporary U.S. and Latin American Fiction* (Cambridge: Cambridge University Press, 1989), pp. 176–92.

SELECTED BIBLIOGRAPHY

Alazraki, Jaime. "Neofantastic Literature—A Structuralist Answer." In *The Analysis of Literary Texts: Current Trends in Methodology.* Ed. Randolph Pope. Ypsilanti: Eastern Michigan University, Bilingual Press, 1980. Pp. 286–90.

————. "The Fantastic as Surrealist Metaphor in Cortázar's Short Fiction." *Dada/Surrealism* 5 (1975): 28–33.

Alexis, Jacques Stéphén. "Du réalisme merveilleux des Haitiens." *Présence Africaine: Revue Culturelle du Monde Noir/Cultural Review of the Negro World* 8–10 (1956): 245–71.

Anderson Imbert, Enrique. *El realismo mágico y otros ensayos.* Caracas: Monte Avila, 1975.

Anhalt, Nedda-G. de. "Amor brujo: Una lectura de *El hombre de los hongos* de Sergio Galindo." *La Palabra y el hombre: Revista de la Universidad Veracruzana* 73 (1990): 272–77.

Arango-L., Manuel Antonio. "Relación social e histórica afro-espiritual y el 'realismo mágico' en ¡Ecué-Yamba-O! de Alejo Carpentier." *Cuadernos Americanos* 234, 1 (1981): 84–91.

Baker, Suzanne. "Magic Realism as a Postcolonial Strategy: The Kadaitcha Sung." *SPAN: Journal of the South Pacific Association for Commonwealth Literature and Language Studies* (1991): 55–63.

Bakker, Martin. "Magic Realism and the Archetype in Hubert Lampo's Work." *Canadian Journal of Netherlandic Studies/Revue Canadienne d'Etudes Neerlandaises* 12, 2 (1991): 17–21.

Barella, Julia. "El realismo mágico: Un fantasma de la imaginación barroca." *Cuadernos Hispanoamericanos: Revista Mensual de Cultura Hispánica* 481 (1990): 69–78.

Barroso, Juan. 'Realismo mágico' y 'lo real maravilloso' en *El reino de este mundo* y *El siglo de las luces.* Miami: Ediciones Universal, 1977.

Bartlett, Catherine. "Magical Realism: The Latin American Influence on Modern

Chicano Writers." *Confluencia: Revista Hispánica de Cultura y Literatura* 1, 2 (1986): 27–37.

Bautista, Gloria. "El realismo mágico en *La casa de los espíritus*." *Discurso Literario: Revista de Temas Hispánicos* 6, 2 (1989): 299–310.

———. *Realismo mágico, cosmos latinoamericano: Teoría y práctica*. Bogotá: América Latina, 1991.

Bayles, Martha. "Special Effects, Special Pleading." *The New Criterion* 6, 5 (1988): 34–40.

Ben-Ur, Lorraine Elena. "El realismo mágico en la crítica hispanoamericana." *Journal of Spanish Studies: Twentieth Century* 4, 3 (1976): 149–63.

Benevento, Joseph. "An Introduction to the Realities of Fiction: Teaching Magic Realism in Three Stories by Borges, Fuentes, and Márquez." *Kansas Quarterly* 16, 3 (1984): 125–51.

Bessière, Irène. *Le récit fantastique: La poétique de l'incertain*. Paris: Larousse, 1974.

Bontempelli, Massimo. "Analogies." *900* (Novecento) 4 (1927): 7–13.

Bravo, José Antonio. *Lo real maravilloso en la narrativa latinoamericana actual*. Lima: Ediciones Unifé, 1984.

Brooke-Rose, Christine. *A Rhetoric of the Unreal: Studies in Narrative and Structure, Especially of the Fantastic*. Cambridge: Cambridge University Press, 1981.

Carillo, Germán. "Del surrealismo al realismo mágico en *Hombres de maíz* de M. A. Asturias." *Sin Nombre* 14, 1 (1983): 53–60.

Castro-Amorim, Beatriz-de. "Del mágico realismo de Mario de Andrade hasta el realismo mágico de Moacyr Scliar." *Romance-Languages-Annual* 1 (1989): 366–71.

Chamberlain, Lori. "Magicking the Real: Paradoxes of Postmodern Writing." In *Postmodern Fiction: A Bio-Bibliographical Guide*. Ed. Larry McCaffery. New York: Greenwood, 1986. Pp. 5–21.

Chanady, Amaryll. *Magical Realism and the Fantastic: Resolved Versus Unresolved Antinomy*. New York: Garland, 1985.

Chiampi, Irlemar. "Carpentier y el surrealismo." *Revista Lingua e Literatura* 9 (1980): 155–74.

Chiampi, Irlemar. *El realismo maravilloso*. Caracas: Monte Avila, 1983.

Ciplijauskaite, Birute. "Socialist and Magic Realism: Veiling or Unveiling?" *Journal of Baltic Studies* 10 (1979): 218–27.

Cixous, Hélène. "La fiction et ses fantômes: Une lecture de *l'Unheimliche* de Freud." *Poétique* 10 (1972): 199–216.

Cluff, Russell M. "El realismo mágico en los cuentos de Uslar Pietri." *Cuadernos Americanos* 204, 1 (1976): 208–24.

Colomines, Gabrielle. "Convergencias y divergencias: De Gabriel García Márquez a Isabel Allende." In *La narrativa de Isabel Allende: Claves de una margina-lidad*. Ed. Adriana Castillo de Berchenko and Pablo Berchenko. Perpignan: Centre de Recherches Ibériques et Latine-Américaines, Université de Perpignan, 1990. Pp. 39–68.

Conniff, Brian. "The Dark Side of Magical Realism: Science, Oppression, and Apocalypse in *One Hundred Years of Solitude*." *Modern Fiction Studies* 36, 2 (1990): 167–79.

Costa Lima, Luiz. *Control of the Imaginary: Reason and Imagination in Modern Times*. Trans. Ronald W. Sousa. Minneapolis: University of Minnesota Press, 1988.

Cros, Edmond. "Space and Textual Genetics: Magical Consciousness and Ideology in *Cumandá*." *Sociocriticism* 4–5 (1986–87): 35–72.

Dash, J. Michael. "Marvellous Realism—The Way Out of Negritude." *Caribbean Studies* 13, 4 (1973): 57–70.

Durix, Jean-Pierre. "Magic Realism in *Midnight's Children*." *Commonwealth* 8, 1 (1985): 57–63.

Fama, Antonio. *Realismo mágico en la narrativa de Aguilera Malta*. Madrid: Playor, 1977.

Flores, Angel, ed. *El realismo mágico en el cuento hispanoamericano*. Tlahuapan, Mexico: Premia, 1985.

Forster, Leonard. Ueber den 'Magischen Realismus' in der heutigen deutschen Dichtung." *Neophilologus* 43 (1950): 86–99.

García Márquez, Gabriel. "Fantasía y creación artística en América Latina y el Caribe." *Texto Crítico* 14 (1979): 3–8.

González Echevarría, Roberto. "Isla a su vuelo fugitiva: Carpentier y el realismo mágico." *Revista Iberoamericana* 40, 86 (1974): 9–64.

———. *Alejo Carpentier: The Pilgrim at Home*. Ithaca: Cornell University Press, 1977. Pp. 108–29.

Hancock, Geoff. "Magic Realism, or, The Future of Fiction." *Canadian Fiction Magazine* 24–25 (1977): 4–6.

Hancock, Geoff, ed. *Magic Realism*. Toronto: Aya Press, 1980.

Hart, Stephen. "Magical Realism in Gabriel García Márquez's *Cien años de soledad*." *INTI: Revista de Literatura Hispánica* 16–17 (1982–83): 37–52.

Hébert, Pierre. "Le Roman québecois depuis 1975: Quelques aspects saillants." *French Review* 61, 6 (1988): 899–909.

Hennens, Franz. *Le fantastique réel*. Bruxelles-Paris-Amiens: Sodi, 1967.

Herrmann, L. "Hat Magischer Realismus Gegenswartswert?" *Aufbau* 4 (1948): 924–26.

Hinchcliffe, Peter, and Ed Jewinski, eds. *Magical Realism and Canadian Literature*. Waterloo: University of Waterloo Press, 1986.

Irish, James A. "Magical Realism: A Search for Caribbean and Latin American Roots." *Revista/Review Interamericana* 4 (1974): 411–21.

Jameson, Fredric. "On Magic Realism in Film." *Critical Inquiry* 12, 2 (1986): 301–25.

Kalenic-Ramsak, Branka. "El realismo mágico, lo real-maravilloso y el surrealismo: una estética parecida." *Verba Hispánica* 1 (1991): 27–34.

Kalogeras, Yiorgos. "Magic Realism in American Literature: The Case of Ethnic and Minority Literatures." *Porphyras* 41–42 (1987): 305–9.

Kanev, Venko-Asenov. "Lo real maravilloso: Un método definidor en las letras hispanoamericanas." *Alba de América: Revista Literaria* 9, 16–17 (1991): 181–96.

Kirk, John M. "Magic Realism and Voodoo: Alejo Carpentier's *The Kingdom of this World*." *Perspectives on Contemporary Literature* 5 (1979): 124–30.

Lérat, Christian. "Ultime va-et-vient entre l'ici et l'ailleurs dans *The Road to Tamazunchale*." In *L'ici et l'ailleurs: Multilinguisme et multiculturalisme en Amérique du Nord*. Ed. Jean Béranger. Bordeaux: Presses de l'Université de Bordeaux, 1991. Pp. 189–202.

Levitt, Morton P. "From Realism to Magic Realism: The Meticulous Modernist Fictions of García Márquez." In *Critical Perspectives on Gabriel García Márquez*. Ed. Bradley Shaw and Nora Vera-Godwin. Lincoln, Nebraska: Society of Spanish and Spanish American Studies, 1986. Pp. 73–99.

Mabille, Pierre. *Le Miroir du merveilleux*. Paris: Minuit, 1940.

Marcone, Jorge. "Lo 'real maravilloso' como categoría literaria." *Lexis: Revista Lingüística y Literaria* 12, 1 (1988): 1–41.

Márquez-Rodríguez, Alexis. "Alejo Carpentier: Teorías del barroco y de lo real maravilloso." *Nuevo Texto Crítico* 3, 1 (1990): 95–121.

———. "Deslinde entre el realismo mágico y lo real-maravilloso a próposito de la novelística de García Márquez." In *En el punto de mira: Gabriel García Márquez*. Ed. Ana María Hernández de López. Madrid: Pliegos, 1985. Pp. 337–44.

———. "El surrealismo y su vinculación con el realismo mágico y lo real maravilloso." In *Prosa hispánica de vanguardia*. Ed. Fernando Borgos. Madrid: Orígenes, 1986. Pp. 77–86.

Martin, Gerald. "On 'Magical' and Social Realism in García Márquez." In *Gabriel García Márquez: New Readings*. Ed. Bernard McGuirk and Richard Cardwell. Cambridge: Cambridge University Press, 1987. Pp. 95–116.

Martínez-Sanz, María Ester. "Lo real maravilloso en el *Quijote* y en *La tía Julia y el escribidor*." *Taller de Letras* 16 (1987): 31–41.

Mathieu, Corina S. "El paisaje americano de Alejo Carpentier: Una visión de lo real maravilloso." *Cuadernos de Aldeeu* 1, 2–3 (1983): 355–63.

McHale, Brian. *Postmodernist Fiction*. New York and London: Methuen, 1987.

McMurray, George. "Magical Realism in Spanish American Fiction." *Colorado State Review* 8, 2 (1981): 3–20.

Mena, Lucila-Inés. "Hacia una formulación teórica del realismo mágico." *Bulletin Hispanique* 77, 3–4 (July–December 1975): 395–407.

Menton, Seymour. "Jorge Luis Borges, Magic Realist." *Hispanic Review* 50, 1 (1982): 111–26.

———. *"The Last of the Just:* Between Borges and García Márquez." *World Literature Today* 59, 4 (Autumn 1985): 517–24.

———. *Magic Realism Rediscovered, 1918–1981.* Philadelphia: Art Alliance Press, 1983.

Merrell, Floyd F. "The Ideal World in Search of Its Reference: An Inquiry into the Underlying Nature of Magical Realism." *Chasqui: Revista de Literatura Latinoamericana* 4, 2 (February 1975): 5–17.

Parra, Teresita. "Perspectiva mítica de la realidad histórica en dos cuentos de Arturo Uslar Pietri." *Revista Iberoamericana* 52, 137 (1986): 945–50.

Pinsker, Sanford. "Magical Realism, Historical Truth, and the Quest for a Liberating Identity: Reflections on Alex Haley's *Roots* and Toni Morrison's *Song of Solomon.*" In *Studies in Black American Literature Volume I: Black American Prose Theory.* Ed. Joe Weixlmann and Chester Fontenot. Greenwood, Fl.: Penkevill, 1984. Pp. 183–97.

Planells, Antonio. "El realismo mágico ante la crítica." *Chasqui* 17, 1 (1988): 9–23.

———. "La polémica sobre el realismo mágico en Hispanoamérica." *Revista Interamericana de Bibliografía/Inter-American Review of Bibliography* 37 (1987): 517–29.

Pohl, G. "Magischer Realismus?" *Aufbau* 4 (1948): 650–53.

Preble-Niemi, Oralia. "Magical Realism and the Great Goddess in Two Novels by Alejo Carpentier and Alice Walker." *Comparatist* 16 (1992): 101–14.

Punter, David. "Essential Imaginings: The Novels of Angela Carter and Russell Hoban." In *The British and Irish Novel Since 1960,* ed. James Acheson. New York: St. Martin's Press, 1991.

Rabinowitz, Paula. "Naming, Magic, and Documentary: The Subversion of the Narrative in *Song of Solomon, Ceremony,* and *China Men.*" In *Feminist Re-Visions: What Has Been and Might Be.* Ed. Vivian Patraka and Louise Tilly. Ann Arbor: Women's Studies Program, University of Michigan, 1983. Pp. 26–42.

Ricci della Grisa, Graciela. *Realismo mágico y conciencia mítica en América Latina.* Buenos Aires: Cambeiro, 1985.

Rincón, Carlos. "Nociones surrealistas, concepción del lenguaje y función ideológico-literaria del realismo mágico en Miguel Angel Asturias." *Escritura: Revista de Teoría y Crítica Literarias* 3, 5–6 (1978): 25–61.

Rodríguez Monegal, Emir. "Surrealism, Magical Realism, Magical Fiction: A Study in Confusion." In *Surrealismo/Surrealismos: Latinoamérica y España*. Ed. Peter G. Earle and Germán Gullón. Philadelphia: Department of Romance Languages, University of Pennsylvania, 1977. Pp. 25–32.

Rodríguez-Luis, Julio. *The Contemporary Praxis of the Fantastic: Borges and Cortázar*. New York: Garland, 1991.

Rogmann, Horst. " 'Realismo mágico' y 'negritude' como construcciones ideológicas." In *Actas del Sexto Congreso Internacional de Hispanistas*. Ed. Alan Gordon and Evelyn Rugg. Toronto: University of Toronto Press, 1980. Pp. 632–35.

Roh, Franz. "Rückblick auf den Magischen Realismus," *Das Kunstwerk* 6, 1 (1952): 7–9.

———. *Nach-Expressionismus. Magischer Realismus. Probleme der neusten Europäischen Malerei*. Leipzig: Klinkhardt und Biermann, 1925.

Romeu, Raquel. "La Mancha: Tierra propicia al realismo mágico." *Cuadernos de Aldeeu* 1, 2–3 (1983): 435–41.

Saldívar, José David. "Postmodern Realism." In *The Columbia History of the American Novel*. Ed. Emory Elliott, Cathy N. Davidson, Patrick O'Donnell, Valerie Smith, and Christopher Wilson. New York: Columbia University Press, 1991. Pp. 521–41.

Sanchez, Napoleon N. "Lo real maravilloso americano o la americanización del surrealismo." *Cuadernos Americanos* 119, 4 (July–August 1976): 69–95.

Scheel, Charles. "Les Romans de Jean-Louis Baghio'o et le réalisme merveilleux redéfini." *Présence Africaine: Revue Culturelle du Monde Noir/Cultural Review of the Negro World* 147, 3 (1988): 43–62.

Scheffel, Michael. *Magischer Realismus: Die Geschichte eines Begriffes und ein Versuch seiner Bestimmung*. Stauffenburg Colloquium Band 16. Tübingen: Stauffenburg Verlag, 1990.

Serrano Plaja, Arturo. *Magic Realism in Cervantes: Don Quixote as Seen through Tom Sawyer and the Idiot*. Berkeley: University of California Press, 1970.

Slattery, Dennis P. "Narcissus Inverted: Fantastic-Realism as a Way of Knowing in *The Idiot*." In *Dostoyevsky and the Human Condition after a Century*. Ed. Alexij Ugrinsky, Frank S. Lambasa, and Valija K. Ozolins. New York: Greenwood Press, 1986. Pp. 61–69.

Slowik, Mary. "Henry James, Meet Spider Woman: A Study of Narrative Form in Leslie Silko's *Ceremony*." *North Dakota Quarterly* 57, 2 (1989): 104–20.

Stempel, Daniel. "Coleridge's Magical Realism: A Reading of the *Rime of the Ancient Mariner*." *Mosaic* 12, 1 (1978): 143–56.

Suárez-Murias, Marguerite C. "El realismo mágico: una definición étnica." In Marguerite C. Suárez-Murias. *Essays on Hispanic Literature/Ensayos de literatura hispana: A Bilingual Anthology*. Washington, D.C.: University Press of America, 1982. Pp. 95–114.

Todd, Richard. "Convention and Innovation in British Literature 1981–84: The Contemporaneity of Magic Realism." In *Convention and Innovation in Literature*. Ed. Theo D'haen, Rainer Grubel, and Helmut Lethen. Utrecht Publications in General and Comparative Literature 24. Amsterdam/Philadelphia: John Benjamins, 1989. Pp. 361–88.

Ude, Wayne. "Forging an American Style: The Romance-Novel and Magical Realism as Response to the Frontier and Wilderness Experiences." In *The Frontier Experience and the American Dream: Essays on American Literature*. Ed. David Morgan, Mark Busby, and Paul Bryant. College Station: Texas A & M University Press, 1989. Pp. 50–64.

———. "North American Magical Realism." *Colorado State Review* 8, 2 (1981): 21–30.

Uslar Pietri, Arturo. *Letras y hombres de Venezuela*. Mexico City: Fondo de Cultura Económica, 1949.

———. "Realismo mágico." In *Godos, insurgentes y visionarios*. Barcelona: Seix Barral, 1986.

Valbuena Briones, Angel. "Una cala en el realismo mágico." *Cuadernos americanos* 166, 5 (1969): 233–41.

Valdivieso, Jorge H. "Realismo mágico en la *Relación del nuevo descubrimiento del famoso Río Grande de las Amazonas* de Fray Gaspar de Carvajal." *Letras de Deusto* 19, 44 (1989): 327–34.

Van de Putte, Chr. *De Magisch-Realistische romanpoetica in de Nederlandse en Suitse literatuur*. Louvain: Nauwelaerts, 1979.

Vax, Louis. *La Séduction de l'étrange: Etude sur la littérature fantastique*. Paris: Presses Universitaires de France, 1965.

Vejar, Carlos. "Entre Luis Barragán y Juan Rulfo: El realismo mágico en la arquitectura y las letras mexicanas." *Plural: Revista Cultural de Excelsior* 209 (1989): 32–44.

Verzasconi, Ray. *Magical Realism and the Literary World of Miguel Angel Asturias*. Seattle: University of Washington Press, 1965.

Volek, Emil. "Alejo Carpentier y la narrativa hispanoamericana actual (dimensiones de un 'realismo mágico')." *Cuadernos Hispanoamericanos* 99, 296 (1975): 319–42.

———. "*El hablador* de Vargas Llosa: Del *realismo mágico* a la postmodernidad." *Cuadernos Hispanoamericanos* 509 (1992): 95–102.

———. "Hacia un concepto cultural postmoderno del realismo mágico en la narrativa hispanoamericana actual." In *Critical Essays on the Literatures of Spain and Spanish America*. Ed. Luis T. González and Julio Baena. Boulder: Society of Spanish and Spanish American Studies, 1991. Pp. 235–43.

———. "Realismo mágico: notas sobre su génesis y naturaleza en Alejo Carpentier." *Nueva Narrativa Hispanoamericana* 3, 2 (1973): 257–74.

————. "Realismo mágico entre la modernidad y la postmodernidad: Hacia una remodelización cultural y discursiva de la nueva narrativa hispanoamericana." *INTI: Revista de Literatura Hispánica* 31 (1990): 3–20.

Weisgerber, Jean, ed. *Le Réalisme magique: roman, peinture et cinéma*. Brussels: Le Centre des Avant-gardes littéraires de l'Université de Bruxelles, 1987.

————. "Métamorphoses du réalisme: Dostoevskij et Faulkner." *Russian Literature* 4 (1973): 37–50.

Williams, Mary Frances. "Ammianus Marcellinus and Gabriel García Márquez: *One Hundred Years of Solitude* and The House of Constantine." *Classical and Modern Literature* 14, 3 (1994): 269–96.

Williamson, Edwin. "*Magical Realism* and the Theme of Incest in *One Hundred Years of Solitude*." In *Gabriel García Márquez: New Readings*. Ed. Bernard McGuirk and Richard Cardwell. Cambridge: Cambridge University Press, 1987. Pp. 54–63.

Wilson, Robert. "On the Boundary of the Magic and the Real: Notes on Inter-American Fiction." *The Compass* 6 (1979): 37–53.

Yates, Donald A., ed. *Otros mundos, otros fuegos: Fantasía y realismo mágico en Iberoamérica*. Memoria del XVI Congreso Internacional de Literatura Iberoamericana. East Lansing: Michigan State University, Latin American Studies Center, 1975.

Young, Robert, and Keith Hollaman, eds. *Magical Realist Fiction: An Anthology*. New York: Longman, 1984. (Available through Oberlin College Press.)

Zamora, Lois Parkinson. "The Magical Tables of Isabel Allende and Remedios Varo." *Comparative Literature* 44, 1 (1992): 113–43.

————. "Magic Realism and Fantastic History: Carlos Fuentes's *Terra Nostra* and Giambattista Vico's *The New Science*." *Review of Contemporary Fiction* 8, 2 (1988): 249–56.

Zeitz, Eileen, and Richard Seybolt. "Hacia una bibliografía sobre el realismo mágico." *Hispanic Journal* 3, 1 (1981): 159–67.

CONTRIBUTORS

Amaryll Chanady is Professor of comparative literature at the Université de Montréal, Quebec. She is the author of *Magical Realism and the Fantastic: Resolved versus Unresolved Antinomy* (Garland, 1985), and editor of *Latin American Identity and Constructions of Difference* (University of Minnesota Press, 1994). She has published numerous articles on Latin American literature, cultural identity in Latin America and Quebec, the representation of Amerindians, discursive marginalization, indigenist discourse, ethnic minorities, multiculturalism, and postcolonial society.

Jeanne Delbaere-Garant is Professor of English literature at the Université Libre de Bruxelles, Belgium. She is the author of *Henry James: The Vision of France* and many articles on American, English, and Commonwealth fiction. She has recently edited *Multiple Voices: Recent Canadian Fiction* (1990), *William Golding: The Sound of Silence* (1991), and *The Ring of Fire: Essays on Janet Frame* (1992). She has also published three articles on magic realism in British literature and the new literatures in English.

Theo D'haen is Professor of English and American Literature at Leiden University in the Netherlands. He has published *Text to Reader* (Amsterdam, 1983) and numerous articles on contemporary literature in European languages, particularly in the field of postmodernism. He edits the series *Postmodern Studies*.

John D. Erickson is Professor of French at the University of Kentucky. He has most recently taught as visiting Professor at the Université de Provence (1987–88) and Rice University (1988–89). He is founder and editor of *L'Esprit Créateur* and founder in 1983 of the Center for French and Francophone Studies at Louisiana State University. He has published numerous essays in the area of Comparative Literature, nineteenth- and twentieth-century French literature, and Francophone studies. He has coedited three volumes (including *Marcel Proust et le texte producteur*, 1980, with Irène Pagès). He has authored two books: *Nommo: African Fiction in French* (1979) and *Dada: Performance, Poetry and Art* (1984).

Wendy B. Faris teaches Comparative Literature in the English Department at the University of Texas at Arlington. She is the author of *Carlos Fuentes* (Frederick Ungar, 1983), *Labyrinths of Language: Symbolic Landscape and Narrative Design in Modern Fiction* (Johns Hopkins, 1988), and articles on modern and contemporary fiction. At present she is completing a book on magical realism as shamanistic narrative.

P. Gabrielle Foreman teaches African American and nineteenth-century American literature at Occidental College. Her articles have appeared in *Representations, Feminist Studies, Callaloo,* and *Black American Literature Forum.* She is currently working on a manuscript entitled *Sentimental Subversions: Reading, Race, and Sexuality in the Nineteenth Century.*

John Burt Foster Jr. is a comparatist at George Mason University, and has written widely on nineteenth- and twentieth-century literature and thought. He is the author of *Heirs to Dionysus: A Nietzschean Current in Literary Modernism* and of *Nabokov's Art of Memory and European Modernism,* both published by Princeton University Press. In an earlier form, his essay in this volume received a Hoepfner Award from Auburn University in 1986.

Irene Guenther is a Ph.D. candidate in nineteenth- and twentieth-century history at the University of Texas in Austin. She has published essays on early French modern painting, German Expressionism, and the German occupation of France during World War II. She is currently working on her dissertation, a study of the political and gender roles of women as they may be seen in women's fashion during the Third Reich.

Patricia Merivale, Professor of English and Comparative Literature at the University of British Columbia, is the author of *Pan the Goat-God: His Myth in Modern Times* (Harvard University Press) and numerous articles on comparative topics. At present she is studying apocalyptic fictions, working on a book about narrative structures in the modern and postmodern artist parable, and co-editing a collection of essays on the metaphysical detective story.

David Mikics is Associate Professor of English at the University of Houston. He has published articles on James Joyce, Ishmael Reed, Alfred Hitchcock, and other twentieth-century figures; *The Limits of Moralizing: Pathos and Subjectivity in Spenser and Milton* was published by Bucknell University Press in 1994. He is currently writing a book on poetry and history in Emerson and Nietzsche.

Susan J. Napier is Associate Professor of Japanese Literature and Culture at the University of Texas at Austin. She is the author of *Escape From the Wasteland: Romanticism and Realism in the Works of Mishima Yukio and Oe Kenzaburo* (Harvard University Press, 1991) and *The Fantastic in Modern Japanese Literature: The*

Subversion of Modernity (Routledge, 1995). She has written numerous articles on postwar Japanese literature and culture, particularly in relation to women's studies and popular culture. She is currently writing a book on Japanese comics and animation entitled *Manga: A Cultural Investigation into the New Japan.*

Scott Simpkins, Assistant Professor of English at the University of North Texas, has published essays on Romanticism, modern literature, and semiotics in journals such as *Semiotica, Style, European Romantic Review, Versus: Quaderni di studi semiotici, Reader: Essays in Reader-Oriented Theory, Criticism, and Pedagogy, Twentieth Century Literature, Comparative Literature Studies,* and the *James Joyce Quarterly.* He is currently preparing studies on the Romantics' subversion of the book and their representations of stigma.

Stephen Slemon is Associate Professor in English at the University of Alberta, and teaches postcolonial literatures and theory. With Helen Tiffin, he has edited a volume entitled *After Europe: Critical Theory and Post-colonial Writing* (1989) and is working on a book tentatively titled *Figuring Out Colonialism.*

Melissa Stewart has just finished an M.A. in English from the University of Texas at Arlington, where she has also taught and tutored students in composition. The essay in this volume was taken from her recently completed thesis on magical realism and the American city.

Jon Thiem, who received his Ph.D. in Comparative Literature at Indiana University, is Professor in the Department of English at Colorado State University. Among his numerous essays in cultural history and literary criticism are "The Library of Alexandria: Towards the History of a Symbol," in the *Journal of the History of Ideas* (1979) and "Borges, Dante, and the Poetics of Total Vision," in *Comparative Literature* (1988). He is also the author of *Lorenzo de' Medici: Selected Poems and Prose* (Pennsylvania State University Press, 1991).

Richard Todd studied at University College London, where he received his Ph.D. in 1977. Since 1976 he has worked in the Netherlands and is currently Reader in English Literature at the Vrije Universiteit Amsterdam. Visiting posts include the 1988–89 Netherlands Chair at the University of Michigan, Ann Arbor, and an Honorary Research Fellowship at University College London for 1994–95. Among his publications are books on Iris Murdoch and George Herbert, several coedited collections of essays, and numerous articles and reviews.

Steven F. Walker, who received his Ph.D. in Comparative Literature from Harvard, is Associate Professor of Comparative Literature at Rutgers University. He is the author of *Theocritus* (1980) and *A Cure for Love: A Generic Study of the Pastoral Idyll* (1987), as well as of numerous articles, including essays on the Indian authors Kalidasa, Vivekananda, and R. K. Narayan. His book, *Jung and the Jungi-*

ans on Myth, was published in the Garland series on major theoreticians of myth in 1995. He is currently working on a book on tragedy and symbolic images of male initiation.

Rawdon Wilson teaches in the English Department of the University of Alberta. His primary research interests are in literary theory, narrative theory, recent fiction (including Australian and Canadian) and Renaissance literature. He has published articles in a variety of journals, and written three books: (with Shirley Neuman) *Labyrinths of Voice: Conversations With Robert Kroetsch* (1982), *In Palamedes' Shadow: Explorations in Play, Game, and Narrative Theory* (1990), and *Shakespearean Narrative* (1995). He has completed a study of the representation of disgust in literature and film called *The Hydra's Breath: Imagining Disgust.*

Lois Parkinson Zamora is a comparatist at the University of Houston; her area of specialization is comparative literary relations in the Americas, particularly contemporary U.S. and Latin American fiction. Her books include *Writing the Apocalypse: Historical Vision in Contemporary U.S. and Latin American Fiction* (Cambridge University Press, 1989) and *Image and Memory: Latin American Photography, 1880–1992* (University of Texas Press, 1997).

INDEX